PITT SERIES IN POLICY AND
INSTITUTIONAL STUDIES

RESEARCHING THE
Presidency

VITAL QUESTIONS, NEW APPROACHES

GEORGE C. EDWARDS III, JOHN H. KESSEL,

AND BERT A. ROCKMAN, EDITORS

UNIVERSITY OF PITTSBURGH PRESS

PITTSBURGH AND LONDON

Published by the University of Pittsburgh Press, Pittsburgh, Pa.,15260
Copyright © 1993, University of Pittsburgh Press
All rights reserved

Manufactured in the United States of America
Printed on acid-free paper

LIBRARY OF CONGRESS CATALOGING-IN-PUBLICATION DATA

Researching the presidency : vital questions, new approaches / George C.
Edwards III, John H. Kessel, and Bert A. Rockman, editors.
    p.   cm—(Pitt series in policy and institutional studies) Includes
bibliographical references.
    ISBN 0–8229–3737–9 (ALK. PAPER).—ISBN 0–8229–5494–X (pbk. : alk.
paper)
    1. Presidents—United States—Congresses. 2. Presidents—
United States—Research—Congresses. I. Edwards, George C.
II. Kessel, John H. (John Howard) III. Rockman, Bert A.
IV. Series.
JK515.R45 1993
353.03 13—DC20   92-24940
                                                                CIP

A CIP catalog record for this book is available from the British Library.

Contents

Preface

In November 1990, a three-day conference sponsored by the National Science Foundation was held at the University of Pittsburgh to evaluate existing research on the U.S. presidency and to foster new ideas and theoretical perspectives that could lead to innovative ways of studying the presidency. The design of the conference was to highlight two goals, which brought together two somewhat different sets of scholars.

One goal was to evaluate some major areas of current presidency scholarship. The group of scholars who were asked to prepare papers to evaluate particular domains of research on the presidency consisted of people currently active in presidency research. The second goal was to generate new approaches to research on the presidency. The idea here was to examine how approaches, theories, or methods associated with streams of scholarship not directed at the study of the presidency could be made useful to it. Many (though not all) of the scholars charged with the task of bringing these ideas to our attention are individuals whose previous work had not directly focused on the presidency. Without the benefit of the conference, it is unlikely that the individuals charged with fulfilling the two goals would have met in the same room on the subject of research on the U.S. presidency.

Our hope was that the first set of scholars (presidency specialists) would acquaint members of the second set (the nonspecialists) with some of the problems involved in doing research on the presidency. We also anticipated that the second set of scholars (mostly nonspecialists), who were associated with certain theoretical or methodological perspectives, would then be able to suggest innovative ways of studying the presidency. Linking novelty to experience was our goal for the conference and the resulting book. Neither would be sufficient by itself. Experience alone begets mere inertia. Novelty alone begets flights of fancy. When experience and novelty are linked together, however, real progress becomes possible. That was, and remains, our overarching goal.

This book conveys to a wider audience a conference that brimmed with intellectual zest, perhaps even combativeness. The chapters represent each individual author's second sober thought, produced in response to the comments of, above all, the conference participants and also the volume editors and the external reviewers. We hope that the book reflects fully the sense of intellectual engagement and vitality of the conference that shaped it.

A project of this magnitude could not happen without the assistance and cooperation of both institutions and people. An award from the National Science Foundation allowed this project to come to fruition. The University Center for International Studies and the Department of Political Science at the University of Pittsburgh, the Center for Presidential Studies at Texas A&M University, and the Department of Political Science at Ohio State University all played important roles in the support of this project. The University of Pittsburgh Press nurtured the development of the book stemming from the conference in just about every way imaginable.

We would be remiss if we failed to single out the enormous contributions of Fred I. Greenstein to this project. Fred was a coinvestigator on the NSF proposal. He provided a constant stream of excellent advice from the point of conception of the conference through its final outcome. Only a scholar of Fred's accomplishments would ask that he not be listed as an editor because he felt his direct contributions did not warrant that status. His self-assessment is far too modest. We honor his request. But we recognize that Fred was nothing less than a full partner in ensuring the success of both the conference and the book.

We are foremost indebted, of course, to the conference participants, who contributed to its intellectual ferment and in both direct and indirect ways to its published contents. Aside from Fred Greenstein and the editors, the conference participants included

John Aldrich, Duke University
Jonathan Bendor, Stanford University
Larry Berman, University of California, Davis
John Burke, University of Vermont

Colin Campbell, S.J., Georgetown University
Thomas Cronin, Colorado College
Martha Feldman, University of Michigan
Morris Fiorina, Harvard University
Susan Fiske, University of Massachusetts, Amherst
Erwin Hargrove, Vanderbilt University
Richard Herrmann, Ohio State University
Karen Hult, Virginia Polytechnic Institute and State University
Jonathan Hurwitz, University of Pittsburgh
Charles Jones, University of Wisconsin, Madison
Anthony King, University of Essex
Gary King, Harvard University
Paul Light, University of Minnesota
Frank Mackamen, The Gerald R. Ford Foundation
Gary Miller, Washington University
Terry Moe, Stanford University
Morris Ogul, University of Pittsburgh
Joseph Pika, University of Delaware
Richard Rose, University of Strathclyde
Robert Shogan, *The Los Angeles Times*
Barbara Sinclair, University of California, Riverside
Norman Thomas, University of Cincinnati
Marie-France Toinet, Fondation Nationale des Sciences Politiques
Stephen Wayne, Georgetown University
M. Stephen Weatherford, University of California, Santa Barbara

The logistics of the conference could not have been put together without the talents of Renee Abrams, who handled all matters pertaining to the conference flawlessly, and Glema Burke of Pitt's University Center for International Studies, who provided superb support and sage advice. All of this meticulous organizing went on while Bert Rockman, the local conference organizer, was in Washington. There is a message in this for would be micromanagers.

We need also to single out names behind institutions. Frederick Hetzel, director of the University of Pittsburgh Press, provided personal commitment to this project. Frank Moone, the Press's acquisitions editor, was enthusiastic about and involved in this project from beginning to end. Several University of Pittsburgh graduate students provided crucial support in keeping the conference (quite literally) on the move. We are appropriately thankful to them. They are Patrick Altdorfer, Buba Misawa, James Van Laningham, Susan Corbesero, and Mary Green.

Two anonymous reviewers of the book's chapters gave us confidence that we, and particularly the authors, achieved much of what we set out to do.

RESEARCHING THE
Presidency

Introduction

THE AMERICAN presidency is a topic that attracts both widespread and intense interest. As the central feature on the American political landscape, it is a magnet for writers of various kinds, including political scientists, historians, journalists, and foreign commentators. The visibility of the presidential office also entices undergraduates into classes on the presidency and gets some of us onto radio or television.

Yet these attractions may have had inhibiting effects on the scientific and theoretical development of the subfield. Ironically, the detachment needed for theoretical and methodological innovation in studying the presidency can be hindered by its popularity as a subject. The prominence of the presidency as a topic of commentary lies, to some extent, in its ability to be personalized. It seems that we are never far from thinking of the presidency as merely the president. Perhaps more than any other subfield, the issues of the conduct of the president and the presidency seem stuck in a temporal context that constrains larger generalizations or inquiries. Attention tends to focus on incumbent presidents, often emphasizing normative judgments and ad hoc descriptions about their behavior.

When this occurs, we fail to make comparisons across presidents and other political executives, study changes in the presidency or the environment in which the presidency operates, and exploit theoretical groundings from the experimental and theoretical sciences of human behavior. Thus, the range of theoretical and empirical possibilities becomes limited. The purpose of this volume quite self-consciously is to expand that range.

The Status of Presidency Research

The status of presidential scholarship is relatively easy to document. The first wave of scholarship on the presidency largely focused on the legal structures and roles of the presidency, exemplified in the work of Edward S. Corwin. Corwin's tradition of scholarship was put into modern dress by scholars such as Clinton Rossiter and Louis Koenig, who saw presidential roles responding to external conditions and thus expanding beyond strictly legal definitions.

A second set of presidential studies reflected an emphasis on political psychology, although, strictly speaking, the psychology was more on the order of political psychoanalysis. This line of psychological work on individual presidents was exemplified by Alexander George's study of Woodrow Wilson and later, if differently, by James David Barber's efforts to define and predict presidential character.

A third type of work has been the provocative and insightful essay regarding the exercise of presidential power and the operation of the White House written by astute former White House staff members who are also political scientists. The work of Richard Neustadt and Thomas Cronin exemplifies this type of analysis. Their efforts contain the basis for broader-scale theories and have stimulated important and valuable research on the presidency.

Many of these works contained potential hypotheses to be investigated but tended to shy away from explicit efforts to theorize. Few political scientists called attention to this situation. One who did, Donald Stokes, wrote in a 1966 paper that "it would indeed be possible to formulate Richard Neustadt's insistence that competing sources of information be built into the organization of the Executive Office in terms of much more general theories of information" (Stokes, 1966, 5). Such broader theoretical concerns were rarely voiced in the field of presidential studies, however. Scholars trained in scientific techniques chose to hone their methodological skills on legislative and voting questions, where theoretical formulation and systematic data seemed more accessible. The subfield of the presidency, on the other hand, seemed tied either to an unchanging subject, that is, formal powers, or to an idiosyncratic one, that is, presidents. The richer subfields continued to prosper while less developed subfields continued in their traditional ways.

As a consequence, the presidency was an underdeveloped subfield. Beginning a review published in 1975, Anthony King wrote:

> To read most general studies of the United States presidency . . . is to feel that one is reading not a number of different books but essentially the same book over and over again. The same sources are

cited; the same points are made; even the same quotations . . . appear again and again. In addition, the existing literature is mainly descriptive and atheoretical: general hypotheses are almost never advanced, and, when advanced, almost never tested. (A. King, 1975, 173)

In a report for the Ford Foundation written two years later, Hugh Heclo concluded,

Political observers have written excellent interpretations of the Presidency. Important questions about Presidential power have been raised. But considering the amount of such writing in relation to the base of original empirical research behind it, the field is as shallow as it is luxuriant. To a great extent, presidential studies have coasted on the reputations of a few . . . classics . . . and on secondary literature and anecdotes produced by former participants. (Heclo, 1977, 30)

At the end of the decade, George Edwards commented:

Research on the presidency too often fails to meet the standards of contemporary political science, including the careful definition and measurement of concepts, the rigorous specification and testing of propositions, the employment of appropriate quantitative methods, and the use of empirical theory to develop hypotheses and explain findings. (Edwards, 1981, 146)

Yet the presidential subfield was changing even as these pessimistic statements were being written. Some scholars felt the presidency ought to be studied with data and explicit methodologies to test propositions. The need to anchor the study of the presidency in broader theoretical contexts also was making headway. Efforts to change the character of presidential research may or may not have been self-conscious, but they did have impact. A list of such work might include those writings of the editors. For example, Edwards's *At the Margins: Presidential Leadership of Congress* (1989) and *Presidential Approval* (1990); Rockman's *The Leadership Question: The Presidency and the American System* (1984); and Kessel's *The Domestic Presidency* (1975) and *Presidential Parties* (1984) are very different from one another, both in the facets of the presidency on which they focus and in the methods of analysis. They are, however, commonly guided by some larger theoretical concerns and include systematically gathered data.

Two books that explicitly aim to stimulate further presidential research have also appeared. George Edwards and Stephen Wayne's *Studying the Presidency,* published in 1983, contains chapters on the methodologies of case studies and quantitative analysis, the techniques of using libraries, legal sources, and interviews, and the role of concept development (Edwards and Wayne, 1983). Gary King and Lyn Ragsdale's *The Elusive Executive* provides statistical data on the presidency comparable to that which has been available for some time about the Congress (King and Ragsdale, 1988).

As Wayne writes in *Studying the Presidency,* "the existence of this methodological guide and commentary indicates that some of the problems [besetting presidential research] can be overcome. Not only do the contributors believe that more social science research is desirable, but their contributions demonstrate that it is possible" (1983, 8–9). King and Ragsdale write that they also "believe that research into the presidency should be conducted in a more rigorous, systematic, and, when possible, quantitative manner" (1988, 483). Both of these books aid in achieving these goals.

The community of modern presidency researchers has taken on some institutional form. The Presidency Research Group, organized under the leadership of Fred Greenstein in 1978, has become the Presidency Research Section of the American Political Science Association. By 1987, the Presidency Research Section had 310 members, making it the sixth largest of the APSA's organized sections. During the past decade, it has published a newsletter containing short articles and guides to research, and the program chairs of the Presidency Research Section and the relevant members of the regular program committee have worked closely together to ensure ample opportunity to present research results. And the amount of research has grown. In 1978 there were only two panels on the presidency at the annual meeting of the APSA. In the early 1990s there are five times as many.

Our view of the present status of presidential scholarship is that, although developments are promising, we are still short of a well-developed subfield that meets standards of cumulativeness and theoretical consistency. But much ground has been gained. Description is inevitable in work on the presidency, given new administrations every four or eight years, and there are now more developed data bases and models of their use for answering descriptive questions. To be sure, however, we do need more theoretical direction.

In the 1980s, a similarly NSF-sponsored conference on legislative studies yielded a *Handbook of Legislative Research* (Loewenberg, Patterson, and Jewell, 1985). We have not tried to provide the same encyclopedic completeness here, in large part because of differences between the extensiveness and rigor of the legislative and presidency literatures. The greater need, we feel, is to catalyze further research on the presidency. Thus, we have avoided duplicating work already done in the volumes by Edwards and Wayne and by King and Ragsdale. Our effort, instead, has been to capitalize on the momentum that has been achieved, call attention to particularly important substantive areas, and suggest theories that can be usefully incorporated into presidency research.

What Should We Study?

The most critical question in any research endeavor is to choose the focus of study. This may be what we seek to explain (a dependent variable) or a phenomenon whose consequences seem vital (an independent variable).

THE INDIVIDUAL OR THE INSTITUTION?

Views about the contribution of the individual to the presidency and about the analytical payoffs from studying individuals are quite divergent. A recent trend in political science has been the adoption of formal theoretical approaches to studying politics that deemphasize the study of individual variability. In addition, a substantial amount of work done from a variety of research traditions concludes that the president is frequently confined by environmental constraints, profoundly limiting his latitude to make a difference as an individual.

Further, we have begun to differentiate among the arenas in which the president is operating, (e.g., making decisions, implementing policy, or dealing with the public, the press, the Congress, or other nations). The arena of presidential operations turns out to be a critical variable in understanding the impact of the individual personality.For example, for years commentators have attributed Lyndon Johnson's success with Congress to his legislative skills, but there is now plenty of evidence that these skills, although certainly not unimportant, were not nearly so overpowering as folklore had made them out to be (Edwards, 1989, chap. 9). Johnson's personality, broadly defined, seems to have had a more substantial difference in his decision making and decisional processes regarding Vietnam than in his relations with Congress (Burke and Greenstein, 1989).

Several chapter authors in this book raise issues about the role of the individual as president that are often left implicit in presidency research. Erwin Hargrove, for example, does not simply ask whether individuals make a difference, but asks under what circumstances they make a difference? The task of scholarship, according to Hargrove, is to integrate the study of individuals with the web of social and institutional forces that move them and which they, in turn, may influence.

Hargrove finds plenty of opportunity for the expression of individuality in the presidency. He suggests that the fit between personality and role tasks is important to understanding the individual as president. Leaders define and play their roles in ways that favor their strengths, and they seek out and respond in congenial ways to situations, tasks, problems, and challenges that favor those strengths. Different roles and situations evoke different elements of style in the same person.

Thus, he suggests we need to explain the dynamic relations between personality, role, and situations, which are inextricably linked. This requires us to clarify the relevant aspects of individuality; what makes a difference in political behavior and what elements of the environment can personality affect? In addition, Hargrove proposes that the best way to capture the political personality of a president is to delineate the recurring styles of leadership over time. His emphasis, therefore, is on operative leadership style, the explanation of which lies in strategic interactions between situational incentives, role experiences, and individual propensities. Hargrove's focus, thus, shifts away from earlier "political personality" studies that found the genesis of political personality in childhood.

Terry Moe views things differently. He concludes that there has been too much attention focused on the personal presidency, which he thinks has little theoretical payoff. The personal presidency promotes enormous complications in theory and research, opening a Pandora's box of individual motivation and behavior and orienting the field around causal mysteries that we are unlikely to solve. For example, leadership (or management) style has been the subject of intensive analysis by organizational theorists for decades. Yet, in Moe's view it has produced few generalizations that can be applied to the presidency or to the link between leadership style and organizational performance. Conclusions typically are contingent on a wide range of variables. Thus, Moe concludes that research on style, personality, and other aspects of the personal presidency fails to provide a foundation for constructing theory.

Ironically, as Moe sees it, scholarly attention shifted from the institution of the presidency to the individual president at the same time as the presidency was becoming highly institutionalized. He argues that all presidents, whatever their personalities, styles, or backgrounds, behave similarly in basic respects. Consequently, Moe proposes building institutional theories of the presidency around interests, structures, roles, authority, control, hierarchy, incentives, and other general properties of organizations that shape presidential behavior regardless of who is president.

A similar view is echoed by Martha Feldman, who feels that it is important to separate presidents from the presidency, because offices as well as persons have power and there *is* some continuity across administrations. Employing concepts like roles lead us to think of what presidents have in common, the functions they perform because of the position they occupy, the history of the presidency as an organization, and the continuity in expectations about it. Feldman sees in the presidency the needs of other organizations—the struggle to reduce uncertainty, the development of routines, the effort to bound problem sets. Unlike Moe, however, Feldman is more agnostic as to whether the presidency or presidents ultimately are more important.

PUBLIC POLICY

Paul Light approaches the issue of what we should study in a different way. He argues that what is missing in the debate between leadership-based and institutional explanations of presidential behavior has been a strong dependent variable. He proposes that researchers adopt policy as that variable.

Light believes that policy is the most important product of the presidency and provides a baseline against which to assess competing explanations of presidential behavior. Being a visible expression of a president's ideology and world view, focusing on policy becomes a

way of tackling the impact of personal belief systems in shaping outcomes. As a variable, policy also is useful for studying the role of process and the rule of law, identifying players and procedures, and
determining what difference they make. Policy also provides an avenue for testing the impact of presidential resources as a set of variables that affect presidential control of policy making.

Almost everyone agrees that policy differences matter. John Aldrich argues that the four "seasons" of presidential elections—aspirants choose to run, parties select candidates, the candidates selected
campaign in the fall, and the victor attempts to govern—are only
temporarily distinct stages. To understand the relationship between
the governors and the governed requires an integration of campaigns
and governance. In other words, we need to connect politics with
policy.

For example, one model of how candidates conduct nomination
campaigns emphasizes the dynamics of the campaign, the other focuses on substantive concerns, notably policy. The first predicts outcomes but does not indicate how candidates use their resources to
generate support or why voters support them. The second looks at
the role of issue stands and provides a possible way of linking the
nomination process to the general campaign.

Apparently paralleling the two views of campaign strategy are two
streams of empirical research on the primary electorate. The first presents voters as ill-informed, attuned to the horse race, possibly capricious, and perhaps vulnerable to manipulation. The second finds a
somewhat more substantive basis for voter choice. Aldrich suggests
that we may be able to bridge the gap between these different approaches to both the candidates and the electorate with the concept
of expected utility accounts. He warns that it is important to recognize that more than the election imperative is involved in elections;
policy is important as well. Thus, when we study presidential selection, we need to make sure that we are sensitive to the fact that candidates seek to make and implement public policy and that voters
have policy concerns. Moreover, it is important to focus on the impact of campaign strategy on governance.

Yet other authors raise the importance of policy as a variable in
analyzing the presidency. Along with Paul Light, Richard Rose also
proposes that we employ policy as a variable to test theories of pres-

idential success. He further suggests that success needs to be evaluated across a number of policy areas and dimensions. Karen Hult argues that we should not study presidential advising in isolation from the impact of advice and advisory systems on presidential policy decisions. She also suggests the need to look for differences in advisory networks, for example, their stability, level of conflict, and degree of access to, and influence on, the president across policy areas involving routine and "adaptive" decisions. Barbara Sinclair also focuses attention on policy by stressing that the ultimate purpose of studying leadership is to assess its affect on policy outcomes.

How Should We Study the Presidency?

Presidency research lacks a powerful consensus on appropriate methodological and theoretical approaches. Diversity can be a strength as long as it contributes to advancing our understanding of the presidency, but it becomes an obstacle to progress if it creates a Tower of Babel that diminishes our capacity to recognize the value of alternative paths of scholarship and thinking. The objective of this book is to juxtapose the tried and true with the new by assessing where the former has led us and seeing where the latter might lead. We see no reason why existing scholarship cannot coexist with more recent developments in theory and methods. Indeed, we see no way to enrich our understanding if it does not. Ultimately, of course, the readers of this volume will judge for themselves which approaches have the most promise.

METHODOLOGY

No issue has plagued research on the presidency more than that of methodology. One of the principal challenges in researching the presidency has been dealing with the problem of "uniqueness," the infamous $N = 1$ issue. This apparent obstacle to systematic study has traditionally inhibited serious thinking about quantitative measurement, data generation, and data analysis. Much of the literature, consequently, has been qualitative and of a historical or biographical nature.

There may be less to the quantitative-qualitative distinction than meets the eye, however. Gary King convincingly argues that there is no inherent difference between quantitative and qualitative research. The rules of inference are the same, as is the need for both rigor and relevance. Indeed, several other chapters, including those by John Aldrich, Barbara Sinclair, and Paul Light, stress the importance of doing rigorous and systematic research, regardless of analytic mode. They agree with Gary King that it takes more than a cogently argued point, perhaps illustrated with a case study, to verify an empirical assertion about the presidency. Theoretical rigor comes from an explicit logical structure of propositions, and empirical rigor comes from variables that are precise, valid, and reliable.

Light emphasizes careful measurement of specific outcomes, which in his case are public policies. In the first instance, the discriminating classification of policies along several dimensions, he argues, helps us sort out the large volume of case studies on the presidency, reveals the gaps and overlaps in presidency research, and provides another tool for indexing and cross-referencing our conclusions. He also demonstrates the utility of classifying policies with an analysis of presidents' policy agendas. He is able to compare administrations and propose tests of various explanations for success and for what presidents propose and why they do so.

We require systematic descriptive work to provide the basis for more parsimonious explanations of presidential behavior and its consequences. The traditional literature, emphasizing history and thick description, is most useful, Gary King argues, for mining what needs to be explained by theory-driven research and for providing texture to more austere explanations and theories. It is less helpful, however, in providing useful explanations or theories. A principal problem with qualitative research is that it often fails to note the degree of uncertainty in results. Levels of uncertainty are especially relevant for those making prescriptions for the presidency, and King cautions us against making prescriptions on a weak basis. Since the number of presidents is too small to ever provide us an acceptable level of certainty, King advises us to turn from employing presidents as units of analysis and to focus on decisions or other observable consequences of the theory being tested or to examine observable implications of the theory at other levels of aggregation.

Anthony King suggests we do more than compare across presidents. He recommends that we make comparisons across chief executives in the democracies of economically developed nations. He illustrates the utility of this approach by comparing the power of these chief executives within their own government systems. Such analyses will not be easily accomplished, however. As King points out, there are three difficulties in studying the American presidency in a comparative context: the lack of literature on chief executives in other nations, the paucity of comparative case studies of executive leadership, and the uniqueness of the American presidency.

One of the key concerns of several of the authors is parsimonious explanation. Terry Moe argues that it is better to focus on a few variables that can explain a great deal about the presidency than to attempt to study the presidency in all its individual complexity. Gary King warns us that theories cannot be so broad or so comprehensive that they cannot be falsified and that we cannot identify research methods capable of distinguishing whether a theory is true or false.

Barbara Sinclair suggests we study leadership by focusing on a limited number of variables and a few key actors. She does not want to incorporate the president's entire psyche into an analytical framework. Instead, she proposes that we include only the president's skill and goals in order to avoid overly complicated models of presidential behavior. Although Karen Hult offers an inductive strategy for studying advisory networks, which naturally focuses on the identification of relevant independent variables for conceptual mapping, she still recommends striving for parsimony in explanation.

THEORIES

Almost everyone agrees that research on the presidency should be more theoretical. *Theory,* however, turns out to be a remarkably plastic term, so different authors have different agendas when they make this assertion. For example, some, such as Karen Hult and Gary King, are broadly concerned with moving beyond description to an emphasis on explanation in research. Other authors have more specifically focused concerns. Most studies of individual presidents have been based on motivational theories rather than cognitive theories, yet presidents act on the basis of the information they can comprehend. There has been much recent activity in schema theories, social cognition, and information processing models. Many of these also are relevant to neoinstitutionalist approaches to political behavior.

Susan Fiske proposes that certain types of social cognitive explanations may provide new integrative themes and perhaps a fresh unifying theory. She believes the complex interplay between motivation and cognition provides fertile ground for understanding the presidency and accompanying political phenomena. Moving beyond the traditional focus on consistency seekers from cognitive dissonance theory, the naive scientists of attribution theory, and the cognitive misers of schema theory, Fiske suggests that a motivated tactician who chooses between various cognitive strategies as the situation demands would be a better balanced approach. This would not commit an observer to any single interpretation of an actor's probable cognitive strategy, as it assumes that an actor will choose a more accurate type of processing if the situation demands it.

She also calls attention to a distinction between category-based thinking and attribute-based thinking that has wide application to problems facing presidential scholars. The former is top-down, often faster, and relies on short cuts such as stereotyping; the latter is bottom-up, inductive, and driven more by data. A less concerned voter, a White House decision maker who is subject to time pressure, or a member of an advisory network who has little regard for members of outgroups is more likely to use the more expeditious category-based processing. An issue-oriented voter, a president who expects to be held accountable and is aware of the cost of being wrong, or an expert in a specific domain will be motivated to use more comprehensive attribute-based processing.

Martha Feldman focuses on the presidency from an organization theory perspective that is cognitive and cultural in nature. She suggests that such an approach will help us answer important questions of organizational identity, how identities are developed, maintained, and communicated, and how organizational identities influence other decisions and actions. It will aid us in understanding what kind of information is available to those involved in the institutionalized presidency and how it is understood by the actors.

Some of our authors propose to employ theories based on rational choice. Terry Moe argues for the application of rational choice theory to understand institutional development in the presidency. Barbara Sinclair employs a "purposive behavior" approach inspired by rational choice theory that posits that individuals rationally (loosely defined) pursue specified goals. She, like John Aldrich (who also argues for the use of the notion of utility maximization), warns, however, that we should be careful not to posit a single-goal assumption. Attributing multiple goals to actors is more realistic.

Formal modeling, usually associated with rational choice, has made substantial headway in political science in the past decade. Formalization may help presidency research in two ways. First, an experienced modeler may be able to identify areas in presidential research that are ready for formal statement. Second, the resulting models may point to critical questions on which further empirical work is needed.

Gary Miller illustrates the use of a formal approach to studying the presidency. He suggests that we know more about why presidents are weak than about why they succeed and why their power varies over time. He finds that abnormal politics serves as an important check on the more typical politics of stalemate. If a large exogenous shock informs and arouses the public, moving it from its normal state of rational ignorance, the president has a greater opportunity for change. Once the status quo is vulnerable, presidents can attempt to exploit these opportunities for leadership.

The president's dominant position in the free flow of information provides him the opportunity to gain access to the public and communicate his intentions to everyone. This unique potential to overcome the rational ignorance of the public creates the possibility for mass mobilization on an issue that may spark great changes in American politics. Thus the president has the potential to be the most powerful issue entrepreneur. He may also legitimize and motivate the efforts of those seeking change, such as civil rights protestors.

Miller argues that in such circumstances the president is positioned to direct media attention, elicit public support, coordinate social action, and direct extraordinary legislative coalitions. He can fill the crucial role in games of coordination by serving as a focal point and by influencing the pace and timing of social movements. He also can serve as a contract enforcer in legislative coalitions by facilitating the market for exchange of political support.

Evaluating the Presidency

Evaluating presidents is ubiquitous, whether in the worlds of journalism or of academia. Yet the prevalence of the activity has not led to conceptual clarification of the standards of evaluation. How can social scientists move beyond individual presidents and focus on the presidency? What should be taken into consideration when evaluating individual presidents?

Richard Rose answers that there are inevitably normative and empirical dimensions to evaluating the presidency, and we should begin by recognizing their relationship. For example, we have substantial data on the president's standing in the public, including electoral results and public opinion polls, but the interpretation of these data in evaluating presidents requires us to apply normative standards. Thus, he suggests we apply both normative and empirical criteria in presidential evaluation.

We need to be as aware of the empirical implications of normative assumptions as of the normative implications of empirical data. Otherwise, we are likely to be blinded by normatively driven empirical preconceptions, such as the president is at the center of the political universe and has the potential to influence anyone (or any country) to support him. Instead, scholars should place the president's performance in office in a perspective that includes activity outside both Washington, D.C. and the nation's boundaries. Questions of the centrality of the president should be subject to empirical test, not assumed.

Susan Fiske raises another normative issue in evaluating presidents: the problem of setting the standards for good decision making. Who sets them? What is the optimal solution? What is accuracy? The normative criteria are wanting and deserve more attention. At the very least, they should be explicit. Richard Rose argues that ultimately scholars should employ the presidents' job definitions, their goals in office, and the environmental constraints on their influence as standards against which to evaluate their achievements. Presidents differ as to the ends and means of office, and our evaluations ought not to reflect a bias toward activism.

Barbara Sinclair agrees, contending that whether the president advances his goals is important for gauging success, and that we should consider both what a president attempts as well as what he accomplishes. We can evaluate presidents on both dimensions, but we should distinguish between them. Susan Fiske adds that we must evaluate presidents against their own performance goals as well as against others' agendas.

Outline of the Book

The next four chapters present critical reviews of the literature on some central areas of presidential scholarship. John Aldrich focuses on the literature on presidential selection, organizing his discussion around four central questions reflecting the temporally distinct stages of the selection process: Who runs? Who is nominated? Who is elected? And how do elections shape governance?

Erwin Hargrove addresses the time-honored question of whether leaders make a difference in political life. Thus, he reviews the literature on presidential personality and political style, seeking to understand the relative importance of individuality in the presidency.

One of the central issues in the study of the presidency is how presidents make decisions. Advising the president, the subject of Karen Hult's review chapter, is one of the most discussed and least understood aspects of presidential decision making. Hult asks, "Who advises the president? What do presidents do with the advice they receive? What explains continuities and discontinuities in presidential advising? To what extent can presidents control advising? And what effect does advising have on decision outcomes?"

Presidential policy making is the focus of Paul Light's contribution. He argues that public policy is what is most important about a presidency and thus should receive more rigorous attention from scholars. He divides the literature on presidential policy making into five areas; the substance of policy, the key players and their positions, the process and structure of policy making, the policies of individual presidencies, and the measurement of specific outcomes. He then offers a focus for future work on presidential policy making based on comparing policy differences among presidential administrations.

Part II of the volume departs from the focus of Part I. It is composed of essays by distinguished scholars who typically do not research the presidency. Our goal is to enrich presidential scholarship with perspectives that have proven fruitful in other areas. Barbara Sinclair begins this process from her background of expertise on Congress. She applies a framework developed for the study of congressional leaders to the analysis of presidential leadership.

Presidential scholars have frequently borrowed from the discipline of psychology, sometimes indiscriminately. Psychologist Susan Fiske reviews four basic views of the social thinker in social cognition research: the person as consistency seeker, the naive scientist, the cognitive miser, and the motivated tactician (who chooses among the other cognitive strategies, depending on motivation). She then applies social cognition perspectives to problems within scholarship and argues that the complex interplay between motivation and cognition provides a fertile ground for understanding the president and surrounding political phenomena.

Martha Feldman brings her expertise in organization theory to the study of the presidency. There are three perspectives on how organizations produce products, one focusing primarily on outcomes, one on structures, and the third on meaning. She applies the third perspective, concerned with questions of organizational identity and how identities are developed, maintained, and communicated and asks how these organizational identities influence presidential decisions and actions.

Formal theory is playing an increasingly prominent role in the study of American politics, and Gary Miller illustrates an application to the study of the presidency. He shows how many of the concepts of importance to presidential scholars, such as communication, leadership, and the symbolic trappings of office, can be employed in formal theory to illuminate important aspects of presidential politics.

Terry Moe argues that it is most productive to view the presidency as an institution. He rejects the focus of the traditional presidential literature on individuals, arguing that all presidents, whatever their personalities, styles, or backgrounds, should tend to behave similarly in basic respects. He then employs theory anchored in rational choice in general and the economics of organization in particular to explain institutional choice in the presidency.

Gary King finds that most of the work on the presidency has not reached the point where concepts are to be measured and theories tested systematically. He does not argue that qualitative research work should be abandoned, however but rather, that it be done systematically and rigorously. The rules of scientific inference should apply to qualitative as well as quantitative research. He also suggests that it will not be productive to increase the richness of description and the inclusiveness of theoretical perspectives, nor is it useful to use the president as the unit of analysis. What we need, he contends, are less inclusive and more specific theoretical concepts.

Part III presents two essays that engage in comparisons. The first, by Anthony King, brings perspective to the study of the presidency by comparing the president with the heads of government in other economically developed democracies. He is concerned with the extent to which the head of government is in a position to assert his or her will over the rest of the cabinet, the bureaucracy, and the national legislature. In other words, how does the power of the president within the American system of government compare with the power of heads of government in other countries, within the national systems of government in those countries? His approach is to compare chief executives on the basis of potential sources of power.

Finally, Richard Rose examines one of the thorniest—and most common—issues in presidency research: evaluating presidents. He finds that there are both normative and empirical dimensions to evaluating the presidency and that scholars are subject to several pitfalls. One is to view the president's performance in office too narrowly, ignoring activity outside both the nation's capital and the nation's boundaries. Another pitfall is to impose a bias toward presidential activism rather than the standard of a president's own goals in office. Finally, of course, we need always to systematically delineate the political and policy constraints that affect the capacity of a president to exert influence, whether these constraints be endogenous to the U.S. political system or exogenous to the system.

References

Burke, John P., and Fred I. Greenstein. 1989. *How Presidents Test Reality: Decisions on Vietnam, 1954 and 1965.* New York: Russell Sage Foundation.

Edwards, George C., III. 1981. "The Quantitative Study of the Presidency." *Presidential Studies Quarterly* 11 (Spring): 146–50.

————. 1989. *At the Margins: Presidential Leadership of Congress.* New Haven: Yale University Press.

Edwards, George C., III, and Stephen J. Wayne, eds. 1983. *Studying the Presidency.* Knoxville: University of Tennessee Press.

Heclo, Hugh. 1977. *Studying the Presidency.* New York: Ford Foundation.

King, Anthony. 1975. "Executives." In *Handbook of Political Science,* vol. 5, ed. Fred I. Greenstein and Nelson W. Polsby. Reading, Mass.: Addison-Wesley.

King, Gary and Lyn Ragsdale. 1988. *The Elusive Presidency: Discovering Statistical Patterns in the Presidency.* Washington, D.C.: Congressional Quarterly Press.

Loewenberg, Gerhard, Samuel C. Patterson, and Malcolm E. Jewell. 1985. *Handbook of Legislative Research.* Cambridge: Harvard University Press.

I

Assessments

I

Presidential Selection

JOHN H. ALDRICH

*T*HE PRESIDENT is, of course, the most important individual—and office—in the American polity. As such, knowing who seeks the office, how he or she succeeds in attaining it, and the constraints this office seeking places on the victor is critical to understanding the presidency. Or, at least, that is the assumption of electoral democracy.

Access to the presidency has assumed a well-defined pattern with temporal regularity, and I use this regularity to organize this review. Sometime between the last presidential election and January 1 of the current election year, presidential ambitions, presumably harbored by many, are translated into firm decisions. The first section of this review examines the question of who does and who does not run for president. In this case, I suggest that there is something approaching a scholarly consensus on the answer to this question and, more important, on the theoretical account, the rational-choice-based theory of political ambition.

Elected presidents, all but Washington in the past and all in the foreseeable future, must first receive the endorsement of their (major) political party. Many methods of nominations have been used, and each differs greatly in the constraints it may place on its nominees. Therefore I examine nominations under the current method, the "new nomination system" largely in place for the 1972 campaign. This is a candidate-centered process, conducted through the media to the public. Two major views of this process have been advanced at both the candidate and public levels. These two views are remarkably different in appearance. One focuses on the dynamic properties of the extended primary season, the "horse race" among candidates, and the associated fluctuations in the public's preferences, all too often making them appear capricious and politically insubstantial. The second view rests on assuming that there is a firmer political, often policy, basis to candidate action and to citizen behavior. I consider the possibility that these two views are not necessarily incompatible, hopeful that a more general theoretical foundation will provide a richer and more realistic account.

The general election campaign is, of course, by far the most studied. In general, this means the study of public opinion and choice, with a rich array of theoretical perspectives to consider. Put alternatively, there is less theoretical—and to an extent empirical—consensus. My overview is focused on aspects of this field that seem to have the most to say about the interaction between candidates and voters. One important question here is whether candidate behavior in the campaign, per se, has much consequence on voter choice. Another question is how, if at all, theory can be comprehensive across the three campaign stages.

The final section asks the question of how these campaign stages affect governance for the successful candidate. In one sense, this section is similar to the first, in which there is relatively less research and, perhaps relatedly, a fairly general scholarly consensus. In another sense, however, the two differ, because the consensus here is over a much smaller scope of theory and evidence.

Candidacy: Who Runs?

There is a single question asked in this section: Who chooses to run for the presidential nomination of a major party? To be sure, the candidates and their staffs do much more in this period, but this "much more" can be considered as part of the next section, asking how candidates run for nomination.

Who runs? is one of the few questions in political science in which there is, as far as I can tell, something approaching consensus, both theoretical and substantive. All scholars employ some version of Schlesinger's ambition theory (1966), often explicitly, or they write in ways that are entirely consistent with it. Substantively, the patterns of candidacy are so well structured that all agree on the empirical regularities. Disagreement, therefore, is over normative questions (e.g., Why don't the great run anymore?) or projections about future trends (e.g., When will a black [woman, Jew, etc.] run and win?) or new rules (e.g., What consequences would a national primary have?). Schlesinger's theory is of ambition—meant in the sense of ordinary, career ambition—applied to the elective political career in particular. Thus, he developed the idea of an opportunity structure, or loose hierarchy of offices, with the presidency at the pinnacle.

Most empirical attention has been given to the manifest office in this structure that is, the office held immediately before running for president. Typical empirical findings are reported by Abramson, Aldrich, and Rohde (1990, table 1), documenting the importance of the Senate, the governorship, and the vice presidency as manifest offices. The last is a new entrant since about World War II; the former two have been shown to be presidential incubators since at least 1876 (Aldrich, 1987a). Peabody, Ornstein, and Rohde (1976) analyze the Senate closely in these terms. The House has never been a major source of candidates (at least since 1876). Aldrich (1987a) also presents evidence on the number and type of offices held by candidates, on the length of time spent in politics, and on the presidential vitae in general (including age, background, etc.) beginning in 1876, thus going deeper into the opportunity structures. The dominant (and surprising) conclusion is how little change there has been since then. The other major contribution Schlesinger makes of relevance is his categorization of types of ambition. Presidential candidacy is, by definition, progressive ambition (excepting only, perhaps, vice presidents who attain the presidency through the death or resignation of the incumbent).[1] Thus, there is no variance here.

Ambition theory is essentially a rational choice theory. It could be considered, in fact, a generalization of the theory underlying those works that assume that reelection is the primary, if not exclusive, goal of elective politicians. Since the effect of the reelection imperative has been studied primarily in the legislative arena (e.g., Mayhew, 1974) rather than the presidential office, little more will be said of this connection. The exceptions are those who study the political-business cycle (e.g., Tufte, 1978; Chappell and Keech, 1985). Here, the argument is that the president or government might manipulate the economy to generate enhanced approval ratings and increased reelection prospects. An analogous cycle might be found in foreign affairs or in rally points (see Mueller, 1973; Ostrom and Job, 1986).

It is not a surprise that a rational choice account of candidacy has become the consensual choice of scholars. The decision to run for a high political office has the characteristics that make rational choice assumptions particularly compelling. It is a decision of great importance to the chooser. The aspirant generally has a great deal of time to consider the decision (compared to crisis decision making, for example). While there are, of course, important unknowns, many of the variables of choice are well known. Experts can be and are consulted, and information is carefully gathered. This or comparable decisions have been made by many others, so learning should be relatively likely. In short, there are means, motives, experience, and regular repetition that all point toward this being a rational choice.[2] I suspect, therefore, that candidates would understand—perhaps even agree with—the assumptions of the theory.

Rohde (1979, building on Black, 1972) formalized ambition theory, casting it into an expected utility maximization problem. Since the Downs (1957) and Riker and Ordeshook (1968) calculus of voting is nearly an exact template, this model can be called the calculus of candidacy. Rohde's formulation explicitly changes one central element of the original theory. Instead of Schlesinger's types of ambition being exogenously given, Rohde endogenizes "static" and "progressive" ambition. He assumes that all officeholders have ambition, per se. Some act as though they held Schlesinger's static ambition because their expected utility calculation (and, therefore, particular circumstances they faced) yields running for reelection to the current office as maximal. Others display apparently progressive ambition simply because running for higher office yields greater expected utility than staying put. Rohde also adds a variable measuring risk-taking proclivities, which he justifies on the grounds that running for a higher office (to the Senate from the House, in his data) is inherently risky.

Tests of Schlesinger's and of Rohde's formulations have consistently yielded strong empirical support, and theoretical plausibility combined with this empirical corroboration explains the scholarly consensus. Direct tests of this model on presidential candidacies (e.g., Aldrich 1980a; Abramson, Aldrich, and Rohde, 1987b) also give strong corroboration of the account.

Many empirical observations, even when not put directly in ambition-theoretic terms, are easily compatible with the theory. For example, the number of serious contenders has been between six and nine since 1972, when the incumbent is not running for nomination in that party. No one has derived nine as a maximum, but it seems a reasonable number (the next entrant would almost certainly have a probability of success under .1, for example). More important, the difference between this "large" number and the one or none who challenge the incumbent is quite compatible with the core model. Also consistent with the core model are the frequencies of candidates in the manifest offices, the high likelihood that senators and governors run when not up for reelection, and the relatively high proportion who run for president unencumbered by currently holding office.[3] The predictions flowing from the ambition theory typically predict the type of person most likely to run, often fairly narrowly defined. The variables employed are generally narrowly political (e.g., current or most recent office, reelection status, etc.). Who does run is, therefore, pretty well understood. Who does *not* run (e.g., Mario Cuomo and Sam Nunn in 1988) is less clear.

The larger set of considerations often invoked—particularly gender, race, religion, and ideology—are also easily consistent with the account. An otherwise similarly situated woman, black, or Jew, for example, faces an additional liability that the comparable white, male Christian does not. Liability can be interpreted as a lower probability of victory or as a greater cost to the candidacy, whether in personal terms or in terms of greater effort and resources needed to convince elites they can win and to convince the public to support them. In sum, there is about as great a consensus around both theory and empirical conclusion in answering Who runs? as there is in any questions in political science. This is, in effect, about as close to an accepted scientific explanation as this discipline is likely to achieve. It is even fair to conclude that there has been cumulation and progress.

I'd like to suggest, however, that the core model is at least partially wrong. First, the election imperative is, like the reelection imperative in the study of Congress, a good but limited approximation. When scholars cite Mayhew (1974), they ordinarily caveat that immediately by citing Fenno (1973) in support of the position that other goals (policy and position or status in Congress) are also material. This is true for presidential candidacies as well. Most candidates have, I believe, strong policy goals (or other, similar nonelection-specific, goals). To be sure, some have them more clearly than others. Certainly, Jesse Jackson's candidacies and campaign actions are incompletely understood by the election imperative but so, too, are the choices of, say, Barry Goldwater, Eugene McCarthy, and George McGovern. A better account, therefore, is of a multivalued set of goals or utilities, with candidates having to face trade-offs (Wittman, 1983, provides a formal structure). Some (many?) may willingly trade off other goals for electoral gain, but not all or not always.

Further, the calculus of candidacy must be transformed from its current decision-theoretic to a true game-theoretic formulation. Banks and Kiewiet do so for a specialized problem in House elections (1989), and this approach may prove a useful template.[4] The reason this may be important is that aspirants decide in part based on strategic considerations. Whether Ted Kennedy would or would not run for nomination in 1972 and 1976 was frequently asked, for example, in part because of the impact his decision would have on the choices of others. Perhaps that decision affected only the probability of success. More likely, it would alter decisions in more fundamental ways, shaping genuine strategies in game-theoretic terms. Finally, and perhaps most important, it would permit a theoretical integration of the twin questions: Who runs? and How do they run? That is, it would make it possible to provide a theoretical basis for analyzing the campaign as a whole. As of now, the decision to run is one question, nomination strategy is a second and all too unrelated question.

Nomination

All agree that the reforms of the presidential nomination process so greatly altered the strategies appropriate for seeking nomination that a new system was created for 1972. The most important change was in greatly increasing the ratio of delegates selected in primary elections to those selected in caucuses or conventions (along with changing financial and other rules). The dramatic increase in the use of primaries has made the seeking of delegate support much more like any other election campaign and much less like an intraparty organizational effort. So profound is this difference that many view it as a new system for nominations. It is a system that, while greatly modified many times since 1972, remains effectively intact.[5] The nomination system is rich and varied, unlike its general election counterpart, which is relatively constant for long periods of time and, at least from the voter's perspective, quite sparse. Much of the work reviewed below is quite comparable with, and in the spirit of, the new institutionalism in political science (whether of the strictly rational choice type, e.g., Shepsle, 1979; or of the more general sort, e.g., March and Olsen, 1984). The nomination system has not been studied in those terms, however, and such a project would be valuable.

The new nomination system has many changeable properties (for overviews, see Crotty and Jackson, 1985; Crotty, 1983; Wayne, 1988). The most salient characteristics, however, are its relative openness to a great variety of candidates and its openness to public participation. Campaigns in the system are long, drawn out, and often highly dynamic—some would even say capricious—affairs. While participation rates are low (25–40 percent turnout is typical in primaries, 5–10 percent in caucuses) and while the nomination is determined by a roll call vote of convention delegates, the effective campaign is between candidate and voter, often conducted through the mass media. Financial reforms have had the much the same effects, accentuating the public nature of nominations.

ANALYSES OF THE SYSTEM, PER SE

One of the most important critiques of the new system is also particularly relevant. The McGovern-Fraser Commission recommendations and subsequent reforms that altered nomination policies, it is claimed, have undermined the political party. (See Polsby, 1983; Kirkpatrick, 1976; and Ranney, 1975, who provides an excellent and more general analysis of the political party. These analyses are a major part of the "decline of parties" literature. See also Broder, 1972; Wattenberg, 1990.) The central argument was that these reforms removed influence entirely from the hands of party leaders and placed it in the hands of the public. At about the same time that the public's identification with parties was weakening, party-line voting in Congress was declining, and legislative power was devolving to subcommittee chairs, the most fundamental act of any party—selection of its standard bearer—was taken from party leadership by their own actions.

There is a great deal of power in these critiques. Historically, our national parties were created around national politics in general and the presidency in particular (see McCormick, 1982). Most important, Andrew Jackson and Martin Van Buren created the first modern mass party in history for the purpose of winning the White House. Loss of leadership influence over the presidential nomination is therefore of great moment. No one disagrees with the claim that party leaders do not exert much influence over presidential nominations, but the remarkably low proportions of Democratic leaders even able to become convention delegates in 1972 and 1976 dramatically documented the assertions.[6] Finally, the consequences of impotent parties are clear. In addition to the above cited critiques, Fiorina (1980) and Jacobson (1987) argue eloquently the consequences of lost collective responsibility in government. The recent interest in, and concern over, the lengthy and unprecedented current run of divided government is another manifestation of parties too weak to carry national elections (see Fiorina, 1990, for a fine recent analysis).

But, did the party reforms really weaken the party? In an underappreciated study, Reiter (1985) demonstrates that virtually all of the alleged indicators of lost influence of party leaders predated the McGovern-Fraser Commission reforms.[7] Thus, the reforms cannot be the *cause* of party decline.

Could the reforms be the *consequence* of party decline? Perhaps. A central feature of national elections, usually thought to have begun in the mid-1960s, is that they are candidate centered. Presidential and congressional candidates alike develop personal campaign organizations for nomination and for election. The formal party apparatus is therefore systematically bypassed. Fund raising, polling, mass mailing (in short, the whole technology of the modern campaign), is led by the candidate and his personal or hired staff. Most important, the candidate-centered campaign is a high-tech, capital-intensive media campaign that needs very little from the traditionally labor-intensive but capital-poor political party.

Nomination campaigns necessarily have a fundamentally candidate-centered nature. Still the idealized image of old, "strong party" presidential nomination campaigns was of a candidate appealing for the support of state and local party leaders who could deliver their delegates, en bloc, for their nomination favorite. To the extent that a presidential contender made a public campaign, it was done through a leader's machine. The quaint-sounding strategy of "going over the heads of the party to the people" was reserved for the party outsider. And it was a losing strategy.

In the decades following World War II, a series of innovations and improvisations fundamentally changed the nature of nomination campaigns. John Kennedy's and Barry Goldwater's campaigns illustrate that, by the 1960s, candidate-centered rather than party-centered campaigns were technologically possible and were potentially successful. Kennedy, for example, used polling extensively, employed media strategies effectively, and developed a massive list of Kennedy supporters throughout the nation for mailings, recruitment, and mobilization. Primary victories, especially in Wisconsin and West Virginia, were important parts of his march toward nomination. Unlike others, such as Estes Kefauver in 1952, who sought primary victories, these were not designed as a strategy of going over the heads of party leaders but as evidence for convincing leaders such as Mayor Richard J. Daley and Governor David Lawrence to support him by demonstrating that his youth, wealth, and religion were not insurmountable electoral liabilities. Four years later, Goldwater's campaign demonstrated that a nationwide network of committed, ideological supporters, coupled with a victory in the California primary, were sufficient to win the nomination in spite of opposition from many Republican leaders (see Kessel, 1968).

The point is not that Kennedy or Goldwater invented the techniques we now associate with candidate-centered campaigns. The point is that they demonstrated that the balance was shifting so that it was no longer necessary to build coalitions of party elites through wheeling and dealing in smoke-filled rooms to win nomination. Candidate-centered methods had come of age and were viable alternatives to the older, party-centered methods. While Hubert H. Humphrey could still win nomination the old-fashioned way in 1968, the resulting costs and divisions were too high. Reforms were needed to create a nomination process compatible with the growing reality of candidate-centered, rather than party-centered, campaigns.

The truth is, perhaps, that nomination reforms postdated weakened parties and reflected the media-dominated, candidate-centered realities, but they also furthered the deterioration. Two of Polsby's consequences of the new nomination system are of particular relevance (1983). First, public contests accentuate intraparty conflict. As Wattenberg (1988) shows, the party with the more divisive nomination campaign loses the general election. Division also may take its toll in governance for the victorious candidate. Second, a public, candidate-centered campaign, even if not bitterly divisive, is an independent campaign. It might be valuable to run as one independent of Washington politics and the party and government establishments, as Polsby suggests, and as Carter and Reagan took pride in articulating. Even so, it places remarkably little value in building alliances with and establishing the support, respect, and trust of those with whom the president must share governance.

CANDIDATE STRATEGY

The new nomination system does not seem to have changed the kinds of candidates who run.[8] Unquestionably, it has changed how they run. Two very different accounts have been proposed: one emphasizes the dynamics of campaigns; the other focuses on substantive concerns, notably policy.

The first stream of research is associated with Aldrich (1980a, 1980b), Bartels (1988), and Brady (1984a, 1984b). The central notion is that the sequential arrangement of primaries creates a dynamic system. Resources invested in a primary increase electoral return. A strong or weak electoral showing, in turn, leads to increased or decreased resources, such as media attention, financial support, campaign volunteer effort, public credibility, and public support. Increased or decreased resources can then be invested in future primaries. The result is a spiral of momentum or decay. This account seems to fit with the broad characteristics of the campaign: emphasis on early primaries, rapid winnowing out of contenders, leaps from unknown to major candidate status, media emphasis on the "horse race," and, perhaps most important, decisiveness.[9] On the latter, it is not obvious why crowded fields of plausible candidates lead, nonetheless, to outright nomination victory in the primary season. Momentum provides the explanation. Gurian (1986) provides a more refined testing, arguing that lesser candidates maximize momentum while front runners maximize delegate acquisition and showing that such an argument is empirically corroborated.

The dynamic account appears to fit well with the surprising victory of the little-known candidate and thus seems to explain Carter's and perhaps McGovern's victories. Some feel that more recent nominations, in which the initially strongest have won, are inconsistent with the account. That is not necessarily so, even in the simplest model of

Aldrich (1980a, 1980b), let alone the more refined models, such as Brady's (1984a, 1984b), It is not an account that predicts that unknowns win. It is an account that predicts that dynamic properties are ever present and that a campaign will ordinarily be decisive before the convention. Front-runners, that is, can benefit from momentum, much as Bush did in 1988.

This basic model, however, is not based on substantive politics. It does not say, for example, how the candidates use the resources to generate support or why voters back the candidates fortunate enough to have momentum. I will return to this topic in considering analyses of voting behavior. For now, it suffices to point out that these models are developed assuming rational candidates. They can, in principle, be compatible with a variety of models of citizens, rational or not.

The second approach emphasizes more substantive concerns. This account is a set of separate pieces, but the outlines of a coherent account are clear enough. Kessel's analysis of presidential "seasons" provides a good introduction (1977). From careful analysis of campaign (and in-office) speeches, Kessel argues that the primary, the general election, and governance seasons are quite distinct. Of most relevance here, he shows that candidates speak about a much greater variety of policy concerns in the primary than in the general election campaign. The primary season looked more like a State of the Union address than the more general platitudes of the fall campaign (see also Page, 1978, for supporting evidence on the fall campaign).

Aranson and Ordeshook (1972) examine a Downsian spatial model of two-party elections in which a candidate adopts a (unidimensional) policy platform for both the nomination season and the general election. Assuming that the two sets of partisans who choose in the nomination season are relatively homogenous liberals and conservatives (that is, ideal points concentrated toward the two extremes relative to the full electorate), their model analyzes the trade-off, for candidates and for partisans, of the competing pressures to nominate a candidate toward the center of the party versus nominating one at the center of the full electorate.[10] That the best strategy is moderate divergence (that is, location between the party's and electorate's centers) fits well with Page's evidence that presidential nominees reflect varying degrees of these party cleavages (1978). It is also consistent with the evidence of how state convention delegates decide (e.g., Stone and Abramowitz, 1983), but whether that prediction extends to models with less restrictive assumptions (notably to multidimensional policy spaces) is unclear. Brams (1978) examines Downsian spatial models with multiple candidacies. One of the more interesting cases he analyzes is of how candidates near the center of their party (ideal for nomination in a two-candidate race) can lose by being squeezed from right and left.[11]

The importance of such models lies in two areas. First, they provide an account in which substance plays a major role in campaign strategy. Second, they provide a possible method for linking the nomination campaign with the general election campaign—and even with the Who runs? decision.[12] Before proceeding further, however, let us turn to the voter, for these two approaches to candidate strategy in nomination campaigns seem to rest on vastly different views of the public.

PRIMARY VOTERS

Apparently paralleling the two views of campaign strategy, empirical research on the primary electorate can be grouped into two different camps.[13] One stream of research sees the voter as ill informed, attuned to the horse race, possibly capricious, and perhaps vulnerable to manipulation. The other research finds a more substantive basis for voter choice.

The rapid fluctuations in candidate's standings in public opinion polls provides a plausibility to the first account. Keeter and Zukin (1983) wrote what I believe to be the first extended analysis of voting in primaries. Sordid details need not detain us. That they titled their book *The Failure of the New Nominating System* and that they wrote that they considered entitling it *The Random Voter* indicates their point of view. Central features include rapidly fluctuating preferences, low indicators of knowledge of candidates and what they stand for, the apparent desire to back winners, per se, and the willingness to offer evaluations (e.g., rate candidates on "feeling" thermometers) without much knowledge underlying those evaluations. Others also seek a policy or general ideological basis for primary voter choice—and find little (e.g., Gopoian, 1982; Shanks et al., 1985).

The other stream of research finds a more substantive basis for voter choice. No one argues for an enlightened voter. Wattier (1983) applies the Kelley-Mirer "simple act of voting" model (1974; see also

Kelley, 1983) to the primary voter and finds that it works about as well in the primary as in the general election.[14] Others produce evidence that, at least from time to time and place to place, issues or ideology are related to primary choice. Aldrich and Alvarez (1990), for example, apply a model drawn from the social-cognitive, political psychology perspective (see Rahn et al., 1990), finding that it fit primary choices in 1988 nearly as well as it did for the Reagan-Mondale vote. Abramson, Aldrich, and Rohde (1987a) suggest that the Democratic public could see (sensible) differences between Walter Mondale and Gary Hart on policy emphasis and in terms of who would best solve particular problems but did not see much difference between their issue stances, per se. They also suggest that these differences were related to choice.

Brady and Conley (1988) provide a slightly different view. They test an expected utility model in which voters have fairly stable preferences of candidates and shift voting intentions as candidates' probabilities of nomination shift. Abramson et al. (1992) also provide evidence of this kind of sophisticated voting, using data from the NES survey of the Super Tuesday electorate. Abramowitz (1989) finds support for an expected utility model based on exit poll data from the 1988 Georgia primary. These cases, then, provide a possible method of combining substantive politics with the horse race. What is unclear is whether utility models are well grounded in politics. Each author, however, provides some evidence that preferences over candidates are relatively stable over time, suggesting they may be less ephemeral than Keeter and Zukin find them to be.

The most important work on the primary votes has been done by Bartels (1988). His work is also a mixture of expectations and political bases of choice. For example, he argues that evaluations of Walter Mondale in 1984 were rather well formed and predictable from the usual political variables from the beginning. Evaluations of Gary Hart, however, were originally (that is, through New Hampshire and Super Tuesday) *not* based on Hart or his campaign positions. Instead, those who evaluated Hart most highly were Democrats who most disliked Mondale. In effect, Hart was the repository of anti-Mondale sentiment. Later, however, evaluations of Hart became more sensible—and based on factors different from those used in evaluating Mondale. Perhaps, then, Democrats learned something over the course of the campaign and turned support for Hart from its anti-Mondale base to support based on Hart's own appeals.

It should be noted that Bartel's equations predicting candidate evaluations are rather weak (that is, have rather low R^2s), and this kind of finding is echoed in other work (e.g., Aldrich and Alvarez, 1990). There may be a good reason for this. The NES primary electorate surveys use questions drawn from the general election survey, for the most part. Issue scales are identical in the two. The instrument, therefore, is appropriate for interparty competitions. If intraparty differences (among candidates and perhaps among voters) are small on these essentially party-cleaving concerns, then the instrument will reveal little substantive bases of choice. An instrument designed around intraparty differences would be a better bet.

It may be that the primary voter's choice is which representative of a fairly homogenous party is the best nominee. Perhaps, then, different criteria are relevant in primaries and in general elections. Position on issues, for example, may be less relevant. In its place, the primary voter may be more likely to back the contender who comes closest to sharing the voter's concerns. Mondale and Hart, in this analysis, may have stood similarly on policy, but they did—and may have been seen to—differ in their priorities. Such an analysis reconciles the Abramson, Aldrich, Rohde (1987a) results, for example, with those who claim insubstantial bases of choice. It would also explain why the open-ended results of Wattier or the more candidate-centered results of Aldrich and Alvarez paint a picture of the primary voter more nearly on a par with the general election voter.

The expected utility accounts, then, provide a bridge at the level of the electorate between the fluctuating, horse-race-attuned voter and the substantively political voter. Such a bridge is also possible at the level of candidate strategy. Momentum and substance need not be considered incompatible. Bartel's account of Mondale and Hart, for instance, may be that the well-known and strong candidacy of Mondale attracted his potential support from the outset. The anti-Mondale vote, therefore, went to Hart for two reasons: he quickly became the strongest alternative, and he was clearly different from Mondale politically. Thus, John Glen failed the first test; he wasn't successful enough. Others, Alan Cranston or other Mondale-like liberals also failed the second test: they weren't different enough from

Mondale. Had Hart articulated Mondale-like positions, he might not have benefited from support from those opposed to what Mondale stood for. Philip Crane in 1980 pronounced himself a younger Reagan conservative. Anti-Reagan votes went to George Bush or John Anderson, not to Crane. Thus, in the spirit of expected utility calculations, viability and substance may interact.

The General Election Campaign

The general election campaign, or at least voting behavior in it, is far more studied than the topics already covered, and it is much less consensual. It is impossible to summarize voting behavior, so my review is much more selective. Fortunately, good reviews already exist (e.g., Converse, 1975; Asher, 1983, 1988).

Candidate strategy, per se, is not exceptionally well studied. To be sure, there are analyses of where candidates compete, such as in tests of the impact of the electoral college on candidate resource allocations (see Brams and Davis, 1974; Colantoni, Levesque, and Ordeshook, 1975; Hinich and Ordeshook, 1974), what they say (notably Page, 1978), and how they say it (e.g., Wayne, 1988; West, 1984, who examine nomination and general election campaigns). These sorts of studies, while useful (and excepting Page's analysis) tend to have relatively little of general interest to say to political science because campaign strategy and tactics are broadcast (or at least candidates know they might be broadcast) nationwide. Media studies are much more extensive (e.g., Arterton, 1984; Graber, 1984; Iyengar and Kinder, 1987; Shapiro et al., 1990), but I'll have little to say beyond noting them. My focus is on candidate, voter, party, and governance.

There are a few studies that try to relate candidate strategy and voter choice. Gant (1983), Aldrich and Weko (1988), and Weko and Aldrich (1990), for example, seek such a correspondence. Their results suggest that there is a correspondence observable in public opinion surveys. These are essentially systematic versions of more general, sometime even journalistic accounts of candidates and voter strategies, sometimes accompanied by fairly careful poll analysis designed to illustrate such a correspondence (e.g., Hershey, 1989).

Kessel has produced a series of works (1968, 1980, 1984, 1988) that provide the most systematic studies of the relationship among candidate strategy, campaign coalitions, and public response. His work is systematic both in covering all campaigns from 1964 through 1988 (and covering elections from 1952 through 1988) and in covering an array of the elements of candidate strategies followed within campaigns. Often based on interviews with campaign managers and always based on surveys of voters' evaluations and choices, he is able to link the intended strategy with public reaction. Moreover, by adroit use of likes or dislikes questions, he is able to make comparisons over the last ten presidential elections. Given, for example, his constant measurement procedures, his demonstration is convincing that policy evaluations and their impact on voter choice have grown significantly over the last four decades. Later, I review findings that show that the candidates' presentations of policy choices are related to actions taken by victors in office. Kessel's demonstration of increased policy sensitivity and issue voting by the public, therefore, implies that the relevance of candidate strategy to governance is perhaps increasing the linkage between the public's policy preferences and actions taken by the federal government.

Many journalists and academics argue that campaigns are irrelevant. Lichtman and DeCell (1990), for example, make a strong empirical argument that the determinants of voter choice are well in place before the campaign gets going. Theirs is perhaps the strongest version of this account. They correctly "predict" all presidential winners from 1860 to 1988 based almost entirely on precampaign variables (most of which are actions of the incumbent or his party over the preceding two to four years). Their theory is consistent with many theories of voter choice that finds most of the action precedes the campaign. The earliest empirical voting studies (Berelson et al., 1954; Lazarsfeld et al., 1948) find most of the sample voters knew (correctly) for whom they would vote before the campaign began.

Theories based on partisanship, on political business cycles, and on retrospective voting all leave room for some campaign effects, but all are based on early socialization or on actual political events that go far in explaining voters' choices before the campaign begins. Social, psychological, and the recent spate of social-cognitive accounts are not, at least at this point, strongly connected with candidate strategy. At present, they are stronger in accounting for the world inside the voter's mind then with the external world. Only Downsian spatial models are developed around the question of how candidates and voters interact, and their empirical pedigree is suspect (but see Erikson and Romero, 1990). At best, the basic spatial premise (one votes for the closer candidate) is taken to be but one of many forces affecting voters' choices. So except, perhaps, for a Goldwater or a McGovern, only at the empirical extremes is there a clear connection between candidates and voters (and even these instances have been challenged).

Generally, it would seem likely that a campaign strategy will be more successful the more heavily it is based in, and drawn from, the political world voters have encountered. Moreover, if both candidates are employing the best available strategies, they well may be confronting each other's strategies, point by point, thus tending to cancel out each other's strongest points. Only if one candidate employs an effective strategy and the other does not (or cannot, having no good one available) may we then observe effects attributable to the campaign itself. I return to this question in the concluding section.

VOTERS AND PARTISANSHIP

The core concept of the work of Campbell et al. (1960, 1964) has been challenged in many ways. Partisanship nonetheless remains as a central feature of the electoral landscape—and is undoubtedly why it remains the concept to challenge. While each has been questioned, the central properties of the core concept retain force: its transmission and early acquisition, its relative stability and durability, its relationship to other attitudes and perceptions, and its consequential, if largely indirect, role in behavior.

Early voter choice models of the statistical sort modeled party identification as purely exogenous of and prior to short-term attitudes, notably issues and candidates' evaluations. Richer statistical models (e.g., Page and Jones, 1979), however, were some of the best demonstrations that it is endogenous. MacKuen et al. (1989) provide a powerful and eloquent demonstration of its dynamic endogeneity at the aggregate level.[15] This analysis lends itself especially to the retrospective interpretation of partisanship. Of even more importance, and presumably related, is the declining strength of attachment of partisanship (see, esp., Wattenberg, 1990). Playing an integral role in the decline of party or dealignment thesis, the rise of independence and decline of strong partisanship conspire, not to change the impact of party, but to make that impact slighter for larger numbers of voters.

Endogeneity and declining significance help to mute the empirical consequences of partisanship and, of course, raise theoretical questions. Other scholars propose alternative theories of partisanship. The social cognitive approach views the electorate as cognitive misers. It is led, therefore, to search for informational shortcuts and other methods of reducing decision costs (see Fiske and Taylor, 1984; Hastie, 1986). Partisanship, therefore, may be seen as a schema or other cognitive structure to achieve these ends (see Hamill, Lodge, and Blake, 1985; Lodge and Hamill, 1986). It is not clear at present that this account leads to much different theoretical analysis, but its cognitive, instead of the original affective, basis may result in significantly different arguments. At very least, it leads to a different interpretation of the same evidence.

Fiorina (1981) has developed the most elaborate theoretical alternative and provides a great deal of evidence in support of his rational choice account. In developing the theory of retrospective voting (discussed more fully below), he views partisan affiliation as a long-term running tally of political memories of partisan relevance. Achen (1989) extends and sharpens this model, viewing partisanship as a part of a Bayesian decision. He calls this a prospective theory, but it should be seen as an elaboration of Fiorina's retrospective account. The difference hinges on Fiorina's relative emphasis on the Bayesian prior distribution (although that's not how he puts it) and Achen's and Fiorina's use of the prior distribution in reaching new decisions. Achen's more precise model allows him to deduce a large array of hypotheses that are often empirical regularities long observed.

It is unclear just what all this means for the candidate. If partisanship is endogenous, cognitively based, or subject to reevaluation retrospectively and prospectively, a candidate—especially a presidential candidate—can be assumed to be able to modify partisanship in the electorate. It is unlikely this could be done rapidly, except in the entirely sensible (rational?) case of black partisanship in the 1960s. Over the course of a four- or eight-year incumbency, however, there may be enough time to move partisanship consequentially. Indeed, it seems the Reagan years did just that. Partisanship did not change permanently in 1980–1981, but it did change substantially around

1984 in a pro-Republican direction (see Norpoth, 1987). Abramson, Aldrich, and Rohde (1990), for example, calculate that had Bush faced the same partisan distribution as Gerald Ford faced in 1976 (and as Reagan faced in 1980), he would have received about the same vote as Ford, ceteris paribus. At least, then, Bush appears to owe his comfortable margin to Reagan's impact on an endogenous partisanship.[16] Thus, it is unlikely that even a powerful presidential candidate can change partisanship in the short run (but see Allsop and Weisberg, 1988), and be able to manipulate it for election or re-election ends. Under some conditions, however, a successful president may be able to manipulate endogenous partisanship to the long-term advantage of his party.

ISSUES

The relative decline in importance of partisanship that began in the mid-1960s meant that something had to replace it in our theories. Issues appeared a likely possibility, and indeed, studies of issue voting took off at that time (see Kessel, 1972, for a measure of their volume). While issue voting remains a staple topic, it seems not to have filled the void. Pomper (1975), for example, shows that issue voting did increase—but only modestly.

Part of the interest in issues was due to the new, seven-point scale, measurement. It was this measure, for example, that Page and Jones (1979) use to show partisanship's endogeneity to issue evaluations (and vice versa). Certainly, the heightened salience of civil rights, urban problems, and the Vietnam War mattered—and these issues lent themselves to positional measurement. The economic and foreign concerns of the 1970s and 1980s seem more appropriate for retrospective voting, since neither candidates nor voters disagree over the desired outcome—they disagree over how to achieve them. And since means in these cases are especially complex (and uncertain) a "what has worked (or failed)" retrospective outlook is plausible. These positional issue scales, however, lent themselves to demonstrations of rationalization in ways open-ended measures could not (see Brody and Page, 1972; Page and Brody, 1972).

Theory also affected the study of issue voting. This was the time of most intellectual progress in spatial modeling (e.g., Davis, Hinich, and Ordeshook, 1970). While spatial modeling continues (see

Enelow and Hinich, 1984; Erikson and Romero, 1990) early enthusiasm passed. Even rational choice modelers turned to other accounts, such as political-business cycles or retrospective voting.

Issue voting in general and spatial modeling in particular are nearly unique in electoral research in developing close connections between candidate and voter behavior. At the very least, it provided a theoretical understanding of the importance of the policy center for winning votes. It also laid out precisely the trade-offs facing candidates with more refined objectives than merely winning the general election, such as policy motivations (Wittman, 1983; Calvert, 1985), the need to win nomination (Aranson and Ordeshook, 1972), and the value of party support in general (Aldrich and McGinnis, 1989).

Moreover, spatial modeling changed our understanding of the relationship between issues and the vote. The proximity measurement—how close is one candidate's (or party's) position to the voter's desired policy compared to the opponent's proximity to the voter—is now the discipline standard. Direct correlation between the respondent's issue position and the vote, the originally preferred measure, is now seen only as the best approximation when candidates' positions are unavailable.

Rabinowitz and Macdonald (1989) challenge the proximity model of issue voting and therefore the Downsian spatial model. They argue for a directional model in which voters choose the candidate or party promising to move policy in the direction favored by the voter, regardless (within broad limits) of how far. This model has several important differences from the proximity model. A moderate liberal, for example, might be closer (that is, more proximate) to a moderately conservative candidate but would, in their model, vote for a more extreme liberal, because that candidate would move policy in the preferred direction. Indeed, moderate liberals would vote for an extreme liberal (within their imposed bounds, at least) even in favor of a candidate who adopts their own position. Second, they show that the best position for candidates or parties is toward extremes, not in the policy center. Indeed, the center may be the worst place for a candidate or party. Third, their empirical tests of the directional and proximity models yield consistently greater empirical support for their formulation than for proximity measures in a variety of electoral data, including the standard NES data for presidential elections.[17]

More recently, Macdonald and Rabinowitz (1989) proposed a probabilistic basis for directional voting in which issues are valence rather than proximity issues. This model (transforming seven-point issue measures into a form more congenial to voters' perceptions of issues, if their model is correct) bears some resemblance to retrospective models, at least in one sense. Retrospective voting models generally assume that there is a general consensus on ends (all want peace and prosperity, honesty, etc.) and that voters are choosing the candidate or party that seems more likely to deliver on that end. The newer formulation by Macdonald and Rabinowitz might, therefore, be seen as a generalization of this aspect of retrospective voting to include new issues lacking a track record of performance.[18]

RETROSPECTIVE VOTING

Downs (1957) and Key (1966) offer two very different versions of retrospective voting. Key's theory is essentially a pure retrospective model in which the voter is a rational god of vengeance or of reward, whose vote is strictly based on the incumbent's performance in office. In this view, at least in its extreme form, the challenger does not matter at all, only the voter's view of the incumbent. Moreover, the campaign and its promises matter not at all (at least at the extreme), nor even the incumbent's intentions or circumstances. Of course, Key would not hold to this extreme an interpretation, but the extreme presentation highlights its central features. Lichtman and DeCell (1990) use something similar to this model to "predict" every election since 1860 correctly. Key's view also fits fairly closely to Riker's (1982) version of "Madisonian liberal democracy" in contrast to populist democracy.

The Downsian view (also Fiorina's, 1981) is that prior performance is good, hard evidence about at least one of the options and evidence that is easily and cheaply acquired. For both of these reasons, then, retrospective evaluations should tend to be weighed very heavily in voter decision making. Decision making, however, is both comparative (i.e., involves comparing one candidate or party with the other) and prospective (i.e., trying to choose which option will be the better choice for the coming term). Thus, the dominance of retrospective evaluations is, essentially, an empirical claim in the Downs-Fiorina view about what evidence tends to predominant in a choice between alternatives for determining who appears to be the better president for the next four years.

Fiorina (1981) adds a great deal to the original, terse, Downsian concept. In particular, he argues that prior performance is an even more likely empirical basis for evaluation in areas in which policy is unusually complex (e.g., how to control inflation), in which there is agreement on ends but not (complex) means (e.g., would the MX or Midget Man missiles be a superior deterrent, given that all want to deter nuclear war), and for which "prospective" and "means" information may be unavailable (e.g., classified). Again, this is basically an empirical claim about the nature of issues and of information and its. processing.

Whether Key's or Down's view of retrospective evaluations is more plausible is also an empirical question. Fiorina (1981) supplies a great deal of empirical support for the Downs-Fiorina version. The Abramson-Aldrich-Rohde series (1983, 1987a, 1990) also consistently provides evidence that the Downsian formulation fares well. The Lichtman-DeCell (1990) estimates are largely Key-like and impressive, if based on aggregate data. They do, however, include some room for comparison between contenders directly (and, presumably, more so indirectly), and their results may be taken as a demonstration of the empirical dominance of retrospective information.

Retrospective models have generally focused on policy concerns, in general, and on economic and (to a lesser extent) foreign policy concerns, in particular. Neither policy nor economic and foreign policy focuses are required by the theory. Indeed, the Fiorina-Achen version of partisanship and Fiorina's use of "mediated" evaluations, such as presidential approval, implicitly open the account to virtually any kind of evaluations. For example, Democratic beneficiaries of the 1974 (Watergate) congressional election owed their victories in some degree to the corruption of the opponent's presidential administration. It also appears that Carter benefited in some measure from Watergate—and Ford's pardon of Nixon. Especially under Fiorina's view of partisanship, other kinds of policies can be understood in this fashion. For example, any Democrat (at least outside the South) might be perceived initially as in favor of civil rights until, and unless, voters are given good reason to the contrary. This comes quite close to Key's idea of partisanship as a standing decision—to favor the candidate of one's party, under the assumption that the two contenders hold traditional party stances, until and unless given good reasons (that is, from being exposed to and attending to information to the contrary) to believe otherwise. George Bush's use of the "*L* word" strategy appears consistent with a candidate basing strategy on this view.

Retrospective evaluations appear to be more consequential in predicting voters' choices than prospective proximity-based issues. A possible implication of this is that the campaign, or at least the parties' and candidates' policy platforms (i.e., promises for the future), are of relatively lesser consequence then events that actually transpired over the last term. There are two caveats, however. First, as Miller and Wattenberg (1985) remind us, virtually any policy measure is likely to be a complex combination of what has been done and what candidates say they are going to do, making pure measures hard to come by. Of course, the Downs-Fiorina view is that retrospective evaluations are used for inferences about platforms and future performance, so that, theoretically, pure measures should be nearly impossible to come by. Second, the campaign may, in larger or smaller part, be conducted in terms of retrospective evaluations. It may be that the relative impact of particular retrospective or prospective measures within any given election and the absolute level of them across elections vary, in part based on the strategies of the candidates in the campaign. Prior performance may be part of the raw material of a campaign, but it may affect voter choice in varying degrees, to the extent that one or both candidates make prior performance central to their campaign.

CANDIDATE EVALUATION

The third of the "big three" electoral forces is the voter's evaluations of the two candidates. This has been noted virtually from the outset of survey research on voter choice (e.g., Stokes, Campbell, and Miller, 1958), just as it has long been argued that the net impact of candidate evaluations is probably the largest and most variable of the three sets of electoral components (e.g., Stokes, 1966). For example, an alternative explanation of McGovern's landslide defeat to his relatively extreme policy position is the unfavorable evaluations held of him as compared to Nixon (Miller et al., 1976; indeed, unfavorable opinions of McGovern might have led to overly extreme perceptions of his policy positions; see Page, 1978).

For a long time, however, candidate evaluations were seen as the most malleable of short-term forces. While there was, of course, a belief that the candidate's actual personal characteristics shaped those evaluations (e.g., Dwight Eisenhower *was* a war hero who was not greatly experienced in politics), there was also the possibility that candidate evaluations were "images," vulnerable to manipulation by clever campaign strategy (often with reference to McGinnis, 1969). Moreover, there was relatively little theoretical work in this area, compared to the theoretical development of party identification and of issue voting. Thus, while elections were understood to be increasingly candidate centered, there was less development of the most candidate-centered evaluations of all.

The transference of social cognition in (social) psychology to political psychology offered a theoretical approach to candidate evaluation. Social cognition is not a theory of candidate evaluation, per se. Indeed, it has been fruitfully employed in the study of partisanship (Hamill, Lodge, and Blake, 1985; Lodge and Hamill, 1986), issues and ideology (Aldrich, Sullivan, and Borgida, 1989; Conover and Feldman, 1984; Feldman and Conover, 1983), and even as a full, information-processing theory of voter choice, per se (Lodge, McGraw, and Stroh, 1989; Rahn et al., 1990). The impact of social cognition on the study of candidate appraisal has been especially consequential, however. One reason for its importance is that it is, effectively, the only theory of candidate evaluations. In addition, an important context for applying social cognition was "person perception," and that easily could be transferred to "candidate perception."

This theory has been used to address two kinds of questions about candidate evaluations. First, what are the dimensions of candidate evaluations? Kinder, alone and with associates, has done a lot of work in this area, from empirically mapping the terrain derived from a battery of questions about candidate attributes included in NES surveys, to developing a prototype of the ideal president (Kinder, 1978, 1986; Kinder and Fiske, 1986; see also Lau, 1986). A second question is how substantial and political (or politically relevant) are these evaluations. In effect, this latter question is a response to the McGinnis-like notion that "candidates can be packaged and sold like soap flakes." In general, the kinds of evaluative dimensions that emerge, their stability, and the seeming importance of task-oriented evaluations over the more purely personal evaluations, among other indicators, suggest that there is a strong (although certainly far from complete) substantive and political component to these evaluations overall.

The recency of serious application of social cognitive approaches to electoral behavior may make it understandable that applications tell us more about individual voters than about their aggregation and about the connections, if any, to what politicians and candidates actually do. Of course, psychologists' natural emphasis on individual differences and on true experimentation may make such a leap methodologically more difficult. We can, however, imagine (and with some evidence) how a social cognitive account might indeed result in a clearer understanding of the impact of a campaign, or political events more generally, on an electorate composed of social cognition theory's "cognitive misers" or its more recent formulation as "motivated tacticians" (see Fiske, chap. 6). I'll explore this set of possibilities in the conclusion, along with a more general view of candidates' campaigning and voter response.

The Campaign and Governance

The relationship between electoral choice and governance is at the very heart of democratic theory. It is very difficult, however, to study this in a specific and concrete way. Thus, it has not received a great deal of attention. A number of specific accounts and a large volume of general work are relevant. One distinction that should be kept in mind is whether the analysis focuses on whether (or to what extent) electoral opinion and behavior shape or constrain the actions of the victor directly or whether (or to what extent) the president or candidate chooses in light of expected electoral response and, thus, are constrained more indirectly. Presidential and perhaps candidate actions also may shape electoral response more actively. Further, of special relevance for the more general concerns is whether the focus is on the president, per se, or the president as a key actor in government (especially in congressional-presidential relations), or seeing the president as the party's standard-bearer (and therefore potentially constrained by, say, party voting).

Most analyses focus on the relationship between campaign promises and actions taken by the victor or on relationships forged between the candidate and other partisan or political figures in nomination and general election campaigns and their consequences for facilitating or hindering the formulation of effective governing coalitions. Other relationships, however, are often mentioned. One is how much the campaign reveals about the candidate as a decision maker. It is common, for example, to wonder whether decisions made during the campaign provide insight into the patterns and styles that will be followed in the White House. McGovern's handling of the revelation that his running mate in 1972, Thomas Eagleton, had undergone electroshock therapy is alleged to have revealed flaws that may have proven costly in a president. It is also attributed as a central reason for the declining public evaluations of him as a candidate. This sort of concern also raises the question of whether the trials endured in the nomination and general election campaigns provide a useful diagnostic test of the qualities needed to be a successful president. Polsby's concern (1983) that current campaign processes undervalue the coalition-building skills needed to work effectively with Congress and the bureaucracy is one important illustration.

A second example is that key campaign advisers often become key presidential advisers, much as James Baker and John Sununu did in the Bush campaign and presidency. Thus, it is widely suspected that the organization and staffing of a campaign are likely to provide a strong indication of who will be consequential actors in the victor's administration. What is less systematically investigated is whether the way these people operate the campaign translates into how the White House will operate. In addition, some campaign operatives do not go to Washington, and many new (and often important) people are hired who did not play a key, if any, role in the campaign. It is therefore unclear how these people will be organized and what procedures they will use to reach decisions.

What has been more systematically investigated than style, management, and personnel is whether the candidate's actions in the campaign constrain his conduct in office. Are campaign promises taken seriously by the victor when in office? Here, both Pomper and Lederman (for executive elections generally, 1980) and Fishel (1985) provide convincing evidence that presidents do tend to take action, often substantial steps, to implement a large majority of their campaign promises. This set of empirical observations does not tell us, of course, whether presidential candidates are simply telling us what they want to do or whether they feel a special obligation to honor public commitments when in office. Whatever the reasons, however, we can take this as evidence that the elected president does ordinarily try to take action on a great deal of that which he claimed he would do in the campaign (for evidence that public opinions seems to drive governmental decisions, see Page and Shapiro 1983, 1990). This question is, of course, of genuine substantive importance. It has also been addressed systematically, in part because platforms and party cleavages on policy transcend individual cases. This systematic nature contrasts with style, management, and personnel decisions, which are likely to vary in a random way from president to president.

Taking action on campaign promises does not mean, of course, that the president succeeds in this effort. There are a great variety of institutional constraints that will modify the smooth transition from promise to action to outcome. To address this systematically is to write an essay on virtually all of American government, so I'll only illustrate some of these concerns briefly.

First, there is the presidency as an office, constraining power in and of itself. Neustadt's famous dictum (1980), that presidential power is the power to persuade, has long shaped our understanding of the presidency. More recently Lowi (1985) has argued of the growing complexity of a decentralized government and party system for making the president at once more central to the systems' expectations of action and also more powerless to move a complex government. Heclo's analysis of bureaucracy (1977) reminds us that the chief executive faces difficulty in getting even his erstwhile subordinates to act in line with his desires. Light (1982) points out the irony that the president is most likely to be effective early in his term (e.g., during the honeymoon period) but is least likely to know precisely what to do and how to do it at that time. In short, this most powerful office yields highly constrained power by its own institution and by its relationship to other institutions. Countering this set of arguments is Kernell's argument (1986) of the increasing effectiveness of going public—marshaling public opinion directly and, through approval ratings, indirectly—to bend the rest of government to the president's will.

Historically, political parties were organized for the purpose of capturing the presidency, primarily, and the rest of government, secondarily. This, at least, is the claim of many political historians, an argument made most forcefully by McCormick (1982). The party, in this view, was in part a vehicle for presidential leadership, but it was also, and probably in greater part, a major constraint on the president. Electorally, the president owed much of his success to the party as it shaped electoral opinion and behavior. Nomination was frequently secured due to the support of key party leaders, and they often placed demands on the victor that limited his freedom to act as he saw fit. If these indicate constraints due to the party-in-the-electorate and the party-as-organization, the party-in-government also helped constrain the president. Indeed, as Kernell points out (1986), Neustadt's "power to persuade" makes the most sense when the president must negotiate with a relatively small number of clearly defined leaders, especially in Congress, and that is most likely in a party-dominated Congress.

Today, if it is true that the party shapes electoral opinion and behavior less, if there are fewer and less powerful party organizational leaders, and if partisan or any other source of power in Congress is highly decentralized, then the party constrains the president much less. Indeed, Lowi's and Kernell's and related arguments can be seen as, in effect, the consequences of a dealigned or declined party era for the president. So, the good news is that the president has much greater room to maneuver. For one example, a strong, successful presidential candidate can shape how the electorate perceives the political party. Perhaps this is best illustrated by Reagan on the positive side and McGovern and Carter on the negative. The bad news is that greater room to maneuver is accompanied by a more muddled, decentralized government. The complexity of such a system overwhelms the president, as it does all others, making freedom to choose unaccompanied by ability to succeed. Of course, much of this literature on the extended consequences of too-weak parties was based on experience through 1980. The resurgence of the party in Congress (see Rohde, 1991) and as a formal organization (see Cotter et al., 1984) presents a different mix of good and bad news for presidents.

If there is general consensus that (1) campaign promises are related to presidential actions and (2) parties and other institutions constrain the ability of presidents to succeed in those actions, there is one more observation about which consensus seems high. The campaign creates an opportunity for the president to shape governance in important ways. This ability, however, depends on two further conditions. First, the campaign helps the president succeed only with promises that were central to the campaign. In other words, the campaign promises must have been clearly made and must have been central to the victor's campaign themes. Part of the postelection aftermath is a battle, conducted via propaganda and internal politics, to define just what the mandate was. There is some room, for example, for a president to claim which of his campaign emphases was the reason for his victory. Thus, Reagan was successful in 1981 in claiming a mandate for increased defense spending, decreased spending for domestic policies, and cuts in income tax rates. He did not try as hard to translate social concerns, such as his set of profamily and prochoice positions, into an electoral mandate. He may not have been able to do so. To claim an electoral mandate, a candidate must emphasize a policy in the campaign and have it apparently receive a favorable response from the electorate.

Second, a significant number of members of Congress must have seen the pledges as central to the president's campaign—and equally important to their own fortunes (see Jacobson,1985). Thus, for example, Johnson's 1964 landslide was based on the promise of a Great Society, and that landslide brought many into Congress who could reasonably believe that the Great Society was an important part of their victory. The same may have been true in 1980. The Boll Weevils also could have concluded that opposition to the central elements of Reagan's 1980 platform might cost them their seats in 1982. Reagan in 1984 and Bush in 1988 could claim sweeping victory but not a mandate, since neither were promises made in the campaign (at least centrally) nor were there presidential coattails then or any expected in the next election.

Recently, a number of scholars have examined the lengthy experience we have been having with divided government. To be sure, divided government depends upon weak parties, but these analysts are really studying the relationship between the president and Congress. Some of these models simply begin with the assumption that officeholders do what they promise in the campaign (e.g., Fiorina, 1988). Divided government in these models is the consequence of intentional electoral choice. Given, for example, a conservative president, the rational response of key swing voters in the center will be to vote liberals into Congress so that the net effect is a compromise between a conservative president and a liberal Congress, yielding moderate policies. While there is a huge hole in these models (why don't or won't candidates moderate?), they at least present a case for divided government being more than the confusion that follows from weak parties—that is, a reasoned action for the purpose of intentionally moderating policies.

Conclusion: Toward an Integrated Account of Presidential Selection

The temporal nature of presidential selection provides a tidy partition of the literature. From a theoretical perspective, the partitioning is too tidy, because not just the empirical results but theoretical developments are partitioned into the presidential season being studied. That is, there is too little theory that ties together the four parts reviewed in this chapter. By way of conclusion, therefore, I propose a theoretical framework for uniting these seasons into a more unified and integrated account. I do so in three steps. The first step focuses on what I believe to be the central problem in studying the presidency in general, as well as in studying presidential selection in particular. This is the problem of specifying the goals of presidential contenders and victors in a way that is sufficiently general to unite the various seasons and yet sufficiently precise for adequate theorizing. The second step is to propose a way to think about campaign strategy and its effects based on a mixture of rational choice and cognitive psychological theories. The final step, supposing goals have been specified adequately, is to work backward from the campaign to the decision to run and to work forward to an accounting of the impact of campaign strategy on governance.

The first step, then, is to consider the problem of goals. Mayhew's study of Congress (1974) has been influential because of the persuasiveness of his argument that the imperatives of election and reelection shape not only candidate behavior but also the behavior of incumbents when in office. Indeed, he argues that it shapes the nature of congressional institutions. The electoral connection is a valuable theoretical foundation precisely because so many incumbents do seek reelection regularly and often. The same cannot be said for presidents. Formally, all second-term presidents cannot be understood as reelection seekers. First-termers could be so understood in principle. It is certainly true that first-term presidents (almost) invariably seek reelection, and it is undoubtedly the rare instance when major decisions are not considered, in part, in terms of their electoral consequences. But that is only one part and often not the most important one. An explanation of, say, Bush's decision to strike a budget compromise that included new taxes, or an explanation of his decisions about the war in the Persian Gulf based exclusively, or even primarily, on reelection considerations would, to say the least, strain credulity.

An attraction of the study of presidential approved ratings is that it is reasonable to assume that presidents desire higher approval ratings, ceteris paribus. In some measure, then, approval ratings provide a sort of continuous "election by other means." But the value of high approval ratings is rarely understood as an end in itself but is, instead, understood as an instrumental end. Going public is useful for persuading Congress or the bureaucracy to do what the president desires. It does not tell us what it is the president desires. It is also common to suppose that presidents, particularly in their second term, are concerned about their "place in history," but that is far too ambiguous to analyze directly.

Presidential approval studies often suggest that the president is held accountable for peace, prosperity, and tranquility. Perhaps presidents are so motivated themselves. If not so directly, then securing those three aims is likely to yield reelection, high approval ratings, and a solid (or better) place in history. Peace, prosperity, and tranquility are at least more specific standards for evaluating presidential actions, thus representing some progress, albeit too little for genuine theorizing. Much remains for more exact study, through, for example, attention to the role of ideology, partisan beliefs, and the like. The trick is more usefully to specify these three aims.

Moving backward, campaign platforms and themes can be seen as twofold concerns; how to win election and how to argue that the candidate will secure peace, prosperity, and tranquility when in office. While these two concerns may be harmonious, they may also conflict, especially in light of the opposition, but the trade-offs—here between the immediate needs of winning elections and the longer-term goals for conduct in office—are precisely what rational choice models of decision making are designed to analyze. Nomination adds a third immediate goal, requiring the study of trade-offs among what is best for winning nomination, for winning election, and for choosing, when in office.[19]

Finally, the value of office in the calculus of candidacy could be specified as more than the usual (large) constant. To be sure, peace, prosperity, and tranquility are not precise, and they are outcomes over which the president (and government) have limited control. If citizens do hold presidents accountable for them, however, that should induce presidents to be as responsive to the electorate and its concerns as Mayhew's electoral connection and Schlesinger's ambition.

Within this broad, unifying framework, consider next what candidates might be doing in a campaign to shape electoral choice. I believe that the campaign is relevant to voter choice, and the following is an argument that rests on that assumption. And yet, it also can lead to the conclusion that candidates' campaign strategies will not be easily observable in a variety of circumstances, especially if they choose reasonable strategies.

Most accounts of elections indicate that events that precede the campaign itself are consequential, if not determinative. In my view, this is the (preexisting) electoral context that provides the raw material from which campaign strategies must be devised. We can think of candidate strategies, then, as drawing from this context, in which the candidates then choose first, in a sort of Stackleberg or "leader-follower" game, with voters responding to those strategies. Obviously, the strategic choice of the two candidates is itself an instance of strategic interaction between the two contenders.

The context or raw material is the beginning. It includes two aspects. The first is the historical context, per se, such as actions already taken by the incumbent, rates of unemployment, economic growth and inflation, and the extent of peace, prosperity, and tranquility. These constrain candidate choice sets in a nearly logical fashion. Bush cannot run in 1992 as a president who gave the public no new taxes, for example, nor can either candidate in 1992 choose strategies that are predicated on an incumbent who kept us out of war. Neither constraint, of course, need be negative for Bush or his challenger, a priori. We cannot know at this time what kinds of constraints the challenger may impose without knowing the challenger's identity. Nonetheless, the background and characteristics of the challenger will provide some constraints on feasible strategies, as Michael Dukakis was, for example, constrained from running as a southern Democrat.

The second, and likely more consequential, aspect of the context is the set of distributions of public opinion, prior to the campaign, over the context; that is, the preexisting conditions and actions taken (perhaps this is one way to interpret such successful forecasting exercises as Rosentone's, 1983). Thus, the campaign begins with a distribution of partisanship, with its variable intensities and base, in the electorate. There are prior distributions of opinions and evaluations on policy and on economic and foreign policy outcomes. The public begins the campaign with a set of evaluations of the incumbent, both personally and politically, and may visit them more or less strongly on the incumbent party's nominee (e.g., how Ford was affected by Watergate before the campaign). The challenger may or may not begin with preexisting evaluations of consequence.

These a priori distributions of evaluations and beliefs may be seen as analogous to Bayesian prior distributions over likely vote choices. This is essentially the same as a generalized version of Converse's "normal vote" for party identification (in Campbell et al., 1964). The normal vote can be understood as how partisanship would lead to behavior in a "faceless, nameless, issueless" campaign. More generally, the Bayesian prior distribution indicates what would happen in a campaign devoid of all strategy by candidates. Strategies, then, can be seen as attempts to shape the choices of the people, given their prior beliefs, or in the Bayesian metaphor, as a Bayesian game to shape the likelihood functions. The result of the campaign strategies or likelihoods combine with prior distributions to determine the posterior distribution of evaluations of the two candidates, leading to the final choice on election day.

This view is then of a two-person (two-candidate) Bayesian game of strategy selection, with voters responding to the two strategies chosen by these Stackleberg "leaders." The impact of strategies followed in the campaign is reduced by the strength of the priors, which varies by how diffuse these priors are. Since one party is always that of the incumbent president, it is reasonable to infer that prior distributions are often far from diffuse. Thus, preexisting conditions will not only reduce the range of feasible strategies in the nearly logical sense, but they will also shape in large part the strategies chosen in the campaign from that feasible set. Moreover, increasingly precise priors reduce the impact of any given pair of strategies chosen.

Since the choice of strategies is competitive, it would not be surprising if optimal strategies do little more than modify prior distributions. Put alternatively, in a two-candidate competitive situation, the best strategies in equilibrium may do little more than ensure that the final outcome is not much different from what one would have predicted before the campaign began. The analogy is to the Downsian spatial model, in which, if both candidates choose optimally on issues, issues won't matter empirically in the vote and neither candidate gets an edge from issues at equilibrium. Only when one candidate chooses an inferior strategy (e.g., a noncentrist position in the Downsian model) will issues be evident in vote choice. So too does it seem likely that only when a candidate chooses an inferior strategy and the opponent chooses a relatively superior one will the campaign appear to have an impact. If not, the a priori overall evaluations will be, more or less directly, translated into choice. It will appear that rational candidates have expended resources on strategies that matter little, but that will only be so because both chose wisely. Moreover, empirical studies that find that retrospective evaluations of incumbent performance of the economy are consequential in voter choice should not be interpreted to indicate that the campaign did not matter. Instead, they may be indicating that the incumbent party's nominee devised a strategy that translated strong a priori evaluations into vote choices on economic performance instead of using a strategy that translated other prior evaluations (perhaps partisanship or foreign affairs) into votes.

Strategically, the idea for a candidate is to select a strategy that will make the posterior distribution (and therefore voters' choices) most favorable, given the prior distribution in the public and the opponent's strategy. At the same time that this is a game-theoretic problem between the two candidates, it is also a problem of choosing strategies that convey information to shape and modify the information held and evaluated by the public. In this respect, it is also an information processing account, amenable to analysis by social cognitive theories.

Consider strategies of policy appeals. While spatial models focus on positions advanced, the general phenomenon is the communication from candidate to voter that the candidate more nearly approximates what the voter values and thinks the government should do. Retrospective evaluations of the Downs-Fiorina version pose the question, Have prior actions of, and campaign appeals by, the incumbent permitted voters to infer that the incumbent will come closer to the voter's ideal than the opposition? Candidate evaluations, especially of Kinder's "ideal" president (1986), ask a similar question of voters, Does this candidate have the personal and professional qualities to come closer than the opposition to approximating the voter's view of the ideal qualities in a president? Thus, candidate strategies can be seen as generalized proximity measures, whether on policy, candidate evaluations, or whatever, where proximity means coming closer than the opposition to what the voter believes best for the next presidential administration.

The actual elements of strategy are messages of varying credibility (and as filtered by the media) about how closely a candidate approximates the best possible candidate for president in light of the circumstances and in comparison to the opponent. Issues stances are one such message. So, too, are priorities. Candidates spend a great deal of time attempting to convince the public that they have identified the most important problems. In spatial terms, this is attempting to match or even to manipulate the salience of problems the public sees as most pressing. The second crucial step is to convince the public that the candidate is the better choice. This can be done by taking positions on policy solutions to these problems. It can also be done by convincing voters that the candidate has the "right stuff" to solve the most pressing problems, which is the role of candidate evaluations. Retrospective strategies are powerful, for what better way to demonstrate that a candidate has that right stuff than to point to past accomplishments (or, for the opponent, to point to past failures).

Social cognitive theories seem most useful for analyzing how strategies impact on voter evaluations (i.e., by modifying or reinforcing prior beliefs). In these theories, it is assumed that the range of electoral "raw material" for decision making by any voter is vast. Voters are cognitive misers (or "motivated tacticians," to use Fiske's newer conception; see Fiske, chap. 6) who can possibly attend to only a small portion of that raw material for choice, and who will attend to far less. As a simple example, these theories conclude that voters will employ a particular factor only if its is available to them in memory and only if it is accessible (that is, more or less on their minds). Allocation of candidate emphasis (see Page, 1976, 1978) may be thought of as a strategy to prime voters (see Iyengar and Kinder, 1987), thereby making that factor more accessible (see Aldrich,

Sullivan, and Borgida, 1989). Cognitive structures such as schemas, scripts, and stereotypes seem to fit smoothly into this perspective.

The potential for a more general theory of candidate campaign strategy and candidate-voter interaction seems to lie in a combination of rational choice and social cognition. To put it simply, rational choice theory can tell us what candidates seek to do, while social cognition can tell us how they do it and with what effect. Such a syllogism is, of course, too simple. Choice of strategies, for example, depends on the ability to implement them effectively. But the general point is clear.

This Bayesian view can be applied to candidate strategy in either nomination or general election campaigning, although it is likely easier to "solve" such a game for two candidates. The sequential nature of the two campaigns fits easily, at least in principle, to the Bayesian metaphor. Nomination strategies are one set of likelihoods, aimed at a subset of the total electorate but, presumably, modifying the prior distribution of the general electorate. In this way, both the strategies of a candidate in the nomination and general election campaigns are related.

An additional virtue of the Bayesian metaphor is that it is possible to imagine the probability of nomination and of election in the "calculus of candidacy" as at least partially determinable a priori. As a result, these terms provide connections to, and constraints on, the feasible range of presidential behavior. There are two critical terms in the calculus of candidacy—the value of the office and the probability of winning. The probability-of-winning terms can be seen as ex ante forecasts of the consequences of alternative campaign strategies and their impact on Bayesian evaluations in the public. The value of office for each candidate depends on solving the central problem of studying the presidency, determining the goals of presidents, and thus candidates and aspirants for that office. In this fashion, they need not be merely some large, positive constant.

Finally, there are some implications for the new president. The evaluations of the victor held by the public at the end of the campaign provides one sort of constraint for in-office behavior, since they presumably help determine public approval of the president. If that connection can be made, then the Bayesian metaphor can be seen to continue, as public approval may well be based in part on their campaign-determined evaluations of the victor.

The point of this exercise is not to argue that the above solves the problems that affect the literature on presidential selection. It is designed, instead, to direct the attention of scholars to addressing the theoretically important questions in presidential research. These are: What are the goals of the president, and how can presidential selection be linked to presidential action in office? Until these two questions are addressed, the presidential literature will be incomplete and its scholarship will be partitioned into discrete segments that lack cumulation and intellectual coherence in the study of the presidency. Not only the campaigns and elections literature, but the study of the presidency, suffers from a lack of discernment.

Notes

This research was conducted while I was a fellow at the Center for Advanced Study in the Behavioral Sciences and was supported in part by a grant from the National Science Foundation, #BNS87-00864. I would like to thank these institutions for their support and participants in the Presidency Research Conference for their comments and suggestions. I would especially like to thank John Kessel and Stephen Wayne for their valuable suggestions. I retain full responsibility for the contents of this research, including remaining errors.

1. Gerald Ford makes an interesting case, however, of one who seemed to be the archetypical case of static ambition when in the House, suggesting Rohde's reformulation of ambition types (below) is correct, at least this level of office.

2. Moreover, those who have chosen poorly in the past are likely to have been screened out well before considering a presidential race.

3. Even the exceptional senators who run for president when their seat is also up for reelection typically conform to the model. For example Aldrich (1980a) points out that Bentsen (1976) benefited from the "Johnson rule" (in which a Texas candidate can stand for election to two offices, such as Lyndon Johnson did in 1960 and Lloyd Bentsen did in 1988), while Henry Jackson (1976) benefited from a change in Washington's caucus date (made for him) to a date after the presidential convention. Others (e.g., Fred Harris in 1976 and Jack Kemp in 1988) had decided to retire from their current office.

4. Aldrich (1987b and forthcoming) does so in a quite different fashion to explain the rise of the Republican party to major party status (and presidential victory in 1860). This approach is less likely to be useful in the contemporary case, however.

5. Aldrich (1989) provides a historical overview of systems for nominating presidential candidates and argues that the regular changes in methods are due to fundamentally incompatible normative values. Change occurs when the clash of incompatible values is manifested in conflict over particular candidates.

6. The Democratic party recognized the problem, too, and reduced the specific problem by creating "super delegate" positions, ensuring that leaders would be represented on the floor. It did not ensure true influence, however.

7. Reiter examines measures of delegates and conventions. Other indicators of party decomposition, notably those in the electorate, also were well under way before these reforms.

8. It is interesting in this light that the three nominees most often cited as beneficiaries of the new system, and thought least likely to have been chosen in the prereform era—McGovern, Carter, and Reagan—had presidential vitae (i.e., length of political careers, background, and political offices) remarkably typical of contenders and nominees in earlier eras. See Aldrich, 1987a.

9. Fred Harris used the term "winnowing" to describe how he had been "winnowed in" due to modest success in the Iowa caucuses in 1976. Matthews (1978) is the first I know of to use that term in an academic setting.

10. The distinctiveness of party activists has a long empirical pedigree (for a theoretical account that deduces such "party cleavages" see Aldrich, 1983; Aldrich and McGinnis, 1989).

11. This is apparently consistent with how Henry Jackson in 1976 may have been squeezed in the New York and Pennsylvania primaries by Morris Udall on the left and Jimmy Carter on the right, leading him to do less well than expected—and to quit.

12. This is roughly the problem of entry into elections, and it may serve to make the probability terms of the calculus of candidacy endogenous.

13. I ignore here two important topics. The first is turnout, which given its low levels, presumably looms even larger than usual to the candidate. See Rothenberg and Brody (1988) and Norrander (1989) for examples of this sort of research. I also ignore differences between primaries and caucuses. As Abramson, Aldrich, and Rohde (1990) argue, Jesse Jackson's victory in the 1988 Michigan caucuses and Pat Robertson's strong showing in the Iowa caucuses appeared to be due more to effective organization than to mass popularity. Quite different candidate strategies, therefore, seem to apply.

14. This means that the model worked very well, indeed, predicting about seven of eight votes correctly.

15. Abramson and Ostrom (1990) modify this claim significantly. They argue that its short-term responsiveness is exaggerated in the Gallup poll data MacKuen et al., use and is there, but much less pronounced, in NES data.

16. This account of Republican gains around 1984 is quite consistent with the Clubb, Flanigan, and Zingale (1980) account of changing partisanship in realignments such as in the New Deal. That 1984 is not a realignment (or perhaps, following Norpoth, 1987, not a realignment of New Deal magnitude) is due to the (fortunately) lesser crisis of the 1980s.

17. Directional voting also places lesser informational demands on the voter than the proximity model.

18. Their newer model may also be more nearly consistent with a spatial model for "dimensions" that are dichotomous, although this is but a conjecture on my part. I also conjecture that their model applies as easily to (approximately) dichotomous issues for which there is not a valance-issue-like consensus (e.g., abortion).

19. This pat formula ignores the two obvious complications that some or all of these involve game-theory rather than decision-theory settings and of ignoring the question of commitment (e.g., why, if at all, the president is committed to taking action on his electoral promises).

References

Abramowitz, Alan I. 1989. "Viability, Electability, and Candidate Choice in a Presidential Primary Election: A Test of Competing Models." *Journal of Politics* 51(4): 977–92.

Abramson, Paul R., and Charles W. Ostrom, Jr. 1990. "Macropartisanship: An Empirical Reassessment." Unpublished paper, Michigan State University, March 21.

Abramson, Paul R., John H. Aldrich, and David W. Rohde. 1983. *Change and Continuity in the 1980 Elections.* Rev. ed. Washington, D.C.: Congressional Quarterly Press.

Abramson, Paul R., John H. Aldrich, and David W. Rohde. 1987a. *Change and Continuity in the 1984 Elections.* Rev. ed. Washington, D.C.: Congressional Quarterly Press.

Abramson, Paul R., John H. Aldrich, and David W. Rohde. 1987b. "Progressive Ambition Among United States Senators: 1972–1988." *Journal of Politics* 49(1): 3–35.

Abramson, Paul R., John H. Aldrich, and David W. Rohde. 1990. *Change and Continuity in the 1988 Elections.* Washington, D.C.: Congressional Quarterly Press.

Abramson, Paul R., John H. Aldrich, Phil Paolino, and David W. Rohde. 1992. " 'Sophisticated' Voting in the 1988 Primary Season." *American Political Science Review* (March 1992): 55–69.

Achen, Christopher H. 1989. "Prospective Voting and the Theory of Party Identification." Unpublished paper, University of Chicago, August 26.

Aldrich, John H. 1980a. *Before the Convention: Strategies and Choices in Presidential Nomination Campaigns.* Chicago: University of Chicago Press.

———. 1980b "A Dynamic Model of Presidential Nomination Campaigns." *American Political Science Review* 74(3): 651–69.

———. 1983. "A Downsian Spatial Model with Party Activism." *American Political Science Review* 77(4): 974–90.

———. 1987a. "Methods and Actors: The Relationship of Processes to Candidates." In *Presidential Selection,* ed. Alexander Heard and Michael Nelson. Durham: Duke University Press.

———. 1987b. "The Rise of the Republican Party, 1854–1860." Paper prepared for the annual meeting of the Midwest Political Science Association, Chicago, April.

———. 1989. "Presidential Nomination Processes and a Clash of Values." In *The Presidency in American Politics,* ed. Paul Brace, Christine B. Harrington, and Gary King. New York: New York University Press.

———. Forthcoming. *A Theory of the American Political Party* (tentative title).

Aldrich, John H., and R. Michael Alvarez. 1990. "Voting in the 1988 Presidential Primaries." Unpublished paper, Duke University.

Aldrich, John H., and Michael M. McGinnis. 1989. "A Model of Party Constraints on Optimal Candidate Positions." *Mathematical and Computer Modelling* 12(4/5): 437–50.

Aldrich, John H., and Thomas Weko. 1988. "The Presidency and the Election Process: Campaign Strategy, Voting, and Governance." In *The Presidency and the Political System,* ed. Michael Nelson. 2d ed. Washington, D.C.: Congressional Quarterly Press.

Aldrich, John H., John L. Sullivan, and Eugene Borgida. 1989. "Foreign Affairs and Issue Voting: Do Presidential Candidates 'Waltz Before a Blind Audience'?" *American Political Science Review* 83(1): 123–41.

Allsop, Dee, and Herbert F. Weisberg. 1988. "Measuring Change in Party Identification in an Election Campaign." *American Journal of Political Science* 32(4): 996–1017.

Aranson, Peter H., and Peter C. Ordeshook. 1972. "Spatial Strategies for Sequential Elections." In *Probability Models of Collective Decision Making,* ed. Richard G. Niemi and Herbert F. Weisberg. Columbus, Oh.: Merrill.

Arterton, F. Christopher. 1984. *Media Politics: The News Strategies of Presidential Campaigns.* Lexington, Mass.: Lexington Books.

Asher, Herbert B. 1983. "Voting Behavior Research in the 1980s: An Examination of Some Old and New Problem Areas." In *Political Science: The State of the Discipline,* ed. Ada W. Finifter. Washington, D.C.: American Political Science Association.

———. 1988. *Presidential Elections and American Politics: Voters, Candidates, and Campaigns Since 1952.* 4th ed. Chicago: Dorsey.

Banks, Jeffery S., and D. Roderick Kiewiet. 1989. "Explaining Patterns of Candidate Competition in Congressional Elections." *American Journal of Political Science* 33(4): 997–1015.

Bartels, Larry M. 1988. *Presidential Primaries and the Dynamics of Public Choice.* Princeton: Princeton University Press.

Berelson, Bernard R., Paul F. Lazarsfeld, and William N. McPhee. 1954. *Voting: A Study of Opinion Formation in a Campaign.* Chicago: University of Chicago Press.

Black, Gordon. 1972. "A Theory of Political Ambition: Career Choices and the Role of Structural Incentives." *American Political Science Review* 66(1): 144–59.

Brady, Henry E. 1984a. "Knowledge, Strategy, and Momentum in Presidential Primaries." Paper prepared for the Weingart Conference, California Institute of Technology.

———. 1984b. "Chances, Utilities, and Voting in Presidential Primaries." Paper prepared for the Annual Meeting of the Public Choice Society, Phoenix.

Brady, Henry E., and Patricia D. Conley. 1988. "Do Strategies Come and Go While Preferences Remain the Same?" Unpublished paper, University of Chicago. August 21.

Brams, Steven J. 1978. *The Presidential Election Game.* New Haven: Yale University Press.

Brams, Steven J., and Morton D. Davis. 1974. "The 3/2's Rule in Presidential Campaigning." *American Political Science Review* 68(1): 113–34.

Broder, David S. 1972. *The Party's Over: The Failure of Politics in America.* New York: Harper and Row.

Brody, Richard A., and Benjamin I. Page. 1972. "Comment: The Assessment of Policy Voting." 66(2): 450–58.

Calvert, Randall C. 1985. "Robustness of the Multidimensional Voting Model: Candidate Motivations, Uncertainty, and Convergence." *American Journal of Political Science* 29(1): 69–95.

Campbell, Angus, Philip E. Converse, Warren E. Miller, and Donald E. Stokes. 1960. *The American Voter*. New York: John Wiley and Sons.

Campbell, Angus, Philip E. Converse, Warren E. Miller, and Donald E. Stokes. 1964. *Elections and the Political Order*. New York: John Wiley and Sons.

Chappell, Henry, and William Keech. 1985. "A New View of Political Accountability for Economic Performance." *American Political Science Review* 79(1): 10–27.

Clubb, Jerome M., William H. Flanigan, and Nancy H. Zingale. 1980. *Partisan Realignment: Voters, Parties, and Government in American History*. Beverley Hills, Calif.: Sage.

Colantoni, Claude S., Terrence J. Levesque, and Peter C. Ordeshook. 1975. "Campaign Resource Allocations Under the Electoral College." *American Political Science Review* 69(1): 141–54.

Conover, Pamela J., and Stanley Feldman. 1984. "How People Organize the Political World: A Schematic Model." *American Journal of Political Science* 28(1): 95–126.

Converse, Philip E. 1975. "Public Opinion and Voting Behavior." In *Handbook of Political Science*, vol. 4, ed. Fred I. Greenstein and Nelson W. Polsby, Reading, Mass.: Addison-Wesley.

Cotter, Cornelius P., James L. Gibson, John F. Bibby, and Robert J. Huckshorn. 1984. *Party Organizations in American Politics*. New York: Praeger.

Crotty, William. 1983. *Party Reform*. New York: Longmans.

Crotty, William, and John S. Jackson III. 1985. *Presidential Primaries and Nominations*. Washington, D.C.: Congressional Quarterly Press.

Davis, Otto A., Melvin Hinich, and Peter C. Ordeshook. 1970. "An Expository Development of a Mathematical Model of the Electoral Process." *American Political Science Review* 64(2): 426–48.

Downs, Anthony. 1957. *An Economic Theory of Democracy*. New York: Harper and Row.

Enelow, James M., and Melvin J. Hinich. 1984. *The Spatial Theory of Voting: An Introduction*. New York: Cambridge University Press.

Erikson, Robert S., and David W. Romero. 1990. "Candidate Equilibrium and the Behavioral Model of the Vote." Unpublished paper. March.

Feldman, Stanley, and Pamela Johnston Conover. 1983. "Candidates, Issues, and Voters: The Role of Inference in Political Perception." *Journal of Politics* 45(4): 810–39.

Fenno, Richard F., Jr. 1973. *Congressmen in Committees*. Boston: Little, Brown.

Fiorina, Morris P. 1980. "The Decline in Collective Responsibility in American Politics." *Daedalus* 109(3): 25–45.

———. 1981. *Retrospective Voting in American National Elections*. New Haven: Yale University Press.

———. 1988. "The Reagan Years: Turning to the Right or Groping Toward the Middle?" In *The Resurgence of Conservatism in Anglo-American Democracies*, ed. Barry Cooper, Allan Kornberg, and William Mishler. Durham,: Duke University Press.

———. 1990. "An Era of Divided Government." In *Developments in American Politics*, ed. Bruce Cain and Gillian Peele. London: Macmillan.

Fishel, Jeff. 1985. *Presidents and Promises: From Campaign Pledge to Presidential Performance*. Washington, D.C.: Congressional Quarterly Press.

Fiske, Susan T., and Shelley E. Taylor. 1984. *Social Cognition*. Reading, Mass.: Addison-Wesley.

Gant, Michael M. 1983. "Citizens' Evaluations of the 1980 Presidential Candidates: Influence of Campaign Strategies." *American Politics Quarterly* 11(3): 327–48.

Gopoian, J. David. 1982. "Issue Preferences and Candidate Choice in Presidential Primaries." *American Journal of Political Science* 26(3): 523–46.

Graber, Doris. 1984. *Mass Media and American Politics* 2d ed. Washington, D.C.: Congressional Quarterly Press.

Gurian, Paul-Henri. 1986. "Resource Allocation Strategies in Presidential Nomination Campaigns." *American Journal of Political Science* 30(4): 802–21.

Hamill, Ruth, Milton Lodge, and Frederick Blake. 1985. "The Breadth, Depth, and Utility of Partisan, Class, and Ideological Schemas." *American Journal of Political Science* 29(4): 850–70.

Hastie, Reid. 1986. "A Primer of Information-processing Theory for the Political Scientist." In *Political Cognition*, ed. Richard R. Lau and David O. Sears. Hillsdale, N.J.: Lawrence Erlbaum.

Heclo, Hugh. 1977. *A Government of Strangers*. Washington, D.C.: Brookings.

Hershey, Marjorie Randon. 1989. "The Campaign and the Media." In *The Election of 1988: Reports and Interpretations*, ed. Gerald M. Pomper et al. Chatham, N.J.: Chatham House.

Hinich, Melvin J., and Peter C. Ordeshook. 1974. "The Electoral College: A Spatial Analysis." *Political Methodology* (1): 1–29.

Iyengar, Shanto, and Donald R. Kinder. 1987. *News That Matters*. Chicago: University of Chicago Press.

Jacobson, Gary C. 1985. "Congress: Politics After a Landslide Without Coattails." In *The Elections of 1984*, ed. Michael Nelson. Washington, D.C.: Congressional Quarterly Press.

———. 1987. *The Politics of Congressional Elections*. 2d ed. Boston: Little, Brown.

Keeter, Scott, and Cliff Zukin. 1983. *Uninformed Choice: The Failure of the New Presidential Nominating System*. New York: Praeger.

Kelley, Stanley, Jr. 1983. *Interpreting Elections*. Princeton: Princeton University Press.

Kelley, Stanley, Jr., and Thad W. Mirer. 1974. "The Simple Act of Voting." *American Political Science Review* 68(2): 572–91.

Kernell, Samuel. 1986. *Going Public: New Strategies of Presidential Leadership*. Washington, D.C.: Congressional Quarterly Press.

Kessel, John H. 1968. *The Goldwater Coalition: Republican Strategies in 1964*. Indianapolis: Bobbs-Merrill.

———. 1972. "Comment: The Issues in Issue Voting." *American Political Science Review* 66(3): 459–65.

———. 1977. "The Seasons of Presidential Politics." *Social Science Quarterly* (December): 418–35.

———. 1980. *Presidential Campaign Politics: Coalition Strategies and Citizen Response*. Homewood, Ill.: Dorsey.

———. 1984. *Presidential Campaign Politics: Coalition Strategies and Citizen Response*. 2d ed. Chicago: Dorsey.

———. 1988. *Presidential Campaign Politics: Coalition Strategies and Citizen Response*. 3d ed. Chicago: Dorsey.

Key, V. O., Jr. 1966. *The Responsible Electorate: Rationality in Presidential Voting, 1936–60.* Cambridge: Harvard University Press.

Kinder, Donald R. 1978. "Political Person Perception: The Asymmetry in Influence of Sentiment and Choice on Perceptions of Presidential Candidates." *Journal of Personality and Social Psychology* 42: 859–71.

———. 1986. "Presidential Character Revisited." In *Political Cognition,* ed. Richard R. Lau and David O. Sears. Hillsdale, N.J.: Lawrence Erlbaum.

Kinder, Donald R., and Susan T. Fiske. 1986. "Presidents in the Public Mind." In *Political Psychology,* ed. Margaret G. Hermann. San Francisco: Jossey-Bass.

Kirkpatrick, Jeane J. 1976. *The New Presidential Elite.* New York: Russell Sage Foundation.

Lau, Richard R. 1986. "Political Schemata, Candidate Evaluations, and Voting Behavior." In *Political Cognition,* ed. Richard R. Lau and David O. Sears. Hillsdale, N.J.: Lawrence Erlbaum.

Lazersfeld, Paul F., Bernard Berelson, and Hazel Gaudet. 1948. *The People's Choice: How the Voter Makes Up His Mind in a Presidential Election Campaign.* 2d ed. New York: Columbia University Press.

Lichtman, Allan J., and Ken DeCell. 1990. *The Thirteen Keys to the Presidency.* Lanham, Md.: Madison Books.

Light, Paul. 1982. *The President's Agenda.* Baltimore: Johns Hopkins University Press.

Lodge, Milton, and Ruth Hamill. 1986. "A Partisan Schema for Political Information Processing." *American Political Science Review* 80(2): 505–19.

Lodge, Milton, Kathleen M. McGraw, and Patrick Stroh. 1989. "An Impression-driven Model of Candidate Evaluation." *American Political Science Review* 83(2): 399–419.

Lowi, Theodore. 1985. *The Personal President: Power Invested, Promise Unfulfilled.* Ithaca: Cornell University Press.

McCormick, Richard P. 1982. *The Presidential Game: Origins of American Politics.* New York: Oxford University Press.

Macdonald, Stuart Elaine, and George Rabinowitz. 1989. "Directional Theory as a Probability Model of Mass-elite Linkages." Paper prepared for the annual meeting of the American Political Science Association, Atlanta, Ga.

McGinnis, Joe. 1969. *The Selling of the President 1968.* New York: Trident.

MacKuen, Michael B., Robert S. Erikson, and James A. Stimson. 1989. "Macropartisanship." *American Political Science Review* 83(4): 1125–42.

March, James G., and Johan P. Olsen. 1984. "The New Institutionalism: Organizational Factors in Political Life." *American Political Science Review* 78(3): 734–49.

Matthews, Donald R. 1978. " 'Winnowing': The News Media and the 1976 Presidential Nominations." In *Race for the Presidency: The Media and the Nominating Process,* ed. James David Barber. Englewood Cliffs, N.J.: Prentice-Hall.

Mayhew, David R. 1974. *Congress: The Electoral Connection.* New Haven: Yale University Press.

Miller, Arthur H., and Martin P. Wattenberg. 1985. "Throwing the Rascals Out: Policy and Performance Evaluations of Presidential Candidates, 1952–1980." *American Political Science Review* 79(2): 359–72.

Miller, Arthur H., Warren E. Miller, Alden S. Raine, and Thad H. Brown. 1976. "A Majority Party in Disarray: Policy Polarization in the 1972 Election." *American Political Science Review* 70(3): 753–78.

Mueller, John E. 1973. *War, Presidents, and Public Opinion*. New York: John Wiley and Sons.

Neustadt, Richard. 1980. *Presidential Power from Kennedy to Carter.* New York: John Wiley.

Norpoth, Helmut. 1987. "Under Way and Here to Stay: Partisan Realignment in the 1980s?" *Public Opinion Quarterly* 51(Fall): 376–91.

Norrander, Barbara. 1989. "Alternative Models of Turnout in Presidential Primaries." Unpublished paper, San Jose State University, August.

Ostrom, Charles W., Jr., and Brian L. Job. 1986. "The President and the Political Use of Force." *American Political Science Review* 80(2): 541–66.

Page, Benjamin I. 1976. "The Theory of Candidate Ambiguity." *American Political Science Review* 70(3): 742–52.

————. 1978. *Choices and Echoes in Presidential Elections: Rational Man and Electoral Democracy.* Chicago: University of Chicago Press.

Page, Benjamin I., and Richard A. Brody. 1972. "Policy Voting and the Electoral Process: The Vietnam War Issue." *American Political Science Review* 66(3): 979–95.

Page, Benjamin I., and Calvin C. Jones. 1979. "Reciprocal Effects of Policy Preferences, Party Loyalties, and the Vote." *American Political Science Review* 73(4): 1071–89.

Page, Benjamin I., and Robert Y. Shapiro. 1983. "Effects of Public Opinion on Policy." *American Political Science Review* 77(1): 175–90.

Page, Benjamin I., and Robert Y. Shapiro. 1990. *The Rational Public: Fifty Years of Trends in Americans' Policy Preferences.* Chicago: University of Chicago-Press.

Peabody, Robert L., Norman J. Ornstein, and David W. Rohde. 1976. "The United States Senate as a Presidential Incubator: Many Are Called but Few Are Chosen." *Political Science Quarterly* 91(3): 237–58.

Polsby, Nelson W. 1983. *Consequences of Party Reform*. New York: Oxford University Press.

Pomper, Gerald M. 1975. *Voters' Choice: Varieties of American Electoral Behavior.* New York: Dodd, Mead.

Pomper, Gerald M., and Susan S. Lederman. 1980. *Elections in America: Control and Influence in Democratic Politics.* 2d ed. New York: Dodd, Mead.

Rabinowitz, George, and Stuart Elaine Macdonald. 1989. "A Directional Theory of Issue Voting." *American Political Science Review* 83(1): 93–121.

Rahn, Wendy, John H. Aldrich, Eugene Borgida, and John L. Sullivan. 1990. "A Social-Cognitive Model of Candidate Appraisal." In *Informatin and Democratic Processes*, ed. John F. Ferejohn and James Kuklinski. Urbana: University of Illinois Press.

Ranney, Austin. 1975. *Curing the Mischiefs of Faction: Party Reform in America.* Berkeley and Los Angeles: University of California Press.

Reiter, Howard L. 1985. *Selecting the President: The Nominating Process in Transition.* Philadelphia: University of Pennsylvania Press.

Riker, William H. 1982. *Liberalism Against Populism: A Confrontation Between the Theory of Democracy and the Theory of Social Choice.* San Francisco: W. H. Freeman.

Riker, William H., and Peter C. Ordeshook. 1968. "A Theory of the Calculus of Voting." *American Political Science Review* 62(1): 25–43.

Rohde, David W. 1979. "Risk-bearing and Progressive Ambition: The Case of Members of the United States House of Representatives." *American Journal of Political Science* 23(1): 1–26.

———. 1991. *Parties and Leaders in the Postreform House.* Chicago: University of Chicago Press.

Rosenstone, Steven J. 1983. *Forecasting Presidential Elections* New Haven: Yale University Press.

Rothenberg, Lawrence S., and Richard A. Brody. 1988. "Participation in Presidential Primaries." *Western Political Quarterly* 41(2): 253–71.

Schlesinger, Joseph A. 1966. *Ambitions and Politics: Political Careers in the United States.* Chicago: Rand McNally.

Shanks, J. Merrill, Warren E. Miller, Henry E. Brady, and Bradley J. Palmquist. 1985. "Viability, Electability, and Presidential 'Preference': Initial Results from the 1984 NES Continuous Monitoring Design." Paper prepared for the 1985 annual meeting of the Midwest Political Science Association, Chicago.

Shapiro, Robert Y., John T. Young, Kelly D. Patterson, Jill E. Blumenfeld, Sara M. Offenhartz, and Ted E. Tsekerides. 1990. "Media Influences on Candidate Support in Primary Elections." Paper prepared for the 1990 annual meeting of the Midwest Political Science Association, Chicago, April 5–7.

Shepsle, Kenneth A. 1979. "Institutional Arrangements and Equilibrium in Multidimensional Voting Models." *American Journal of Political Science* 23(1): 27–59.

Stokes, Donald E. 1966. "Some Dynamic Elements of Contests for the Presidency." *American Political Science Review* 60(1): 19–28.

Stokes, Donald E., Angus Campbell, and Warren E. Miller. 1958. "Components of Electoral Decision." *American Political Science Review* 52(2): 367–87.

Stone, Walter J., and Alan I. Abramowitz. 1983. "Winning May Not Be Everything, but It's More Than We Thought." *American Political Science Review* 77(4): 945–56.

Tufte, Edward R. 1978. *Political Control of the Economy.* Princeton: Princeton University Press.

Wattenberg, Martin P. 1988. Paper prepared for the 1988 annual meeting of the American Political Science Association.

———. 1990. *The Decline of American Political Parties: 1952–1988.* Cambridge: Harvard University Press.

Wattier, Mark J. 1983. "The Simple Act of Voting in the 1980 Democratic Presidential Primaries." *American Politics Quarterly* 11(3): 267–92.

Wayne, Stephen J. 1988. *The Road to the White House: The Politics of Presidential Elections.* 3d ed. New York: St. Martin's.

Weko, Thomas, and John H. Aldrich. 1990. "The Presidency and the Election Campaign: Framing the Choice in 1988." In *The Presidency and the Political System,* ed. Michael Nelson. 3d ed. Washington, D.C.: Congressional Quarterly Press.

West, Darrell M. 1984. *Making Campaigns Count: Leadership and Coalition Building in 1980.* Westport, Conn.: Greenwood.

Wittman, Donald. 1983. "Candidate Motivation: A Synthesis of Alternative Theories." *American Political Science Review* 77(1): 142–57.

2

Presidential Personality and Leadership Style

ERWIN C. HARGROVE

O LEADERS make a difference in political life? We usually assume so without asking for proof. But consider the evidence against it. Theodore Roosevelt hoped to be nominated as the Republican candidate for president in 1920. Had he not died he might have been nominated and elected. Would the politics of the policies of the 1920s been more "progressive" in his presidency than under Warren Harding and Calvin Coolidge? Or would the forces of "normalcy," to repeat Harding's misreading of his inaugural text, have been too strong even for Theodore Roosevelt? To consider another case, Harry Truman was bold and decisive in resisting Communist encroachment in Greece and Turkey, Western Europe, and Korea in the postwar years, but would not Thomas Dewey or Dwight Eisenhower, had either one been president, have made the same decisions? On the other hand, if the Democrats had nominated the conservative Newton D. Baker in 1932, would the New Deal policies and political coalition have been created or were these the unique achievements of Franklin D. Roosevelt? Or, would a president with a less conspiratorial mind than Richard M. Nixon have been able to build a new Republican majority on the very real achievements of those years?

Such hypothetical questions cannot be definitively answered, but in posing them we clarify the questions to be asked about the relative importance of individuality in the presidency. The impact of individual leaders on events and institutions is greater or lesser depending upon the historical situation and the opportunities available to them. Historians are comfortable with these questions and resolve them empirically in given cases. Political scientists have a more difficult problem. If individuality makes a difference, I would like to generalize about that difference, and the conditions that make it possible, across historical situations.

Political Science and the Study of Leaders

Many political scientists are uncomfortable with the conclusion that leaders matter, because the analysis of individuals is thereby required. Our research methods are designed to discover regularities in the behavior of aggregates of people, whether groups or institutions. We wish to generalize about these aggregates. The individual is lost in the search for statements of probability about groups and institutions that can be replicated and used for prediction (Edinger, 1964). The study of political leadership is not regarded as real political science by many of our number, and this helps explain the uncertain status of presidential studies within the discipline. Individuality is too great a wild card for many. I share that view regarding any hope of developing theories about political leadership. Leadership is ubiquitous in political life but is related to so many varying factors that general theories are not possible. The study of political leadership must therefore be historically and institutionally specific. However, the insight that individuality is important for understanding leadership is also an admission that individuality may be important for understanding the presidency. One cannot have it both ways, arguing that individuals are not important and then in the same breath arguing that the importance of individuals in the presidency precludes systematic study.

Surely the issue is not, Do individuals make a difference? but Under what conditions do they make a difference? The relative importance of leaders varies across institutions and across time and place. Congressional leaders are important in understanding parts of congressional life. Individual presidents may be important for understanding important historical events and institutional changes. The task of scholarship is to integrate the study of individuals with the social and institutional forces that move them and that they, in turn, may influence.

A second objection to the study of leadership is that it is like quicksilver; it slips through your hands. Robert Dahl puts it very well: Political skill "is generally thought to be of critical importance in explaining the power of different leaders. . . . However, despite many attempts at analysis, from Machiavelli to the present day, political skill has remained among the more elusive aspects of power" (1969). It is difficult to establish measurable links between the actions of leaders and possible consequences for institutions or society. The debate about whether presidential skill is important for influencing legislation is one example of the difficulty (Edwards, 1989). The relation between public support for presidents and their influence in Washington is somewhat clearer, but there are many intervening factors (Peterson, 1990). Presidential style of authority appears to shape decision-making processes within the circle of lieutenants, but the impact on the actual decisions taken is not easy to calculate (Burke et al., 1989). One could cite such difficulties endlessly, but they are not unique to the study of leadership in political science. Many of the most interesting aspects of government do not lend themselves to measurement and disaggregation, because the phenomena are configurative and cannot be pulled apart into independent and dependent variables. Clarity may come from precise conceptual frameworks by which varying leadership situations may be compared.

A third objection to the emphasis upon individuals is that the concept of institutional role will suffice. The political pressures on and incentives of presidents will cause different individuals to act in much the same way in common situations. Thus Terry Moe concludes that political pressures on successive modern presidents have forced a "centralization" of policy formation in the White House and a "politicization" of upper reaches of the executive branch so that presidents might increase "responsiveness" to their goals. Nixon's much criticized efforts in this direction are described by Moe as part of the logic of institutional development, and Ronald Reagan's strategies are seen as the culmination of the long-term trend (Moe, 1985).

Theodore Lowi argues that the strong political incentives arising from an entrepreneurial system of presidential selection tempt presidents to substitute public grandstanding for governing. Thus Reagan's invasion of Grenada was designed to increase his political capital in time for reelection (Lowi, 1985, 167). Lowi sees this "pathology" of imagery as virtually a necessity in the contemporary presidency: "An institutionalist approach does not deny the relevance of individual psychology but treats it as marginal in the context of the tremendous historical forces lodged in the laws, traditions and commitments of institutions" (20, 136). He goes on to argue that the aim of institutions is to make the behavior of its members more predictable. People who occupy the same jobs over time behave predictably as a result of the expectations, obligations, and rational strategies that adhere to their roles (137–38). Lowi both makes and misses a point here. Much of a president's job may be structured by fixed expectations and incentives. The budgetary process, congressional liaison, and perhaps the White House media operation appear to be very much institutionalized at the operating level across presidencies, even though individual presidents lend their touch. But one can point to many things that presidents do that are not institutionalized, such as the presentation of self to a mass audience, the initial choice of a policy agenda, management of decision processes, and methods of persuasion of independent power holders.

There is plenty of opportunity for the expression of individuality. We have not done a good job in presidential studies in sorting out stable role patterns from individually shaped actions. Fred Greenstein suggests areas of action that permit the individuality of leaders to find expression (Greenstein and Polsby, 1975, 19–21):

1. Ambiguous situations leave room for personality to express itself.
2. The absence of standardized "mental sets," whether role expectations or ideology, leave room for variability according to personality.
3. If sanctions are not attached to given courses of action the possibility of variability is greater.
4. High intensity of feelings in the leader may override standard expectations.
5. The greater the demands on the leader to act at high levels of skill the more likely individuality will be expressed.

Personality, role, and situation are thus inextricably joined. The task of analysis is to explain the dynamic relations among them. It is simplistic to see leadership as always a function of personality, role, or situation (Edinger, 1964, 437). But, of course, one factor may be more important in given cases than others. Richard Ellis and Aaron Wildavsky argue that James Madison's difficulties with Congress are explained more by the character of his political followers than by any lack of skill on his part. On the other hand, Thomas Jefferson's skillful leadership of a congressional caucus was a combination of skill and a favorable situation (1989, 68–78). Skill will have more scope in some situations than others.

The effort to assess the relative importance of individuality to the impact of leadership requires clarification of the relevant aspects of individuality. We need a model of political personality that specifies the aspects of individuality that may make a difference in political behavior. We must also be clear about what it is we wish to explain. What elements of the political environment do we expect the political personality to affect? The relation between personality and environment is dynamic, and our propositions must capture dynamic variations.

I analyze three configurations in which personality and environment interact in dynamic fashion in the presidency: (1) the relation of political skill to historical context, (2) the triggering of self-defeating ego-defensive actions in leaders by environmental factors, and (3) the management of decision making. The first task is to set out a model of political personality and then illustrate its utility for these three configurations.

Political scientists are not particularly interested in the study of political personality and leadership style for the sake of understanding individuals, as a biographer might be. But even a biographer wishes to assess the historical importance of the subject of the biography. So in each of these three areas, we wish to know the extent to which personality not only shaped the playing of presidential roles, but actually influenced decisions and events. But before we pursue those questions, I must set out the model of political personality.

A Model of Political Personality

Most of the writing by political scientists upon political personality is psychoanalytic in character and focuses upon ego-defensive behavior in individuals. For example, Woodrow Wilson is said to have personalized political conflicts and thereby acted in self-defeating ways. Lyndon Johnson's great defensiveness about his Vietnam commitment was, some argue, actually personal defensiveness in its great rigidity. Richard Nixon conceived of political life as an arena for testing his toughness and may have sought conflict in a lifelong ritual. This approach to explaining the particular actions of particular presidents emphasizes pathology and is not suited to explaining role playing in which style and skill are brought to bear upon tasks of leadership. We need a model of political personality that will permit comparison of presidents, and other political leaders, in ordinary language and that will also permit the introduction of insights from personality theory. This is a big order: there is no definitive model of personality, and the links between predispositions and action are not strong in any theory. Uniqueness of person and situation stand in the way.

Below, I offer a model of political personality that will provide a framework for individual biography and comparison of styles of presidential leadership. The model has been developed through the experience of trying to understand political leaders.[1] Political style develops through experience. Figure 1 demonstrates how leadership skills and style are a result of the congruence of the elements of the political personality as mediated by the ego. Figure 2 shows that both policy purpose and political and administrative style are extensions of political personality. The model has been useful to me because the variables in the model help me identify the elements of leadership style. Of course one is involved in a circular argument here, because the model guides interpretation and a different model might lead one to see different factors and thus to develop different interpretations. My response is to say that my model satisfies me, that it permits the organization of raw data about a person's life and work in a way that leaves nothing out, and that it permits the personality to be seen as a whole.[2]

The ego is that agency in personality that mediates among elements of personality and searches for congruence among them. In this sense, much behavior is overdetermined, and one finds congruence among motives in action that serve more than one purpose. The ego also mediates between the elements of personality and the external environment, again seeking congruence between internal needs and receptive

FIGURE I

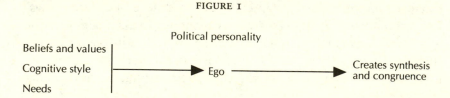

Political personality

Beliefs and values

Cognitive style ———————▶ Ego ————————————▶ Creates synthesis and congruence

Needs

FIGURE 2

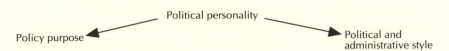

external avenues of action to the extent that such congruence is possible. As an example of internal congruence, a need for attention could stimulate the development of self-dramatizing skills, which are then employed in political life for the dramatization of particular policy goals. To carry the example further, such a dramatizing leader would seek out opportunities in the political environment to exhibit self-dramatizing skills, meet the need for attention, and serve larger policy goals, all at the same time.

Leadership style is understood to be the characteristic ways in which a political leader deals with recurring tasks of leadership such as persuasion, the management of conflict, and administration. The term *skill* refers to the degree of virtuosity with which those tasks are accomplished. There are no absolute standards for evaluating skill. The requirements may change across time and place. Individuals with quite different skills, such as Franklin Roosevelt and Dwight Eisenhower, may both be skillful politicians, but in different ways. We sometimes understand the importance of skill by its absence in leaders who have difficulty carrying out the tasks of leadership. However, there is, perhaps, general agreement among presidency scholars that the repertoire of presidential skills includes the ability to present oneself to the public in ways that gain support for presidential policy as well as person; the ability to manage conflict, within the administration, with Congress, and with other domestic and international groups; and the ability to set up and direct an effective executive establishment for policy making and implementation. All of these skills are enhanced by a more fundamental ability to assess the possibilities for action in a historical situation and devise concrete strategies for realizing those possibilities. These are quite general characterizations, and different presidents approach these tasks differently. There is no a priori skill test. But skill and effectiveness can be judged comparatively and historically.

The model enables us to link political personality to situations in the environment of the leader. Individuals play institutional roles in ways that favor their strengths and seek out and respond in congenial ways to situations, tasks, problems, and challenges that favor those strengths. It follows that they seek to avoid situations for which they are not well suited. If one is good at negotiation and bargaining, such tasks are sought, for example. Of course, political life does not arrange itself so conveniently for leaders, and a central theme of leadership is that strengths and weaknesses are opposite sides of the coin. This becomes apparent over the course of a career as politicians face congenial and uncongenial tasks.

It is only a first step to sketch style across time in a linear way. Diverse roles and situations evoke different elements of style in the same person. An accurate portrait of the presidential leadership of one individual must move from analysis of central predispositions to explanation of the complex configurations of personality, role, and situation. The analysis of style and skill cannot fully explain what presidents will do in particular situations. Nor can past actions be fully explained, even by historians and biographers. There is a freedom, or indeterminacy, in human life that precludes final explanation of action. This indeterminacy permits both political creativity and failure in leaders. Leadership behavior is something more than rational choice of intelligent strategies. To a great extent it is intuitive and is an expression of personality, in the fullest sense.

Political leaders, such as presidents, are recognizable across their careers as distinctive personalities with limits to their range of style and skill. We are ourselves, even as we adapt to changing conditions. The initial task of analysis is to develop portraits of the style and skills of politicians, the strongest predispositions, the strengths to which they play, and the weaknesses they avoid as these factors are displayed in a variety of roles and situations. This approach avoids simplistic explanations that explain behavior by any one factor, whether it be need striving, beliefs, and so forth. Most behavior is overdetermined in the sense that we act for more than one reason. The idea of congruence among forces in personality, as mediated by the ego, permits explanation of action in terms of more than one factor.[3] The strength of a given element in personality, in relation to others in a given case, is an empirical question. The ego must also perform the task of matching political personality to changing situations in the political environment. Again, one sees a search for congruence among the elements of political personality and environmental situations. Political creativity consists of linking elements of oneself to situations in ways that win the support of others. The actions of leaders cannot often be reduced to single factors in personality or to characteristics of the situation alone but must be explained in terms of the efforts of leaders to join beliefs and talents to situations in the search for solutions to political and policy problems.

This formulation does not preclude explanations in terms of single factors. Institutional role may explain a whole set of actions for a given person, time, and place. Unconscious needs may be very important in cases of ego-defensive behavior. Convincing explanations of the reasons for behavior will not come from the model but from the insight of the observer. The model only names important variables. It can be used by scholars with competing interpretations of an individual. It is also easier to explain style and favorite ways of acting, using the idea of congruence, than it is to explain particular actions in specific situations. The political scientist must follow the methods of biographers and historians in explaining past events, and no explanation is ever final or definitive.

The conception of personality that underlies the model is psychodynamic. It draws on the psychoanalytic perspective with a strong element of ego psychology (Hartmann, 1963). One must admit the possibility of competing models drawn from other schools. In the concept of personality presented here, people are accorded the capacity to test reality and chart their course through life in varying degrees of independence from unconscious forces. But such forces are presumed to exist. They are manifested as ego-defensive behavior that protects vulnerability. Ordinary political style is also, in part, a manifestation of deeply rooted, unstated goals, such as the need for mastery over problems, the desire for affection or respect. But there is plenty of room in the model for beliefs and values, for conscious purposes, and for learning about roles, institutions, and problems that permit variations in style. This model does not explicitly incorporate concepts of the stages of life as seen in the work of Erik Erikson and Daniel Levinson (Erikson, 1963; Levinson, 1978; Renshon, 1980, chap. 6). There are rich possibilities here, but I have not developed them. For example, in my study of Jimmy Carter, I interpret his way of coping with defeat in his first race for governor in terms of Levinson's idea of the midlife crisis, in which a man must cope with the fact of failure (Hargrove, 1988, chap. 4 and 5). But I do not present alternative explanations; the idea is simply given as an insight in passing.

Research Strategy

The best way to capture the political personality of a president is to delineate the recurring styles of leadership as seen over time. One builds a portrait of style. This strategy is fully developed in my study of Jimmy Carter (Hargrove, 1988, chaps. 1 and 2). He had a need for mastery of problem solving, the rationalistic cognitive style of an engineer, the optimism of a believer that with God all things were possible, and the belief in rational programmatic action of a southern progressive. These characteristics reinforced each other. His confidence in his own intelligence was strengthened by two successful careers (in the navy and in business) before he entered politics. His first political success was winning election to the Georgia state senate over the opposition of a crooked local machine. He entered office as an outsider who developed a strategy of leadership that posited public goods to which people could subscribe, thus bypassing the politics of bargaining between politicians and interest groups. His leadership style as governor emphasized all of these factors in their congruence: mastery of problems, intelligence, belief in progress, and appeal to the public over the heads of the legislature. His beliefs, cognitive style, and personal needs reinforced each other in his political style.

This style and the political appeals that it engendered were well matched to the post-Watergate period of American politics. Carter promised morality and problem solving and anticipated the public goods character of many emerging issues, such as the energy problem. As president he played to his strength for problem solving. This worked well when he could control the situation, as in the Camp David accords or perhaps even the Strategic Arms Limitation Talks (SALT). But his style was less effective in situations requiring anticipation of political pitfalls and bargaining, especially with Congress. By the same token, he organized White House decision making along collegial lines, and it worked well when his goals were clear. But if he was uncertain and his lieutenants were in disagreement, he often found it difficult to control executive politics.

The analysis of Carter's leadership in any given policy area reveals a congruence of beliefs, mode of thinking, and personal needs in his purposes and strategy of leadership. Policy leadership is explained as a blend of presidential purpose, joining purpose to political strategies, and matching decision-making processes to purpose and politics. For example, in his economic policies, Carter tried to ward off inflation and unemployment in alternating zigs and zags in a period of stagflation, not only for policy reasons but as a balancing act within the Democratic coalition. Decision-making processes were correspondingly collegial and balanced among liberal and conservative advisers to the president. He pulled it all together, more or less. An analysis of this kind avoids oversimple explanations in terms of any one factor.

Ronald Reagan is a mirror image of Carter in many respects. An exponent of traditional American values, with an impressionist cognitive style and strong needs for attention and applause, he developed a mature style of leadership that inspired and obscured and made his persona the centerpiece of his appeal. This style and the attendant skills were well matched for the watershed opportunity that presented itself in 1980 as the liberal policy regime that began in 1961 collapsed (Wills, 1988). Reagan seized the opportunity to use rhetoric and persona to articulate a new policy agenda and to clarify an ambiguous historical situation.[4] Again, one sees congruence in political personality and in strategies of leadership.

One may analyze and compare Carter and Reagan with ordinary language, using the model of political personality as a touchstone. One may go deeper and use personality theory to suggest that specific needs influenced particular actions. Carter's need for mastery of problems had compulsive qualities and was a strength in its tenacity but a weakness in its insensitivity to political factors. Reagan's perennial optimism, which often seemed blind to reality with regard to (SDI) or supply-side economics, may reflect the denial of the dark side of life by the child of an alcoholic. Such strong needs could have been responsible for both the creativity and the failures of these two politicians. This is not to suggest the validity of these hypotheses but to illustrate that the model of political personality can be used for comparison of political leaders to explain their general styles of leadership and also for uncovering particular actions that rely upon personality theory. The evidence for any interpretation would never be definitive, but the model is a framework both for matching hypotheses to the available evidence and for debate. Differences in interpretation can diverge from a common point of origin, and the degree of agreement or disagreement about the consequences of personality for action may be assessed in terms of the model. One need not identify the genesis of political personality in childhood to describe and analyze adult political style. One can infer that Carter had a need for mastery and Reagan had a need for attention and see these needs expressed in private feelings and political life, without explaining the origins of the needs in childhood experiences. A biographer may wish to suggest how needs and cognitive style developed in complementary ways, and such an approach must account for values and beliefs acquired along the way, but my model stops short of genesis. However, it is at that point that personality theory, with hypotheses about genesis, may be invoked to explain some feature of personality and action.

This approach is called a "coherent whole" strategy of biography by Faye Crosby and Travis Crosby, as distinct from a "causal" approach (1981, 199). One looks for repetitive patterns in the coherent whole approach and identifies the contexts in which they recur (ibid., 219). The Crosbys contend, and I agree, that causal analysis, which relies on psychoanalysis, encounters the difficulty of obtaining adequate evidence to support the hypotheses made (199–200). For example, they argue that the excellent study of Woodrow Wilson by Alexander and Juliette George, which probes Wilson's self-defeating behavior, is adequately treated by the coherent whole approach, in which Wilson is shown to have become rigid and defensive on those rare occasions when he interpreted political opposition as challenging his identity and integrity (221). The Georges richly document the emotional insecurities that underlay Wilson's need for office and greatness and draw plausible inferences about the relation of those insecurities to his ego-defensive rigidity in given cases. Their additional hypothesis that his rigidity arose out of childhood conflicts with his authoritarian father is reasonable, but it cannot be proved nor do they so claim (George and George, 1956). The Georges were assisted by personality theory in their analysis of Wilson, and such theory can be helpful to biographers by suggesting possible dynamic relations among personality traits—and this can be done without examining childhood. For example, Richard Bushman's psychologically sensitive biography of Benjamin Franklin illustrates that Franklin's desire to avoid hostility prompted him to choose negotiating roles as an adult (Crosby and Crosby, 1981, 222). Bushman's insights were psychoanalytically inspired, as were those of the Georges, in the sense of looking for a psychologically coherent pattern to a person's life. This is what I try to do with Jimmy Carter (Hargrove, 1988, chaps. 1 and 2).

The Crosbys rate psychobiographies with coherent whole explanations in terms of criteria of good biography: that is, are concepts operationalized, are the principles of analysis clear, are alternative explanations considered? They conclude that the studies that best matched their criteria were written by political scientists (Crosby and Crosby, 1981, 226–33). They do not speculate as to why, but I suggest that the intention to avoid psychological reductionism is perhaps one reason. The Crosbys also compare biographies that rely on explanations of adult behavior in terms of developmental causes with the coherent whole biographies and conclude that the latter meet the standards of good biography more thoroughly (ibid., 233).

William Runyan advocates a "life course" orientation to the study of lives and careers, which he sees as broader than the study of personality per se (1984, 82–85). The life course approach is ecological in its concept of the dynamic relation among person, situation, and behavior. One is shaped by formative influences over the entire course of one's life, including situations and experiences. For Runyan, neither psychological traits nor situations are sufficient to explain behavior, because neither remains fixed over time. Dynamic person-situation configurations continually develop (94–96). I posit a greater stability to political personality after young adulthood than Runyan might, but the difference is not fundamental—and the question is empirical in any case. Runyan's idea is consistent with the coherent whole approach in the desire to avoid reductionism.

In my judgment, ego psychology, as one variant of psychoanalytic theory, helps the biographer to see individual patterns and relations in the life course of an individual that one might not otherwise see (Woods, 1987, chap. 8). This is the framework most appropriate for the study of leadership style. It is assumed that the leader being studied has the ego strength to test "reality" with sufficient accuracy to permit actions designed to cope with problems in a "realistic" manner. But the implicit premises of style that shape the choice of particular strategies are also identified. Thus Carter's need for mastery or Reagan's need for attention are depicted along with the consequences for style. A president may be both following a set of preconscious intuitions that animate his entire political life and coping realistically with objective policy problems. The intuitions may be the basis of effective coping, but they may also lead him astray.

It is often argued that models of political personality are not really necessary. An astute observer will see a given individual clearly without the baggage of a model as a checklist to follow. Certainly a model is no guarantee of insight. But empiricism unguided by an explicit framework surely contains an implicit one. It is best to be explicit as long as the model does not blind one to empirical complexity. I find my model to be particularly helpful in two respects. It helps me avoid reductionist explanations and reveals the degree to which actions are motivated by more than one factor—thus the idea of the search for congruence among the grounds of action by the actor. The model also assists comparison of presidents so that one may ask how different personality characteristics contribute to the playing of presidential roles in different ways. One may also find that personality is not a factor in some cases because the role overrides individuality. However, I do not use the model for comprehensive comparisons of presidential role playing, because I lack a complete taxonomy of roles. This is work to be done.

The ultimate test of the use of models of personality or of personality theory in explaining the actions of political leaders is whether the propositions generated appear to explain the actions in question better than alternative hypotheses. There are no definitive explanations in biography, but some analyses square with the evidence better than others, even though all are incomplete. The use of models and theories of personality require the observer to develop a coherent whole understanding of the subject in a way that may lead to nonobvious insights about a political career and style of leadership. But to be convincing, such insights must be stated in ordinary language and with evidence that can be appraised by those who do not use psychology for their work.

Skill in Context

I have engaged in a study of executive leaders in which the relation of leadership skills to the tasks attempted was analyzed (Doig and Hargrove, 1987a, chap. 1) Effectiveness in achieving goals was enhanced if skill and task were congruent. For example, David Lilienthal's rhetorical skills were just what the new Tennessee Valley

Authority needed to sell the merits of publicly provided electricity to the people of the valley (ibid., chap. 2). But when Lilienthal became chairman of the Atomic Energy Commission in 1946 there was little scope for such skills. A third element in success or failure is the degree of potential political support in the society for the goals of the leader. Lilienthal was able to link the TVA with Roosevelt and the New Deal. But the AEC became embroiled in the politics of security risks and anticommunism, which placed it under congressional attack and hampered Lilienthal's leadership.

It is plausible to ask these same questions of presidents—the kinds of questions with which I began this essay—in order to assess the relative importance of political skill or its absence in varying historical contexts. Political science descriptions of presidential policy leadership are too often content with describing the impact of individual presidents on role playing without asking about the effects on policy. We should widen our lenses to ask how presidents affect history in significant ways through strategies of leadership. The table below suggests a crude combination of possibilities in the match of individual political skill to favorable or unfavorable political conditions as a means of comparing the impact of presidents on history.

	Favorable political conditions	Unfavorable political conditions
High political skill	1	2
Low political skill	3	4

The criteria for high and low skill are not going to fall on one continuum. For example, both Franklin Roosevelt and Dwight Eisenhower were skillful presidents, but in different ways. However, most experts would contend that Roosevelt had a greater repertoire of skills than Eisenhower and that the latter was a more skillful leader in the White House than Gerald Ford. But still, the specifics of skill—manipulative ability, rhetoric, strategic sense—would have to be spelled out to a greater extent than I do here. By the same token, the specification of favorable and unfavorable political conditions for the exercise of skill requires a careful identification of the key variables, such as public support, confirming events, the strength of governing coalitions, and the character of policy problems. Again, I will not pause here to do that work, but it should be clear to the reader what is needed.

This framework can be used to assess one president by asking about his contribution, through skill or ineptness, to his own successes and failures. Thus Jimmy Carter experienced very few cases in either cells 1 or 3. He was not president at a propitious time for the exercise of skill, and his skills were limited. But there is little evidence that ineptness sabotaged favorable receptivity to his goals. Most of his successes fell in cell 2, in which he could infuse his vision, tenacity, and capacity for homework on obstacles to change, such as the Panama Canal treaties, the Camp David Accords, and passage of comprehensive energy legislation. But Carter also became mired in cell 4 and may have contributed to his own undoing by his handling of the Iranian revolution, the Soviet invasion of Afghanistan, and the high inflation of his last year. Such assessments would require studying a number of Carter cases, looking at both what the president did and did not do in relation to contextual support and impediments (Hargrove, 1988, chap. 6).

The framework is most useful for the comparison of presidents. It permits the analysis of skill in context so that we can assess the actual contribution of individuality to presidential success and failure in specified conditions. Great skill and favorable conditions reinforce each other—for example, Franklin Roosevelt in his first term. Highly skilled leaders may fail in unfavorable conditions; Roosevelt's second term was less successful legislatively in the face of the anti–New Deal conservative coalition in Congress. Presidents who are not highly skilled may achieve successes because of very favorable conditions, such as Truman's initial cold war policies. And finally, one can imagine a president who is favored by neither ability nor or context, but presidents of limited ability are rare. The table admits a number of variations within cells. The inept may turn favorable situations into failure. Talent may extract success from adversity. Skill, as an attribute of personality, may be matched to the historical context. Such an approach opens the door to the comparative study of many aspects of strategic and tactical leadership.

Greenstein contends that leaders have an impact on the environment to the degree that it admits of restructuring (1969, 42–45). He concludes that the greater a leader's skill, the less his or her initial need for a favorable or manipulable environment and "the greater the likelihood that he himself will contribute to making his subsequent position and his environment manipulable" (45). I agree with this, but there are limits to what talent can accomplish. This sense of a dynamic relation between leader and environment must be captured.

The most important skill in politicians, as defined by this matrix, is the capacity to discern where history may go and to reinforce that direction by skillful action. I call this "strategic leadership" (Hargrove and Nelson, 1984, chap. 4). Such talent transcends the sensitivity to political resources in the bargaining arena of Washington that Richard Neustadt requires of presidents.[5] The discernment required is insight into the central dilemmas of a period and, if it is to have an effect, must be joined to the ability to form and articulate plausible remedies for those dilemmas that will win support in the country. I am not speaking of heroic leadership here. Even muddle and confusion require leadership, as does the desire for peace and stability. The bargaining and manipulative skills required for effective work in Washington are very important, but they will be enhanced if complemented by articulated historical discernment.

George Edwards makes a very clear distinction in this regard between a president who is a facilitator in contrast to the president who seeks to be the director of change (1989, 221–24). He predicts that the facilitator provides more effective leadership than the director because he understands the limits of the political resources available to him.[6] According to Edwards, and I agree, effective presidents do not usually create the political resources on which they rely; rather, they take advantage of those resources and the opportunities created by them. Thus, both Franklin Roosevelt and Lyndon Johnson understood the importance of striking hard and quickly to win in Congress while support was high, in the knowledge that it would also be temporary. John Kennedy introduced a program knowing that much of it would not pass but hoping to win a mandate for action in his second term. Carter failed to follow Kennedy's example and perhaps tried to do too much too early without the necessary support. Reagan profited from that lesson and pressed only one or two big issues in his first year.

Presidential leadership has three components: (1) policy purposes, (2) consideration of the politics of action in relation to purpose, and (3) the management of decision making. Presidents seek a congruence among these three factors. Carter's economic policies, for example balanced the dangers of inflation and unemployment, consistent with Democratic politics, through an advisory process that gave equal weight to liberal and conservative economic advisers. Reagan, who had much clearer economic goals, fueled by the political appeal of supply-side economics, could permit a more centralized decision process. Presidential political personality is the catalyst of style that joins purpose, politics, and process (Hargrove, 1988, chap. 4).

What kinds of generalizations might one expect from thus anchoring skill in historical context? A few possibilities come to mind: explanation of significant achievements and failures; understanding the relation of skill to presidential role playing and the resultant impact on events; identification of the presidential roles in which individuality is less important. Gary King argues in his chapter in this book that the individual president should not be the unit of analysis for research because the N is simply too small. That is true if one wishes to understand the presidency as an institution, to the degree that it is one. But King fails to see that the purpose of my essay is to ask about the conditions under which individuality matters for the presidency. Small N or not, it is an important question, even though it is only one of many approaches to studying the office. King is correct that regularities of various kinds might be discovered from focusing, for example, upon large numbers of decisions, although he underestimates the difficulty of the task. But at the end of the day, the study of presidential decisions may send one in search of presidential personality and leadership style as one explanation for the patterns discerned.

Structural Analysis

The approach to studying presidents proceeds necessarily by induction insofar as we lack deductive theories by which to explain presidential actions. It is possible to proceed deductively with theories of presidential behavior that rely on political and institutional variables and then to ask whether personality adds to the understanding of behavior. For example, Stephen Skowronek has developed a typology of party regimes in American history—the Jeffersonian, Jacksonian, Republican, and New Deal regimes (1984, chap. 4). Each regime has reproduced four types of presidencies: those who construct a new regime, such as Thomas Jefferson, Andrew Jackson, Abraham Lincoln and Franklin Roosevelt; those who close out a regime, such as John Quincy Adams, James Buchanan, Herbert Hoover, and Jimmy Carter; those who revive a flagging regime, such as Theodore Roosevelt,

John Kennedy, and Lyndon Johnson; and, finally, minority presidents who are elected and achieve significant goals, such as Grover Cleveland and Woodrow Wilson.

The important point here is that Skowronek explains presidential actions and achievements primarily in terms of the political resources provided by the structure of politics in each type of regime rather than by presidential leadership and style. For example, presidents who come at the end of a regime cannot rely on a strong party coalition for support in Congress, since an alternative alignment is emerging. These presidents are blamed for lacking political skill, but they are prisoners of conflicts they cannot reconcile. They may even become scapegoats for the nation's problems. This kind of president may have a strong determination to pull the regime into the new era but will approach great national issues as technical, nonpolitical problems. They are problem solvers. Compare Hoover and Carter, the two engineer presidents, who are much alike in these respects. Individuality seems to wash out. But how does that explain Carter's very real achievements? Did not political personality have a place? The presidents who create new regimes would seem to have the opportunity for personal creativity, as would those who revive coalitions or become effective minority presidents. The virtue of Skowronek's framework is that it permits one to ask what style contributes to the structural variables in his typologies. Such an approach is a useful antidote to explanations of presidential action that rely solely on personality, without considering such structural factors.

The study of presidential leadership of Congress is particularly congenial to schema that specify variations in the political conditions for presidential success. Political personality may play a role here, at the margins. George Edwards and Mark Peterson create such schema in their studies of presidential leadership of Congress. Edwards seeks to relate three sources of presidential influence in Congress—party strength, public support, and presidential skill—to presidential effectiveness. His general conclusion is that leadership skill makes a difference at the margins; party strength and public support are more important (Edwards, 1989, 7, 124–25, 135, 143). Presidents seldom have public mandates, and such mandates are the results of historical forces that presidents do not create or control (164). But they can claim a mandate and thus set the terms of congressional debate in their favor, as Reagan did in 1981 (160–61, 166). Even so, presidential legislative skills, which may change a few votes, are less important than the larger historical context (185). Edwards equates skill in the presidency with what I call strategic leadership—knowing what is possible and making the most of one's opportunities (216). Strong party and public support enhance the exercise of presidential skill (217–18). Edwards may neglect the value-added element of skill in favorable circumstances, in contrast to my formulation. But he does recognize that the facilitator of change, aware of the limits on action, is still a skillful leader (223).

Peterson assesses the relative strength of contextual variables—institutional, political, economic, and policy character—to presidential strategies of leadership (1990, chap. 6). The key to presidential success is the strategic decisions presidents make about what kinds of and how many proposals to send to Congress in relation to contextual factors (215). This finding suggests that discernment of the historical situation is the cardinal virtue of presidential leadership. Peterson suggests that this skill is, in large part, a result of the important choices presidents have made about their careers and life-style, which have shaped their talents in understanding others and knowing how "to understand and exploit the human element that rests at the heart of politics" (230). This is an argument for understanding political personality.

Ego-Defensive Behavior and
the Political Science Tradition

One can go further than the delineation of style and attempt to explain particular actions in terms of theories about the effects of unconscious forces on action. This approach is most applicable to the study of ego-defensive behavior, in which the person responds more to internal vulnerabilities, or defenses against such vulnerabilities, than to the realities of the situation. There is a political science tradition of such explanations directed primarily at the study of presidents, and I will now consider that approach.

The questions that political scientists ask are whether ego-defensive behavior can be predicted and detected in presidents and whether such behavior, if it occurs, is harmful to the nation by leading to policy actions more reflective of personality needs than of objective realities. The detection of ego-defensive action requires the isolation and assessment of the strength of unconscious forces that may cause a president to act in response to private needs, imposing that response on his interpretation of the situation faced. This is not an easy assignment. It risks reductionist error. And yet such an explanation is inherently reductionist.

In 1930, Harold Lasswell invented the idea of "political man," one who entered politics in order to win power, attention, and other values as a means of overcoming low estimates of the self. Since the roots of low self-esteem are unconscious, the drive for a response from others to meet the need is insatiable and is pursued relentlessly (Lasswell, 1930). Lasswell sketches a model of political man in which private needs are rationalized into political goals and displaced onto public objects. Thus the "agitator" uses all his skill and energy to win favorable responses from audiences. Agitators are actors in politics. "Administrators" have strong compulsive needs that take the political form of imposing order and structure on the flux of governmental life. "Theorists" displace hidden aggression onto dogmas to justify their political work. These portraits are reductionist, as Lasswell admits in a later edition.[7] Such "nuclear types," as Lasswell characterizes them, are driven solely by unconscious forces without reliance upon beliefs, values, and realistic coping with political situations.

Lasswell contributed two legacies: the concept of a nuclear type of political personality and the insight that private needs might be displaced onto public objects. The idea of ego-defensive behavior, in which the most vulnerable parts of the self virtually rush onto the political stage, was implicit in his formulation. But he wrote before ego psychology was fully developed. His rather primitive types give the impression of politicians who can hardly control the unconscious forces impelling them into political life. My model of political personality, derived from ego psychology, permits the politician to deal with reality most of the time without intense infusions from the unconscious.

Alexander and Juliette George enrich Lasswell's theoretical structure in their study of Woodrow Wilson (George and George, 1956). Wilson was a highly successful university president, governor, and president of the United States, but a pattern of self-defeating behavior occurred three times in crucial episodes, the most dramatic being his refusal to compromise with Senate Republicans on revision of the League of Nations proposal, thus destroying any hope for U.S.

participation in the League. This action, and conflicts with the graduate dean at Princeton and the New Jersey legislature, are seen by the Georges as ego-defensive behavior in which Wilson saw his integrity as a person at stake. The Georges build on Lasswell's hypothesis that power may be used to overcome low estimates of the self. In their words: "Power was for [Wilson] a compensatory value, a means of restoring the self-esteem damaged in childhood" (320).

The Georges probe the three levels of analysis necessary for good psychobiography. They first delineate Wilson's recurring styles of leadership in academic and political life: his use of eloquent rhetoric, his drive for reform through forceful leadership of faculty and legislative party, his willingness to compromise on details when he was winning, and in the three key episodes, his refusal to compromise, to his own detriment. They move to the second level of analysis and build a model of the psychodynamics of Wilson's political personality. Single traits are depicted in a unified portrait of a leader whose need for power was matched with skills of rhetoric and manipulation and accompanied by strong subjective feelings of uncertainty and insecurity and a need for deference that drove both the private and public man. In this respect, they create a more plausible understanding of Wilson's motivations as a political man than biographers who are not informed by personality theory. For example, the historian Paige Smith complains that the Georges tell us what we already know about Wilson's stubbornness. But Smith fails to understand that stubbornness is best understood in terms of psychodynamics that explain why Wilson was flexible in some situations and rigid in others (Greenstein, 1969, 71).

The Georges then move to a third level and present evidence for the hypothesis that Wilson's ego-defensive rigidity was the legacy of a difficult relationship with a loving but authoritarian father. The adult Woodrow Wilson may have resolved never to bend to the will of another who challenged him in a way to stimulate the painful memories of his father's authoritarian control (George and George, 1956, chap. 1). The authors provide rich evidence for such a relation, with the possible negative effects on Wilson. They do not sufficiently develop the idea that his strengths as a politician were rooted in compensatory striving to overcome low estimates of the self. Wilson's very insecurities, combined with his talents and considerable ego strength, were the motivational basis for his political successes. But the Achilles heel of insecurity may have ultimately provided for his undoing and made him a tragic figure, brought low by a crucial weakness in character.

Critics of the Georges' thesis about the genesis of Wilson's insecurity and the attendant consequences either accept the pattern of self-defeating action but attribute a different cause, or argue that Wilson acted as he did, especially in the League fight, for tactical political reasons. This is not the place for an analysis of the debate about whether Wilson's rigidity in key cases was the result of a series of strokes, especially the serious illness of 1918 (Weinstein, Anderson, and Link, 1987, chap. 12). In my judgment, those who contend that Wilson's rigidity had biological causes fail to take account of the psychological detail developed by the Georges about Wilson's need for deference, thirst for office, and strong drive to dominate. A stroke in 1918 surely contributed to his refusal to compromise, but earlier possible strokes, if they occurred (and the evidence is not strong), were not so consistently timed so as to explain earlier episodes. Arthur Link, Wilson's biographer, cites Wilson's "nervous strain" as one cause of his inability to compromise with the dean of the graduate school at Princeton (Link, 1987, 74, 84–85). This is simply putting a name on something without explaining it. Jeffrey Tulis denies the psychological approach altogether when he criticizes the Georges' failure to understand that rhetorical leadership, in which the political leader appeals to the public over the heads of intermediaries like Congress, was Wilson's stock and trade as a politician and an expression of his theory of political leadership (1987, 149–61). This is surely true of Wilson, but Tulis cannot explain why Wilson was flexible at times, even when appealing to the public, and inflexible at other times, nor does he address the emotional intensity of the self-defeating behavior.

In short, the Georges observe the rules of good psychobiography, as set out by the Crosbys, better than their critics. They try to avoid reductionism. Their critics would reply that this is not the case, because the Georges rely too heavily on psychodynamic explanations for Wilson's behavior. I think that the Georges could have depicted Wilson's talents and his leadership style as products of the same personality needs that lay beneath his self-defeating behavior. It is quite possible that an interpretation of Wilson's actions based upon the hypothesis of congruence among needs, skills, and beliefs might incorporate a number of insights about motivation in a way that would accept, but mute, the Georges' hypothesis about ego-defensiveness. Or, their thesis might be sustained as a sufficient explanation for self-defeating behavior. In the final analysis, the question of whether Wilson became rigid under specified conditions cannot be fully tested because, as in all biography and history, the incomplete available evidence about complex decisions is subject to competing explanations without any possibility of a scientific resolution of the disagreement.

Even so, we must take seriously the possibility that presidents may engage in ego-defensive behavior and therefore respond in inappropriate ways to challenge. Such behavior is most likely to occur in crises when presidents feel the greatest stress and the greatest threats to their own self-esteem and sense of efficacy. Harold Lasswell does not address this issue directly, but he draws the distinction between "political man" and "democratic character" (1948). Earlier (Lasswell, 1930), he set out three nuclear types of political man. By implication, all three types—agitator, administrator, and theorist—are capable of projecting personal needs onto public goals, sometimes constructively, but also potentially in ego-defensive ways. The democratic character, in contrast, did not need or desire political power or adulation. Lasswell's democratic character is actually more citizen than leader, for in a polity of such people, leadership is less important. We outgrow the need for political men.

James David Barber joins these insights from Lasswell to his own perceptiveness about the presidency to formulate a typology of presidents that combines ego-defensive action with normal and legitimate ranges of behavior (Barber, 1985). Barber's typology originally emerged from the study of Connecticut state legislators (Barber, 1965). He was a student of Lasswell, knew the work of the Georges, and was in a good position to adapt the insights of this work to the study of presidents. Barber improved on earlier work of mine that came from the same tradition of Lasswell and the Georges. A comparison of the work illustrates the impact of the Johnson and Nixon presidencies on Barber and on ideas about ego-defensiveness in political leaders. In 1966, I set out a typology of presidents of action—the two Roosevelts and Wilson—and presidents of restraint—Taft, Hoover, and Eisenhower (Hargrove, 1966). The presidents of action were said to have channeled needs for attention and power into the skillful playing of leadership roles. Their talents served and were guided by a belief in the positive role of government in reforming society. The presidents of restraint lacked such political needs and skills and believed in limited government. Political virtuosity was less important to them. They were therefore judged to be less skillful in achieving their goals than presidents of action.

My presidents of action have antecedents in Lasswell's agitator, broadened to mean a political man who could function well within a democratic system of checks and balances. Ego-defensive impulses, even with Wilson, following the Georges, were contained by institutions. I worked backward from Neustadt's model of Franklin Roosevelt as the president of exemplary political skill to ask what personality characteristics might accompany such skills. In this regard, I found the work of Henry Murray extremely helpful. Murray's studies find a dynamic connection between personality "needs" and "skills." For example, the need for attention could stimulate the development of exhibitionist skills to serve that need, in both private life and political life. The need for dominance could nurture the development of power-maximizing skills. And the causal relation might be reversed, in that abilities stimulate needs. Murray introduces a third concept, that of "press," which is an environmental stimulus that evokes the need-skill dynamic in action. This is the initial basis for my insight that political leaders seek out problems and situations that permit them to play to their strengths (skills) and also to meet their needs.

My intent in positing a congruence of needs, skills, and beliefs is to avoid reductionism, to permit needs and skills to shape styles of action without dictating the content of action, and to accept the overdetermination of the actions of political leaders. Beliefs, needs, and skills are congruent, as mediated by the ego. Thus, Roosevelt believed in strong, active government, had the political skills necessary to extend the power of government, and served personal needs for attention and power by doing so. Eisenhower's restraint was, by the same token, ideological and personal. No one factor in a political personality is less weighty than others. Style is explained, but specific behaviors are not predicted. However, the complexity of motivation limits the typology's scope. Presidents Nixon and Reagan confounded the assumption that conservatives are presidents of restraint. Presidents

Johnson and Nixon also disturbed the assumption that the needs of presidents of action are not destructive of themselves or institutions. Barber (1985) profits from the history of Johnson and Nixon in his formulation of a typology of presidents.[8] His four types are characterized by terms that are strictly neither psychological nor political, but link the two. There are two dimensions: active-passive and positive-negative. A president brings high or low levels of energy and enthusiasm to the job and has positive or negative feelings about himself in relation to that activity. These two dimensions yield four types: active positive, active negative, passive positive, and passive negative. The fourteen most recent presidents fall into these categories:

ACTIVE POSITIVE	PASSIVE POSITIVE
F. Roosevelt	Taft
Truman	Harding
Kennedy	Reagan
Ford	
Carter	

ACTIVE NEGATIVE	PASSIVE NEGATIVE
Wilson	Coolidge
Hoover	Eisenhower
Johnson	
Nixon	

Barber had a greater sensitivity in 1972 than I had in 1966 to the fact that presidents of action might have destructive as well as constructive personalities; he therefore divides them into active positives and active negatives. The examples of Johnson and Nixon were there to consider. His concept of the active negative, the leader who is a prisoner of joyless compensatory striving, is a contemporary reformulation of Lasswell's political man. Barber's active positive, who has high self-esteem, ego strength, and a good sense of reality, is close to Lasswell's formulation of the democratic character who is the opposite of political man in his lack of drivenness and his capacity for openness, learning, and flexible adaptations to the beliefs and needs of others. The passive positives are presidents who wish to please, to be popular, and to be adulated. The passive negatives serve out of duty; they are prisoners of conscience. Barber predicts the general style of leadership of each type of president. The active positives will lead realistically with optimism and buoyancy. The active negatives are driven by their needs to develop political skills and become ego-defensive and rigid in situations in which their self-esteem is challenged by opposition; the Georges' hypothesis about Wilson is extended to Hoover, Johnson, and Nixon. The passive positives court popularity. The passive negatives limit the possibilities of presidential leadership by canons of right conduct.

Barber's model of political personality is based on three elements: character, world view, and style; each individual is a blend of the three elements (Barber, 1985). Character consists of needs, drives, and sense of self in relation to others "and is the force, the motive power, around which the person gathers his world view" (501). Barber tilts in favor of character as the organizing principle of personality; beliefs, style, and contextual analysis are introduced in the individual studies, but character dominates the schema and is the basis for prediction of what individuals will do. Simplicity is both the strength and weakness of Barber's typology; his achievement is to have produced a comprehensive typology were none existed before. But the work also illustrates the difficulties of building typologies. The following views are expressed by several of Barber's critics: Alexander George (1974), Daniel Katz (1973), Jean Blondel (1987), Paul Conkin (1986), and John Blum (1980).

First, the four types are not grounded in personality theory. Barber adds theory about adaptation, compulsion, and so on, to the individual profiles, but such theoretical insights are not derived from the typology itself. Nor does he establish that the traits attributed to each type go together according to personality theory. A theory of political personality must be able to link personality variables with political behavior. But there are few ready-made psychological types in personality theory that can be applied to the study of politicians. Barber tries to build bridging categories that are neither fully psychological nor fully political, and he deserves credit for attempting the link. The hard question is what one does to ground the schema in psychology or whether it is necessary to do so.

Second, the four types are pure types and are only a starting point for the study of an individual. But Barber also uses the typology to explain specific cases and thus may distort individual profiles. Eisenhower and Reagan are so presented in terms of the models of passive negative and passive positive, respectively, that one begins to wonder if Barber has not selected illustrations to fit the categories. Ike was a much wilier politician and Reagan a much tougher and dedicated ideologue and partisan than Barber admits. In other cases, he does admit the possibility of hybrids; for example, the active positive Truman had strong active negative tendencies. The development of subtypes might ease this difficulty if the small number of cases permits it. Hoover, Johnson, and Nixon are all pressed into the Wilson mold as active negatives who ultimately arrange for their own defeat. But it is not at all clear that the other three presidents engaged in recurring self-defeating behavior, as Wilson did. Hoover may not fit the type at all. Johnson and Nixon did enter politics, in part, to overcome low self-estimates through compensatory striving. Insatiable unconscious needs drove them with a restlessness and compulsive ambition that could never be satisfied. But the leap from style to the prediction and explanation of self-defeating actions is too great to be convincing.

Third, Barber shows how personality expresses itself in political behavior, but it does not follow that psychological forces are the primary cause of substantive policy commitment or political action. Contextual factors of role and situation add to style and beliefs and values to influence the content of action. Barber traps himself in reductionist explanations at times, because the typology, based solely on character, cannot carry the burden of multicausal explanation. For example, his analysis of Johnson's intensity and rigidity in the Vietnam commitment does not explore possible political explanations.

Fourth, active positive presidents vary so as individuals that the category lacks the capacity to analyze and explain actions of political leadership. A schema that puts Franklin Roosevelt and Jimmy Carter in the same cell tells us that they shared high self-esteem and the capacity to learn and adapt to circumstances, but it says nothing about the great difference in political skill between them or the psychological bases for such differences. In fact active positives, Barber's favorite type, are primarily men without the personality quirks that might lead them into ego-defensive actions.

We understand the active negatives because of Lasswell's early insights, and this is Barber's contribution to Lasswell's concept. We do not know what sends the active positives into politics. Barber's typology does not include political skill as a variable and, therefore, does not permit us to ask how active positives and active negatives, who are both high in skill, may differ with regard to democratic character—and with what consequences. For example, there may be a relation between needs and skills that explains the presence or absence of political talent. Theodore Roosevelt needed attention and developed the skills to get it, whereas his chosen successor, William Howard Taft, had no such needs or abilities and was poor at dramatizing himself as president. But character, understood in terms of high or low self-esteem, appears to be an important distinction among highly politically skilled politicians. Franklin Roosevelt and Lyndon Johnson were both very skillful politicians, but the latter may have been deficient in self-esteem—with consequences for leadership style and policy decisions (see Hargrove, 1974, chap. 2, for comparisons of presidents in these terms).

These criticisms are not intended to slight Barber's contribution. Rather, they illustrate the difficulty of creating a comprehensive typology of political personalities. I suggest a simpler schema for the comparison of presidents (and other political leaders) that does not attempt such comprehensiveness. The principal purpose is to uncover the links in personality between high political skill and high democratic character and high political skill and low democratic character, since this is the context of ego-defensive behavior:

	High democratic character	Low democratic character
High political skill	1	2
Low political skill	3	4

I have discussed the difficulties of placing quite different presidents on the same skill continuum. The same work must be attempted in assessing high and low democratic character, as judgments about the degree of ego strength and self-esteem. The democratic character has less need to respond to the world in ways that quell private fears, and therefore such a person can deal with events realistically and has the capacity to learn from experience. The leader who lacks a democratic character may be highly skilled in serving his need for attention and dominance but is likely to interpret challenges as threats to the self and to act accordingly.

Franklin Roosevelt surely possessed both high skill and high democratic character. I place Eisenhower and Kennedy as high in character and at a midpoint in skill. I put Carter, certainly a democratic
character, a bit lower on the skill continuum. Reagan is at the midpoint of both continua. Johnson and Nixon have high political skills
and uncertain democratic characters. (One is not going to find occupants of cell 4 in the presidency. It takes some skill or character to get
there.) These judgments need not be defended here. They illustrate that
it may be possible to compare presidents in this way. The framework
is consistent with the model of political personality presented earlier.

Comparisons of Presidential Management
of Decision Making

The best work on the relation of personality to presidential leadership is in the study of foreign policy decision making. The limited
number of variables, in comparison to domestic politics and policy,
and the relatively closed decision process and limited number of presidential advisers, permit analysis of the effects of a president's style of
authority upon a decision-making group. Insights from personality
theory may be joined with ideas from social psychology about the impact of leaders upon small groups. Such analyses must be understood
in terms of the beliefs of decision makers and their efforts to take account of the political and policy problems they face. For example, one
cannot establish a direct causal link from either presidential style or
the character of a group process to specific historical decisions; beliefs and strategies of action intervene. However, one may generalize
about the relation among leadership style, group process, and the
general characteristics of decisions taken in different combinations of
leadership and decision making. This is the goal of a comparison of
presidential styles. Foreign policy making has taken on the character
and complexity of domestic policy making because of the interlacing
of foreign and domestic problems and politics.

Marginal Comparisons

Joseph de Rivera illustrates three approaches to measuring personality: the nomothetic approach classifies; the ideographic approach
describes individuality; and the phenomenal approach attempts to

understand individuals in terms of processes common to all people. He believes that the phenomenal approach is best suited to the study of complex decision making (de Rivera, 1968, 168).

One nomothetic approach, suggested in the work of Murray, is to group subjects in terms of behavior that suggests underlying needs. If a way can be found to measure the need, one would hope to predict its effects on behavior in specified situations. But laboratory efforts to predict the effects of the need for achievement on risk taking, for example, produce very limited predictions. De Rivera concludes that "we are ill prepared to predict the behavior of a normal individual" (175). Some individuals in a test group are more or less cautious or confident about taking risks; individuals do not show consistent risk-taking styles but tailor their predispositions to changing situations. A personality test of a number of individuals show greater and lesser needs across the board but does not predict what any given person will do: "When it comes to accurately describing the personality of an individual, the best battery of personality tests is a poor substitute for a skillful biography" (181). The attempt to describe Abraham Lincoln, for example, may use variables that are not relevant to most politicians. Not all politicians undergo Lincoln's transformation from ambitious politician to moral leader. Few politicians have the historical opportunity available to Lincoln. This is not to reject the nomothetic approach, which has the problems of all typology, but to emphasize how that typology does not do justice to either individuality or context.

The ideographic approach begins with the effort to understand an individual in terms of a number of traits by examining the relation of those traits within the individual. One then attempts to group that individual with others with similar clusters of traits. Descriptive labels are used to type rather than to understand behavior. The ideographic classification is more complex than the nomothetic, which usually singles out only one factor as the basis for classification. The pattern of action, which can be observed "from the outside" can be the basis for typing (182–83). An illustration of this approach is the adaptation of the Meyer-Briggs test of psychological types to politicians. If they cannot take the test, one can take it for them by matching their expressed feelings and actions to the typology. Thus Jimmy Carter appears to be an INTJ (introvert, intuitive, thinking, judging), as opposed to the opposite polar type of ESFP (extrovert, sensate, feeling, perceiving; Keirsey and Bates, 1978, 180–83). There are sixteen possibilities in these combinations. Carter matches the attributed characteristics of INTJs. He seeks competence, values intelligence, is skeptical of authority, works at play, sends contradictory messages, provides no redundancy for communication, seeks to rearrange the environment, focuses on the future, may miss direct experience, and is not always sensitive to the complexity of interpersonal relations (48–57). Reagan is perhaps an ENFJ (extrovert, intuitive, feeling, judging). He operates by charm, intuition, feeling, and strong beliefs. Mrs. Reagan could be an ISTJ (introvert, sensate, thinking, judging) and, therefore, is sensitive enough to his weaknesses to protect him from them (167–70, 189–92). I am more confident of my characterization of Carter, having studied him, than I am of these suggestions about the Reagans.[9]

De Rivera's point is that the ideographic approach, like the nomothetic, permits typing but is not sufficient to explain what makes the individual tick. The INTJ label provided a shock of recognition about Carter when I came upon it after my portrait of his personality had been etched. But it is no substitute for my understanding of his individuality (Hargrove, 1974, chaps. 1 and 2). However, typing may be useful in comparing presidents and should be explored.

The phenomenal approach studies individuals from a subjective viewpoint as they cope with issues common to all people in the universe studied. From example, we can compare Wilson, Roosevelt, and Truman in regard to their degree of self-confidence as president and the effects on their leadership styles. Wilson was very confident when he saw himself as pursuing a great ideal. Roosevelt thought of the presidency as himself in the White House. Truman made a sharp distinction between official and personal authority. Each president's strength was also his weakness. Wilson's great drive in behalf of ideals helps explain both his achievements and failures. Roosevelt's confidence could and did lead to hubris. Truman's respect for the authority of his office was a resource that had to be invoked to fire lieutenants who infringed on his uncertain personal authority (de Rivera, 1968, 183–88). De Rivera suggests that presidents can be compared according to the emotional predispositions they bring to presidential tasks and roles in ways that illuminate their actions. The phenomenal approach rests on the premise that the common function being used as a base for comparison—crucial decision, modes of thinking, interests, developmental stages—is valuable for understanding and comparing individuals. For example, the idea of Erikson that individuals pass through developmental stages in their lives, which must be explicitly confronted for growth to occur, provides specific questions to be asked in studying individual lives and in comparing individuals (ibid., 186). The phenomenal approach, with particular attention to the emotions, is a promising point of departure for comparing presidents. This is illustrated in the material that follows.

The Management of Decision Making

Alexander George posits the importance of three factors for the way presidents manage decision making (George, 1980, 139; Johnson, 1974): (1) The president's cognitive style (the way he defines his informational needs and goes about getting information) influences what he learns. (2) The president's sense of efficacy about managing decision making affects his authority in a group. (3) The president's personal orientation to conflict among his advisers influences what they will tell him and their relations with each other. The combination of these three elements of personality tends to define the norms and decision rules that an executive imposes on his advisers. Their group dynamics are attendant on his style (George, 1980, 99–100).

Carter had the cognitive style of an engineer. He liked to factor problems into pieces and to understand the relation of details to the whole. He also had great confidence that he could personally master difficult intellectual tasks. He did not immediately ask about the politics of a problem but sought solutions. Such problem solving, as a mode of thought, was congruent with Carter's belief that the best policies were those that articulated the public good, values shared in common, rather than appealed to interests or coalitions. He wished to organize the world according to basic principles. The messy politics of pluralism and incrementalism did not appeal to him. Finally, he wished his relations with his advisers to be collegial, a band of brothers. He did not think of his relationships with lieutenants as political in the sense that there might be conflicts over values and interest among them. His feel for order, purpose, and process was more technocratic than political. Leadership style was a composite of congruent forces (Hargrove, 1988, chap. 2).

Style of authority is useful for comparing how presidents manage decision making. The comparisons can be in phenomenal terms. George, borrowing from Richard Tanner Johnson, classifies presidents according to whether they initiate formalistic, competitive, or collegial processes of decision making. Truman, Eisenhower, and Nixon preferred orderly structures with well-defined procedures, hierarchical lines of communication, and a structured staff system. Franklin Roosevelt liked to pit his advisers against each other, giving them overlapping responsibilities and using multiple channels of communication. Johnson began with such a competitive system and gradually moved toward a formalistic one. Other modern presidents have preferred variations of the collegial model, which seeks to blend diversity and unity (George, 1980, 148–49).

One difficulty with these three models is that they do not capture the informal elements of decision process; for example, Greenstein believes that Eisenhower built informal collegiality into a formal structure (1982, chap. 4). Another difficulty is that individual presidents who favor variations on the formal model vary greatly in their political personalities, including George's three traits. We keep gravitating back to individuality. The problem with using models to differentiate the authority styles of presidents is similar to the problem of psychological types. The closer one comes to deductive abstraction, the further one is from empirical reality. Models of authority style are only points of departure for understanding individual presidents. George's detailed comparisons of presidents, using the models, illustrate the point (1980, 149–64). However, George generalizes about the benefits and costs of each model; for example, other things being equal, an orderly decision process enforces a more thorough analysis than a competitive one but may screen out highly innovative ideas that would bubble up in competition (165). Such generalizations have moved a long way from the personalities of individual presidents, particularly since quite different personalities may adhere to the same general model. The impact of personality is crucial and may be discerned but must be joined to contextual factors.

Irving Janis thinks it possible that the three elements of leadership style cited by George may interact with situational factors to reveal consistent differences among policymakers in "vigilant problem solving." Drawing upon psychological research, he posits that attention to careful organization, openness to information of a variety of kinds, and emotional security are related to a willingness to probe beyond group consensus, organizational routine, and conventional wisdom to discover and explore fresh remedies for problems (1989, 206–09). Janis admits that the measures of these attributes for empirical research have yet to be developed, and it is not clear how they would be applied to presidents except in historical case studies. He is less interested in comparisons than in identifying the kinds of people who will not practice vigilant problem solving. His goal is to construct a prototype of an exemplary "grand master" at policy making (210–28). Work of this kind on executives and problem solving by psychologists may contribute in time to our understanding of presidential decision making.

In the meantime, what can be done to compare presidents in order to assess the importance of personality for the management of decision making? John Burke and Fred Greenstein (1989) tackle the issue head-on in their comparative study of Eisenhower and Johnson and two periods of decision about Vietnam. In 1954, the United States did not intervene militarily to help France in its losing battle in Vietnam. In 1965 the United States escalated the war in Vietnam by introducing American troops to combat on a large scale. The authors do not attempt to explain these decisions as a result of decision processes but compare the two cases to assess the effects of presidential style upon such processes. Each president is assessed in terms of criteria for good decision making developed by George, Janis, and others. Three questions are asked about each president. (1) What core personal attributes of the president influence decision making? (cognitive style, emotional resources, political ties). (2) What dispositions of the president influence the way he works with advisers? (use of delegation, reward and punishment, openness to new ideas). (3) What dispositions of the president explain how he responds to the political environment? (the politics of policy choices, presidential skills, and resources in influencing the environment). The most important question in this last area is, How malleable is the environment to presidential leadership? (ibid., 21–24).

A careful analysis in great detail of the two cases reveals that the two men had very different influences on the decision process by virtue of their different leadership styles (261–68). Eisenhower reformulated questions brought to the table and reframed alternatives. He made net judgments about the proper course of action as he went along, clearing the decks for new sets of questions. He was not seen as intimidating by his advisers and encouraged them to speak frankly. Nor was there any evidence of anger or stress. He managed his advisers as a planner and conceptualizer. Johnson did not reformulate questions or reframe alternatives. He would often let a policy question dangle while he shifted attention to the politics of the issue and never got back to the prior analysis. He was intimidating to his advisers and apparently used his critics as devil's advocates only as window dressing. While Eisenhower was steady and calm, Johnson showed signs of fear, panic, and hypervigilance (for example, in getting up in the middle of the night to oversee bombing raids). He managed the members of the advisory group as if they were a bunch of senators from whom he was seeking a consensus on a course of action that would broker out differences; in the process, he stifled debate and muffled issues.

Burke and Greenstein believe that, in both cases, the political environment was open to presidential leadership in directions other than the one taken (268). Eisenhower and his lieutenants had created a climate of domestic opinion that would have supported U.S. air strikes to help the French. Johnson may by July have been trapped by the escalation of the U.S. military role since January, but he had fewer political constraints in January and might have chosen a different course. Presidential decisions were the decisive ones in relation to the advisory group; the record does not support the thesis that either president was simply following his advisers. One must then ask whether presidential management of the advisory process assisted or impeded the president in making these crucial personal decisions (271–73).

Burke and Greenstein conclude that the formal, analytic process constructed by Eisenhower had great strengths for the articulation, through staff analysis, of choices. The absence of such coherence in the more informal and iterative process of Johnson's decisions seemed to preclude systematic consideration of alternatives. Johnson was acting like a Senate leader, keeping his advisers apart and off balance. These writers also see some evidence of ego-defensiveness in Johnson, such as we-they thinking about the "enemy." As the two presidents shaped the dynamics of each group, they each became dependent upon those dynamics for information and analysis. It cannot be proven that different presidents and different patterns of advising and discussion would have led to different decisions in the political environments of the time, but Johnson's failure to develop the choices before him more analytically might have caused him to fail to take advantage of the available political latitude, at least early in the day. Nothing is said about the world view of Johnson and his associates, which shaped their commitments and actions, but presumably a better decision process might have questioned premises in their worldview, even though there are limits to the degree a policy debate can shake a strong worldview (276–95).

It is also possible that the presidential worldview shapes the decision process. For example, if presidents and their advisers share a world view, they may see less need for debate. As suggested, Carter and his economic advisers were uncertain about the relation of economic theory to practice, and perhaps as a result, the decision process was open and somewhat disjointed. Reagan and his advisers thought that they knew the truth about economics, and the decision process was correspondingly centralized and disciplined, at least in the first year. A formal typology of decision systems would not have been helpful in understanding the two Vietnam cases: the three categories, formalistic, competitive, and collegial, are too simple. The typology is based on formal arrangements but leaves out the mix of formal and informal. An effort to broaden the typology would become particularistic and lose its purpose (274–75).

The comparison of executive styles of presidents is probably best attempted in twos and threes, grouping like and unlike presidents to explore the consequences for policy making of similar and different leadership styles. The Carter-Reagan contrast is instructive, but Carter is also usefully compared to Truman, whom he admired and with whom he shared characteristics. Roosevelt and Johnson reveal interesting similarities and differences, and Ford and Bush appear to share much in common as men who learned to be politicians rather than natural political men like Roosevelt and Johnson. Knowledge of this kind will be iterative and serial in character because of the great number of contextual wild cards. Therefore, it is best to hold as many factors constant as possible and compare at the margins. Critics may say that approach gives up the hope of broad generalizations about the impact of individuality on presidential leadership, and it does to a certain extent. But we must suit our method to the material being studied, and the presidency does not lend itself to broad generalizations. However, we do learn about effective and ineffective leadership, under varying conditions, by marginal comparisons. The model of political personality introduced at the beginning of this essay is useful for research in each of the three areas of inquiry set out here. The model forms the point of departure for analyzing skill in context, assessing ego strength and defensiveness, and understanding the relation of style to policy making.

Conclusion

Other essays in this volume recommend deductive approaches to the study of the presidency as an institution. For example, Gary Miller contends that presidents can prevail over Congress on certain kinds of public goods issues, under given conditions. Terry Moe believes that the presidency, as an institution, is characterized by recurring behavior patterns. This is the insight that impels Gary King to ask for simpler variables and more cases. I commend these suggestions. Such work might bring the study of the presidency closer to work on Congress and bureaucracy in political science. But it might also miss a great deal of importance in the presidency, because the office is also an individual. In fact, in all three institutions, there is a place for the study of leadership that asks about the conditions under which individuals make a difference.

Gary King asks that qualitative presidency research be precise in estimating the uncertainty of generalizations about the office. This is a reasonable request, but I doubt that King would accept the conventional methods of biographers and historians in which competing hypotheses are matched against evidence. But this is what presidency researchers do, or should do. King also wants many more cases in the hope of providing evidence for propositions of greater generality. But the presidency, whether conceived as institution or individual, may not yield the kind of general statements he would like. This is certainly true of the study of presidential personality. The research approach must be clinical in that it produces generalizations that emerge inductively from historical experience, which are inevitably superseded by fresh cases and generalizations. Any hope for broad theoretical formulations may be naive.

One constructive path toward theory would be to do more work on the study of political leadership in general, under which presidency research might fall. We might then see the presidency in a wider theoretical context. But that begs the question of whether the study of leadership is susceptible to generalization—and is an essay for another day.

Notes

I wish to thank my Vanderbilt colleagues Paul Conkin, a historian, John Glidewell, a psychologist, and Volney Gay, a psychoanalyst, for their helpful advice. Kristy Thompson wrote an M.A. thesis on the literature on psychological biography, which was most useful. Fred Greenstein has given good suggestions along the way, and George Edwards was a trenchant editor. The faults of the essay are all mine.

1. See Hargrove, 1966. The book that helped me develop my idea of the relation between needs and skills was Murray et al. (1938).

2. I believe that my model captures shared perspectives among leading personality theories as set out by Hall and Lindzey (1978), 702–05.

3. My psychologist colleague John Glidewell has urged me to develop my model of political personality more fully. He thinks that I do not trace the path of influence from needs and cognitive style through ego and experience to full political personality and thus policy purposes. I call the ego a mediator but do not develop the various ways in which it might mediate: to match internal and external variables as a bulwark against unconscious forces into creative political action. He is correct, and these issues should be addressed—but the collaboration of a psychologist would be required to do it.

4. Tucker (1981) sees leadership as the clarification of historical ambiguities and the articulation of a sense of direction.

5. The attention to bargaining was stronger in Neustadt's first edition in 1960, and he has gradually moved toward a greater emphasis on rhetorical leadership (Neustadt, 1990).

6. Hargrove and Nelson (1984), chap. 4. See the comparison of Roosevelt, who understood limits, and Johnson, who did not.

7. A paperback edition with "Afterthoughts Thirty Years Later" was published by Viking in 1961.

8. Barber identifies serious flaws in Nixon's political personality. It is not clear that the several Watergate offenses were a Nixon seeking a new and challenging fight or a Nixon who was so fearful of opposition that he broke the law to make sure that he won in policy and politics. His rigidity once discovered was not the deliberate precipitation of a crisis but the actions of a guilty man who wished to stay in office. The 1992 edition of Barber's *Presidential Character* seeks clarification of skill differences within the active-positive category (personal communication).

9. A new book classifies all American presidents according to the Meyers-Briggs categories (Choiniere and Kiersey, 1992)

References

Barber, James David. 1965. *The Lawmakers: Recruitment and Adaptation to Legislative Life*. New Haven: Yale University Press.

———. 1985. *The Presidential Character: Predicting Performance in the White House*. Englewood Cliffs, N.J.: Prentice-Hall.

Blondel, Jean. 1987. *Political Leadership: Towards a General Analysis*. London: Sage.

Blum, John Morton. 1980. *The Progressive Presidents*. New York: W. W. Norton.

Burke, John P., and Fred I. Greenstein, with Larry Berman and Richard Immerman. 1989. *How Presidents Test Reality: Decisions on Vietnam, 1954 and 1965*. New York: Russell Sage Foundation.

Choiniere, Ray, and David Kiersey. 1992. *Presidential Temperament*. Del Mar, Calif.: Prometheus Nemesis.

Conkin, Paul K. 1986. *Big Daddy from the Pedernales: Lyndon Baines Johnson*. Boston: Twayne.

Crosby, Faye, and Travis L. Crosby. 1981. "Psychobiography and Psychohistory." In *Handbook of Political Behavior*, vol. 1, ed. S. Long. New York: Plenum.

Dahl, Robert A. 1969. "Power." In *The Presidency*, ed. Aaron Wildavsky. Boston: Little, Brown.

de Rivera, Joseph H. 1968. *The Psychological Dimension of Foreign Policy*. Columbus, Oh.: Charles E. Merrill.

Doig, Jameson W., and Erwin C. Hargrove, eds. 1987. *Leadership and Innovation: A Biographical Perspective on Entrepreneurs in Government*. Baltimore: Johns Hopkins University Press.

Edinger, Lewis J. 1964. "Political Science and Political Biography: Reflections on the Study of Leadership." *Journal of Politics* 26:423–43.

Edwards, George C., III. 1989. *At the Margins: Presidential Leadership of Congress*. New Haven: Yale University Press.

Ellis, Richard, and Aaron Wildavsky. 1989. *Dilemmas of Presidential Leadership: From Washington through Lincoln*. New Brunswick: Transaction.

Erikson, Erik H. 1963. *Childhood and Society*. New York: W. W. Norton.

George, Alexander L. 1974. "Assessing Presidential Character." *World Politics* 26:234–82.

———. 1980. *Presidential Decisionmaking in Foreign Policy*. Boulder, Colo.: Westview.

George, Alexander L., and Juliette L. George. 1956. *Woodrow Wilson and Colonel House: A Personality Study*. New York: John Day.

Greenstein, Fred I. 1969. *Personality and Politics*. Chicago: Markham.

———. 1982. "The Two Faces of Organization." In *The Hidden Hand Presidency*. New York: Basic Books.

Greenstein, Fred I., and Nelson Polsby, eds. 1975. *The Handbook of Political Theory: Micro-Political Theory*. Vol. 2. Reading, Mass.: Addison-Wesley.

Hall, Calvin S., and Gardner Lindzey. 1978. "Personality Theory in Perspective." In *Theories of Personality*. New York: John Wiley.

Hargrove, Erwin C. 1966. *Presidential Leadership, Personality and Political Style*. New York: Macmillan.

———. 1974. *The Power of the Modern Presidency*. New York: Knopf.

———. 1988. *Jimmy Carter as President: Leadership and the Politics of the Public Good*. Baton Rouge: Louisiana State University Press.

Hargrove, Erwin C., and Michael Nelson. 1984. "Presidential Leadership." In *Presidents, Politics and Policy*. Baltimore: Johns Hopkins University Press.

Hartmann, Heinz. 1963. *Essays on Ego Psychology*. New York: W. W. Norton.

Janis, Irving L. 1989. *Crucial Decisions: Leadership in Policymaking and Crisis Management*. New York: Free Press.

Johnson, Richard Tanner. 1974. *Managing the White House: An Intimate Study of the Presidency*. New York: Harper and Row.

Katz, Daniel. 1973. "Patterns of Leadership." In *Handbook of Political Psychology*, ed. Jeanne K. Knutson. San Francisco: Jossey-Bass.

Keirsey, David, and Marilyn Bates. 1978. *Please Understand Me: Character and Treatment Types*. Del Mar, Calif.: Prometheus.

Lasswell, Harold D. 1930. *Psychology and Politics*. Chicago: University of Chicago Press.

———. 1948. *Power and Personality*. New York: W. W. Norton.

Levinson, Daniel J. 1978. *Seasons of a Man's Life*. New York: Ballantine.

Link, Arthur S. 1987. "The Battle of Princeton." In *Wilson: The Road to the White House*. Princeton: Princeton University Press.

Lowi, Theodore J. 1985. *The Personal President, Power Invested, Promises Unfulfilled*. Ithaca: Cornell University Press.

Moe, Terry M. 1985. "The Politicized Presidency." In *The New Directions in American Politics*, ed. John E. Chubb and Paul E. Peterson. Washington, D.C.: Brookings.

Murray, Henry A., et al. 1938. *Explorations in Personality*. New York: Oxford University Press.

Neustadt, Richard E. 1990. *Presidential Power and the Modern Presidents: The Politics of Leadership from Roosevelt to Reagan*. New York: Free Press.

Peterson, Mark A. 1990. *Legislating Together: The White House and Capitol Hill from Eisenhower to Reagan*. Cambridge: Harvard University Press.

Renshon, Stanley A. 1980. "Life History and Character Development: Some Reflections on Political Leadership." In *New Directions in Psychohistory: The Adelphi Papers in Honor of Erik H. Erikson*, ed. Mel Albin. Lexington, Mass.: Lexington Books, D. C. Heath.

Runyan, William McKinley. 1984. *Life Histories and Psychobiography*. New York: Oxford University Press.

Skowronek, Stephen. 1984. "The Presidency in Political Time." In *The Presidency in the Political System*, ed. Michael Nelson. Washington D.C.: Congressional Quarterly Press.

Tucker, Robert C. 1981. *Politics as Leadership*. Columbia: University of Missouri Press.

Tulis, Jeffrey K. 1987. *The Rhetorical Presidency*. Princeton: Princeton University Press.

Wills, Garry. 1988. *Reagan's America*. New York: Penguin.

Weinstein, Edwin A., James William Anderson, and Arthur S. Link. 1987. "Woodrow Wilson's Political Personality: A Reappraisal." In *Psycho/History: Readings in the Method of Psychology, Psychoanalysis and History*, ed. Geoffrey Cocks and Travis L. Crosby. New Haven: Yale University Press.

Woods, Joseph M. 1987. "Some Considerations on Psycho-History." In *Psycho/History: Readings in the Method of Psychology, Psychoanalysis, and History*, ed. Geoffrey Cocks and Travis L. Crosby. New Haven: Yale University Press.

3

Advising the President

KAREN M. HULT

IN 1977, Almond and Genco observed that "the essence of political science is the analysis of choice in the context of constraints" (1977, 522). Looking more narrowly on presidency scholarship, Quirk contends that its "central issue is how presidents make policy decisions" (1989, 10). Clearly, one-sentence definitions of entire disciplines, or even disciplinary subfields, can be both trivializing and dangerous. Yet they also can serve as catalysts for helping orient and focus analysis. The observations of Almond, Genco, and Quirk arguably fall in the latter category. Whether or not one believes that these scholars point to the only or the best ways of approaching political science or the study of the presidency, they do direct attention to significant dimensions of political and presidential activity and suggest topics for sustained exploration.

When one focuses on presidential policy decisions, one such topic is advising, which most expect to play an important part in explaining presidential choice. If one is interested in learning more about presidential advising, several questions ensue. First, and most commonly addressed: Who advises presidents? Simply knowing who has access to the president, however, tells one little about that adviser's influence. The second question, then, is; What do presidents do with the advice they receive?

As social scientists and presidency scholars, we expect to discover not only patterns in presidential advising but also much diversity and change; the goal is to be able to identify such patterns and to explain what we find. Thus the third questions is, What explains continuities and discontinuities in presidential advising? The fourth question raises one of the most bedeviling issues in the study of the presidency: presidential agency. To what extent can presidents control advising?

The fifth and final question looks for a link between advising and government performance: What effects does advising have on decision outcomes?

This chapter explores these five questions and, in the process, examines and assesses the state of existing understanding of presidential advising and sketches possible directions for further work. Before beginning, however, some of the ideas guiding the discussion need to be introduced.

Conceptual Underpinnings

"Advising" is treated here as a task rather than as a property of particular individuals or of units whose staffs are often referred to in shorthand as *advisers*.[1] *Advising* refers to providing input into or support for presidential decision making—as opposed to, for example, overseeing executive branch activities, lobbying members of Congress, or running a cabinet department. Most of what follows emphasizes the more cognitive aspects of advising: providing information, defining problems, structuring choices, generating alternatives, and communicating viewpoints (cf. Light, 1984, 18). Yet, advising also may involve more socioemotional dimensions; it may, for instance, reinforce presidential values or offer reassurance for particular presidential positions (cf. Meltsner, 1990, 8ff).

Finally, the emphasis is on policy-relevant advising—that is, advising bearing on presidential policy choice. Policy-relevant advising can involve counsel on the articulation and selection of substantive policy objectives or the means of achieving them, on decisions about whether and when to take action, and on the choice of strategies for preserving or enhancing presidential capacity to achieve policy goals. Thus, policy-relevant advising encompasses both "policy" advice (for example, input on the likely effects on economic growth of a capital gains tax cut) and "political" counsel (the possible impact of such a tax cut on presidential approval levels or on the support of particular constituencies). Excluded from the discussion is advising on strictly electoral or party maintenance matters.[2]

Because this chapter focuses on advising, not decision making, the examination of scholarly work is complicated, since much of the relevant literature is more concerned with decision making. Yet, the distinction seems to be one worth making. Those from whom presidents receive information, counsel, and support may not be those who are actively involved in the choice process itself; advisory and decision processes may (or may not) be quite different. These possibilities suggest a range of empirical questions, the answers to which analysts arguably ought to examine rather than assume. Moreover, itseems reasonable to expect that advisory arrangements and participants will be more inclusive than those directly relevant to decision making.[3]

Finally, this chapter examines advising in terms of advisory networks. A network—the concept is borrowed from organization theory—links actors at several levels of analysis, ranging from the individual to the interorganizational. It pays particular attention to the relationships among those actors. A presidential advisory network encompasses the president and individuals (e.g., the national security assistant), subunits (such as the White House Office of Political Affairs), and organizations (for example, the CIA) that provide input into presidential decisions.[4] The interaction among members of a presidential advisory network—or the absence of such interaction—may affect, for example, the nature and timing of the advice a president receives, the president's views of the credibility and importance of that advice, and the impact of the advice on presidential decisions and decision outcomes. A given administration may have multiple advisory networks, varying according to, for example, the policy area, the point in a president's term, or the routineness of the decision to be made.

Networks are at an intermediate level of analysis between individuals and structures, on the one hand, and systems, on the other hand. Typically, an advisory network is made up of several individuals operating in different advisory structures; both individuals and structures may have a distinctive way of providing advice to the president (for elaboration, see Hult and Walcott, 1990, chap. 7). The advice a secretary of state gives a president, for instance, may be the product of a hierarchical chain of internal checking of information within the State Department, while the national security assistant may offer advice reflecting collegial discussion among National Security Council staffers. Meanwhile, White House aides may find themselves refereeing among advocates of competing positions. Examining only one or some of these actors and structures might well lead one to overemphasize their importance or to miss critical interplay and dynamics.

More commonly employed is the concept of advisory systems (e.g., Paul Anderson, 1985; Barilleaux, 1988; Burke and Greenstein, 1989; Campbell, 1986; Cronin and Greenberg, 1969; Destler, 1977; George, 1980; Pika, 1981–1982). Only rarely, however, do scholars clearly define the term. Most seem to have in mind the classifications of Johnson (1974), which describe characteristic patterns of getting information and counsel to the president, as well as the degree of presidential involvement. Such patterns are typically assumed to describe most advisory tasks within a given administration. Although these works have been influential and fruitful, they risk overlooking the significant diversity in advisory arrangements within any particular administration (cf. Burke and Greenstein, 1989).

Focusing at the network level largely avoids the problems both of overgeneralizing and of missing the possible impact of diverse structures and multiple participants. The network concept provides a useful way to organize much of the unwieldy literature on presidential advising and to attempt to answer the questions about advising posed at the beginning of this chapter.

Who Advises Presidents and What Do Presidents Do with the Advice?

Network notions are most helpful in highlighting the complex interplay among multiple actors and structures and the dynamics and evolution of patterns of relationships. A first step when using network ideas, however, is to identify the possibly relevant network actors.

In fact, much work on presidential advising has focused on network actors. Many studies examine particular advisers and advisory units, while others begin with the president as the focal actor and examine which other actors offer advice with what apparent effect on presidential action (or inaction). As a prelude to examining advisory networks more directly, this section reviews analyses bearing on who gives advice and on what influence that advice seems to have on presidents.

NETWORK ACTORS

Considerable work seeks to trace the activities of given network actors and traces changes in their participation in advisory networks;

less often does it adequately confront the issue of influence. What follows treats mainly those actors who have been examined in isolation: the cabinet, the vice president, and members of the White House staff. Others (e.g., the chair of the Council of Economic Advisers, the national security assistant) are more commonly—and more usefully—discussed in terms compatible with the fuller scale network-based analysis introduced in later sections.[5]

The Cabinet. It is almost a truism that the cabinet as a collectivity rarely serves in an advisory capacity (cf. Campbell, 1986, 25). Indeed, Hess (1988) no longer counsels presidents to consider using the cabinet as an advisory or deliberative body but instead concentrates on the qualities and potential contributions of individual cabinet members. Similarly, Cronin (1975) distinguishes between the activities of inner and outer cabinet members, and J. Cohen (1988) emphasizes the representative function of the cabinet by focusing on the characteristics of individual members. Meanwhile, Riddlesperger and King (1986, 1989) explore presidential objectives in selecting cabinet members; they find that inner cabinet members tend to be either specialists in a particular field or presidential ambassadors with personal relationships with the president.

These works reach few conclusions about the nature or the influence of the advice cabinet members give presidents. Cronin's distinction does point to the differential access to the president enjoyed by inner and outer cabinet members. Riddlesperger and King also find that presidents, during the course of their administrations, tend to appoint officials more on the basis of their loyalty to the president and their Washington experience, which presumably affects the kind of advice presidents receive. In addition, the breadth and nature of cabinet representation might influence the range of viewpoints available to presidents, although much of the diversity in demographic characteristics (e.g., gender, race, previous occupation) is found among those furthest from the president (see Riddlesperger and King, 1986). And Wyszomirski (1989) argues that the appointment of more policy specialists to cabinet positions has weakened cabinet members' political capabilities, diminishing another kind of useful advice.[6] Finally, cabinet members' access to and their influence on presidents may vary according to the stage in the term (White House access becomes more difficult as a term proceeds) and the organization of the White House staff (which can block or inhibit access, permit direct links with the president, or insist upon White House staffers serving as intermediaries).

At the same time, the cabinet as a collectivity has not been completely ignored. Campbell (1986), for example, traces cabinet structures and areas of specialization from Franklin Roosevelt through Ronald Reagan's first term. He expects that the increasing use Jimmy Carter and Reagan made of subunits of the cabinet will continue, reflecting both the power of precedent in presidents' organizational decisions and the evident usefulness of the subunits in economic and national security policy (78–79). Pfiffner (1990) agrees, pointing to Bush's establishment of three cabinet councils.

Others, however, caution that even relatively visible cabinet bodies may not be significant sources of information and counsel for presidents. Dwight Eisenhower, for example, evidently used his cabinet less to provide advice than to promote coherence in administration activities, to provide a sense of participation in decision making, and to build support among those consulted (e.g., Greenstein, 1982; Henderson, 1988). Similarly, Reagan's cabinet councils were closely guided and monitored by White House staffers, considered mostly second-level issues, emphasized implementation rather than policy formulation, and became less important over the course of the administration (J. Cohen, 1988; Newland, 1984; Walker and Reopel, 1986; Warshaw, 1990). Apparently, the Bush White House even "more often bypasses the cabinet council system in resolving key issues" (Campbell, 1991, 211).

Still, in addition to their other contributions, cabinet bodies may be useful sounding boards for presidential ideas and arenas in which presidents can hear diverse views and debate (J. Anderson, 1986b; Greenstein, 1982; Henderson, 1988). Overall, though, while individual cabinet members may be important advisers, the cabinet and cabinet committees most often are not, whatever their other activities.

The Vice President. The vice presidencies of Nelson Rockefeller and, especially, Walter Mondale convinced many observers that the vice presidency was growing to be worth more than the proverbial "bucket of warm spit." A number of works point to the emergence of the vice president as a significant member of presidential advisory networks (e.g., Barilleaux, 1988; Goldstein, 1982; Pfiffner and Hoxie, 1989; Light, 1984; Natoli, 1985; Pika, 1990). Light traces the growing role of vice presidents from 1961, when Lyndon Johnson moved from a Capitol Hill office to the Executive Office Building, thereby increasing his visibility and proximity to the president. Over the next fifteen years, the political system grew increasingly complex and fragmented, making vice presidential political and policy advice potentially more valuable (Light, 1984, 140). By 1977, Vice President Mondale had acquired an office in the West Wing of the White House, and his staff was fully integrated into the White House policy process. Such institutional development evidently has persisted through later vice presidencies (Pika, 1990).

Unlike many other students of advising, Light (1984) usefully distinguishes between the extent to which vice presidents have access and offer advice to presidents and the influence they have on presidents. The vice president's role as adviser may well become part of the job description, given the practices and precedents of the last three decades (Pika, 1990). Still, a vice president's advisory tasks depend on more administration-specific factors, such as his or her resources and skills, personal and political compatibility with the president, and his or her relationship with the White House staff (Goldstein, 1982; Light, 1984; Natoli, 1985). Key, too, are the backgrounds of the president and vice president. A president with little Washington experience is probably most in need of the input of an insider vice president with ties to actors in relevant Washington networks; insider presidents like George Bush already have those relationships and can be expected to pay less attention to outsider vice presidents (Light, 1984, 139).[7]

Vice presidential influence is even less assured. It depends on vice presidential resources like information, "persuasive expertise, image in the White House, and presidential persuadability" (ibid., 224). Light also contends that influence is linked to electoral and policy cycles and to the comparative effectiveness of the presidential and vice presidential staffs (238–47). In general, vice presidents may be more influential as generalist advisers who move from issue to issue and refuse line responsibilities (ibid.; Pika, 1990). Still left to be explored are the interplay among the determinants of vice presidential influence, presidential and vice presidential strategies for achieving their political and policy goals, and the nature of the advice provided to and considered by presidents (cf. Light, 1984, 257).

The White House Staff. Relatively little of the work on the White House Office as a whole focuses explicitly on the staff's advisory activities. Still, White House units can affect the volume, nature, and timing of the advice that reaches presidents, and at least some of the staffers perform advisory tasks. Emphasized here are actors not always thought of as advisory—those with explicit policy responsibilities are examined in later sections.

Although presidential chiefs of staff are often highly visible, few works explicitly examine their involvement in and effect on presidential advising. Instead, much of the discussion revolves around whether the White House Office is (or should be) organized using a chief of staff arrangement or a spokes-of-a-wheel arrangement. Most of the conclusions about which is more appropriate reflect the experiences of particular administrations. After the experiences of the Ford and Carter White Houses and Reagan in his first term, many declared the spokes-of-a-wheel model unworkable, given the expectations and constraints confronting presidents, and urged presidents to hire a chief of staff (e.g., Barilleaux, 1988, 107–12; Henderson, 1988, 75; Kernell and Popkin, 1986; Pfiffner, 1988). Yet, the problems of the second-term Reagan White House prompted others to note the trade-offs associated with centralization and to distinguish among a small, competitive top staff like Reagan's troika and the pyramidal management system imposed by Donald Regan (Kernell, 1989, 236–37). John Sununu's stormy reign also underscores the significance of the person serving as chief of staff. At the very least, though, Hess (1988, 7–8ff) contends that there needs to be a *primus inter pares* to serve as a process manager and honest broker (cf. NAPA, 1988).

Less systematically examined in most works are the extent of advising these senior staffers actually engage in, the degree to which they block or distort advice flowing to the president from other sources, or their ultimate influence on presidential decisions (cf. Walcott and Hult, 1987a).

The involvement in advising of staff units other than those with explicit policy responsibilities (such as the domestic policy staff) has been tracked only sporadically. For example, Hult and Walcott (1989b; cf. Walcott and Hult, forthcoming) argue that, since the Hoover administration, White House press secretaries (with the significant exception of Jody Powell) have been progressively less involved in advising presidents and have spent more time managing a burgeoning White House press office. They link this decline to a changing political environment, the organizational imperatives of an increasingly specialized White House staff, and presidential strategies. Meanwhile, Pika (1989) suggests that, at least in the Nixon administration, some of the political advising once done by White House press aides shifted to the Office of Communications (see, too, Grossman and Kumar, 1981).

More generally, one should expect that staff units that span White House boundaries (e.g., press and congressional liaison) will be less influential in White House discussions, since the president and other staffers frequently view contacts with outsiders with some suspicion (Pika, 1986). Whether this is so has not been systematically tested, since much of the work on such units tends to focus on their links with external actors (see, e.g., Davis, 1979; Hart, 1983, on congressional liaison).

The involvement of the more political units in presidential advising also is not clear. Several scholars have highlighted the increased centralization of the appointments process in the White House (e.g., Pfiffner, 1988; Weko, 1990; on Bush, though, see Aberbach, 1991). Presumably, this means that White House staffers participate more in advising presidents on possible executive branch appointments than do, for example, party leaders and members of Congress (cf. Weko, 1990). Less clear is the extent to which these staffers influence presidential decisions or merely collate suggestions from external groups (e.g., the Heritage Foundation and the National Women's Political Caucus) and other powerful presidential aides.

Still others have pointed to the growing influence of pollsters in the White House. Although systematic tracing of their advice and influence is not yet available, some work is beginning (e.g., Altschuler, 1990; Jacobs, 1992).

RELATIONSHIPS BETWEEN THE PRESIDENT AND OTHER NETWORK ACTORS

Instead of focusing on specific advisers and advisory units, some scholars begin with presidents and examine presidential relationships with other actors in advisory networks. Although relatively little systematic information exists on these ties, this work suggests that presidential relationships might be characterized by their volume, directness, diversity, and salience and offers tentative explanations for variation along these dimensions.

Best (1988a, 1988b) and R. Thompson (1989), using scheduled presidential appointments and samples from presidents' daily diaries, respectively, trace the volume of interactions between presidents and a variety of executive and legislative branch actors. Even though the data reveal little about the substance of the meetings or the participants' influence on the president, they do point to differential patterns of interactions among types of actors and across administrations. Campbell (1986) reports that interviews with Carter and Reagan appointees show that Carter met more frequently and more directly (rather than in committees) with his appointees than did Reagan. Again, though, little can be discovered about the impact of any advice.

Other scholars direct attention to independent variables that need to be considered when examining network relationships. For instance, Greenstein (1982) underscores the significance of informal as well as formal ties; applied to Eisenhower, this dramatically increased the range of those with whom he interacted, diversifying his network tie and presumably the advice he received. Others stress the importance of a president's organizational style to understanding advisory links (e.g., Cottam and Rockman, 1984; Wyszomirski, 1985). And Kessel's (1975) study of the Nixon Domestic Council points to decision complexity and political importance as variables, that make presidential involvement more likely and ties with advisers more salient.

Still, despite the numerous characterizations of and explanations for presidential relationships with other network actors, few sources demonstrate that the links actually involved advising or that presidents were influenced by any of the advice they did receive. Hargrove (1988) seeks to establish such influence relationships by tracing the streams of advice Carter relied upon and links them to his ultimate actions. In examining the vice presidency, Light (1984) supplements this approach by asking other participants how influential Rockefeller and Mondale were. Memoirs often provide the clearest concrete evidence of the interplay between advisers and presidents and of the perceived effect of advice on presidents (see, e.g., Ehrlichman, 1982; Kissinger, 1979; Menges, 1988; Stockman, 1986). Yet, like most other work, they contribute little to generalizations about the influence of advice.

What Explains the Continuities and Discontinuities in Presidential Advising?

Part of the reason that generalizing about presidential advising is so difficult is that advising arrangements and dynamics vary so dramatically, both within and across administrations. Indeed, that is the rationale for examining advisory networks rather than advisory systems. If one casts existing studies in network terms, among the factors scholars use to explain continuities and discontinuities in advisory networks are the type of policy, the type of decision, the point in the president's term, cross-administration dynamics, and the particular president and administration. Many of the analyses include several of the explanatory factors listed above.[8]

TYPE OF POLICY

Foreign Policy. Foreign policy has received the most scholarly attention. This reflects both its perceived importance and the tendency for presidents to be more interested and involved in foreign policy. Perhaps, too, the greater boundedness and centralization of the foreign policy arena (Hargrove, 1988; Porter, 1986) make it easier for systematic study.

It should be noted at the outset that, just as in Washington, the national security concerns that most of the sources in this area refer to actually encompass foreign policy more generally (cf. Hart, 1987, 71). Since World War II, most presidents have received foreign policy advice from a variety of actors (Destler, 1977, 145). The evident significance of these actors in advisory networks has changed over time.

Considerable attention has been trained, for example, on the evolving influence of the National Security Council and the NSC staff (see, e.g., Bundy, 1982–1983; Destler, 1980–1981; Destler, Gelb, and Lake, 1984; Falk, 1964; Lord, 1988; Nelson, 1981; Steiner, 1977). Although the NSC was a major (though not the dominant) advisory body through the 1950s (see, e.g., Henderson, 1988), since then presidential use of the council as a regular, major advisory forum has been the exception (Destler, 1977, 148). Instead, the NSC staff has grown in importance as decision making became centralized in the White House (e.g., Destler, Gelb, and Lake, 1984; Mann, 1990; Mulcahy, 1990; Nathan and Oliver, 1987) in the midst of increased fragmentation and rising dissensus in government. A key figure in these dynamics is the national security assistant, who became a principal policy adviser for the first time under Kennedy (Bock and Clark, 1986; Hart, 1987). No longer the neutral facilitator and coordinator of Eisenhower's time, most national security assistants have been substantive advisers and policy advocates, with ready access to presidents and often high public visibility.

Receiving less systematic attention have been the rest of the NSC staff and the other actors in the foreign policy arena. Allison and Szanton (1976, 39) claim that the secretary of state was a weak participant in advisory networks, but the experiences of recent administrations suggest that that need not always be true (cf. Clarke, 1987). Others contend that the quality of the advice presidents receive often suffers from insufficient interaction among key actors. According to Lord (1988), both intelligence and military officials operate along critical "fault lines" in the executive branch; these gaps in the links among major actors arguably yield inferior advice.

The actual operation of advisory networks is less well understood than the involvement of particular actors. George (1980) developed models of policy decision arrangements (distinguishing between, for example, White House–oriented and State Department–centered mechanisms), which have implications for tracing flows of advice and influence. Yet, what models are likely to be operative under what circumstances is less clear. Similarly, Crabb and Mulcahy's (1986, 323–28) efforts to formulate typologies based on the relative influence of the president, the national security assistant, and the secretary of State produce a different pattern for virtually every president since Franklin Roosevelt, and seemingly do not allow for advisory networks to shift, depending on the issue or the point in the aaministration (cf. Mulcahy, 1987).

Kohl (1975) addresses these concerns by examining patterns within a single administration. He introduces several models of foreign policy making, each of which implies certain kinds of advisory networks. In the "royal court" view, for example, relatively few officials with close links to the president dominate advising; in the better known multiple-advocacy situation (cf. George, 1972, 1980), more diverse points of view are represented, with a custodian ensuring equal access to the president. Kohl finds elements of each model in the foreign policy processes of the Nixon administration. Although

Kohl ends with several more general propositions (e.g., similar diversity will be present in all administrations, and major policy shifts will involve fewer actors), few of the models have actually been applied to other presidencies (or to other policy spheres).

After the publication of Allison's *Essence of Decision* (1972), however, several authors sought to demonstrate that bureaucratic politics explanations of advisory dynamics and decision outcomes were not compelling (see, e.g., Art, 1973; Freedman, 1976; Perlmutter, 1974). And, of course, multiple advocacy continues to receive considerable empirical and normative attention.

For all of its strengths, much of the literature that seeks to generalize about patterns of foreign policy advising mentions but does not focus upon the sources, credibility, or influence of the advice presidents receive (though on the impact of intelligence, see, e.g., Betts, 1980; Lord, 1988). More helpful are case studies (e.g., Allison, 1971; Berman, 1982; Kissinger, 1979). The trade-off, of course, is a frequent absence of generalization.

Many question whether such generalization is even possible given the degree of control presidents have over foreign policy advisory networks. Presidential style may help shape the advisory mechanisms presidents construct, as well as whether and how they are used (e.g., Barilleaux, 1988, 25–26; Cottam and Rockman, 1984; Henderson, 1988; Kissinger, 1979, 40). Destler (1977, 160ff) lists several presidential-level factors that may shape the foreign policy advice chief executives receive; among them are the clarity of a president's organizational sense, the president's view of formality and regularity in the flow of analysis and advice, the degree of personal substantive or operational involvement the president seeks, and the president's attitude toward divided counsel or interpersonal disputes among advisers. Destler believes that only one of these factors—the interplay among the principals—is beyond the president's full control.

Others argue that volatility in advisory networks also reflects a changing foreign policy environment. Not only is the global system a source of constant turbulence, but U.S. politics has become more fragmented while dissensus on foreign policy objectives and strategies has grown (see, e.g., Bloomfield, 1984; Crabb and Mulcahy, 1986; Destler, Gelb, and Lake, 1984). In such settings, presidents struggle for control, resulting not only in White House centralization but also in ongoing experimentation with the design of advisory networks.

Perhaps, too, this turbulence accounts for the ongoing efforts at prescription that occupy many writers. Some argue for greater continuity across administrations, proposing, for example, a permanent secretariat for the NSC (Barilleaux, 1988, 35) or permanent undersecretaries in the State Department (Bloomfield, 1984). Bundy (1982–1983) points to the need for more systematic interjection of advice from those with experience and expertise, and Mulcahy (1987) suggests that vice presidents may be particularly well suited for coordinating foreign policy advice. Whether multiple advocacy is an appropriate type of advisory network has been the subject of considerable discussion, with George (1972, 1980) continuing to emphasize its utility and others (e.g., Destler, 1977; Nathan and Oliver, 1987, 75) expressing concern that it may well exacerbate uncertainty and problems of accountability and authority.

Debate revolves around the overall nature of the president's foreign policy advisory arrangements: Should they be president centered or State Department centered? Former national security assistant and Secretary of State Henry Kissinger (1979), for example, advocates a stronger role for the secretary of state, while Carter's national security assistant Zbigniew Brzezinski (1983, 1987–1988) and Carnes Lord (1988), a former member of the Reagan NSC staff, can be described as presidentialists. Others occupy more of a middle ground. Destler, Gelb, and Lake (1984, 278) maintain that design depends on the president and the situation; Destler (1977) advocates a hybrid system including "a team of 'presidential' officials combining line and staff roles," which would be headed by the secretary of state.

Many of these differences can be traced to divergent views of the role of the national security assistant and the NSC staff. George (1980), for example, calls for the national security assistant to be a "custodian" of the advisory process; similarly, Allison and Szanton (1976) recommend that the NSC staff help ensure that the advisory process has "balance, depth, and integrity" and that no substantive adviser plays a role in managing the flow of advice. In contrast, others contend that to be perceived as an effective and influential actor, the national security assistant needs to be more than a custodian or neutral broker. Clarke (1989) calls for him or her to be a substantive adviser (cf. Lord, 1988), while Destler (1977) suggests that he or she manage the president's daily foreign policy business and oversee implementation in order to get a better impression of what the president wants.

In sum, discussions of networks of foreign policy advice tend to point to a relatively stable set of actors and a limited number of recurring prescriptions. Although the national security assistant has grown in importance and advisory processes have become more centralized in the White House, presidents have relied upon a variety of specific mechanisms for channeling information and counsel into the policy process. The determinants, dynamics, and impact of such advisory networks may provide fertile ground for additional exploration.

Domestic Policy. Domestic and economic policy advising are "organizationally more congested and messy than national security advice" (Porter, 1986, 867). Yet, perhaps because of this greater complexity, works relevant to domestic policy advising seem to concentrate somewhat more on issues of structure and process and considerably less on policy substance, providing more systematic guidance in examining advisory networks.

This is not to argue that a flood of generalizations emerges from such investigations. As Walcott and Hult observe in their analysis of White House domestic policy organization from 1929 through 1968, "few coherent developmental patterns" can be identified; "much more evident instead are continuous presidential experimentation and a distinct lack of structural stability within and across administrations" (1989, 2). The creation of the Domestic Council and its staff in 1970 (a successor to Joseph Califano's staff in the Johnson White House) introduced some stability: every president since then has relied on some sort of domestic policy staff. Yet these units have varied considerably in their structures, activities, and status within the White House (Walcott and Hult, 1989, 36). Generalization is further complicated by the larger number and the fluidity of participants in the domestic policy arena; advisory networks can change dramatically, depending on the issue (cf. Hargrove 1988, 27).

Still, works in this area point to some tentative generalizations. A number of metacycles can be identified (Rockman 1984). For example, substantive policy advising and responsibility for coordinating executive branch information have become more centralized in the White House (e.g., Light, 1982; Newland, 1984; Salamon, 1981; Walcott and Hult, 1989). Centralization has brought an increase in the size of White House domestic policy operations, which in turn has reduced the direct access of substantive specialists to presidents. Similarly, specialization of staff units and of staff aides has grown (e.g., Light, 1982; Salamon, 1981; Walcott and Hult, 1989), increasing the potential for more diverse information flowing to the president and for more conflict developing among staffers. In the process, the overall contribution of departmental and agency actors has probably declined.[9]

The involvement of OMB (formerly, the Bureau of the Budget) has been more variable. Having once been a key source of advice for Truman and Eisenhower, the participation of the budget bureau in policy formulation and advising on enrolled bills declined during the 1960s and 1970s (e.g., Hyde and Wayne, 1979; Salamon, 1981; Walcott and Hult, 1989). However, as budget concerns began in the 1980s to drive policy making, OMB's involvement and influence have risen (see, e.g., Porter, 1985). Meanwhile, the budget bureau has become increasingly politicized (e.g., Hart, 1987; Heclo, 1975). In part, this reflects the addition of a new layer of political appointees (the associate directors of the budget examination divisions). Career staff allegedly have less "direct access to the principal policymakers in the OMB and the White House" (Seidman and Gilmour, 1986, 73; cf. Campbell, 1991, 188), which in turn may diminish the extent to which program expertise informs the advice policy makers receive.

At least one term cycle (Rockman, 1984) relevant to domestic advising also can be identified. Conflict in advisory networks should be expected to increase over the course of a president's term as issues multiply, a president's influence resources decline, and presidential attention is diverted elsewhere (e.g., Light, 1982).

As White House domestic policy units have grown more visible, they have attracted additional scholarly attention. Most extensive is Kessel's (1975) book on the Nixon Domestic Council. Based on structured interviews with Domestic Council staffers, Kessel finds that aides spent much of their time on activities that are closely related to presidential advising, such as clarifying options for the president (84–92). Staffers did little of their own information collecting, generally relying on materials from executive branch activities (100); instead, aides raised questions about this information, sought to assure that gaps were filled (26–27), and served as brokers among competing departments (65). Although the Domestic Council staff was involved in advising (for example, submitting its own recommendations to the president), the views of cabinet members evidently were channeled to the president without being changed (60).

Helmer and Maisel (1978) draw out possible determinants of the influence of the Domestic Council staff in their replication of Kessel's study in the Ford White House. They argue that staff influence increased as access to the president rose, staff cohesion grew, and turnover declined (51–52). Based on an examination of domestic policy staffs from Nixon through Reagan, Wyszomirski (1985) adds staffers' ability and compatibility with the president and the influence and authority of other executive branch units to the list of determinants of staff influence (cf. Hart, 1987, 86).

Most observers agree that the extent of presidential involvement in domestic policy networks is key to understanding the influence of executive branch actors on decisions and, hence, the volume and significance of any advisory activity (see, e.g., Kessel, 1975; Light, 1982; Salamon, 1981). Unlike the foreign policy arena, presidential interest in domestic policy tends to be sporadic, varying within and across administrations. The effects of this variability are less clear. Presidential inattention may permit domination of the advisory process by a small set of players, the outbreak of immobilizing conflict, or the development of "traffic jams" caused by too many underdirected participants (Helmer, 1981). All three can lead to the "exit of qualified advocates" (Light, 1982, 201), reducing the scope of involvement in advising, the influence of particular actors, and the diversity of information and counsel that presidents receive. Alternatively, presidential indifference or distraction may turn participation in domestic policy processes from advising to actual policy formulation, removing the president from the scene altogether.

Economic Policy. As with foreign and domestic policy, difficulties in tracing network relations also characterize the economic policy arena. In part, this evidently is because, like scholarship on foreign policy advising, much of the relevant work focuses on policy substance (e.g., Norton, 1985; much of Pfiffner, 1986; Stein, 1984). Even so, economic networks appear to be somewhat better defined and more bounded than those handling domestic policy. Meanwhile, White House economic policy aides are less important actors than are their counterparts in foreign and domestic policy (Porter, 1981, 217).

Among the major actors in the economic policy arena, the Council of Economic Advisers is often singled out for attention. Formed in 1946, its influence increased during the Eisenhower years; its halcyon days, though, came during the Kennedy and Johnson administrations (Hart, 1987, 55ff). Beginning with Walter Heller in the Kennedy administration, the CEA chair increasingly played the role of policy advocate (see, e.g., Rose, 1989). By the end of the 1960s, CEA influence waned as other executive units developed more professional economic staffs and began to compete more effectively for the president's ear. The council's significance has varied across administrations. The key factors are familiar: CEA influence rises, for example, when its advice is both compatible with presidential values and politically relevant and when it has relatively constructive relationships with the White House staff (e.g., Hart, 1987; Seib and Wessel, 1990; Sloan, 1990a; Stein, 1985; Zwicker, 1989). Naveh (1981, 501–07) adds that the CEA's reputation for superior analysis and its perception as an honest and neutral broker also can enhance its standing with presidents. At the same time, the CEA chair arguably must be skilled at "opportunistic accommodation" (Flash, 1965).

More generally, Hargrove and Nelson (1984, 186–89) detect metacycles in post–World War II economic advising arrangements. Until 1960, the CEA chair, the BOB director, and the secretaries of Treasury, Commerce, and Agriculture interacted in fairly informal, ad hoc ways. From 1961 until the mid-1970s, economic advising became institutionalized in the president's Troika. Beginning with the Ford administration, however, the advisory network expanded, and formal structures multiplied.

Few stable patterns, however, have emerged in this last period. Ford's Economic Policy Board was replaced by Carter's weaker and more diffuse Economic Policy Group, which in turn gave way to Reagan's cabinet councils (e.g., Porter, 1980, 1981, 1983). Moreover, Porter contends that, although these bodies may be important on particular issues, presidents typically rely more on informal groups of advisers rather than on such "general purpose formal entities" (1981, 215; on Johnson, cf. J. Anderson, 1986a; on Reagan, see, e.g., Newland, 1984).

For the most part, Weatherford (1988) seems to be right in his claim that scholars have neglected economic advisory processes, making influence difficult to determine. However, there are significant exceptions—for example, Porter's (1980) careful examination of the Economic Policy Board, Sloan's (1990a) study of the relationships between the president and the CEA during the Johnson and Ford administrations, and Weatherford's (1987) use of advisory organization to help account for the differences in Eisenhower's and Nixon's approaches to particular economic problems. Weatherford and McDonnell (1990) try to generalize from Reagan's experience, suggesting that presidents differ in the consistency of their economic ideologies, the strength of their drive for policy coherence, and the relative weight they accord to expert economic and political advice. Ideological consistency and the pursuit of policy coherence lead to greater centralization and hierarchy in economic advising; presidential receptivity to economic versus political advice helps determine patterns of influence. The capacity to make additional generalizations awaits the emergence of more such studies.

Network characteristics—for example, the range of actors, stability, degree of conflict, extent of access to and influence on the president—can vary dramatically within and between policy arenas. To some extent, such variation may reflect the analytical and empirical problems associated with drawing boundaries around policy arenas (see, e.g., Hart, 1987, 62–63; Walcott and Hult, 1989, 29ff). There may be a danger of overlooking relevant actors and relationships if they seem not to belong in a particular policy sphere; for example, Destler (1977) comments on the general absence of ties between domestic and foreign policy aides, though it is unclear that any studies have systematically probed for such links. Perhaps, too, analytical policy types (e.g., distributive, redistributive, regulatory) rather than categories based on policy substance may be more useful.

Still, some comparison across policy realms is possible. For instance, foreign policy networks tend to be smaller and somewhat more durable than those in either the domestic or the economic policy spheres. Although the participants are more consistent in economic policy networks than in the domestic policy arena, advisory networks change frequently in both cases.

TYPE OF DECISION

Different advisory networks also may be associated with different kinds of decisions. For example, Kozak (1985) distinguishes between routine decisions, in which networks populated by cabinet and

bureaucratic officials are particularly influential, and adaptive decisions, dominated by Executive Office staff and White House aides.
Crises typically lead presidents to turn to more ad hoc networks made
up of an inner circle or kitchen cabinet (cf. Walcott and Hult, 1989,
20). Sigelman and McNeil's (1980) study of advising during the Tet
offensive suggests that during crises, networks do not necessarily
shrink in size, or become more interactive or likely to be dominated
by a few individuals (cf. Best and DesRoches, 1991).

OTHER FACTORS

Other variations in networks can be traced to term cycles other
than those associated with specific types of policy. In general, presidents tend to activate and rely upon formal networks more frequently
earlier in their terms; more ad hoc mechanisms become more prominent as relationships solidify. Moreover, advisory networks evidently
shrink over the course of a term, as presidents become less interested
in seeing multiple advisers or in hearing debate in the face of more
fixed agendas and growing constraints (e.g., Light, 1984, 57). As
mentioned earlier, presidents also turn to their cabinets less frequently as the term goes on. Meanwhile, the White House staff typically increases in size, and the significance of its input mounts.

Still other aspects of advisory networks persist across administrations. Some of these metacycles may reflect partisan learning, in
which presidents follow strategies of predecessors of the same party
and react against approaches of presidents from the opposing party
(see, e.g., Hult and Walcott, 1989b). Republican presidents, for example, have been more likely than Democratic presidents to appoint
special economic advisers to their White House staffs (Porter, 1981).

Other similarities and differences in advisory networks may be ac-
counted for by continuities and discontinuities in what Kessel (1983,
1984) calls White House "communication structures," which tap the
volume of interaction and the degree of centralization and hierarchy
in staff communication patterns. On the basis of his analyses of the
Carter and Reagan White Houses, Kessel expects such structures to
be relatively stable within and across administrations, though with
some variation reflecting the management predispositions of particular presidents (e.g., whether a president opts for a strong chief of
staff). Communication structures may well affect, for example, the

volume, timing, and range of advice that reaches a president, as well as the amount of conflict and competition to which the chief executive is exposed.

Additional metacycles highlight the importance of precedent in presidential activities (e.g., Kernell, 1989). Campbell (1986, 263) points to the increased use of special cabinet-level bodies in the Carter and Reagan administrations and argues that such an approach is likely to continue. More broadly, advising and soliciting and coordinating advice evidently have become more centralized in the White House (cf. Moe, 1985). Meanwhile, the growth, differentiation, and politicization of the Executive Office of the President may be fostering denser, more specialized, and more conflictual advisory networks.

Relatively few generalizations can be made about the use presidents make of such networks or the influence of particular network actors. Kessel's (1983, 1984) analyses of "organizational structures" in the Carter and Reagan White Houses, however, suggest that the relative influence of certain network actors persists across administrations.[10] In addition, evidence of growing centralization and politicization indicates that presidents may have greater access to diverse expert information and counsel, be less well-informed on more operational matters perhaps best discussed with departmental officials, and be subject to overload and increased demands for conflict resolution.

Finally, the advisory networks presidents rely on and how they use them also may depend on particular presidents and their administrations. Individual characteristics of presidents—their management styles, predispositions, or strategies—may well affect advisory networks. George Bush, for example, seems to consult widely, often on an informal basis, with one or a few individuals at a time, without necessarily telling the various actors of each other's existence. Richard Nixon, in contrast, sought the input of only a few on many matters, while Dwight Eisenhower relied both on formal, highly structured advisory processes and on more ad hoc mechanisms. The extent to which presidents listen to those they consult also varies. Lyndon Johnson, for example, evidently paid attention only to those with whom he agreed (e.g., Berman, 1982).

Kessel's work (1983, 1984) again points to possible generalizations, this time about the significance of particular administrations in explaining variation in advisory networks. In his framework, "issue structures" tap the extent of policy agreement among staffers, and "influence structures" measure the concentration of and the bases for perceived staff influence. In comparing the Carter and Reagan White Houses, Kessel finds that issue structures are the most variable and influence structures the second most variable of the four structures he examined. Both issue and influence structures can be expected to vary across and, often, within administrations as staffers and their perceived standing with the president change. And both may affect, for example, the diversity of the advice presidents receive, the amount of conflict to which they are exposed, and their own views of the credibility of their sources of advice.

Can Presidents Control Advisory Networks?

Rather clearly, one can spot both significant diversity in presidential advisory networks and numerous potential explanations for that diversity. But how much control do presidents have over the networks that bring them advice? This issue has received perhaps more attention from scholars than any other single concern. For the most part, though, it remains largely unresolved.

In examining work in this area, one must consider at least two general issues. The first concerns the kinds of variables that may affect advisory networks; scholars have examined factors at the individual presidential, the organizational, and the environmental levels of analysis. Second, and more directly relevant for a discussion of network manipulability, is the extent of presidential control over key variables.

The most systematic work focuses on presidential-level variables and their impact on advisory networks. Some scholars point to the significance of particular dimensions such as the degree of presidential involvement in generating and evaluating options (e.g., Paul Anderson, 1985; Destler, 1977; Edwards and Wayne 1990), the breadth of the search for advice (Destler, 1977; Edwards and Wayne, 1990), the extent of presidential activity or passivity in the advising process (Best, 1985); Greenstein, 1990; Salamon, 1981), and the form of the advice presidents wish to receive (e.g., Edwards and Wayne, 1990; Porter, 1986, 868).

Other studies trace the effects of clusters of presidential characteristics. Receiving perhaps the most attention are presidential management styles (e.g., George, 1980; Hess, 1988; Johnson, 1974; Porter, 1981). Although there is little agreement on the political and policy consequences of different management styles (Pika, 1988, 8), they typically are said to reflect the cognitive needs, management preferences, and experiences of individual presidents and to shape the management models (e.g., formal, competitive, ad hoc) presidents select. Similarly, a president's political style (Hargrove, 1988)—his or her character, cognitive skills, and values—may affect how the president seeks out and responds to advice. George (1980) also draws attention to a president's efficacy and ability to tolerate conflict, while Janis (1989) suggests that a range of cognitive, egocentric, and affiliative factors may inhibit presidential openness to and use of advice. Cottam and Rockman (1984) attempt to link what they call a president's psychological style to his or her organizational style (the extent and nature of presidential involvement, the locus of key advisers, and presidential preferences for adversarial, collegial, or hierarchical advisory mechanisms). Cottam and Rockman hypothesize that both of these clusters of variables in turn affect presidential policy goals.

Presidents' goals are the starting point for still other efforts to examine their use of advisory networks. Rather than focusing primarily on presidential characteristics, these works emphasize presidential strategy: advisory mechanisms reflect, at least in part, presidential efforts to pursue political, policy, and administrative objectives given the constraints and opportunities of the larger political system and the executive branch (e.g., Hult and Walcott, 1989b; Kernell, 1989; Moe, 1985; Walcott and Hult, 1989).

A concentration on strategy moves away from perhaps the most common understanding of presidential advising—the personal contingency perspective (cf. Hult and Walcott 1989a, 6). This latter view argues that presidents both do and should adapt advisory networks to their preferences and needs (see, e.g., Allison and Szanton, 1976; Kernell, 1986; Rockman, 1988b; Williams, 1990). Highlighting strategy, in contrast, involves more of a problem contingency approach, which contends that advisory arrangements ought to respond, at least in part, to the characteristics of problem settings (see Hult and Walcott, 1989a, 7) and points to the impact of both presidential and environmental factors. As we shall see, however, the extent of presidential control over advisory networks remains an open question for both the personal contingency and the more strategic perspectives.

Other analysts emphasize more organizational-level variables. Some of these scholars engage in what has been termed "pure structural prescription" (Hult and Walcott, 1989a, 6), offering counsel for designing advisory networks that is assumed to apply to all administrations. A prime example is the debate over the desirability of a chief of staff mentioned earlier.

More important is the possible impact of existing organizational structures on presidential advising. Bendor and Hammond (1989, 33–34) contend, for instance: "Different structures may cause each piece of advice to [be] compared with, or aggregated with, different pieces of advice. . . . What the top level officials come to believe about the outside world will also be a function of structure." Hierarchical structures may decrease the number of options and the thoroughness of the evaluations forwarded to the president (Helmer and Maisel, 1978, 46); such "uncertainty absorption" (March and Simon, 1958) is a common feature of many bureaucracies.

In addition, structures and processes in place at one point in time may affect later organizational arrangements. Two such patterns were mentioned earlier—partisan learning and the impact of precedent.

The extent and the significance of these more stable arrangements are at the center of much of the discussion of the institutionalization of executive branch structures and practices (see, e.g., Arnold, 1989; Gilmour, 1975; Kesselman, 1970; Moe, 1985; Sander, 1989; Seligman, 1983; Wyszomirski, 1982). Although definitions of institutionalization differ, common to most is a concern with the stability over time of "regular behavior patterns" (Moe, 1985, 236 fn 1; cf. Arnold, 1989). Far less agreement exists on the extent of institutionalization.

Other phenomena are common to most complex organizations. For example, the dynamics of advisory groups—such as pressures for conformity and consensus—may affect the diversity and quality of the information and options that presidents receive (Burke and Greenstein, 1989, 281ff; Janis, 1989). The growing specialization of presidential advisers and advisory networks has already been noted. Such differentiation is common in organizational settings characterized by diverse, complex, and often volatile demands. The specialization in turn often generates growing needs for coordination, direction, and conflict resolution, as the development of the roles of the chief of staff and the national security adviser may suggest. Yet, as we have seen, efforts to respond to specialization may magnify fragmentation and trigger renewed conflict, leading to additional attempts to channel conflict and coordinate activities (which Walcott and Hult, 1987b, have labeled a "differentiation dynamic"; cf. Helmer and Maisel, 1978, 46). In addition, struggles over policy direction and access to the president resemble the conflict characteristic of most organizational settings (see, e.g., Cyert and March, 1963; Pfeffer, 1981). This conflict in turn may influence the operation and evolution of presidential advisory networks.

Finally, many scholars contend that variables in the surrounding social, political, and economic systems also affect (or should affect) presidential advisory networks. Such arguments are another variant of the problem contingency approach introduced above. For example, some maintain that the centralization of advising in the White House reflects the mounting fragmentation in Congress and in Washington, D.C., more generally and the rising demands and expectations focused on the presidency (e.g., Kernell, 1989; Moe, 1985). Paul Anderson (1985) stresses the importance of the relevant policy context (e.g., the type of policy, the extent of goal consensus), which influences where options are framed and the degree of delegation of authority. Others are more prescriptive, contending that advisory networks ought to reflect the character of particular political and policy problems confronting presidents (e.g., Walcott and Hult, 1987b; Lord, 1988).

Underlying most discussions of the factors that potentially shape presidential advisory networks is the issue of presidential control over the design and use of those arrangements. Not surprisingly, those focusing on presidential-level variables are more apt to view advisory networks as subject to presidential control than are those who concentrate on organizational and environmental factors. Yet, even consideration of presidential-level variables points to possible constraints on presidential control. For example, Johnson (1974) paints presidents and those around them as virtual captives of the propensities and limitations of presidential personality. This also seems to be one of the motivations behind Janis's (1989) exploration of the personality requisites for good policy makers. Meanwhile, Rockman (1984, 205) contends that presidential management styles in part reflect both public expectations and precedent. For all his emphasis on individual presidential management preferences and styles, even Hess

(1988) observes that White House staffs grow to resemble each other over the course of a term.

Others note that the extent of presidential influence on advisory arrangements varies with the salience of the issue being considered (Cottam and Rockman, 1984; Destler, 1980–1981; Janis, 1989). It also may be the case that presidents are better able to manipulate more informal advisory mechanisms than they are formal ones (Greenstein, 1982; Burke and Greenstein, 1989); by the same token, of course, these informal mechanisms are probably more susceptible to the manipulation of others.

Many works discuss variables at more than one level of analysis. Some scholars, for example, examine the interplay of presidential, organizational, and environmental variables (eg., Campbell, 1986; Edwards and Wayne, 1990; Kernell, 1989; Walcott and Hult, 1989, forthcoming) and their implications for presidential influence over activities in the executive branch. Others focus more narrowly on the interplay between presidential-level and organizational variables. Arnold (1989, 29–30), for instance, writes of the "dialectical tension [in the EOP] between neutral competence . . . and adaptation to the needs and interests of the incumbent." Similarly, Pika (1988) explores the interaction between presidential management style and the "organizational matrix" (elements associated with the presidency as an office distinguishable from its occupant). More generally, Janis (1989) proposes design strategies for coping with the constraints that participants' personalities place on policy processes. Burke and Greenstein (1989) strive to link the literatures on advising and leadership in explaining presidential use of information. They contend that, although there is a "largely . . . circular" relationship between presidents and their advisory systems, the president has "temporal priority: he establishes his advisory system whether by design or default. And he can say no to advice" (272).

Virtually all of these works point to there being some room for presidential choice in designing and using management structures. As Kernell (1989) notes, the very existence of so much diversity in staffing patterns within and among administrations suggests that such arrangements are at least to some extent manipulable. Still not fully clear, though, is just how much conscious control presidents have over networks. Most scholars temporize, noting that internal and external political dynamics and organizational constraints are important as well. And one must guard against assuming that arrangements reflect any particular actors' objectives: "advisory procedures develop without conscious design" (Paul Anderson, 1985, 162).

What Effect Does Advice Have on Decision Outcomes?

For many considering presidential advising mechanisms, the bottom line is performance. Most seem to agree that relying on desirable processes increases the probability of achieving desirable outcomes (cf. Burke and Greenstein, 1989; Janis, 1989). Analysts have examined the advantages and disadvantages of conventionally used models of presidential advising and management (e.g., George, 1980; Johnson, 1974; Porter, 1980). Others point to particular problems in current arrangements and propose possible solutions (e.g., Allison and Szanton, 1976; George, 1980; Hess, 1988).

Numerous evaluative criteria underpin these assessments. Standards direct attention to advisory networks and to the role of the president. Desirable networks provide reliable information and analysis to presidents and other key policy makers, make available information and counsel from all relevant interests, and work to ensure that presidents see all pertinent materials and are exposed to conflict among advisers (e.g., Allison and Szanton, 1976; Burke, 1984; George, 1980; Johnson, 1974; Porter, 1980). At the same time, desirable processes must be able to reach closure (e.g., Allison and Szanton, 1976, 62). Even more fundamental for some is that advisory networks meet the needs of particular presidents (e.g., Kernell, 1986, 226).

Not surprisingly, given these demanding criteria, scholars point to numerous shortcomings in advising. The hierarchies of more formalistic designs may screen out or distort important information, while the diverse sources of advice and competition characteristic of multiple advocacy arrangements may work against closure. Others point to the frequent absence of neutral policy advice and counsel informed by institutional memory (e.g., Arnold, 1989; Barilleaux, 1988; Covington, 1985; Edwards and Wayne, 1990).

Yet even in well-designed advisory networks, presidents evidently are key actors. For example, the level of presidential attention affects whether advisory arrangements are used at all and whether their inputs are taken seriously (e.g., Burke and Greenstein, 1989; Weatherford, 1987, 945). Presidents also may be rated on their strategic competence (the ability to evaluate policy advice) and their process sensibility (the capacity to spot problems in advisory networks; Quirk, 1990).

Meanwhile, the extent to which presidents should be held accountable for the outcomes of advisory processes—that is, for the impact of advising on decisions and the consequences of those decisions—remains an open question. This depends in part, of course, on one's view of the manipulability of advisory networks and the president's ability to guide them in intended directions. Berman (1982), for example, sharply disagrees with those who view many of Johnson's actions during the Vietnam conflict as the result of flawed advisory networks; rather, Berman claims, Johnson must be held responsible for his poor use of those arrangements. Yet, others caution that one must be wary about too quickly linking process and outcome (Barilleaux, 1988; Burke and Greenstein, 1989; Pika, 1991).

Assessing the Literature

One can point to a great many works that touch on presidential advising. They paint a complex picture of diverse and often volatile advisory networks and of presidents who are at least as constrained as they are assisted by the prevailing advisory arrangements. At best, however, only tentative answers exist for the five questions initially posed about presidential advising. This section assesses the literature on presidential advising with an eye toward identifying shortcomings and, more importantly, suggesting directions for future work.

Underlying all assessments are specific notions of what is desirable. The evaluation that follows is grounded in a particular understanding of political science.[11] In my view, the chief aim of political science is the systematic explanation of political phenomena. Evaluation and prescription are important, but they need to be grounded in a strong explanatory foundation (as well as in explicit, well-justified evaluative criteria). If one accepts explanation as the first and primary objective of inquiry (and not all do), then the question becomes one of strategy: How best to advance toward that goal?

Staking out favored strategies demands that one address both conceptual and methodological issues. Conceptually, moving toward (causal) explanation minimally requires knowing what one wants to explain; that is, being able to specify the dependent variables. Necessary as well is identifying independent variables and their relationships with the dependent variables and with each other. This suggests that some attention should be paid to conceptual mapping as a prelude to formulating testable hypotheses. Certainly, not all potential explanatory variables can be examined (or even known) at any one point, but deciding which to focus on and which to omit necessitates that some thought be given to the range of possibly relevant factors and relationships.

Such an approach to explanation implies a particular logic of theory construction and development. In the approach just outlined, one begins not from assumptions and axioms (as, for example, social choice theorists do) but rather with the clear identification and justification of variables and proposed relationships—with the logic, that is, of the regression model. Which of these two strategies a given scholar selects is doubtless in part a function of taste and training.[12] Relevant, too, are her or his expectations of social science inquiry. Those who seek simple and elegant theories will be attracted by the first, more deductive strategy. Those whose primary aim is to understand and explain political phenomena may find the strategy outlined here more appealing.[13]

For all their differences, both conceptual strategies suggest that analysis ought to be very rigorous and very careful. That said, scholars pursuing the variable identification approach might well learn from the emphasis of many social choice theorists on parsimony: a research strategy that emphasizes studying simpler problems and fewer variables may yield more and clearer findings than one that delves immediately into a complex tangle of interrelated variables. At the same time, one must be careful not to look, like the mythical drunkard, only under the streetlight for a few easily identified, brightly shining variables—as arduous, complicated, and uncertain as it is to do otherwise. Doing so may well militate against finding the explanations one seeks (see Kaplan, 1964).

More difficult, of course, is actually selecting the variables of interest for any one study. Conceptual mapping may threaten to overwhelm one with numerous, often interrelated variables. Used as a basis for designing particular studies, however, mapping can assist by drawing together previous work, by identifying outstanding questions, and by clarifying one's thinking about possibly relevant variables and relationships. It also can help one avoid the omitted variable problem and the inclusion of variables that merely muddy explanation (see King, 1990) and move toward formulating testable hypotheses.[14]

Finally, explanation can be advanced by paying careful attention to familiar and mundane, but sometimes overlooked, methodological issues. Examples include the importance of specifying testable and competing hypotheses, selecting and justifying research designs, confronting sampling and measurement issues, fitting data collection and analysis techniques to the question being asked, and noting both the potential for and the limits to generalizing from the findings.

If systematic explanation is the primary aim of political science, then much of the literature on presidential advising fits uncomfortably at best. Evaluation and prescription dominate. They also are likely premature: not enough about presidential advising is known or fully understood to permit insightful assessment or useful recommendation. Moreover, if one looks to future evaluation and prescription, existing works offer cautionary tales about how to engage in those activities.

Prescription is a primary objective of many works that touch on advising (see, e.g., Allison and Szanton, 1976; Bundy, 1982–1983; Clark, 1989; Feigenbaum, 1980; Heineman and Hessler, 1980; Hess, 1988; Meltsner, 1990; Sorensen, 1987–1988). Crises often trigger an avalanche of recommendations. Barilleaux (1988), for example, analyzes the role of presidential staffs in the context of events like the Bay of Pigs, the Cuban missile crisis, Watergate, and Iran-contra; and Henderson (1988) offers prescriptions for the national security adviser in the wake of the Iran-contra affair. Such "lurching reaction to the perceived problems of the day" (Pika, 1991) leads scholars and practitioners alike to neglect the broader, more systematic study of advising that would focus more on general understanding and less on immediate responses (Kessel, 1989, 16; cf. Pika, 1981–1982; Quirk, 1989). Moreover, there is evidently great danger in drawing lessons from atypical and dramatic rather than more frequent, routine events.[15]

Other prescriptive efforts reflect gaps in empirical analysis. Organization-level prescription, for example, often is rejected out of hand. Clearly, pure structural prescription, which points to the one best way to organize advisory arrangements, makes little sense. Even the widely acclaimed multiple advocacy networks are not appropriate for all situations; they may lead to presidential overload or to debilitating conflict (see, e.g., Destler, 1977; Light, 1982). Before one undertakes structural prescription, what seems to be needed is more systematic consideration of problem contingency approaches that explore the effects of varying advisory networks under specified conditions (cf. Johnson, 1974, 239; Pika, 1991; Porter, 1980, 252; more generally, see Hult and Walcott, 1990). Of course, to the extent that presidents find themselves in situations of high complexity, controversy, or ambiguity, such matching of problem settings and organizational coping mechanisms may not be very helpful. Needed under those conditions is presidential inspiration or leadership (Hult and Walcott, 1990, 72; cf. J. Thompson, 1967). It may be here that testing propositions from the literature on leadership and presidential advising (Burke and Greenstein, 1989) becomes particularly compelling.

Even if one believes that evaluation and prescription ought to be among the primary goals of students of presidential advising, much contemporary literature falls short in at least three ways. First, some prescriptions conflate what is with what ought to be. For example, simply because advisory networks seem to reflect presidential management styles does not mean that they must or that they should do so. Perhaps instead, advisory arrangements should "compensate for the deficiencies and complement the strengths" of presidents (Rockman, 1988b, 5; cf. Burke and Greenstein, 1989, 293ff; Redford and McCulley, 1986; Yates, 1985, 215).

Second, many prescriptions often contradict each other, much like Simon's notorious proverbs of administration (1946; cf. Heclo, 1977, 41). For instance, some call for the national security adviser and the chief of staff to act as neutral custodians of the advisory process, but others contend that such officials need to be perceived as influential in order for them to have legitimacy and credibility with other network actors. Team building among advisers is important (e.g., Bundy, 1982–1983; Destler, 1977), yet "groupthink" (Janis, 1972) is a significant risk. On the one hand, many place a high premium on adversarial advisory networks that expose presidents to competing viewpoints (e.g., Betts, 1980; Cottam and Rockman, 1984; Newland, 1984; Rockman, 1988b; Yates, 1985); on the other hand, apparent conflict among presidential advisers sends the public disturbing signals of administration disarray (e.g., Edwards and Wayne, 1990).

Third, shared, but often implicit and insufficiently justified normative assumptions seem to underlie many works on presidential advising. For example, some stress the desirability of additional neutral competence. The availability of neutral policy advice seems to be a normative benchmark and, as we have seen, a source of much dissatisfaction with contemporary presidential advising. The loss of institutional memory in the White House and the Executive Office allegedly deprives presidents of a balanced view of policy issues and obscures the lessons of past experience. Of course, enhancing the role of careerists (a common proposal for enhancing institutional memory) hardly guarantees neutral competence. More important, neutrality may be the wrong counterfactual for evaluating advice. Neutral advice may not meet presidents' needs and desires for "responsive competence" (Moe, 1985), and presidents may well receive broader, more diverse, and hence more helpful counsel when those with legitimate stakes in what is being discussed participate in advisory networks (see, e.g., Porter, 1985). Indeed, it is not clear what *neutral* might mean in an advisory context. The very idea of neutral recommendations appears oxymoronic, since advisers' positions, values, and sense of priorities help shape the information they interpret and the options they explore.

A second assumption frequently is present in efforts to assess decision, and by extension advisory, processes. The desired process with which actual ones are compared typically involves a clear formulation of the question to be answered, a careful setting of goals and priorities, a search for relevant information, and an examination and assessment of a range of alternatives (see, e.g., George, 1980; Janis, 1989). An implicit rational actor model seems to lurk behind such an evaluative framework; it is rarely defended, though such a view may be neither plausible nor desirable (see, e.g., Lindblom, 1979; March and Olsen, 1986). Janis (1989, 115ff) is somewhat of an exception, arguing (but not systematically demonstrating) that political scientists have overemphasized the influence of "nonrational" factors; he also may underplay possible organizational and environmental constraints not subject to human control (though see Rockman, 1989). Still, the more general failure to be clearer about the rationales for assessments of advising may obscure understanding and hamper prescription.

That normative approaches can be so readily questioned highlights the need for more careful delineation and, especially, justification of evaluative criteria. Probably even more important, however, is the need for better understanding of presidential advising and of its determinants and effects.

To call for fuller understanding and better explanation of presidential advising raises two questions: What is it we don't know? and Why don't we know it? Heclo (1977, 5) once observed that "a lack of basic empirical research" characterizes the study of the presidency. To a significant extent, that still describes the contemporary understanding of presidential advising (cf. Wayne 1983, 6). As the excursion through the literature relevant to presidential advising reveals, none of the five questions at the beginning of the chapter can be fully answered. Even on the seemingly straightforward issue of who advises presidents, gaps remain. Much work focuses on decision rather than advisory networks and, consequently, pays less attention to the flows of information and counsel to presidents (cf. Quirk, 1989, 21). Studies that do focus on advisory arrangements for the most part neglect some potentially relevant actors (such as White House and NSC staffers below the senior level).

We know even less about the influence of advice on presidents or its impact on policy outcomes. Presidential ability to shape advisory networks—the issue of agency—remains murky. Finally, although numerous tentative generalizations can be advanced about the continuities and discontinuities in advisory networks, it is less clear which variables are most important under what conditions for explaining the determinants, dynamics, and effects of such arrangements. That more needs to be learned about presidential advising seems clear. Why that is the case is less readily apparent. Looking at prevailing conceptual and methodological strategies provides some insight.

CONCEPTUAL ISSUES

A critical component of any explanatory strategy is the ability to specify the dependent variables. Yet, in the presidential advising literature, there is a general failure to consistently identify and justify the choice of dependent variables. The selection of dependent variables often seems to be ad hoc, driven more by available independent variables than by guiding research questions (cf. Hult and Walcott, 1989a). This is a particular problem given the lack of direct attention paid to presidential advising and the analytical blurring between advising and decision making.

At the same time, there is an abundance of independent variables: presidential style, ideology, and strategy; small group interactions and staff structures; the prevailing values in the larger political system; fragmentation in Washington; and the features of the relevant policy arena. For all the diversity, though, relatively little effort has been devoted to explicit conceptual mapping. There have been few systematic attempts to speculate about the relationships of such variables with each other and with possible dependent variables. There are rarely strong grounds, then, for justifying decisions to focus on particular variables or specific research questions.

Such neglect may have significantly stunted what we know about presidential advising. Many discussions stop at either too high or too low a level of analysis. For example, numerous works on individual actors examine their various roles (e.g., Dexter, 1977; Kellerman, 1981; Light, 1984; Mulcahy and Crabb, 1988; Wyszomirski 1984, 1985). Such analyses run the risk of providing only classifications, offering little insight into the advice actors bring to presidents or their involvement in the more general dynamics of advisory networks. "It is as if we used the categories of theatrical performance without reference to the drama that alone explains their development and interrelationships" (Seligman, 1980, 354; cf. Hart, 1987, 188).

Other efforts to categorize whole advisory systems and to classify presidential management styles fail to "capture the complexity and variation in advisory practices" (Greenstein, 1988, 351) that are apparent in most accounts of actual presidential activity (such as those discussed in Campbell, 1986; Redford and McCulley, 1986). In addition, despite the richness of proposed presidential, organizational, and environmental factors, much work concentrates on only one cluster of variables.[16] Moreover, presidential variables tend to dominate analysis with little clear rationale (cf. Pika, 1981–1982); most common is a personal contingency view of presidential advising.

Receiving far less attention are the possible independent effects of organizational variables on presidential advising. Yet, as we have seen, existing structures and processes may have a significant impact on the nature and range of advice policy makers receive. Organizational precedents, growing specialization, and the dynamics of conflict and efforts at conflict resolution also may constrain the evolution and use of advisory networks. The extent to which presidents can manipulate such organizational variables, or other factors in the surrounding political and policy environments, remains very much an open question.

These varying emphases may in part reflect an implicit assumption about human agency that evidently underlies much of the literature. In this view, individuals (whether they be presidents or other actors) are (or can be) shapers of advisory networks and of the ways in which advice is requested, gathered, communicated, and used. Such an understanding may in fact be accurate in many cases. Nonetheless, other interpretations—for example, those offered by organized anarchy theorists (e.g., Cohen, March, and Olsen, 1972)—are possible. At the very least, assumptions about human, institutional, and systemic capacities and dynamics could be more clearly articulated and defended. Competing hypotheses about the determinants of network design, operation, and impact based on varying assumptions might then be tested (see, e.g., Pfeffer, 1981).

Underlying all of these conceptual weaknesses is the lack of an explicit theoretical foundation on which to ground variable selection and hypothesis formulation, which could in turn guide empirical investigation. This reflects the general absence of agreement on the major questions about advising as well as a gap and a lack of iteration between theorizing and data gathering (though see, e.g., Kessel, 1975, 1983, 1984).

METHODOLOGICAL CONCERNS

Not all of the issues surrounding strategies for studying presidential advising are conceptual. Others are methodological. In this realm, more progress seems to have been made. Over the last several years, students of presidential staffing and advising have heeded Heclo's (1977) call to expand their data sources. Scholars have increasingly used interviews with participants (e.g., Bock and Clarke, 1986; Campbell, 1986; Covington, 1985; Helmer and Maisel, 1978; Kessel, 1975, 1983, 1984; Light, 1984), oral histories (e.g., Hargrove, 1988), and documents housed in presidential libraries (e.g., Best, 1988a, 1988b;

Burke and Greenstein, 1989; Henderson, 1988; Redford and McCulley, 1986). At the same time, many works still rely heavily on more traditional sources of information, such as journalistic coverage, memoirs, and casual observation. Indeed, Quirk (1989, 23) contends that greater use needs to be made of easily available and generally reliable journalistic coverage, saving archival research for investigating narrowly focused research questions. And Jones (1989) encourages scholars to make additional use of memoirs, always being careful to "mistrust but verify." Although access to documents and to participants, perhaps especially those currently in office or involved in national security advising (cf. Lord, 1988, 124), continues to pose difficulties, the absence of usable data is evidently not a major barrier to doing work on presidential advising.

The systematic collection and analysis of these data have been more problematic. In large part, of course, such difficulties can be explained by conceptual weaknesses—the relative poverty of available theory and the lack of clearly specified dependent variables. At the same time, research design remains a major challenge. Scholars have used a variety of approaches to address issues relevant to presidential advising: for example, case studies of decisions and organizations (e.g., Barilleaux, 1985; Kessel, 1975), comparative case studies (e.g., Burke and Greenstein, 1989; Weatherford, 1987), analyses that trace the activities of a particular unit or the performance of a certain task over time (e.g., Hult and Walcott, 1989b; Weko, 1989), and efforts to track relationships within and between administrations (e.g., Best, 1988a, 1988b; Kessel, 1983, 1984). A critical concern in much of this research is sampling—in terms of choosing cases for examination and comparison and of selecting respondents to be interviewed, documents to be surveyed, or activities to be counted. More self-conscious sampling, and explicit justification of those decisions can only improve these endeavors (cf. Paul Anderson, 1985, 167).

Perhaps the greatest methodological challenge is that of measurement. Although some notable quantitative work has been done (e.g., Best, 1988a, 1988b; Helmer and Maisel, 1978; Kessel, 1975, 1983, 1984; Sigelman and McNeil, 1980; R. Thompson, 1989), most problems do not easily lend themselves to such treatment. For instance, knowing who met with the president how often in what size groups reveals little about the purpose of the meetings, the extent and nature of any information or counsel exhanged, or the influence of the participants on the president's thinking or actions. Nor are these likely to be short-term weaknesses of quantitative indicators: the complexity and dynamics of advisory networks and relationships demand more qualitative measures. Indeed, the best quantitative work (such as that of Kessel) relies heavily on qualitative data in interpreting its findings. Qualitative indicators deserve more careful development, justification, and analysis.

An even greater difficulty is determining how to operationalize some variables in the first place. For example, measuring the influence of advice on presidents—like tapping influence more generally—is a continuing problem. Many scholars use multiple indicators (a strategy recommended by, e.g., Sullivan and Feldman, 1979), searching for evidence of influence in the match between advice and presidential action, the testimony of those around the president, and the more generalized reputation of particular actors (e.g., Crabb and Mulcahy, 1986; Hargrove, 1988; Light, 1984; Sloan, 1990b). Even so, advice and outcome need not be causally linked, and the imputation of influence may be post hoc rationalization or effective public relations (cf. Rockman, 1989, 786).

Despite these problems, methodological sensitivity seems to be growing in works on presidential advising. What remains critical is to harness this mounting methodological sophistication to address more clearly framed and better justified research questions.

Next Steps

If current strategies for understanding presidential advising are inadequate, what should be done to improve matters? Initially, explicit conceptual mapping would help clarify the range of variables and relationships that possibly are relevant to presidential advising. Network notions might well be useful at this stage. Examining networks emphasizes the need to consider the potential contributions of numerous actors, directs attention to relationships among those actors, and raises the possibility that advisory networks may be distinguishable from other kinds of networks (e.g., those for decision making and implementation) and may vary across decision settings and policy arenas as well as within and between administrations. The numerous propositions derived from existing work provide a strong start for such mapping.

Clearly, however, mapping is at best pretheoretical (Pika, 1981–1982; Rosenau, 1966) and not an end in itself. The next step is to formulate propositions that can be converted to testable hypotheses. As suggested above, a conceptual framework can help guide variable selection and the development of competing explanations. Even so, difficult questions remain: Which variables are most important? and Which propositions are worth pursuing? Also important is a clear (though flexible) idea of research priorities, reflecting not only what needs to be done but also what reasonably can be done in a particular area of inquiry.

Two clusters of dependent variables seem especially critical for improving understanding of presidential advising: the nature of presidential advisory relationships and networks[17] and the influence of those relationships and networks on presidential decisions (and nondecisions) and on decision outcomes. Tracing and seeking to explain the extent of variation in these clusters of variables could take scholars a long way toward answering the questions posed at the beginning of this chapter, while also better focusing inquiry.

In such study, presidential policy decisions would appear to be the most often appropriate units of analysis (cf. Quirk, 1989; King, 1990), permitting comparison within and across presidencies and policy spheres. In selecting independent variables, it might be well to pay special attention to variables that tap both environmental and organizational factors. First, these variables may be easier to conceptualize, operationalize, and measure than more idiosyncratic presidential variables (such as presidential personality or presidential style). In addition, individual-level factors have received considerably more attention. Focusing on environmental and organizational variables not only compensates for this likely overemphasis but also converts the assumption of presidential agency into an issue for empirical examination.

Quite clearly, these suggestions constitute neither a step-by-step guide to explanatory success nor an elegant theory of presidential advising. Rather, much like presidential advising and policy making themselves, explaining the determinants, dynamics, and impact of advising and, ultimately, of presidential choice is likely to be complex, ambiguous, full of disagreement, and frequently downright frustrating. Yet, as Morris Ogul observed, strategies that promise to be "long and dirty" may well be the most fruitful for enhancing understanding.[18]

Notes

I am grateful for the comments and suggestions of Larry Berman, John Burke, George Edwards, David Elliott, John Kessel, Joseph Pika, Charles Walcott, Thomas Weko, and the anonymous referees. I also benefited greatly from the stimulating and provocative discussion at the Pittsburgh conference. In addition, I appreciate the research assistance of Bruce Snyder, the secretarial help of Evelyn Khalili and Terry Kingrea, and the institutional support of Pomona College, the Claremont Graduate School, and Virginia Tech.

1. The more popular books on presidential advising, in contrast, often focus on individual advisers. See, for example, Patrick Anderson (1968) and Medved (1979).

2. In contrast, Meltsner includes "policy for getting the ruler elected or reappointed" (1990, 6) in his examination of advising. To include this here would not only lengthen the discussion but also threaten to obscure the arguably useful analytical distinction between campaigning and governing.

3. A final, more pragmatic reason for focusing on advising was the initial division of review assignments for this volume: advising and decision making were originally conceived as topics for two separate chapters.

4. Cronin (1969), J. Anderson (1986a), Riddlesperger and King (1989), and Weatherford and McDonnell (1990) all refer at least in passing to advisory networks. For more general background on network ideas, see, for example, Hult and Walcott, 1990, 96ff; Perrow, 1986, 192ff; and Wellman and Berkowitz, 1988.

5. Still other potentially important actors have received little sustained attention. Although some scholarly work has examined presidential families (most notably, Kellerman, 1981), little focuses on the nature and influence of any advice given go the president. Exceptions tend to emphasize specific individuals like Eleanor Roosevelt (e.g., Lash, 1971) and Milton Eisenhower (e.g., Greenstein, 1982). Similarly, "presidential friends, kitchen cabinets, former presidents, and Washington icons" (Rockman, 1988a, 63) are rarely the objects of systematic examination. In general, none of these actors may be very important members of presidential advisory networks. If one is interested in identifying relevant network actors, however, their significance (or insignificance) in advising arguably should be demonstrated rather than ignored or assumed away.

In contrast, presidential task forces and advisory commissions have been examined more thoroughly. Used extensively by Kennedy and Johnson for policy formulation and external input, they evidently are now less important in generating ideas and evaluating policy options for presidents (Light, 1982).

6. In network terms, these changing characteristics of cabinet members might be hypothesized to affect the make-up of presidential advisory networks, as presidents look elsewhere for more politically informed advice.

7. Vice President Dan Quayle, however, has proved to be a valuable emissary to various conservative groups.

8. What follows stresses the spheres of foreign, domestic, and economic policy. Other works emphasize more specialized areas of advising, typically with a

focus on particular units in the Executive Office. Science advising, for instance, has received a fair amount of attention (e.g., Beckler, 1974; Burger, 1980; Golden 1989; Katz, 1978; Lambright, 1985; more generally, see Walcott and Hult, 1989, 25–27, and forthcoming). For the most part, these studies reach conclusions and have weaknesses similar to those sketched in the text.

9. During the Reagan administration, for example, the White House Office of Policy Development helped set the agenda for and closely monitored the domestic cabinet councils (see, e.g., Newland, 1984; Warshaw, 1990).

10. Kessel uses "organizational structures" to refer to White House aides' perceptions of the importance of recommendations made by particular staff units.

11. The epistemological and methodological underpinnings of this assessment largely reflect what Diesing (1991, chap. 4) calls pragmatism. In Diesing's categorization, "pragmatists treat science as a process of inquiry or search for truth. The emphasis is on process, method, correction, change, not definitive and permanent results" (75).

12. There are, of course, other worthwhile strategies. See, for example, Tulis, 1990.

13. A good deal of the contention and evident miscommunication among advocates of these two strategies seems to revolve around the significance of parsimony as a criterion with which to assess theory (however theory is defined). I enter that debate only to observe that, from the second perspective (variable identification), parsimony is an important, but not the most important, evaluative standard. (Other criteria might include a theory's contribution to understanding a political phenomenon, its apparent progressivity in adding to cumulative knowledge, or its prescriptive utility.) If the ultimate aim of inquiry is explanation, parsimony becomes, as Occam's razor suggests, essentially a tie breaker: when two explanations yield equal insight, the simpler one is preferred.

14. The omitted variable problem arises when independent variables that are excluded from an analysis are related to both the independent variables that are included and the dependent variable. When related variables are omitted, some of the apparent effect of the included independent variables on the dependent variable will actually reflect the influence of the excluded variables, thus distorting any findings. If the excluded variables are not related to the included variables, then the estimates of the effects of the included variables will be unbiased. Of course, including variables to address the omitted variables problem leaves one vulnerable to the problem of multicollinearity, making it difficult to determine the unique contribution of independent variables that are related to each other.

15. Not all work suffers from these problems. The prescriptions of scholars like Destler (1977) and George (1980), for example, are informed by the complexities and turbulence in which presidential advising networks are embedded.

16. Exceptions include Burke and Greenstein, 1989; Cottam and Rockman, 1984; Pika, 1988; Walcott and Hult, 1989.

17. Included in this cluster of variables might be the kinds of advice conveyed; the stability, intensity, and degree of conflict of particular advising relationships; and the degree of conflict, diversity, stability, and tightness of the coupling characteristic of specific advisory networks.

18. Ogul's observation was made at the Presidency Research Conference, November 1990.

References

Aberbach, Joel D. 1991. "The President and the Executive Branch." In *The Bush Presidency: First Appraisals*, ed. Colin Campbell, S. J. and Bert A. Rockman. Catham, N.J.: Chatham House.

Allison, Graham T. 1971. *Essence of Decision*. Boston: Little, Brown.

Allison, Graham T., and Peter Szanton. 1976. *Remaking Foreign Policy: The Organizational Connection*. New York: Basic Books.

Almond, Gabriel A., and Stephen J. Genco. 1977. "Clouds, Clocks, and the Study of Politics." *World Politics* 29:489–522.

Altshuler, Bruce E. 1990. *LBJ and the Polls*. Gainesville: University of Florida Press.

Anderson, James E. 1986a. "Developing Fiscal Policy." In *The President and Economic Policy*, ed. James Pfiffner. Philadelphia: Institute for the Study of Human Issues.

——— . 1986b. "A Revised View of the Johnson Cabinet." *Journal of Politics* 48:529–37.

Anderson, Patrick. 1968. *The President's Men*. New York: Doubleday.

Anderson, Paul A. 1985. "Deciding How to Decide in Foreign Affairs: Decision-Making Strategies as Solutions to Presidential Problems." In *The Presidency and Public Policy Making*, ed. George C. Edwards III, Steven A. Shull, and Norman C. Thomas. Pittsburgh: University of Pittsburgh Press.

Arnold, Peri E. 1989. "Strategic Ambition and the Institutional Presidency." Paper prepared for the annual meeting of the American Political Science Association.

Art, Robert. 1973. "Bureaucratic Politics and American Foreign Policy: A Critique." *Policy Sciences* 4:467–90.

Barilleaux, Ryan. 1985. *The President and Foreign Affairs: Evaluation, Performance, and Power*. New York: Praeger.

——— . 1988. *The Post Modern Presidency: The Office After Ronald Reagan*. New York: Praeger.

Beckler, David Z. 1974. "The Precarious Life of Science in the White House." *Daedalus* 103:115–34.

Bendor, Jonathan, and Thomas H. Hammond. 1989. "Rethinking Allison's Models." Paper prepared for the annual meeting of the American Political Science Association.

Berman, Larry. 1982. *Planning a Tragedy: The Americanization of the War in Vietnam*. New York: W. W. Norton.

Best, James J. 1988a. "Presidential Learning: A Comparative Study of Carter and Reagan." *Congress and the Presidency* 15:25–48.

——— . 1988b. "Who Talked to the President When? A Study of Lyndon B. Johnson." *Political Science Quarterly* 103:531–45.

Best, James, and Kim DesRoches. 1991. "Learning from Crises: An Empirical Analysis of Crisis Situations in the Kennedy and Johnson Administrations." Paper prepared for the annual meeting of the Midwest Political Science Association.

Betts, Richard K. 1980. "Intelligence for Policy-Making." *Washington Quarterly* 3:118–29.

Bloomfield, Lincoln P. 1984. "What's Wrong with Transitions." *Foreign Policy* 55:23–39.

Bock, Joseph G., and Duncan L. Clarke. 1986. "The National Security Assistant and the White House Staff: National Security Decision-Making and Domestic Political Considerations." *Presidential Studies Quarterly* 16:258–79.

Brzezinski, Zbigniew. 1983. *Power and Principle: Memoirs of the National Security Adviser, 1977–81.* New York: Farrar, Straus, Giroux.

———. 1987–1988. "The NSC's Midlife Crisis." *Foreign Policy* 69:80–99.

Bundy, William P. 1982–1983. "The National Security Process." *International Security* 7:94–109.

Burger, Edward J., Jr. 1980. *Science at the White House.* Baltimore: Johns Hopkins University Press.

Burke, John P. 1984. "Responsibilities of Presidents and Advisers: A Theory and Case Study of Vietnam Decision Making." *Journal of Politics* 46:818–45.

Burke, John P., and Fred I. Greenstein, with Larry Berman and Richard Immerman. 1989. *How Presidents Test Reality: Decisions on Vietnam, 1954 and 1965.* New York: Russell Sage Foundation.

Campbell, Colin, S. J. 1986. *Managing the Presidency: Carter, Reagan, and the Search for Executive Harmony.* Pittsburgh: University of Pittsburgh Press.

———. 1991. "The White House and Cabinet under the 'Let's Deal' Presidency." In *The Bush Presidency: First Appraisals,* ed. Colin Campbell, S. J., and Bert A. Rockman. Chatham, N. J.: Chatham House.

Clarke, Duncan L. 1987. "Why States Can't Lead." *Foreign Policy* 66:128–42.

———. 1989. *American Defense and Foreign Policy Institutions.* New York: Harper and Row.

Cohen, Jeffrey E. 1988. *Politics of the U.S. Cabinet: Representation in the Executive Branch, 1789–1984.* Pittsburgh: University of Pittsburgh Press.

Cohen, Michael D., James G. March, and Johan P. Olsen. 1972. "A Garbage Can Model of Organizational Choice." *Administrative Science Quarterly* 17:1–25.

Cottam, Richard W., and Bert Rockman. 1984. "In the Shadow of Substance: Presidents as Foreign Policy Makers." In *American Foreign Policy in an Uncertain World,* ed. David P. Forsythe. Lincoln: University of Nebraska Press.

Covington, Carey. 1985. "Organizational Memory in Presidential Agencies." *Administration and Society* 17:171–96.

Crabb, Cecil B., Jr., and Kevin V. Mulcahy. 1986. *Presidents and Foreign Policy Making: From FDR to Reagan.* Baton Rouge: Louisiana State University Press.

Cronin, Thomas E. 1969. "Political Science and Executive Advisory Systems." In *The Presidential Advisory System,* ed. Cronin and Sanford D. Greenberg. New York: Harper and Row.

———. 1975. *The State of the Presidency.* Boston: Little, Brown.

Cronin, Thomas E., and Sanford D. Greenbert. 1969. Ed. *The Presidential Advisory System.* New York: Harper and Row.

Cyert, Richard M., and James G. March. 1963. *A Behavioral Theory of the Firm.* Englewood Cliffs, N.J.: Prentice-Hall.

Davis, Eric L. 1979. "Legislative Liaison in the Carter Administration." *Political Science Quarterly* 94:287–301.

Destler, I. M. 1977. "National Security Advice to U.S. Presidents: Some Lessons From Thirty Years." *World Politics* 29:143–76.

————. 1980–1981. "National Security Management: What Presidents Have Wrought." *Political Science Quarterly* 95:573–88.

Destler, I. M., Leslie H. Gelb, and Anthony Lake. 1984. *Our Own Worst Enemy: The Unmaking of American Foreign Policy*. Rev. ed. New York: Simon and Schuster.

Dexter, Lewis A. 1977. "Court Politics: Presidential Staff Relations as a Special Case of a General Phenomenon." *Administration and Society* 9:267–84.

Diesing, Paul. 1991. *How Does Social Science Work?: Reflections on Practice*. Pittsburgh: University of Pittsburgh Press.

Edwards, George C., and Stephen J. Wayne. 1990. *Presidential Leadership: Politics and Policy Making*. 2d ed. New York: St. Martin's.

Ehrlichman, John D. 1982. *Witness to Power: The Nixon Years*. New York: Simon and Schuster.

Falk, Stanley L. 1964. "The National Security Council Under Truman, Eisenhower, and Kennedy." *Political Science Quarterly* 79:403–34.

Feigenbaum, Edward D. 1980. "Staffing, Organization, and Decision-Making in the Ford and Carter White Houses." *Presidential Studies Quarterly* 10:364–77.

Flash, Edward S. 1965. *Economic Advice and Presidential Leadership: The Council of Economic Advisers*. New York: Columbia University Press.

Freedman, Lawrence. 1976. "Logic, Politics and Foreign Policy Processes: A Critique of the Bureaucratic Politics Model." *International Affairs* 52:434–49.

George, Alexander L. 1972. "The Case for Multiple Advocacy in Making Foreign Policy." *American Political Science Review* 66:751–85.

————. 1990. *Presidential Decision-Making in Foreign Policy*. Boulder, Colo.: Westview.

Gilmour, Robert A. 1975. "The Institutional Presidency: A Conceptual Clarification." In *The Presidency in Contemporary Context*, ed. Norman C. Thomas. New York: Dodd, Mead.

Golden, William T. 1980. *Science Advice to the President*. New York: Pergamon.

————. 1989. "Presidential Science and Technology Advising." In *The Presidency in Transition*, ed. James P. Pfiffner and R. Gordon Hoxie. New York: Center for the Study of the Presidency.

Goldstein, Joel K. 1982. *The Modern American Vice Presidency*. Princeton: Princeton University Press.

Greenstein, Fred I. 1982. *The Hidden-Hand Presidency: Eisenhower as Leader*. New York: Basic Books.

————. 1988. *Leadership in the Modern Presidency*. Cambridge: Harvard University Press.

————. 1990. "Ronald Reagan—Another Hidden-Hand Ike?" *PS* 23:7–13.

Grossman, Michael Baruch, and Martha Joynt Kumar. 1981. *Portraying the President: The White House and the News Media*. Baltimore: Johns Hopkins University Press.

Hargrove, Erwin C. 1988. *Jimmy Carter as President: Leadership and the Politics of the Public Good*. Baton Rouge: Louisiana State University Press.

Hargrove, Erwin C., and Michael Nelson. 1984. *Presidents, Politics, and Policy*. New York: Alfred A. Knopf.

Hart, John 1983. "Staffing the Presidency: Kennedy and the Office of Congressional Relations." *Presidential Studies Quarterly* 13:101–10.

————. 1987. *The Presidential Branch*. New York: Pergamon.

Heclo, Hugh. 1975. "OMB and the Presidency—The Problem of 'Neutral Competence.' " *Public Interest* 38:80–98.

————. 1977. *Studying the Presidency: A Report to the Ford Foundation*. New York: Ford Foundation.

Heineman, Ben W., and Curtis A. Hessler. 1980. *Memorandum for the President: A Strategic Approach to Domestic Affairs in the 1980s*. New York: Random House.

Helmer, John. 1981. "The Presidential Office: Velvet Fist in an Iron Glove?" In *The Illusion of Presidential Government*, ed. Hugh Heclo and Lester M. Salamon. Boulder, Colo.: Westview.

Helmer, John, and Louis Maisel. 1978. "Analytical Problems in the Study of Presidential Advice: The Domestic Council Staff in Flux." *Presidential Studies Quarterly* 8:45–67.

Henderson, Phillip G. 1988. *Managing the Presidency: The Eisenhower Legacy: From Kennedy to Reagan*. Boulder, Colo.: Westview.

Hess, Stephen. 1988. *Organizing the Presidency*. 2d ed. Washington, D.C.: Brookings.

Hult, Karen M., and Charles Walcott. 1989a. "Studying the White House: Some Observations and a Brief Argument. *Presidency Research* 11 (Spring): 5–17.

Hult, Karen M., and Charles Walcott. 1989b. "To Meet the Press: Tracing the Evolution of White House Press Operation." Paper prepared for the annual meeting of the Midwest Political Science Association.

Hult, Karen M., and Charles Walcott. 1990. *Governing Public Organizations: Politics, Structures, and Institutional Design*. Pacific Grove, Calif.: Brooks/Cole.

Hyde, James F. C., and Stephen J. Wayne. 1979. "White House—OMB Relations." In *The Presidency: Studies in Public Policy*, ed. Steven A. Shull and Lance T. LeLoup. Brunswick, Oh: King's Court Communications.

Jacobs, Lawrence R. 1992. "The Recoil Effect: Public Opinion in the U.S. and Britain." *Comparative Politics* 24: 199–217.

Janis, Irving L. 1972. *Victims of Groupthink*. Boston: Houghton Mifflin.

————. 1990. *Crucial Decisions: Leadership in Policymaking and Crisis Management*. New York: Free Press.

Johnson, Robert Tanner. 1974. *Managing the White House*. New York: Harper and Row.

Jones, Charles O. 1989. "Mistrust But Verify: Memories of the Reagan Era." *American Political Science Review* 83:981–88.

Kaplan, Abraham. 1964. *The Conduct of Inquiry*. New York: Chandler.

Katz, James Everett. 1978. *Presidential Politics and Science Policy*. New York: Praeger.

Kellerman, Barbara. 1981. *All the President's Kin*. New York: Free Press.

Kernell, Samuel. 1986. "The Creed and Reality of Modern White House Management." In *Chief of Staff: Twenty-Five Years of Managing the Presidency*, ed. Samuel Kernell and Samuel Popkin. Berkeley and Los Angeles: University of California Press.

————. 1989. "The Evolution of the White House Staff.' In *Can the Government Govern?* eds. John E. Chubb and Paul E. Peterson. Washington, D.C.: Brookings.

Kernell, Samuel, and Samuel Popkin. 1986. Editors. *Chief of Staff: Twenty-Five Years of Managing the Presidency*. Berkeley and Los Angeles: University of California Press.

Kessel, John. 1975. *The Domestic Presidency: Decision-Making in the White House*. North Scituate, Mass.: Duxbury.

———. 1983. "The Structure of the Carter White House." *American Journal of Political Science* 27:431–63.

———. 1984. "The Structure of the Reagan White House." *American Journal of Political Science* 28:231–58.

———. 1989. "White House Structure During Reagan's Second Term." In *The Presidency in American Politics* ed. Paul Brace, Christine B. Harrington, Gary King. New York: New York University Press.

Kessselman, Mark. 1970. "Overinstitutionalization and Political Constraint." *Comparative Politics* 3:21–44.

King, Gary. 1990. "The Methodology of Presidency Research." Paper prepared for the Presidency Research Conference.

Kissinger, Henry. 1979. *The White House Years*. Boston: Little, Brown.

Kohl, Wilfred. 1975. "The Nixon-Kissinger Foreign Policy System and U.S.-European Relations: Patterns of Policy Making." *World Politics* 28:1–43.

Kozak, David C. 1985. "Decision Settings in the White House." In *The American Presidency*, ed. Kozak and Kenneth N. Ciboski. Chicago: Nelson-Hall.

Lambright, W. Henry. 1985. *Presidential Management of Science and Technology: The Johnson Presidency*. Austin: University of Texas Press.

Lash, Joseph P. 1971. *Eleanor and Franklin*. New York: New American Library.

Light, Paul C. 1982. *The President's Agenda*. Baltimore: Johns Hopkins University Press.

———. 1984. *Vice Presidential Power: Advice and Influence in the White House*. Baltimore: Johns Hopkins University Press.

Lindblom, Charles E. 1979. "Still Muddling, Not Yet Through." *Public Administration Review* 39:517–525.

Lord, Carnes. 1988. *The Presidency and the Management of National Security*. New York: Free Press.

Mann, Thomas E., ed. 1990. *A Question of Balance: The President, The Congress, and Foreign Policy*. Washington, D.C.: Brookings.

March, James G., and Johan P. Olsen. 1986. "Garbage Can Models of Decision Making in Organization." In *Ambiguity and Command*, ed. James March and Roger Weissinger-Baylon. Marshfield, Mass.: Pitman.

March, James G., and Herbert A. Simon. 1958. *Organizations*. New York: Wiley.

Medved, Michael. 1979. *The Shadow Presidents*. New York: Times Books.

Meltsner, Arnold J. 1990. *Rules for Rulers: The Politics of Advice*. Philadelphia: Temple University Press.

Menges, Constantine C. 1988. *Inside the NSC: The True Story of the Making and Unmaking of Reagan's Foreign Policy*. New York: Simon and Schuster.

Moe, Terry M. 1985. "The Politicized Presidency." In *The New Direction in American Politics*, ed. John E. Chubb and Paul E. Peterson. Washington, D.C.: Brookings.

Mulcahy, Kevin V. 1987. "Presidents and the Administration of Foreign Policy: A New Role for the Vice President." *Presidential Studies Quarterly* 17: 119–31.

———. 1990. "Bush Administration and National Security: Process, Programs, Policy." *Public Administration Review* 50:115–19.

Mulcahy, Kevin V., and Cecil V. Crabb, Jr. 1988. "What Oliver North Has Wrought: The Lessons of Irangate for National Security Policymaking." Paper prepared for the annual meeting of the American Political Science Association.

NAPA (National Academy of Public Administration). 1988. *The Executive Presidency: Federal Management for the 1990s.* Washington, D.C.: NAPA.

Nathan, James A., and James K. Oliver. 1987. *Foreign Policy Making and the American Political System.* 2d ed. Boston: Little, Brown.

Natoli, Marie. 1985. *American Prince, American Pauper: The Contemporary Vice Presidency in Perspective.* Westport, Conn.: Greenwood.

Naveh, David. 1981. "The Political Role of Academic Advisers: The Case of the U.S. President's Council of Economic Advisers, 1946–76." *Presidential Studies Quarterly* 11:492–510.

Nelson, Anna. 1981. "National Security I: Inventing a Process (1945–60)." In *The Illusions of Presidential Government,* ed. Hugh Heclo and Lester M. Salamon. Boulder, Colo.: Westview.

Newland, Chester A. 1984. "Executive Office Policy Apparatus: Enforcing the Reagan Agenda." In *The Reagan Presidency and the Governing of America,* ed. Lester M. Salamon and Michael S. Lund. Washington, D.C.: Urban Institute.

Norton, Hugh. 1985. *The Quest for Stability: Roosevelt to Reagan.* Columbia: University of South Carolina Press.

Perlmutter, Amos. 1974. "The Presidential Political Center and Foreign Policy: A Critique of the Revisionist and Bureaucratic-Revisionist Orientations." *World Politics* 27:87–106.

Perrow, Charles. 1986. *Complex Organizations: A Critical Essay.* 3d ed. New York: Random House.

Pfeffer, Jeffrey. 1981. *Power in Organizations.* Marshfield, Mass.: Pitman.

Pfiffner, James, ed. 1986. *The President and Economic Policy.* Philadelphia: Institute for the Study of Human Issues.

Pfiffner, James. 1988. *The Strategic Presidency: Hitting the Ground Running.* Chicago: Dorsey.

———. 1990. "Establishing the Bush Presidency." *Public Administration Review* 50:64–73.

Pfiffner, James P. and R. Gordon Hoxie. Editors. 1989. *The Presidency in Transition.* New York: Center for the Study of the Presidency.

Pika, Joseph A. 1981–1982. "Moving Beyond the Oval Office: Problems in Studying the Presidency." *Congress and the Presidency* 9:17–36.

———. 1986. "White House Boundary Roles: Marginal Men Amidst the Palace Guard." *Presidential Studies Quarterly* 16:700–15.

———. 1988. "Management Style and the White House." *Administration and Society* 20:3–29.

———. 1989. "The Nixon White House and the Mobilization of Bias." Paper prepared for the annual meeting of the Midwest Political Science Association.

———. 1990. "Bush, Quayle, and the New Vice Presidency." In *The Presidency and the Political System,* ed. Michael Nelson. 3d ed. Washington, D.C.: Congressional Quarterly.

————. 1991. "White House Staffing: Salvation, Damnation, and Uncertainty." In *The Executive Establishment and Executive Leadership: A Comparative Perspective*, ed. Colin Campbell and Margaret Jane Wyszomirski. Pittsburgh: University of Pittsburgh Press.

Porter, Roger B. 1980. *Presidential Decision Making*. New York: Cambridge University Press.

————. 1981. "The President and Economic Policy: Problems, Patterns, and Alternatives." In *The Illusion of Presidential Government*, ed. Hugh Heclo and Lester Salamon. Boulder, Colo.: Westview.

————. 1983. "Economic Advice to the President: From Eisenhower to Reagan." *Political Science Quarterly* 98:403–26.

————. 1985. "Roger B. Porter on How the White House Works." *Brookings Review* (Fall):37–40.

————. 1986. "Advising the President." *PS* 19:867–69.

Quirk, Paul. 1989. "What Do We Know and How Do We Know It? Research on the Presidency." *Presidency Research* 12:9–30.

————. 1990. "Presidential Competence." In *The Presidency and the Political System*, ed. Michael Nelson. 3d ed. Washington, D.C.: Congressional Quarterly Press.

Redford, Emmette S., and Richard T. McCulley. 1986. *White House Operations: The Johnson Presidency*. Austin: University of Texas Press.

Riddlesperger, James W., Jr., and James D. King. 1986. "Presidential Appointments to the Cabinet, Executive Office, and White House Staff." *Presidential Studies Quarterly* 16:691–99.

Riddlesperger, James W., Jr., and James D. King. 1989. "Jimmy Carter and the Administrative Presidency." Paper prepared for the annual meeting of the Southern Political Science Association.

Rockman, Bert A. 1985. *The Leadership Question: The Presidency and the American System*. New York: Praeger.

————. 1988a. "The American Presidency in Comparative Perspective." In *The Presidency and the Political System*, ed. Michael Nelson. 2d ed. Washington, D.C.: Congressional Quarterly.

————. 1988b. "The Style and Organization of the Reagan Presidency." In *The Reagan Legacy: Promise and Performance*, ed. Charles O. Jones. Chatham, N.J.: Chatham House.

————. 1989. "What Didn't We Know and Should We Forget it? Political Science and the Reagan Presidency." *Polity* 21:777–92.

Rose, Richard. 1989. "Changing Markets." In *The Presidency in Transition*, ed. James P. Pfiffner and R. Gordon Hoxie. New York: Center for the Study of the Presidency.

Rosenau, James N. 1966. "Pre-theories and Theories of Foreign Policy." In *Approaches to Comparative and International Politics*, ed. R. Barry Farrell. Evanston: Northwestern University Press.

Salamon, Lester M. 1981. "The Presidency and Domestic Policy Formulation." In *The Illusion of Presidential Government*, ed. Hugh Heclo and Lester Salaman. Boulder, Colo.: Westview.

Sander, Alfred Dick. 1989. *A Staff for the President*. Westport, Conn.: Greenwood.

Seib, Gerald F., and David Wessel. 1990. "The Troika: Three Free-Marketers Shape Bush's Domestic and Economic Policy." *Wall Street Journal*, April 27.

Seidman, Harold, and Robert Gilmour. 1986. *Politics, Position, and Power: From the Positive to the Regulatory State*. 4th ed. New York: Oxford University Press.

Seligman, Lester M. 1956. "Presidential Leadership: The Inner Circle and Institutionalization." *Journal of Politics* 18:410–26.

———. 1980. "On Models of the Presidency." *Presidential Studies Quarterly* 10:353–363.

———. 1983. "The Presidency and Political Change." *Annals of the American Academy of Political and Social Science* 466:179–92.

Sigelman, Lee, and Dixie Mercer McNeil. 1980. "White House Decision-Making Under Stress." *American Journal of Political Science* 24:652–73.

Sloan, John W. 1990a. "Economic Policy Making in the Johnson and Ford Administration." *Presidential Studies Quarterly* 20:111–25.

———. 1990b. "The Management and Decision-Making Style of President Eisenhower." *Presidential Studies Quarterly* 20:295–314.

Simon, Herbert A. 1946. "The Proverbs of Administration." *Public Administration Review* 6:53–67.

Sorensen, Theodore C. 1987–1988. "The President and the Secretary of State." *Foreign Affairs* 66:231–48.

Stein, Herbert. 1984. *Presidential Economics*. New York: Simon and Schuster.

Steiner, B. H. 1977. "Policy Organization in Security Affairs: An Assessment." *Public Administration Review* 37:357–67.

Stockman, David A. 1986. *The Triumph of Politics*. New York: Harper and Row.

Sullivan, John L., and Stanley Feldman. 1979. *Multiple Indicators: An Introduction*. Beverly Hills: Sage.

Thompson, James D. 1967. *Organizations in Action*. New York: McGraw-Hill.

Thompson, Robert J. 1989. "Juggling the President's Time: Constitutional vs. Operational Roles." Paper prepared for the annual meeting of the Southern Political Science Association.

Tulis, Jeffrey K. 1990. "The Interpretable Presidency." In *The Presidency and the Political System*, ed. Michael Nelson. 3d ed. Washington, D.C.: Congressional Quarterly Press.

Walcott, Charles, and Karen M. Hult. 1987a. "Institutionalizing the Presidency: The Structural Development of the White House Staff." Paper prepared for the annual meeting of the American Political Science Association.

Walcott, Charles, and Karen M. Hult. 1987b. "Organizing the White House: Structure, Environment, and Organizational Governance." *American Journal of Political Science* 31:109–25.

Walcott, Charles, and Karen M. Hult. 1989. "The Domestic Policy Conundrum: White House Domestic Policy Organization." Paper prepared for the annual meeting of the American Political Science Association.

Walcott, Charles, and Karen M. Hult. Forthcoming. *Governing the White House: The Presidency as an Organization, 1929–1969*. Lawrence: University Press of Kansas.

Walker, Wallace Earl, and Michael R. Reopel. 1986. "Strategies for Governance: Transition and Domestic Policymaking in the Reagan Administration." *Presidential Studies Quarterly* 16:734–60.

———. 1990. "The Reagan Experience With Cabinet Government." Paper prepared for the annual meeting of the Midwest Political Science Association.

Wayne, Stephen J. 1983. "An Introduction to Research on the Presidency." In *Studying the Presidency*, ed. George C. Edwards and Stephen Wayne. Knoxville: University of Tennessee Press.

Weatherford, M. Stephen. 1987. "The Interplay of Ideology and Advice in Economic Policy-Making: The Case of Political Business Cycles." *Journal of Politics* 49:925–52.

———. 1988. "An Agenda Paper: Political Business Cycles and the Process of Economic Policymaking." *American Politics Quarterly* 16:99–136.

Weatherford, M. Stephen, and Lorraine M. McDonnell. 1990. "Ideology and Economic Policy." In *Looking Back on the Reagan Presidency*, ed. Larry Berman. Baltimore: Johns Hopkins University Press.

Weko, Thomas. 1989. "A Good Man Is Hard to Find: Presidents and Their Political Executives." Paper prepared for the annual meeting of the Midwest Political Science Association.

———. 1990. "Taming the Welfare State: Nixon, Reagan, and the Social Service Bureaucracy." Paper prepared for the annual meeting of the Midwest Political Science Association.

Wellman, Barry, and S. D. Berkowitz. 1988. Eds. *Social Structures: A Network Approach*. New York: Cambridge University Press.

Williams, Walter. 1990. *Mismanaging America: The Rise of the Anti-Analytic Presidency*. Lawrence: University Press of Kansas.

Wyszomirski, Margaret Jane. 1982. "The Deinstitutionalization of Presidential Staff Agencies." *Public Administration Review* 42:448–58.

———. 1984. "A Domestic Policy Office: Presidential Agency in Search of a Role." *Policy Studies Journal* 12:705–18.

———. 1985. "The Roles of a Presidential Office for Domestic Policy: Three Models and Four Cases." In *The Presidency and Public Policy Making*, ed. George C. Edwards III, Steven A. Shull, and Norman C. Thomas. Pittsburgh: University of Pittsburgh Press.

———. 1989. "The Waning Political Capital of Cabinet Appointments." In *The Presidency in Transition*, ed. James P. Pfiffner and R. Gordon Hoxie. New York: Center for the Study of the Presidency.

Yates, Douglas. 1985. *The Politics of Management*. San Francisco: Jossey Bass.

Zwicker, Charles H. 1989. "The President's Council of Economic Advisers." In *The Presidency in Transition*, ed. James P. Pfiffner and R. Gordon Hoxie. New York: Center for the Study of the Presidency.

4

Presidential Policy Making

PAUL C. LIGHT

*P*OLICY IS one of the most important products of the presidency. Long after the parades are over, the appointees gone, and the speeches recorded, a president's policy achievements, or lack thereof, remain. Franklin Roosevelt's New Deal, Lyndon Johnson's Great Society, Richard Nixon's New Federalism, and the Reagan Revolution will structure the political debate far into the next century.

Whether policy is narrowly defined as legislative requests cleared by the Office of Management and Budget as in accord with the president's philosophy or more broadly interpreted as other executive maneuvers, invasions, orders, and assorted exercises of presidential power, policy is the stuff of which a president's place in history is made, the end result against which to assess an administration's impact. Although policy is hardly the only product of an administration, it is one of the most stable for purposes of studying different presidents in different eras.

More importantly for the study of the presidency, policy can be viewed as the standard against which to test a host of competing theories about presidential success. Like a new car coming off an assembly line, the president's policy tells scholars a great deal about the overall operation, productivity, and quality of a given administration, all of which reveal something in turn about a president's design, manufacturing, and marketing sense.

Thus, whatever one's preferred theory of presidential success, policy can be viewed as a critical test of predictive success. If personality, leadership, and style are the most important factors, the president's policies should show the impact. If institutional constraint, the advisory web, and historical forces are the key determinants, policy should show the predictive power, too. What has been missing from the debate between those who favor leadership-based versus institutional explanations of presidential behavior has been a strong dependent variable against which to measure impact.

For policy to play this more prominent role, however, scholars must be much more precise about the variable. Thus, after reviewing the state of the literature in more detail, this chapter will recommend that scholars push forward on a common front, using the concept of policy differences to specify their advance.

The Role of Policy in Presidency Research

As noted above, policy is not the only product of the presidency nor the only device for separating theoretical wheat from chaff. Public approval, election results, and congressional support are equally valuable dependent variables, as are presidential appointments and administrative style. Interestingly, George Edwards (1989, 1990) has authored the most valuable reference volumes on both public approval and congressional support.[1]

This said, if our concern is with developing theory that predicts actual performance, what better outcome as a testing ground than policy? What else is there, short of uncomfortably broad questions of regime stability and human well-being? Policy is certainly up to the task, offering at least five ways to measure the validity of our theories of presidential success or failure.

First, as noted above, policy provides a baseline against which to assess competing explanations of presidential behavior. If it does not matter whether a president organizes collegially or hierarchically—that is, if the policies a president selects are essentially similar in both situations—then those who maintain that management style is important vis-à-vis other hypotheses are hard pressed to answer why. Perhaps style is irrelevant. If policies do not differ whether the president is in a cycle of consolidation or expansion, then those who maintain that there is order in the political universe are hard pressed to explain how. Perhaps cycles are but a figment of a search for stability in an otherwise chaotic political world. Policy may be a necessary, if not quite sufficient, tool for validating our theory.

Second, policy acts as a visible expression of a president's ideology and world view and, therefore, serves as a way to tackle a systematic study of the impact of personal belief systems in shaping outcomes. Those who suggest that scholars have spent too much time taking the Neustadian pulse of the White House while neglecting the ideological imperative should be able to find clear patterns of differences in the policy approaches of, say, Johnson versus Reagan, the two most ideological of America's recent presidents. Those who argue that history is the true constraint on a president's choice ought to be able to demonstrate policy stability across even the most hidebound of administrations. Policy again becomes a central barometer for testing important hypotheses about the presidency.

Third, policy offers a reasonable tack for studying the role of process and the rule of law. Simply put, it is a trace element in a frequently invisible, often opaque process, helping scholars identify players and procedures alike. Just because the president believes that a regulatory review system will affect regulatory policy does not make it so. It is always possible that such central controls make little difference in the net amount of regulations promulgated. Just because a given White House staff believes that large numbers of political appointees will somehow make the bureaucracy more responsive does not make this true either. It is equally plausible that counterweights such as appointee turnover blunt the impact of politicization.

Here, policy generates insights into the true impact of administrative holy grails such as cabinet government, while placing White House structure in its proper context as a means to some end besides organizational neatness or goodness of fit to personality. The legislative clearance process may be interesting to describe, but it may be unimportant, too.

Transitions planning? Same issue. Much as presidents, staffs and their literary agents believe that what they do is important to policy outcomes, perhaps the institutional and historical constraints are too great. Policy provides the tool to ask the tough research question.

Fourth, policy creates a method for testing the market value of the essential resources of the presidency: public approval, electoral margin, seats in Congress. Assuming these resources are more than aesthetic, differences among presidents should produce policy differences. Once again, just because presidents spend increasing amounts of time going public does not mean that public approval has any bearing on White House policy success. If declining support produces no measurable shift in policy, perhaps our scholarly interest is misplaced.

Fifth, policy exists as an independent intervening variable in its own right. For example, policy differences may help scholars understand how abstract variables such as public approval get translated into winning coalitions in Congress. As public approval determines the kinds of policy a president pursues, in turn, policy may determine the president's success on Capitol Hill. If true, presidency scholars might then turn to the issue of how public approval is "fixed" or attached to specific policy proposals through a given legislative process or decision-making system, asking whether leadership, legislative skill, or personality somehow explain how presidents estimate the potential for success. In other words, defining policy as an intervening variable may push the presidency subfield toward needed specification of cause-and-effect models.

Ultimately, policy provides a critical tool for assessing the predictive power of presidency research. Consider, for example, James David Barber's (1985) study of presidential character. Long remembered for its prediction of Nixon's downfall, Barber's work might be much more aggressively tested for its value in predicting presidential policy differences. After all, Barber's subtitle, *Predicting Performance in the White House,* invites just such a test.

It is Barber's earlier article, "The Interplay of Presidential Character and Style," that throws down the empirical gauntlet. Focusing on the advisory system as the key to a president's success, Barber suggests that it is the good fit between personality and structure that produces the optimal outcome. "The structure must fit the man if it is to be effective," Barber writes. "The hard question is how to produce that fit. That requires a way of anticipating the ways a President's needs, values, and habits are likely to connect with alternative advisory relationships. In turn, that calls for concepts which will highlight, amidst the flux of individual idiosyncrasies, those characteristics most relevant for discerning regularities in the man's links with his friends at the office" (1971, 383).

For presidency scholars, the hard question is not whether style is interesting. Obviously, Barber's sales figures show that style and personality are best-sellers. Rather, the hard question is how to measure the goodness of fit through some objective indicator. That leads inevitably to the search for dependent variables that might validate Barber's typology of presidential personality, built from two dimensions, one dealing with the amount of energy directed toward the job, the other addressing the president's personal attitude toward the presidency, posits four different presidential types: active-positive (F. Roosevelt, Truman, Kennedy, Ford, Carter), active-negative (Wilson, Hoover, Johnson, Nixon), passive-positive (Taft, Harding, Reagan), and passive-negative (Coolidge, Eisenhower).

Of the two descriptors, the active-passive dimension has always been the easiest to validate, whether through hunch or simple measures of policy. The active-passive dimension is based on a rather simple assessment of productivity. Not surprisingly, therefore, Barber's active presidents are more active in proposing legislation to Congress than Barber's passive presidents, though by no means in a uniform sense. Nixon was far less active than Johnson, largely given his much weaker political base. Nevertheless, as a simple dichotomy, the active-passive dimension stands. Thus does policy offer a tool for assessing the between-cell strength of Barber's approach while, at the same time, introducing room for within-cell variation.

Alas, Barber's positive-negative dimension does not fare as well. Designed to tap a president's deep-seated attachment to the job, it has always been suspect as far too simple to capture true differences. As goes the dimension, so goes the typology. Johnson and Nixon had very different policy agendas, both in terms of scope and intended impact, while Eisenhower apparently operated through an entirely different process, according to Fred Greenstein (1982). Looking at policy outcomes, as opposed to, say, management style, it is exceedingly difficult to distinguish between Nixon in one cell and Kennedy and Carter in the other.

As this interlude suggests, policy proves a reasonable test of a president's attitude toward the office, exerting itself as a trace element of the impact of style and personality, a trace element that shows little variation among Barber's types. In contrast to those who have found Barber's approach lacking in theoretical content or specificity (see Nelson, 1988; Qualls, 1977), the policy approach simply asks whether the typology has any predictive value. It fails this test.

A Brief Overview of the Literature

Much as policy offers great potential for sorting myriad theories of presidential performance, the study of policy has produced more chaos than clarity. Despite an overwhelming body of research, patterns are rare, and summative research rarer still, largely because of our tendency toward specialization.

Unfortunately, our greatest problem may also be our greatest strength. If the field of presidential policy studies can be characterized at all, it is best viewed as a collection of research entrepreneurs who work in relative isolation in one of five distinctive specializations: (1) the substance of presidential policy, (2) the key players and their positions, (3) the process and structure, (4) individual presidencies, and (5) the measurement of specific outcomes. In that regard, we may have taken on too much of the character of the presidency itself.

Although this specialization has generated a great volume of research, it is inchoate nonetheless, linked more by a general interest in the presidency than a search for broad theory. As the automobile industry has learned, the more that assembly-line workers operate in isolation, the less each one knows and cares about the final product. More importantly, merely speeding up the assembly line does not necessarily assure greater quality. Unfortunately, we appear to be producing more and more research with less and less integration.

Thus, the question is where to invest our future energies, a question that calls for a brief review of each subspecialization in the policy assembly line. There are some areas where the field is overstocked with research, others where there is still room for additional work, and at least one—the measurement of outcomes—where we face a significant shortage.

THE SUBSTANCE OF POLICY

Start with the first specialization identified above, the substance of policy, where presidency scholars may have an oversupply of high-quality, overlapping work. This is no surprise, however, if only because key policy decisions provide such fertile ground for the kind of detective work so many scholars rightly enjoy. Delving into cases such as Social Security (see Light, 1985) or veterans policy tests one's ability to separate real clues from red herrings. Writing a good case study is a Sherlock Holmesian task, putting us as close to the policy process as possible.

Nor would anyone question the strategic importance of Kennedy's Cuban Missile Crisis or Johnson's Vietnam escalation, Nixon's Family Assistance Plan, Carter's Program for Better Jobs and Income, Reagan's disability initiative, or the ongoing struggle for regulatory reform. In writing about these watershed decisions, Graham Allison (1971), Larry Berman (1982), Martin Anderson (1978), Larry Lynn and David Whitman (1981), and Martha Derthick, working alone (1991) and with Paul Quirk (1985) have not only authored enormously satisfying case studies (albeit from very different perspectives), they have catalogued decisions that profoundly affected the course of American foreign and domestic policy.

The problem with further investment in this stage of production is that case studies may not sum well toward general theory. After all, even the broadest case studies are based upon single snapshots of presidential policy choice. No matter the breadth of the decision, a book on Social Security is ultimately a book on Social Security, generalizable only through a broader theory. It may be that we have entered a period where general theory is more important than new case studies. Again, this is not to suggest that our past case studies are poorly done or uninformative, just that our shelves may be almost full.

PLAYERS AND POSITIONS

The problem continues at the second stop, players and positions research, where presidency scholars also have an overstock. Again, no wonder. Presidency scholars are rightly interested in political characters and can spend entire careers cataloguing the rise and fall of specific advisers like former National Security Advisor Henry Kissinger. Probing the influence of an office and its occupants can be remarkably interesting. There is certainly nothing more entertaining, if not always immediately digestible, than sitting down for lunch in the White House mess with a respondent.

This work involves much more than political voyeurism, however. Few would question the policy impact of the national security adviser and the domestic policy staff, the rising activism of the vice presidency, the changing fortunes of the Office of Management and Budget (OMB), and the rise, fall, and rise of the administrative presidency. In cataloguing the strategies and tactics of specific White House advisers and their offices, Alexander George (1980), Larry Berman (1979), Michael Turner (1982), John Kessel (1975), Roger Porter (1980), and

Emmette Redford and Richard McCulley (1986) have not only produced compelling stories of individual advisers and offices, they have
identified the dramatis personae in presidential policy.

Again, I doubt further investment here will add great value to our
knowledge base. We now have the key players identified, and short
of tracking their relative strength, it is time to ask whether these
players and positions actually matter. There may still be one or two
missing pieces, but my hunch is that we now need to build our inventory elsewhere.

PROCESS AND PROCEDURES

Scholars at the third stop in the production process, process and
procedures, are also in a bear market for further research. Much of
this work rightly worries about the institutional constraints and standard operating procedures that constrain policy decisions. Moreover,
describing basic operations may be a central first step toward theoretical progress. The effort to define a process such as presidential
agenda setting can offer valuable insights into the key components of
individual decisions. And, for those scholars who like to solve puzzles, there may be little more rewarding than finally figuring out just
how a class of decisions get made.

Clearly, there are plenty of puzzles to solve, for the literature on
presidential policy process and management is deep and wide. In
theory, there are procedures for almost every kind of substantive
policy. Taken to an extreme, there is a different process for virtually
every decision—welfare reform may be just enough different from,
say, energy policy to warrant a separate description. Moreover, virtually everything a president does in the day-to-day business of governing affects policy. Hence, the long list of edited volumes on the
presidency that either implicitly or explicitly address policy process,
starting with Aaron Wildavsky's venerable 1975 text, *Perspectives
on the Presidency,* and continuing with Michael Nelson's 1985 *Politics of the Presidency* and George Edwards, Steven Shull, and Norman Thomas's 1985 *The Presidency and Public Policy Making.*

Of the most recent edited texts, none is more process oriented vis-
à-vis policy than James Pfiffner's excellent 1991 volume *The Managerial Presidency,* perhaps reflecting his long-term concern with

transitions and presidential planning. The book clearly views policy as a problem of managing the levers of policy, from presidential appointments to congressional relations to various subpresidencies. Policy appears more the outcome of what presidents do to shape, mold, and knead problems and solutions through process than the reverse.

Indeed, as Pfiffner argues in his preface, the book is designed to gather together an emerging subfield that combines presidency scholarship with public administration. Consider a sampling of the chapter titles as indicative of the range of research that falls into this presidential policy management literature:

- Can the President Manage the Government? Should He?
- Constrained Diversity: The Organizational Demands of the Presidency
- Organizing Issues In and Organizing Problems Out
- Presidentializing the Bureaucracy: From Kennedy to Reagan
- Mandates or Mandarins? Control and Discretion in the Modern Administrative State
- Political Appointees and Career Executives: The Democracy-Bureaucracy Nexus
- Political Direction and Policy Change in Three Federal Departments
- Presidents and Agendas: Who Defines What for Whom?
- Presidential Management of the Economy
- Presidential Management of National Security Policy Making, 1947–1987.

Pfiffner's volume builds on the long stream of process-oriented work before him, which contributed to the base knowledge on how presidents make decisions. Few would second-guess the decision by scholars like Stephen Wayne (1978), Stephen Hess (1988), G. Calvin Mackenzie (1981), Richard Nathan (1983), or I. M. Destler (1980) to invest research energy in describing the critically important procedures involved in developing a legislative agenda, organizing the White House, making presidential appointments, or setting foreign economic policy. More importantly, perhaps, for political science in general, this literature occasionally crosses between academic discourse and actual presidential performance as new administrations draw upon a Mackenzie or a Hess to refine existing processes.[2]

Yet we may have gone about as far as we can in this area. Short of updating our existing work and cataloguing entirely new processes—for example, commissions and summits—it may be time to move on.

INDIVIDUAL PRESIDENTS AND PRESIDENCIES

Moving on takes scholars into a subspecialization, individual presidents and presidencies, that will always have room for continued work, though perhaps not major new investment. As long as there are new administrations there will be a need for study of the individuals who occupy 1600 Pennsylvania Avenue, the policies they pick, and the stories they produce. Although this turf is customarily reserved for historians like Robert Caro, presidency scholars have hardly been shy about weighing in with their own snapshots.

Again, who can blame them. Students clamor for material on the latest scandal, sometimes showing painfully limited tolerance for ancient history like Vietnam or Watergate, while publishers scramble to print the postelection or postadministration books as quickly as possible. Chatham House has become particularly skilled at getting these books to press, bringing the latest volume out seemingly moments after inauguration.

This does not mean the authors take their projects less seriously. In fact, what makes these books particularly important is their strong policy content. Larry Berman's *Looking Back on the Reagan Presidency* (1990) offers a compelling snapshot of the administration's policy agenda, including six policy chapters (out of fourteen), while Charles Jones (1988) offers an equally sophisticated treatment in *The Reagan Legacy*, although with only two policy chapters out of ten. Nevertheless, since policy is the most visible product of most administrations (or at least a close second to image), those who write in this genre have little choice but to include policy as one quick indicator of success or failure.

Because of their essentially descriptive nature, these books suffer in comparison to more detailed efforts—for example, Fred Greenstein's 1988 edited compendium on presidential leadership. Built around chapters on each of the past nine presidents, Greenstein's effort is very much within the presidential policy literature, a conclusion clearly demonstrated by the index entry (sans page numbers) on Carter:

Carter, James E., failure; as chief legislator; commitment to comprehensive solutions; presidential personality; and public goods politics; and advisers; and Camp David agreement; and Panama Canal
treaties; decision-making style; leadership style; economic policy;
domestic policy; and national health insurance; and welfare reform;
energy program; and regulatory reform; foreign policy; and China;
and Strategic Arms Limitations Talks (SALT II); and Iran hostage
crisis; and National Security Council; and OMB; staff and organization; as public leader; political ineptitude, as chief diplomat; relations with media. (1988, 442)

Of the twenty-seven areas, eleven deal with specific Carter policies,
and another seven with policy-making style and organization.

Yet, in turn, even Greenstein's book suffers in comparison to much
more detailed work on single presidencies—for example, Charles
Jones's (1988b) book on the Carter administration. Not only is the
book a revealing portrait of what went both wrong and right with the
Carter legislative agenda, it provides a model for presidential policy
scholarship. Using detailed interviews with White House and congressional staff, legislative box scores, case studies, primary documents, and a host of secondary sources, Jones builds a compelling
portrait of the Carter policy agenda as a reflection of the substantive
issues confronting the governor-turned-president, the institutional
and staff structure, and basic changes in the political process.

The book is organized around a simple theme: Carter's legislative
strategy was the natural product of his view of the president as a
trustee of the people. As Jones writes, Carter's policy agenda was
grounded in a cogent, if politically naive, belief system, one that was
very different from Reagan's.

To evaluate a policy option primarily from the standpoint of possible electoral consequences was considered wrong by the president.
That is not to say that he and his advisers never evaluated such consequences, particularly during an election year when the trusteeship
was established or renewed. It is simply to emphasize the tendency
and preference of the president as chief executive to perform as a
trustee rather than as a constituency-bound, election-oriented delegate. And further, his concept of the president's ideal role naturally
led to an unflattering evaluation of the policy behavior of members of Congress, which fortified even more the need to perform as
a trustee. Indeed, by selecting certain issues, for example, the elimination of water projects, the president could demonstrate in bold
relief his trusteeship and their constituency-bound delegate status.
(1988b, 6)

The value of Jones's book for presidency research lies in its comprehensive, integrative tone. Although he does not settle the nature-nurture dispute between institution and leadership, he does place the variables in the proper order. Although personality affects how steady is the hand at the levers, the determining factors are more the president's institutional and political horsepower.

MEASUREMENT OF SPECIFIC OUTCOMES

Contrary to the generally bearish outlook on presidential policy studies thus far, there is ample need for substantial investment at the fifth and final stop in this review of subspecializations, measurement of specific outcomes. Whether defined as analytic capital (e.g., data archives, new statistical tools, or content analysis of presidential papers) or human capital (e.g., training), investment in measurement can only improve the overall infrastructure of policy research.[3] Outside a small number of scholars led by George Edwards (1989, 1990), John Kessel (1985), and Jeff Fishel (1985), this is one area where the field has clearly not done enough.

It is not that measurement is the be-all and end-all of effective scholarship. Nor is it that Edwards, Fishel, or Kessel aspire to solve our intellectual debates once and for all through a statistical equation (although Edwards in particular offers more than a few carefully drawn hypotheses about the relative importance of personality, skills, and leadership, hunches that he tests out with hard data). Rather, what these authors demonstrate is that measurement can push the discussion of policy toward a much more concrete level. And where they do not have easily available data—such as congressional support scores—they create it through careful specification. Kessel, for example, uses a structured survey of White House advisers to build a revealing portrait of changing White House politics, while Fishel creates his data set promise by promise.

What is particularly interesting about this work is that Edwards, Kessel, and Fishel focus on very different steps in the presidential policy process. Fishel's work centers on the president's campaign promises and the degree to which those preelection utterances shape postelection choice; Edwards's research focuses on congressional support for the president's policy program at the very tail end of the legislative process, during roll call votes; while Kessel looks at the internal debates in between. Yet, all three scholars are able to effectively measure their chosen phenomenon and, in so doing, provide some of the building blocks for a new research infrastructure.

The Search for Policy Differences

All in all, presidency scholars have produced an impressive stock of policy literature. We know a great deal about a great number of key topics. The notion, for example, that presidency research is somehow lagging behind congressional studies is simply not supported within the policy literature.

Yet, the literature also supports the notion that our policy research is chaotic and disjointed. Those who study tax policy may find it nearly impossible to talk with those who study Eisenhower; those who work on the budget process have almost nothing to share with those who research the National Security Council; those who study executive orders or the president's cabinet have little to say to those who study welfare reform. Simply put, we may have spent too much time studying trees and too little studying the forest.

SPECIFYING THE DEPENDENT VARIABLE

The first step toward unifying the subfield may involve nothing more than a more precise definition of the dependent variable, policy. Like five blindfolded inspectors touching a Buick (to continue my earlier automotive analogy), presidency researchers can easily lose sight of the overall product.

Luckily, this is not a difficult problem to address, particularly given what we have already learned about differences among policies. Much of the credit for this research goes to John Campbell, whose work on Japanese aging policy led to the creation of the large/small and new/old policy distinctions, as well as the combination thereof discussed later in this chapter. According to Campbell,

> Large-new decisions are the sort one reads about in case studies and the agenda-setting literature; a good example for the aging policy area in America is Medicare. . . . At the extreme, these decisions have a large fiscal impact and they significantly alter the relations among social groups or between state and society. Accordingly, they are controversial and receive considerable publicity; participation is relatively broad (interest groups, political parties or subgroups, chief executive, perhaps several agencies); and the outcome in some

sense will represent the political balance of power for the society as a whole.

Small new decisions do not have as broad an impact and probably will receive little publicity; participation is often confined within a "subgovernment" of officials, interest groups, representatives, and the few politicians directly and routinely concerned with a specific policy area; outcomes depend on the balance of power or views within the subculture. (1978, 3)

Simply put, all policy proposals are not created equal, a point well illustrated in Mark Peterson's recent study of Congress and the presidency (1990).

The usefulness of classifying policy into categories is threefold. First, it helps us sort through the growing volume of case studies. Just as we already sort by genus (economic, foreign, domestic) and species (economic-budget, taxation, monetary), we can also sort by size (large, small), and scope (new initiative or old). Second, classifying policy shows the gaps and overlaps in our work and, therefore, helps target future research. We may have enough work on the federal budget but not enough on small-scale policy experiments, enough on large-scale reforms but not enough on more routine reauthorizations of existing programs. Third, classification gives us another tool for indexing and cross-referencing our conclusions. My view is that the presidency subfield has produced a deeper research inventory than most of our colleagues believe. One problem may be that we do not classify our findings well, limiting the transferability of presidency research findings into other subfields.

This focus on policy differences actually dates back to Theodore Lowi's 1964 study of distributive, redistributive, and regulatory policy. Most presidency scholars will also remember Aaron Wildavsky's 1966 article on the two presidencies of domestic and foreign policy, which sets forth the most frequently attacked typology in the field. "The President's normal problem with domestic policy is to get congressional support for the programs he prefers," Wildavsky argues. "In foreign affairs, in contrast, he can almost always get support for policies that he believes will protect the nation—but his problem is to find a viable policy" (1966, 7).

Whatever one thinks of the merits of the case, Wildavsky's argument provided just what the subfield needed: a healthy controversy to provoke the development of increasingly sophisticated models.[4]

Moreover, to this day, Wildavsky's initial hunch appears to hold: policy differences do matter, though not of the kind nor in the way that Wildavsky once thought. Peterson (1990), for example, uses a much more elegant model of policy differences both to show that presidents are most successful with proposals that are neither the most nor the least consequential and to predict how Congress will react to a given approach.

My own work on the president's domestic agenda may illustrate the potential value of policy differences in describing how presidents select among the many alternatives they might attach to a given policy problem (Light, 1991). Think of the agenda-setting process as a set of choices, first, on the problems a president will address, second, on the solutions to those problems, and third, on the relative priorities among final proposals.

Although this simple outline may seem rudimentary to some, in part because it may be difficult to imagine problems and solutions moving toward the agenda in relative isolation, it well describes the mechanism that recent presidents have used to build their legislative programs. In fact, interviews with senior White House staff suggest that solutions often search for a problem, any problem, that might ensure eventual passage, while problems often get "coupled," as John Kingdon (1984) calls it, to an inappropriate solution in the haste to do something, anything to address a crisis.

Moreover, even when the choice of a problem and its solution, or a solution and its problem, occurs in a single White House meeting, different forces explain each decision.[5] Problems are generally evaluated on the basis of potential benefits to the president from either taking action or not deciding, while solutions are almost always discussed in terms of costs—political, budgetary, or bureaucratic.

Although the choice of problems is certainly important, I believe that the definition of alternatives is the single most important step in the presidential policy process. It is also the most difficult.

> More than any other choice, the choice of alternatives determines who gets what, when, where, and how. Though Presidents are granted considerable flexibility in choosing the domestic issues, the definition of alternatives is fraught with conflict. Indeed, my argument is that the search for acceptable alternatives has become more difficult over the past decade, that the kinds of programs that can survive the legislative process are increasingly limited. The search

for alternatives may now be the most difficult task of the domestic agenda process. (Light, 1991, 105)

The key variable in the choice among competing solutions is the president's political capital, a kind of policy checking account, as former Vice President Walter Mondale described it, to be spent down over time. Although the account can be replenished somewhat through careful investment in midterm elections and the second-term campaign, it does not appear that bursts in the public's presidential approval alone become spendable assets on Capitol Hill. On the domestic policy agenda, political capital is best viewed as a moving tally of committee and floor votes, which starts with party margin in Congress, adjusted somewhat for the president's public approval in each member's home district.

However measured, capital clearly affects the president's ability to "afford" given alternatives. Presidents with less capital cannot afford the same kinds of choices as presidents with more, a hypothesis illustrated by the Ford presidency. Limited by the lowest number of party congressional seats available to a sitting president in this century, as well as by lingering public resentment toward Watergate and the pardon of Richard Nixon, and operating with no electoral margin at all as the first appointed president in U.S. history, Ford could not afford much in the way of large-scale policy initiatives, choosing instead a defensive strategy based on sixty-six vetoes in his two years in office.

Although presidents are always free to ignore the cost of policy, there is considerable evidence that they do make rough calculations of the odds of success and act accordingly.[6] Whether the initial choice is between formal legislation (more expensive) and vetoes (less) or administrative gambits (even less), or between large-scale initiatives (more expensive) and small-scale initiatives (less), or between new initiatives (more expensive) and old initiatives (less), presidents build their agenda through a reasonably careful allocation of their political capital; at least, that is how the participants explain it. Thus do policy differences mirror the president's political strength, becoming a way to distinguish one agenda from another.

THE REAGAN POLICY AGENDA

One way to illustrate the value of policy differences as an organizing device is to look at the Reagan domestic agenda. Admittedly, the following overview examines only one genus of policy (domestic) at only one stage of the process (agenda setting). However, if illustration is the aim, such limitations may be excused.

If, for example, political capital constrains legislative choices, Reagan's agenda should look more "expensive" than Nixon's and Ford's, but less than Carter's, Kennedy's, and Johnson's. As Thomas Mann notes in one of the Reagan volumes referenced earlier, "Reagan faced enormous obstacles that were not unusual in the American political system. With a permanent Democratic majority in the House, he was never in a dominant position on Capitol Hill" (1990, 21). This is not to argue that Reagan was without advantages. Holding a Republican majority in the Senate and an implied mandate to govern, Reagan appeared to have the capital to purchase more than his two Republican predecessors, Nixon and Ford. Yet, lacking a majority in the House, he had much less than did Democrats John Kennedy, Lyndon Johnson, and Jimmy Carter, all three of whom worked with much larger accounts on Capitol Hill.

Before turning to the agendas, it is useful to note that the Reagan data do not come from the same source as the Kennedy through Carter data. The Kennedy-Carter list is drawn from all legislation (1) cleared "i/a" or "in accord" with the president's program by the Office of Management and Budget, and (2) mentioned in the president's State of the Union message.[7] Unfortunately, under the Reagan administration, access to the OMB clearance records became impossible. Indeed, it is not even clear that the records, and the tracking system that once produced them, still exist.[8]

Thus, in adding the Reagan agenda to the earlier data on agenda setting, I had to rebuild the clearance records by hand, using an entirely different set of materials and guessing somewhat at Reagan's priorities. Lacking the formal clearance materials, I defined the Reagan agenda to include any legislation (1) mentioned in either the Inaugural Address or the State of the Union message, and (2) later found as a legislative initiative in Congressional Quarterly's *Congressional Almanac*. As a result, there are limitations to comparisons across the six presidents. Readers should note, therefore, that these data are intended for illustration. This caveat noted, table 1 offers some interesting insights on the timing and content of the Reagan agenda.

Three conclusions emerge from table 1. First, Reagan's agenda is the smallest in recent experience, averaging four proposals per year

TABLE I
Presidential Requests for Legislation

President	Total new requests	Repeats from previous years	President	Total new requests	Repeats from previous years
Kennedy/			Ford		
Johnson			1975	10	3
1961	25	0	1976	6	7
1962	16	8	Carter		
1963	6	12	1977	21	0
1964	6	11	1978	8	3
Johnson			1979	8	5
1965	34	4	1980	4	7
1966	24	7	Reagan I		
1967	19	8	1981	8	0
1968	14	12	1982	7	1
Nixon I			1983	11	3
1969	17	0	1984	4	5
1970	12	9	Reagan II		
1971	8	12	1985	0	7
1972	3	14	1986	0	5
Nixon II			1987	0	5
1973	20	3	1988	0	4
1974	5	11			

Source: Kennedy through Carter, OMB Legislative Reference Division clearance records, coded according to Light (1991); Reagan, State of the Union messages and legislative records as summarized by *Congressional Quarterly Almanac* for each year.

over the eight-year term, making Ford look like a veritable activist. Reagan's agenda looks even smaller considering the fact that seven of his eight first-year proposals appeared in the same omnibus budget resolution. Remember, however, that my coding of the Reagan agenda may understate his overall activitism.

Second, Reagan's agenda is the latest, peaking in the third, not first, year of the term. Reagan's third-year surge is not led by the social agenda, however, but by a mix of the old and new, the large and small: a Social Security rescue plan alongside the first call for tax simplification, reauthorization of the Civil Rights Commission side by side with tuition tax credits and child support enforcement. In many ways, Reagan's third year is fairly similar to most other first years.

Third, Reagan's agenda is the most repetitive, with the second term consisting entirely of repeats from his first four years, including tax reform (first offered in 1983), urban enterprise zones (1982), the line

TABLE 2
Presidential Requests for Legislation:
New Programs versus Old Programs

President	New programs		Old programs		Percentage of new programs
	Total	Average per year	Total	Average per year	
Kennedy/Johnson	33	8	20	5	62
Johnson	55	14	36	9	60
Nixon	46	12	19	5	71
Ford	6	3	10	5	44
Carter	25	6	16	4	61
Reagan	18	2	12	2	60

Note: Does not include repeats.

item veto (1984), prayer in school (1984), and the continuing efforts to cut the federal budget using many of the same proposals tried in 1981. With the 1988 presidential campaign under way almost immediately after his second inaugural, his White House in almost constant turmoil, his executive appointees establishing new turnover records, and the Senate lost to the Democrats in 1986, Reagan had precious little to propose and almost no chance of legislative success.

Whatever the lessons in this broad overview, Reagan's legislative strategy becomes much clearer in tables 2 and 3, which compare two key policy differences: (1) new versus old, and (2) large versus small. Recall that new proposals involve departures from the status quo that either expand or reduce the government's role in society. Also note that decisions on what is new or old and large or small often involve tough judgment calls and reflect the substance of the actual proposals, not the rhetoric.

Most importantly, the general rule is not to give the benefit of the doubt to the president. Even if a proposal contains an especially novel idea—for example, the Sentencing Guidelines Commission in the 1983 criminal justice reform—it must be coded as an old initiative if the overall weight of the initiative falls within the boundary of existing ideas. Thus, tables 2 and 3 may generally understate the number of new ideas.

The tables reveal the peculiar problems of comparing presidents across the same decade, let alone a quarter century or more. Looking at the percentage of his agenda devoted to large and new proposals,

TABLE 3
Presidential Requests for Legislation:
Large Programs versus Small Programs

President	Large programs		Small programs		
	Total	Average per year	Total	Average per year	Percentage of large programs
Kennedy/Johnson	28	7	25	6	53
Johnson	50	12	41	10	55
Nixon	23	4	42	7	35
Ford	8	4	8	4	50
Carter	22	6	19	5	54
Reagan	13	2	17	2	43

Reagan looks more like a Democrat than a Nixon or a Ford, but looking at the absolutes, he looks passive by comparison. Legislative packaging may explain the difference. The Reagan budget package, for example, touched virtually every entitlement program on the books, established new user fees for dozens of government services, reduced federal contributions to a host of spending programs (school lunches, student aid, and housing finance), and proposed the consolidation of seventy-seven categorical programs in social, education, and health services into five block grants.

Thus, had each item in the omnibus budget been presented as a separate proposal through the normal OMB clearance process, Reagan's first-year agenda might well appear as the most active since Johnson. Presented as a unified package—albeit in one of the longest bills ever considered by Congress—it looks much more passive.

These packaging decisions notwithstanding, Reagan understood the need to get his new ideas into the process as quickly as possible—eleven of Reagan's first eighteen proposals, or 61 percent, were new ideas. Presenting the new ideas fast was hardly unique to Reagan, however. Twenty-three of Kennedy's first forty-one proposals were new (56 percent); thirty-six of Johnson's first fifty-eight in 1965–1966 (62 percent); twenty of Nixon's first twenty-nine (69 percent); seventeen of Carter's first twenty-nine (59 percent). New ideas may be the heart and soul of the president's honeymoon, an expected phenomenon in either the change of administrations or the renewal of power.

TABLE 4
The Reagan Agenda:
Large/Small versus New/Old Programs,
by Congress

Congress	Large/New	Large/Old	Small/New	Small/Old
1981–82	6	0	5	4
1983–84	5	2	2	6
1985–86	0	0	0	0
1987–88	0	0	0	0
Total	11	2	7	10
Percentage of total	36	6	23	33

The Reagan legislative strategy becomes clearer when the two categories of policy—large-small and new-old—are combined in table 4. In Reagan's first two years, eleven of his fifteen total proposals (73 percent) were either large/new or small/new, and none fell into the large/old category. In his second two years, only seven of fifteen (47 percent) were large/new or small/new, with a significant increase in the number of initiatives dealing with existing, or old, programs like Social Security.

Comparing the six presidents on the percentages only, Reagan's agenda actually looks more Democratic than Republican, perhaps suggesting his higher initial political capital. Large/new programs averaged 38 percent of the combined Kennedy, Johnson, and Carter agendas, 27 percent of the combined Nixon and Ford agendas, and 36 percent of Reagan's; small/new programs averaged only 18 percent of the combined Democratic agenda, 37 percent of the two Republicans, and 23 percent of Reagan's. If there is a pattern in these figures, it would appear that political capital has less of an impact on the absolute number or percentage of new ideas but a very significant impact on the size of those new ideas.

As table 4 also suggests, Reagan faced a normal share of reauthorizations and extensions of existing programs, what Richard Rose (1989) calls "inheritances" in his study of British policy, and what I define as old proposals. Yet, to the extent possible, he held these necessary evils to small, not large, expansions—for example, more money for environmental protection following the Gorsuch-Burford scandal, an extension of revenue sharing. In fact, of Reagan's twelve "old" initiatives, only two were large scale—the 1983 Social Security compromise built from the ashes of Stockman's initial disaster, and a sweeping revision of the criminal statutes that actually originated in the Senate, not the White House.

As this brief review should demonstrate, policy differences can put a president's domestic agenda into clearer historical and political focus. By examining the differences in size and scope, the Reagan agenda can be more easily compared with those of his predecessors, allowing scholars who study substantive policy, individual players, processes, or presidencies some way to judge the Reagan administration more systematically. Although such comparisons involve some risks—particularly across longer time horizons—policy differences allow us to separate the various explanations of success through a reasonably objective measure.

Missing Differences

This brief review of the Reagan agenda hardly exhausts all the policy differences presidency scholars might tackle. Consider, for example, the following list of variables that might be used to describe a president's policies:

- Symbolic/substantive
- Spending/nonspending
- Regulatory/deregulatory/nonregulatory
- Administrative/legislative
- Individualized/group benefits
- Tax side/spending side
- Public/private
- Federal/state/local delivery

Obviously, my portrait of the Reagan agenda might look very different through the lens of a federal/state/local delivery or a regulatory/deregulatory measure. Although such research is yet to be done, even a cursory reading of the Reagan history would suggest that he had a much deeper focus on state/local and deregulatory policy than his immediate predecessors.

What one decides to measure depends, of course, upon what one wants to test. As noted earlier, those of us interested in presidential-congressional relations have been drawn to measures that allow us to test for the impact of political capital on agenda depth. Unfortunately, measures of size or scope may be much less valuable in assessing the role of ideology or personality, where the direction and content of policy may matter more. As is clearly demonstrated elsewhere in this volume, there is ample room for hypothesis testing in this area. What is still lacking is a set of content measures that might display the relative weight of personality versus politics in explaining presidential policy outcomes.

Ultimately, there is plenty of room for a more precise specification of policy as a dependent variable. Those who are interested in the role of ideology or personality might be attracted to very different measures than those interested in politics or organization, but both schools might well invest in measures of policy as a first step toward rigorous hypothesis testing.

AN ILLUSTRATION

Consider as an illustration of the pitfalls and potentials involved in such endeavors the question of *durability*—that is, whether a presidential policy is short term or long term. That presidency scholars might look for differences in the time horizons of policy emerges from a stream of recent research. There is considerable agreement, for example, that presidents are increasingly "going public," as Samuel Kernell argues, "displaying exceptional sensitivity to the breezes that blow into Washington." According to Kernell, going public has inevitable policy consequences:

> There is a compelling rationale for suspecting that the more presidents rest their leadership on going public, the more volatile policy outcomes in Washington will be. The public can be assumed to be more fickle in its assessments of politicians and policies than will be a stable community of Washington elites, whose business it is to make informed judgments. As the former becomes more important and the latter less, political relations will be more easily disrupted. (1986, 233)

By itself, however, going public does not necessarily mean that the president's agenda will be more short term than long. Rather, going public may cement the reciprocal relationship between public opinion and presidential policy, each one reinforcing the other over time. The more volatile the public, the more volatile the policy, and vice versa— a vicious circle that may eventually corrode the president's ability to think much beyond the next three months, let alone three decades. According to Dennis Simon and Charles Ostrom, Jr., the president faces a dilemma between improving the quality of outcomes (long term) or engaging in high politics (short term):

> The long-term approach will direct the president's actions and energies toward the solution of principal problems of the day. . . . To the extent that such attempts fail to solve problems, the president's resource reservoir will become increasingly shallow as the vicious circle begins to undermine his influence on the policy process. This explains the attractiveness of the short-term approach. The president is relatively unconstrained in relying upon political drama and will welcome the bursts in support which actions on the political stage trigger. However, the impact of such actions are short-lived and, by themselves, can do little but provide bumps and wiggles on the downward course of approval. Therein lies the dilemma. (1985, 65–66).

Assuming such trade-offs exist, it seems reasonable to test the Reagan agenda for differences between short-term and long-term policy, distinguishing between intentions, proposals, and consequences. This distinction is central for understanding the president's policy horizons. Simply put, long-term intentions do not necessarily lead to either long-term legislation or ultimate long-term success. A president such as Reagan can be undeniably committed to long-term change yet incapable of developing a long-term legislative agenda. Indeed, the American policy landscape is littered with well-intended programs that failed to produce the desired long-term consequences—the War on Poverty, Model Cities, the War on Drugs, energy conservation, and so on. Some failed because the problems were too tough, others because the legislation was poorly drafted, still others because the world failed to perform as predicted.

Consider at least two places where a long-term intention might go astray. First, the president may be unable to either locate or develop a long-term proposal to match the intention. Second, the proposal itself may fail to work as designed, whether because of unfavorable external conditions or because of bureaucratic opposition. These two potential failures are summarized in tables 5 and 6. The examples in cells 2 and 3 of each table may well constitute a unique class of presidential policy decisions, for they show "disconnects" between intentions and proposals and proposals and consequences. In short, they

TABLE 5
Intentions versus Proposals

Proposal	Intention	
	Short term	Long term
Short term	1981 Social Security rescue	1981 budget and tax package
Long term	1974 national health insurance	1983 Social Security rescue

TABLE 6
Proposals versus Consequences

Consequence	Proposal	
	Short term	Long term
Short term	1981 accelerated tax depreciation	1977 Social Security rescue
Long term	1981 budget and tax package	1983 Social Security rescue

indicate policy failures of one kind or another—errors in forecasting, design, or implementation.

Reagan's 1981 budget and tax package, for example, emerges in each table as a policy disconnect, first as a failure to link the longterm intention with a long-term proposal, next as a failure to match a short-term proposal to the intended long-term consequence. In contrast, Reagan's 1983 Social Security reform emerges in both tables as a successful match, first as a long-term intention tied to a long-term proposal, next as a long-term proposal that yields a long-term consequence.

However interesting these policy failures, the operative question is not whether presidents and their staffs sometimes make mistakes. Nor is it whether the policy process sometimes mismatches intentions to proposals or proposals to consequences. All in all, most short-term intentions convert easily into short-term proposals and short-term consequences. And, at least until the late 1970s, most long-term intentions converted smoothly into long-term proposals and long-term consequences. Rather, the question is whether the prospects for long-term policy have decreased over the past three decades. Although intentions and outcomes are important pieces of the durability question, the following discussion focuses only on the specific tactics chosen to link the two.

Making decisions about what constitutes a short-term or long-term proposal is no small task, particularly since many proposals contain elements of both. The challenge is to make reasonable judgment calls based on questions about the legislative specifics, for example:

- What is the phase-in and phase-out schedule for the specific proposal?
- What does the legislative record reveal about the hoped for timetable for results?
- What sunsets, if any, or triggers constrain the life of the proposal?
- What kind of administrative structure, if any, was envisioned for implementation; was it already built?
- What are the expectations for the proposal en route to passage?

The purpose here is not to produce a perfect interval measure, but to gather enough information about the legislative content to distinguish the overall structure of a given proposal. Unlike some of our existing measures of size and scope (e.g., spending/nonspending) where coding decisions are remarkably easy, measures of direction are inherently more difficult and might be best developed through intercoder reliability tests of the kind used in survey research and content analysis. Toward that end, consider the following list of proposals from the Kennedy, Nixon, Carter, and Reagan administrations as a sample.

Short Term: postal rate increases, Kennedy's area redevelopment, juvenile crime control, accelerated public works, water projects, Carter's hospital cost containment, the windfall profits tax, emergency strike controls, special revenue sharing, standby gas rationing, cuts in food stamps and Aid to Families with Dependent Children, Social Security reform (1981), and Reagan's acceleration of the 1980 Disability Insurance review.

Long Term: Hatch Act Reform (civil service political participation) Medicare, civil rights, Clean Water, Alaska Lands Protection, Clean Air Act, indigent legal aid, Social Security reform (1977 and 1983), airline, banking, and transportation deregulation, Nixon's family assistance plan, Carter's program for better jobs and income, Reagan's welfare demonstration projects, catastrophic health insurance, the balanced budget and school prayer amendments, establishment of a Department of Veterans Affairs, and the proposed dismantling of the departments of Energy and Education.

This is not to suggest that long-term proposals such as Medicare and civil rights are pure types—that is, that long-term proposals do not contain elements of short-term and vice versa. Nor is this to suggest that short-term proposals cannot become "immortal," as many government programs do. Rather, the judgment calls must be based on the weight of the legislative record at the launch of the proposal—for example, was the legislation timed for immediate impact, does the bill involve changes in the basic statute, does it lead toward more lasting reform?

Ultimately, such judgments are best treated as rough clues to potential trends in the president's agenda. However, even accepting the potential for disagreement over the specific examples offered above, the data presented in table 7 suggest that the president's agenda may be becoming short term. Looking back to Kennedy-Johnson (1961–65), Nixon's first and only full term (1969–73), Carter (1977–81), and Reagan (1981–89), the percentage of short-term proposals has risen by one-third.

THE SHORT-TERM AGENDA

Imperfect though the data are, table 7 suggests that presidential policy horizons may have changed over the past two decades, if not significantly, at least provocatively. Not only does the proportion of short-term policy increase over time, the greatest shift appears to have occurred in 1978, when Carter turned away somewhat from the trusteeship presidency and toward a precarious reelection campaign.

From a statistical standpoint, however, the tables can only be said to reveal slight trends, mainly in distinguishing Reagan's legislative strategy from his predecessors—a strategy of short-term policy that runs precisely opposite to Kennedy, Nixon, and Carter. Facing a set of first-year economic and social problems that would have been difficult to solve even with carefully crafted long-term proposals, Reagan opted instead for a series of short-term cuts, caps, and accounting gimmicks, moving his short-term policy at the beginning, not the end, of the term. Like his predecessors, Reagan was clearly committed to striking fast. However, striking fast does not mean striking fast only with short-term policy. In that regard, Reagan was very different indeed.

This is not to suggest that Reagan was consumed by short-term intentions. Quite the contrary. He held very strong beliefs about taxes,

TABLE 7
Presidential Requests for Legislation:
Short-term versus Long-term Proposals

President	Short term	Long term
Kennedy		
1961	11	14
1962	7	9
1963	2	4
Johnson		
1964	3	3
Total	23	30
Percentage	43	57
Nixon I		
1969	6	11
1970	4	8
1971	4	4
1972	1	2
Total	15	25
Percentage	38	62
Carter		
1977	6	15
1978	6	2
1979	4	4
1980	3	1
Total	19	22
Percentage	46	54
Reagan[a]		
1981	7	1
1982	3	4
1983	4	7
1984	3	1
Total	17	13
Percentage	57	43

a. Reagan had no additional legislative requests in 1985–88.

spending, and the proper role of government. With "no new taxes" as his rallying cry, Reagan espoused one of the most uncompromising, perhaps even rigid, ideologies in recent presidential history. Given the rhetoric of revolution, it may seem all the more surprising that his administration failed to craft a revolutionary set of first-year proposals to match. Despite several notable long-term initiatives later in his term—taxes, welfare reform, and a new version of Nixon's New Federalism—the Reagan agenda had an overall thrust toward legislation timed for immediate returns.

While there is little doubt that a president as conservative as Reagan would want to do significant "weed cutting" at the start of the term, there is a difference between weed *cutting* and weed *pulling*. The fact that Reagan and his budget director opted for quick, if deep, cuts meant they would have to cut again and again over time to realize the president's broad plan of limited government. To carry the analogy further, most weeds grow back.

The question, of course, is how a president as tenaciously ideological as Reagan could be drawn to an agenda of short-term proposals. The answer may be that ideology takes a back seat to political reality in the choice of specific legislative tactics. No matter how ideological, Reagan may have had no other choice but to go short term. Simply put, the decision to opt for short-term proposals reflected a series of both tactical and strategic problems early in the Reagan administration.

On the one hand, Stockman had little time to consider lasting reforms in America's permanent government, not with a budget due in three weeks. Such a package would have taken months to develop, let alone pass in a single omnibus bill. Thus, the best Stockman could do was cut and paste, keeping track of the running total on the back of an envelope. "The reason we did it wrong—not wrong but less than the optimum," Stockman admitted at the time, "was that we said, Hey, we have to get a program out fast. And when you decide to put a program of this breadth and depth out fast, you can only do so much. We were working in a twenty to twenty-five-day time frame, and we didn't think it all the way through" (Greider, 1982, 65).

Moreover, a first-year package laden with more permanent reform might have faced endless delays in the congressional authorizing committees. Unlike Carter, who spent his first two years trying to figure out which committee was responsible for his omnibus energy package, Reagan was right to worry about how to secure passage of anything in a highly fragmented Congress.

On the other hand, there were few ready proposals to be found on Capitol Hill, especially for a president as conservative as Reagan. Unlike Kennedy, who could borrow or steal an entire legislative agenda from his Democratic colleagues in 1961, Reagan had no ready-made party program. The lack of a House or Senate Republican majority in the years before Reagan's election may have fore-doomed his agenda to short-term proposals in the first years after his election.

Even had there been a Republican majority in Congress, it would likely not have been of much use to a conservative president. Yet, coming into office as the consummate outsider, and a former governor to boot, Reagan had few detailed alternatives of his own. Absent an adoptable Republican agenda on Capitol Hill, the best the new administration could do was draw upon conservative think tanks for overly broad recommendations, hardly a substitute for fully developed legislation in reserve on Capitol Hill.

Finally, even had there been a deep Republican agenda at the ready, it was not clear that Reagan had the political capital for a package of first-year reforms. Despite Reagan's working majority of House Republicans and boll weevil southern Democrats in the House, it was a fragile coalition at best. Perhaps an assortment of short-term cuts was all he could afford. In this regard, dismantling or repealing programs is a very different task from zeroing out, or sharply cutting, the budget in a given fiscal year. The former raises even greater constituency counter pressure, greater legislative review, and greater risk of delay than budget cuts. Hard as liberals fought to stop the Reagan budget and tax package, at least their programs would live to fight another day.

Ultimately, however, Reagan's first-year agenda reflected his own distaste for detail. Ignoring the sometimes painful process of translating broadly sculpted intentions into highly specific proposals, Reagan left the fine print to his budget director and Congress. In this regard, Reagan may have avoided details too much. Left to his own devices, Stockman drifted toward short-term proposals. While some might rightly argue that Reagan achieved his aim of limited government through creation of a persistent budget crisis, surely that is not what he originally intended. As Stockman also admitted,

> We should have designed those pieces to be more compatible. But the pieces were moving on independent tracks—the tax program, where we were going on spending, and the defense program, which was just a bunch of numbers written on a piece of paper. And it didn't quite mesh. That's what happened. But, you see, for about a month and a half we got away with that because of the novelty of all these budget reductions. (Greider, 1982, 37)

TABLE 8
Presidential Requests for Legislation:
New/Short Term versus New/Long Term

President	New/Short term		New/Long term	
	Total	Percentage	Total	Percentage
Kennedy	11	33	22	67
Nixon, first term	7	28	18	72
Carter	12	48	13	52
Reagan	9	50	9	50

Unfortunately for Reagan, by the time his long-term proposals came on line, his political capital was gone. Thus, what remains of the administration is largely what passed in 1981. Although Reagan can claim some credit for tax simplification and welfare reform in his second term, he did not have the political support—nor, for that matter, a continued Senate majority—to shape outcomes as he had five or six years before.

THE SIZE AND SCOPE OF SHORT-TERM POLICY

Ultimately, these data are not particularly significant in any statistical sense until they are combined with the earlier measures of size and scope in tables 8 and 9. The combination of the three policy differences—large/small, new/old, and short-term/long-term—is particularly important for understanding where presidents invest their capital. It might be, for example, that presidents only go short term on old issues, reserving their long-term vision for new proposals. It might also be that presidents go short term only on small items, reserving their long-range ideas for large opportunities.

TABLE 9
Presidential Requests for Legislation:
Large/Short Term versus Large/Long Term

President	Large/Short term		Large/Long term	
	Total	Percentage	Total	Percentage
Kennedy	13	46	15	54
Nixon, first term	2	14	14	86
Carter	10	45	12	55
Reagan	5	39	8	61

According to these tables, neither argument is true. Kennedy and Nixon both used their nonincremental opportunities for long-term policy, while Carter and Reagan were much more likely to go short term. As a proportion of their agendas, Carter and Reagan both offered roughly twice as much new/short-term policy as Kennedy and Nixon. Again, however, the key difference between Carter and Reagan is the timing of the short-term proposals. Of Carter's 1977 new proposals, only two of twelve were short term; of Reagan's 1981 new proposals, five of six were short term.

Table 9 is more difficult to interpret. Roughly half of Kennedy, Carter, and Reagan's large proposals are long term, compared to 86 percent of Nixon's. One explanation is that the size of a president's short- and long-term initiatives is not always subject to choice. When old ideas hit the agenda—for example, the two recent Social Security financing crises—the president has little option but to go large.

However, Nixon's agenda also reflects pure political reality: he simply did not have the political capital to secure passage of his program, whether short- or long-term, large or small, new or old. Facing such limited legislative prospects, Nixon may have simply been in the business of developing proposals for his second term, showing the public that he was, indeed, a great thinker, even as he asked his campaign team to win by the biggest landslide possible.

One might even argue that Nixon's long-term agenda reflects his obsession with a place in history. In this regard, the content of his policy agenda may be just another manifestation of the same psychological impulse that led to the secret White House taping system. Just as Nixon wanted a perfect historical record for the future, perhaps he also wanted the perfect policy agenda. Intriguing though this hypothesis may be, it pales in comparison to simple political realities for explaining the Nixon agenda. Believing that 1972 would produce a landslide realignment on the order of 1932, Nixon's long-term policy agenda may reflect nothing more than his own judgment that the second term would present ample opportunity for legislative achievement.

Ultimately, it is table 10 that raises the greatest questions about the Carter and Reagan eras. Comparing the mix of short and long term on each president's nonincremental agenda, table 10 suggests that Kennedy and Nixon may have operated in a very different policy period from Carter and Reagan. Whereas Kennedy and Nixon averaged only one short-term nonincremental proposal out of five, Carter and

TABLE 10
Presidential Requests for Legislation:
New Large/Short Term versus New Large/Long Term

President	New Large/Short term		New Large/Long term	
	Total	Percentage	Total	Percentage
Kennedy	4	21	15	79
Nixon, first term	1	8	11	92
Carter	8	50	8	50
Reagan	5	45	6	55

Reagan averaged one out of two. Moreover, in absolute terms, the number of large-new/long-term proposals steadily declines over time, perhaps suggesting that government may have become saturated at some point, incapable of absorbing any new major programs. As above, however, there are timing differences between Carter and Reagan, with all five of Reagan's large-new/short-term proposals arriving on Capitol Hill before his first large-new/long-term request. In contrast, six of Carter's first seven large-new proposals were long term, perhaps explaining why Congress was choked by his agenda.

Conclusion

Reagan was hardly the first American president to make choices among short-term and long-term proposals. Every president from George Washington to George Bush has faced a similar tension. It is inherent in the very structure of the presidency.

Nor was Reagan the first president to offer short-term proposals. He had two hundred years of precedent. Indeed, many, if not all, of America's celebrated long-term domestic programs—Social Security, Medicare, unemployment compensation, the interstate highway system, wilderness preservation—carry some element of short-term politics. The growing power of the gray lobby no doubt crossed Lyndon Johnson's mind as he signed Medicare into law.

Rather, Reagan may have inherited a presidency less capable of converting long-term intentions into long-term proposals, and, as I argue elsewhere, he most certainly left behind a weaker presidency. It has always been one thing for a president to intend long-term impact, quite another to draft and secure passage of long-term legislative proposals, and still another to assure successful implementation that produces the intended long-term results. However, what makes the current era different is that public patience for long-term programs may have worn thin, the proposals themselves may not be readily available, and the prospects for successful implementation may have been severely weakened. Intentions notwithstanding, today's president may simply be less able to go long term.

Ultimately, the question is whether the rise in short-term policy is merely a passing phenomenon—the simple artifact of temporary budgetary and political volatility and oversaturation of the federal system—or a more durable feature of the modern policy process. Several trends suggest that short-term policy may be at the fore in the presidential policy process for some time to come.

First, the political culture bracketing the president's agenda may have become more impatient since the 1970s, characterized by declining long-term attachments to the political system and shallow investments in the electoral process. When coupled with a general disengagement from civic life, the erosion of party identification among younger Americans in general and the baby boom generation specifically, has created an environment in which presidents have very few incentives for addressing long-term policy issues. Although studies of the national mood are risky, it is clear that presidents do pay attention to swings in public commitment.

Second, the supply of long-term policy proposals may have been affected by America's increasingly fragmented legislative process. The sources of ideas that fueled the president's agenda in the 1950s and 1960s either no longer exist or have been weakened significantly and cannot be replaced by the proliferation of boutique interest groups— the highly specialized organizations that have blossomed in recent years. Moreover, disinvestment in government's analytic capacity has reduced the president's ability to develop policy with long-term horizons. The lost ability to understand how programs work has a clear impact on the president's ability to both develop policy proposals and sell them to Congress and the public.

Third, the implementation of long-term proposals may have become more difficult in an era of scarce resources and declining management capacity. And if implementation is unlikely, presidents and the assorted entrepreneurs who surround them are wise to focus on the short term. Ironically, many of these constraints were self-inflicted by past presidents, reflecting efforts to gain control of the executive branch. As the National Commission on the Public Service (Volcker Commission) argued in its final report in 1989, two decades of pay freezes, bureaucrat bashing, budget crises, political turnover, and an ever-tightening noose of internal regulation may have so demoralized the career work force that presidents cannot be sure that even the shortest-term policies will be successfully implemented.

One of the advantages of looking at policy differences is the ability to sort through these and competing explanations of presidential choices. Walter Williams, for example, might argue that Reagan's agenda was merely another manifestation of his antianalytic bias:

> One point driven home to me over nearly a decade of study is how much individual political leaders matter. Reagan, central to the study, was the first truly charismatic president since Franklin Roosevelt. Despite innumerable misstatements, gross mismanagement, and significant policy failures that would have destroyed other presidents, Reagan thrived. . . . The most ideological president in memory, certain of the rightness of his policies without needing facts and figures, became the first modern anti-analytic president. (1990, x)

Yet, while Williams is no doubt correct regarding the administration's disinvestment in analytic capacity, the data suggest that Reagan was not the first modern short-term president. Carter established the pattern three years earlier. Carter may have been the trustee president, but he clearly began moving toward the short term from his second year onward.

Thus, declining analytic capacity may be only a small part of a complex explanation for changing policy outcomes in which political context and institutional structure matter most. By being more deliberate about defining our dependent variables and by focusing on essential presidential products like policy, we may yet be able to settle these kinds of questions.

The national mood, as John Kingdon calls it, may be a much more significant predictor of policy outcomes than White House analytic capacity. First, the president's agenda may reflect the attachments of citizens as voters. The decline in party identification among all Americans in general, and among the under-forty-five electorate in particular, has a profound impact on the kinds of policies presidents prefer.

Second, the agenda may also reflect the social attachments of citizens as clients. Political attitudes are but a small part of the overall geography of public opinion a president faces in building a policy agenda. Basic life-style changes may be far more important in understanding the fragile balance of presidential policy than the erosion of party identification. The fact that the seventy-five million baby boomers born between 1946 and 1964 have separated from traditional social roles as spouses, parents, and workers may not automatically spring to mind as an important indicator for those who study presidential policy. Nevertheless, as presidents survey the political and social landscape upon entering office, they cannot help but see the broad emphasis on short-term returns. They face an exceedingly volatile electorate, as well as a broadly disengaged public, both of which affect the cost of going public.

Ultimately, analytic capacity and political culture are both important additions to a long list of variables designed to explain presidential performance. The only way, short of divine intervention, to know which of the myriad theories matters more is to test each against a reasonable dependent variable. I nominate presidential policy for the task.

Notes

I wish to thank Larry Berman, George Edwards, Charles O. Jones, Robert Katzmann, John Kessell, Bert Rockman, and Norman Thomas for their insights and suggestions on this chapter.

1. See George Edwards, III, working alone (1989) and with Alec Gallup (1990). See also Gary King and Lyn Ragsdale (1988) for an exhaustive attempt to develop measures of presidential behavior and performance.

2. Hess drafted transition memos on White House organization for both Carter and Reagan. See Stephen Hess (1988).

3. See, for example, Gary King and Lyn Ragsdale (1988).

4. The most effective, and what once seemed to be the final nail in the argument, came from George Edwards and Alec Gallup (1990). Donald Peppers drove the first nail in 1975 with "The Two Presidencies"; Lance LeLoup and Steven Shull drove the second in 1979 with "Congress versus the Executive"; while Lee Sigelman drove the third in 1979 with "A Reassessment of the Two Presidencies Thesis." It is a sign of the respect for Wildavsky's work that the hypothesis survived as long as it did, for Edwards was able to successful prove that it was clearly an artifact of the 1950s and early 1960s.

5. In the Carter domestic policy process, the agenda-setting mechanism actually required presentation of ideas in a sequence, starting with memoranda on the

general problem, then moving forward with specific proposals, with each decision memorandum carefully structured to give the president a go or no go option.

6. See Stephen Wayne (1978) for a description of how presidents go about making these calculations.

7. See Light (1991, 40–41) for a description of the Kennedy-Carter data.

8. The OMB Library, for example, which was open to the public during the late 1970s when I first conducted this research, was closed to the public immediately following the attempted assassination of Reagan in 1981. Heightened security concerns dovetailed with a much greater sensitivity to the value of information to render academic access almost impossible. Even upon gaining access to the library through a cumbersome set of rules, the clearance data was no longer available. Nor was it available through my sources in the Legislative Reference Division, who had become much more reluctant to open their files to curious researchers.

References

Allison, Graham. 1971. *Essence of Decision: Explaining the Cuban Missile Crisis*. Boston: Little, Brown.

Anderson, Martin. 1978. *Welfare: The Political Economy of Welfare Reform in the United States*. Palo Alto: Hoover Institution Press.

Barber, James David. 1971. "The Interplay of Presidential Character and Style: A Paradigm and Five Illustrations." In *A Sourcebook for the Study of Personality and Politics*, ed. F. I. Greenstein and M. Lerner. Chicago: Markham.

————. 1985. *The Presidential Character: Predicting Performance in the White House*. 3d ed. Englewood Cliffs, N.J.: Prentice-Hall.

Berman, Larry. 1979. *The Office of Management and Budget and the Presidency, 1921–1979*. Princeton: Princeton University Press.

————. 1982. *Planning a Tragedy: The Americanization of the War in Vietnam*. New York: Norton.

————. 1990. *Looking Back on the Reagan Presidency*. Baltimore: Johns Hopkins University Press.

Campbell, John. 1978. "The Old People Boom and Japanese Policy Making." *Journal of Japanese Studies* 5 (2): 329–50.

Derthick, Martha. 1991. *Agency Under Stress*. Washington, D.C.: Brookings.

Derthick, Martha, and Paul Quirk. 1985. *The Politics of Deregulation*. Washington, D.C.: Brookings.

Destler, I. M. 1980. *Making Foreign Economic Policy*. Washington, D.C.: Brookings.

Edwards, George, III. 1989. *At the Margins: Presidential Leadership of Congress*. New Haven: Yale University Press.

Edwards, George, III, with Alec M. Gallup. 1990. *Presidential Approval: A Sourcebook*. Baltimore: Johns Hopkins University Press.

Edwards, George, III, Steven Shull, and Norman Thomas, eds. 1985. *The Presidency and Public Policy Making*. Pittsburgh: Pittsburgh University Press.

Fishel, Jeff. 1985. *Presidents and Promises: From Campaign Pledge to Presidential Performance*. Washington, D.C.: Congressional Quarterly Press.

George, Alexander. 1980. *Presidential Decisionmaking in Foreign Policy : The Effective Use of Information and Advice*. Boulder, Colo.: Westview.

Greenstein, Fred. 1982. *The Hidden-Hand Presidency: Eisenhower as a Leader.* New York: Basic.

———, ed. 1988. *Leadership in the Modern Presidency.* Cambridge: Harvard University Press.

Greider, William. 1982. *The Education of David Stockman and Other Americans.* New York: Dutton.

Hess, Stephen. 1988. *Organizing the Presidency.* 2d ed. Washington, D.C.: Brookings.

Jones, Charles O. 1988a. *The Reagan Legacy: Promise and Performance.* Chatham, N.J.: Chatham House.

———. 1988b. *The Trusteeship Presidency: Jimmy Carter and the United States Congress.* Baton Rouge: Louisiana State University Press.

Kernell, Samuel. 1986. *Going Public: New Strategies of Presidential Leadership.* Washington, D.C.: Congressional Quarterly Press.

Kessel, John. 1975. *The Domestic Presidency.* Boston: Duxbury.

———. 1985. *Presidential Parties.* Homewood, Il.: Dorsey.

King, Gary, and Lyn Ragsdale. 1988. *The Elusive Executive: Discovering Statistical Patterns in the Presidency.* Washington, D.C.: Congressional Quarterly Press.

Kingdon, John. 1984. *Agendas, Alternatives, and Public Policy.* Boston: Little, Brown.

LeLoup, Lance, and Steven Shull. 1979. "Congress versus the Executive: The 'Two Presidencies' Reconsidered." *Social Science Quarterly* 59 (1):704–19.

Light, Paul. 1983. *Vice Presidential Power: Advice and Influence in the White House.* Baltimore: Johns Hopkins University Press.

———. 1985. *Artful Work: The Politics of Social Security Reform.* New York: Random House.

———. 1991. *The President's Agenda: Domestic Policy Choice from Kennedy to Reagan (With Notes on George Bush).* Rev. ed. Baltimore: Johns Hopkins University Press.

Lowi, Theodore J. 1964. "American Business, Public Policy, Case Studies and Political Theory." *World Politics* 16, (2): 677–715.

Lynn, Lawrence Jr., and David deF. Whitman. 1981. *The President as Policymaker: Jimmy Carter and Welfare Reform.* Philadelphia: Temple University Press.

Mackenzie, G. Calvin. 1981. *The Politics of Presidential Appointments.* New York: Free Press.

Mann, Thomas. 1990. "Thinking About the Reagan Years." In *Looking Back on the Reagan Presidency,* ed. L. Berman. Baltimore: Johns Hopkins University Press.

Nathan, Richard. 1983. *The Administrative Presidency.* Rev. ed. New York: Wiley.

Nelson, Michael, ed. 1985. *The Presidency and the Political System.* 1st ed. Washington, D.C.: Congressional Quarterly Press.

———. 1988. "The Psychological Presidency." In *The Presidency and the Political System,* 2nd ed., ed. M. Nelson. Washington, D.C.: Congressional Quarterly Press.

Peppers, Donald. 1975. "The Two Presidencies: Eight Years Later." In *Perspectives on the Presidency,* ed. A. Wildavsky. Boston: Little, Brown.

Peterson, Mark. 1990. *Legislating Together: The White House and Capitol Hill from Eisenhower to Reagan*. Cambridge: Harvard University Press.

Pfiffner, James. 1991. *The Managerial Presidency*. Pacific Grove, Calif.: Brooks Cole.

Porter, Roger. 1980. *Presidential Decision Making: The Economic Policy Board*. Cambridge: Harvard University Press.

Qualls, James H. 1977. "Barber's Typological Analysis of Political Leaders." *American Political Science Review* 71 (1):182–211.

Redford, Emmette, and Richard McCulley. 1986. *White House Operations: The Johnson Presidency*. Austin: University of Texas Press.

Rose, Richard. 1989. *Inheritance Before Choice in Public Policy*. Studies in Public Policy 180. Glasgow, Scotland: Centre for the Study of Public Policy.

Shull, Steven. 1987. *The President and Civil Rights Policy: Leadership and Change*. Westport, Conn.: Greenwood.

Sigelman, Lee. 1979. "A Reassessment of the Two Presidencies Thesis." *Journal of Politics* 41 (4):1195–1205.

Simon, Dennis, and Charles Ostrom, Jr. 1985. "The President and Public Support: A Strategic Perspective." In *The Presidency and Public Policy Making*, ed. G. Edwards, S. Shull, and N. Thomas. Pittsburgh: University of Pittsburgh Press.

Spitzer, Robert. 1983. *The Presidency and Public Policy: The Four Arenas of Presidential Power*. University: University of Alabama Press.

Turner, Michael. 1982. *The Vice President as Policy Maker: Rockefeller in the Ford White House*. Westport, Conn.: Greenwood.

Wayne, Stephen. 1978. *The Legislative Presidency*. New York: Harper and Row.

Wildavsky, Aaron. 1966. "The Two Presidencies." *Trans-action* 4 (2).

———. ed. 1975. *Perspectives on the Presidency*. Boston: Little, Brown.

Williams, Walter. 1990. *Mismanaging America: The Rise of the Anti-Analytic Presidency*. Lawrence: University of Kansas Press.

II

Approaches

5

Studying Presidential Leadership

BARBARA SINCLAIR

*D*ESPITE its concern with leadership, political science has not yet developed anything that can in the strict sense of the term be labeled leadership theory. Congressional scholars have, however, devoted considerable attention to studying and theorizing about leadership and related issues—the changing distribution of influence within the chambers, most particularly (see Mackaman, 1981; Sinclair, 1990; Rohde and Shepsle, 1987). This chapter's purpose is to assess what that body of work might contribute to the study of presidential leadership. Given the lack of a fully developed leadership theory in congressional studies, the contribution is in the form of strategies for research. Some of the conceptualizations and methodological approaches found useful by congressional scholars may also prove fruitful in the presidential field; in particular, I will argue that the theoretical framework that is increasingly prevalent in congressional work offers a promising approach to the study of the presidency.

Why might one expect that research strategies fruitful in the study of congressional leadership would transfer successfully to the study of presidential leadership? Certainly some of the basic methodological problems are similar, most especially the problem of a very small N (at least if one focuses upon the top party leader in one's study of congressional leadership). More importantly, the "big" questions that ultimately motivate and give broader meaning to the study of presidential and congressional leadership are much the same. Rockman begins his book-length treatment of what he calls the leadership question with the generalization that "much of the literature on the American presidency unavoidably focuses on the dilemmas of generating leadership in a system not designed to endure much of it" (1984, xv). The study of congressional leadership likewise focuses upon the difficulties central leaders face in providing any sort of direction and locates the ultimate source in the constitutionally prescribed governmental structure and its electoral consequences. Yet students of both branches are very much aware that at times strong leadership does get exercised. Explaining why and when thus becomes the ultimate task. As the questions have commonly been formulated, what are the traits of those holding leadership positions and what are the environmental conditions that make the exercise of leadership possible?

Conceptualizing the Focal Variable

Leadership, like *power,* has given social scientists immense definitional problems. The proliferation of definitions attests to our failure to conceptualize the term in a broadly satisfactory way (Bass, 1990). Remarking that "there are almost as many different definitions of leadership as there are persons who have attempted to define the concept," Stogdill, in his *Handbook of Leadership,* classifies those definitions into eleven categories: leadership as a focus of group processes (the "centralization of effort in one person as an expression of the power of all"); leadership as personality and its effects ("a combination of traits which enables an individual to induce others to accomplish a given task"); leadership as the art of inducing compliance ("the process by which an agent induces a subordinate to behave in a desired manner"); leadership as the exercise of influence ("the process of influencing the activities of an organized group in its efforts toward goal setting and goal achievement"); leadership as act or behavior ("the behavior of an individual while he is involved in directing group activities"); leadership as a form of persuasion ("the activity of persuading people to cooperate in the achievement of a common objective"); leadership as a power relationship ("a form of relationship between persons [that] requires that one or several persons act in conformance with the requests of another"); leadership as "an instrument of goal achievement ("the human factor which binds a group together and motivates it toward goals"); leadership as an emerging effect of interaction ("a process of mutual stimulation which, by the successful interplay of individual differences, controls human energy in the pursuit of a common cause"); leadership as a differentiated role ("leadership is a role within the scheme of relations and is defined by reciprocal expectations between the leader and other members"); and leadership as the initiation of structure ("the initiation and maintenance of structure in expectation and interaction") (in ibid., 1990, 11–17).

A number of these definitions contain theoretically suggestive elements that point us toward potentially fruitful ways of thinking about political leadership. That the phenomenon involves moving (others, the group) toward an objective or goal, and that it in some way is a function of the interaction between leader and followers, seem useful insights. What none of these definitions does is clearly identify the phenomenon to be studied. None tells us how to identify leadership with sufficient clarity that trained observers will agree on what is and what is not leadership. Those definitions that appear closest to what students of politics seem to mean by leadership—leadership as the art of inducing compliance, as the exercise of influence, as a form of persuasion, or as a power relationship—just shift the definitional problem; they define leadership using concepts such as power or influence, which are themselves not well defined and certainly do not clearly identify observable phenomena.

In the study of Congress, this definitional problem, when combined with scholars' interest in questions of leadership strength, led to global judgments based upon fuzzy criteria without clear empirical referents. When differences are stark—between "Czar" Reed, Speaker of the House in the 1890s, and John McCormack, Speaker in the 1960s, for example—such labeling of leaders as strong or weak is unproblematical but also not in and of itself particularly enlightening. When dealing with a figure like Sam Rayburn, however, such global characterizations have led to confusion and, I would contend, to misunderstanding.

In Washington during the 1950s Sam Rayburn had a reputation as a strong Speaker, and that reputation has only grown since then (see Hardeman and Bacon, 1987; Bolling, 1968). The longest-serving Speaker in American history, he was respected, admired, and even revered. His willingness and ability to help out members who needed it became legend. Yet, in the last and one of the most important

battles of his legislative life—the packing of the Rules Committee—
he barely won. He had, in fact, strenuously tried to avoid the battle
but had finally been pushed into it by a segment of his membership
and by circumstances. Furthermore, in other confrontations with
committee chairmen during the 1950s, Rayburn often lost. So was he
a strong or a weak leader?

Only when congressional scholars turned to a consideration of
what leaders do, did a basis of cumulative and comparative research
begin to emerge. By focusing upon leadership activities—upon the
type of activities and rate of performance—we can make comparisons across leaders with some hope of precision. If conceptualized in
terms of observable behavior and activities, leadership style becomes
a variable upon which some agreement among scholars and across
leaders may be possible (see Cooper and Brady, 1981; Sinclair, 1992).

When Rayburn's leadership is examined from this perspective, it
becomes clear that the institutional structure of the House during the
period of his speakership constricted the activities of central leaders
narrowly. By the standards of earlier and later eras, the policy role of
speakers of the committee government era (approximately 1920–
1970) was restricted, consisting almost solely of building winning
floor coalitions on legislation written by autonomous committees.
Furthermore, given the system of intercommittee reciprocity, which
protected committee bills from attack on the floor, committee leaders
only rarely needed the Speaker's help to pass their legislation. Consequently, even the rate of coalition-building activity was not high, at
least by later standards.

The institutional structure of the committee government era severely constricted the activities of rank and file members. The attribution of power to Rayburn was undoubtedly due, in part, to the
differential between central leader and rank and file. It may also be
the case that Rayburn got the most out of his meager resources, and
he certainly seems to have been adept at picking his fights carefully,
avoiding to the extent possible those he would likely lose. While these
are factors that a comprehensive examination of Rayburn's leadership would undoubtedly want to consider, the core data are those
on activities. When we know what activities (e.g., organizing party
and chamber via appointments, agenda setting, shaping policy at
the pre-floor stage, building floor majorities) the central leadership

engaged in and with what frequency, we have the basis for making comparisons across time and for assessing the impact of leadership upon outcomes.

To what extent are these lessons from congressional scholarship applicable to presidential studies? The broader stage on which the president performs and the much greater amount of information available about presidents make it even more important that the phenomenon on which inquiry centers be clearly conceptualized and operationalized. Global judgments are seldom based upon precise criteria with clear empirical referents; consequently, scholars frequently disagree in their judgments—even worse, the basis of their disagreement (or agreement) is often unclear—and as a result, research has not cumulated into a body of broadly accepted generalizations.

Because the presidency is a constitutionally specified position, our inability to define leadership in a clearly operationalizable way need not be fatal to systematic inquiry. Students of the presidency, like students of congressional party leadership, are interested in what the holders of the position do, why they do it, and with what effect. Given that interest, the argument for focusing on concrete observable variables such as activities or decisions seems very strong. By doing so, we can expect to achieve agreement on the characteristics of the phenomenon we are studying (e.g., the values of the focal variable over a number of cases), which is a precondition to cumulative scholarship.

One's specific research question will, of course, influence just how one conceptualizes the focal variable or variables. Decisions, types of activities, patterns of behavior (which one can also label *styles*) are the sort of reasonably concrete and at least potentially observable variables that could serve as focal variables. In a simple and highly abstract model, this behavioral variable can be seen as an intervening variable; it is the result of a set of determinants; it, together with other factors, determines the outcome, which can be characterized substantively or in terms of winning-losing or success-failure (see figure 3).

This model is too general to provide any analytic leverage; its value is in clarifying some relationships that in such a simple model are obvious but become less so when an actual research question is dealt

FIGURE 3
An Abstract Model

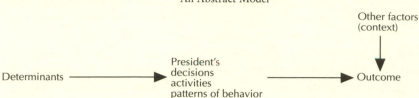

with in all its complexity. First, the analytic separation of a president's decisions, activities, and patterns of behavior from the outcome, reminds us that we are interested in the president's decis ions *because* of their presumed effect upon outcomes of some broadly consequential sort. Not all presidential behavior is necessarily of scientific interest. However fascinating a certain behavior may be to journalists, if no reasonable hypothesis links variations in such behavior to variations in outcomes, its study is unlikely to prove scientifically fruitful.

Second, factors other than the president's behavior influence such outcomes, whether defined substantively or in terms of winning or losing. If, for example, the focal variable is presidential legislative requests and his activities on their behalf, or major foreign policy decisions, or presidential efforts to influence public opinion, outcomes are not solely a function of the president's behavior. Whether Congress passes the president's proposals and in what form, the geopolitical results of foreign policy decisions in the near as well as the longer term, or the extent to which the president is able to move public opinion all certainly depend on factors other than the president's behavior. The relative weight of such other factors and of the president's behavior in any given area is, of course, an empirical question. Even a cursory consideration of these examples suggests that sometimes presidents influence outcomes by influencing these other contextual factors and, thus, that an arrow between those variables should be added to the figure. However, in such a highly abstract model, that increased complexity yields no added insights and consequently the link is omitted.

The simple model does suggest a way of bringing the concept of leadership back into our scholarly enterprise. If abandoning the concept altogether and focusing upon concrete activities exclusively seems too extreme, one might want to define leadership in terms of outcomes and the link between presidential behavior and outcomes. That is, one might say leadership has occurred when the outcome was what the president intended and his behavior had some significant effect in bringing about the outcome. (One might want to limit the label to some subset of such instances—ones in which the outcome reaches some minimum level of importance, for example.) Leadership thus conceptualized may seem rather pedestrian and unglamorous; it is, however, a conceptualization that lends itself to operationalization. What follows does not, in any case, depend upon accepting this conceptualization of leadership.

Within the structure provided by the model, three broad questions are central to an understanding of the phenomenon. First, what are the determinants of presidential behavior? Within the voluminous literature on leadership and related topics, two general classes of determinants can be distinguished—contextual or environmental variables and presidential traits (see Bass, 1990; Jones, 1981). Second, what are these other factors—contextual variables by assumption—that affect outcomes directly? Third, what is the relative weight of presidential behavior and of these other factors as determinants of outcomes? The model provides no basis for answering these questions. For that we need a theory or at least a theoretical framework.

Theoretical Approaches

Since the 1970s, the rational choice approach has increasingly influenced congressional scholarship, including studies of leadership. Although some full-blown deductive models mathematically stated have been developed, more frequently the fundamental assumption that individuals rationally pursue specified goals is the basis for a looser verbal model, and rationality is not strictly defined. (The two seminal studies are Fenno, 1973; and Mayhew, 1974; for a review of the formal literature see Krehbeil, 1988.) As another chapter in this book is devoted to formal models and as, given our current state of knowledge, these looser formulations are likely to have wider applicability, I restrict my attention to what I call the purposive behavior approach. I use that label to emphasize the centrality that purposive, goal-seeking behavior has in this approach and to distinguish it from the more rigorous rational choice approach (Sinclair, 1983). It is certainly not intended to imply that other approaches assume nonpurposive behavior.

However labeled, this approach has proved to be quite fruitful in helping us understand a wide range of phenomena: from aggregate congressional election outcomes (Jacobson and Kernell, 1981) to the differences among committees (Fenno, 1973) to policy outcomes (Arnold, 1990) to institutional change (Sinclair, 1989). The applicability of a particular theoretical approach depends upon both the character of the subject matter and the status of scholarship at a given time. In the study of Congress, we are dealing with the behavior of professionals in their area of expertise; consequently the rational choice assumption, especially in the weak form in which it is usually employed, is a reasonable one. Congressional scholars already know a good deal about the electoral and institutional environment; consequently one can base one's verbal models upon propositions about how behavior and outcomes are linked for which considerable empirical support exists. These seem to be prerequisites to the fruitful use of the approach.

The purposive behavior approach requires assumptions about the goals of the actors. Some true rational choice models simply posit a mathematical utility function and assume utility maximization. For the looser purposive behavior models, such an abstract approach provides no analytic leverage. Concrete assumptions for which there are empirical referents are necessary. Congressional scholars have approached this task in one of two distinct ways. Many, following Mayhew, have posited a single goal for members of Congress—almost always reelection. Others, following Fenno, have posited multiple goals. The advantages of the single-goal approach are simplicity and, if that goal is reelection, measurability. The multiple-goal approach, in contrast, is more realistic and, in its consideration of trade-offs among goals, leads to more interesting conclusions. The number of goals posited must be sufficiently limited that deductions, albeit loose verbal ones, about expected behaviors are possible. Fenno's assumption of three goals—reelection, power in the chamber, and good public policy—or a variant thereof is most frequently used and seems to work well.

The analytic leverage of the purposive behavior approach derives from its predictions about what elements of a very complex environment an actor will attend to. Theoretically ambitious studies of congressional leadership—those that employ an explicit theoretical framework and aim to generalize and explain—have long put heavy emphasis upon context as the shaper of congressional leadership (see Jones, 1981; Sinclair, 1990). However, the assumption that context or environment shapes behavior does not, by itself, provide much research guidance. The environment in which members and leaders of Congress operate is highly complex; presumably not all aspects are equally influential. The purposive behavior approach predicts that an actor will attend to those aspects that affect the advancement of his or her goals. Much of the environment consists of other actors, many of whom want something from the actor who is the focus of inquiry. The purposive behavior approach predicts that an actor will attempt to satisfy such other actors in the order and to the extent that those actors influence his ability to attain his goals.

Thus congressional party leaders are subject to demands from a myriad of sources—from the president, interest groups, leaders of the other chamber, members and leaders of the other party in the chamber, and from their own party colleagues in the chamber. How do leaders respond? From the fact that congressional party leaders must be elected and reelected by their chamber party colleagues and from the assumption that party leaders want to hold onto their positions, it follows that leaders will give precedence to the satisfaction of their members' demands. The expectations and demands of their members are, thus, the most important determinants of leadership behavior. Members in turn are dependent upon their constituents for their positions; and, assuming they desire reelection, members give precedence to constituents' demands over those of others, including those of their party leadership.

The purposive behavior approach has been applied to questions of institutional change as well as to narrower questions of leadership behavior and, while our understanding is far from complete, has very significantly advanced our knowledge. A brief sketch of the argument will demonstrate how the relatively modest assumptions discussed above provide order to and make sense out of a highly complex historical process.

If the most important determinant of congressional leadership behavior is member expectations and demands, and if member expectations are, in turn, highly influenced by the expectations of their constituents upon whom they depend for reelection, then the character of the link between members and their constituents should be key. What members want their leaders to do, the extent to which members' expectations are congruent or conflicting, and the resources members are willing to grant their leaders should all be a function of the character of that link, which, in turn, is heavily dependent upon the character of the party system. (For a more detailed presentation of the following argument with substantiating citations, see Sinclair, 1990.)

When parties are strong—when they play an important role in the recruitment and election of members, and when party identification is the primary determinant of voting behavior—members of Congress are linked to their constituencies via party and are dependent on party success for their own reelection. Both the homogeneous mass base characteristic of strong parties and the strong organizational role (in recruitment, for example) of such parties contribute to a congressional party membership that is ideologically like-minded. That is, there is likely to be a high degree of intraparty consensus on the legislation members need to satisfy their reelection and policy goals. Because the congressional majority party membership is like-minded and because reelection depends on party success, members place great weight on successful coalition building. They expect their leaders to devote their efforts to passing legislation and are willing to behave in a way that furthers that end. Furthermore, if leaders do not possess resources sufficient to insure legislative success, members are willing to support institutional changes that provide them with the necessary resources. The establishment and maintenance of the strong speakership of the 1890–1910 period can be thus explained.

When the party system weakens and parties play a lesser role in elections, the link between members of Congress and their constituencies becomes direct. Individual efforts and personalized appeals become more important to members' reelection than party success. A weak party system in which the link between members of Congress and their constituencies is less dependent on party success is less likely than a strong party system to produce congressional party memberships that are ideologically like-minded.

Members who perceive their reelection to be primarily dependent on their own efforts and less so on party success will expect leaders to facilitate their district-pleasing endeavors, even if this comes at the expense of coalition-building success. Such members will be leery of giving leaders great powers and resources for fear that they might be used to induce behavior not conducive to maximizing their individual reelection chances. Thus the strong speakership system broke down when parties weakened. It was replaced with a system in which members had greater autonomy to engage in district-pleasing behavior even if that entailed opposing party majorities and their party leadership. Within this committee government system, the role of party leaders was restricted; service activities and bargaining rather than policy leadership is what members expected and received from their central party leaders.

Although phrased here a little differently, this explanation of change from the strong speakership to the committee government era is a relatively familiar one. Recent congressional change offers the purposive behavior approach a greater challenge. Given the relative weakness of contemporary American political parties, why did a more active and more decisive—a stronger—majority party leadership emerge in the House of Representatives in the 1980s? Briefly stated, I argue that the costs and benefits to majority party House members of strong leadership and of the behavior on their part that makes such leadership possible have changed significantly (Sinclair, 1992). The 1970s reforms that increased the vulnerability of legislation to attack on the floor combined with the constraints of the 1980s political climate (these constraints being split control; a conservative confrontational president who threatened Democrats' policy, power, and reelection goals; the big deficits) greatly increased the difficulty of enacting legislation, especially legislation Democrats find satisfactory. The majority party leadership possesses critical resources—control over the Rules Committee, for example—that, if Democratic members acquiesce in their use, can significantly increase the probability of legislative success. Consequently, the benefits of strong leadership in terms of legislative outputs—to the Democratic membership, to Democratic committee contingents, to Democratic committee leaders—were considerably higher in the 1980s and into the 1990s than they were in previous decades.

Changes that reduced the costs of strong leadership also occurred during the 1980s and continue into the 1990s. Most important, the effective ideological homogeneity of the Democratic membership increased as the election constituencies of southern Democrats became more like those of their northern party colleagues and as the big deficits shrank the feasible issue space. In addition, the 1980s political environment, especially the deficit, made free-lance policy entrepreneurship, as practiced in the 1970s, much less feasible for moderates and liberals. Consequently, when Democratic members practice the sort of restraint that makes strong leadership possible—by giving up the right to offer floor amendments on selected legislation, for example—they are not giving up very much.

The purposive behavior framework suggests that it is not the strength of the external party system per se but how it affects the costs and benefits to members of strong internal leadership that is key. Consequently, changes in internal leadership strength may be the result of factors other than external party strength that influence those costs and benefits, and thus it is upon the costs and benefits themselves that one must focus. The purposive behavior approach thus is capable of dealing with change and, in fact, with complex processes of change. Within the framework, congressional leadership behavior should change in response to changes in member expectations, which, in turn, should be traceable to environmental alterations that affect members' pursuit of their goals. The inability or unwillingness of the leadership to respond to new member expectations in a way members find satisfactory may lead to institutional change.

Within congressional studies, the purposive behavior approach has proven its utility. It identifies a limited number of crucial variables and specifies how those variables are linked, with the rational choice assumption linking goals and behavior and propositions gleaned from the extensive empirical literature linking behavior and outcomes. The approach provides an interpretive framework for understanding congressional phenomena as complex as institutional change and, in some areas of study, can be fleshed out into a model from which testable hypotheses can be derived.

Purposive Behavior and the Presidency

In assessing the applicability of the purposive behavior approach to presidential studies, one must begin with a consideration of whether the two preconditions for fruitful use are met. First, does the assumption of rational behavior make sense? Most presidents do have considerable previous political experience and are, in fact, professional politicians. Although all undergo some on-the-job learning, presidents themselves possess or can command a great deal of information about the office and the political environment. Obviously a president has a huge stake in the outcomes of the decisions he makes. Presidents possess both information and a stake in the outcome, and thus the minimum requirements for assuming rational behavior are met.

The second precondition, that the scholar know enough about the relevant environment to formulate empirically supported propositions about the relationships among its key elements, seems reasonably well met in a number of the aspects of the presidency in which we are most interested. We know, for example, a good deal about the determinants of congressional responsiveness to presidential attempts to set the agenda and to influence policy content. Certainly we know enough to make attempts at formulating clear and specific propositions about how behaviors and outcomes are linked. In this and other areas, the attempt to formulate such propositions will, at minimum, pinpoint areas of ignorance that require research.

The analytic leverage of the purposive behavior approach derives, I have argued, from its ability to predict which elements of a very complex environment an actor will attend to. Given the incredibly complex environment within which the president operates, such prediction would provide a powerful analytic tool for bringing order and meaning to that complexity. By assumption, an actor will attend to aspects of the environment to the extent and in the order that they affect his ability to attain his goals. That assumption allows the scholar to single out and often order a set of actors in the environment that are key to the advancement of the focal actor's goals.

The assumption serves the critical function of identifying a limited number of key variables to be dealt with. A model's usefulness in scientific inquiry depends heavily upon the variables included being limited to a tractable number. To be sure, one can also argue that human beings, even presidents, have limited time and capacity and thus can take into account only the actors most key to achieving their goals— and, thus, that a model with a limited number of key variables is, in fact, realistic (see Sperlich, 1969). However, even if one believes that the number of relevant variables is legion, the argument for simplicity still holds. Only if the number of variables is limited can relationships among them be stated with sufficient clarity to make deductions of propositions about behaviors and outcomes possible; only then can the kind of careful operationalization and data gathering needed for testing hypotheses be undertaken.

Returning to the highly abstract model posited earlier, we can now begin to flesh it out. In that model, some form of presidential behavior was the focal variable and was posited to be the result of determinants unspecified though broadly classifiable as context variables and presidential traits. Within the purposive behavior framework, the key trait variable is goals; the key context variables are the expectations, demands, and expected behaviors of those actors in the environment whose behavior significantly affects the president's chances of furthering his goals. In the initial model, outcomes were determined by presidential behavior, decisions, and activities and also by a set of unspecified context variables. Within the purposive behavior framework, these context variables that directly affect outcomes consist by assumption largely of the same set of key actor variables posited to influence presidential behavior. It is because of their influence over outcomes that the president takes these actors into account in determining his behavior.

These key actors are themselves assumed to be rational actors pursuing specified goals; their behavior is posited to be a function of their goals and of the behavior of actors who are key to their goal achievement. Depending upon who those actors are and what sort of behavior the pursuit of their goals dictates, a basis for presidents to influence the behavior of their key actors may be present. That is, the relationship between a president's behavior and that of key actors in his environment may be reciprocal. (See figure 4.)

Presidential resources—and those of other key actors—affect the relationships of interdependence among actors and are thus incorporated in the model. The president's possession of the veto, for example, gives him the ability to affect the goal achievement of all actors seeking legislation and therefore the opportunity to influence their behavior.

Thus, the purposive behavior framework provides a basis for identifying a set of actors that are key to explaining the president's behavior. By using the same assumption about rational, goal-directed behavior to analyze these key actors' likely behavior, this strategy of analysis should enable the scholar to identify the major empirical determinants of such actors' behavior and answer questions about the conditions under which such actors, in pursuing their own goals, will

FIGURE 4
A Purposive Behavior Model

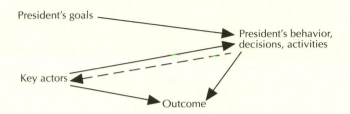

advance or hinder the president's pursuit of his goals and the extent to which he can in turn influence their behavior.

The purposive behavior approach can be employed in two distinct ways and for two different purposes. First, it can provide an interpretive framework for a case study. A scholar studying Bush's decision to go to war with Iraq, for example, could use the approach to identify a limited number of key determinative factors and to offer an interpretative explanation based upon the relationships specified in the model. One might posit that Bush's goals were to exert world leadership and to attain reelection; that the key actors were the U.S. electorate and a set of foreign states; that over an extended period of time, the key actors in pursuing their own goals would likely act in a way inimical to Bush's achievement of his goals (or at least this was Bush's perception); and that, therefore, Bush decided to attack quickly.

In the second use, the basic framework can be fleshed out into a verbal model from which hypotheses can be derived. If the necessary data can be gathered for an adequate number of cases, the hypotheses can then be tested in the conventional way. Instead of attempting to account for a specific foreign policy decision, the scholar would attempt to specify a model of foreign policy decision making based upon the framework and then test the propositions about decisions and outcomes derived from that model. It is this second use that offers the hope of yielding broadly accepted generalizations. The first can, however, provide the data for the second.

The specific empirical question or area of interest will, of course, determine how the framework is fleshed out, who the key actors

are posited to be, and what the character of the relationships are between those actors and the president. Nevertheless, a cursory and, of
necessity, loose application of the approach to presidential behavior
generally does provide some perspective on a core question in presidential research. Within this framework, what is the relative importance of context variables and of presidential traits as determinants of
presidential behavior and of outcomes?

After examining that question, I consider three other important
questions about the framework. What sorts of assumptions about
presidential goals are most likely to be analytically and empirically
fruitful? What is the role of presidential skill, and can the framework
incorporate skill differences in an analytically tractable way? Does
the framework provide a basis for judging presidential success and
failure?

KEY ACTORS AND THE IMPORTANCE
OF CONTEXT VARIABLES

Which actors does the approach single out as key to the president's
achieving his goals? What does it suggest about the types of variables
that determine these actors' behavior? In particular, to what extent
can the president influence these actors' behavior? To what extent is
their behavior—and therefore the president's chances of attaining his
goals that depend upon it—a function of determinants beyond the
president's control?

Although questions concerning the most fruitful assumptions
about the president's goals will be considered in more depth later,
even a cursory application of the approach requires an assumption
about goals. Let us begin by assuming that presidents desire reelection and that they also have other goals, either the desire to see
certain policies enacted, or the desire to exert leadership or power,
or both.

The assumption that an actor attends to aspects of the environment
to the extent and in the order that they affect the pursuit of his goals
does not result in as clear and simple a prediction for the president
as for congressional leaders. The assumption that presidents, like
congressional party leaders, desire reelection seems safe enough;
however, even aside from the two-term limit, the character of the relationship between president and voters is very different from the
character of the relationship between leaders and members in Con-

gress. The frequency of personal interaction between members and leaders in Congress results in leaders obtaining a fairly clear notion of what members expect and in members obtaining a fairly detailed knowledge of what leaders have, in fact, done. The relationship between president and voters is much less information-rich. The president has less information about voter expectations—beyond peace and prosperity—in large part because those expectations are often ill formed, and voters have much less information about actual presidential behavior. Consequently, even if reelection were the president's sole goal, his behavior would still be less tightly constrained by voter expectations and demands than is the behavior of congressional leaders by the expectations of their members.

This weaker constraint complicates the analytic task but does not lessen the usefulness of the approach. Clearly, reelection is a powerful motivating goal during a president's first term, and that does dictate attention to voters. Compared to congressional leaders vis-à-vis their members, presidents appear to have and believe they have a greater ability to influence voters' judgments of how adequately they have performed.

Research, scholarly and applied, in the areas of public opinion and voting behavior has produced a wealth of data, numerous low- to middle-level generalizations, and some understanding of the dynamics of opinion formation and opinion change. (For a summary, see Kinder and Sears, 1985.) Nevertheless, the extent to which and the ways in which the president can influence public opinion are still unclear. In particular, we do not know the extent to which presidential influence upon voters' perceptions depends upon context or upon characteristics of the president, especially communications skills. Does the character of the situation or problem—clear-cut or ambiguous, complex and technical or easily understood, directly experienced or remote—largely determine whether voters' perceptions can be significantly influenced by the president, or is the president's skill a more important determinant? It is clear that while a president may be able to influence his image with the voters, he certainly cannot control it (Lanoue, 1988). Also, conditions that adversely affect people directly—a recession or high inflation, for example—are very difficult to explain away.

Presidents are aware there are limits to their influence on public opinion and there are uncertainties about its exercise. Yet because of its importance to the pursuit of their goals, they have every reason to attempt to influence voters' judgments of how adequately they are performing. Certainly, presidents attempt to influence such judgments and not only by satisfying voters' demands and expectations when these are clear and it is possible to do so. Presidents all attempt to promote and maintain prosperity. In addition, however, presidents attempt to influence voters' judgments by seeking to shape the interpretation of information and events voters receive. Presidential media strategies appear to be becoming more sophisticated and more central to presidents' leadership styles (Grossman and Kuman, 1981; Kernell, 1986). The greater amount of information available about public opinion and the seemingly greater ability to gauge the effect of a president's influence attempts and of other events—through tracking polls, focus groups, and so on—appear to have contributed to the increasing importance of media strategies by making them technically feasible. So, very likely, did the decline in party identification in the electorate and the failed presidencies of the 1970s, which made evident the need for presidents to develop new or at least more sophisticated strategies vis-à-vis the voters in order to attain reelection.

The purposive behavior framework thus predicts that, of the multitude of actors in the president's environment, the voters will receive high priority. Given the voters' inattentiveness, however, the president's strategy vis-à-vis the voters is not a straightforward attempt to satisfy well-formed, stable demands and expectations. Rather, much effort—and, given changes in the environment in recent times, increasingly much effort—is devoted to influencing voters' perceptions of presidential performance.

If voters are critical to a president's reelection but are often inattentive and perhaps manipulable, Congress is critical to the attainment of most goals one might posit a president as pursuing and (unlike the voters) is highly attentive and not easily manipulated. Anything the president wants that requires legislation—including everything that requires money in appreciable amounts—depends upon the assent or acquiescence of Congress. Consequently, the purposive behavior framework suggests that Congress should be seen overall as the first or second most important actor in the president's environment. To be sure, in some areas of presidential decision making Congress might loom less large and other actors take precedence. Foreign policy crisis decision making may be such an area, though presidents must concern themselves with congressional reactions to their decisions. Noncrisis foreign policy and defense policy decision making are areas in which contemporary presidents are highly dependent upon Congress for attaining their policy objectives.

If to accomplish his objectives, whatever they may be, a president is heavily dependent upon Congress, to what extent, if at all, can the president influence the likelihood of Congress giving him what he wants? Is the congressional response largely determined by context variables beyond the president's control, or can presidential skill make a difference?

How will the Congress respond to presidential requests? The purposive behavior approach suggests that members make their decisions on the basis of whether giving the president what he wants will advance or hinder the pursuit of their own goals. Clearly the most critical limitation upon the president's ability to influence members of Congress is his limited influence on their reelection chances. He cannot guarantee or deny renomination to members of his party, and, in fact, his and their electoral fates are only tenuously linked. Nevertheless, whether one posits that members of Congress are motivated by reelection only or by policy as well, reactions to presidential requests should usually differ by party. Most of the time, supporting the president's requests is much more likely to advance both the reelection and the policy goals of members of the president's party than those of the other party. Consequently, the party balance in the chambers is critical to the president. Clearly, that is a context variable over which he has little control.

Members of Congress of the other party may disagree with the president for policy reasons, but if they believe that their constituents strongly want them to support the president, the reelection goal may well take precedence over the policy goal. An election perceived to carry a mandate, as those of 1932 and 1980 were, will produce this sort of support for a president (see Edwards, 1989, chap. 8; Sinclair, 1985). However, although the mandate interpretation is to some extent a creation of the political community, it does not appear to be manipulable ex post facto by the administration. (Attempts after the elections of 1984 and 1988 were dismal failures.)

Empirical findings on whether or under what conditions presidential popularity translates into congressional support are equivocal

(Edwards, 1989, chap. 7). The purposive behavior framework predicts that only when members read the president's popularity as resting, at least in part, upon their constituents' support for his policy proposals is this popularity likely to significantly increase congressional support. Congress's lack of support for President Bush's positions in 1989–1990, despite his high popularity, is consonant with the model's prediction.

Nevertheless, a president is better off being popular than unpopular with the public at large, whatever the basis of the popularity. Members of Congress can seldom be completely sure about the basis of a president's popularity and so may give him the benefit of the doubt in close call situations. A popular president can certainly help members of his own party more than an unpopular president with reelection; he can, for example, make an important contribution via fundraising, and he may help and will not hurt the member in the voting booth. Members of the other party are less likely to perceive electoral benefits from attacking a popular president and opposing his proposals. Clearly a president has incentives to maintain high popularity for reasons other than reelection. However, as the discussion earlier indicated, although a president may be able to influence his popularity, he certainly cannot control it.

On the basis of an exhaustive analysis of presidential support scores of members of the House and Senate, Edwards argues that context variables are determining and that the role of presidential skill is, at best, marginal (Edwards, 1989, chap. 11). The purposive behavior approach both suggests that context variables, particularly the party balance in the chambers and whether the election was perceived to carry a mandate, are central and provides a theoretical rationale for the importance attributed to those variables as well.

SPECIFYING GOALS

The purposive behavior framework depends for its analytic leverage upon the assumption that actors rationally pursue specified goals. The framework itself cannot, however, provide guidance in the specification of the goals. Decisions about what goal or goals to posit must be based upon prior knowledge. Presidential scholars are best equipped to make those decisions, but certain analytic questions can be addressed here.

At our current state of knowledge, the most fruitful assumptions are likely to vary across areas of research. It seems more important to posit goals that are sufficiently concrete that they provide analytic leverage than to worry about a lack of uniformity. If goals are too abstractly stated, it becomes impossible to formulate propositions about which actors are key and which strategies are most conducive to the advancement of the president's goals.

Whatever one's judgment of the single-goal assumption in congressional studies, it would seem to be almost always inappropriate in presidential studies. The simplicity that the assumption of a single goal brings will almost always be bought at too high a price, not just in verisimilitude but also in analytic leverage. The environment in which the president operates is not only complex but also not easily compartmentalized; presidential behavior in one arena has impacts in others. The president's election strategy may affect Congress's responsiveness to his policy proposals. The president's strategic moves aimed at influencing the behavior of foreign powers may affect the voters' perceptions of him. The trade-offs that characteristically confront presidents in their decision making seem best conceptualized as trade-offs across or the balancing of multiple goals.

Although presidential scholars may find quite different research assumptions useful depending upon their research question, Light's typology or some modification of it seems broadly applicable (1982, 64). Basing his typology on that of Fenno, Light suggests that reelection, historical achievement, and good policy are the goals that presidents pursue. One might want to expand the reelection goal into a broader electoral goal, where not only the president's personal fate but also that of his party is at issue. One might add a current power goal distinct from historical achievement; presidents, one might assume, desire to be powerful, to be movers and shakers, to be, and be recognized as, leaders, quite apart from their wish to be remembered as great, consequential presidents. While one might modify Light's typology at the margins, it does meet some important criteria for usefulness: it specifies a limited number of goals and ones with considerable face validity.

Substantively and analytically, it makes sense to assume that presidents' goals may vary, at least in salience, over the course of their terms in office. Most obviously, the reelection goal will be highly salient for most presidents during their first term but becomes irrelevant in the second. Such variation may provide some useful analytic leverage for sorting out reelection-directed strategies from those aimed at the advancement of other goals.

Finally, should one assume that all presidents pursue the same goals or that one of the factors that distinguishes presidents from one another is the set of goals each pursues? Undoubtedly there are research questions for which the assumption of goal uniformity is the only appropriate one. The selection process and the office itself, including the expectations surrounding it, exert pressures toward uniformity. Yet, if we seek to understand the effect of individual differences among presidents upon how presidents act in office and subsequently upon outcomes, assuming that goals vary across presidents seems advisable. By doing so one incorporates individual variation in the research in a way that furthers rather than retards analysis.

Reducing individual differences among presidents to differences in goals (and perhaps skills, as is discussed later) may seem unrealistic in the extreme. Why not incorporate the full psyche of the president in our analysis? Assume that scholars agree upon the variables that constitute personality and that they develop generally accepted ways of ascertaining their values for presidents—both wildly optimistic assumptions. The likely number of such variables and the lack of a clearly stated framework from which could be deduced propositions about the behavioral consequences of various combinations of values of those variables (that is, different personalities) would still make such an approach scientifically untractable.

If important differences among presidents can be conceptualized in terms of (a limited number of) differences in goals, ultimate or proximate, such differences will actually provide analytic leverage rather than make systematic analysis difficult, as is now so often the case. The framework provides an analytic handle for attacking Hargrove's key question (in chapter 2 of this book)—do leaders make a difference? The framework suggests that, to gauge the extent to which leaders do make a difference, one should examine similarly situated presidents with different goals and differently situated presidents with similar goals.

INCORPORATING PRESIDENTIAL SKILL

Popular wisdom holds that presidents differ greatly in skill and that such differences affect outcomes. Does the purposive behavior approach allow for the possibility that the president's skill may make a difference? And, more importantly, does it provide an analytically tractable way of incorporating that variable into the research?

If context sets the parameters of the possible, one can argue that individual differences, especially skill, determine the extent to which presidents take advantage of the possibilities open to them. One may have no control over the hand one is dealt, but one can play it badly or well. Specifying the range of the possible in any given situation and judging whether a particular president could have done better is an inevitably controversial enterprise. No one would argue that Carter, had he possessed the skills of FDR, could have induced Congress to pass a legislative program as ambitious as the New Deal. Though the environment in which Carter operated precluded such an outcome, was it so constraining that, no matter what he did, Carter was doomed to failure? Was he dealt an inevitably losing hand, or, had he played it with more skill, might the outcome have been different?

Although the purposive behavior approach cannot provide simple answers to such questions, it does provide an analytic handle by which one can deal with them systematically and perhaps even rigorously. The key again is first to identify the actors who are critical to the president's attaining his aims; second, to assess whether, in pursuing their own goals, these actors will act as the president wants and needs them to; and third, if not, to consider whether the president has available strategies to alter those actors' goal-related calculus.

Returning to the example of presidential-congressional relations, presidential success in getting a proposal passed by Congress is largely dependent upon enough members of Congress perceiving that the proposal will facilitate the advancement of their own goals, and this is largely dependent upon environmental factors outside the president's control. Certainly spectacular success such as FDR's One Hundred Days and Lyndon Johnson's Great Society requires a congressional membership that by wide margins is prepared for its own reasons to act as the president needs and wants it to act. In both instances, congressional majorities saw passage of the president's program as furthering both their reelection and their policy goals. When, in contrast, solid majorities perceive passage of the president's program as clearly detrimental to their goal advancement, there is not much the president can do to engineer the support necessary for passage. If, for example, members perceive the president's program as seriously threatening their reelection or see it as antithetical to their notion of good public policy, what the president can do to or for a member will seldom be sufficient to alter the goal-related calculus of many members. Given the relatively meager resources the system bestows upon the president (especially vis-à-vis the Congress), he has available few strategies for altering members' goal-relevant calculus wholesale, even if that calculus is less heavily weighted against support of the president's program than in the above example. Nonpolicy quid pro quo bargaining—an appointment, a project, or an appearance at a fund-raiser for a vote—is only feasible for picking up support at the margins.

The attractiveness to presidents of going public as a strategy for influencing Congress is that it offers the possibility of altering the goal-relevant calculus of sizable groups of members. Yet context very much influences whether that strategy has much probability of success, and conducive circumstances are relatively rare (Kernell, 1986).

If a president is not blessed with a Congress that for its own reasons wants to pass his program, if neither quid pro quo bargaining nor going public are feasible as everyday strategies, are there other strategies a president can employ? A president can adjust what he asks Congress for. Clearly, the closer the president's requests are to the preferences of congressional majorities, the more likely Congress is to give the president what he requests. The president can also bargain on the substance of policies at the postproposal stage. Again, the closer the president moves toward the preferences of congressional majorities in what he will accept or settle for, the more likely Congress is to comply.

Such strategies of adjustment are commonplace in presidential-congressional relations. They are important in other areas of presidential involvement as well. In dealing with foreign powers, for example, presidents often engage in prior adjustment of their positions or in later bargaining over substance. In the design of such strategies, the president's individual characteristics, certainly including skill but also goals, may make a difference. The gauging of just how and how much an initial position should be adjusted and what sorts of substantive compromises to offer is an art, not a science. The purposive behavior framework does provide a basis for assessing the extent of the constraints imposed by the context and the range of the possible; it therefore provides an explicitly stated standard for assessing the level of presidential skill and its contribution to the outcome. I am not claiming that the framework is so powerful and its application so unambiguous that scholars will necessarily agree in a particular case upon just how constrained a president was by factors outside his control, what his options were, and, therefore, the extent to which he maximized the possibilities inherent in the situation. Rather, the framework's requirement that the scholar base his or her judgment upon an explicit, logical argument grounded in empirical evidence will clarify where the differences among scholars lie, which is the first step toward resolution.

Presidential skill is usually thought of as skill in strategy and maneuver. If we define skill as unusual proficiency at using the resources available to advance one's goals within the contraints of the environment, how presidents organize and then make use of their advisory networks should probably also be considered a central element of skill. Hult, in her review of that literature (chap. 3), finds "the lack of an explicit theoretical foundation on which to ground variable selection and hypothesis formulation." The purposive behavior framework directs the researcher to ask about the fit between a president's goals and his advisory system. Are certain systems better suited to advancing some goals rather than others? What are the environmental constraints—the key environmental actors—on the form of advisory systems? Do some presidents create advisory systems well suited to advancing their goals, while others, similarly situated, do not? That is, do some display more of this sort of skill than others?

ASSESSING SUCCESS AND FAILURE

Questions of presidential success and failure are both empirically and normatively important; yet scholarly writing in that area suffers from a lack of clear criteria. The purposive behavior framework's requirement that presidential goals be explicitly posited offers a way of dealing with the empirical question that may at least clarify the issues involved in the normative one. Certainly whether or not a president advances his goals is a solid initial basis for gauging degree of success or failure. If a president accomplishes what he sets out to achieve, if he attains his own goals whatever they happen to be, he is a success according to one standard. To take an extreme example, a president who has no policy goals should not, according to this initial standard, be judged by his administration's policy output. For him,

Light's arguments (as outlined in this volume) taken in empirical terms are not relevant. Of course, normatively, those arguments about the primacy of policy are far from irrelevant. The approach advocated here clarifies the normative question by making it obvious that both what the president tries to do and what he actually accomplishes must be considered. One can judge a president on whether he achieves his own goals or ours or does both, but if one does not distinguish the two bases, only confusion will result.

Implications for Research Design

The purposive behavior approach offers an analytic framework, not a true theory. It provides a useful analytic structure for dealing with specific empirical research questions. It cannot shed much light on highly abstract, globally conceived questions about presidential leadership. My reading of the presidential literature, although certainly not exhaustive, convinces me that progress lies in focusing upon theoretically interesting but reasonably concrete and not too broadly defined questions. Thus, in his study of the president's agenda Light focuses upon a set of questions circumscribed enough to enable him to carry out a convincing empirical study from which significant generalizations emerge (1983). Rose worries about "a series of unrelated studies that do not contribute to cumulative understanding" (1990, 24). Overly broad studies, where the breadth is purchased at the expense of precision in conceptualization and rigor in marshaling empirical substantiation, contribute even less. A common theoretical approach can provide the linkage among methodologically sound but inevitably narrower studies that is necessary for cumulation.

The purposive behavior approach is most likely to prove fruitful when relatively concrete and empirically observable presidential decisions, activities, or patterns of behavior are the focal variable. An advantage of this approach not previously discussed is its amelioration of the small-N problem. If our cases are presidents, we almost always have more explanatory variables than cases, a methodologically untenable situation. If, in contrast, our cases are decisions or instances of certain types of behavior or situations that elicit presidential activity, the small-N problem is often less acute. For example, in studying presidential-congressional relations, the president's requests or the items on the congressional agenda, variously defined, might be the cases. In studying the relationship between the president and the public, presidential influence attempts might be the cases. To be sure, these cases are not statistically independent of one another. We cannot, via this approach, obtain the statistical leverage that an actual increase in the number of presidents would bring; this is not magic. Yet for many research questions this approach will increase statistical and analytic leverage over a presidents-as-cases approach and will encourage a much needed rigor in the operationalization of variables.

In the presidency field as in others, rigor, when not bought by simple-mindedness, has a high payoff, because only rigor ensures that our findings are replicable and thus intersubjectively valid. On the theoretical end of the research enterprise, rigor means our propositions are derived from an explicitly stated logical structure—a theoretical framework, if not a theory; on the empirical end, rigor means that operationalizations of variables be clear and replicable, and that implies quantification where possible.

The lack of data that are quantitative in their "natural state" has long been considered a problem in presidency research. If presidency scholars do focus upon decisions, behavior, or other relatively concrete and observable phenomena, and if they approach their task with imagination and a certain amount of daring, considerable progress in quantitative operationalization of key variables seems possible. Some presidency scholars have pursued such a research strategy, Peterson (1990), Light, and Edwards being notably successful examples.

Here again the history of congressional scholarship may offer some lessons. For years, congressional roll call data, which are "naturally" quantitative, were quantitatively analyzed by scholars to answer questions about voting alignments at the aggregate level and member voting decisions at the individual level. Other research questions for which no naturally quantitative data existed were studied qualitatively. Over time, however, scholars began to realize that other, not quite so "naturally" quantitative, data could nevertheless be quantitatively analyzed (e.g., committee assignment request data; Shepsle, 1978). Scholars began to use roll call data differently and to shed light on a very different set of questions (e.g., about norm abidance in the Senate, patterns of floor decision making in both houses, institutional change; Smith, 1989; Sinclair, 1989). They became increasingly innovative about generating quantitative data from elite interviews and from the documentary record to answer difficult questions, such as who within the legislature influenced the shaping of legislation, who (the president or his congressional adversaries) prevailed on a given piece of legislation, or how legislatively active has the majority party leadership been over time (Hall, 1987; Sinclair, 1992). To be sure, a certain amount of daring is needed in such an enterprise; the decisions one makes in quantitatively operationalizing these variables are difficult and never unassailable. Yet, by proceeding in this manner we are forced into a precision that, at minimum, allows us to pinpoint where our differences lie. And that is a prerequisite to the sort of fruitful exchange that leads to progress.

Conclusion

The presidency field is replete with historically rich accounts, careful detailed descriptions, and perceptive ideas. What is lacking is a set of broadly accepted generalizations; even sharp, clearly defined controversies are few. Too many scholars have attempted to deal with questions of presidential decision making and presidential leadership in all their complexity; inevitably, the myriad of variables dealt with have not been clearly conceptualized, and relationships among the variables have not been clearly specified. Consequently, such work has not cumulated into a body of commonly accepted generalizations.

The purposive behavior approach outlined here provides a framework for studying the presidency that offers the hope of cumulation. It identifies a limited number of crucial variables and specifies how they are linked. The assumption that the president rationally pursues specified goals together with an understanding based upon previous empirical work of the context allows the scholar to identify a limited number of key actors in the president's environment. The president attends to those actors because their behavior significantly affects the president's chances of attaining his goals. The president's behavior is a function of his goals and of (his reactions to) the key actors. The outcome is a function of the president's behavior and of the key actors' behavior, which in turn is a function of their own goals and of the actors key to the achievement of their goals, which may, of course, include the president. The approach can be used as an interpretative framework for case studies; it can also provide the infrastructure for a model yielding testable hypotheses.

As illustratively applied here, the framework suggests that context variables are major shapers of presidential decisions and also are heavily determinative of outcomes directly. The framework does, however, make it possible to incorporate individual variation across presidents—in skill, in aims—in one's research in an analytically tractable way. Earlier, I suggested conceptualizing leadership as having occurred when the outcome was what the president intended (that is, it was consonant with his goals, ultimate or proximate) and the president's behavior had some significant effect in bringing about the outcome. The purposive behavior approach makes possible the identification of leadership thus defined—a considerable virtue. As here applied, the approach also suggests that leadership depends to some extent upon the skillful exploitation of opportunities but ultimately much more upon what sorts of opportunities the context presents, and over that the president has little control.

Note

I would like to thank George Edwards, Bert Rockman, John Kessel, Fred Greenstein, the other participants at the Pittsburgh conference, and two unnamed reviewers for their helpful comments and suggestions.

References

Arnold, R. Douglas. 1990. *The Logic of Congressional Action*. New Haven: Yale University Press.
Bass, Bernard. 1990. *Bass and Stogdill's Handbook of Leadership*. 3d ed. New York: Free Press.
Bolling, Richard. 1968. *Power in the House*. New York: Dutton.
Cooper, Joseph, and David W. Brady. 1981. "Institutional Context and Leadership Style: The House from Cannon to Rayburn." *American Political Science Review* 75:411–25.
Edwards, George C. 1989. *At the Margins*. New Haven: Yale University Press.
Fenno, Richard. 1973. *Congressmen in Committees*. Boston: Little, Brown.
Grossman, Michael, and Martha Kuman. 1981. *Portraying the President: The White House and the News Media*. Baltimore: Johns Hopkins University Press.
Hall, Richard L. 1987. "Participation and Purpose in Committee Decision Making." *American Political Science Review* 81:105–27.
Hardeman, D. B., and Donald C. Bacon. 1987. *Rayburn: A Biography*. Austin: Texas Monthly Press.

Jacobson, Gary, and Samuel Kernell. 1981. *Strategy and Choice in Congressional Elections*. New Haven: Yale University Press.

Jones, Charles O. 1981. "House Leadership in an Age of Reform." In *Understanding Congressional Leadership*, ed. Frank H. Mackaman. Washington, D.C.: Congressional Quarterly Press.

Kernell, Samuel. 1986. *Going Public: New Strategies of Presidential Leadership*. Washington, D.C.: Congressional Quarterly Press.

Kinder, Donald, and David Sears. 1985. "Public Opinion and Political Behavior." In *Handbook of Social Psychology*, 3d ed., vol. 2, ed. G. Lindzey and E. Aronson. New York: Random House.

Krehbiel, Keith. 1988. "Spatial Models of Legislative Choice." *Legislative Studies Quarterly* 13:259–320.

Lanoue, David J. 1988. *From Camelot to the Teflon President: Economics and Presidential Popularity Since 1960*. New York: Greenwood.

Light, Paul. 1982. *The President's Agenda*. Baltimore: Johns Hopkins University Press.

Mackaman, Frank, ed. 1981. *Understanding Congressional Leadership*. Washington, D.C.: Congressional Quarterly Press.

Mayhew, David. 1974. *Congress: The Electoral Connection*. New Haven: Yale University Press.

Peterson, Mark. 1990. *Legislating Together*. Cambridge: Harvard University Press.

Rockman, Bert A. 1984. *The Leadership Question: The Presidency and the American System*. New York: Praeger.

Rhode, David, and Kenneth A. Shepsle. 1987. "Leaders and Followers in the House of Representatives: Reflections on Woodrow Wilson's 'Congressional Government.' " *Congress and the Presidency* 14:111–33.

Rose, Richard. 1990. "Evaluating the Presidency." Prepared for the Presidency Research Conference, University of Pittsburgh, 12–14 November.

Shepsle, Kenneth. 1978. *The Giant Jigsaw Puzzle: Democratic Committee Assignments in the Modern House*. Chicago: University of Chicago Press.

Sinclair, Barbara. 1983. "Purposive Behavior in the U.S. Congress: A Review Essay." *Legislative Studies Quarterly* 8 (February): 117–31.

———. 1985. "Agenda Control and Policy Success: The Case of Ronald Reagan and the 97th House." *Legislative Studies Quarterly* 20 (August): 291–314.

———. 1989. *Transformation of the U.S. Senate*. Baltimore: Johns Hopkins University Press.

———. 1990. "Congressional Leadership: A Review Essay and a Research Agenda." In *Leading Congress: New Styles, New Strategies*, ed. John Kornacki. Washington, D.C.: Congressional Quarterly Press.

———. 1992. "Strong Party Leadership in a Weak Party Era—The Evolution of Party Leadership in the Modern House." In *The Atomistic Congress*, ed. Ronald Peters and Allen Herteke. Armonk, N.Y.: M. E. Sharpe.

Smith, Steven. 1989. *Call to Order: Floor Politics in the House and Senate*. Washington, D.C.: Brookings.

Sperlich, Peter W. 1969. "Bargaining and Overload: An Essay on *Presidential Power*." In *The Presidency*, ed. Aaron Wildavsky. Boston: Little, Brown.

6

Cognitive Theory and the Presidency

SUSAN T. FISKE

*P*SYCHOLOGY underwent a revolution nearly two decades ago, and the new regime, with a few adjustments, is apparently here to stay. B. F. Skinner's last public remarks to the contrary, most psychologists now do not view cognitive science as the "creationism of psychology." Quite the contrary. After many years of relentless domination by behaviorism, which suppressed all discussions of the mind as scientific treason, American psychology overthrew that perspective in favor of cognitive approaches that embrace the mind. Through the years of behaviorist rule, however, there were pockets of resistance, many of them sheltered within social psychology. Social psychology has always provided a home for cognition, with an emphasis on attitudes as variables that intervene between social stimulus and individual response. Now that cognition enjoys a position of respect—some would say imperialistic and dictatorial power—social psychology's longstanding loyalty to cognition makes it an appropriate discipline to act as ambassador to other fields. Social cognition theory and research borrow heavily from cognitive psychology, but they adapt it to real-world interpersonal settings, which makes social cognition an able translator of cognitive insights for other disciplines further afield, such as politics.

This chapter selectively applies social cognition perspectives to problems within current scholarship on the presidency. In doing so, it argues that certain types of social cognitive explanation potentially provide new integrative themes, and perhaps a fresh unifying theory, to the well-established field of research on the presidency. In particular, it suggests that the complex interplay between motivation and cognition provides a fertile ground for understanding the president and surrounding political phenomena. The chapter commences with a précis of social cognition metatheory; that is, what views of the thinking person have been advanced within social cognition research, and what are the roles of motivation and cognition in each? Next, it addresses five broad topics within research on the presidency and applies major social cognitive frameworks to each, showing how they might give new perspectives to old problems.

A Social Cognition Cram Sheet

Social cognition research and theory have entertained four basic views of the social thinker (Fiske and Taylor, 1991), each of which has relevance to research on the American presidency. These evolving views of the social thinker provide sharply differing roles for motivation's interactions with cognition. The four basic views include the person as consistency seeker, trying to minimize cognitive discrepancies; naive scientist, searching for unbiased truth; cognitive miser, looking for a good enough understanding with minimal effort; and the motivated tactician, choosing among more and less effortful cognitive strategies, depending on motivation.

CONSISTENCY SEEKERS

Initially, people were viewed primarily as consistency seekers, an approach perhaps reflective of the political and social climate of the 1950s during which it was proposed. Essentially, the consistency seeker was seen as unable to tolerate inconsistency among the components (cognitive, affective, behavioral) of any given attitude. Cognitive dissonance theory (Festinger, 1957) is the best example of this approach, and it has certainly been applied to political analysis (e.g., Bronfenbrenner, 1961). With regard to the president and presidential advisers, for example, the consistency seeker approach would predict that, having taken a risky course (e.g., invading Grenada or Iraq), the decision makers would resist evidence that the move was ill-advised. Many readers are doubtless familiar with consistency theory and its various spin-offs. (For a contemporaneous survey, see Abelson et al., 1968; for a current evaluation, see Abelson, 1983.)

The role of motivation in the consistency seeker was central, in that the experience of psychological inconsistency was posited to be inherently aversive, driving people to rearrange their thoughts to fit together more comfortably. Consistency theories proliferated, but it became clear both that thinkers tolerate a fair amount of inconsistency and that other motives, such as accuracy, fairness, or efficiency, can intervene.

NAIVE SCIENTISTS

In reaction to the overarching (and oversimplifying) framework provided by consistency theories, attribution theories emerged as midrange theories making more modest claims. In essence, these theories portrayed people as naive scientists, in dogged and neutral pursuit of the truth about other people and themselves. Given complete information and careful calculation, people were posited to attain fairly accurate answers. The best example of such a theory is Kelley's (1972) analysis-of-variance model of attribution processes, whereby people seek to know which potential causal dimensions covary with which outcomes, in order to attribute causality to actors, circumstances, or objects, all by following standard scientific methods. With regard to presidential policy making, for example, Kelley's attribution theory would predict that an outcome such as a particular group's disproportionate unemployment would be analyzed thus: Do other disadvantaged groups have trouble finding jobs? (the consensus question). Does this group always have trouble finding jobs? (the consistency question). And does this group have troubles in areas other than employment? (the distinctiveness question). If the answer is no to the first and yes to the last two, then the causes of the phenomenon (unemployment) lie in the group (that is, inadequate family structure, inherent laziness), according to this logic. If, however, other disadvantaged groups also have trouble finding jobs, and this group's only major problem is consistent unemployment, then the cause may be something about the broader employment situation.

This example illustrates how one's (perhaps ideological) motivation to believe in one cause or the other might influence one's interpretation of the attributional data (e.g., Jervis, Lebow, and Stein, 1985, 164). Similarly, motivation was viewed in the naive scientist theories primarily as a potential source of error intruding on otherwise objective processes. As such, this type of naive scientist theory was posited more as a normative standard than as a fully descriptive theory.

COGNITIVE MISERS

It rapidly became clear that people are not such careful scientific thinkers in everyday reasoning and that our lives require far more cognitive coping than scientific analysis. Enter the cognitive miser viewpoint. The errors and biases in people's ordinary thought processes more descriptively portray us as doing well enough ("satisficing"), given our limited brains for confronting complex information environments. The best examples are the inferential heuristics (Kahneman and Tversky, 1973; for a review, see Kahneman, Slovic, and Tversky, 1982, or Nisbett and Ross, 1980) and the schema theories (for a review, see Fiske and Taylor, 1991, chaps. 4–5, or Higgins and Bargh, 1987). These cognitive shortcuts allow people to make rapid but not necessarily accurate judgments, and motivation has nothing to do with it. The cognitive miser perspective predicts that presidents and other people rely on historical scripts (for example, avoiding "another Vietnam" or "another Munich"), familiar stereotypes (for example, Saddam Hussein as Hitler), and other schemas noted by previous analysts of schema-based political decision making (Lau and Sears, 1986).

MOTIVATED TACTICIANS

However, the cognitive miser viewpoint tilted too far in emphasizing people's theory-driven processing over their attention to the information given. Consequently, the current generation of approaches presents a more balanced view of the social (and political) thinker as a motivated tactician (Fiske and Taylor, 1991), with a variety of cognitive strategies available, choosing among the more effortful and complete strategies or easy and approximate ones, as the motivational situation demands. Thus, in the current view, people who are appropriately motivated do not neglect the data in favor of their schemas; they combine their prior expectations with the available information, making adjustments to fit.

This viewpoint predicts an important role for motivated involvement in the degree of processing exerted by the thinking person. This is not to say that effort necessarily begets accuracy, for people often think hard only to construct elaborately justified biases. This perspective does suggest that people make cognitive choices in the heat of the cognitive battle to manage the barrage of information, but the choices are not so purposeful as to constitute a priori battle strategies; hence I have chosen the term *tactician,* not *strategist,* here and elsewhere.

Applications to Political Science

The basic message here is that political scientists may want to take a hard look at the usefulness of this fourth generation in social cognition research, viewing the thinking person as motivated tactician. It has much to recommend it. It acknowledges the variety of cognitive processes posited by the earlier approaches: the discrepancy reduction of the consistency seeker, the potential for the careful analysis exemplified by the naive scientist, and the shortcuts taken by the cognitive miser. But it also emphasizes a new role for motivation so far missing in social cognition research and perhaps, also, in political research that borrows from it. People are flexible thinkers, responsive to the demands of particular situations, and any complete account of their social (and political) behavior has to acknowledge both the variety of strategies at their disposal and the extent of their control over their strategies.

To this point, this motivated tactician perspective is illustrated in political analyses, as far as I know, mainly in terms of the flexible approaches available to political experts, as compared to novices (for an early review of such work, see Showers and Cantor, 1985; for a collection of such work in politics, see Krosnick, 1990). But discussing expertise as a kind of motivation does not entirely capture the point of the motivated tactician perspective.

Many different motives are potentially relevant to political decision making: accuracy, self-presentation, self-esteem, accountability, ideological biases, time pressure, to name a few. One question, of course, is which motives operate when, and another question is which take precedence when several are present. These are not easily answered in studying either an individual or an aggregate. However, what the motivated tactician perspective does suggest is that one analyze the goals of the particular decision maker (whether president, staffer, or voter) in the particular situation. Both the individual and the situation are important here. One can often predict or explain which goals have highest priority in a particular setting or for a particular individual, and this then accounts for the cognitive strategies followed by that decision maker. A goal-based analysis is more specific than a general, motivationally oriented analysis, because it requires a careful analysis of the task immediately before the person in question. The immediate stimulus is often a better predictor of behavior than is some global background variable (e.g., Ajzen and Fishbein, 1977). The same is true of predicting cognitive strategies, which is of course the business of social cognition research and its applications.

The cognitive strategies may be more or less careful, broadly speaking. In the next section of this chapter, I introduce a distinction between two types of decision making, category based and attribute based. This distinction comes up throughout the remaining sections, as well, for it has general applicability. Category-based thinking is top-down, theory-driven, expectancy-driven thinking. It looks for patterns that fit prior knowledge and then applies the content, decisions, evaluations, rules, and patterns associated with that prior knowledge to the understanding of the new information deemed to fit. As long as the fit is good enough, the decision maker has a ready-made set of responses to the new information, without having to overanalyze it. Such efficiency has obvious benefits in an information-rich environment. But it has obvious costs as well: one may apply the wrong prior category, or the new instance may be a poor fit to even the most applicable prior category.

Decision makers are no fools; they do check the fit of the selected category to the new information, and if the fit is blatantly poor, or if they sufficiently scrutinize the new information, they may recategorize or subcategorize the new instance. Given sufficiently poor fit, people can move to an altogether different type of processing, attribute-based thinking. In this case, information is processed bottom-up, data driven, piecemeal. This has the potential to be a more accurate type of processing, as each attribute is assessed separately, but of course perceptions of individual attributes can be distorted, whether alone or within a gestalt. More discussion of these two types of thinking (as well as relevant references and examples) follow in subsequent sections, but for the moment, the point is that people have available different styles of thinking, and the flexibility to use them under different circumstances: hence the appellation *motivated tactician.*

There is much room for growth here, in applying various types of motivation to these different kinds of political thinking in research on the presidency. The next sections of this chapter represent some first efforts in that direction, based almost entirely on five essays' worth of introduction to scholarship on the presidency. The motivated tactician perspective is applied to each area of research, and the category-based/attributed-based distinction is another central theme in much of the work. The overall goal is to illustrate a social-cognitive analysis of these issues.

Presidential Selection, as the Motivated TacticianDoes It

As John Aldrich (chap. 1) points out, social cognition approaches have already informed some work on presidential selection; indeed, most of my own limited work in politics comes from an understanding that candidate perception is in part a kind of person perception. Beyond this type of prior work, a social cognition perspective nevertheless has a broader point to contribute, based on the motivated tactician viewpoint that has recently supplemented the cognitive miser viewpoint.

The cognitive miser perspective begins by suggesting that people hoard their overtaxed cognitive capacity, and one important type of savings is people's reliance on already organized prior knowledge, which often goes by the term *schema* (although the terms *category, expectancy, prototype, script,* and *stereotype* can each fit too; see Fiske and Taylor, 1991, chap. 4, for a discussion of the differences). If one can apply generic prior knowledge to a new instance, so the argument goes, one need not examine the new instance quite as thoroughly. How might this help to explain the process of presidential selection?

At the candidacy stage, there are certain categories of people who fit the party's candidate schema, and such people are more likely to be encouraged to run than those who do not. Apart from demographic features (age, sex, ethnicity), the candidate schema doubtless has other features (appearance, personality, background, not to mention competencies and policies; see Kinder and Fiske, 1986). Finally, resemblance to or difference from previous officeholders and candidates can be an important, specific property of a schema (it was an advantage to Gary Hart that he was not another Walter Mondale; it was a disadvantage to Mondale that he was seen as fitting the Carter schema).

Why call a collection of features a schema? Because the premise is that this cluster allows rapid categorization of people who do and do not fit. And, once categorized, the perceiver fills in the gaps where information is incomplete or ambiguous. Moreover, the features themselves are interconnected and interactive (in a prospective candidate, being a wealthy male—upper crust, powerful, sophisticated—may not have the same implications as being a wealthy female—pampered, dilettante, socialite). In short, party members' organized preconceptions of who is a prototypical candidate doubtless influence who is encouraged to run.

Similar phenomena occur during the primaries and general election campaign. As Aldrich notes, people's schemas for party and ideology influence their reception of information during a campaign (and this is more than the old model of party identification as a filter for campaign information). Elsewhere, my colleagues and I argue that people's prototype or schema for the ideal president—responsive in part to the shortcomings of the previous president—significantly influences their evaluations of the candidates (Kinder, et al., 1980). Again, how does this differ from the rational person's measured list evaluating a candidate's pros and cons? Schema-based thinking shortcuts the details of the particular instance for the broad outlines of the generic case. Some might even argue that it generates rapid, schema-triggered emotional responses that apply the affect associated with the category to the particular instance (for the general model, see Fiske, 1982; Fiske and Pavelchak, 1986). Affective responses to candidates have been shown to outweigh considerations of personality and even party identification (Abelson et al., 1982). Hence the voter's schemas for candidates, parties, and issues can trigger relatively spontaneous affective reactions to the candidates.

Obviously, this argument holds a brief for the schema- or category-based view of candidate selection. But, in line with the motivated tactician view of voters and politicians, I argue that people do not inevitably operate in this category-based fashion. Under some circumstances, people also operate in accord with the rational actor mode of decision making, which I have elsewhere termed *piecemeal* or *attribute-based* processing (for examples with social psychology, see Ajzen and Fishbein, 1980; Anderson, 1981). In impressions formed of candidates, this type of process might resemble the summed cross products of the evaluations of relevant attributes (personality traits, party, issues, appearance, etc.) by their relative importance. This type of processing better fits the predominant views of candidate evaluation, as I understand them, whereby candidate positions are compared one by one with the voter's positions. One major problem is how psychologically realistic such a process might be; do people really evaluate each attribute in isolation, weight it, combine the weight and the evaluation, and then add it to some running total? A more plausible psychological model has been proposed, using a serial anchoring and adjustment process (Lopes, 1982), but it has never been tested. Whatever the exact computational method people might use, the attribute-by-attribute process is an effortful, capacity-consuming way to evaluate a candidate, so it is unlikely to be used except when people are highly motivated, are not in a hurry, and have complete information.

In short, a psychologically realistic view of candidate selection processes best fits a continuum model, running from category-based processes at one end to attribute-based processes at the other. People are predisposed to use the easier, category-based processes, unless motivations intervene to encourage intermediate processes that retain the category but modify it slightly to fit better. If that effort fails, and people are highly motivated, they will turn to the taxing, attribute-oriented type of process now emphasized in the voting literature. This continuum model provides a richer view of human decision making, for it suggests an interaction of actor characteristics and the decision at hand. In particular, involvement in the outcome will encourage more complex decision making, while indifference encourages the easier category-based type of decision making. Dual-mode models of this type have been proposed for person perception (Brewer, 1988; Fiske and Neuberg, 1990; Fiske and Pavelchak, 1986) and persuasion processes (Chaiken, 1980; Chaiken, Liberman, and Eagly, 1989; Petty and Cacioppo, 1984, 1986; see Fiske, 1986, for an earlier application to politics).

What kinds of motivations are likely to encourage the more effortful type of decisions traditionally favored by the presidential selection literature? A growing catalog of motivations can be roughly indexed by those that increase the costs of being wrong and those that increase the cost of being indecisive (for a review, see Fiske and Taylor, 1991, chap. 5). When the potential cost of being wrong is increased, people make more complex (but not necessarily more accurate) judgments. The perceived costs of being wrong are increased by explicit accuracy motivations (Neuberg, 1989; Neuberg & Fiske, 1987), by accountability to third parties (Tetlock, 1983a, 1983b, 1985; Tetlock and Boettger, 1989; Tetlock and Kim, 1987), by interdependence between the perceiver and the target of a decision (Erber and Fiske, 1984; Neuberg and Fiske, 1987; Ruscher and Fiske, 1990), by concerns about self-presentation to others and fear of public invalidity (Freund, Kruglanski, and Shpitzajzen, 1985; Kruglanski and Freund, 1983; Kruglanski and Mayseless, 1988), by deliberative decision making prior to implementation (Gollwitzer and Kinney, 1989), and by emphasizing the potential harm to the other person (Freund, Kruglanski, and Shpitzajzen, 1985). On the other hand, when the potential costs of being indecisive are increased, people make rapid, good-enough decisions. The perceived cost of being indecisive is increased by time pressure (Jamieson and Zanna, 1989; Kruglanski and Freund, 1983; Kruglanski and Mayseless, 1988), having to communicate information to others, as opposed to receiving it (e.g., Cohen, 1961; Higgins, McCann, and Fondacaro, 1982; Hoffman, Mischel, and Baer, 1984; Leventhal 1962; Zajonc, 1960), generally operating in a narrative, as opposed to scientific, mode (Zukier, 1986; Zukier and Pepitone, 1984; cf. Leyens, 1983), threats to high self-esteem (Crocker et al., 1987), and anxiety from public criticism or embarrassment (Wilder and Shapiro, 1989a, 1989b).

To what extent are ordinary voters' decisional motivations likely to emphasize the costs of being wrong over the costs of being indecisive? Politics being a sideshow in the circus of life, most voters are more likely to be concerned about making efficient, rather than totally justifiable, decisions. Most voters are not accountable to others and not especially worried about the self-presentational implications of their choices nor the impact of their decision on the candidate. On the other hand, voters do have to make up their minds at some point, may communicate their decisions briefly to others, but do not have to meet the standards of scientific discourse. In short, the typical voter probably worries more about being indecisive as the election approaches than about being wrong. This will differ from voter to voter, and perhaps from campaign to campaign, but it all fits with the idea of decision makers as motivated tacticians who have the flexibility to use different tactics as needed. It is ultimately an empirical question, which may help to specify better how presidents are actually selected at each step of the process.

Personality and Leadership Style: Who Is Graceful Under Pressure?

Just as individual voters selecting the president can make their decisions in relatively categorical or relatively rational, attribute-driven ways, so too the individual occupying the Oval Office can make relatively category-based or attribute-based decisions. In the case of the president, we are seeking to explain the behavior of an individual, so the appropriate methods obviously differ from those used to understand the aggregate behavior of voters. Although social cognition research is not well-equipped to predict the behavior of individuals, a few approaches might lend themselves to a sample of presidents in which N ranges from one to about forty (depending on one's purposes and data). These speculations assume an affirmative answer to Erwin Hargrove's first question (chap. 2), namely that leaders do matter. And in particular, they address the person-by-situation interaction that places the individual president in context, as Hargrove urges. The cognitive approach has most to say about presidential motivations and cognitive processes (an excellent contemporary illustration of this type of approach may be found in Cantor and Kihlstrom, 1987). Here, I simply want to suggest a few ways to explain a president's proclivity to make decisions in one of the two modes outlined just previously.

RIGID VERSUS FLEXIBLE THINKING

Because we seek to explain the behavior of an individual rather than a huge aggregate, we have the luxury of examining individual differences that predict decision-making style. For example, consider the dimension rigid versus flexible thinking. Ever since work on the authoritarian personality (Adorno et al., 1950), psychologists have hypothesized a relationship between a general style of rigid thinking and prejudice. Accordingly, one might expect a more general relationship between a rigid style of thinking and category-based thinking specifically. Psychologists have proposed various personality differences that affect category-based thinking: category width (Pettigrew, 1958, 1982); dogmatism (Rokeach, 1960; Troldahl and Powell, 1965); ambiguity tolerance (Norton, 1975); right-wing authoritarianism, which covers authoritarian submission, conventionalism, and authoritarian aggression (Altemeyer, 1981); categorical thinking (a subscale of the constructive thinking inventory, Epstein and Meier, 1989); and need for structure (Neuberg and Newsom, 1990; Thompson, Naccarato, and Parker, 1989). Each of these personality dimensions, in one way or another, assesses people's propensity to think in well-defined, category-based ways or in loose, flexible ways, and this has obvious bearing on a president's leadership style.

MOTIVES TO THINK

Consider, as another example, motives to think at all. Rational choice processes require more time and effort than do category-based processes, as indicated by research on two-mode models of social cognition as well as other work indicating the category-driven effects of time pressure (e.g., Jamieson and Zanna, 1989; Kruglanski and Freund, 1983). Some people are typically more motivated than others to think, and perhaps this proclivity carries over to a president's leadership style. (Popular depictions of recent occupants of the Oval Office might seem to anchor the extremes of a president liking to think too much, in Carter's case, and liking to think too little, in Reagan's case.) A number of well-established individual differences potentially describe this dimension: cognitive complexity (Bieri, 1955; Scott, 1966), need for achievement (McClelland, et al., 1958), repression-sensitization (Epstein and Fenz, 1967), need for cognition (Cacioppo and Petty, 1982), and uncertainty orientation (Sorrentino and Hewitt, 1984; Sorrentino, Short, and Raynor, 1984). People's motives to think much (these dimensions) are correlated with their tendency to think in rigid or flexible ways (the previous set of dimensions). Nevertheless, the two are conceptually distinct.

DYSPHORIC THINKING

To say that someone who thinks rigidly or does not like to think is more likely to make decisions in a category-based fashion seems like a safe bet. Nevertheless, there may be other less obvious types of predispositions that would lead to category-based versus rational leadership. Dysphoric thinking is one. There is some evidence that dysphoric thinking—that is, thinking with a negative emotional outlook—is correlated with narrow, category-based thinking. For example, positive moods lead to broader, looser, more inclusive, and novel categories (Isen, 1987), which suggests that relatively optimistic leaders might include more attributes in their decisions. People in the pit of their circadian cycle stereotype more (Bodenhausen, 1990), which suggests that leaders feeling depleted (and more likely to experience negative feelings) might categorize more freely. The point here is not simply that presidents in bad moods will focus on negative categories, although that may be the case (Erber, 1991). Rather, presidents in habitually dysphoric states may not trouble to think so carefully and hard about others. Richard Nixon comes to mind as a recent example of a president who may have been depressive and certainly stereotyped his enemies. Although the relationship is doubtless complex (Mackie et al., 1989), it is worth exploring further. Accordingly, one might consider individual differences in self-esteem (Janis and Field, 1959; Rosenberg, 1965), depression (Beck, 1967), negative attitudes toward people in general (Christie et al., 1973), optimism in general (Scheier and Carver, 1985), or optimism and future (planning) orientation (Epstein and Meier, 1989).

TRADITIONAL STEREOTYPING

Finally, combining these ideas about lack of thought and negative thinking, a social psychologist naturally thinks of traditional stereotyping. People who stereotype one group tend to stereotype other groups, as psychologists have known for decades (Adorno et al., 1950; Allport, 1954). Similarly, one might find that individual differences in the tendency to stereotype specific groups spill over to predict leaders' tendencies toward more category-based impressions generally. Examples include anti-Semitism (Adorno et al., 1950), attitudes toward women (Spence and Helmreich, 1972), modern or subtle racism (McConahay, 1983), more direct pro-black and anti-black attitudes (Katz and Hass, 1988), and attitudes toward homosexuals (Hudson and Ricketts, 1980; Larsen et al., 1980).

These approaches do not uniquely subscribe to any one personality theory. Rather, these researchers work in various theoretical frameworks, but all their work bears on thinking styles, which fits the

charge of this chapter. These personality dimensions illustrate proclivities to make decisions in certain styles, and many of these dimensions have sound empirical literatures behind them. Hence, as a way
to examine leadership styles—both the president's own decision making and presidential management of decision making among advisers—they would seem to have some promise. Unfortunately, we
cannot administer these personality scales to presidents, but one
might examine the historical record for evidence that they would fit
the tendencies suggested by these scales. Although designed to quan-
tify individual differences among aggregates of people, these personality differences also provide rich material for the narrative
explanations more typical of presidential biography. As a whole, this
approach is probably closest to that of I. L. Janis's (1989) work on
policy makers' degree of vigilant problem solving.

A social psychologist would be remiss not to add a note about social context and its impact on thinking styles. Each of these personality factors has analogous contextual factors, some of which were
noted earlier. Just as the motivational situation can affect ordinary
decision makers (e.g., voters), so too it can affect presidents. Thus,
certain motivational factors were described earlier as increasing the
costs of being wrong (such as perceived accountability, important interdependence, worries about being perceived as careful, need for accuracy, extended deliberation, and salient possibilities of harming
others); these situationally based motivations can promote "rational"
or at least complex thinking in presidents as much as in anyone else.
And just as surely, factors related to stress (time pressure, having to
tell a good story, avoiding technical or scientific thinking, anxiety
about public humiliation, and self-esteem threats) must have the opposite effect, encouraging category-based thinking.

It would be reasonable to ask how these various contextual motivations balance each other and the personality factors described earlier. How do we know which motives operate when? The relative
salience of the cues that spark the various motives, along with the
cognitive accessibility of motives, help determine which predominate
in any given situation for any given person. As the next section indicates, social cognition researchers know a thing or two about how to
predict the focus of people's attention, which in turn shapes people's
motivations. The issue of attention also takes us into another topic in
research on the presidency.

Policy Making off the Top of One's Head

What grabs the attention of a president, or anyone else, for that matter? In a provocative essay, Paul Light argues that, for a variety of reasons, short-term goals are becoming more prominent in presidential policy making (chap. 4). In effect, he argues that only in recent times have presidents been top-of-the-head policy makers. Social cognition research might argue that presidents, like other people, very often make decisions and policy on the basis of whatever catches their attention but that what specific issues capture their attention differs in potentially predictable—or at least explicable—ways.

People's attention generally is captured by whatever or whoever is novel in context or relative to expectations (for reviews of this literature, see McArthur, 1981; Taylor and Fiske, 1978; Fiske and Taylor, 1991, chap. 7). The seemingly trivial factor of salience that happens to catch one's eye or ear has profound effects on cognitive processes. People make more extreme judgments about salient stimuli; people are more likely to view salient stimuli as causal; salient stimuli receive more weight in judgments. In short, just because something happens to capture attention, it is assumed to be important (see Iyengar and Kinder, 1987, for a political application of these principles). One might imagine that presidents, overwhelmed as they are by one of the most demanding jobs in the world, would be especially vulnerable to the dynamics of salience. Hence, the latest poll result, the sudden international crisis, and the late-breaking domestic issue all predictably dominate longer-term concerns. The news carries what is new (novel); as the news media carry ever greater quantities of novel information, long-term perspectives recede.

The only way to overcome these cognitive tendencies to focus on novelty is to have a conscious goal that overrides simple salience. Much of the time, when people do not have explicit goals, they are at the mercy of salience, and they make salience-driven judgments. If presidents are human (often rumored to be the case), then they too must have the most compelling of goals in order to override the effects of moment-to-moment salience. In managerial terms, it is the difference between putting out fires and taking the time to design a firebreak. Another way to frame Light's complaint is that presidential attention has been captured by novelty and short-term political salience, to the exclusion of long-term goals. To the extent that the presidency is a job characterized by constant information overload, it is not surprising that the president's attention focuses on the short term. Instead, from the perspective of social cognition, one needs theories to explain the generation of long-term goals that override the more common case of salience.

Perhaps social cognition theories can be helpful here as well. Goals, like other mental constructs, are maintained by what has been activated recently or frequently in the past (Bargh, 1990; Higgins and King, 1981; Wyer and Srull, 1981; for a review, see Higgins and Bargh, 1987). If many other inputs activate competing goals, then the original goal is pushed into the background. Again, we see the importance of information overload in leaving a president (or anyone else) at the mercy of momentary salience and other trivial influences. As William James described it, "attention with effort is all that any case of volition implies" (1983, 264). Intentionality demands the "hard choice" of sustained attention to the one goal (Fiske, 1989). If attentional capacity is strained, maintaining a focus on chosen goals is jeopardized. Jimmy Carter's notorious attention to detail probably prevented his ability to implement long-term planning, except for lifelong agendas tied into his religious values (e.g., his focus on human rights violations), which would have been more resistant to contextual factors. In contrast, Ronald Reagan's notorious lack of attention to detail probably enabled him to concentrate on implementing broad ideological goals. Such simplifying strategies enable a focus on long-term goals.

Of course, goals can reflect short-term or long-term concerns. Suppose that a particular goal is indeed kept in the foreground by recent and frequent activation, due to intent or circumstances. It will tend to shape the interpretation of ambiguous stimuli into concepts relevant to the person's goals. Presidents who assimilate all and sundry matters into their core preoccupations illustrate this process. Hence, the short-term politician will view every issue as a public relations opportunity; the long-term prophet will view every issue as a stepping-stone to history. Biographers of particular presidents doubtless use their subjects' slanted interpretations as evidence of the most salient and accessible issues. Scholars who focus on the broader role demands of presidents could use such biased assimilation as evidence of the ebb and flow of particular presidential concerns over the decades. Such interpretational biases could be readily coded from public records of speeches, press conferences, and memoirs.

Thus far, we have seen that attention may influence policy making in two ways. First, factors that attract attention are given more weight in decision making. Second, attention determines which goals are most accessible and therefore more influential. A third role of attention is to influence categorization processes. That is, attention determines which of many available categories are applied to a given person, problem, or event. Much as attention determines the weight of particular attributes in a decision and of particular goals within an array of possible goals, so attentional focus determines which categories are used when. The principles of recent and frequent activation, temporal primacy, and novelty are all attentional principles that predict category use.

A final note about policy making and attention: presidents and other people do differ in their attentional capacity, not just as a function of native intelligence. In domains of their own expertise, people have the ability to organize details into larger chunks of information (Chase and Simon, 1973), leaving them more capacity for complex understanding (Fiske and Kinder, 1981; Fiske, Kinder, and Larter, 1983; Fiske, Lau, and Smith, 1990). Experts in a particular domain are simply more efficient and organized in their attentional capacities and consequently stay more informed, more organized, and more opinionated (see Krosnick, 1990, for a collection of essays on political expertise). Hence, many effects of temporary salience and accessibility may be diminished for a domain-specific expert. What, then, shapes the cognitive processes of domain-specific experts in the White House? The next section addresses another set of cognition-motivation interactions.

Advisory Networks as Protective In-groups

The coterie of people surrounding the president only rarely serve the rational actor model of advising, according to the literature reviewed by Karen Hult (chap. 3). Indeed, the impression that emerges is dominated by in-group politics, rather than reasoned expertise. For example, the description of Eisenhower's cabinet—as promoting coherence, a sense of participation, and support—suggests more socioemotional than task functions. Similarly, moving the vice president closer to the Oval Office encourages the boundaries that define "us" (executive branch) versus "them" (Congress, the judiciary, the media, the citizens, or whoever the relevant out-group is). Similarly, the idea that staff units spanning White House boundaries are suspect and less influential again reinforces the idea of the White House as protected in-group. The president's centralized control over the advisory network is apparently especially important in the turbulent foreign policy arena, which is typically more involving to presidents than domestic policy. All these interpretations fit the notion of the advisory network functioning as a protective in-group.

An in-group is defined by the interdependence of its members, and presidential relationships with other network actors vary in their volume, salience, diversity, directness, and nature, according to Hult. This list uncannily resembles the list of ways that interdependence structures differ in other types of relationships (Kelley et al., 1983). Moreover, the preoccupation with inner and outer circles within the in-group characterizes groups with a centralized focus, as does the lack of interaction among key actors apart from the president. That is, the interdependence structure of the advisory network revolves entirely around proximity to the president, who ultimately controls the most important outcomes in the system.

Attention follows power (Dépret and Fiske, in press). People scrutinize others on whom their outcomes depend, in order to enhance their own sense of prediction and control (Erber and Fiske, 1984; Neuberg and Fiske, 1987; Ruscher and Fiske, 1990). In particular, outcome-dependent people attend to the most informative cues about the powerful other, and they make dispositional (personality) inferences about them. Hence, it makes sense that advisory networks revolve around the president. And I wager that network members spend an inordinate amount of cognitive energy analyzing the president's personality, in order to predict future behavior as it relates to their own concerns. Moreover, to the extent a group is interdependent, the members examine each other closely, to determine who is reliable and who is not (Ruscher et al., 1991).

The in-group presupposes an out-group, us versus them. It is a fundamental example of category-based thinking. People's understanding of out-groups is that they are all alike, different from us, and bad besides. Any given *us* category is preferred to any given *them* category, under most circumstances (Brewer, 1979; Brewer and Kramer, 1985; Tajfel, 1978, 1982; Wilder, 1981, 1986; one historical precedent is Sherif et al., 1961). Merely labeling people as a group leads them to want to reward their own group more and to see its members as superior, less responsible for any failures, and more responsible for successes. For example, the in-group's failures follow the "self-serving attributional bias" (for reviews, see Brewer and Kramer, 1985; Deaux, 1976; Hamilton and Trolier, 1986; Hewstone and Jaspers, 1984; Pettigrew, 1979). Our group's failures are due to external circumstances beyond our control, while our successes are our own doing; their group's failures show how incompetent they really are, while any successes must be due to chance or extraordinary effort. Does this sound like any presidential press conferences or memoirs you have ever encountered?

In the psychological evidence on these points, the striking point is that even arbitrary in-groups create the sense of members being similar to oneself (e.g. Billig and Tajfel, 1973; Hamilton, 1979; Wilder and Cooper, 1981); the apparent ease with which intergroup bias can be created is surprising. In-group bias does not stem, contrary to what one might think, from pure unmitigated self-interest; it occurs even when people do not personally benefit or did not personally contribute to the group (Brown, Schmidt, and Collins, 1988). People apparently are motivated to give the in-group as a whole a relative advantage over the out-group (Wilder, 1986). In-group favoritism is a clear and persistent bias, probably stronger in the real world than in the laboratory. Competition and status differences between groups (typical in the political world) exaggerate in-group favoritism, as does being outnumbered (Gerard and Hoyt, 1974) or drawing attention to group membership (Abrams, 1985). All these factors tend to exaggerate in-group biases among the White House advisory network.[1]

Moreover, such real world factors are likely to have important effects on intragovernmental interactions. In intergroup negotiations, coercion is perceived to influence the out-group, but conciliation is perceived to influence the in-group (Rothbart and Hallmark, 1988). This finding may have special relevance to the tactics chosen by the White House to influence the relevant out-group, as in the often months-long budget negotiations between the White House and Congress in a divided government.

In-group members use several well-established cognitive strategies to support their in-group favoritism and to set themselves apart from relevant out-groups. Each of these standard social cognitive effects has advisory network parallels, some of which have been apparently documented, and some of which await support in what would be a fruitful line of inquiry. For example, memory is affected by in-group/out-group status; people recall more details about an in-group member than an out-group member (Park and Rothbart, 1982). And people tend to recall negative things about out-groups (e.g., Howard and Rothbart, 1980). They also recall how the out-group differs from the in-group, more than their similarities (Wilder, 1981). Memory for the out-group thus tends to support people's in-group biases.

Categorizing and labeling the out-group also makes them seem more uniform than would otherwise be true, thus minimizing the variability within the out-group. Simply categorizing people into groups minimizes within-group variability and maximizes between-group differences (e.g. Tajfel, Sheikh, and Gardner, 1964; Tajfel and Wilkes, 1963; Wilder, 1978, 1981). People are particularly sensitive to new information that enhances between-group differences (Krueger, Rothbart, and Sriram, 1989).

Hence, this in-group/out-group perception exaggerates the differences between the White House and outsiders (whether the opposition party, the Congress, the media, or the citizenry). People more generally perceive themselves and their own group to be different from the out-group (Allen and Wilder, 1979), and they seek information that confirms this perception (Wilder and Allen, 1978). Categorization's effect of reducing perceived variability is even stronger when people are considering groups to which they do not belong. A group of outsiders appears less variable than one's own group. This out-group homogeneity effect occurs across a wide range of groups. The out-group homogeneity effect is larger and more reliable than the in-group heterogeneity effect, and it is even stronger for preexisting, real world groups than for artificially created laboratory groups (for a review, see Mullen and Hu, 1989). Perceiving the out-group as relatively less variable may serve to make them seem more predictable, even as individuals.

People not only perceive out-group members as less variable than in-group members, they also have less complex conceptualizations of them, which result in more polarized evaluations of the out-group members (Linville, 1982; Linville and Jones, 1980; see also Judd and Lusk, 1984). People's simple-minded views of out-groups may be reflected in their knowing well only a few members of the out-group. As a consequence, one bit of favorable or unfavorable information has much more impact when little else is already known about the out-group, but because a lot is already known about the in-group, one bit of information is only minor by comparison and has limited impact. Thus, a bad out-group member is worse and a good out-group member is better than comparable in-groupers. Thus, out-group members elicit unreasonably extreme evaluations.[2] It is discouraging to consider the implications of these cognitive mechanisms for politics between the executive and legislative branches in a divided government.

To summarize, the cognitive-motivational dynamics of in-group/out-group perceptions include an array of category-based thinking: in-group favoritism in resource allocation and memory structure, maximizing between-group differences, minimizing within-group variability, viewing the out-group as homogeneous, having less complex conceptualizations of out-group members, and evaluating them in extreme terms. In this context, it makes good psychological sense, both cognitively and motivationally, that presidents would turn to the core of the in-group under crisis and that the network tends to shrink over the course of a term. Both mechanisms provide the protection of a tested in-group as outside pressures mount.

The extent to which the president, as motivated tactician, uses the advisory network as a protective in-group doubtless depends on the individual president's goals; in her chapter, Hult lists involvement, breadth of search, and activity, which are good motivational variables that affect the degree of category-based (schematic) versus attribute-based (rational actor) information processing. More explicit presidential strategies in pursuing certain goals also motivate network use, according to Hult, a problem contingency approach that equally fits the motivated tactician viewpoint.

The in-group/out-group phenomena have both interpersonal and task implications, as interpersonal relationships may impede the flow of information or may bias the information that does get through. There are, as well, other, more narrowly task-related cognitive factors to consider in advisory networks. Earlier, I noted that experts may be less prone to some effects of arbitrary attentional factors than are nonexperts. The White House staff is of course composed of domain-specific experts, whose job it is to inform the president, who is typically less expert in each specific arena. Each staff unit is responsible for scanning some segment of the political environment, picking up relevant information, and channeling it upward toward the president, where it may feed into decisions. Most staff members are (or soon become) expert in their particular domain, and the head of a given unit may have dealt with the subject matter for a lifetime. The key link in the information chain for presidential decisions is between the unit head and the president, therefore typically between an expert and a generalist.[3]

One major implication is that the expert will have to simplify and frame the information for the president, especially because the president is the hub receiving information along many spokes around the wheel. The president's information overload must be managed by those who communicate on behalf of a given domain. Accordingly, the unit head's particular framing of an issue is likely to be extremely important. The unit head's categories are likely to be the president's categories. And it is only with unusual urging by the unit head that the president may think in a more attribute-oriented way about any given domain. More typically, the unit head's limitations and biases are likely to be communicated in their entirety to the president, who may not have the time or the expertise to notice or challenge them. Hence, the unit heads as individuals are inordinately crucial cognizers in the White House advisory network because they define the categories of thinking that go into policy making. Of course, they are picked by presidents to be knowledgeable and trustworthy representatives of their fields, so they ordinarily reflect the president's initial biases as well.

In short, there are both interpersonal (in-group/out-group) and informational factors among advisory networks that potentially benefit from a cognitive-motivational analysis.

Evaluating the Presidency: A Question of Standards

In chapter 12, Richard Rose rightly notes that both normative standards and positive empirical criteria must combine in evaluating the presidency. Implicit in a cognitive approach are particular normative standards, in, for example, the stages of information processing. One can evaluate the adequacy of sampling data, gathering it, combining it, and reaching a decision in line with the information. But who or what sets the standards for accuracy here? Many cognitive models implicitly compare human decision making to some compulsively programmed computer. Compared to the hypothetical computer, ordinary people commit many errors in such inferential processes. Even experts commit many of the same errors. But who sets the standards for accuracy when experts disagree? The normative computer has to be programmed by somebody, but most political decisions and decision making processes do not have a single optimal solution (for example, an activist versus a guardian approach). In short, the normative criteria themselves are wanting.

Even assuming reasonable people could agree on certain criteria for information gathering and inferential decision making, do we expect the president to be an extraordinary decision maker? Given the consequences of the president's decisions, we might like to say yes, but given the standards of normal human cognitive capacities, how can we? On the basis of existing research, we can expect the president as a human decision maker to rely on prior theories when deciding what data are relevant to a given decision. Sampling is likely to be biased, and biases in existing samples are likely to be ignored. Strong inferences may be drawn from small and unreliable samples. When good population norms (base rates) are available, they may be ignored in favor of less reliable anecdotal information. Estimates and combinations of probabilistic information, characteristic of political judgments under uncertainty, are often wrong. Weighting the whole range of inputs is likely to be inadequate, instead using only a few cues. Estimating the covariation of events, necessary for judgments of causality, will fare no better (for reviews, see Fiske and Taylor, 1991, chap. 9; Nisbett and Ross, 1980).

Does this mean that presidents will, more often than not, stumble into any old decision that fits their cognitive convenience? Not entirely. The motivated tactician makes some decisions more carefully than others, especially when explicitly considering alternative courses of action, when validating the decision process against the inputs of other people, and when prior theories are not strong. Moreover, the heuristics and other convenient strategies that presidents and other people do use often produce good-enough decisions. If we consider accuracy not from the perspective of some humanoid computer, but rather from the perspective of the limited domains in which a particular decision has to operate, people, including presidents, fare better (Swann, 1984; see also Fiske, 1993; Funder, 1987).

As a final note, social cognition researchers and their forebears in person perception research have wrestled with the notion of accuracy for a long time. Early on, researchers noted that one may evaluate different types of accuracy, on an analysis of variance model (Cronbach, 1955; Kenny, 1991). For example, a president may be generally more or less accurate than other people, more or less accurate in some domains than others (e.g., foreign, as opposed to domestic policy), more or less accurate on some dimensions regardless of domain (e.g., interpersonal diplomacy, as opposed to technical matters), and more or less accurate on particular combinations of domains and dimensions. I suspect that presidential scholars typically consider only the first kind of accuracy (the grand mean of accuracy), as person perception researchers typically did. However, the motivated tactician has his or her own standards; one must evaluate the president against what the chief executive is trying to accomplish, as well as against other people's agendas. In either case, of course, the standards have to be made explicit.

Conclusion

This chapter argues for attending to the interaction between cognition and motivation, examining cognitive strategies used in the service of particular goals. In responding to chapters on presidential selection, leadership style, policy making, advising, and evaluation, I have applied the framework of the motivated tactician at different levels of analysis. That is, one can consider presidents as motivated tacticians, using flexible cognitive strategies depending on particular aims. One can also view people who respond to the president as motivated tacticians with goals of their own, within the executive branch or within mass publics.

Finally, one can also view scholars as motivated tacticians, who use different intellectual strategies to meet different theoretical objectives. As an outsider to this area of research, I am impressed with the range of intellectual approaches to the president as subject matter.

Some scholars take a more holistic, narrative approach, focusing on crafting an in-depth and coherent portrait. Their approach might be termed more category based, in the sense of identifying the relevant category and specifying how its contents fit together. Other scholars take a more scientific, analytic approach, focusing on accurate quantitative prediction. Their approach might be termed more attribute based, in the sense of focusing one by one on single indicators to construct an overall equation. These two prototypical strategies of scholars parallel the prototypical strategies of ordinary social cognition described earlier, namely category-based or theory-driven thinking, and attribute-based or piecemeal thinking. I argue for a middle ground occupied by scholars as self-consciously motivated tacticians, who use some of each strategy as their task requires.

Notes

1. This discussion does not begin to touch infighting within the in-group. In that case, the relevant in-group is no longer the entire advisory net but the individual actor and any perceived allies. The current discussion presupposes a case where the most relevant in-group/out-group dynamics concern the president's people against some other group or groups.

2. Under particular circumstances, negative in-groupers are more decisively rejected than are comparable out-groupers (and positive in-groupers are more extremely valued), a phenomenon termed the Black Sheep Effect (Marques, Yzerbyt, and Leyens, 1988; Marques and Yzerbyt, 1988; cf. Brewer et al., 1987).

3. For this analysis, I am indebted to John Kessel.

References

Abelson, R. P. 1983. "Whatever Became of Consistency Theory?" *Personality and Social Psychology Bulletin* 9:37–54.

Abelson, R. P., E. Aronson, W. J. McGuire, T. M. Newcomb, M. J. Rosenberg, and P. H. Tannenbaum, eds. 1968. *Theories of Cognitive Consistency: A Sourcebook.* Chicago: Rand McNally.

Abelson, R. P., D. R. Kinder, M. D. Peters, and S. T. Fiske. 1982. "Affective and Semantic Components in Political Person Perception." *Journal of Personality and Social Psychology* 42:619–30.

Abrams, D. 1985. "Focus of Attention in Minimal Intergroup Discrimination." *British Journal of Social Psychology* 24:65–74.

Adorno, T. W., E. Frenkel-Brunswik, D. J. Levinson, and R. N. Sanford. 1950. *The Authoritarian Personality.* New York: Harper.

Ajzen, I., and M. Fishbein. 1977. "Attitude-Behavior Relations: A Theoretical Analysis and Review of Empirical Research." *Psychological Bulletin* 84:888–918.

Ajzen, I., and M. Fishbein. 1980. *Understanding Attitudes and Predicting Social Behavior.* Englewood Cliffs, N.J.: Prentice-Hall.

Allen, V. L. and D. A. Wilder. 1979. "Group Categorization and Attribution of Belief Similarity." *Small Group Behavior* 10:73–80.

Allport, G. W. 1954. *The Nature of Prejudice.* Reading, Mass.: Addison-Wesley.

Altemeyer, R. A. 1981. *Right-wing Authoritarianism.* Winnipeg: University of Manitoba Press.

Anderson, N. H. 1981. *Foundations of Information Integration Theory.* New York: Academic Press.

Bargh, J. A. 1990. "Auto-motives: Preconscious Determinants of Social Interaction." In *Handbook of Motivation and Cognition: Foundations of Social Behavior,* vol. 2, ed. E. T. Higgins and R. M. Sorrentino, 93–130. New York: Guilford.

Beck, A. T. 1967. *Depression: Clinical, Experimental, and the Theoretical Aspects.* New York: Harper and Row.

Bieri, J. 1955. "Cognitive Complexity-Simplicity and Predictive Behavior." *Journal of Abnormal and Social Psychology* 51:263–68.

Billig, M., and H. Tajfel. 1973. "Social Categorization and Similarity in Intergroup Behavior." *European Journal of Social Psychology* 3:27–52.

Bodenhausen, G. V. 1990. "Stereotypes as Judgmental Heuristics: Evidence of Circadian Variations in Discrimination." *Psychological Science* 1:319–22.

Brewer, M. B. 1979. "In-group Bias in the Minimal Intergroup Situation: A Cognitive-Motivational Analysis." *Psychological Bulletin* 86:307–24.

Brewer, M. B. 1988. "A Dual Process Model of Impression Formation." In T. K. Srull and R. S. Wyer, Jr., eds., *Advances in social cognition,* vol. 1, 1–36. Hillsdale, N.J.: Erlbaum.

Brewer, M. B., H. K. Ho, J. Y. Lee, and N. Miller. 1987. "Social Identity and Social Distance among Hong Kong School Children." *Personality and Social Psychology Bulletin* 13:156–65.

Brewer, M. B., and R. M. Kramer. 1985. "The Psychology of Intergroup Attitudes and Behavior." *Annual Review of Psychology* 36:219–43.

Bronfenbrenner, U. 1961. "The Mirror-Image in Soviet American Relations." *Journal of Social Issues* 17:45–56.

Brown, J. D., G. W. Schmidt, and R. L. Collins. 1988. "Personal Involvement and the Evaluation of Group Products." *European Journal of Social Psychology* 18:177–79.

Cacioppo, J. T., and R. E. Petty. 1982. "The Need for Cognition." *Journal of Personality and Social Psychology* 42:116–31.

Cantor, N., and J. F. Kihlstrom. 1987. *Personality and Social Intelligence.* Englewood Cliffs, N.J.: Prentice-Hall.

Chaiken, S. 1980. "Heuristic versus Systematic Information Processing and the Use of Source versus Message Cues in Persuasion." *Journal of Personality and Social Psychology* 39:752–66.

Chaiken, S., A. Liberman, and A. H. Eagly. 1989. "Heuristic and Systematic Information processing Within and Beyond the Persuasion Context." In *Unintended Thought,* ed. J. S. Uleman and J. A. Bargh, 212–52. New York: Guilford.

Chase, W. G., and H. A. Simon. 1973. "The Mind's Eye in Chess." In *Visual Information Processing,* ed. W. G. Chase, 215–81. New York: Academic.

Christie, R., et al. 1973. "Machiavellianism." In *Measures of Social Psychological Attitudes,* ed. R. Robinson and R. Shaver, 590–602. Ann Arbor: Institute for Social Research, The University of Michigan.

Cohen, A. R. 1961. "Cognitive Tuning as a Factor Affecting Impression Formation." *Journal of Personality* 29:235–45.

Crocker, J., L. L. Thompson, K. M. McGraw, and C. Ingerman. 1987. "Downward Comparison, Prejudice, and Evaluation of Others: Effects of Self-esteem and Threat." *Journal of Personality and Social Psychology* 52:907–16.

Cronbach, L. J. 1955. "Processes Affecting Scores on 'Understanding of Others' and 'Assumed Similarity'. " *Psychological Bulletin* 52:177–93.

Deaux, K. 1976. *The Behavior of Women and Men*. Monterey, Calif.: Brooks/Cole.

Dépret, E. F., and S. T. Fiske. In press. "Social Cognition and Power: Some Cognitive Consequences of Social Structure as a Source of Control Deprivation." In *Control Motivation and Social Cognition*, ed. G. Weary, F. Gleicher, and K. Marsh. New York: Springer-Verlag.

Epstein, S., and W. Fenz. 1967. "The Detection of Emotional Stress Through Variations in Perceptual Threshold and Physiological Arousal." *Journal of Experimental Research in Psychology* 2:191–99.

Epstein, S., and P. Meier. 1989. "Constructive Thinking: A Broad Coping Variable with Specific Components." *Journal of Personality and Social Psychology* 57:332–50.

Erber, R. 1991. "Affective and Semantic Priming: Effects of Mood on Category Accessibility and Inference." *Journal of Experimental Social Psychology* 27:480–98.

Erber, R. and S. T. Fiske. 1984. "Outcome Dependency and Attention to Inconsistent Information." *Journal of Personality and Social Psychology* 47:709–26.

Festinger, L. 1957. *A Theory of Cognitive Dissonance*. Stanford: Stanford University Press.

Fiske, S. T. 1982. "Schema-triggered Affect: Applications to Social Perception." In *Affect and Cognition: The 17th Annual Carnegie Symposium on Cognition*, ed. M. S. Clark and S. T. Fiske, 55–78. Hillsdale, N.J.: Erlbaum.

———. 1986. "Schema-based versus Piecemeal Politics: A Patchwork Quilt, but not a Blanket, of Evidence." In *Political Cognition: The 19th Annual Carnegie Symposium of Cognition*, ed. R. R. Lau and D. O. Sears, 41–53. Hillsdale, N.J.: Erlbaum.

———. 1989. "Examining the Role of Intent: Toward Understanding its Role in Stereotyping and Prejudice." In *Unintended Thought*, ed. J. S. Uleman and J. A. Bargh, 253–83. New York: Guilford.

———. 1993. "Social Cognition and Social Perception." *Annual Review of Psychology* 44: 155–94.

Fiske, S. T., and D. R. Kinder. 1981. "Involvement, Expertise, and Schema Use: Evidence from Political Cognition." In *Personality, Cognition, and Social Interaction*, ed. N. Cantor and J. Kihlstrom. Hillsdale, N.J.: Erlbaum.

Fiske, S. T., D. R. Kinder, and W. M. Larter. 1983. "The Novice and the Expert: Knowledge-based Strategies in Political Cognition." *Journal of Experimental Social Psychology* 19:381–400.

Fiske, S. T., R. R. Lau, and R. A. Smith. 1990. "On the Varieties and Utilities of Political Expertise." *Social Cognition* 8:31–48.

Fiske, S. T., and S. L. Neuberg. 1990. "A Continuum of Impression Formation, from Category-based to Individuating Processes: Influences of Information and Motivation on Attention and Interpretation." In *Advances in Experimental Social Psychology*, vol. 23, ed. M. P. Zanna, 1–74. New York: Academic.

Fiske, S. T., and M. A. Pavelchak. 1986. "Category-based versus Piecemeal-based Affective Responses: Developments in Schema-triggered Affect." In *Handbook of Motivation and Cognition: Foundations of Social Behavior*, ed. R. M. Sorrentino and E. T. Higgins, 167–203. New York: Guilford.

Fiske, S. T., and S. E. Taylor. 1991. *Social Cognition*, 2d ed. New York: McGraw-Hill.

Freund, T., A. W. Kruglanski, and A. Shpitzajzen. 1985. "The Freezing and Unfreezing of Impression Primacy: Effects of the Need for Structure and the Fear of Invalidity." *Personality and Social Psychology Bulletin* 11:479–87.

Funder, D. C. 1987. "Errors and Mistakes: Evaluating the Accuracy of Social Judgment." *Psychological Bulletin* 101:75–90.

Gerard, H. B., and M. F. Hoyt. 1974. "Distinctiveness of Social Categorization and Attitude Toward Ingroup Members." *Journal of Personality and Social Psychology* 29:836–42.

Gollwitzer, P. M., and R. F. Kinney. 1989. "Effects of Deliberative and Implemental Mind-sets on Illusion of Control." *Journal of Personality and Social Psychology* 56:531–42.

Hamilton, D. L. 1979. "A Cognitive-attributional Analysis of Stereotyping." In *Advances in Experimental Social Psychology*, vol. 12, ed. L. Berkowitz, 53–84. New York: Academic.

Hamilton, D. L., and T. K. Trolier. 1986. "Stereotypes and Stereotyping: An Overview of the Cognitive Approach." In *Prejudice, Discrimination, and Racism*, ed. J. F. Dovidio and S. L. Gaertner, 127–63. Orlando, Fla.: Academic.

Hewstone, M., and J. M. F. Jaspars. 1984. "Social Dimensions of Attribution." In *The Social Dimension: European Developments in Social Psychology*, ed. H. Tajfel, 379–404. Cambridge: Cambridge University Press.

Higgins, E. T., and J. A. Bargh. 1987. "Social cognition and Social Perception." In *Annual Review of Psychology*, vol. 38, ed. M. R. Rosenzweig and L. W. Porter, 369–425. Palo Alto: Annual Reviews.

Higgins, E. T., and G. A. King. 1981. "Accessibility of Social Constructs: Information-processing Consequences of Individual and Contextual Variability." In *Personality, Cognition, and Social Interaction*, ed. N. Cantor and J. F. Kihlstrom, 69–122. Hillsdale, N.J.: Erlbaum.

Higgins, E. T., C. D. McCann, and R. Fondacaro. 1982. "The 'Communication Game': Goal-directed Encoding and Cognitive Consequences." *Social Cognition* 1:21–37.

Hoffman, C., W. Mischel, and J. S. Baer. 1984. "Language and Person Cognition: Effects of Communicative Set on Trait Attribution." *Journal of Personality and Social Psychology* 46:1029–43.

Howard, J. W., and M. Rothbart. 1980. "Social Categorization and Memory for Ingroup and Outgroup Behavior." *Journal of Personality and Social Psychology* 38:301–10.

Hudson, W. W., and W. A. Ricketts. 1980. "A Strategy for the Measurement of Homophobia." *Journal of Homosexuality* 5:357–72.

Isen, A. M. 1987. "Positive Affect, Cognitive Processes, and Social Behavior." In *Advances in Experimental Social Psychology*, vol. 20, ed. L. Berkowitz, 203–53. New York: Academic.

Iyengar, S., and D. R. Kinder. 1987. *News That Matters: Television and American Opinion.* Chicago: University of Chicago Press.

James, W. 1983. *The Principles of Psychology*. Cambridge: Harvard University Press. (Original work published 1890).

Jamieson, D. W., and M. P. Zanna. 1989. "Need for Structure in Attitude Formation and Expression." In *Attitudes Structure and Function*, ed. A. R. Pratkanis, S. J. Breckler, and A. G. Greenwald, 383–406. Hillsdale, N.J.: Erlbaum.

Janis, I. L. 1989. *Crucial Decisions: Leadership in Policymaking and Crisis Management*. New York: Free Press.

Janis, I. L., and P. B. Field. 1959. "Sex Differences and Personality Factors Related to Persuasibility." In *Personality and Persuasibility*, ed. C. I. Hovland and I. L. Janis. New Haven: Yale University Press.

Jervis, R., R. N. Lebow, and J. G. Stein. 1985. *Psychology and Deterrence*. Baltimore: Johns Hopkins University Press.

Judd, C. M., and C. M. Lusk. 1984. "Knowledge Structures and Evaluative Judgments: Effects of Structural Variables on Judgmental Extremity." *Journal of Personality and Social Psychology* 46:1193–1207.

Kahneman, D., P. Slovic, and A. Tversky, eds. 1982. *Judgment under Uncertainty: Heuristics and Biases*. New York: Cambridge University Press.

Kahneman, D., and A. Tversky. 1973. "On the Psychology of Prediction." *Psychological Review*, 80:237–51.

Katz, I., and R. G. Hass. 1988. "Racial Ambivalence and American Value Conflict: Correlational and Priming Studies of Dual Cognitive Structures." *Journal of Personality and Social Psychology* 55:893–905.

Kelley, H. H. 1972. "Attribution in Social Interaction." In *Attribution: Perceiving the causes of behavior*, ed. E. E. Jones, D. E. Kanouse, H. H. Kelley, R. E. Nisbett, S. Valins, and B. Weiner, 1–26. Morristown, N.J.: General Learning Press.

Kelley, H. H., E. Berscheid, A. Christensen, J. H. Harvey, T. L. Huston, G. Levinger, E. McClintock, L. A. Peplau, and D. R. Peterson. 1983. "Analyzing Close Relationships." In *Close Relationships*, ed. H. H. Kelley, E. Berscheid, A. Christensen, J. H. Harvey, T. L. Huston, G. Levinger, E. McClintock, L. A. Peplau, and D. R. Peterson, 20–67. New York: W. H. Freeman.

Kenny, D. A. 1991. "A General Model of Consensus and Accuracy in Interpersonal Perception." *Psychological Review* 98:155–63.

Kinder, D. R., and S. T. Fiske. 1986. "Presidents in the Public Mind." In *Handbook of Political Psychology*, vol. 2, ed. M. G. Hermann, 193–218. San Francisco: Jossey-Bass.

Kinder, D. R., M. D. Peters, R. P. Abelson, and S. T. Fiske. 1980. "Presidential Prototypes." *Political Behavior* 2:315–38.

Krosnick, J. A. 1990. "Expertise and Political Psychology." *Social Cognition* 8:1–8.

Krueger, J., M. Rothbart, and N. Sriram. 1989. "Category Learning and Change: Differences in Sensitivity to Information that Enhances or Reduces Intercategory Distinctions." *Journal of Personality and Social Psychology* 56:866–75.

Kruglanski, A. W., and T. Freund. 1983. "The Freezing and Unfreezing of Lay-inferences: Effects of Impressional Primacy, Ethnic Stereotyping, and Numerical Anchoring." *Journal of Experimental Social Psychology* 19:448–68.

Kruglanski, A. W., and O. Mayseless. 1988. "Contextual Effects in Hypothesis Testing: The Role of Competing Alternatives and Epistemic Motivations." *Social Cognition* 6:1–20.

Larsen, K. S., M. Reed, and S. Hoffman. 1980. "Attitudes of Heterosexuals Toward Homosexuality: A Likert-type Scale and Construct Validity." *Journal of Sex Research* 16:245–57.

Lau, R. R., and D. O. Sears, eds. 1986. *Political Cognition*. Hillsdale, N.J.: Erlbaum.

Leventhal, H. 1962. "The Effects of Set and Discrepancy on Impression Change." *Journal of Personality* 30:1–15.

Leyens, J. P. 1983. *Sommes-Nous Tous des Psychologues? Approche Psychosociale des Théories Implicites de la Personnalité* Bruxelles: Mardaga.

Linville, P. W. 1982. "The Complexity-extremity Effect and Age-based Stereotyping." *Journal of Personality and Social Psychology* 42:193–211.

Linville, P. W., and E. E. Jones. 1980. "Polarized Appraisals of Outgroup Members." *Journal of Personality and Social Psychology* 38:689–703.

Lopes, L. L. 1982. *Towards a Procedural Theory of Judgment*. Tech. Rep. no. 17, pp. 1–49. University of Wisconsin, Madison: Information Processing Program.

Mackie, D. M., D. L. Hamilton, H. A. Schroth, C. J. Carlisle, B. F. Gersho, L. M. Meneses, B. F. Nedler, and L. D. Reichel. 1989. "The Effects of Induced Mood on Illusory Correlations." *Journal of Experimental Social Psychology* 25:524–44.

Marques, J. M., and V. Y. Yzerbyt. 1988. "The Black Sheep Effect: Judgmental Extremity Towards Ingroup Members in Inter- and Intra-group Situations." *European Journal of Social Psychology* 18:287–92.

Marques, J. M., V. Y. Yzerbyt, and J. P. Leyens. 1988. "The 'Black Sheep Effect': Extremity of Judgments Towards Ingroup Members as a Function of Group Identification." *European Journal of Social Psychology* 18:1–16.

McArthur, L. Z. 1981. "What Grabs You? The Role of Attention in Impression Formation and Causal Attribution." In *Social Cognition: The Ontario Symposium*, vol. 1, ed. E. T. Higgins, C. P. Herman, and M. P. Zanna, 201–46. Hillsdale, N.J.: Erlbaum.

McClelland, D. C., J. W. Atkinson, R. A. Clark, and E. L. Lowell. 1958. "A Scoring Manual for the Achievement Motive." In *Motives in Fantasy, Action and Society*, ed. J. W. Atkinson, 179–204. Princeton, N.J.: Van Nostrand.

McConahay, J. B. 1983. "Modern Racism and Modern Discrimination: The Effects of Race, Racial Attitudes, and Context on Simulated Hiring Decisions." *Personality and Social Psychology Bulletin* 9:551–58.

Mullen, B., and L. Hu. 1989. "Perceptions of Ingroup and Outgroup Variability: A Meta-Analytic Integration." *Basic and Applied Social Psychology* 10:233–52.

Neuberg, S. L. 1989. "The Goal of Forming Accurate Impressions During Social Interactions: Attenuating the Impact of Negative Expectancies." *Journal of Personality and Social Psychology* 56:374–86.

Neuberg, S. L, and S. T. Fiske. 1987. "Motivational Influences on Impression Formation: Outcome Dependency, Accuracy-driven Attention, and Individuating Processes." *Journal of Personality and Social Psychology* 53:431–44.

Neuberg, S. L., and J. T. Newsom. 1990. *Individual Differences in Chronic Motivation to Simplify: Personal Need for Structure and Social-cognitive Processing*. Unpublished manuscript, Arizona State University.

Nisbett, R. E., and L. Ross. 1980. *Human Inference: Strategies and Shortcomings of Social Judgment*. Englewood Cliffs, N.J.: Prentice-Hall.

Norton, R. W. 1975. "Measurement of Ambiguity Tolerance." *Journal of Personality Assessment* 39:607–19.

Park, B., and M. Rothbart. 1982. "Perception of Out-group Homogeneity and Levels of Social Categorization: Memory for the Subordinate Attributes of In-group and Out-group Members." *Journal of Personality and Social Psychology* 42:1051–68.

Pettigrew, T. F. 1958. "The Measurement and Correlates of Category-width as a Cognitive Variable." *Journal of Personality* 26:532–44.

———. 1979. "The Ultimate Attribution Error: Extending Allport's Cognitive Analysis of Prejudice." *Personality and Social Psychology Bulletin* 5:461–76.

———. 1982. "Cognitive Style and Social Behavior: A Review of Category-width." In *Review of Personality and Social Psychology*, vol. 3, ed. L. Wheeler, 199–233. Beverly Hills: Sage.

Petty, R. E., and J. T. Cacioppo. 1984. "The Effects of Involvement on Responses to Argument Quantity and Quality: Central and Peripheral Routes to Persuasion." *Journal of Personality and Social Psychology* 46:69–81.

Petty, R. E., and J. T. Cacioppo. 1986. "The Elaboration Likelihood Model of Persuasion." In *Advances in Experimental Social Psychology*, vol. 19, ed. L. Berkowitz, 123–205. New York: Academic.

Rokeach, M. 1960. *The Open and Closed Mind*. New York: Basic.

Rosenberg, M. 1965. *Society and the Adolescent Self-image*. Princeton: Princeton University Press.

Rothbart, M., R. Dawes, and B. Park. 1984. "Stereotyping and Sampling Biases in Intergroup Perception." In *Attitudinal Judgment*, ed. J. R. Eiser, 109–134. New York: Springer-Verlag.

Rothbart, M., and W. Hallmark. 1988. "Ingroup-outgroup Differences in the Perceived Efficacy of Coercion and Conciliation in Resolving Social Conflict." *Journal of Personality and Social Psychology* 55:248–57.

Ruscher, J. B., and S. T. Fiske. 1990. "Interpersonal Competition can Cause Individuating Impression Formation." *Journal of Personality and Social Psychology* 58:832–42.

Ruscher, J. B., S. T. Fiske, H. Miki, and S. Van Manen. 1991. "Individuating Processes in Competition: Interpersonal Versus Intergroup." *Personality and Social Psychology Bulletin* 17:595–605.

Scheier, M. F., and C. S. Carver. 1985. "Optimism, Coping, and Health: Assessment and Implications of Generalized Outcome Expectancies." *Health Psychology* 4:219–47.

Scott, W. A. 1966. "Brief Report: Measures of Cognitive Structures." *Multivariate Behavioral Research* 1:391–95.

Sherif, M., O. J. Harvey, B. J. White, W. R. Hood, and C. W. Sherif. 1961. *Intergroup Conflict and Cooperation: The Robbers' Cave Experiment*. Norman: University of Oklahoma Press.

Showers, C., and N. Cantor. 1985. "Social Cognition: A look at Motivated Strategies." *Annual Review of Psychology*, 36: 275–305.

Sorrentino, R. M., and E. Hewitt. 1984. "Uncertainty-related Properties of Achievement Tasks as a Function of Uncertainty-orientation and Achievement-related Motives." *Journal of Personality and Social Psychology* 47:884–99.

Sorrentino, R. M., J. C. Short, and J. O. Raynor. 1984. "Uncertainty Orientation: Implications for Affective and Cognitive Views of Achievement Behavior." *Journal of Personality and Social Psychology* 46:189–206.

Spence, J. T., and R. Helmreich. 1972. "The Attitudes Toward Women Scale: An Objective Instrument to Measure Attitudes Toward the Rights and Roles of Women in Contemporary Society." *Journal Supplement Abstract Service Catalog of Selected Documents in Psychology* 2:66–67.

Swann, W. B., Jr. 1984. "Quest for Accuracy in Person Perception: A Matter of Pragmatics." *Psychological Review* 91:457–77.

Tajfel, H., ed. 1978. *Differentiation Between Social Groups*. London: Academic.

———. 1982. "Social Psychology of Intergroup Relations." In *Annual Review of Psychology* 33: 1–39.

Tajfel, H., A. A. Sheikh and R. C. Gardner. 1964. "Content of Stereotypes and the Inference of Similarity Between Members of Stereotyped Groups." *Acta Psychologica* 22:191–201.

Tajfel, H., and A. L. Wilkes. 1963. "Classification and Qualitative Judgment." *British Journal of Psychology* 54:101–14.

Taylor, S. E., and S. T. Fiske. 1978. "Salience, Attention, and Attribution: Top of the Head Phenomena." In *Advances in Experimental Social Psychology*, vol. 11, ed. L. Berkowitz, 249–88. New York: Academic.

Tetlock, P. E. 1983a. "Accountability and Complexity of Thought." *Journal of Personality and Social Psychology* 45:74–83.

———. 1983b. "Accountability and the Perseverance of First Impressions." *Social Psychology Quarterly* 46:285–92.

———. 1985. "Accountability: A Social Check on the Fundamental Attribution Error." *Social Psychology Quarterly* 48:227–36.

Tetlock, P. E., and R. Boettger. 1989. "Accountability: A Social Magnifier of the Dilution Effect." *Journal of Personality and Social Psychology.* 57:388–98.

Tetlock, P. E., and J. I. Kim. 1987. "Accountability and Judgment Processes in a Personality Prediction Task." *Journal of Personality and Social Psychology* 52:700–709.

Thompson, M. M., M. E. Naccarato, and K. Parker. 1989. *The Development of the Need for Structure and Fear of Invalidity Scales*. Unpublished manuscript, University of Waterloo.

Troldahl, V. C., and F. A. Powell. 1965. "A Short-form Dogmatism Scale for Use in Field Studies." *Social Forces* 44:211–14.

Wilder, D. A. 1978. "Perceiving Persons as a Group: Effects on Attributions of Causality and Beliefs." *Social Psychology* 1:13–23.

———. 1981. "Perceiving Persons as a Group: Categorization and Intergroup Relations." In *Cognitive Processes in Stereotyping and Intergroup Behavior,* ed. D. L. Hamilton, 213–58. Hillsdale, N.J.: Erlbaum.

———. 1986. "Social Categorization: Implications for Creation and Reduction of Intergroup Bias." *Advances in Experimental Social Psychology* 19:291–355.

Wilder, D. A., and V. L. Allen. 1978. "Group Membership and Preference for Information about Others." *Personality and Social Psychology Bulletin* 4:106–110.

Wilder, D. A., and W. E. Cooper. 1981. "Categorization in Groups: Consequences for Social Perception and Attribution." In *New Directions in Attribution Research,* vol. 3, ed. J. Harvey, W. Ickes, and R. Kidd, 247–77. Hillsdale, N.J.: Erlbaum.

Wilder, D. A., and P. Shapiro. 1989a. "Effects of Anxiety on Impression Formation in a Group Context: An Anxiety-assimilation Hypothesis." *Journal of Experimental Social Psychology* 25:481–99.

Wilder, D. A., and P. Shapiro. 1989b. "The Role of Competition-induced Anxiety in Limiting the Beneficial Impact of Positive Behavior by an Outgroup Member." *Journal of Personality and Social Psychology* 56:60–69.

Wyer, R. S. Jr., and T. K. Srull. 1981. "Category Accessibility: Some Theoretical and Empirical Issues Concerning the Processing of Social Stimulus Information." In *Social Cognition: The Ontario Symposium,* vol. 1, ed. E. T. Higgins, C. P. Herman, and M. P. Zanna, 161–98. Hillsdale, N.J.: Erlbaum.

Zajonc, R. B. 1960. "The Process of Cognitive Tuning in Communication." *Journal of Abnormal and Social Psychology* 61:159–67.

Zukier, H. 1986. "The Paradigmatic and Narrative Modes in Goal-guided Inference." In *Handbook of Motivation and Cognition,* ed. R. M. Sorrentino and E. T. Higgins, 465–502. New York: Guilford.

Zukier, H., and A. Pepitone. 1984. "Social Roles and Strategies in Prediction: Some Determinants of the Use of Base Rate Information." *Journal of Personality and Social Psychology* 47:349–60.

7

Organization Theory and the Presidency

MARTHA S. FELDMAN

*T*HIS VOLUME and the conference that spawned it are testimony to the fact that the presidency may be usefully viewed from many different perspectives (see, e.g., Meltsner, 1981; Rockman, 1986; and Wildavsky, 1975). The disciplines of psychology, history, and political science all play important roles in the study of the presidency. Many have studied the presidency from the perspective of the psychology and personality of the individuals occupying the office (George, 1974; Hargrove, 1966, 1973; Shogan, 1991). Some view the presidency as an office with certain rights and obligations that have evolved over the years in response to particular events and pressures (Kessel, 1975; Moe, 1985). Still others have studied the presidency in relation to other institutions, like Congress (Light, 1981, 1982; Manley, 1978), and other heads of state, like prime ministers (Rose and Suleiman, 1980). We have learned from all of these perspectives.

The presidency, however, is both a complex and an important phenomenon. Accordingly, we may want to ask if there are other perspectives that may help us further understand the phenomenon. In this chapter I suggest a relatively unexplored perspective that is a variant of organization theory. I discuss briefly the field of organization theory and the particular variant of this theory upon which I have chosen to focus. I then describe several concepts from this variant of organization theory that may be useful in thinking about the presidency.

Organization Theory

Organization theory is a field that draws on many disciplines. All of the social sciences make major contributions to this field. As a result, there are numerous ways to describe the field.[1] Much of organization theory has been concerned with the way organizations produce products. One way to categorize this study is to say that there are three perspectives on how organizations produce these products. One perspective focuses primarily on outcomes; another primarily on structures; the third primarily on meaning. I use the term *primarily* to emphasize a point. Though I separate these three perspectives, I do not want to suggest that any one of them makes sense alone. Indeed, students of organizations often combine elements of each of these in describing organizational actions. Studies do, however, tend to have a primary focus because of the need for parsimony.

The first perspective is well represented by the rational actor theories (e.g., Arrow, 1974; March and Simon, 1958; Simon, 1957; Taylor, 1911; Thompson, 1967; and Williamson, 1975). Goals are given, organizations are judged by their abilities to achieve the goals, and efficiency is a major objective. Organizations are seen as unitary actors or as entities with power strongly held by a person at the top. Control is an important element of this perpective.

The second perspective is represented by theories of incrementalism or organizational process (e.g., Chandler, 1962; Cyert and March, 1963; Galbraith, 1967; Lawrence and Lorsch, 1967; Lindblom, 1977; Merton, 1957; and Schumpeter, 1947). Structures direct organizational action and constrain possible outcomes. Structures are generally perceived as promoting certain values such as equality or pluralism. Structures are often seen as being efficient in routine situations and ineffencent in novel ones. From this perspective, the actions of an organization may be quite predictable, though not necessarily easily controlled.

The third perspective is cognitive and cultural in nature (e.g., March and Olsen, 1976; and Weick, 1979). It is concerned with questions of organizational identity, how identities are developed, maintained, and communicated, and how organizational identities influence other decisions and actions. Organizations are seen as having cultures of varying degrees of uniformity. Organizations and organizational members learn from external pressures and internal dialogues and behaviors. Many people who view organizations from this perpective are interested in what kind of information is available to the people inside the organization and how they make sense of it. It is from this third perspective that I will be viewing the presidency in this chapter.

Presidents, the Presidency, and the Presidential Organization

In writing about organization theory and the presidency, it is necessary first to define some terms. This is, in part, because it is not clear what we are talking about when we talk about the presidency as an organization. On the one hand, the presidency is tightly linked to the particular people who have been president. On the other hand, it is related to many organizations in many different ways. Consequently, it is not at all clear what we consider to be organizational about the presidency.

The first issue is to separate the presidents from the presidency. Much of the literature about the presidency has focused on the personal presidency (Lowi, 1985; Moe, 1985; Neustadt, 1980). That is, it has focused on the particular people who occupy the office of the president and the particular capabilities and propensities of these people. This is not surprising—the people who have occupied this position often have quite strong personalities and are often very powerful or charismatic people. The office also gives them considerable latitude to express their preferences and get them enacted. Furthermore, since there is only one president at a time, it is methodologically difficult to separate the person's power from that of the office or the person's preferences from the demands of the environment on the office.

Nonetheless, it must be true that the office as well as the person have power. After all, Ronald Reagan was charismatic before he became president. He did not, however, have the power to affect public policies in the ways that he did and the degree to which he did before he occupied the office of the president. Furthermore, other presidents have been charismatic, perhaps equally so, and they have not had the powers that had accrued to the presidency over the years that gave Reagan, for example, so much control over appointments. Therefore, we need to separate the person from the office. I do that here by referring to the people who have occupied the office as the presidents and the office or roles as the presidency.

The second distinction that needs to be made is what organization or organizations we are talking about when we speak of the presidency as an organization. There are, in fact, a large number of organizations of which the president is a member. These include the executive branch, the military, the cabinet, the White House staff, the National Security Council, the Council of Economic Advisers, the policy-making network that includes Congress, the nation as a whole, the group of national leaders who meet for economic summits, and so forth. While there are many interconnections among these organizations, they are not all hierarchically linked in the way they might be if we were talking about the president of General Motors or some other very large corporation.

There is, however, a set of these organizations that one can separate as being formally under the control of the president and as being linked to one another through their hierarchical links to the presidency. We might think of these as the staff and line organization of a large corporation. They consist of the White House staff, the various councils that advise the president, the cabinet, and the departments and bureaus of the executive branch. In general, every group in this list down to the departments and bureaus can be thought of as the president's staff. The departments and bureaus are the line organizations. There may be exceptions to this statement. For example, the Office of Management and Budget may be thought of as staff in at least some of its functions. Also, some of the parts of the presidential organization, such as the congressional liaison unit or the appointments unit, may have line functions. The distinction between line and staff, however, may be useful if we are going to talk about the organization of the president as opposed to the entire executive branch of the government. In the following, the *organization of the president* or the *presidential organization* refers to the office of the president and the staff that serves that office. The *executive branch* includes the departments and bureaus.

The Question of Continuity

Using organization theory to understand the presidency assumes that there is a presidential organization. The substantial and highly visible changes from one administration to another tend to focus attention on the distinct nature of each administration. This raises the question of whether there is a continuing phenomenon. For instance, some say, with some measure of wisdom, that there is no staff that serves the office of the president. There are, instead, particular people who serve particular presidents. The composition of the staff, both in terms of people and structure, changes substantially from one administration to another. These facts, however, do not necessarily mean that there is no continuity to the organization. Other examples exist of organizations that have changed their leadership, their membership, their functions, and even their names while still maintaining enough continuity to be considered "the same organization." Indeed, Herbert Kaufman suggests that these facts may account for the perception that government organizations are immortal (Kaufman, 1976).

There is evidence of continuity in the presidency (Moe, 1985). While acknowledging the individual influence of presidents, the chapters by Hult and Moe in this volume both recognize the institutional nature of the presidency as well. Both note that features external to any particular president drive behaviors resulting in institutional tendencies. Moe suggests that power cannot be fully understood outside of the institutional context from which it emerges and in which it is exercised. He goes on to note that the institutional context is, in part, endogenous. It conditions the presidential behavior we observe and is also a dynamic product of that behavior. Indeed, previous presidential behavior helps to form the institutional context of current and future presidencies.

Hult's chapter on presidential advisory networks in this volume provides several examples of presidential continuity. She cites her work with Walcott (1989) and their argument that, since the Hoover administration, White House press secretaries (except Jody Powell) have been increasingly less involved in advising presidents and spend more time managing a burgeoning White House press office. Hult and Walcott link this decline to a changing political environment, the organizational imperatives of an increasingly specialized White House staff, and presidential strategies (Hult, chap. 3). Another example concerns the role of the vice president. Hult notes that from 1961 to 1977, the political system grew increasingly complex and fragmented, making vice presidential political and policy advice potentially more valuable (Light, 1984, 140). By 1977, Vice President

Mondale had acquired an office in the West Wing of the White House, and his staff was fully integrated into the White House policy process. Hult claims that such institutional development of the vice presidency has continued to the present time. Other continuities in the presidency may not be so directly tied to changes in the external environment. Some changes are standard observations in the field of public administration (Parkinson, 1987). Hult notes that the White House has become increasingly centralized and increasingly specialized with a resulting increase in the size of staffs and a decrease in the link between substantive specialists and presidents.

These examples are not intended to constitute an argument that the most appropriate way to view the presidency is as one continuous organization. I intend only to make the point that there are some respects in which the presidency does appear to be a continuous organization. Organization theory provides several tools for exploring the organizational or continuous aspects of the presidency. In the following pages, I suggest several concepts that focus attention on features of organizations that tend to be cumulative rather than discrete. Since I am an organization theorist rather than a presidency scholar, I focus on describing the concepts from the perspective of organization theory rather than on arguing their implications for the presidency. At several points in the text, I suggest questions that might be useful to ask in applying the concepts to the presidency, though I leave this latter step to experts in the field.

This section is divided into four subsections, each of which present a cluster of concepts. The first cluster is more individually oriented than the other clusters and is about roles and associated ideas. The second cluster is about institutional memory, the third about learning processes, the fourth about decision making.

ROLES

Weber described an organization as being made up of offices. Offices have fixed powers and limitations, embedded in a structure of interlinked offices. Responsibilities are distributed throughout the organization in such a way that the offices are interdependent. The people assigned to an office must have the skills to perform the tasks assigned to the office. In the ideal, the personalities and individual characteristics of these people are not relevant to the way the duties of the office are performed (Weber, 1947). This ideal has been substantially debunked over the years. The human relations movement in organization theory helped to show that, in fact, the characteristics of people in general, the interactions within groups of people, and even, at times, the specific characteristics of individuals do matter (Scott, 1981, 86–90).

The concept that Weber articulated, however, has lived on in a more subtle form. We now speak of roles rather than offices. The distinction I make between roles and offices is conceptual rather than empirical. The office exists on paper and can be conceived of as separate from the individuals who inhabit the office.[2] Role refers to "the expectations for or evaluative standards employed in assessing the behavior of occupants of specific social positions" (Scott, 1981, 14). Role combines the concept of office with the concept of people. There are at least three categories of people who are important to the formation of a role. There are the people who currently inhabit the office, the people who have inhabited the office in the past, and the people who have expectations and assessments of the inhabitants of the office. These expectations and assessments are influenced by the behaviors of people, both past and present, occupying the office as well as by other aspects of the external environment. Thus, the role is constantly evolving even when the office remains substantially the same. Take, for example, the influence of the Watergate scandal on the role and the office of the presidency. The office has changed little, if at all, while the role has been greatly affected.

This move away from the strict Weberian notion of organizations to a more humanized version has allowed us to add social pressure to the more mechanized pressures of the Weberian organization. Thus, the strength of roles is perceived to be very great (see Pfeffer, 1982, 98–102, for a description of several studies that make this point). Role expectations are widely reported to have a strong influence on the behavior of individuals (Thomas and Biddle, 1966; Van Maanen, 1973; Wilson, 1989). They are even reported to produce behaviors that are the opposite of what one would expect of the individual prior to occupying the role (Dean, 1976). This phenomenon has been associated, for instance, with Supreme Court justices who became increasingly liberal or conservative after taking office despite their original leanings in the opposite direction (Woodward and Armstrong, 1979).

Many features of the concept of role may be useful in understanding the presidency. There are formal and informal features of roles.

For instance, there are legal constraints on what the president can and cannot do. There are sanctions for transgressing those limits. While the role is bound by these constraints, it may be just as much defined by unwritten norms and expectations. Though the sanctions for transgressing these tacit limits may not be as clearly defined as the sanctions for transgressing the formal limits, they may, nonetheless, be very powerful. Sufficient transgression may even result in the codification of the norm in a formal requirement.[3]

Often roles are defined by the existence of other roles (Goffman, 1959). For instance, the role of parent is defined by the existence of children. The role of teacher is defined by the existence of students and vice versa. The role of the president seems to depend on the relation to the nation, to the other branches of government, and to the other parts of the executive branch. How does the existence of these other entities influence the role of the presidency? How do changes in their roles influence the definition of the presidency?

In general, the notion of role and the related concepts of expectations, norms, performance, sanction, status, and so forth lead us to think about what presidents have in common rather than how they differ. A large part of what they have in common is a function of the position they occupy and its history. The position is, in part, defined by the formal and informal expectations of people and institutions outside the presidential organization. If we assume that these expectations change incrementally and cumulatively, then many of the expectations are quite similar from administration to administration.

INSTITUTIONAL MEMORY

When an organization acts, it is often influenced by institutional or organizational memory (March and Olsen, 1976, 1989). That is, in some way, it "remembers" what has been done in the past and repeats it or avoids repeating it if it was a clear disaster. One of the ways that an organization remembers is that members of the organization remember. Another way is that current members can ask former members. A third way is for members to consult the files or the paper or electronic memory of the organization. A study of continuity in the presidential organization might focus on which members of the organization remain from administration to administration. In conditions of high turnover, people in otherwise unimportant positions may have great influence because they represent institutional memory. For this reason, documents and files from previous administrations may also have surprising influence.

All of the above ways for organizations to remember past actions are similar in that they involve individual cognition. There is, however, another way that organizations remember, which involves imitative behavior rather than cognitive absorption. Organizations may "remember" to behave in certain ways because their members engage in behaviors that, in essence, reproduce past actions. The actors need not be aware of the reasons for the actions that they are taking. The following story is a somewhat comical example taken from Elting Morison.

> During World War II the British military mounted on mobile units a piece of light artillery that had been used as far back as the Boer War. Though these units worked well, "it was felt that the rapidity of the fire could be increased. A time-motion expert was, therefore, called in to suggest ways to simplify the firing procedures. He watched one of the gun crews of five men at practice in the field for some time. Puzzled by certain aspects of the procedures, he took some slow-motion pictures of the soldiers performing the loading, aiming, and firing routines.
>
> "When he ran these pictures over once or twice, he noticed something that appeared odd to him. A moment before the firing, two members of the gun crew ceased all activity and came to attention for a three-second interval extending throughout the discharge of the gun. He summoned an old colonel of artillery, showed him the pictures and pointed out this strange behavior. What, he asked the colonel, did it mean. The colonel, too, was puzzled. He asked to see the pictures again. 'Ah,' he said when the performance was over, 'I have it. They are holding the horses.'" (Morison, 1966, 17f)

Though examples such as this one may be easier to discern because the actions are no longer functional, the same dynamic can result in behaviors that produce useful outcomes. Indeed, behaviors may have antecedents that were never consciously thought out but that may simply emerge as reactions to the various constraints and pressures in a given situation (Merton, 1936; Nelson and Winter, 1982; Sandelands and Stablein, 1987; Sheil, 1981; Suchman, 1983). In such situations the actors may not even be aware that they are reproducing organizational behavior (Feldman, 1989). One of the means through which organizational behavior is unconsciously reproduced is through the repetition of interdependent behaviors. These might be called routines (Feldman, 1988), situated practices, or typified action sequences (Brown and Duguid, 1991; Jordan, 1990; Suchman, 1987). Interdependence is crucial to the process because it ensures that the actions of one person will be constrained by the actions and expectations of others. The maintenance of institutional memory through interdependent actions makes it possible for organizations to "remember" ways of behaving even when members of the organization leave. Of course, if all of the people involved in the routine or practice leave, there are no other actions or expectations to define "proper" behavior.

The high rate of turnover in the presidential organization leads me to speculate about the possible existence of institutional memory that is outside the organization. While this suggestion substantially extends the concept of institutional memory beyond its normal boundaries, the extension may be appropriate in this situation. I argued above that institutional memory may be sustained by the existence of interdependent behaviors of people within the organization. The behaviors of organizational members may be intertwined with those of people outside the organization as well. Thus, the continuity of behaviors may be the result not of expectations from other organizational members but of expectations from members of other organizations with whom one is engaged in interdependent actions. This effect may be rather negligible in some relatively self-contained organizations. The organization of the presidency, however, can hardly be so characterized. Thus, one of the main places we would look for sources of continuity in the presidential organization is in the behaviors that are influenced by external expectations. These may be "grand" expectations about how a president should act and what a president should know. They may also be less grand, such as expectations of legislators about when the budget will be ready for review.[4] While these expectations surely change, they do not necessarily change in connection with the changes of administration.

ORGANIZATIONAL LEARNING

The issue of learning is one of potentially great importance in the study of the presidency. After all, every few years most of the people in the organization are new. They may have experience that qualifies them for the positions they take, but no position is quite like the one they will fulfill in the presidential organization. The scope is different, the problems and potential solutions are different, the relevant actors are different. How is it that they learn all they need to know? How do these processes contribute to the continuities and discontinuities of a presidential organization?

Before further discussing learning processes, I should make clear that organizational learning does not necessarily imply any absolute increase in successes or decrease in failures. Some refer to this as "valid learning" (March, Sproull, and Tamuz, 1991). Nor does organizational learning imply that everyone learns the same thing. This has been called "reliable learning" (ibid). The term *organizational learning* generally refers to the processes of acquiring new ways of thinking about the organization and its work or new ways of doing tasks. It also refers to increasing the consensus on these matters. I discuss three forms of organizational learning: trial and error, imitation, and enactment. I do not, here, discuss conscious processes of analysis and choice. To the extent that learning occurs in these processes, they belong here, but I believe they are more appropriately dealt with in a separate section.

Trial and error is perhaps the best known process. It consists of taking an action and interpreting the feedback associated with the action. The major complications of the process come in determining what is feedback and whether it is associated with the action and in making sense of the feedback (March and Olsen, 1976). How, for example, does one understand no response? Possible sources of continuity or discontinuity may be found in three elements: the audiences to whom one looks for feedback, the substance of the feedback, and the interpretations made of the feedback. In varying circumstances any of these elements may change or stay the same. For example, if a relatively conservative and a relatively liberal administration were each to make the same policy proposal, they may get the same response from the conservative (for example) electorate, but they may interpret that response differently. Likewise, these two administrations may simply pay attention to different audiences. There are many variations on this theme, but the point is the same: what is learned depends on these three elements. Continuity or discontinuity in the substance of what is learned from trial and error depends on the similarities and differences in these elements.

Another means of learning is to gain information from people who were in or associated with previous administrations. This information can be acquired either directly or indirectly. New occupants of positions in the presidential organization may consult with people from previous administrations (Hess, 1976; Moe, 1985). They may learn by analyzing previous administrations (Hult, chap. 3). They may also learn by attempting to imitate what others in the same position have done (Nelson and Winter, 1982). Indirect learning from the successes (and failures) of previous people with the same responsibilities is imitation or reverse imitation (i.e., doing that which someone else did or did not do).[5] One of the critical questions in understanding the process of imitation is understanding how choices are made about who or what to imitate. How do people determine on what or whom to pattern their behavior?

Understanding how choices about imitation are made involves first acknowledging that some of these choices are conscious decisions and some are not. Much behavior is taken for granted as the only reasonable way to act. For instance, most people who work for the president would occupy the offices they are assigned, answer the telephone when it rings, respond to questions put to them, and so forth, without much consideration of whether these are reasonable actions to take. Much of everyday behavior is constituted in this unreflective way (Schutz, 1970; Garfinkel, 1967). Even behaviors that may be quite important to the operation of the president's organization may be of this sort. There are, however, other behaviors upon which people reflect before they act.[6] These behaviors are dependent upon interpretations of who exemplifies success or failure and of what they did that constituted or brought about their success or failure. Such interpretations may be made by individuals, but they are often created by groups of people who develop a common way of viewing the world (Seidman, 1980; Van Maanen and Barley, 1985).

The question of whom or what to imitate (or avoid imitating) is just one in a myriad of questions that may be explicitly or implicitly answered by the development of a perspective shared among groups of people in the presidential organization. Such a perspective is one feature of what people have called organizational culture (Frost et al., 1985, 1991; Ott, 1989; Smirchich, 1983, 1985; Van Maanen and Barley, 1985). The perspective may be developed through and carried by stories, norms, rituals, routines, jargon, and other uses of language and behavior (Beyer, 1981; Martin et al., 1983; Ott, 1989; Sproull, 1981; Trice and Beyer, 1984). The perspective is likely to deal with questions such as, Who are we? (How are we different from and similar to previous groups who have held these positions? What do we want to be known for or not known for? What are the characteristics that we have that are relevant to our current positions?), and What are we doing? (Who did what, when, and how? What do particular actions mean? What do actions mean when taken by different people?). While these questions seem likely, the perspective may deal with a very different set of questions instead of or in addition to these. Only through research can one ascertain what questions are being addressed and which of them are the subject of conscious deliberation and which are taken for granted.

Such a perspective seems destined to include an orientation to previous administrations.[7] Groups of people who have performed similar jobs in the past seem likely to be objects that are either emulated or not. The process of this emulation, however, is not likely to be straightforward. Under what conditions does a group of people designate another group as one they want to emulate? Party ID may be one defining characteristic, resulting in what Hult refers to as partisan learning (Hult, chap. 3); national popularity may be another. Other characteristics are likely to be much more idiosyncratic. Groups may want to identify themselves as tough on crime or as fiscal conservatives or as social liberals. Even relatively straightforward characteristics such as party affiliation and national popularity require a theory (either implicit or explicit) to connect the characteristics with appropriate behaviors (Sproull, 1981). Where do members of the presidential organization look for appropriate models or antimodels? How do they translate the successes or failures of previous groups into behavior appropriate for the present?

A third means of learning that has been associated with organizations involves learning by doing or enactment (Eden, 1990; Leavitt and March, 1988; Weick, 1979). This line of research suggests that organizations do not necessarily decide what they are going to learn or even what they need to learn. Instead, they act and then they attribute meaning to these actions. Through this process, the actions become meaningful. An example of this enactment process comes from the institute in which I teach. The students have for the past five or six years sponsored a conference. The first conference was simply something that a group of students was interested in doing. The institute provided minimal though significant support. Since the first conference, the student conference has taken on many meanings. It is seen by many of the students as an obligation; a class that did not sponsor a conference would be seen by many as a failure; there is a subtle (or not so subtle) competition among classes for producing better and better conferences; the choice of a topic for the conference is often a matter of considerable dissension, with the attendant opportunities for the class as a whole to come to a new consensus; the institute now provides a faculty sponsor for the conference. All of this has occurred despite the fact that the conference makes only a minimal contribution to the education of most members of the class and despite the fact that the first conference was never undertaken with these changes in mind and despite the fact that no one is being overtly rewarded or punished for participation in or failure to participate in the conference. The best description of the phenomenon is that it is a series of events to which people inside the organization have attached meaning.

Enactment is related to trial and error learning in that something happens and then meaning is attributed to it. In trial and error learning, however, the meaning is attributed by an external force in the form of success or failure. The distinctive feature of the enactment conception of learning is that the attribution of meaning comes from within the organization and is based on values internal to the organization. Thus, this form of learning is closely associated with the notions of organizational culture presented earlier.

The scholar relating these ideas to the office of the presidency might want to ask the following questions: Are there traditions that have developed in the office of the president that would take on great meaning if they were ceased? What are the values that are placed on these traditions? How are these values related to other values held by people who occupy the presidential organization? What other sets of values could be associated with these traditions? The answer to such questions may help the scholar to find an underlying layer of values and perceptions that unites the different administrations that occupy the presidency or to identify the depth of differences between one administration and another.

ORGANIZATIONAL DECISION MAKING

The presidential organization produces many decisions. There are many features of decision making that could be explored and many that have been. In what follows, I focus on the way people think about the issues that are the subject of the decisions. Though there are many ways of categorizing decisions, the one I describe is particularly relevant to choices about the process of decision making. Exploring this categorization and its implications may provide scholars of the presidency with a way to think about such issues as how and when experts are used in policy making. I propose dividing issues into two categories: uncertainty and ambiguity (of course, all issues do not fall neatly into these two categories). Issues of uncertainty can be resolved by specific pieces of information. These pieces of information may be very difficult or even impossible to obtain. One can, however, specify what information one would need in order to resolve the uncertainty. Issues of ambiguity, by contrast, cannot be resolved through the use of information alone. In fact, while information is often useful in resolving ambiguity, it also often confounds the ambiguity (Feldman, 1989).

Let's take the national budget as an example. There are many issues of uncertainty in the budget. For instance, if entitlements are increased yearly by the cost of living adjustment, what percentage of the national budget will entitlements constitute in the year 2000? This is an issue of uncertainty because we know exactly what information we need to resolve it, and ultimately, we can know the answer; we just don't have all this information now. For instance, we don't know what the cost of living adjustment will be for the coming years. We can, however, specify that we need that piece of information. While it is not important to the definition of this question as an issue of uncertainty, it is true that we have ways of estimating the cost of living adjustments for the coming years. Because we are often unwilling to wait until the answer is known for sure, these means of estimation are an essential part of our ability to deal with uncertainty.

The budget also illustrates issues of ambiguity. There is the issue of national health care, for instance. One issue that the budget raises is, What is the appropriate level of national health care? Should the government be involved in the provision of health care at all? Should the government provide a safety net for those people who cannot pay for their own health care? Should the government require employers to provide health insurance? Should there be national health insurance? Should there be national health care? These are just a few of the questions that could be raised about this issue. Though we may each have our own answers to the above questions, we know that there are reasonable arguments for alternative approaches. Furthermore, no particular information can be summoned to resolve these questions. Information may be useful in developing a way of thinking about these questions that enables us to make decisions and implement proposals. The information, however, will just be one part of a process of determining the appropriate action (Feldman, 1990, 1991).

Whether an issue is perceived as ambiguous or uncertain can have an effect on how decisions are made about it. The two kinds of issues tend to be resolved differently. In general, we tend to use problem solving and analysis to make decisions where issues of uncertainty are involved. We are more likely to use political processes where issues of ambiguity are concerned. These political processes include, for example, assigning the decision to a hierarchical authority and voting.[8]

I've talked about uncertainty and ambiguity as if they were characteristics of the issues themselves. It is more appropriate, however, to portray them as perceptions of the issues. That is, we perceive issues as uncertain when we have agreed on ways of thinking that put to rest possible ambiguities. Specifically, we agree on the creation of particular categories and on what phenomena should be considered part of the category. For example, the question of how much the federal government will pay for entitlements in the year 2000 is an issue of uncertainty only if we agree on what an entitlement is. This means that we have to have defined a category called *entitlements* and we have to have certain programs that fall in that category and other programs that do not.

Underlying most, if not all, issues of uncertainty are issues of potential ambiguity. Making decisions or even thinking about issues requires us to develop categories and definitions and to consider some phenomena relevant and others not (Cicourel, 1968; Garfinkel, 1967; Weick, 1979). For many issues there is such widespread agreement about what is relevant that we may forget that the categories and definitions are our own creations. They become reality. Many categories and definitions have attained the status of reality or of being unquestioned most of the time. For instance, for the purpose of counting how many people are in the room or in the city or in the state, we generally agree on what constitutes a person as well as on the boundaries that define the room, the city, or the state.[9] There are other categories and definitions that have not attained this status and over which there is a great deal of debate. For example, there is much disagreement about whether to classify abortion as a murder or as a right. Then there are categories and definitions that are not hotly disputed but that have not attained the status of unquestioned reality. For instance, our standard way of counting the number of unemployed people stops counting them if they have been unemployed for a long period of time. This leads to a situation in which people who consider themselves unemployed because they do not have jobs are not considered in the official count of the unemployed. Similarly, the definition of full employment could be questioned. Some might wonder how it can be defined differently during different periods. It has, for example, risen from 3 percent to 6 percent joblessness between the 1940s and the 1980s (Stone, 1988). Some might even find it odd that full employment is not defined as 0 percent unemployment.

Issues that are clearly ambiguous (e.g., abortion) and issues that are clearly not ambiguous (e.g., what is a person) are not readily changed. The third group discussed above, however, constitutes a gray area in which political officials have an opportunity to intervene. The definition of full employment can be redefined; how unemployment is defined can be changed. The presidential organization has virtually sole jurisdiction over many issues that fall into this grey area. As a result, it has many opportunities to influence the definitions and categories that are used to construct understandings about the policies it proposes and the actions it takes. There are limits to how much any administration can avail itself of these opportunities. One of the limits is simply that such changes require some expenditure of attention, which is a limited resource. Thus, we would expect presidential organizations to make some changes in this grey area and to leave much of it the same.

Some of the areas of inquiry that might help to explore the continuity and discontinuity from one administration to another are suggested by the following questions. What are the differences and similarities among administrations regarding which gray areas they choose to focus on? Do different administrations become more or less involved in the process of redefinition? To what extent are the political elements of different administrations involved in the development of analyses?

Conclusion

I have described four concepts from organization theory, and each can be used to learn more about the ways in which the presidency is or is not continuous from one administration to another. This analysis can help students of the presidency to understand when it is appropriate to treat presidencies as separate and independent phenomena and when it is more appropriate to view them as continuous and cumulative. I have endeavored to provide a sufficient introduction to each of these concepts that students of the presidency will be interested in finding out how they relate to actual presidencies, presidential organizations, and the executive branches under different administrations. How these phenomena look through the lens of these concepts remains to be seen.

Notes

1. For two excellent though quite different maps of the field, see Scott (1981) and Pfeffer (1982).

2. In fact, this distinction between the person and the office is one of the principle attributes of modern organizations, according to Weber.

3. The War Powers Act may be an example of putting into writing what was an unwritten norm.

4. Note that it is not necessary for the expectation to be fulfilled. It is only necessary that it be known.

5. Hult's chapter in this volume discusses a form of imitation in her section on cross-administration dynamics.

6. This distinction is not nearly so neat as I suggest here.

7. The development of such a perspective is also destined to encompass the past experiences of the people in the current administration. This, however, is more of a psychological issue and less of an organizational issue. Therefore, I concentrate on the relation to previous administrations.

8. This is not an exhaustive list of political processes. For a more through discussion of the relation of uncertainty and ambiguity to decision processes see Feldman (1990, 1991).

9. The counting process may leave much to be desired, particularly in the case of the homeless, but the problems are not overtly problems of defining who counts as a person.

References

Arrow, Kenneth. 1974. *The Limits of Organization*. New York: Norton.

Barley, Stephen P. 1983. "Semiotics and the Study of Occupational Cultures." *Administrative Science Quarterly* 28 (3): 393–413.

Beyer Janice M. 1981. "Ideologies, Values and Decision Making in Organizations." In *The Handbook of Organizational Design*, vol. 2, ed. Paul C. Nystrom and William H. Starbuck. New York: Oxford University Press.

Brown, John Seeley, and Paul Duguid. 1991. "Organizational Learning and Communities-of-Practice." *Organizational Science* 2 (1): 40–57.

Chandler, Alfred D. Jr. 1962. *Strategy and Structure: Chapters in the History of American Industrial Enterprise*. Cambridge: MIT Press.

Cicourel, Aaron. 1968. *The Social Organization of Juvenile Justice*. New York: Wiley.

Cyert, Richard M., and James G. March. 1963. *A Behavioral Theory of the Firm*. Englewood Cliffs, N.J.: Prentice-Hall.

Dean, John. 1976. *Blind Ambition*. New York: Simon and Schuster.

Eden, Lynn. 1990. "The Hypothetical Organization: Organizational Learning and Interpretation in U.S. Strategic Nuclear Targeting." Paper prepared for the American Political Science Association meetings, August 29–September 1.

Feldman, Martha S. 1988. "Understanding Organizational Routines: Stability and Change," Norwegian Research Center in Organization and Management Working Paper 88/35 (LOS Senter Notat 88/35), University of Bergen, Bergen, Norway.

————. 1989. *Order Without Design: Information Production and Policy Making*. Stanford: Stanford University Press.

————. 1990. "Alternative Uses of Information in Organizations." Paper prepared for the Conference on Understanding and Improving Public Decision Making, Institute of Government and Public Affairs, University of Illinois, April 19–20.

————. 1991. "Perceptions of Uncertainty and Ambiguity and the Effects on Choice Processes." Talk delivered at XeroxPARC, April 25.

Frost, Peter J., Larry F. Moore, Meryl Reis Louis, Craig C. Lundberg, Joanne Martin. 1985. *Organizational Culture*. Beverly Hills: Sage.

Frost, Peter J., Larry F. Moore, Meryl Reis Louis, Craig C. Lundberg, Joanne Martin. 1991. *Reframing Organizational Culture*. Beverly Hills: Sage.

Galbraith, John Kenneth. 1967. *The New Industrial State*. Boston: Houghton Mifflin.

Garfinkel, Harold. 1967. *Studies in Ethnomethodology*. Englewood Cliffs, N.J.; Prentice-Hall.

George, Alexander. 1974. "Assessing Presidential Character." *World Politics* 26 (January):234–82.

Goffman, Erving. 1959. *The Presentation of Self in Everyday Life*. New York: Doubleday.

Hargrove, Erwin. 1966. *Presidential Leadership: Personality and Political Style*. New York: Macmillan.

————. 1973. "Presidential Personality and Revisionist Views of the Presidency." *American Journal of Political Science* 17 (November): 819–36.

Hess, Stephen. 1976. *Organizing the Presidency.* Washington, D.C.: Brookings.

Hult, Karen M. 1992. "Advising the President: Making Sense of Presidential Advisory Networks." In *Researching the Presidency,* ed. G. Edwards, J. Kessel, and B. Rockman. Pittsburgh: University of Pittsburgh Press.

Hult, Karen M., and Charles Walcott. 1989. "To Meet the Press: Tracing the Evolution of the White House Press Operation." Paper prepared for the Midwest Political Science Association Meetings, April.

Jordan, Brigitte. 1990. "The Organization of Activity and the Achievement of Competent Practice in a Complex Work Setting." Prepared for the Symposium on Transformation and Cognition at Work, 2d International Congress for Research on Activity Theory, Lahti, Finland, May 21–25.

Kaufman, Herbert. 1976. *Are Government Organizations Immortal?* Washington, D.C.: Brookings.

Kessel, John H. 1975. *The Domestic Presidency: Decision Making in the White House.* North Scituate, Mass: Duxbury.

Leavitt, Barbara, and James G. March. 1988. "Organizational Learning." *Annual Review of Sociology* 14:319–40.

Lawrence, Paul R., and Jay Lorsch. 1967. *Organization and Environment: Managing Differentiation and Integration.* Boston: Graduate School of Business Administration, Harvard University.

Light, Paul. 1981. "The President's Agenda: Notes on the Timing of Domestic Choice." *Presidential Studies Quarterly* 12:67–82.

———. 1982. *The President's Agenda: Domestic Policy Choice from Kennedy to Carter.* Baltimore: Johns Hopkins University Press.

———. 1984. *Vice Presidential Power: Advice and Influence in the White House.* Baltimore: Johns Hopkins University Press.

Lindblom, Charles E. 1977. *Politics and Markets.* New York: Basic.

Lowi, Theodore J. 1985. *The Personal Presidency.* Ithaca: Cornell University Press.

Manley, John F. 1978. "Presidential Power and White House Lobbying." *Political Science Quarterly* 93:255–75.

March, James G., and Johan P. Olsen. 1976. *Ambiguity and Choice in Organizations.* Bergen, Norway: Universitetsforlaget.

March, James G., and Johan P. Olsen. 1989. *Rediscovering Institutions: The Organizational Basis of Politics.* New York: Free Press.

March, James G., and Herbert Simon. 1958. *Organizations.* New York: Wiley.

March, James G., Lee S. Sproull, and Michal Tamuz. 1991. "Learning from Samples of One or Fewer." *Organizational Science* 2 (1): 1–13.

Martin, Joanne, Martha S. Feldman, Mary Jo Hatch, Sim B. Sitkin. 1983. "The Uniqueness Paradox in Organizational Stories." *Administrative Science Quarterly* 28 (3): 438–53.

Meltsner, Arnold J. 1981. *Politics and the Oval Office.* San Fransisco: Institute for Contemporary Studies.

Merton, Robert K. 1936. "The Unanticipated Consequences of Purposive Social Action." *American Sociological Review* 1:894–904.

———. 1957. *Social Theory and Social Structure.* 2d ed. Glencoe, Ill: Free Press.

Moe, Terry M. 1985. "The Politicized Presidency." In *The New Directions in American Politics,* ed. John Chubb and Paul Peterson. Washington, D.C.: Brookings.

————. 1992. "Presidents, Institutions, and Theory." In *Researching the Presidency*, ed. G. Edwards, J. Kessel, and B. Rockman. Pittsburgh: University of Pittsburgh Press.

Morison, Elting E. 1966. *Men, Machines and Modern Times*. Cambridge: MIT Press.

Nelson, Richard R., and Sidney G. Winter. 1982. *An Evolutionary Theory of Economic Choice*. Cambridge Mass.: Belknap.

Neustadt, Richard E. 1980. *Presidential Power*. New York: Wiley.

Ott, Stephen J. 1989. *The Organizational Culture Perspective*. Pacific Grove, Calif.: Brooks/Cole.

Parkinson, C. Northcote. 1987. "Parkinson's Law or The Rising Pyramid." In *Classics of Public Administration*, 2d ed., ed. Shafritz and Hyde. Chicago, Ill.: Dorsey.

Pfeffer, Jeffrey. 1982. *Organizations and Organization Theory*. Boston: Pitman.

Rockman, Bert A. 1986. "Presidential and Executive Studies: The One, the Few and The Many." In *Political Science: The Science of Politics*, ed. Herbert F. Weisberg. New York: Agathon.

Rose, Richard, and Ezra Suleiman, eds. 1980. *Presidents and Prime Ministers*. Washington, D.C.: American Enterprise Institute.

Sandelands, Lloyd E., and Ralph E. Stablein. 1987. "The Concept of Organizational Mind." *Research in the Sociology of Organizations* 5:135–61.

Schumpeter, Joseph A. 1947. *Capitalism, Socialism and Democracy*. 2d ed. New York: Harper.

Schutz, Alfred. 1970. *Reflections on the Problem of Relevance*. New Haven: Yale University Press.

Scott, W. Richard. 1981. *Organizations: Rational, Natural, and Open Systems*. Englewood Cliffs, N.J.: Prentice-Hall.

Seidman, Harold. 1980. *Politics, Position, and Power*. 3d ed. New York: Oxford University Press.

Sheil, B. 1981. "Coping with Complexity." Working paper, Xerox Palo Alto Research Center Laboratory for Artificial Intelligence.

Shogan, Robert. 1991. *The Riddle of Power: Presidential Leadership from Truman to Bush*. New York: Dutton.

Simon, Herbert. 1957. *Administrative Behavior*. New York: Macmillan.

Smirchich, Linda. 1983. "Concepts of Culture and Organizational Analysis." *Adminstrative Science Quarterly* 28 (3): 339–58.

————. 1985. "Is The Concept of Culture a Paradigm for Understanding Organizations and Ourselves?" In *Organizational Culture*, ed. Peter J. Frost, et. al. Beverly Hills: Sage.

Sproull, Lee S. 1981. "Beliefs in Organizations." In *The Handbook of Organizational Design*, vol. 2, ed. Paul C. Nystrom and William H. Starbuck. New York: Oxford University Press.

Stone, Deborah A. 1988. *Policy Paradox and Political Reason*. Glenview, Ill.: Scott, Foresman.

Suchman, Lucy. 1983. "Office Procedures as Practical Action: Models of Work and System Design." *ACM Transactions on Office Information Systems* 1:320–28.

————. 1987. *Plans and Situation Actions: The Problem of Human Machine Interaction*. Cambridge: Cambridge University Press.

Taylor, Frederick W. 1911. *The Principles of Scientific Management*. New York: Harper.

Thomas, Edwin J., and Bruce J. Biddle. 1966. "Basic Concepts For Classifying The Phenomena of Role." In *Role Theory: Concepts and Research*, ed. Bruce J. Biddle and Edwin Thomas. New York: Wiley.

Thompson, James D. 1967. *Organizations in Action*. New York: McGraw Hill.

Trice, H. M., and Janice M. Beyer. 1984. "Studying Organizational Cultures Through Rites and Ceremonials." *The Academy of Management Review* 9 (4): 653–69.

Van Maanen, John. 1973. "Observations on the Making of Policemen." *Human Organization* 32 (4): 407–18.

Van Maanen, John, and Stephen R. Barley. 1985. "Cultural Organization: Fragments of a Theory." In *Organizational Culture*, ed. Peter J. Frost, et. al. Beverly Hills: Sage.

Weber, Max. 1947. "Bureaucracy." In *From Max Weber*, ed. H. H. Gerth and C. Wright Mills. New York: Oxford University Press.

Weick, Karl E. 1979. *The Social Psychology of Organizing*. New York: Random House.

Wildavsky, Aaron. 1975. *Perspectives on the Presidency*. Boston: Little, Brown.

Williamson, Oliver E. 1975. *Markets and Hierarchies: Analysis and Antitrust Implications*. New York: Free Press.

Wilson, James Q. 1989. *Bureaucracy: What Government Agencies Do and Why They Do It*. New York: Basic.

Woodward, Bob, and Scott Armstrong. 1979. *The Brethren: Inside the Supreme Court*. New York: Simon and Schuster.

8

Formal Theory and the Presidency

GARY J. MILLER

I N *The Semi-Sovereign People,* E. E. Schattschneider argues that "the outcome of all conflict is determined by the scope of its contagion" (1960, 2). Some contestants gain by broadening the scope of conflict, others by keeping conflict private. "If a fight starts, watch the crowd, because the crowd plays the decisive role" (3).

Schattschneider refers to "pressure politics" as that relatively private game of politics in which small organizations seek quietly to procure action in their members' interest. "Party politics," on the other hand, is that much more socialized brand of politics that mobilizes a much larger number of unorganized voters to win elections. In a chapter titled "Whose Game Do We Play?" Schattschneider argues that it makes a very big difference whether a given public policy issue is resolved through pressure politics or party politics. With party politics, the scope of conflict is broadened, and the "crowd plays the decisive role."

Schattschneider has not been used as a source of inspiration either by presidential scholars or formal theorists. However, I would argue that Schattschneider's insights are important to both literatures.

The best applications of formal theory to American politics (Ferejohn, 1986; Fiorina, 1977; Shepsle and Weingast, 1981; Weingast, 1984) have done an outstanding job of providing insight into what Schattschneider calls pressure politics. In this game, people are rationally ignorant, members of Congress seek reelection by providing benefits to organized minorities, congressional committees provide the mechanism for stable bargains within Congress, and bureaucracies are trained to respond to changes in committee structure. This is the normal world of American politics, and political parties and the president play only a marginal role in it.

However, the purpose of this chapter is to argue that abnormal politics serves as an important check on the normal world of pressure politics. Abnormal politics begins with that abnormal player in American politics: the (relatively) informed voter. While the relatively informed voter is not a normal feature in American politics for very good reasons, she carries a great deal of impact when she appears. As Schattschneider argues, when the passive crowd is provided with free information on a salient issue, it changes the nature of the game considerably. In American politics, the arousal of the crowd triggers a series of institutional responses that feature the two-party system and the presidency. I argue that the key to understanding the role of presidential leadership in American politics rests with Schattschneider's insights about the socialization of conflict. Given the extraordinary contingency of an aroused and involved general public, the president has the opportunity to play a crucial role as focus of coordination and nexus of contracts. In short, the president emerges from the constraints to which he is consigned by the formal analysis of normal politics and weighs in as the two-ton gorilla.

This chapter begins by reviewing a few well-known cases of presidential leadership and weakness. It continues by suggesting that current formal theories of presidential influence do not capture the dynamic nature of presidential leadership. The chapter then proceeds with an analysis of presidential leadership based primarily on the president's symbolic and communicative powers, rather than his formal and legislative powers.

Case Studies of Presidential Strength and Weakness

The record of presidential influence and passivity seems to support a number of positions about the presidency. An interesting case of presidential influence was the 1933 bank crisis.

ROOSEVELT AND THE BANK CRISIS

The four months between the election of Franklin Roosevelt and his inauguration in March 1933 were the worst months of the Great Depression: national income had been cut in half, fifteen million workers had lost their jobs, and Congress failed to produce a single piece of legislation to deal with the crisis. Banks all over the country were in trouble by the end of February. By March 4, Inauguration Day, the governors of thirty-eight states had closed their banks, Richard Whitney announced the closing of the Stock Exchange, and the Chicago Board of Trade locked its doors for the first time since 1848 (Leuchtenberg, 1963).

Roosevelt wondered aloud in February if the country would last until he assumed office (ibid., 39). Yet his inauguration speech conveyed a feeling of courage and confidence. On Sunday, March 5, he approved two presidential edicts, one halting transactions in gold and proclaiming a national bank holiday, and one calling Congress into special session for the following Thursday. At one o'clock on that day, the Speaker read aloud the one available copy of Roosevelt's banking bill, a rather conservative document extending assistance to bankers and giving the president control over gold movements. The House approved it, essentially sight unseen, by a unanimous voice vote.

On Sunday night, March 12, sixty million people listened to Roosevelt over the radio assuring them that it was now safe to return their savings to the banks. The next morning, people were more eager to deposit cash than withdraw it. In every city, deposits exceeded withdrawals, despite the fact that everyone had done without cash for eight days. One observer wrote in her diary, "The people trust this admin. as they distrusted the other. This is the secret of the whole situation" (ibid., 44).

REAGAN AND TAX REFORM

The progressive income tax instituted after 1913 offered infinite possibilities for legislative logrolling. After the tariff reform of the Depression era, the income tax became perhaps the most important source of distributive benefits that members of Congress could hand out to their constituents.

With inflation and economic growth, a tax system pegged to income levels naturally generated more and more revenues, some of which could be turned back to the public in the form of tax breaks. Congress chose to return tax revenues in the form of tax breaks to targeted (and politically active) interest groups, in a way that would bring credit to specific tax committee members or other legislators.

Tax reform—the elimination of tax breaks and generalized lower-ing of tax rates—was of course regarded unenthusiastically by legis-lators having influence on tax policy. It was the kind of issue that politicians could symbolically support in the safe and sure knowledge that it would never happen and that they would not be held account-able for its failure by any politically active or influential lobby.

Ronald Reagan claimed that tax reform was his major domestic is-sue in the 1984 reelection. Members of Congress and tax lobbyists were sure this was only a symbolic, not to mention cynical, attempt to create a pleasing public image of the populist Reagan. However, in May 1985 Reagan made a strong televised address for support of tax reform. This initiated a chain reaction.

The Democrats decided that they could not be known as the party that killed tax reform, so Ways and Means Chairman Rostenkowski supported Reagan's initiative. "If he allowed the bill to die in the House, President Reagan and the Republicans would never let the Democrats, who were in control there, live it down" (Birnbaum and Murray, 1987, 103). Rostenkowski committed himself to getting a bill through the House. When House Republicans defeated the rule that would bring it to the floor for a vote, Reagan appeared person-ally before the Republican caucus and reminded them that "tax re-form was important to him and important to the Republican party" (ibid., 170). A sufficient number of House Republicans then decided that they could not buck a president who had the ability to mobilize the nation behind the tax reform issue.

After passage through the House, the most unlikely switch oc-curred. The chair and members of the Senate Finance Committee, who had made quite comfortable careers out of catering to the special interests demanding tax breaks, now were faced with the same fact that had faced the House Republicans: they could not afford to take the blame for killing a measure that their president had made the number one domestic issue for their party. Although they had wanted tax reform to die in the House, they had to vote in favor of a version offered by Chairman Packwood, who was up for reelection that year. In doing so, they had to vote against the lobbyists whose interests they had cheerfully supported throughout their careers. "At each step President Reagan threatened to label lobbyists' friends in Congress as toadies to the special interests and enemies of rate cuts for the people, and that was a threat that could not be taken lightly" (ibid., 287). As in the bank crisis, it was the symbolic and extraconstitutional powers of the president that seemed to make the difference.

PRESIDENTIAL POWERLESSNESS: THE CORPS OF ENGINEERS

The two cases just mentioned contrast sharply with the history of the presidency as it relates to a different issue: the water control projects sponsored by the Corps of Engineers. The Corps has had a very close relationship with Congress and especially with the House Appropriations Committee. Members of Congress have regarded the Corps' public works projects as sought-after reelection benefits, perfect for claiming credit with contractors, developers, and unions. The activities of the Corps are supported by strong interest groups such as the National Rivers and Harbors Congress, which includes in its membership contractors, officers of the Corps, and members of Congress (Seidman, 1975, 152).

Against the tight coalition of legislators, bureaucrats, and interest groups, the president has had little influence. In 1923, President Harding thought it would be nice to move the Corps into the Department of the Interior, in order to achieve more effective executive coordination. Congress rejected the proposal. In 1932, President Hoover issued an executive order effecting the same transfer; Congress nullified the order. Franklin Roosevelt used his hierarchical authority as the head of the military establishment (of which the Corps is presumably a part) to direct that the controversial Kings and Kern river projects be built by the Bureau of Reclamation rather than the Corps, but Congress insisted that it be built by the Corps. In 1976, Carter ran on a platform that included the necessity of greater control of the bureaucracy, but his plan to scrap seven of the Corps' more inefficient projects provoked the first big battle of his administration. In 1985, Reagan tried to consolidate the Corps of Engineers and the Bureau of Reclamation, only to have his proposal rejected by the bureaus themselves and their congressional supporters.

"If the Corps had been responsive to the wishes, even the orders, of the presidency, a quite different pattern of power would have existed, and the consequences in distribution of benefits of the Corps'activities within various areas might also have been different"

(McConnell, 1966, 216). Unlike the bank crisis of 1933 or the tax re form of 1986, the pork barrel projects of the Corps have been an arena of enduring presidential passivity and powerlessness.

Is there a theoretical rationalization for the variability in presidential impact across issues, across time, and across incumbents in the White House? At present we have a very good theoretical justification for presidential powerlessness; we have less understanding of those occasions when the president seems to have great impact on the flow of decisions in Washington; we have least of all an explanation for why the president should be powerful on some occasions and not others. The next section begins with a discussion of normal politics and why the president is not a featured player in it.

Rational Ignorance and Normal Politics

Normally, individuals have an incentive to become relatively informed about the qualities of alternative private goods available for purchase. At the local public library, for example, one can find potential car buyers using resource materials that reveal the safety record, repair record, and other merits of different styles of automobiles.

On the other hand, individuals have little reason to become equally informed about public goods. Wise public decisions regarding Social Security or environmental pollution benefit everyone; they are public goods. The efforts necessary for the public to become informed, however, are private and costly. As a result, each individual citizen would most prefer to free-ride on everyone else's costly efforts to inform themselves about technical issues like the environment, social security, and the positions and qualifications of candidates. If everyone else free-rides, then it does no good for any one individual to inform himself. Whether or not the rest of the public is informed, everyone has a dominant strategy to stay uninformed.

The net result is that most of the public is uninformed about most public policy issues most of the time.

PRESSURE POLITICS

Weingast captures concisely and accurately the connection between rational ignorance and pressure politics:

While rational ignorance pervades the political system, that does not imply that the interests of constituents are irrelevant for representatives or that the latter are free to pursue their own interests. Rather, rational ignorance underpins interest group advantage in politics. Because most voters have only a dim awareness of an incumbent's actions, rational ignorance biases political response toward those who do form impressions. Thus interest groups, because they have greater individual stakes in particular issues, monitor congressmen and provide them with information (Weingast and Marshall, 1988, 136).

Organized special interest groups are thus often able to obtain "access" to legislators and regulatory agencies by means of campaign contributions or expertise. The most influential interest groups are those that are organized around rather narrow, precise interests. They are often trade associations or individual firms. Those groups that try to represent too broad a spectrum of the public often lose influence in policy formation. The reasons for this are clear: the interests they represent are too often at odds on particular issues, the bureaucracy becomes too cumbersome, individuals find it expedient to free-ride on other members when it comes to grassroots lobbying efforts, and the staff finds it necessary to spend too much of its time providing selective incentives just to keep the organization alive.

In order to serve the narrow, often quite parochial interests necessary for election of individual congressmen in their districts, legislators must construct majority coalitions. As Weingast and Marshall discuss, this requires a mechanism for negotiating and enforcing contracts. This problem is compounded because noncontemporaneous benefit flows and nonsimultaneous exchange of political support provide ample opportunities for opportunism—reneging on political bargains (ibid., 140–41). Weingast and Marshall correctly focus on the committee system as the principal means by which bargains are enforced. As illustrated by Ferejohn (1986), rural control of the House Agriculture Committee and liberal control of the Rules Committee provided the basis for two hostile groups to maintain a stable coalition over a very long period of time.

Special interest groups, congressional committees, and regulatory agencies constitute what Schattschneider calls the "pressure system" and what others call "policy subsystems" or "cozy triangles." One of the distinguished features of the pressure system is that the public policies that result tend to provide benefits that are concentrated in the special interests that are most involved in the formation of the policy. This is true for milk price supports, maritime policy, and Corps of Engineers projects. A second distinguishing characteristic is that no actor in the pressure system has anything to gain from greater public awareness of the issues in their domain. Neither the Department of Agriculture nor the tobacco lobby is trying to publicize the fact that the American public is supporting tobacco subsidies. The Corps of Engineers did not seek greater public involvement in its decision making, although that was forced on it as a result of the environmental crisis.

Several institutions of American politics are rarely mentioned in this analysis. Weingast and Marshall dismiss the political party system altogether: "Parties place no constraints on the behavior of individual representatives" (1988, 137). The empirical support for this view is quite strong (Fiorina, 1980). On a day-to-day basis, political parties play little role in the bargaining and negotiation of agriculture bills, water projects, and so on. Similarly, the president is not even mentioned in Weingast and Marshall and only rarely in other formal theoretical analyses of normal politics. But doesn't the president's veto power make him a crucial player in legislative politics?

THE FORMAL POWERS OF THE PRESIDENCY AND ITS LIMITS

What impact does the presidential veto have on legislative decision making? As a thought experiment, imagine that Congress is voting in a two-dimensional policy space as shown in figure 5. The Senate is composed of three equal voting blocs with concentric indifference curves around the three ideal points labeled S. The House is composed of five equal voting blocs with concentric indifference curves around the five ideal points labeled H. The president has concentric indifference curves around the point labeled P.

If these nine actors constituted a simple majority rule game, there would be no core—that is, no outcome that could not be upset by a majority coalition preferring a different alternative. McKelvey (1976) and Schofield (1976) show that such simple majority rule games are chaotic—any outcome could occur. Does the constitutional veto power give the president any power to provide closure to this game? Will the president be able to influence the outcome? Would a change

FIGURE 5
Legislative Instability Allows for Presidential Leadership

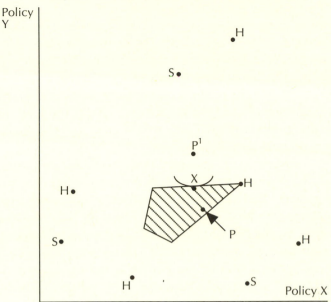

in presidential preferences (or a new incumbent in the White House) make a difference in the outcome? The formal analysis of the presidential veto provides the basis for some answers to these questions and in so doing suggests that the president who relies only on the veto power will not be a legislative success.

The Presidential Power Index. Beginning with Shapley and Shubik (1954), there has been a small but important literature on formal theory and the presidency. Shapley and Shubik try to determine the relative power of the president vis-à-vis individual members of Congress and the House and Senate as a whole. Their analysis uses the characteristic function form of an *N*-person cooperative game; their index of an individual's power is determined by the additional value that the individual brings to each possible coalition. The power indexes indicate an overwhelming advantage for a president as compared to any individual member of the Senate or the House; specifically, the proportions are reflected by a 350:9:2 ratio. This indicates an overwhelming advantage for a president as compared to any individual legislator. However, they also analyze the collective House and Senate against the president and find that each chamber has a 5:2 power ad vantage against the president. This suggests a bargaining weakness of the president, but it doesn't explain why the president should seem weaker on some issues than on others.

SPATIAL ANALYSIS AND THE ASYMMETRICAL IMPACT OF THE VETO

Kiewiet and McCubbins (1991) go far beyond Shapley and Shubik by discussing how the president's influence could systematically vary across issues. The central difference is the relative budgetary preferences of the president and Congress. Their model shows that presidential budgetary influence is asymmetrical. As long as the president prefers less money for a program than the Congress, then the veto can constrain congressional appetites. However, when the president wants more of something than Congress, then the veto provides no presidential leverage.

The Kiewiet-McCubbins model represents a significant advance over earlier analyses of the president's formal powers, and Kiewiet and McCubbins provide empirical support for the primary implications of the model. While the Kiewiet-McCubbins model recognizes the asymmetrical effect of the veto, however, it maintains a false symmetry by positing both the executive and legislature as monolithic bargainers.

MAJORITY RULE CYCLES AND TRICAMERAL STABILITY

Hammond and Miller argue that the president's power depends on his ability to play off alternative coalitions in the legislature. While it is reasonable to speak of the presidential position on a given policy issue, the notion of a congressional position is a myth in the absence of majority rule equilibrium. There are a very large number of majority coalitions possible in either chamber, and the president can hope to use his agenda and veto power to build and protect the most favorable of those congressional coalitions. Furthermore, given the bicameral nature of Congress, the president's veto power is very likely to create a stable, undominated outcome (a core) in what would otherwise be an unstable legislative game.

For example, in figure 5, Hammond and Miller (1987, 1160–61) argue that, *absent a committee system*, the president's veto can make him a limited dictator. Let us define a legislative core as the set of outcomes that no decisive legislative coalition can replace with a preferred outcome, given the rules of procedure in the legislature. There is no legislative core to the game in figure 5, even allowing for the necessity of obtaining a concurrent majority in both chambers. For any policy proposal, there is a different outcome preferred by a majority of both chambers. For instance, a majority of both chambers would upset point x in favor of a point to the south.

However, the presidential veto creates stability where the legislature is unstable. With the president, there are two kinds of decisive coalitions: a simple majority of both chambers plus the president, or an override coalition. Let us assume that a presidential veto may be overridden by a coalition of two of the three Senate blocs and *four* of the five House blocs.

The shaded region in figure 5 constitutes a set of policy proposals that cannot be upset by any override coalition. If the president's ideal point is located anywhere in this region (say at P), then his ideal point will be the unique core; there is no override coalition that can impose any other point over the presidential veto. If the president's ideal point is outside of this region (say at P'), then he can always impose his most preferred point from within the region. For instance, if the president's ideal point is at P', then his most preferred stable point is x. Any change the president would prefer could only be upset by a subsequent override coalition, but the president could effectively veto any move that he dislikes. In other words, the president can be a limited dictator within the confines of the shaded region; the absence of a legislative core means that the president has the power to play one competitive legislative coalition off against another, until his most preferred point within the no-override set is reached.

Furthermore, Greenberg (1979) shows that in a two-dimensional space there will *always* be a region of policy outcomes that cannot be overcome by a $^{67}/_{100}$ or greater majority. If the policy space facing the country is essentially two-dimensional, as demonstrated by Poole and Rosenthal (1985), then there must always be a set of outcomes (like the shaded region in figure 5) that the president can impose without fear of being upset by a coalition capable of overriding the veto.

In general, then, the absence of a majority rule equilibrium creates an opportunity for presidential influence. The more diverse the preferences of the legislature, the larger will be the region of policy alternatives in which he may be a dictator.

However, this analysis assumes that the legislature has unstable preferences, so that the president can play one majority coalition off another. As the next section shows, with a committee system, the legislature can in fact create for itself undominated core outcomes; in fact, the set of core outcomes may be quite large. This limits the ability of the president to have any policy impact, as any outcome in a legislative core may not be upset by the formal powers of the president. The primary effect of the committee system will be to limit presidential influence on the legislative process.

THE COMMITTEE SYSTEM AND
PRESIDENTIAL INFLUENCE

The gatekeeping powers of committees allow committees to table over 90 percent of the legislation that is introduced into Congress. Inevitably, this means that the committees can prevent legislative majorities from imposing outcomes that they would prefer. Any legislative change in a policy dimension in the jurisdiction of a committee must include a majority of that committee, as well as a majority of each chamber.

Some bicameral majorities, in other words, are not going to be able to enforce their majority preferences, simply because they do not include the correct committee member composition. This means that some outcomes that would be dominated by means of bicameral majority rule are going to be undominated—they will be elements of a legislative core. As shown in a recent paper by Hammond and Miller (1990, 225–26), the committee system may create a core by creating a deadlock between committee members and chamber majorities.[1]

As an example, imagine that just one of the two chambers in figure 6—in particular, the House—has a gatekeeping committee system. One voting bloc (H_x) constitutes a committee with jurisdiction over policy dimension X, and one voting bloc (H_y) constitutes a committee with jurisdiction over policy dimension Y. In order to institute a change in the X dimension, a coalition requires a majority of both chambers and the votes of H_x. This means that any outcome that is not between X_c (the committee's preferred X-policy) and X_m (the median House member's preferred X-policy) may not be in the core. The committee, a majority of the House, and a majority of the Senate could agree to a change in the X dimension to keep it in that range.

FIGURE 6
The Committe System Induces a Large Legislative Core
that Constrains the President

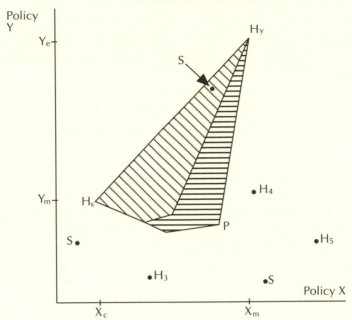

Similarly, any change in the Y dimension requires a majority of both chambers and the votes of H_y.

Any policy change involving a simultaneous change in both X and Y requires the votes of a majority of both chambers and the support of H_x and H_y; for instance, two senate members, the two House committees, and H_3 could agree to upset anything to the right of the contract curve between H_3 and H_y. This rules out all possible alternatives but the lightly shaded region in figure 6, which is the core of the game *even without a presidential veto*. None of the policy choices in the shaded region can be upset by any decisive coalition.

The existence of this large legislative core means that presidential influence is extremely limited. The committee system creates stable outcomes, which make it impossible for the president to play one coalition off against another. When the committee system induces a deadlock, then the president is unable to play alternative majority coalitions against each other; the coalitions he needs to reach his ideal point are not decisive.

By definition, any status quo point in the legislative core is stable; the requirement of a presidential veto can simply add more stability. For example, point S is stable despite the fact that the president plus a majority of the House and the Senate would prefer to move toward the president's ideal point; the reason, of course, is the ability of the H_y committee to table any such proposed legislation. A newly elected president cannot use his constitutional role in legislation (the veto) to move the legislature from S, no matter what his own preferences are. The president has no constitutional means to overcome the committee gatekeeping role. The presidential veto can create *more* undominated outcomes, but the president is powerless to upset any core outcome that was imposed before he came to office.

The only time the president may have the ability to change the status quo is if the status quo point is exogenously determined and extremely unpopular. This might occur as a result, for example, of a surprise Supreme Court decision. In this case, the president may pit his agenda power and coalition-forming abilities to achieve the most favorable outcome in the core of the game; but there are no guarantees. The presidential veto, combined with the committee system, adds the darkly shaded region in figure 6 to the set of stable outcomes. That is, from an unpopular status quo, an outcome in either the lightly or darkly shaded region may be attainable. Once attained, any point in the shaded region would be stable: either the relevant committees would table any proposed change, or the president would issue a (sustainable) veto. Thus, when considering the multiplicity of veto points in a bicameral legislature with gatekeeping committees and an executive veto, the most likely outcome is not instability but deadlock.

FORMAL THEORY AND
PRESIDENTIAL POWERLESSNESS

This analysis serves as a possible model for understanding the kind of presidential powerlessness evidenced in areas such as agricultural subsidies or Corps of Engineers projects. When the status quo has reached the core (as would be expected short of exogenous shocks like court decisions), incoming presidents have very little influence on policy. They cannot play off alternative bicameral majorities to reach preferred outcomes. By creating stable outcomes, the committee system serves as a block to any executive manipulation of cross-cutting legislative coalitions.

In our system of divided powers, creating a decisive coalition requires putting together a large number of actors with potentially quite different preferences, including everyone from the House Rules Committee, the Senate majority leader, the members of the conference committee, and the president. As Hammond and Miller (1990) show, this can create quite a large core, resulting in static, unresponsive government. Presidents find it unprofitable to try to score points with either the electorate or the history books by promising momentous policy reform in such unresponsive areas as taxation, energy policy, or agricultural policy.

This does not mean that the president has an negligible role in the normal politics of countervailing checks and balances. The Congress will be a continuing source of potential policy opposition to the president. The president will have to use (or threaten) his veto power, appointment powers, and budgetary powers simply to keep from being done in by these opponents. Not doing unto others, but keeping others from doing unto you, would be a central ingredient of this version of the presidential role.[2]

However, it may take a very large shock resulting in a very unfavorable status quo to give the president the opportunity to take significant action. Presidents historically seek to provide leadership in exactly those policy arenas in which some exogenous shock has resulted in a status quo that is clearly outside the core and, therefore, unstable—and therefore susceptible to leadership. When the Santa Barbara oil spill clearly indicates that the current policy is unacceptable to a decisive majority of government, then President Nixon seeks to influence exactly which policy will replace the newly vulnerable status quo. When an oil shock makes some action in the energy area imperative, then presidents discover that they are very interested in providing leadership in a previously ignored policy arena.

In the rest of this chapter I examine what positive political theory has to offer about the world of "abnormal politics," where it seems to me presidents hope to do more than serve as one of many countervailing (and mutually restricting) veto points in a static policy process.

Rational Awareness and Abnormal Politics

When we start with the assumption of rational ignorance on the part of most voters, we end up with a picture of normal politics in which special interest groups dominate the re-election calculations of legislators and in which the committee system serves as the means for stable legislative bargains to serve coalitions of parochial interests. But is it ever rational for voters to be informed about public policy issues?

For individuals in large groups, being informed is rational only when the costs of getting informed are close to zero or negative. Although people will not read a book about the savings and loan crisis, they will accept whatever information on the subject is "free." Information is free when it is heard over the radio while commuting, when it is heard over the television news while getting the kids' supper, or when it is noticed in the headlines as one turns the newspaper pages toward the sports section.

In a very few special cases there may even be private consumption benefit to be derived from becoming informed about the public policy issue. This occurs when the news is highly dramatic, novel, or personal—when it has the same attraction held by a TV serial, a sensational murder case, or a gossip column. Issues that hold this degree of popular interest will be discussed with animation at the hair styling salon, the office water cooler, or the bar.

The vast majority of public policy issues—for example, rate and entry regulation before a utility commission—never rise to this level. But a few public policy issues can be this salient, for short periods of time. I denote the decision-making processes that surround these globally salient issues as abnormal politics. At any given time, there are two or three such issues filling the communication networks in the country and hundreds more issues that most of the public is not thinking about at the time.

Labor's spontaneous sit-down strikes of 1936 and 1937 spread across the country because there was an excited awareness on the part of the general public that it was being done elsewhere. Another such issue was civil rights in May 1963, when people watched their television sets as children were fire-hosed by the Birmingham police. Natural resource conservation was once a technical issue with as much popular awareness and interest as utility rate regulation, but the Santa Barbara oil spill, followed by the nuclear plant accident at Three Mile Island, raised the issue to one which virtually 100 percent of the public was aware of in the early seventies. The 1991 Senate hearings on Clarence Thomas generated millions of small group discussions on the subject of sexual harassment—many of them serious and thoughtful.

If Johnny Carson can tell jokes about a certain issue, night after night, then it may confidently be regarded as being one about which the public is getting a lot of free (although not necessarily accurate) information. The *Exxon Valdez* spill raised the issue of Alaskan oil to this exalted status for over a year.

The same thing can be said for individual politicians. Wilbur Mills was never better known than when he landed in the Tidal Basin with a stripper. Ralph Nader was an intrinsically boring reforming lawyer, with a little-read book about auto safety, until the auto industry tried to find out whether he had any sexual proclivities that could be used against him. Then he sued General Motors and became a very well-known, intrinsically boring lawyer with a little-read book about auto safety.

Political economy can do very little to explain which public issues and politicians are able to develop this high level of intrinsic public interest. That lies in the psychological realm of explaining preferences, the only social scientific area that economists have doggedly refused to imperialize. The economic technique has always been to regard preferences as given and to derive implications from those preferences. This chapter will proceed along these lines, with the aside that sex and violence seems to have a great deal of value in predicting what aspects of politics are provided as free information to the public by newspapers, television, and *People* magazine.

The result is that the public is much more erratically intense about political issues than about private issues. The overall demand for private goods is relatively constant; the demand for bread does not take dramatic swings. Not so with public goods. The level of demand for civil rights legislation was negligible throughout the fifties; it was the single domestic issue that most voters were most concerned about as they voted in the 1964 presidential election; and it subsided to the background again by the end of the decade. Politicians ignored the environment as a public issue throughout the sixties; in the early seventies environmental organizations succeeded in unseating several incumbent members of Congress on this issue; it declined as a result of the energy crisis by the end of the seventies.

A high level of public salience (and the abnormal style of political decision making) may be more likely in some policy areas than in others, but it is not intrinsic in any given issue, contrary to the views of policy taxonomists. Lowi (1964), for instance, argues that different styles of politics accompany redistributive, regulatory, or distributive policy issues, with high, moderate, and low levels of visibility, respectively, and distinctively different styles of decision making. It may be true that redistributive policies, involving the intense interests of large groups of people, are more likely to generate the kind of interest and conflict that typifies abnormal politics, and when this happens, the decision-making style resembles that described by Lowi.

However, most redistributive issues (such as Social Security) are not at the forefront of public attention most of the time (the political system probably could not handle such an overload of conflict); when out of the limelight, the decision-making style for redistributive issues looks more like regulatory bargaining. And some regulatory issues (such as regulation of the environment) can become intensely salient to the general public at times—looking much like a redistributive issue. Even a distributive issue, which is normally cloaked in anonymity for all but the small groups lobbying for pork barrel benefits, can become a salient issue in the aftermath of scandal—witness the Teapot Dome or Pentagon cost overrun scandals. It is not the policy issue area that determines the style of politics; for any given issue, the style of political decision making is transformed as a result of public awareness and involvement, as argued by Schattschneider.

WHEN THE PUBLIC IS AWARE: THE PARTY SYSTEM

When the vast majority of the American public is made aware of a public policy issue, the characteristics of political decision making are vastly different than in the case of normal pressure politics. A case in point is civil rights.

Support for the civil rights bill was in no way analogous to support from a pressure system or cozy triangle. Throughout the fifties, several key committees were chaired by senior southern officials who had sworn to stop civil rights legislation. The NAACP and other organized interest group had tiny memberships, underpaid staffs, and no campaign funds. There were no bureaucratic sponsors for civil rights; indeed, the FBI was headed by a powerful opponent of Martin Luther King and the civil rights movement.

With congressional committees and bureaucracies closed to them, and with no ability to mount a strong pressure group lobbying presence, civil rights advocates had to formulate an outsider political strategy. But the Republican party was indifferent to civil rights, and the Democratic party was convinced that the Solid South was essential for success. As a result, even Adlai Stevenson had soft-pedaled the civil rights issue, trying to maintain the legacy of New Deal support from northern blacks without losing the South. Up until the midfifties, the public in general was uninformed about and uninvolved in civil rights. In response to Gallup's question, What do you think is the most important problem facing the entire country today?, the issue of civil rights did not appear as a response in May 1950, October 1951, and April 1954 (Gallup, 1972).

With all the normal routes of political access closed to it, the civil rights movement used a strategy that was nearly the opposite of pressure politics. Operating on a shoestring, the NAACP secured the Brown school desegregation victory in 1954, which provided the opening for nonviolent protests and civil disobedience in furtherance of school desegregation. By January 1955, 4 percent of the population thought that segregation and discrimination was the most important problem facing the new Congress. That increased to 10 percent by September 1957, at which time the violence at Little Rock broke out. This got the nation's attention and sympathy, resulting in 29 percent of the public telling Gallup pollsters just two months later that civil rights was the most important problem facing the nation (ibid.).

Public interest in civil rights declined after Little Rock. In April 1963, only 4 percent of the public felt that civil rights was the most important national concern. But by October 1963, civil rights was for the first time perceived as the most important issue by a majority of Americans—52 percent. What had occurred between April and October was the Birmingham campaign, in which high-pressure water hoses were used to break the legs and cave in the rib cages of youthful protestors. President Kennedy said privately, "the civil rights movement should thank God for Bull Connor. He's helped it as much as Abraham Lincoln" (Sorenson, 1965, 550). But he said little publicly, recognizing the necessity of dealing with southern committee chairmen if he was to have any legislative success.

On June 11, 1963, the attention of the nation was focused on the drama of Governor Wallace standing in the doorway of the

Tuscaloosa registration building. At that time, realizing that his policy of conciliation with southern congressmen had resulted in little in
the way of legislative accomplishments anyhow, Kennedy made a
break. He made an unprecedented televised presidential appeal on
June 11 for a civil rights bill, "while attention was focused on the
subject. . . . By June 11 the country was listening—and the bills previously proposed were insufficient" (ibid., 554–56). He put his personal reputation behind a stronger civil rights bill to Congress, a bill
that was sitting in the Rules Committee when he was assassinated in
November.

By 1964, both parties were aware that there were a large number
of voters who in previous years might have gone to the polls thinking
about the Russian menace or unemployment but who in 1964 were
thinking about the civil rights movement. These voters were unorganized, they had no large campaign fund, and they didn't have any
special access to congressional committees; but the simple fact that
they were voting in 1964 forced both political parties to compete for
their votes on the issue that was important to them: civil rights.

Thus, Schattschneider (1960) argues that party politics is a very
different brand of politics than pressure politics. Pressure politics represents the narrow interests of those groups of people who manage to
overcome free-rider problems and maintain a political presence in
Washington. Party politics is able to represent those broad interests
that the general public is (momentarily) aroused about as the result
of being inundated by free information from the news media. While
pressure groups (such as the sugar lobby) generally count on the public's passivity on the issues of most importance to them, the civil
rights and similar movements are absolutely dependent on being able
to arouse the public through actions that get the attention of the news
media. Legislative decision making in pressure politics is characterized by nonpartisan logrolling and committee sponsorship of special
legislation. Legislative decision making in party politics transcends
the bounds of committees as the party leadership jockeys for the support of the aroused mass electorate, forcing issues (like civil rights
legislation) out of committee and using party discipline to get it
passed.

As a result, the Rules Committee opposition to civil rights, which
had earlier been an insuperable obstacle, was simply brushed aside in
the supercharged atmosphere of 1964. As Ripley and Franklin write,

"There was no quiet subgovernment at work in this policy area" (1980, 169). The negotiations regarding the bill were at the highest level, with President Johnson, leading Democratic forces, finding an opportunity for Republican leader Dirksen to save face with some minor amendments to the bill. The result was a 71 to 29 vote on cloture in the Senate and a 73 to 27 vote on the bill.

As Schattschneider predicted in 1960, the ability of civil rights protesters to involve the general public through the party system changed the outcome. The civil rights movement became a model for outsider groups seeking to influence policy: the formula was to get media attention, public sympathy, and the eventual support of one or both political parties. It was a formula that was to be followed bythe women's movement, the consumer movement, the environmental movement, and eventually the antiabortion movement and the tax revolt.

ISSUE ENTREPRENEURSHIP:
THE SOCIALIZATION OF CONFLICT

Thus, the most important determinant of a policy decision is the scope of the conflict surrounding it. If organized interests, congressional committees, and bureaucracies make the decision through normal pressure politics, the outcome is very likely to be different than if the conflict is broadened to include the two major parties clashing for the votes of the general electorate. Consequently, the "losers" in any pressure politics decision have everything to gain and nothing to lose by changing the scope of conflict.

One name for someone who tries to change the scope of conflict by involving a larger public is *political entrepreneur* (Wilson, 1980; Pertschuk, 1982). The drug regulation reforms in the sixties provide a clear example of how entrepreneurs can use public attention to change outcomes. At that time, Senator Estes Kefauver held hearings on drug regulation, his primary concern being the relatively dry and unappealing monopoly pricing tendencies of the drug industry. He earned little public response or public support. All of the organized interests heard daily on Capitol Hill were opposed to reform; the consumers whom Kefauver hoped to help through lower drug prices were untouched and unheard from.

This left Kefauver with little base of support for his proposals among the actors in the pressure system. It made a great deal of sense for him to try to broaden the scope of conflict. When his staff learned that the sedative thalidomide was causing gruesome birth defects in Europe, they decided this was an issue that could be used to attract the attention of the large segments of the American public that were rationally ignorant on the subject of drug regulation. In fact, rational ignorance was crucial to their strategy, since the thalidomide crisis in Europe had nothing to do with monopoly pricing, and since American safety regulation had been sufficient to protect the American public from the drug. However, they hoped that the gruesome effects of the crisis in Europe would be sufficient to attract public concern about American drug regulation and to change the configuration of political forces on this issue.

The Kefauver staffers withheld publicizing the news until the drug bill would benefit the most and then passed the story on to the news media.

> The ensuing national publicity and public horror were then skill-fully exploited to generate support for the proposed amendments. The thalidomide episode was politically useful despite the lack of any substantial connection between the disaster and the proposed legislation. . . . But neither public opinion nor politicians were interested in fine distinctions concerning the policy significance of the scandal. After thalidomide, enactment of Kefauver's bill was virtually a foregone conclusion (Quirk, 1980, 199).

The configuration of organized interests did not change significantly with the dissemination of free information about the thalidomide issue; nor was the connection between thalidomide and monopoly pricing practices in the drug industry ever made clear. But spreading free information about a salient issue like the thalidomide crisis guaranteed that drug reform became a focal point of public concern and attention. Since legislators must respond to issues of public concern, entrepreneurial actions like Kefauver's can be seen as actually changing the preferences of legislators. The median legislator in both chambers and in oversight was much more sympathetic to drug regulation after the thalidomide scandal than before.

A similar story is told about shifts in the preferences of members of legislative committees with oversight of the SEC (Weingast, 1984) and the FTC (Weingast and Moran, 1983). By this process, status quo alternatives that are stable and undominated may actually become dominated as the legislative core shifts ground.

THE PRESIDENT'S DOMINANT POSITION IN THE FLOW OF FREE INFORMATION

The greatest amount of entrepreneurial activity in American politics is no doubt centered in Congress. Like Kefauver on drug reform, there are always members of the U.S. Senate who are seeking not just legislative success but to mobilize publics around high-impact issues (often in preparation for a presidential election). One thinks readily of Ted Kennedy and civil rights legislation, Warren Magnuson and consumer protection, and Abraham Ribicoff and auto safety.

While Congress can be a wellspring of entrepreneurs, the presidency offers a great advantage to those presidents who are inclined to play the game of mobilizing publics. The president's most important source of power is that he, almost alone in the United States, has the ability to gain immediate and complete access to the flow of free information. He therefore has the potential to be the most powerful issue entrepreneur in the country. For example, when Reagan gave a television address on September 24, 1981, to propose additional federal budget cuts, 59 percent of the public saw or heard about this address (Gallup, 1981, 231). By way of contrast, only 15 percent could tell a Gallup interviewer in late September 1987 that Robert Bork was a nominee for the Supreme Court (Gallup, 1987, 221). These were both major news stories involving national office, but the presidency swamps all other contenders in his ability to get his ideas across to the public.

While representatives and senators are posturing and competing with each other for the opportunity to get a fifteen-second sound bite on the evening news, the president has the luxury of virtually determining which aspect of his day will be the lead story on the evening news every night. As a result of this ability to dominate the flow of free information, the president plays a central role in those highly visible issues that constitute party politics. In the civil rights issue, Kennedy's decision to support King after his arrest did several things. It made the national election of 1960 in part a referendum on civil rights, so that the public could deliver a mandate on that issue. Kennedy's decision was itself news, and thus it accelerated the ability of the civil rights issue to dominate the news and contributed to the flow of free information that was sensitizing the public to the issue.

And (as we shall see later in the chapter), it legitimized and focused the civil rights movement itself.

THE PRESIDENT AS ENTREPRENEUR

In the case of the civil rights movement, Kennedy and then Johnson were able to claim political credit and further their political goals by representing aroused public concern that they themselves did very little to initiate. Because of their position, Kennedy and Johnson were able to assume the mantle of leadership in the civil rights movement quite easily—and gain the political benefits therefrom—despite the fact that they had each been initially reluctant to press the issue for fear of the southern white backlash.

In other cases, the president can actually use his dominant position in the flow of free information to help generate public awareness and concern about issues that might be politically useful to him. Like Senator Kefauver and drug regulation, the president tries to use the news media to get the attention and, in successful cases, the support of the previously apathetic public. This is the theme of Kernell's "going public" hypothesis, which argues that major addresses of the president frequently attempt to mobilize support and build coalitions (Kernell, 1986).

Teddy Roosevelt not only regarded the presidency as a bully pulpit, he also had a very good sense of the kinds of issues that would get a powerful response from the congregation. On the issue of conservation he was at the forefront of the attempt to convert the public to the "gospel of efficiency" in the utilization of natural resources, and by the end of his presidency, "Roosevelt personally embodied the popular impulses which swung behind the conservation movement during the years of the great crusade" (Hays, 1975, 271). While neither television or radio were available to him, he dominated the news media in an inimitable way and was a rousing public speaker. Roosevelt, together with this flamboyant administrator Gifford Pinchot, "collectively produced and performed a series of newsworthy 'events'—speeches, conventions, presidential commissions and visits—that seized the attention of the press and placed conservation on the nation's front pages" (Ponder, 1990, 548). One dramatic victory that resulted from a conscious effort at presidential mobilization of the public was the transfer of control of the nation's forests from the

Department of the Interior to Gifford Pinchot's agency in the Department of Agriculture (ibid., 549–50).

The intimate connection between public arousal and presidential power is demonstrated by the case of post office reform, discussed by Fenno (1978). The Post Office committees of Congress had established a firm alliance of mutual benefit with the postal employees and the business users of subsidized third-class mail. Presidents of various persuasions had been powerless to budge this alliance from a favorable status quo. Then in 1966 postal service broke down during the Christmas rush. As Fenno notes, this event "triggered a public concern over postal issues that eventually shattered the monolithic, clientele-dominated environment of the Committee. Postal reform advocates seized upon the event to wrest the policy initiative from the clientele-Committee alliance" (ibid., 282). This made possible a degree of presidential influence that had not existed before, with Nixon appointing a postmaster general committed to reform and sending a post office reorganization bill to Congress soon after his inauguration. Nixon played a major role in rallying public efforts behind postal reform. The ten-day postal strike in March 1970 confirmed Nixon's decision to move in this area. "The effect of all this activity was to increase the salience of postal issues nationally and to bring the executive branch to leadership of the policy coalition confronting the Post Office Committee" (ibid., 282).

Even if the president is not instrumental in creating the crisis that gets the public's attention, he would be foolish not to exploit it for his own purposes as much as possible. For instance, the central policy issue in the public's mind in the midseventies was inflation. In the presidential race of 1976, both Gerald Ford and Jimmy Carter used the anti-inflationary concerns of the public to justify a platform of regulatory reform. After Carter's election he followed through with deregulation of the Civil Aeronautics Board and other agencies (McCraw, 1984, 259).

Whether the president pursues his agenda because of private policy preferences or out of political opportunism is irrelevant. The point is that an entrepreneurial president and unorganized publics need each other. The mechanism of two-party competition for the White House forces candidates to vie for the support of large blocs of aroused voters, even if those voters do not make another political act for four

years. In the wake of Earth Day 1970, Nixon felt that he was vulnerable to a Democratic contender like Muskie with strong environmental support. Consequently, he moved quickly to earn his share of
environmental votes by creating the EPA, despite the fact that there
is very little evidence that Nixon was an avid and sincere environ-
mentalist.

POPULAR SUPPORT AND PRESIDENTIAL
INFLUENCE IN CONGRESS

Why doesn't the president attempt to mobilize the public on every
issue? There is no firm answer to this problem, but there is clearly
some kind of psychological budget constraint operating. The public
cannot be aroused about an infinite number of issues at the same
time, a fact Franklin Roosevelt was sensitive to (Kernell, 1986, 87).
Concern about Vietnam can crowd out concern about civil rights.
Watergate replaces Vietnam as the lead item on CBS news. Johnny
Carson may find that if his audiences are laughing about Exxon and
the vice president, then they have probably tired of jokes about Reagan sleeping at cabinet meetings.

This means that, even for the president, access to the public is a resource that has to be conserved. If Reagan chose to label tax reform
as his number one domestic issue in 1985, he could not credibly give
that label to the reorganization of the Corps of Engineers. In 1981,
Reagan and his advisers evidently made a conscious decision to focus
on the conservative economic agenda, postponing the conservative
social agenda for later. I would argue that a personally popular president will not automatically have much success in Congress with an
issue that the public is not concerned about (e.g., the departmental location of the Corps of Engineers). The president has to take actions
to mobilize the resource of public support on particular issues.

The president's most powerful weapon, then, is a public aroused
on a specific issue. The successful president does not tell a member
of Congress to vote with him against his constituency; he may tell the
constituency to let members of Congress know how they feel on a
particular subject. This was the strategy used by Franklin Roosevelt
with his fireside chats, by Johnson on civil rights, and by Reagan on
budget cuts and tax reform.

There is a great deal of interest and empirical research on the connection between public support for a president and legislative suc-

cess. Rivers and Rose estimate that a 1 percent increase in the president's public support level increases the president's legislative approval rate by approximately 1 percent, holding program size fixed. They also demonstrate that the rate of presidential success decreases with the number of requests that the president sends to Congress: "For each percentage point the president increases the size of his program, the congressional approval rate falls by between 0.26 percent and 0.33 percent" (1985, 192). Presidential popularity is not a resource that can be automatically used on any number of issues; it is limited by the necessity of arousing public awareness and concern.

As Ostrom and Simon point out, not only is presidential popularity a determinant of legislative success, but legislative success is a determinant of presidential popularity. They do a two-stage least squares estimation of an interdependent model of these two variables. With this model, they argue that "the cumulative rate of roll-call victories will decline by three points for every ten-point drop in approval. This impact is quite substantial" (1985, 349).

In 1989, Edwards did a time-series regression analysis of the effect of presidential approval rates (as measured by Gallup polls) on legislative support for the president by House and Senate members of both parties for the thirty-four years between 1953 and 1986. His most striking finding was that House Democrats tend to be quite responsive to public popularity; their legislative support for the president tends to increase by three or four percentage points for every 10 percent increase in presidential popularity as measured by the Gallup poll. This is true whether the president is Democratic or Republican. Senate Democrats are less responsive. House Republicans are still less responsive and may actually be negatively responsive to the popularity of Democratic presidents. Senate Republicans, on the other hand, are quite sensitive to the popularity of Republican presidents (Edwards, 1989, 120–24).

Mouw and MacKuen demonstrate the effect of a "going public" strategy on legislative bill sponsors. They find that legislative sponsors do *not* change the ideological placements of their bills in response to simple presidential popularity (1990, 14). However, legislative sponsors are responsive to the "going public" speechmaking behavior of presidents. When Eisenhower mobilized the public on behalf of liberal legislation, "he had the effect of deflecting Conservative initiatives in the Liberal direction" (ibid., 14). When

Reagan went public on a conservative issue, liberal bill sponsors had to move their bill placements significantly in the conservative direction.

Mouw and MacKuen (1989) also argue that determining the relationship between presidential popularity and presidential influence in Congress will *underestimate* the president's influence, if the president in fact scales back his efforts at times when he feels his influence is weak. One way to correct for this is to examine presidential influence in an area in which the president cannot adjust his degree of involvement based on his public standing One such arena is Supreme Court nominations, since his involvement is set by the Constitution and determined by the existence of an opening on the Court. Segal and others estimate the effect of presidential popularity on legislative support for Court nominations, controlling for such other variables as constituency, legislator, and nominee ideology. They conclude that, on average, a president with a 40 percent approval rate can expect a 0.5 probability of a yes vote from a legislator, while one with a 60 percent approval rate can expect a 0.73 probability of a legislator's support (1990, 16).

The most compelling evidence for a link between popularity and legislative influence comes from Sullivan (1987, 1988). Sullivan uses the differences between early head counts of proadministration feelings by legislators and their subsequent recorded votes to measure presidential influence. In his 1987 article, Sullivan shows that members of Congress do frequently vote in ways different from their initial predispositions. Some of this, Sullivan shows, is "normal" clarification of their position and that of their constituencies; some legislative change is "conversion" to the presidential coalition. On the difficult Civil Rights Act of 1968, Sullivan estimates that the president managed to build a coalition in support that was a 30.5 percent improvement over initial support (1988, 582).

In another article, Sullivan focuses on how presidents build these coalitions. In a series of roll-call votes having to do with economic regulation, Sullivan estimates a PROBIT model of conversion. His estimates show that the presidential popularity as measured by the Gallup poll is significantly associated with conversion in all kinds of districts. For legislators holding marginal seats, conversion is also aided by a high percentage of Johnson votes in the 1964 election. As Sullivan aptly summarizes this evidence, "presidents who can tap the public's mood in an electrifying way are apt to greatly lessen their troubles with Congress" (1987, 300).

Kernell (1986, 35–38) offers a compelling argument that a "going public" strategy is harmful because it disrupts the effectiveness of the normal bargaining process among the stable institutional actors in Washington. While this is persuasive, it assumes that the stable institutional actors are representative of all major interests in society and that the outcomes of "institutional pluralism," as he aptly terms it, achieve optimality through a low-cost bargaining process, as in the Coase Theorem (Coase, 1960). There is much to be said for this position; however, there are two limitations to Kernell's argument that are suggested by the recent literature on bargaining, transaction costs, and institutions (North 1990a, 1990b, North and Weingast, 1989). One is that some interests are clearly kept from the Washington bargaining table by the costs of organizing to be heard; to the extent that the president can mobilize and represent those interests, then going public can increase the efficiency of policy making. This is discussed in the next section of this chapter. Furthermore, even among those interests that are represented in Washington and present at the bargaining table, the ability to strike an efficient bargain may be limited by opportunism, mistrust, and incomplete contracts. The president may play a beneficial role in addressing these problems, as well, as is discussed later.

The President and Insurgency: A Coordination Problem

The president's dominant position in the flow of free political information allows the president to play other roles. By reviewing briefly the formal theory of coordination games, it is possible to see that the presidency has a unique role in American politics as the focal point of coordination, thus providing a degree of influence that goes beyond his constitutional powers.

AN ILLUSTRATIVE COORDINATION GAME

Imagine that there are a large number of French citizens who would very much like to overthrow the French monarchy. They are

TABLE 11

Collection Action as a Coordination Game

Pierre	Gaston	
	Storm Bastille Today	Storm Bastille Tomorrow
Storm Bastille Today	4, 3	−10, 0
Storm Bastille Tomorrow	0, −10	3, 4

so committed that they would take pleasure, as members of a large crowd, in undertaking a desperate act such as the storming of the Bastille. They disagree on the optimal timing, however. Gaston and his allies would like to storm the Bastille today, and Pierre would like to storm the Bastille tomorrow. However, neither side would like to storm the Bastille alone, as that would lead to certain death. These preferences are illustrated in table 11. There are two Nash equilibria to this game: one in which everyone storms the Bastille today and one in which everyone storms the Bastille tomorrow. As in all such games, the essential step is coordinating individual actions.

The problem can be complex indeed. Suppose Pierre sends a message to Gaston to storm the Bastille today. However, he does not get a confirmation that Gaston received the message. He may then decide to show up tomorrow on the assumption that Gaston didn't receive the message, which may leave Gaston storming the Bastille alone. Or Gaston may receive Pierre's message and send an acceptance that they will in fact storm the Bastille today. However, Gaston may not receive a confirmation that Pierre received his acceptance; if he thinks Pierre did not receive his acceptance, then he may assume that Pierre will wait till tomorrow on the assumption that he (Gaston) did not receive the order.

Such problems ultimately require common knowledge—the mutual recognition by each party that the other party knows exactly what he knows, and knows that the other knows what he knows, ad infinitum. Schelling (1960, 57) introduced the concept of "focal point" as a way of discussing this problem; a focal point is some point that "suggests itself" as the outcome to be coordinated on some given common knowledge of the participants. It is generally recognized that communication is important in creating common knowledge and resolving coordination problems (Calvert, 1987). But if there is a relatively symmetrical ability by different individuals to suggest alternative preferred Nash equilibria, then coordination can fail because of symmetrical bluffs and strategems.

On the other hand, if one individual has a unique ability to communicate his intentions, that becomes an enormous advantage to him. He can state his intentions and then refuse to acknowledge any contrary intentions by other actors. In American politics, the president is virtually the only actor capable of creating such common knowledge.

BANK RUNS AS A COORDINATION PROBLEM

The problem of bank runs that faced the country in early 1933 was of course a coordination problem. Each bank depositor would rather keep her money in the bank earning interest if everyone else will and would rather withdraw her money if everyone else intends to do the same. Once again, there are two Nash equilibria. What is required is the common knowledge that every individual has confidence that everyone else has confidence that everyone will keep their money in the banks. That common knowledge was patently Roosevelt's goal and his major accomplishment in the first weeks of his presidency. An address by any political figure other than the president, no matter how intellectual compelling or emotionally stimulating, could not have created this common knowledge. Using no constitutional power whatsoever, Roosevelt "blessed" the banks in his Sunday fireside chat. This symbolic action can only be understood as a powerful resolution of the coordination problem.

SOCIAL PROTEST AS A COORDINATION PROBLEM

The bank crisis illustrates a pure type of coordination problem in that its resolution was arguably beneficial to everyone. Most coordination problems are what we might call impure or biased in that the coordination of actions among one subset of the population may be beneficial to the members of that subset but harmful to others. The storming of the Bastille is just such a coordination problem: the coordination of Gaston's and Pierre's actions is harmful to the king of France. The king of France will of course do anything he can to impede the solution of the coordination problem among his opponents—by outlawing public assemblies, sending false information to his plotting subjects, or jailing the leaders of the opposition.

Like the French populace before the Revolution, large, unorganized constituencies often have the potential to change a political system—a potential unrealized due to inability to coordinate their actions. The opposition, consisting frequently of more organized and powerful constituencies, will naturally do everything it can to keep unorganized constituencies from acting in a coordinated fashion.

The president can play a key role in the political conflicts engendered by unorganized constituencies seeking to coordinate their actions. The president can discourage such actions, as in the case of nineteenth-century presidents and the Populist movement. Or, by giving his stamp of approval to a social movement, the president can solve the kind of coordination problem that faced Gaston and Pierre. For example, Kennedy's support for King in 1960 proved to be a shot in the arm for the civil rights movement. It meant that the civil rights movement was not a half-hearted false start but an all-out attempt to get "freedom *now*." A civil rights supporter would know, when he put his life on the line by participating in a freedom march, that he was not storming the Bastille alone but that millions of others were doing the same thing all across the South. It is the symbolic legitimization of social action that the president supplied.

Similarly, on the evening of March 13, 1964, when Johnson made his extraordinary appeal for a civil rights bill before both houses of Congress, he was simultaneously representing the civil rights movement to Congress, legitimizing it to the public, and motivating its further actions. Presidential support for civil rights legislation provided an enormous incentive to individuals who might otherwise have been doubtful of participating in the extremely dangerous Selma march, to begin on March 21.

LABOR INSURGENCY: "THE PRESIDENT WANTS YOU TO ORGANIZE"

Another clear example of presidential coordination of social insurgency was the labor revolt of the New Deal. Prior to 1933, the labor movement was hesitant and faltering. Roosevelt's promise to protect industrial workers gave them a sense of immediacy and legitimacy that they had never had before. Just as a bugle call solves a coordination problem by creating a focal point for collective action, Roosevelt's speeches created the sense that workers could rationally take actions with the assurance that, around the country, other workers were taking similar actions.

With the almost immediate passage of the National Industrial Recovery Act, labor felt they had been further legitimized by the president. John L. Lewis committed the entire United Mine Workers treasury and one hundred organizers, dispatching sound trucks to coalfields with the message, "The president wants *you* to organize" (Piven and Cloward, 1977, 114). UMW membership jumped from 60,000 to 300,000 in a period of two months. The same pattern was present with the International Ladies Garment Workers Union (50,000 to 200,000) and the Amalgamated Clothing Workers (7,000 to 125,000). Even in previously unorganized industries, workers spontaneously held mass meetings and sent word to Washington and unions that they wanted to be organized under the NIRA.

This totally unexpected response put Roosevelt in an uncomfortable position, since he spent the first years of his administration trying to construct a coalition that would include business. However, the labor movement of the thirties, like the civil rights movement of the sixties, would not allow fence sitters. A rising chorus of labor protesters pressured Roosevelt from the left, and he responded. His first significant action of the so-called Second Hundred Days was to change course on Wagner's labor bill, shifting from opposition to stating that it was "must" legislation. "Once Roosevelt gave his blessing, the measure had clear sailing" (Leuchtenberg 1963, 151). Given the popularity of Roosevelt and the New Deal, Democrats who had benefited from the landslide of 1934 could not afford to oppose him on an item he labeled a "must."

Once again, presidential support for labor insurgency not only carried an impact in Congress, but it further activated labor insurgents themselves. The number of strikes continued to rise to over two thousand each year in 1935 and 1936 and to 4,740 in 1937. More than half of the strikes were to demand union recognition under the Wagner Act. Like the spontaneous organization of 1933, these actions were not led and organized by unions. As Piven and Cloward point out, the unions continually lagged behind and retarded the labor disruptions of the thirties (1979, 148). The clearest focal point for this seemingly coordinated wave of labor disruption was not the unions, but the presidency.

SUMMARY

The case can be made that the driving force behind changing American politics has been the insurgency of new groups demanding full and equal participation. The Progressives, women, labor, blacks, and environmentalists have all had a profound impact on politics. In many of these cases, social insurgency has also been the means by which American presidents have defined the goals of their administrations, promoted those goals through legislative agendas, and made their mark on American society. Presidential leadership has relied on the abnormal politics of social insurgency.

The Presidency and National Interests: A Cooperation Problem

The president has a special ability to overcome rational ignorance in the general public, creating the potential for mass mobilization on an issue that sparks the great changes in American politics. The president also has the ability to solve coordination problems, serving as a focal point and controlling the pace and timing of social movements. In addition, the president is the primary hope of representation for the large, latent interests that are not organized by means of selective incentives.

Putting these facts together, it is possible to see that the president has a special role to play in the resolution not only of coordination games, but of social dilemmas. Much of the president's influence comes from this extraconstitutional role.

SPECIAL INTEREST REPRESENTATION
AS A SOCIAL DILEMMA

Imagine that the voters in a single district are faced with two candidates. One candidate, Ms. Fiscal Responsibility, says that the federal government is in fiscal trouble because it hands out too many federal dollars to too many inefficient local projects. She commits herself to standing up for fiscal responsibility by opposing funding for such projects across the country. She specifically supports the closing of the local military base, which has been without a significant military mission for some years and has survived simply because of local political support. The other candidate, Mr. Pork Barrel, promises to dedicate himself to guaranteeing that federal funds are provided for local pork barrel programs, no matter how inefficient they might be; he specifically promises to fight for the local military base, he hopes as a member of the Armed Services Committee.

Let us assume that the voters all agree with the first candidate that the federal government should stop all inefficient expenditures. In particular, they would quite happily vote to close all unnecessary military bases, including their own, if there was a national referendum on that issue; they believe they are hurt more by the cost of keeping a large number of such bases in existence across the country than they are helped by the local base. However, the local congressional race is not such a referendum. By supporting Ms. Fiscal Responsibility, they would be eliminating local support for the military base and could easily get the local military base closed; however, they would realistically have no effect on the closing of the other unnecessary military bases around the country. A vote for Ms. Fiscal Responsibility, at the congressional level, is a vote for the "suckers payoff" in a prisoner's dilemma—an outcome in which the local constituency, alone, contributes to the public good while the other districts free-ride. A vote for Mr. Pork Barrel is not a vote for fiscal irresponsibility, it is a quite rational attempt by the local citizenry to contribute their share to the federal budget deficit.

Thus, Mr. Pork Barrel defeats Ms. Fiscal Responsibility in every district in the country, despite the fact that a national referendum would lead to overwhelming support for a balanced budget. In the context of small, single-member districts, neither local voters nor local candidates have the ability to express national interests effectively.

The only arena in which local voters can express their national interests is the presidential race. If the same two candidates, Mr. Pork Barrel and Ms. Fiscal Responsibility, were running at the national level, Mr. Pork Barrel could not win by promising to keep one inefficient military base or even by promising to keep all inefficient military bases. Presidential candidates of both parties have found it expedient to run against the collective fiscal irresponsibility of Congress.

THE CONGRESSIONAL DILEMMA

As many authors point out, this creates a social dilemma for members of Congress. Each is pledged to support vital local interests, but if all achieve this goal, Congress as a whole looks bad. Wildavsky points out that Congress is in a social dilemma, in which the combination of individually rational actions in budgeting leads to an outcome that none of them like:

> A simple way of approaching this complex subject is to say that legislators were unhappy with the collective consequences of their individual choices. They liked voting for spending but not for taxes. They got their way, in a manner of speaking, by riding roughshod over the appropriations committees, by tunneling beneath them through direct drafts on the Treasury ("backdoor spending"), or by getting around them entirely through tax expenditures (spending that allows certain people to reduce their taxes before these taxes get to the Treasury). Individual members of Congress won but Congress as a whole lost; individual and collective rationality were at odds. (Wildavsky, 1979, 223)

This image of Congress as the setting for a prisoner's dilemma game suggests that individual members should evidence some willingness to support a contract that effectively enforces pareto-superior outcomes. That is, individual members should be willing to sacrifice local pork barrel projects and special interests if and only if other districts were forced to do the same thing. There is evidence for this in a variety of areas: committee reform, budget reform, and tax reform, for example.

COMMITTEE REFORM

A large class of reformist freshmen members of Congress, elected in 1974, proposed to put Congress's house in order in the post-Watergate era of public cynicism. One way to do this, they argued, was through committee reform. The committees, it was argued, were too narrowly defined, making it possible for special interests to capture them for their own purposes. The overall outcome was that Congress's image was tarnished, even while members of Congress on the narrow committees earned credit with special interests. Reformers argued that all members of Congress would be better off if the committees were consolidated, providing each with a broader base and a more comprehensive agenda. In other words, reformers offered committee reform as a solution to the congressional dilemma in which individuals were forced to take actions that hurt Congress as a whole.

The reformers were pleased to find that there was a great deal of conditional support for their proposal: conditional in just the way that one would expect if Congress were in fact in a social dilemma. That is, none of the members of the special interest committees wanted to be the only special interest committee legislated out of existence; this would be comparable to the "suckers' payoff" in a prisoner's dilemma. Each special interest committee wanted the other special interest committees legislated out of existence while their own was preserved—this would achieve the "temptation payoff." But— the defining characteristic of a social dilemma—many committee members privately expressed a willingness to see their special interest committees legislated out of existence as long as all the other special committees received the same treatment.

In the Senate, the plan was to reduce the number of committees from thirty-one to fifteen, eliminating such special interest committees as the Small Business Committee, the Veterans Committee, the Committee on Aging, and the Committee on Nutrition and Human Needs. The chairman of the Senate Rules Committee, Howard Cannon, had primary responsibility for the bill and was initially optimistic. He told the *New York Times,* "Several people told me privately that they would support the proposal *as long as nobody was exempted*" (Feb. 9, 1977, emphasis added). To make it easier for senators to support the deal, he asked for unanimous consent to hold a closed bill-drafting session. The Rules Committee gave in to pressure from Iowa's Senator Clark to hold the meetings publicly.

At that point, the quiet agreement to reform the committee system began to unwind. Bowing to strong pressure from veterans groups, the committee voted to save the Veterans Committee. At this point, Senator Claiborne Pell from Rhode Island argued that if the veterans' interests were to be served by protecting their voice in the Senate, then so should the interests of small business. "We are very much a small business-minded state. We don't have any large businesses." Senator Adlai Stevenson, the architect of the plan, warned at this point, "If this committee wants reorganization, this is where you make the decision, right now. Once you have done it in one case, made special exceptions, you are going to do it for other groups, and reorganization goes down the drain. You are going to the bone, and if you cut through the first of those bones, the rest are going to get cut too, and the delicate edifice is going to come down" (ibid.). He was very much aware that partial cooperation in an N-person social dilemma is not a viable outcome.

By a 5 to 4 vote, the Rules Committee saved the Small Business Committee from extinction. On the floor of the Senate, the Committee on Aging, creating in 1961 "to elect Democrats," was reinstated. It was clear at this point that the votes of those senators whose support was conditional on a general reorganization were now gone. Senator Clark noted wryly, "I gather some other exceptions are going to be created" (ibid.). Six more committees were reinstated, in a general collapse of the cooperative solution to the congressional dilemma. The coordinating influence of the Senate leadership was not quite adequate for the scale of cooperation required by this reform attempt.

LEADERSHIP AND COOPERATION

Congressional dilemmas such as these embarrass the institution, limit its ability to provide effective solutions to crises such as the oil embargo and the savings and loan crisis, and make it necessary for legislators to try to divorce themselves as individuals from Congress as an institution. For these reasons, Congress has regularly, although often ineffectually, faced the problem of organizing itself to resolve congressional dilemmas based on parochialism.

Hardin (1982) points out that repeated social dilemma games are in fact coordination games, via an important result in game theory known as the Folk Theorem. The Folk Theorem states that, in a repeated game of perfect information, virtually any outcome that guarantees each player a minimal payoff can be supported as a Nash equilibrium. That is, virtually any outcome (cooperative or not) can be explained by game theory as the result of mutually consistent rational choices of the players. As Miller (1992) and Hechter (1992) point out, game theory simply indicates that cooperation is one possible outcome supportable by rational players; it doesn't explain why cooperation occurs instead of some other outcome. Cooperation in a repeated game thus requires coordination. Game theory must be supplemented by contributions from other social sciences (e.g., social psychology, sociology, anthropology) that explain why and how individuals agree to coordinate on cooperative equilibria in some situations and not in others.

Calvert provides an outstanding analysis of the possibilities of cooperation and coordination through legislative leadership. His argument is that in order to avoid the costs that come with uncoordinated legislative action, legislators often support focal-point inducing norms; that is, they coordinate on norm-indicated behavior and sanction behavior that violates norms. But norms cannot cover all situations; selecting an individual to serve as focal-point indicator can be more comprehensive and easier; "leadership emerges when players substitute a search for focal *players* in place of the original search for focal *strategies*" (Calvert, 1987, 38). These leaders will inevitably have opportunities to claim benefits in the form of favorable legislation; however, the benefits of coordinating on their actions exceed the costs of anarchy. The further discipline legislative action by making promises or threats "to encourage followers to support his proposed division or to support him the next time a leader is selected" (ibid., 45).

As Calvert points out, legislative leadership is fragile in many ways. First of all, "the leader's control over [sanctioning] resources is granted voluntarily by a majority in the legislature, and can be taken away again if the leaders uses them in a manner disagreeable to a majority or fails to provide the desired results (ibid., 49). Furthermore, while no individual by definition has an incentive to violate the actions indicated by the leader, various coalitions may have such an incentive. The main force constraining legislators from upsetting legislative leadership is simply "the knowledge that it is likely to weaken the conventions by which the leader is able to achieve coordination. A new leader, taking over when an old one is overthrown, is almost bound to be weaker than the old one" (ibid.). In other words, the only force holding legislative leadership in place is the Hobbesian recognition that anarchy might be even worse. As might be expected, this is not always sufficient. As Calvert mentions, there have been occasions in which coalitions of legislators preferred to risk the anarchy of revolt rather than put up with the policy outcomes resulting from a given leadership's actions.

Given the fragility of the base for legislative leadership, it is not surprising that legislative leaders have only an imperfect ability to discipline the self-serving and collectively harmful actions of members. It is also not surprising that Congress at times acknowledges the legislative leadership of an actor who is not subject to the limitations that internal leaders act under.

THE PRESIDENT AS LEGISLATIVE LEADER

The president is elected by a process of two-party competition for the national electorate. As Schattschneider writes, "It is nearly impossible to translate pressure politics into party politics" (1960, 53). The significance of this is that, in order to get elected, the president must compete for and represent those large blocks of Americans who do not belong to organized interests but who are concerned about issues such as inflation, tax reform, civil rights, and deficits. Furthermore, the president derives his influence in politics from the fact that he alone represents these latent national constituencies.

The implication of this is that the president, *of either party,* must take a different position than most members of Congress, just because the president represents the national constituency in a way that legislators from small, single-member districts cannot (Moe, 1985). As Mayhew writes, "Presidents are less likely than congressmen to traffic in particularized benefits or to defer to the organized" (1974, 169). Presidents and presidential candidates are required to act as issue entrepreneurs, hoping to get elected by rousing public opposition to the results of legislative pressure politics. They are the natural proponents of cooperative solutions to social dilemmas. Unlike a member of Congress, when a president takes a position in favor of budget-balancing, he does not have to say "except in my district." For example, West describes how Reagan was able to rally Republican activists around his revolutionary budget in 1981: "The unanimity of the activist response was so overwhelming that it at least temporarily convinced many [undecided legislators] to support the president's economic package" (1987, 60).

Furthermore, unlike the legislative leaders discussed by Calvert, presidential power is not founded on a set of sanctions that the legislature can choose to take away. The separation of powers promotes the president as an ideal legislative contract enforcer.

THE PRESIDENT AS CONTRACT ENFORCER

The standard solution to a social dilemma is a contract enforcing the mutually advantageous trades. In a seminal article entitled "The Industrial Organization of Congress," Weingast and Marshall (1988) point out that much of the structure in Congress is facilitative of these contracts. The trouble is that budgetary problems, for example, constitute a social dilemma in which every party in Congress is an interested party. The problems of negotiating and enforcing solutions to major congressional dilemmas such as these are immense; the good offices of the presidency can be very useful in such a situation, for several reasons.

First of all, for reasons described by Schattschneider, the president cannot get elected or reelected by appealing to the kind of narrow constituencies that elect representatives form the dairy districts of Wisconsin or the tobacco districts of North Carolina. As a result, the president can appear as virtually a disinterested party in agricultural politics, for example, although he is of course interested only at a different scale. Furthermore, because he is the focus of political attention, presidential shirking in the enforcement of intracongressional contracts would be very visible.

More importantly, perhaps, the president has the means to act as contract enforcer; side payments make it possible to provide selective incentives for cooperators and to punish contract violators. The president's office certainly did this during the budget battle of 1981.

With the ability to establish a net of side payments in support of his position, the president becomes an arbitrageur or a nexus of contracts. He facilitates a market for the exchange of support that could hardly be reproduced in any other focal point in Washington.

TAX REFORM

An even more striking example of congressional parochialism confronted by presidential power is the case of the 1986 tax reform. Here again, congressional responsiveness to parochial interests had created a tax code that was an embarrassment, rather than a source of credit claiming, for legislators. Even those legislators whose parochial interests were most vigorously enacted into tax legislation found it expedient to divorce themselves from it when speaking to general audiences.

Presidents have long been advocates of tax reform but have had little impact. Why was 1986 different? In this case, the president made a credible commitment to spotlight tax reform, focusing public attention on it in a way that only the president can. Furthermore, when the chips were down, the Reagan administration was willing to use scarce side payments to build and enforce a coalition capable of voting tax reform through.

Reagan's meeting with the House Republicans in December 1985, illustrates the symbolic powers of the presidency very well. The House Republicans were in open revolt, having just voted down the rule allowing it to come to the floor. Speaker O'Neill had refused to move further until Reagan promised fifty Republican votes for the rule. Reagan couldn't use his legislative power to veto a bill; he needed to talk legislators who were opposed to the bill into voting for it so it would get to his desk. "By going to the Capitol, the president was putting his reputation on the line" (Birnbaum and Murray, 1987, 169). When he arrived, Kemp introduced the president with an indictment of the bill. Reagan responded by asking for a moment of silent prayer for 248 army soldiers who had died in a plane crash. After a short plea for support for the bill, and a round of bitter questions in which Reagan admitted he wanted additional changes in the bill himself, Henry Hyde from Illinois said, "Mr. President, if you say you'll fight for the $2,000 exemption, the rate reduction, effective dates, and a lower capital-gains rate, I don't need a letter. I'll vote for it." At this point, "the meeting changed from a debate over the tax bill to a show of loyalty for the popular president" (ibid., 171).

What was happening here? Was it simply the case of the Great Communicator winning over the hearts and minds of simple-minded legislators? There was clearly some of that involved, but it is important to remember what else was happening. The rebel leaders in the House had been coaching reluctant representatives with the following lines:

> QUESTION: How could a good Republican oppose the administration's top domestic priority?
> ANSWER: Since my president said he'd veto this bill if it came to his desk, I voted against it. (Ibid., 169)

In other words, the Republican rebels were basing their strategy on the belief that the president was not committed to coming up with a workable tax reform bill and would therefore not hold them accountable to the public if they voted against this version. The president, in his appearance before the Republican caucus, was eliminating that as a strategy. He was in effect promising to take the heat from opponents of tax reform and demonstrating a commitment to tax reform that was precisely what was in question up to that point.

At the end of the caucus, a secret ballot showed forty-eight of the fifty Republican votes that Reagan needed to deliver. As with the budget reform fight five years earlier, the administration had to deal with marginal voters, promising side payments to come up with the extra two votes. The president as arbitrageur and nexus of contracts came into play. Administrative officials made deals promising support for legislation or campaign assistance (ibid., 172).

If Reagan had not come up with those fifty Republican votes, tax reform would have died. He got the votes by trading on the range of symbolic powers of the president. He constructed a series of side contracts based on these powers that allowed a large proreform coalition to be maintained—one that could resist the parochial forces pulling at the members of Congress to kill tax reform. As is necessarily true in a coordination game, the outcome achieved (together with the distribution of side payments) was a Nash equilibrium—none of the supporters had an incentive to defect given that others were supporting it. Yet it is difficult to imagine internal legislative leadership moving Congress to this outcome. No other nexus of contracts could have brought about a cross-committee coalition of this scope, on an issue as fraught with parochial interests as taxes.

Conclusion

No doubt one of the reasons for the lack of interaction between formal theorists and presidential scholars has been the fact that many concepts of importance to presidential scholars (communication, leadership, the symbolic trappings of office) seem to have had no place in the literature on formal theory. In the past, formal theorists of politics have for the most part been engaged in a search for a deterministic, unique equilibrium driven by little more than economic self-interest and the formal rules of voting.

Formal theories in this mode have been the engine for the development of the field of congressional elections and legislation and provide a very good picture of normal politics in the United States. Serving parochial and economic interests through committee-based negotiations and enforcement of deals is the normal reelection strategy of members of Congress, as portrayed by Weingast and Marshall, Fiorina, and others. It is for the most part a successful strategy, as Mayhew argues: "The organization of Congress meets remarkably well the electoral needs of its members. To put it another way, if a group of planners sat down and tried to design a pair of American national assemblies with the goal of serving members' electoral needs year in and year out, they would be hard pressed to improve on what exists" (1974, 81).

While this is correct, it does not mean that legislators are not hard pressed at times to keep up with the shifting focus of public attention. When a crisis (like the bank crisis of 1933) or an issue entrepreneur (like Martin Luther King) captures media attention and public concern, legislators cannot ignore the glare of public attention. As Schattschneider argues, when the crowd gets involved in a fight, it becomes a different fight. Legislators who want to side with winners may have to switch sides when the crowd pitches in.

The very institutions that allow members of Congress to serve day-to-day parochial demands from their districts make it difficult to respond to demands from the broader public for tax reform or a response to the savings and loan crisis. When this is true, the reelection motivation of members of Congress may make legislators vulnerable to public pressure or open to presidential appeals to form or enforce difficult legislative coalitions. Extraordinary events like these call for abnormal politics, and the president's power is dependent on his ability to direct media attention, elicit public support, coordinate social action, and direct extraordinary legislative coalitions.

Recent developments in game theory and political economy have made it possible to develop a formal theory of the presidency that incorporates many of the traditional concerns of presidential scholars. The Folk Theorem forces an awareness of the multiple possibilities of political life (as opposed to the unique determinacies of economic life); this in turn requires attention to a set of social phenomena that allows political actors to coordinate on one of the many equilibrium possibilities available. The formal theory literature has begun to address previously ignored concerns, such as social norms and conventions (Hardin, 1982), organizational culture (Kreps, 1990), leadership (Calvert, 1987), and commitment (North and Weingast, 1989; Weingast, 1991).

These concepts are newly incorporated into formal theory, but are of long lasting and central concern to presidential scholars. Just as congressional scholars and formal theorists have engaged in a constructive interaction over the past two decades, we can hope that the next decades will see a constructive dialogue between presidential scholars and formal theorists, addressing the possibilities and limitations of presidential influence on legislation, public opinion, and policy making. This should lead to a richer and more sophisticated picture of American politics, which transcends the normal politics of economic interests served by congressional committees and executive agencies. It should allow for the possibility of less intense and less organized constituencies periodically transforming American politics through the extraordinary mechanisms of social protest, party activism, and presidential entrepreneurship.

Notes

1. The legislative core, when it exists, is a subset of Shepsle's "structure-induced equilibrium." The core excludes alternatives that may be upset by logrolling coalitions, including a majority of two or more committees as well as a majority of the chamber. The structure-induced equilibrium includes such outcomes, on the assumption that such logrolling will not occur.

2. My thanks to Bert Rockman for making this point to me.

References

Birnbaum, Jeffrey H., and Alan S. Murray. 1987. *Showdown at Gucci Gulch: Lawmakers, Lobbyists and the Unlikely Triumph of Tax Reform.* New York: Vintage.

Calvert, Randall. 1987. "Coordination and Power: The Foundation of Leadership Among Rational Legislators." Paper prepared for the American Political Science Association meeting at Rochester University.

Coase, Ronald. 1960. "The Problem of Social Cost." *Journal of Law and Economics* 26:1–21.

Edwards, George. 1989. *At the Margins: Presidential Leadership in Congress.* New Haven: Yale University Press.

Fenno, Richard F. 1978. *Congressmen in Committees.* Boston: Little, Brown.

Ferejohn, John. 1986. "Logrolling in an Institutional Context: The Case of Foodstamps." In *Congress and Policy Change,* ed. G. Wright, L. Rieselbach, and L. Dodd. New York: Agathon.

Fiorina, Morris. 1977. *Congress: Keystone of the Washington Establishment.* New Haven: Yale University Press.

———. 1980. "The Decline of Collective Responsibility in American Politics." *Daedalus* 109:25–46.

Gallup, George. 1972. *The Gallup Poll: Public Opinion 1935–1971.* New York: Random House.

———. 1982. *The Gallup Poll: Public Opinion 1981.* Wilmington: Scholarly Resources, Inc.

——. 1988. *The Gallup Poll: Public Opinion 1987*. Wilmington: Scholarly Resources, Inc.

Greenberg, Joseph. 1979. "Consistent Majority Rule over Compact Sets of Alternatives." *Econometrica* 47:627–36.

Hammond, Thomas, and Gary Miller. 1987. "The Core of the Constitution." *American Political Science Review* 81:1155–74.

Hammond, Thomas, and Gary Miller. 1990. "Committees and the Core." *Public Choice* 66:201–77.

Hardin, Russell. 1982. *Collective Action*. Baltimore: Johns Hopkins University Press.

Hays, Samuel P. 1975. *Conservation and the Gospel of Efficiency: The Progressive Conservation Movement, 1890–1920*. New York: Atheneum.

Hechter, Michael. 1992. "The Insufficiency of Game Theory for the Resolution of Real-World Collective Action Problems." *Rationality and Society* 4:33–40.

Holloway, Harry, and John George. 1986. *Public Opinion: Coalitions, Elites, and Masses*. 2d Ed. New York: St. Martin's.

Kernell, Samuel. 1986. *Going Public: New Strategies of Presidential Leadership*. Washington, D.C.: Congressional Quarterly Press.

Kiewiet, Roderick, and Mathew McCubbins. 1991. *The Spending Power: Congress, the President, and the Appropriations Process*. Chicago: University of Chicago Press.

Kreps, David M. 1990. "Corporate Culture and Economic Theory." In *Perspectives on Positive Political Economy*, ed. James Alt and Kenneth Shepsle. Cambridge: Cambridge University Press.

Leuchtenberg, William E. 1963. *Franklin D. Roosevelt and the New Deal*. New York: Harper & Row.

Lowi, Theodore. 1964. "American Business, Public Policy, Case-Studies, and Political Theory." *World Politics* 16:677–715.

Marcus, Alfred. 1980. "Environmental Protection Agency." In *The Politics of Regulation*, ed. James Q. Wilson. New York: Basic.

Mayhew, David R. 1974. *Congress: The Electoral Connection*. New Haven: Yale University Press.

McConnell, Grant. 1966. *Private Power and American Democracy*. New York: Vintage.

McCraw, Thomas K. 1984. *Prophets of Regulation*. Cambridge: Belknap.

McKelvey, Richard D. 1976. "Intransitivities in Multidimensional Voting Models and Some Implications for Agenda Control." *Journal of Economic Theory* 12:472–82.

Miller, Gary. 1992. *Managerial Dilemmas: The Political Economy of Hierarchy*. Cambridge: Cambridge University Press.

Moe, Terry. 1985. "The Politicized Presidency." In *The New Directions in American Politics*, ed. John Chubb and Paul Peterson, 235–271. Washington, D.C.: Brookings.

Mouw, Calvin, and Michael MacKuen. 1989. "The Strategic Configuration, Political Influence, and Presidential Power in Congress." Paper prepared for the annual meeting of the Midwest Political Science Association, Chicago.

Mouw, Calvin, and Michael MacKuen. 1990. "The Strategic Agenda." Paper prepared for delivery at the annual meeting of the American Political Science Association, San Francisco.

Neustadt, Richard E. 1976. *Presidential Power: The Politics of Leadership.* 2d ed. New York: Wiley.

New York Times. February 4, 1977. "Despite McGovern's Pleas, Senate Abolishes His Nutrition Committee."

———. February 9, 1977. "How Senate's Reorganization Plan was Scaled Down After Pressure From Veterans."

North, Douglass. 1990a. "A Transaction Cost Theory of Politics." *Journal of Theoretical Politics* 2:355–67.

———. 1990b. *Institutions, Institutional Change, and Economic Performance.* Cambridge: Cambridge University Press.

North, Douglass, and Barry Weingast. 1989. "The Evolution of Institutions Governing Public Choice in 17th Century England." *Journal of Economic History* 49:803–32.

Ostrom, Charles, and Dennis Simon. 1985. "Promise and Performance: A Dynamic Model of Presidential Popularity." *American Political Science Review* 79:334–358.

Pertschuk, Michael. 1982. *Revolt Against Regulation: The Rise and Pause of the Consumer Movement.* Berkeley and Los Angeles: University of California Press.

Piven, Frances Fox, and Richard A. Cloward. 1977. *Poor People's Movements: Why They Succeed, How They Fail.* New York: Vintage.

Ponder, Stephen. 1990. " 'Publicity in the Interest of the People': Theodore Roosevelt's Conservation Crusade." *Presidential Studies Quarterly* 20: 547–550.

Poole, Keith, and Howard Rosenthal. 1985. "A Spatial Model for Legislative Roll Call Analysis." *American Journal of Political Science* 29:357–84.

Quirk, Paul J. 1980. "Food and Drug Administration." In *The Politics of Regulation,* ed. James Q. Wilson. New York: Basic.

Ripley, Randall, and Grace A. Franklin. 1980. *Congress, the Bureaucracy, and Public Policy.* Rev. ed. Homewood: Dorsey.

Rivers, Douglas, and Nancy L. Rose. 1985. "Passing the President's Program: Public Opinion and Presidential Influence in Congress." *American Journal of Political Science* 29:183–96.

Schattschneider, E. E. 1960. *The Semi-Sovereign People: A Realist's View of Democracy in America.* New York: Holt, Rinehart, and Winston.

Schelling, Thomas. 1960. *The Strategy of Conflict.* Cambridge: Harvard University Press.

Schofield, Norman. 1985. "Anarchy, Altruism and Cooperation". *Social Choice and Welfare* 2:207–19.

Segal, Jeffrey, Charles Cameron, and Albert Cover. 1990. "Spatial Models of Roll Call Voting: Interest Groups and Constituents in Supreme Court Confirmations." Political Economy working paper, Stony Brook University.

Seidman, Harold. 1975. *Politics, Position, and Power: The Dynamics of Federal Organization,* 2d ed. New York: Oxford University Press.

Shapley, L. S., and Martin Shubik. 1954. "A Method of Evaluating the Distribution of Power in a Committee System." *American Political Science Review* 48:787–92.

Shepsle, Kenneth, and Barry Weingast. 1981. "Structure-Induced Equilibrium and Legislative Choice." *Public Choice* 37:503–19.

Sorenson, Theodore C. 1965. *Kennedy*. New York: Bantam.

Sullivan, Terry. 1987. "Presidential Leadership in Congress: Securing Commitments." In *Congress: Structure and Policy*, ed. Matthew McCubbins and Terry Sullivan. Cambridge: Cambridge University Press.

————. 1988. "Headcounts, Expectations, and Presidential Coalitions in Congress." *American Journal of Political Science* 32:567–89.

Weingast, Barry. 1984. "The Congressional-Bureaucratic System: A Principal-Agent Perspective (With Applications to the SEC)." *Public Choice* 44:147–91.

————. 1991. "Political Economy of Slavery: Credible Commitments and the Preservation of the Union." Hoover Institute working paper.

Weingast, Barry, and William Marshall. 1988. "The Industrial Organization of Congress; or, Why Legislatures, Like Firms, Are Not Organized as Markets." *Journal of Political Economy* 96:132–63.

Weingast, Barry, and Mark Moran. 1983. "Bureaucratic Discretion or Legislative Control? Regulatory Policymaking by the Federal Trade Commission." *Journal of Political Economy* 91:765–800.

West, Darrell M. 1987. *Congress and Economic Policymaking*. Pittsburgh: University of Pittsburgh Press.

Wildavsky, Aaron. 1979. *The Politics of the Budgetary Process*. 3d ed. Boston: Little, Brown.

Wilson, James Q. 1980. "The Politics of Regulation." In *The Politics of Regulation*, ed. James Q. Wilson. New York: Basic.

9

Presidents, Institutions, and Theory

TERRY M. MOE

OR A long time now, scholars have understood the presidency in largely personal terms, and they have invested heavily in theory and research intended to lay bare the personal foundations of presidential behavior. This is certainly reasonable. The presidency is built around the leadership of a single individual, and it is well known that personality, style, skills, and the like are important determinants of what individuals do.

But the presidency is also an institution, and the individual who occupies the office at any given time is an institutional actor, his role well specified by law and expectations, his incentives highly structured by the system. Some portion of presidential behavior, then, and perhaps a very large portion, is quite impersonal. All presidents, whatever their personalities or styles or backgrounds, should tend to behave similarly in basic respects.

In recent years, with the rise of the new institutionalism, presidential scholars have been encouraged to devote more serious attention to the institutional side of the equation (Pika, 1981; Heclo, 1977). Their models, it is commonly argued, should strive to take account of the full range of influences on presidential behavior and thus combine and assess the impacts of both personal and institutional variables. Today, there seems to be substantial agreement that this is the path to scientific progress in the field.

In my view, this widely accepted approach to progress is mistaken, and a radically different (and less popular) approach is called for. The first part of this chapter is my attempt to explain why. For reasons I will discuss at some length, I believe presidential scholars are far

more likely to be successful if they concentrate their theoretical resources on the institutional side—essentially omitting personal factors from their theories—and if they move toward a methodology
that values simplicity and parsimony rather than complexity and
comprehensiveness.

In the second part of the chapter, I try to illustrate more concretely
what such an approach might look like by setting out an analysis of
my own that highlights at least some of the basic issues an institutional theory must ultimately address. This is a limited exercise that
is meant to be suggestive, even provocative. My hope is simply that
it may help stimulate a productive debate—about presidents, about
institutions, about theory.

The Personal Presidency

Before the behavioral revolution hit with full force, the accepted
view of the presidency was institutional. Scholars studied the office
and the formal structures and powers associated with it, and they ac-
counted for these things—for the development of the presidency as
an institution—by anchoring them in the constitution, in statutory
law, in practice and precedent, and in history.[1]

By today's standards, their institutionalism appears narrowly legal-
istic and devoid of politics. Edward Corwin's The President: Office
and Powers, for instance, which first appeared in 1940 and served for
years as the bible of the field, was regarded by its author as "primarily a study in American public law" (1957, vii)—hardly the sort of
intensely political analysis one would now expect from institutionalists within the discipline. Yet the important point to make about traditional scholarship is not that it somehow failed to live up to modern
standards, but that it abstracted the presidency from the individuals
who occupied it and, in so doing, promoted a clear, simple view of
what needed to be explained: the institution.

All this changed with the publication in 1960 of Richard Neustadt's Presidential Power (1980), which brought the behavioral revolution to the study of the presidency and, for the last thirty years,
has dominated its theory and research. Neustadt stood traditionalism
on its head. Formal authority and structure, he argued, do not tell us
what we need to know about the presidency. The foundations of pres-

idential leadership are informal and personal, and these are the things that scholars ought to be studying.

The American system of "separated institutions sharing powers" (ibid., 26), as he puts it, grants the president nowhere near enough authority to exercise strong leadership. To achieve his objectives, the president needs support from other political actors, particularly in Congress and the bureaucracy, who have independent bases of power and are not formally required to follow his lead. The only way he can gain their support is through persuasion and bargaining. "Presidential power is the power to persuade" (ibid., 10), and "the power to persuade is the power to bargain" (ibid., 28). Neustadt's analysis is largely about how the president can develop and deploy this kind of power in an institutional world that stacks the deck against him.

The keys to success, by Neustadt's reckoning, are almost entirely personal. A strong president cannot count on others to do the persuading and bargaining for him, nor to safeguard the prime determinants of his power: his reputation within the Washington community and his prestige with the general public. The signal requirement of leadership is self-help. He must do it all himself. He must be his own power expert, his own executive assistant, his own director of intelligence—which in turn means that he must be highly skilled in the political arts, thoroughly informed about issues and strategies and personalities, deeply experienced in the ways of the political world, and enthusiastically involved in political horse-trading. It follows that only a very special person could possibly do all this and do it well, someone who comes to the job with the right psychological makeup: self-confidence, an instinct for power, a sense of purpose and direction. Strong presidential leadership calls for a man of "extraordinary temperament" (ibid., 143).

Almost every aspect of Neustadt's work has had profound influence on the way the presidency is understood and studied. It is difficult to think of any book or article in any area of political science that has had greater influence and staying power than this one. Its most consequential impact is broadly methodological: with *Presidential Power*, the balance of scholarly attention shifted from the formal to the informal, from the impersonal to the personal.

This is not to say that Neustadt ignores institutions. In the first place, his explanation for the personal presidency is, in effect, institutional:

presidents are thrown back on their personal resources precisely because American institutions deny them enough formal authority for effective leadership. Moreover, in the pulling and hauling of politics, authority and structure provide presidents with vantage points that may contribute to the exercise of power.

But Neustadt's analysis, nonetheless, is not about institutions. For the most part, they provide a framework within which the relevant action takes place—and the focus is on the action, not the framework. Institutions are relegated to the background. The driving forces of presidential politics are personal. As Neustadt puts it, "My theme is personal power and its politics: what it is, how to get it, how to keep it, how to use it. . . . This is not a book about the Presidency as an organization, or as legal powers, or as precedents, or as procedures" (ibid., v).

Viewed historically, there is a certain irony in this methodological shift. Neustadt's book is about the modern presidency, which, by his account and most everyone else's, was ushered in by Franklin Roosevelt and the New Deal. Roosevelt also happens to be Neustadt's model of the strong presidential leader—the president who relishes politics, excels at it, has a hand in every pot, and, through his own skill, knowledge, and acumen, amasses power and political success. Roosevelt was the kind of person a president should be. He had the kind of experience and skill and enthusiasm a president should have. His style of organization—flexible, competitive—was the style a president should adopt. He was the standard against which all other modern presidents should be judged. He was the embodiment of the personal presidency.

But here is the irony. At precisely the same time that Neustadt's work was reorienting scholarly thinking around the concept of the personal presidency, the presidency itself was becoming highly institutionalized. Indeed, the hallmark of the modern presidency is its growth and development as an institution. It consists of hundreds of individuals whose various roles and offices fill out a highly differentiated organizational network, the basic structure of which has gained a substantial measure of stability and uniformity across administrations (Moe, 1985; Kernell and Popkin, 1986). "Presidential behavior" is generated by all these individuals, collectively, as they go about their presidential business. It is an institutional phenomenon, not a personal one.

The modern president does not simply decide what his legislative program or budget proposal will be. Most of the decisions are actually made by aides and specialists in the White House, in the Office of Management and Budget, in the Council of Economic Advisers, in Treasury, and elsewhere. Similarly, the president does not rely much on personal lobbying to get his way in Congress. Almost all presidential lobbying is handled by his people in the White House congressional liaison office. Nor does the president have much to do with most presidential appointments. These are handled by a special personnel staff. And so it goes, for virtually all important aspects of the presidency (Arnold, 1986; Hart, 1987; Wayne, 1978).

Today's presidency is vastly different from what it was in Franklin Roosevelt's time. The roots of change can be found in the Progressive activism of Theodore Roosevelt and Woodrow Wilson, as well as in the creation of the Bureau of the Budget in 1921. But the real transformation was initiated by Franklin Roosevelt himself, who, in fashioning his New Deal and leading the nation in war, revolutionized public expectations about the office (Greenstein, 1978). From that point on, all presidents would be held responsible for addressing every conceivable social problem, and they would be expected, through legislative leadership and executive control, to take effective action. While these expectations far outstripped the president's means of meeting them, presidents responded as best they could by incrementally developing their institutional capacity for governance. The result has been a trajectory of change in which, over the decades, policy making has become more centralized in the White House organization and the bureaucracy has become more politicized (or, more accurately, presidentialized) through appointments and top-down control (Moe, 1985; Nathan, 1983).

Probably the most dramatic upsurge in the institutional presidency came right at the beginning, during the Roosevelt years, with the creation of the Executive Office of the President and the spectacular enlargement of the Bureau of the Budget. These reforms were recommended by the Brownlow Committee, whose justification for change is one of the most quoted phrases in public administration: "The president needs help" (President's Committee on Administrative Management, 1937, 5). There is no mystery here. The president really did need help. The responsibilities of the job simply overwhelmed the president as an individual. It was impossible for any person to do it all, or even to do most of the things that successful presidential leadership required. He needed help—an institutional capacity that, appropriately designed, would enable a small army of other people to take effective action on the president's behalf. The whole point of the Brownlow reforms, as well as the next fifty years of institutional change, was to reject the notion that presidents ought to do everything for themselves. The key to a successful presidency was not self-help. It was institutional capacity—which, in a very meaningful sense, is just the opposite of self-help.

By the time Neustadt's book had placed its indelible stamp on the scholarly mind, the personal presidency was already out of date. As scholars extolled the informal, personal aspects of the presidency, the presidency was becoming a large, complex, multifaceted institution whose "presidential behavior" could not adequately be understood in personal terms. The new methodology of the field directed attention to precisely those aspects of the presidency that were declining in importance and distracted attention from the very developments that should have been seen and studied as the essence of the modern presidency.

Struggling with the Personal Presidency

This did not mean that scholars literally began ignoring institutions, any more than Neustadt himself had ignored institutions. In terms of substantive research effort, informal and personal topics gained markedly in prominence, and this represented a genuine sea change in the field. But even during the first decade or two after Neustadt's book appeared, when its influence was greatest, some areas of study—those concerned with congressional relations (Fisher, 1972), bureaucratic politics (Destler, 1972), presidential popularity (Mueller, 1970), and White House organization (Kessel, 1975), for instance—continued to explore institutional issues and point to contextual or environmental (as well as personal) determinants of presidential behavior.

The real burden of the personal presidency, then and now, is not simply that it affects the allocation of scholarly work. It is more deeply rooted than this. It has to do with the way scholars think about the presidency and, in particular, with how they approach their fundamental task as social scientists: the task of explanation.

As a methodology, the personal presidency sets an explanatory standard that the vast majority of scholars throughout the field, even those whose concerns are largely institutional, seems to embrace. The notion is that an acceptable explanation of presidential behavior, whatever its initial level of abstraction, must eventually be anchored in an understanding of why individual presidents make the specific decisions they do. While impersonal theories (institutional or environmental, say) may help in identifying constraints on these decisions, they are incomplete. They must ultimately be grounded in personal theories—theories about values, beliefs, skills, formative experiences, and the like—if presidential behavior is to be fully explained.

This promotes enormous complications in theory and research, opening the Pandora's box of individual motivation and cognitive processes and orienting the field around untold causal mysteries. Explanation cannot center on general issues of organization and structure but must lay bare the behavior of a single person in the full flower of his uniqueness. This is the most vexing theoretical problem in all social science, and it now pervades and stifles the study of the presidency.

Throughout the 1960s and 1970s, presidency scholars took serious aim at issues of personal behavior.[2] To the extent their work can be classified as theoretical, it often relied heavily on existing theories in psychology and social psychology, theories that are tremendously complicated and diverse in what they have to say about the causal foundations of individual behavior. The paths from relevant factors—within the individual, in the individual's past, in the individual's environment—to the individual's behavior tend to be long, confusing, tortuous, and, in the end, quite uncertain. As Alexander George (1974) notes, using these theories to say something definite and systematic about the behavior of specific presidents is extraordinarily difficult and perhaps impossible.

Precisely because there was often a big gap between what these theories were able to say and what political scientists wanted to explain, scholars sometimes supplemented—or simply began—with what we might call sui generis theories of the presidency. Neustadt's theory of how presidents acquire personal power is one version of this: it does not derive from some larger body of theoretical work, nor does it generalize beyond the presidency.

Neither approach to theory has generated much in the way of real progress. Psychology and social psychology are far removed from what political scientists want to explain, and they have done more to complicate and confuse the study of the presidency than to resolve its major issues. Sui generis theories, in compensating for what these others fail to offer, tend to be specialized and logically isolated. They are internal to the presidency. They stand alone.

Most work on the presidency, moreover, cannot really be considered theoretical at all. This was a weakness of traditional political science as a whole, of course, but in most areas of the discipline it was rapidly overcome following the behavioral revolution. Not so for the presidency, and the methodology of personalism is an important reason why. It attached explanatory value to virtually everything that might influence the specific decisions of the unique human being occupying the office; and this overload, in turn, encouraged "explanation" through history, description, anecdotes, and educated judgment.

Thus, while the personal presidency revolutionized the field by rejecting the traditional focus on institutions, it also had a profoundly conservative impact: it reinforced and perpetuated the traditional *style* of analysis within the modern field. In its scholarly style, the study of the presidency continued to have more in common with history or journalism than with the study of Congress or voting behavior. Good work remained, above all else, a matter of good writing— writing so elegant, so interwoven with stories and illustrations, so flush with historical detail, that one might almost overlook its absence of theory, testing, logical rigor, objectivity, or other mainstays of modern social science.

Almost, but not entirely. By the late 1970s and early 1980s, critics were arguing that the traditional style of analysis was hindering theoretical progress and that a more systematic adherence to the scientific method was urgently needed. They also argued that the presidency had become overpersonalized, that many "nonpersonal" variables are at least as important to presidential behavior, and that progress calls for new, more broadly based perspectives that bring together the personal and nonpersonal foundations of the presidency (King, 1975; Pika, 1981; Edwards and Wayne, 1983).

At about the same time that these scientific concerns became salient, political science as a whole was swept by the new institutionalism—adding fuel to the argument that something was wrong with the way the presidency was being studied. In virtually all areas of the discipline, scholars grew skeptical of behavioralism and the perspectives associated with it (pluralism, most notably) and showed renewed interest in the origins, structures, modes of operation, and social consequences of political institutions.

This was not a response to changes in government; institutions had not suddenly become more prevalent or powerful. It is better viewed as a methodological reawakening, a recognition that behavioralism had promoted an unbalanced view of politics and society. For most fellow travelers within the movement, the new institutionalism was an attempt to redress the imbalance by bringing institutions back in. For others, the serious institutionalists, it was more than this. It was a means of showing that institutions are fundamental and behavior largely derivative (March and Olsen, 1989).

Presidential scholars were caught up in all this, but most often as fellow travelers rather than serious institutionalists. In part this was because, unlike their colleagues in other fields, they had a practical reason for shifting course: the presidency had grown dramatically as an institution in a relatively short period of time. No methodological reawakening was necessary to see that theory and research should pay more attention to this. The more basic reason that true institutionalism never took root here, however, is that the personal presidency effectively defused any inclination to see institutions as truly fundamental.

As a result, the institutionalist critique took a form that dovetailed neatly with the scientific critique of the field's traditional style of analysis. Critics pointed out, quite rightly, that the presidency had become overpersonalized and that institutions needed to be taken more fully into account; but this entailed no radical rejection of the personal presidency. Their concern was not to shift attention from the man to the office but rather to encourage more broadly based studies that incorporate both sets of relevant factors and sort out their various effects (Pika, 1981; Heclo, 1977).

The last decade or so, not coincidentally, has been a period of change and modernization within the field. Increasingly, presidency scholars have been formulating testable theoretical models, collecting quantitative data, and carrying out statistical analyses (Edwards, 1980; King and Ragsdale, 1988; Kernell, 1978; Ostrom and Simon,

1985; Moe, 1982). They have also moved aggressively in studying the institutional presidency (Kessell, 1983, 1984; Campbell, 1986; Moe, 1985; Kernell and Popkin, 1986; Arnold, 1986; Hart, 1987) and in arguing the predominance of institutional and environmental influences on presidential behavior (Skowronek, 1984; Pious, 1979; Edwards, 1989; Peterson, 1990; Kerbel, 1991; Bunce, 1981).

But the problem remains: how can intellectual order be imposed on all this? Critics seem to place their faith in "pretheories" and empirical studies that, over a long period of time, might help sort through the geometrically increasing numbers of relevant variables. Meantime, absent an alternative methodology, the personal presidency continues to shape the way most scholars think about explanation. By default, it is the organizing conception that pulls together the mind-boggling array of relevant factors—including institutional factors—into a single framework. And it personalizes them all.

The common notion is that relevant variables help explain presidential behavior to the extent that, via causal chains that are lengthy and complicated, they ultimately affect the thinking of the man who is president. All influences find their translation through personal influences. As Joseph Pika (1981, 23) observes,

> Closely associated with the personalization of research is the causal model employed even in ostensibly "institutional" research; it is, in most cases, president-centered in that environmental influences are significant only to the extent that they are mediated by presidential thinking and decisions. The presidential person is lodged in the neck of our "funnel of causality" with all other influences necessarily passing through this individualizing filter.

Most aspects of the modern institutional presidency, moreover, are doubly personalized. Not only are their effects realized through the president's personal filter, but the institution itself is taken to be highly malleable, its form intricately shaped and reshaped as presidents come and go. Each president, as an individual with a unique personality, background, and style, builds his own system of operation inside the White House and throughout the executive branch, fashioning an institutional presidency in his own image—a personal institutional presidency, as it were (e.g., Hess, 1988).

After more than a decade of intellectual ferment, the field still lacks a solid foundation. The two major lines of criticism, the scientific and the institutional, have succeeded in highlighting weaknesses in the literature and in convincing scholars that something should be done to turn matters around. But the new enlightenment they offer is not in the end very enlightening, and it adds to the field's problems rather than resolving them. While the personal presidency already entails a theoretical perspective of forbidding complexity, the new wisdom is that the presidential world is actually far more complex still, that many more relevant variables need to be taken into account, and that progress means compiling them into comprehensive theories. This is a giant step in the wrong direction.

Presidential Style: Lessons from Organization Theory

Let's take a closer look, for instance, at presidential style. With the triumph of the personal presidency during the 1960s, style quickly emerged as one of the most important of these relevant variables. Neustadt had blazed the trail. The style best suited to strong presidential leadership, he argued, is a loose, informal, highly personalized approach to decision making and administration that ensures the president himself maximal involvement and control.

This, of course, was Roosevelt's style. Although president at a time when ideas about administration were dominated by classical organization theory—emphasizing formal structure, clear lines of authority, and other features of neat organizational hierarchies—he enthusiastically violated every one of its principles.[3] He adroitly juggled subordinates to his own advantage. He gave the same responsibilities to different advisers, cultivating competition and uncertainty among them. He orchestrated everything personally from the center, ensuring that he held all the cards. To Neustadt and those who followed him, this was the way to be a good president.

The way to be a mediocre president was to do what Dwight Eisenhower did. His style—or at least the style scholars uniformly attributed to him until recently (Greenstein, 1982)—was to build his presidency around formal organization, following a nonpolitical model of bureaucratic leadership he picked up in the army. He appointed a chief of staff, Sherman Adams, who sat atop a strict White House hierarchy, managed the president's time, dealt with subordinates, and in myriad ways did what Eisenhower might have done for himself. Specialized units were created within the White House— for press relations and congressional liaison, for examples—that delegated to staffers functions essential to presidential success. Existing units like the National Security Council were reinforced with new structures that formalized their operations. Overall, Eisenhower's approach to the presidency appeared to remove him personally from most of the action—and thus, so the conventional wisdom had it, to deny him the personal resources so necessary for strong leadership.

For many years, this simple comparison of presidential styles was widely accepted. A style built around informal arrangements and personal involvement was good. A style built around formal arrangements, specialization, and delegation was bad. As Bert Rockman (1984, 204) puts it, "The model of organization that Neustadt attributes to Franklin Roosevelt has nearly attained legendary status as a prescribed style for managing the White House."

What exactly was the basis for this belief about formal and informal styles? For the most part, it was an empirical generalization based on assessments—not entirely accurate ones—of Roosevelt and Eisenhower. As time went one, the experiences of subsequent presidents were accommodated without giving up the generalization. Kennedy, whom Neustadt admired almost as much as he did Roosevelt and whom most scholars regard as a reasonably successful president, had a collegial style consistent with the presumed requirements of self-help. Nixon, forever doomed by Watergate to disaster status (whatever his achievements in foreign and domestic policy), created a formal presidency reminiscent of Eisenhower's—a style that contributed, so they say, to his downfall.

More generally, this belief about style survived because of the confluence to two important features of the modern presidency. First, as Theodore Lowi (1985) points out, most modern presidents after Roosevelt (the lionized Kennedy aside) have been regarded as unsuccessful in major respects. Second, as the presidency has become increasingly institutionalized, presidents have naturally moved away from the informal style that Neustadt and others prescribe. Indeed, it is reasonable to suggest that no president will ever again be free to adopt this kind of style, even if he wants to (Kernell and Popkin, 1986). Thus, there are no clear-cut examples of bad presidents with informal styles (although some might try to put Carter in this category), and there are plenty of presidents who have formalized their presidencies in various ways and gone on to perform unsuccessfully.

The result is a correlation, a spurious one, that may appear to buttress the conventional wisdom.

Generalizing from a few cases is hazardous anyway, even under the best of circumstances. The more significant question is: Does this conventional wisdom have a broader theoretical basis? The answer is that it does not, outside of theories that are essentially sui generis to the presidency, and thus, given the inductive approach so characteristic of the literature, formulated with reference to the same small set of cases.

There has never been any justification for such an insular approach to theory within presidential studies, and this applies with a vengeance to issues of style. For within the broader, interdisciplinary field of organization theory, leadership (or managerial) style has been the subject of intensive analysis since the late 1930s. Countless studies have been carried out in a variety of organizational settings, and diverse theories have been proposed, debated, tested, and compared. Throughout, the connection between style and performance has been at the center of inquiry (Bass, 1981).

This body of work is obviously of the utmost relevance for the study of the presidential style. It represents virtually the sum total of what social science has been able to learn over the years about style and, more generally, about the exercise of leadership in organizations. If this were not enough, it also fits in beautifully with the personal presidency, for the literature on style grew out of the human relations school of organization theory, which rejected the formalism of classical theory and insisted on seeing organizations in social and personal terms. Leadership was not a matter of formal powers and roles, but of personal traits and interpersonal relationships. For the personal presidency, a more congruent body of theory and research could hardly have been asked for.

Nonetheless, presidential scholars have paid little or no attention to it (Johnson, 1974; Hess, 1988). Why would this be so? It is partly due to the field's traditional style of analysis, which promotes atheoretical lines of research. It is also due to the inclination, encouraged by the methodology of personalism, to think that presidents, the office, and the institution are all too unique to be subsumed under a more general body of work on leadership and organization. But whatever the full panoply of reasons, the fact is that presidential scholars have failed to take advantage of what organization theory has to offer on these issues (and many others), and this has hindered their efforts to understand the presidency.[4]

What, then, are the lessons that presidential scholars ought to be—but are not—picking up on? My own views on the subject are unorthodox, so let me begin by outlining what the mainstream position would most likely be. A mainstream organization theorist would argue that cumulative scientific research over the past half century has taught us a great deal about style and its consequences and that this knowledge, above all else, is what organization theory has to contribute to the study of the presidency.

In the earliest studies, leadership was thought to be largely a matter of traits inherent in the individual—intelligence, for instance. For the most part, these were things a person either did or did not have, and they could not readily be learned or changed. Subsequent studies disavowed trait theory, arguing that an individual's style of leadership—which could in fact be learned or changed—was an important determinant of his effectiveness. Some of this work, especially in the early going, pursued the simple distinction between authoritarian and democratic styles of leadership, almost invariably showing that the latter (the normative favorite) is the more productive. More nuanced work along similar lines claimed that there are two fundamental dimensions of leadership, one employee-centered (a socioemotional, informal, democratic dimension), the other production-centered (an instrumental, formal, authoritarian dimension), and that both—but especially the former—contribute to organizational performance.

These familiar, timeworn conceptions of style continue to find their reflection in modern ideas about leadership, but several decades of painstaking research have left them hedged about by zillions of caveats and qualifications. The thrust of the modern work is that leadership is highly specific to the situation: it is contingent on the environment, the goals of the group, the nature of the members, and many other relevant variables. No one style, set of traits, or combination of these is necessarily best. Different contexts call for different types of leadership.[5]

The mainstream lesson for presidential scholars, a lesson whose foundations were already established by the 1960s, would appear to go something like this. The connection between presidential style and presidential performance, like that between leader style and organizational performance more generally, is enormously complicated. So forget the fixation on Roosevelt. There is no one best style for presidents, any more than for other organizational leaders. The style that works best in any given situation is contingent on a whole range of relevant variables and the specific values they happen to take on in that situation. The way to understand leadership is to identify all these relevant variables, study them, and figure out how they all operate to shape the president's exercise of leadership.

My own view is less orthodox. Part of the mainstream position, I should emphasize, conveys important lessons for the study of presidential style: no single style is best, there is no theoretical basis for exalting the styles of Roosevelt or Kennedy or anybody else, and efforts to figure out which styles work best in particular situations will be extremely complicated.[6] But these lessons do not take us very far, and they reflect a very limited brand of knowledge.

The fact is that virtually everything organization theorists have learned about leadership style is negative. Myths have been debunked and commonsense notions have been rejected. These simple ideas have been replaced, however, not by a positive understanding of leadership—by a theory that tells us what we should actually expect and why—but by "contingency theory," which is just a label for how desperately little organization theorists have managed to learn about leadership in half a century of trying. Saying that things are complicated and situational is but another way of saying that organization theorists have only the vaguest idea what is going on.

Charles Perrow (1986), in his insightful review of the organizational literature, sums it up this way:

> "Good leadership" is generally described as democratic rather than authoritarian, employee-centered rather than production-centered, concerned with human relations rather than with bureaucratic rules. . . .
> The history of research in this area is one of progressive disenchantment with the above theses and progressive awareness of the complexities of human behavior and human situations. As a result of forty years of intensive research, we have a large body of information on what does *not* clearly and simply affect productivity . . . and a growing list of qualifiers and conditions that have to be taken into account. The size of this list threatens to overwhelm us before we can, with confidence, either advise managers as to what they

should do to increase productivity or develop theories that have much explanatory power. (85–86)

The most important lesson that presidential scholars stand to gain from organizational theory, in my view, is not a lesson about the causal foundations of presidential style. Nor is it about the causal connection between presidential style and presidential performance. Organization theory has very little of positive value to tell us on these scores. The major lesson to be learned, rather, is about how the presidency ought to be studied. It is a methodological rather than a substantive lesson.

What decades of research on organizational leadership have demonstrated is that the conventional methodology will never lead to a clear, coherent theory that makes sense of the encyclopedic list of variables that are supposedly relevant. The lesson is that this line of research is on a path to nowhere. Presidential scholars can learn best and most productively from organization theory by paying close attention to it, recognizing its failures, refusing to repeat them, and insisting upon a new methodology that will take presidential theory and research down a very different path.

Proposal: A New Methodology for Presidential Studies

Like everyone else, I believe that style and other personal variables make a difference for presidential behavior. My considered opinion is that institutions probably have much more to do with it than individuals do. But I cannot be sure about this. As Joseph Pika (1981, 17) has observed, the question of relative explanatory power—of the "relationship between the president and the presidency, the individual and the institution"—has long been perhaps the central analytic problem of the field, and it remains unanswered. All we can say with confidence is that both aspects of the presidency, the personal and the institutional, are important.

By almost any account, however, scholars have been distinctly unsuccessful thus far in building theories anchored in the individuality of presidents. And while it is tempting to think that this is only a temporary problem, a problem that might be solved with a half century's worth of new research, there is little basis for this kind of optimism. The problem is inherent in the enterprise itself, and it cannot be resolved through more study. The only way out is to change the enterprise, to move along a different path.

How can this be done and still allow us to learn as much as we can about the presidency? There are two basic parts to what I consider a reasonable answer. First, I think efforts to build institutional theories of the presidency are far more likely to prove successful over the long haul than are efforts to build personal theories. We need not pretend that institutions are simple or easy to understand. The crucial thing is that they are impersonal. They do not force us to open the Pandora's box of the individual's psyche, nor to engage in endlessly detailed personal comparisons across individuals. Institutions direct our attention instead to structures, roles, authority, control, hierarchy, incentives, and other general properties of organization—properties that shape presidential behavior in distinctive ways regardless of who is president.

Personality, style, and other aspects of the personal presidency are eminently worth studying, and they should continue to be the focus of intensive research. But our expectations should be different. We should expect research along these lines to provide essential facts about the presidency and its occupants over time and thus to build an empirical foundation that promotes sound judgments about what presidents have actually done and why. We should also expect it to be structured, as all good research is, by analytical rigor and theoretical notions of cause and effect. But we should not expect it to generate, somewhere down the road, coherent theories with the degree of generality and explanatory power we are looking for, and we should not design or undertake it with that purpose in mind. The theoretical resources of the field should be invested on the institutional side of the equation, not the personal side.

Second, I think scholars would do well to move away from the conventional methodology of the field, which encourages a fruitless search for relevant variables, and move instead toward the methodology that has worked so well for economics. This does not require a heavy reliance on mathematical models. What it requires is a different orientation to explanation: one that places positive value on *not* being comprehensive, on eliminating rather than proliferating variables, on capturing just the essence of a problem rather than describing the whole thing.

In general, I think presidential scholars must take a more restrictive view of what they want to explain. They cannot explain everything about the presidency that they find interesting or important. They can explain institutional aspects better than they can explain personal aspects, and they can probably explain some properties of institutions—structure, in particular—more readily than others. In the long run, it seems to me that they will learn more about the presidency, produce better theories, and invest their scarce resources more wisely if they concentrate their scientific efforts more narrowly and strategically.

Rational Choice and the Presidency

The methodology I am suggesting here has been influential and productive in other areas of the discipline, especially in the study of legislatures and elections, but it has rarely been applied to the presidency. In part, of course, this has happened because presidential scholars have their own, very different ways of doing things. But another, equally important reason is that the most aggressive proponents of this methodology within the wider discipline, positive theorists, have themselves shown little interest in building a theory of the presidency.

Why did positive theorists invade, quite successfully, the study of legislatures and elections, yet choose to stay away from the study of presidents? The answer is that their analytic tradition is rooted in social choice theory, which centers on voting—and presidents don't vote. Legislators and members of the general electorate do, allowing for elaborately developed positive theories of legislative and electoral behavior. But the same technology cannot readily be applied to presidents. Much the same story, I should add, can be told for public bureaucracy.

This imbalance is slowly being corrected. Positive theorists moved into the era of the new institutionalism by exploring the various ways that institutions bring stability to the inherently unstable world of majority rule voting. Their focus was largely on the U.S. Congress, and their concerns centered on how its internal structures—committees, procedural rules, and the like—constrain the behavior of members, allocate agenda powers, and produce stable outcomes. For these matters, social choice seemed to work fine. Over time, however, they began to ask how the legislature's internal structures might have emerged in the first place, and, more generally, how rational legislators approach and resolve issues of institutional choice. They also began to branch out, concerning themselves with aspects of legislative behavior—political control of the bureaucracy, for instance—that involve nonvoting institutions and nonelectoral types of relationships (Shepsle, 1986; McCubbins, Noll, and Weingast, 1987).

For these sorts of things, positive theorists had to look beyond social choice for other theories that could help them out. They found what they were looking for in the new economics of organization (Moe, 1984), a fast-growing body of work—consisting, roughly speaking, of transaction costs economics, agency theory, and the theory of repeated games—that is revolutionizing not only the way economists think about firms, but also how social scientists think about structure, control, and other issues at the heart of organization theory (Williamson, 1985; Milgrom and Roberts, 1992).

The new economics is not about voting or the instabilities of majority rule, although it can accommodate them. It is about voluntary exchange among actors in the marketplace, and it inquires into the conditions under which they will find it mutually beneficial to cooperate—that is, to organize their behavior. Some of this work focuses on how cooperation, in the form of regularized or tacitly coordinated behavior, can emerge from the "noncooperative" dynamics of strategic interaction. But the bulk of it is about how formal cooperative structures are explicitly arrived at through contractual agreement—and thus, as political scientists might put it, through bargains or deals the relevant players find mutually beneficial. Considered together, then, these strands of theory get at both the informal and formal aspects of cooperation, and they point the way toward a coherent perspective on the rational bases of organization.

In recent years, the trend has been toward a positive theory of political institutions that combines social choice and the new economics. Voting remains of key importance, as it should, but attention is increasingly paid to the conditions affecting the desirability of cooperative deals (conditions having to do, for instance, with transaction costs or asymmetric information), the commitment and enforcement problems that make durable deals so hard to arrange in politics, the

kinds of structures that help mitigate these problems, and the consequences that these deals and structures have for institutional behavior
and outcomes.

Positive theorists are just beginning to sort all this out, and they
have a long way to go. But it is clear even now that rational choice
theory can be extended to a full range of important institutional topics—from congressional procedures to legislative oversight and bureaucratic design to presidential control and the institutional
presidency. Given where the discipline stood just ten years ago, re-
markable headway has been made in putting us on the threshhold of
a broadly based theory of institutions.

What does this mean for the study of the presidency? It means that,
unlike at any time in the past, a powerful theoretical framework is
now available to help us work our way toward an institutional theory
of the presidency. This is an extraordinary opportunity for a field
that has long found theory so elusive, an opportunity that presidential scholars should welcome and exploit.

It also means that an institutional theory of the presidency built
along these lines will not simply be presidential in focus but an integral part of a larger theory of the institutional system. Presidential
scholars who think in institutional terms, then, will really be thinking and studying about institutions more generally. The rational
choice foundation ensures as much by linking everything together,
providing the same explanation for the legislature, the presidency, the
bureaucracy, and the judiciary, and understanding each in connection
with the others.

And finally, it means that, even if presidential scholars are not keen
to embrace this alien methodology, the positive theorists are coming
anyway. They are going to invade presidential studies, just as they invaded legislative and electoral studies, and they will change the field.
How productively it changes depends on the extent to which presidential scholars contribute to its development: to the theoretical ideas
that get proposed, to debates about these ideas, and to research that
puts them the test. This has been the key to progress in legislatures
and elections, where positive theorists and scholars wedded to very
different traditions have learned enormously from one another, and
where, as a result, rational choice has both transformed and been
transformed by the fields it has invaded. Much the same must happen
in the study of the presidency.

Putting Rational Choice to Use

How, then, should we proceed in trying to put rational choice to good use in building an institutional theory of the presidency? It seems to me that there are two basic ways to go about it that, in the end, ought to be quite complementary. The first is to follow the trajectory already set by positive theory, which is expanding outward from its base in legislatures and voting to incorporate other institutions. The emphasis here, at least in the early stages, is on the legislative aspects of the presidency—veto and appointment power, for instance—and their implications for the strategies and outcomes of legislative voting. Theoretical anchoring is largely in the social choice tradition, with some attention to the new economics (Hammond and Miller, 1987; Calvert, McCubbins, and Weingast, 1989). Future developments along this path will presumably integrate presidents more fully into models of legislative choice and then, taking greater advantage of the new economics, begin to explore aspects of the presidency that are less directly related to Congress and voting.

This "normal science" approach has much to recommend it as a way of developing a coherent body of institutional theory. But those of us who are less content in the short term with a Congress-centered view of the world are likely to find a second approach much more attractive—and at least as productive. The theoretical orientation here comes more from the new economics (and political modifications of it) than from social choice, and its emphasis is on understanding the presidency—its basic properties, its development over time, its consequences for behavior—as an integral part of the larger institutional system.

This second approach lacks the well-defined trajectory of the first. But this is also what makes it so exciting. For it is not yet bogged down in technicalities, incremental modifications, and unavoidable baggage. It is just starting out: thrusting new issues to the fore, begging for new ideas, and opening up opportunities for dramatic progress. The tools are available, and, precisely because rational choice theory has so rarely been applied to the presidency, the field is especially fertile ground.

In the remainder of this paper, I want to illustrate what an analysis along this second path might look like. In an article I wrote several years ago (Moe, 1985), I argued that the presidency has become more centralized and politicized during the modern era for reasons that have little to do with individual presidents and a lot to do with forces rooted in American institutions. In more recent work, I have put the new economics of organization to use (with modifications) in an effort to explain the broader structure of government, especially its public bureaucracy (Moe, 1989, 1990a, 1990b). Here I will bring these two strands of argument together.

A mature institutional literature, of course, would speak to a much wider range of topics than I can deal with here. My purpose is simply to raise some basic issues that are central to an institutional theory, address them in a clear, logical fashion, and combine them into a coherent perspective that sheds light on the presidency and its place in the larger system. Whether or not these specific ideas prove to have staying power over time, my hope is that they will help broaden the debate and get the ball rolling.

Institutions and the Politics of Structural Choice

One problem with the new institutionalism, at least within presidential studies, is that institutions tend to be so vaguely conceptualized that, in effect, they are just another way of talking about all the environmental or historical factors that somehow affect the presidency (Pike, 1981; Peterson, 1990). If we are to get a useful handle on how presidential behavior is shaped by its surrounding institutional system, and indeed on how presidents can actually change the system itself, then we need a simple, clear way of thinking about it. Let's try to do this by stepping back from the presidency for a moment and reflecting on the system as a whole.

A useful place to begin is with the most basic building block of any political system: public authority. In politics, people with very different interests engage in a struggle to control and exercise public authority. The struggle arises because public authority does not belong to anyone and because whoever wins hold of it has the right to make law for everyone. The winners can legitimately promote their own interests through policies and structures of their own design, and the losers can be forced by law to accept outcomes that make them absolutely worse off. The power of public authority, then, is essentially coercive and redistributive. This is why political actors value it so much—and, at the same time, fear it.

Most political institutions are instances of the exercise of public authority. They arise out of a politics of structural choice in which the winners use public authority to design new structures and impose them on the polity as a whole. These structures are simply vehicles by which the winners pursue their own interests. Some may administer programs that supply the winners with benefits. Others may extract resources or behavioral adjustments from losers. Still others may impose new constraints on the way the political game will be played in the future, giving today's winners advantages over their opponents in tomorrow's jockeying to exercise public authority.

Consider American bureaucracy in particular. What can we say about the politics of structural choice and the kinds of bureaucratic institutions it is likely to yield? Several very basic forces are at work, all of them anchored in the American separation of powers system and its distinctive scheme of public authority (Moe, 1990a).

The first is what I call *political uncertainty*. A winning group or coalition that gains control of public authority today is in a position to impose whatever structures they like—say, an agency with a particular mandate, organization, and staff. But they do not own what they create. They have no property rights making the agency legally theirs—as, say, economic actors do when they create business organizations. Political structures belong to whoever happens to be in authority, and tomorrow some other group with opposing interests may gain control. They would then become the new "owners" and have the legal right to destroy or undermine what the first group had created (without paying any compensation whatever).

Because the dangers of political uncertainty can be anticipated from the outset, however, today's winners need not leave their creations unprotected. They can fashion structures to insulate their agencies and programs from the future exercise of public authority. In doing so, of course, they will not only be reducing their enemies' opportunities for future control; they will be reducing their own opportunities as well. But this is often a reasonable price to pay, given the alternative. And because they get to go first, they are really not giving up control. They are just choosing to exercise a greater measure of it *ex ante*, through insulated structures that, once locked in, predispose the agency to do the right things. What they are moving away from—because it is dangerous—is the kind of ongoing democratic control that is exercised through the discretionary decisions of public authority over time.

There are various ways of doing this (Moe, 1990a). The most direct is for the winners to specify, in excruciating detail, precisely what the agency is to do and how it is to do it, leaving as little as possible to the discretionary judgment of bureaucrats—and thus as little as possible for future authorities to exercise control over, short of passing new legislation later on (which is usually not possible). Thus, agency goals, decision criteria, procedures, timetables, personnel rules, and virtually anything else affecting agency performance can be specified exhaustively in the original legislation, sinking a vast range of behaviors in formal concrete and shielding them from political influence.

Obviously, this is not a formula for effective organization. In the interests of political protection, agencies are knowingly burdened with cumbersome, technically inappropriate structures that undermine their capacity to do their jobs well. Nor, obviously, is this a formula for effective control by democratic superiors. Insulationist devices are called for precisely because those who create public bureaucracy do not want a truly effective structure of democratic control.

A second force driving the politics of structural choice is what I call, for lack of a better term, *political compromise*. The design of most structures, in or out of politics, involves lots of compromise. In business transactions, for instance, economic actors make compromises all the time as they engage in voluntary exchange, hammer out contracts, and create structures. The key thing about voluntary exchange, however, is that the structures so created should tend to be mutually beneficial. All participants expect to benefit—and if they don't, they are free to leave. In these contexts, organizations are designed by people who want them to succeed.

This is not so in politics. In the American separation of powers system, political victory is exceedingly difficult in the absence of compromise with the losing side. And because everyone knows that whatever structures are chosen will influence the content and effectiveness of public policy, virtually all aspects of structure and policy are up for grabs as separate items for political compromise. The re-

sult is that, if the winners want to shift the status quo, they will usually have to let the losers participate in the design of any organization
being created—and the losers will often press for structures that undermine the organization's performance. Because American politics is
unavoidably a process of compromise, then, public agencies will be
designed in part by their enemies, who want them to fail.

A third basic force driving the politics of structural choice is what
I call *fear of the state*. To see what it is and where it comes from, we
need to distinguish two types of political participants: public officials
(elected and administrative) and social actors (interest groups and
constituents). Public officials occupy positions of public authority
and have the legal right to exercise it. Social actors try to influence
public officials through elections, lobbying, and other means.

When the relationship between the two is construed in principal-
agent terms (Pratt and Zeckhauser, 1985), it is clear that social actors, as principals, cannot perfectly control the public officials who
are presumably their agents. This is perhaps less a problem in the politics of structural choice than in other aspects of politics, because
here the most relevant social actors by far are likely to be organized
interest groups—who, compared to constituents in general, are well
informed about structural issues and endowed with substantial resources for monitoring official behavior, assigning credit and blame,
and bringing their influence to bear. Structural politics is clearly interest group politics. But even though public officials have strong incentives to respond to what the groups want, control will still be
imperfect—and officials, therefore, will still have a measure of autonomy in their exercise of public authority.

This has a profound effect on the way interest groups approach the
design of political structures. While they are afraid of one another,
pressing for structures that protect their own interests from subver-
sion by their group enemies, they are also afraid—quite separately
afraid—of public officials, even those who are presumably their allies. For public officials have their own interests—in money, security,
policy—at heart; and, because political control is imperfect, they can
use the coercive power of public authority in ways that are unwanted
and sometimes even devastating to the groups.

When a winning group creates a new public agency to serve its interests, then, it is creating a new structure of public authority—and
agreeing to be a subordinate in a forbidding authority relationship

that will henceforth be involuntary. There is no exit, even if it has created a monster. Its design problem, therefore, is to protect itself from the dangers of public authority. While there are various ways to do this, one attractive approach is to limit the autonomous exercise of authority *ex ante* through detailed formal requirements—criteria, standards, rules, deadlines—that are written into the law. This maneuver simultaneously protects against political uncertainty: by locking in controls *ex ante,* not only are public officials highly constrained in how they can use their authority, but opposing groups are effectively shut out as well.

In any event, protection against the state will entail structures that make it more difficult for the agency to do its job well—just as protection against political uncertainty does. There is no getting around this. In politics, it is rational for social actors to fear one another, to fear the state, and to use structure to protect themselves—even though it may hobble the agencies that are supposed to be serving them.

Presidents, Legislators, and Structure

All this suggests that American public bureaucracy will tend to be highly "bureaucratic," structured in complex, cumbersome ways that undermine effective performance and insulate against effective political control. To this point, however, we have focused our attention largely on the interest groups that make up the winning and losing coalitions. This is the kind of bureaucracy they would build.

But what about the public officials most directly involved in the politics of structural choice: legislators and the president? They are the ones who exercise public authority, and the groups must act through them. Do they go along with these political forces and thus help create a bureaucracy built more for protection than for performance and accountability? The short answer is that legislators do and presidents don't—and this, I will argue later, is essential to what the institutional presidency is all about.

Legislators go along because of their almost paranoid concern for reelection (Mayhew, 1974). They are not in the business of creating effective organizations that can be held accountable. They are in the business of making themselves popular. And because broad constituency influences are largely absent on arcane issues of structure, their attentions center on the active interest groups.

This does not mean that legislators will simply operate as faithful agents of the groups. There is some basis for autonomous action. The incentive and monitoring mechanisms available to groups are imperfect. Moreover, the fact is that legislators value reelection as a means to more fundamental ends—income, power, policy—and these may give them incentives on occasion to "shirk." But truly autonomous action is likely to be important for legislators only at the margin. The electoral connection ensures that they will be highly responsive to group pressures and, in particular, to the costs groups can impose on them for going their own way.

Congress, then, is receptive to the kind of bureaucracy groups want to create. Legislators are not bound by any overarching notion of what the bureaucracy as a whole ought to look like. They are not driven by efficiency, coordination, management, or any other design criteria that might limit the kind of bureaucracy they can accept. They do not even insist on retaining control for themselves. For the most part, they willingly build, piece by piece—however grotesque the pieces, however inconsistent with one another—whatever makes the groups happy. This "congressional bureaucracy" is not supposed to function as a coherent whole. Only the pieces are important.

Were it not for presidents, this would pretty much be the end of the story. But presidents do not want the kind of bureaucracy that the other players are busily trying to create—and they have the power to do something about it. Because of presidents, the game of structural politics is very different than it would otherwise be, and its outcomes are very different as well.

Presidents pursue interests that are often incompatible with, and indeed threatening to, the interests of most of the other major players. Their heterogeneous national constituency leads them to think in grander terms about social problems and the public interest and to resist specialized appeals. Reelection, moreover, does not loom so large in their calculations (and in the second term, of course, it is not a factor at all). They are more fundamentally concerned with governance.

Unlike legislators, presidents are held responsible by the public for virtually every aspect of national performance. When the economy declines, an agency falters, or a social problem goes unaddressed, it is the president who gets the blame and whose popularity and historical legacy are on the line. All presidents are aware of this, and they respond by trying to build an institutional capacity for effective governance. As a result, they are the only players in the politics of structural choice who are motivated to seek a unified, coordinated, centrally directed bureaucratic system. They want a bureaucracy they can control from the top.

The presidential quest for control is especially troublesome, from the standpoint of the other players, because the president acts with a great deal of autonomy. This is true in two basic respects. The first is that his large, heterogeneous constituency, along with the lower priority he attaches to reelection, gives him freedom to fashion his own agenda and to pursue his own brand of control. In the language of social choice: his constituency constraints are weak, the set of feasible choices large, and he has great flexibility in deciding where in the "policy space" he wants to end up.

The second is more deeply rooted. If there is a single driving force that motivates all presidents, it is not popularity with the constituency, nor even governance per se. It is leadership. Above all else, the public wants presidents to be strong leaders, and presidents know that their success in office and place in history hinge on the extent to which citizens, political elites, academics, and journalists see them as fulfilling these lofty expectations.

What do presidents have to do in order to be regarded as strong leaders? Clearly, they often have to do what is popular, and they have to govern effectively; these aspects of presidential motivation are, in large measure, simply derivative components of strong leadership. But presidents also have to do something else: they have to show the way by charting new paths for American society—even when these paths happen to be *unpopular* at the time. Strong leaders have the capacity for rising above politics when necessary, for pursuing their own vision in the face of political odds, for doing what is right and best rather than what is politically safe and expedient. Strong leaders have to demonstrate their true metal by being selectively *unresponsive*—by being autonomous.

Here again, presidents are dramatically different from legislators. For legislators, autonomy is a form of shirking for which they expect to be electorally punished if caught. Their incentive structure strongly discourages whatever inclinations they may have to go their own way. But almost the opposite is true for presidents. They are expected to take autonomous action—indeed, to be open and bold about it—and their leadership suffers when they fail to do so. Autonomy is an integral part of their institutional incentive structure, part of what it means to be a good president.

The great emphasis presidents place on autonomy is a major threat to most of the organized groups that animate the legislative politics of structural choice. As far as they are concerned, presidents are unresponsive and out of control. Worse, presidents not only want structures of a different kind, they want structures that *give them control* of public bureaucracy—when, of course, what the groups want is to control the various, uncoordinated pieces of the bureaucracy themselves.

Thus, while groups have rational grounds for fearing the state, they do not fear all state actors equally. They fear legislators a little. They fear presidents a lot. As they pursue their best interests in the politics of structural choice, then, they will favor protective structures that are disproportionately aimed at limiting presidential control. There are various ways of going about this. They may favor independent forms of organization, the insulation of personnel through civil service and professionalism, and reduced roles for political appointees, for example. And, of course, they can also seek protection from the president by pushing for all the usual formal restrictions (on procedures, criteria, timing, and the like) that, by reducing the scope for agency discretion, insulate "their" components of the bureaucracy from anyone's *ex post* control.

When the various pieces of the bureaucracy are being created, then, the legislative politics of structural choice tends to reflect an antipresidential bias. The U.S. Constitution may say that the president is the chief executive, but his domain is largely the creation of other powerful players—who incrementally build an executive branch that is both difficult for him to control and ill-suited to effective performance.

Structural Choice and Presidential Power

This is what presidents are up against. It is not just that the American separation of powers system is stacked against them, denying them the power they need for true leadership. It is that they are part of a dynamic system that, by virtue of the politics of structural choice, is continually generating *new* institutional arrangements that are purposely designed to limit and obstruct the very leadership presidents are trying to exercise.

Presidents are driven to do something about this. There is not much they can do to change the basic features of separation of powers. But by weighing into the politics of structural choice, they can alter the dynamics of institutional change and fashion a system more to their liking. In some measure, they can create their own context—and either prevent others from doing so or counteract what others have done.

The simple fact that presidents are the nation's chief executives, endowed by Constitution and statute with certain formal powers, is of great consequence. For these powers enable them to make lots of important structural choices *on their own* without going through the legislative process. They have what economists would refer to as "residual decision rights" (Grossman and Hart, 1986) to take unilateral action at their own discretion: in many spheres of government organization, the absence of specific legal directives about how to proceed means that presidents are able to make authoritative decisions on these matters. They can organize and direct the presidency as they see fit, create public agencies, reorganize them, move them around, coordinate them, impose rules on their behavior, put their own people in top positions, and otherwise place their structural stamps on the executive branch.

Some of these actions, particularly those broadly authorized by statute, might be reversed by legislation later on. But because separation of powers makes legislative victories so difficult to achieve, this is unlikely. The result is that the president has a trump card of great consequence for the institutional system. He can act unilaterally in many matters of structure, while Congress must go through a difficult process of legislation—in which the president gets to participate and, if he disagrees, to veto. Moreover, when Congress does succeed in designing administrative arrangements much to its own liking, the president can subsequently add on new structures that, in qualifying the way these arrangements work, are more conducive to his own interests.

As presidents pursue strong leadership, then, their best strategy is not simply to take structure as given and plunge into the informal politics of bargaining. Nor is it to concentrate their institution-building energies solely on the legislative politics of structural choice. In both, especially the first, presidents are playing on someone else's turf, are prisoners of the prevailing structure, and are acquiescing to an institutional system that is incompatible with their leadership. Their best strategy is to use their comparative advantage—their residual decision rights as chief executive—by taking aggressive action within their own sphere of authority to shift the structure of politics for themselves and everyone else. Doing so allows them to become, as much as they ever will, masters of their own destinies, shaping the institutional system along presidential lines.

This is the rational basis for the institutional presidency. Throughout this century, presidents have struggled to provide themselves with a structural capacity for leadership by building institutions of their own. For all kinds of reasons—political opposition, the pressure of events, the scarcity of resources, imperfect knowledge about what works—this has not been a simple, linear process of development. But the trajectory is clear, and the motive force behind it is the president's drive for leadership in a system largely beyond his control.

At a very general level, the internal organization of the presidency can be understood in much the same way as the internal organization of Congress. Both take forms that facilitate the realization of member interests. Congress, however, is made up of hundreds of coequal individuals, each concerned with bringing home the bacon to his own constituents; and, as a group, they face serious collective action problems in arriving at structures that are stable and mutually beneficial. In large measure, the committees, procedures, and party leadership that organize congressional behavior emerged over time as (imperfect) solutions to these collective action problems. They enable members to have disproportionate influence over issues of relevance to their own districts, to make credible commitments in legislative bargaining, to arrive at durable political deals, and thus to realize gains from trade with their colleagues. They minimize the transaction costs of political exchange (Weingast and Marshall, 1988; Cox and McCubbins, 1990).[7]

The internal organization of the presidency, likewise, reflects the interests of the president. The crucial difference is that the presidency is a unified institution, in the sense that it has one supreme authority: the president. In determining his own preferences and making his own decisions, the president does not suffer from the severe collective action problems plaguing Congress, and he need not resort to complex structural arrangements for mitigating them.[8] The task of institution building, then, even if politically difficult, is conceptually more straightforward here. Presidents create structures that provide them with a capacity for effective leadership.

All sorts of functions are essential to effective leadership in modern times, but most of these the president cannot possibly handle by himself. He cannot carry out his own lobbying with Congress. He cannot recruit, screen, and hire all his own personnel. He cannot maintain constant contact with relevant interest groups. He cannot provide the press with all the information they want (or he wants them to have). He cannot plan and schedule all the details of his day-to-day activities. He cannot know enough, technically or politically, to formulate coherent programs and make wise policy choices. He cannot personally control the bureaucracy.

He is infinitely better able to carry out these functions, and thus to be an effective leader, if he relies on other people to perform them for him—if he relies, that is, on agents. In rational choice terms, the president faces the classic "principal's problem" in building his institution: how to choose agents, and how to structure his relationship to them—via rules, incentive schemes, monitoring and reporting requirements, and the like—in such a way that they are most likely to take actions that enhance his own capacity for leadership (Pratt and Zeckhauser, 1985).

Figuring out how to organize people productively is a complicated business. But the fact that presidents have unchallenged authority within their own realm gives them a great advantage in minimizing the "agency losses" that plague most control relationships in politics. They can choose people who not only have the right kind of training and skills to do their jobs well but who also—by virtue of ideology, partisanship, and loyalty—can be expected to keep the president's own interests uppermost as they go about their tasks. The presidency is not just a hierarchy of employees: it is, more than perhaps any other political institution, a team.[9]

This simplifies the president's job and his organization as well. In most agency relationships, structures proliferate in order to minimize the agency losses associated with opportunism, conflict of interest, and asymmetric information. Rules, incentive schemes, monitoring, and all the rest are necessary to control agents who cannot be counted upon to do the right thing. But to the extent that personnel choices produce a genuine team, opportunism and conflict of interest are greatly reduced, and much of the bureaucratic apparatus designed to reduce agent shirking can be dispensed with. Still, the decisions these agents make are important to the president, they are often politically sensitive, and mistakes can be very costly. So some bureaucracy is still necessary. Its purpose is to mitigate the problems teams face by promoting coordination, information sharing, and suitable expertise among individuals who all want the same thing (what is best for the president) but may not know how to achieve it or how to function productively as a group.

All this applies with most force to what we might think of as the purely presidential part of the institutional presidency. This is the part that provides support services for the president—his closest advisers, the personnel office, the media office, the congressional liaison office, units for outreach to interest groups, and the like. These are clearly internal to the presidential hierarchy, subject to his complete authority. But the boundaries of the institutional presidency are unclear at the margins, more so than those of Congress, because the president as chief executive has rationally extended his own institution to try to control the far-flung federal bureaucracy—which is *not* solely under his authority. This extension of the presidency reaches beyond the president's own special realm. And the problems he faces, as well as the structures needed to deal with them, are different.

Presidential control of the bureaucracy involves a two-step agency relationship. The first step is of the purely presidential sort: the president delegates the task to his own agents, whom he must try to control. Although he cannot do so perfectly, this is nonetheless the easy part. It is the second step, in which the president's people try to control the bureaucracy, that produces real trouble. Opportunism, conflict of interest, and asymmetric information—the bases of willful noncompliance—are rampant at this lower level. The surface reason is that each agency has its own mission, expertise, clientele, linkages with congressional committees, and ways of operating. They do not want to be controlled by the president. The deeper reason is that much of this is built in: legislators and groups design it to be that way.

How can the president employ his residual decision rights as chief executive to mitigate these problems and gain more control for himself? Two institutional strategies stand out: he can politicize and he can centralize. Although dealing with agencies designed and overseen by Congress, he can implement these two strategies on his own authority to target the foundations of agency noncompliance.

The term *politicize,* I should point out, is something of a misnomer (although I sometimes use it myself). The agencies arise out of the politics of structural choice and are thoroughly political from the moment of their conception. Their insulation from presidential control—whether through rules, civil service, professionalism, or whatever—is itself a political act with widespread political consequences, and presidents do not make the agencies more political by trying to do something about it.

Semantics aside, presidents follow this strategy by using their appointment authority to place their own people—loyal, ideologically compatible people—in pivotal positions in the bureaus, the departments, and of course, the Office of Management and Budget and other presidential agencies whose job it is to exercise control. This is a strategy of imperialism: extending the turf of the presidential team by infiltrating alien territory. The idea is to ensure that important bureaucratic decisions are placed in the hands of presidential agents, or at least are directly overseen and monitored by them.

To the extent this can be done, the aggressive use of presidential appointment power goes a long way toward mitigating the most severe problems of opportunism and conflict of interest that prompt agencies willfully to resist presidential control. In addition, especially if appointees bring expertise or experience to their jobs, it also attacks the problem of asymmetric information by providing the presidential team with a pipeline into the private information that agencies might otherwise use to evade control. Thus, it mitigates not only the will to resist, but also the means—for expertise and other types of private information are perhaps the most crucial sources of agency power (Rourke, 1984; Niskanen, 1971).

This does part of the job, but serious problems remain. Political appointees can never know what career bureaucrats know; they will always be at a disadvantage. Moreover, precisely because they are "out there" and need the support of agency personnel to do their jobs well, they are under very real pressures to become advocates for the parochial interests of their agencies. For these and other reasons, as long as effective decision authority rests with the agencies themselves, presidents will have a difficult time gaining control through an appointments strategy alone. And because the parceling out of authority in this manner means that decisions will be decentralized and fragmented, presidents cannot simply rely on appointments to create the kind of coherent, coordinated policy control they need.

This is where the centralization strategy comes in. Instead of infiltrating the agencies to ensure they make the right kinds of decisions "out there," presidents can try to see that most of the important decisions are not made "out there" at all, but inside the presidency proper. They can use structure to shift the locus of effective decision authority to the center. One basic way they can do this, as chief executives, is by imposing managerial rules that constrain agency behavior, and thus by building presidential organizations—the OMB, notably—whose job it is to make and enforce these rules. The rules may vary from the most mundane procedures for budget submissions to the bold Reagan-era requirement that regulatory agencies send proposed regulations to the OMB for prior approval. But all such rules have the effect of limiting agency discretion and shifting decision-making power to the president.

More generally, presidents can move toward coherent central control by setting up their own policy-making structures inside the White House, incorporating people of their own choosing from the departments and agencies (and presidential units like the OMB), and pulling salient issues of public policy into the presidency for consideration, debate, and resolution. In foreign policy, of course, the major centralizing institution is the National Security Council. The president clearly has strong reasons for not wanting the State Department, the Defense Department, and other agencies to make their own foreign policy decisions. And by incorporating them into a central structure run by his own people, he can attempt to make foreign policy truly presidential: hearing their views, enlisting their expertise, coordinating their contributions, and directing policy toward presidential ends.

In domestic policy, much the same applies. Although there is no statutory agency like the NSC to put a formal stamp on their efforts, all modern presidents have rightly feared becoming captives of the bureaus and departments, and they have incrementally moved toward the development of White House structures—for example,

Nixon's Domestic Council, Reagan's cabinet councils—that presidentialize major policy issues. As structures of presidential control, these are the functional equivalents of the NSC.

Even in combination, of course, politicization and centralization cannot give the president the control he really needs for effective leadership. The bureaucracy does not want to be controlled, is structured to prevent it, and has resources to resist. Moreover, even if he could— and the system would stop him far short of it—the president would not want to push these strategies to an extreme. For his leadership obviously benefits from the expertise, experience, and continued operation of public agencies, and he cannot totally circumvent them or deny them discretion without undermining their essential role in governance—and his own capacity for leadership (Heclo, 1975; Aberbach and Rockman, 1988).

The continuing problem for presidents, though, is that they have far too little control, not too much, and they need to build an institution—however inadequate by absolute standards—that allows them to overcome the tremendous obstacles to leadership the system places in their way. This is what the presidential team, the various presidential organizations, and the strategies of politicization and centralization are all about, and it is what the institutional presidency as a whole is all about. This is how presidents fight back against a system that is stacked against them.

Presidents and the Dynamics of System Change

Now let's take another look at the system. Its basic framework is fixed by the Constitution, but within this framework institutions of various sorts are continually being created, modified, and destroyed. There is an ongoing process of institutional development, animated by the politics of structural choice. The system is being changed. What I want to argue here is that, while the basic structure of the system is stacked against the president, the dynamics of system *change* are stacked in his favor.

At the heart of system change is a basic political tension. Legislators and groups, motivated by parochial concerns, routinely go about the piecemeal construction of a bureaucracy buried in formalism, insulated from effective control, and ill-designed for its tasks. Presidents, motivated to lead, find this unacceptable. They take aggressive action to presidentialize the system's institutional makeup by modifying "congressional bureaucracy," developing their own institutions, and putting them to use. The other players resist, the president counters, and so it goes. The central dynamic of the American institutional system comes from this tension between presidents who seek control and the legislative and group players who want to carve out their own small pieces of turf.

The American system has always been fragmented and decentralized. The kind of institutions favored by legislators and groups fit in nicely with the traditional character of the system. What is new and different in the modern period is the presidency and, in particular, the public expectations that drive all modern presidents to seek leadership and control. Presidents are the ones who are out of step, pushing for new institutional arrangements that fly in the face of traditional practice and parochialism. They are the ones, as a consequence, who represent the real driving force for change in the American institutional system. Legislators and groups are essentially protectors of the institutional status quo.

Inevitably, the protectors of the status quo are well equipped to block most attempts at change. But presidents hold pivotal advantages that, over the long haul, allow them to propel the system (however haltingly and intermittently) along a presidential trajectory. Two have already been discussed at some length. The first is a matter of authority: presidents can take unilateral action through their residual decision rights a chief executives to impose structures of their own design. In some measure, they can presidentialize the system on their own, without explicit congressional approval. The second is motivational: presidents are driven to gain coherent, centralized control over government, but legislators are not. Thus, presidents are constantly on the move in building institutions of control—they are imperialistic—while members of Congress are defensive and protective. When change comes, therefore, it is most often presidential.

A third key advantage, at least as important as the others, has only received brief mention so far and deserves greater emphasis. It is that Congress suffers from collective action problems that the president avoids—and can exploit. There is a tendency among scholars and journalists of reify the Congress, to treat it as though it is a unitary decision maker like the president, and to analyze their institutional conflicts accordingly. The president and Congress are portrayed as fighting it out, head to head, over matters of institutional power and prerogative.

But this misconstrues things. Congress is a collection of hundreds of individuals who do their work in committees, who struggle among themselves, and who take action in their own best interests—which may conflict with the best interests of the institution as a whole. When decisions about policy or structure are beneficial to individual legislators (or their group allies) but have negative consequences for the institution—for example, by reducing Congress's power relative to the president—individual interests will often win out. As a collegial organization lacking strong, unifying authority, Congress is simply in a poor position to protect its institutional interests. As an "actor," it will often make choices that are to its own disadvantage. Shifting coalitions of legislators and groups are short-term winners. The institution is the long-term loser.[10]

Presidents are not hobbled by these collective action problems and can simply make authoritative decisions about what is best for the presidency. While their own interests as individuals may sometimes conflict with the interests of the presidency as an institution—their demand for short-term responsiveness, for instance, could undercut the presidency's long-term institutional capacity for expertise and competence—their overriding concern for leadership induces them to promote the power of their institution relative to that of others. Thus, not only is the presidency a unitary institution, but there is also substantial congruence between the president's individual interests and the interests of the institution, far more so than within Congress.

Moreover, because Congress is a collective institution and, specifically, a majority-rule institution, presidents can manipulate outcomes to their own advantage. As positive theorists have already shown, there are typically lots of outcomes that, given the right manipulation of the agenda, could win against the status quo (McKelvey, 1976). Thus, when presidents—whether through appointments, executive order, bureaucratic policy making, or simply the initiation of legislation—are able to exercise agenda control, they can take still greater advantage of Congress's collective action problems by engineering outcomes beneficial to the presidency as an institution and sometimes, for reasons noted above, disadvantageous to Congress as an institution (Hammond, Hill, and Miller, 1986).

To illustrate, let's consider one example. Throughout most of the modern period, Congress has willingly granted reorganization authority to presidents, thus giving them additional means of building their capacity for control. Why would Congress do this? The answer, at least in part, is that presidents have taken advantage of Congress's collective action problems.[11]

If presidents were to propose specific reorganizations that had to be approved through legislation, the interested groups and legislators could use their leverage within the relevant committees to block them. But by asking for general authority without tying it to specific cases, presidents avoid activating the fierce opposition of special interests, and they avoid the decision arenas that those interests control. Instead, they make vague appeals to the broad, relatively indifferent majority, suggesting that they can do good things as chief executives that otherwise wouldn't get done at all by an unwieldy Congress—for example, coordinating services, raising the profile of deserving programs, saving money.

The majority does not simply trust presidents to do good things, of course, and has always insisted on protection through legislative veto (prior to the 1983 Chadha decision). But this is palatable to presidents. For, once they submit a specific proposal, an *affirmative* act by Congress is therefore necessary to *prevent* such proposals from going into effect. All the usual impediments to congressional action are thereby turned to presidential advantage—and special interests threatened by the proposal find themselves facing an uphill battle: they cannot simply block, but must mobilize a majority on their own behalf. Indeed, the latter's job is all the more difficult because, assuming the president's targets (in each instance) are narrowly drawn, most legislators and groups will often not be opposed on substance, and they will typically not see the larger institutional issue—further expansion of presidential control in only these particular respects—as a threat to their individual interests.

Now that Chadha has eliminated the legislative veto as a protection, it appears the whole arrangement surrounding reorganization authority is extinct. But while it operated, faced as they were with a system stacked against their leadership, presidents were only too happy to take what they could get—relatively small victories that, with Congress's "support," shifted the institutional balance a little bit more toward the presidency over time.

This is just the tip of the iceberg, for there are many ways presidents might take advantage of Congress's collective action problems to enhance their own control at Congress's expense. And in each case, once they have done so a ratchet effect takes over: presidents will not give back what they have achieved. They want control, and every president will protect not only what he has won, but what all past presidents have won. Sometimes they cannot succeed in this. Congress may on rare occasions overcome its congenital incapacities and strike a blow for greater congressional control—as it did, for instance, in the War Powers Act (which presidents have largely ignored). But these are the exceptions. Congress will usually be incapable of winning back the ground it has lost.

When it comes to building structures of control, then, the battle between president and Congress is lopsided. The president is a unitary decision maker, he can take unilateral action in imposing his own structures, his individual interests are largely congruent with the institutional interests of the presidency, and he is dedicated to gaining control over government. Congress is hobbled by collective action problems, vulnerable to agenda manipulation by the president, and populated by individuals whose interests diverge substantially from those of the institution. The result is an asymmetry in the dynamic of institutional change, yielding an uneven but steady shift toward a more presidential system.

Once again, I am not saying that presidents are destined to take over. Separation of powers sets up legal impediments to such an extreme shift in the institutional balance. And, in the ongoing politics of structural choice, the growth of presidential control represents an increasing threat to parochial interests and gives them greater incentives to invest in political opposition. The most reasonable expectation is for some sort of equilibrium to be reached in future years, an equilibrium more presidential than what we have now, but still a far cry from what presidents might like.

Conclusion

Scholars often rail against presidents for being imperialistic about institution building and political control. Presidents should stop all this, critics say, and do an about-face. They should rely more heavily on their cabinet. They should decentralize. They should respect the "neutral competence" of the bureaucracy. They should appoint professionals, not loyalists. They should resist creating their own bureaucracy (Hess, 1988; Heclo, 1975; Seidman and Gilmour, 1986; Aberbach and Rockman, 1988).

These sorts of criticisms arise from perspectives in which presidents are understood, in the final analysis, as just people like the rest of us. When they go astray, it is for reasons intrinsic to their own cases: their psyches, backgrounds, skills, relationships, political situations. Scholars do not think they can remake presidents into different individuals, of course. But they do tend to think that, through ideas, evidence, and argument, they might convince presidents to stop their mischief and do a better job of running the presidency.

Consider how strange this would seem if Congress were the target of reform. Viewing members of Congress as just people, we might urge them to stop being so concerned with pushing the parochial interests of their districts and instead to think in terms of the national interest. Or to vote their consciences. Or to stop being so responsive to interest groups. Or to centralize power in a strong congressional leadership. But this is obviously an empty exercise, and congressional scholars rarely waste their time making these sorts of recommendations. They know full well that members of Congress will not heed them.

The reason, of course, is that members of Congress are *not* just people. They are people who occupy distinctive formal roles embedded in an institutional context. Their incentives are strongly shaped by this context, and they behave in very predictable ways because of it. Virtually any individuals placed in the same roles can be expected to behave in the same basic ways, regardless of their personalities or styles or values. Members of Congress are institutional actors, and they conform to their roles.

This does not mean that members of Congress are not open to ideas about reform. They are. But only to ideas asking them to do things that are in their own best interests. Feasible reform proposals therefore require serious attention to what those interests are and how they are embedded in institutions. Congressional scholars are aware of this, and their work reflects it. They know that members of Congress are highly constrained by their roles, they know why, and they do not (usually) prod them to behave otherwise. They have treated members of Congress as institutional actors.

But too often, presidential scholars have not done the same for presidents. Their tradition has been to treat presidents as personal actors. And while they surely recognize that institutions constrain presidential behavior, they have paid far less attention to institutions than congressional scholars have in building their explanations and fashioning their reform proposals. When presidents politicize, centralize, and otherwise offend scholarly sensibilities of what a good presidency ought to look like, scholars "take it personally"—rather than recognizing, as congressional scholars would, that this sort of behavior is likely to arise from institutionally rooted incentives that have nothing to do with presidents as people, are common to all presidents, and are fundamental to an understanding of the presidency. The result is that presidents are not fully appreciated as institutional actors, and they are presented, time and again, with reform proposals that they have absolutely no incentive to follow through on.

When presidents are regarded as institutional actors, our explanations of their behavior are dramatically different than a traditional methodology of personalism would suggest, and even the most basic issues are cast in a different light. To take an obvious example, consider presidential power, which has been central to the presidency literature for decades. Would we want to say with Neustadt—and conventional wisdom in the field—that presidential power is the power to persuade? I don't think so.

Persuasion and bargaining are essential to presidential leadership. But the activities surrounding them are reflections of their institutional setting. Institutions allocate authority, resources, and opportunities—they entail a structure of power. The way this power gets exercised is, to a significant degree, epiphenomenal. It *arises* from structure, and it can be fully appreciated only when its connection to structure is laid bare.

Much of the institutional context, moreover, is itself endogenous. It not only conditions the presidential behavior we observe, but it is also a dynamic product of that behavior. This means that presidents can alter their own power through the politics of structural choice, and that leadership is not simply about the exercise of power, per se, but about developing the structural capacity for its exercise. It is about institution building.

Like the pluralist theories of power that gained prominence during the 1960s (e.g., Dahl, 1961), Neustadt's "power to persuade" directs attention to the action of politics and away from its deeper structure, failing to recognize that the power wielding we observe is but a small part of a larger story. The job of presidential theory, it seems to me, is to tell this larger story—to understand the presidency as an integral part of the institutional system. The best way to do this is to stop thinking about presidents as people and to start thinking of them *generically:* as faceless, nameless, institutional actors whose behavior is an institutional product.

I am not claiming that personal variables are unimportant, nor that we can get away without studying them. The fact is, scholars must attend to many aspects of the presidency, and the balance between institutional and personal influences can vary considerably depending on what is being explained. If the topic is political control or power, for instance, institutional concerns are likely to play a more influential role than if the topic is crisis decision making or White House advisory processes, which often are heavily dependent on the president's personal characteristics. Across the field as a whole, then, there is no substitute for paying attention to the personal side of the equation. An argument can be made, in fact, that personal factors cannot be ignored even in areas that are strongly institutional—for, especially given the autonomy that presidents exercise, personal factors are everywhere relevant in helping us understand why presidents make one choice rather than another. Institutions may push them in a general direction—to politicize, to centralize, and so on—but the specific decisions they make along the way will often be a reflection of their individuality.

The problem is not the relevance of personal factors for presidential behavior. The problem is that the personal side of the presidency lends itself very poorly to theory. When the exercise is taken seriously, personal theories turn out to be extremely complex, difficult to construct, and quite limited in generality and scope. Given their scant progress over the last half century within both presidential studies and organization theory more generally, there is every reason to believe that the enormous scholarly investment in them has simply not been worth it and that further investment is unwarranted. Much the same must be said for the methodology underpinning all this: a methodology that sees everything as worth explaining, proliferates relevant variables, and views progress in terms of endlessly increasing complexity and comprehensiveness.

This is why I have to depart so radically from the mainstream. The standard, widely accepted critique in recent years is that the field is not sufficiently scientific, that we have not paid enough attention to institutions, and that we should be striving to build theories that combine and sort out the personal and institutional influences on presidential behavior. While much of this is well founded, it ultimately keeps us on the same path—and, if we are to succeed, it seems to me that we cannot do this. We need to strike out in a very different and, for the field, unorthodox direction.

The new approach I'm suggesting has two components. First, while recognizing the genuine importance of personal variables, we should nonetheless invest our theoretical efforts far more heavily on the institutional side. Institutional theories, precisely because they are impersonal and deal with generic properties of actors and their contexts, hold out far greater prospects for success than personal theories do. Research on personal factors should continue to be an integral part of the field, but its role should be descriptive, informative, and suggestive.

Second, as this exclusion of personal concerns from theory indicates, we cannot dedicate ourselves to explaining everything. We need to move toward a methodology that, instead of reveling in complexity and universal relevance, places a premium on just the opposite: on simplicity, on parsimony, on stripping away the tangle of relevant variables and capturing just the essence of what is going on. We need to get simple and get basic or we will not get anywhere.

There are perhaps various ways of going about this. The most obvious is to rely on rational choice theory, which is already founded on such a methodology, and which, thanks largely to the new economics of organization, already provides a powerful body of institutional theory, one that political scientists are now exploiting to great advantage in the study of political institutions.

In the latter half of this essay, I have tried to show how rational choice, and the new economics in particular, might be put to use in fleshing out at least one small part of an institutional theory, the part dealing with the development of the institutional presidency and its anchoring in the politics of structural choice. Some readers may disagree with the arguments I make here. Others may claim that this kind of theory can never be extended to much of what is truly important about the presidency. But such reactions are to be expected at this point, and they are healthy for a field in which theory has played too little a role for far too long. I invite these readers to counter with theories of their own. If what I say here stimulates a measure of debate and turmoil over basic issues of theory and method, not to mention substance, I will consider my efforts worthwhile.

Notes

1. For a brief overview, see Wayne, 1983.

2. The best known of these efforts is James David Barber's *Presidential Character* (1985), which, it happens, stands apart from most other work in this tradition by attempting to fashion a simple, potentially powerful theory. Partly for this reason, however, it has been extensively criticized on both theoretical and empirical grounds, especially by those who take a serious interest in psychological explanation (see George, 1974). For an overview of some of the broader, more mainstream literature on the psychological foundations of presidential behavior, see Erwin Hargrove's chapter in this volume.

3. Note that the Brownlow reforms of 1939, which Roosevelt initiated and which signaled the beginning of the modern institutional presidency, were founded on classical principles. Since then, formal structure has grown increasingly important (in fits and starts) in presidential style. See, e.g., Kernell and Popkin (1986).

4. Not all presidential scholars, of course, have ignored the organizational literature on leadership. Two who stand out as having put this work to serious use are James MacGregor Burns and Alexander George. See, e.g., Burns (1978) and George (1981).

5. For overviews of the literature on organizational leadership, see Bass (1981) and Perrow (1986).

6. I should point out here that many political scientists eventually arrived at this conclusion on their own, aided especially by Greenstein's (1982) revisionist analysis of Eisenhower. They would have seen the light much earlier had they looked beyond presidential studies and paid serious attention to organization theory.

7. The internal structure of the legislature has also been shaped by the power politics of winning and losing and not simply by considerations of mutual gains. Rational choice theory clearly has much to say about both, but for convenience I stress only the latter here (which happens to be the standard line these days among positive theorists). See Moe (1990b).

8. I should emphasize that I am making relative statements here. Within the presidency, various players with different interests, ideologies, information, etc. participate in decision making; and collective action problems can surely arise. This is true of any organization (Hammond and Miller, 1985). My point here is simply that the presidency and Congress are fundamentally different in terms of the way formal authority is allocated within them, and, for this reason, Congress is far more vulnerable to collective action problems than the presidency is.

9. Again, I use the team concept here to emphasize very basic differences between the presidency and Congress. It is not meant to be taken literally—e.g., that there are no conflicts of interest among presidential staffers.

10. Congress does, of course, have internal arrangements that help protect its institutional interests—party leadership, most notably—but these are highly imperfect and weak. They mitigate the problem somewhat but are far from solving it. For a sympathetic treatment, see Cox and McCubbins (1990).

11. For overviews of reorganization politics, see Arnold (1986); Fesler and Kettl (1991); Seidman and Gilmour (1986); and Wilson (1991).

References

Aberbach, Joel D., and Bert A. Rockman. 1988. "Mandates or Mandarins? Control and Discretion in the Modern Administrative State." *Public Administrative Review* March/April: 606–12.

Arnold, Peri E. 1986. *Making the Managerial Presidency*. Princeton: Princeton University Press.

Barber, James David. 1985. *The Presidential Character*. Englewood Cliffs, N.J.: Prentice-Hall.

Bass, Bernard M. 1981. *Stogdill's Handbook of Leadership*. New York: Free Press.

Bunce, Valerie. 1981. *Do Leaders Make a Difference? Executive Succession and Public Policy under Capitalism and Socialism*. Princeton: Princeton University Press.

Burns, James MacGregor. 1978. *Leadership*. New York: Harper and Row.

Calvert, Randall L., Mathew D. McCubbins, and Barry R. Weingast. 1989. "A Theory of Political Control and Agency Discretion." *American Journal of Political Science* 33 (August): 588–611.

Campbell, Colin. 1986. *Managing the Presidency*. Pittsburgh: University of Pittsburgh Press.

Corwin, Edward. 1957. *The President: Office and Powers 1787–1957*. New York: New York University Press.

Cox, Gary, and Mathew McCubbins. 1990. "Parties and Committees in the U.S. House of Representatives." Unpublished manuscript, University of California, San Diego.

Dahl, Robert A. 1961. *Who Governs?* New Haven: Yale University Press.

Destler, I. M. 1972. *Presidents, Bureaucrats, and Foreign Policy*. Princeton: Princeton University Press.

Edwards, George C., III. 1980. *Presidential Influence in Congress*. San Francisco: W. H. Freeman.

———. 1989. *At the Margins*. New Haven: Yale University Press.

Edwards, George C., III, and Stephen J. Wayne. 1983. *Studying the Presidency*. Knoxville: University of Tennessee Press.

Fesler, James W., and Donald F. Kettl. 1991. *The Politics of the Administrative Process*. Chatham, N.J.: Chatham House.

Fisher, Louis. 1972. *President and Congress*. New York: Free Press.

George, Alexander L. 1974. "Assessing Presidential Character." *World Politics* 26 (January): 234–82.

———. 1981. *Presidential Decision Making in Foreign Policy.* Boulder, Colo.: Westview.

Greenstein, Fred I. 1978. "Change and Continuity in the Modern Presidency." In *The New American Political System*, ed. Anthony King. Washington, D.C.: American Enterprise Institute.

———. 1982. *The Hidden Hand Presidency.* New York: Basic.

Grossman, Sanford, and Oliver Hart. 1986. "The Costs and Benefits of Ownership: A Theory of Vertical and Lateral Integration." *Journal of Political Economy* 94:691–719.

Hammond, Thomas H., and Gary J. Miller. 1985. "A Social Choice Perspective on Expertise and Authority in Bureaucracy." *American Journal of Political Science* 29:1–28.

Hammond, Thomas H., Jeffrey S. Hill, and Gary J. Miller. 1986. "Presidents, Congress, and the 'Congressional Control of Administration' Hypothesis." Paper prepared for the annual meeting of the American Political Science Association, Washington, D.C.

Hammond, Thomas H., and Gary J. Miller. 1987. "The Core of the Constitution." *American Political Science Review* 81 (December): 115–74.

Hargrove, Erwin C. 1992. "Presidential Personality and Leadership Style." In *Researching the Presidency*, ed. G. Edwards, J. Kessel, B. Rockman. Pittsburgh: University of Pittsburgh Press.

Hart, John. 1987. *The Presidential Branch.* New York: Pergamon.

Heclo, Hugh. 1975. "OMB and the Presidency: The Problem of Neutral Competence." *The Public Interest* 38 (Winter): 80–98.

Hess, Stephen. 1988. *Organizing the Presidency.* 2d ed. Washington, D.C.: Brookings.

Johnson, Richard Tanner. 1974. *Managing the White House.* New York: Harper and Row.

Kerbel, Matthew Robert. 1991. *Beyond Persuasion.* Albany: State University of New York Press.

Kernell, Samuel. 1978. "Explaining Presidential Popularity." *American Political Science Review* 72 (June): 506–22.

Kernell, Samuel, and Samuel L. Popkin. 1986. *The Chief of Staff.* Berkeley and Los Angeles: University of California Press.

Kessel, John H. 1975. *The Domestic Presidency.* North Scituate, Mass.: Duxbury.

———. 1983. "The Structures of the Carter White House." *American Journal of Political Science* 27:431–63.

———. 1984. "The Structures of the Reagan White House." *American Journal of Political Science* 28:231–58.

King, Anthony. 1975. "Executives." In *Handbook of Political Science*, Vol. 5, ed. Fred Greenstein and Nelson Polsby, 173–255. Reading, Mass.: Addison Wesley.

King, Gary, and Lyn Ragsdale. 1988. *The Elusive Executive.* Washington, D.C.: Congressional Quarterly Press.

Lowi, Theodore J. 1985. *The Personal President.* Ithaca: Cornell University Press.

March, James G., and Johann P. Olsen. 1989. *Rediscovering Institutions.* New York: Free Press.

Mayhew, David. 1974. *Congress: The Electoral Connection*. New Haven: Yale University Press.

McCubbins, Mathew D., Roger G. Noll, and Barry R. Weingast. 1987. "Administrative Procedures as Instruments of Political Control." *Journal of Law, Economics, and Organization* 3:243–77.

McKelvey, Richard D. 1976. "Intransitivities in Multidimensional Voting: Models and Some Implications for Agenda Control." *Journal of Economic Theory* 12:472–82.

Milgrom, Paul, and John Roberts. 1992. *Economics, Organization, and Management*. Englewood Cliffs, N.J.: Prentice-Hall.

Moe, Terry M. 1982. "Regulatory Performance and Presidential Administration." *American Journal of Political Science* 26 (May): 197–224.

———. 1984. "The New Economics of Organization." *American Journal of Political Science* (November): 739–77.

———. 1985. "The Politicized Presidency." In *The New Direction in American Politics*, ed. John E. Chubb and Paul E. Peterson. Washington, D.C.: Brookings.

———. 1989. "The Politics of Bureaucratic Structure." In *Can the Government Govern?* ed. John E. Chubb and Paul E. Peterson. Washington, D.C.: Brookings.

———. 1990a. "The Politics of Structural Choice: Toward a Theory of Public Bureaucracy." In *Organization Theory: From Chester Barnard to the Present and Beyond*, ed. Oliver E. Williamson. New York: Oxford University Press.

———. 1990b. "Political Institutions: The Neglected Side of the Story." *Journal of Law, Economics, and Organization* 6:213–54.

Mueller, John. 1970. "Presidential Popularity from Truman to Johnson." *American Political Science Review* 64 (March): 18–34.

Nathan, Richard. 1983. *The Administrative Presidency*. New York: Wiley.

Neustadt, Richard E. 1980. *Presidential Power*. New York: Wiley.

Niskanen, William. 1971. *Bureaucracy and Representative Government*. Chicago: Aldine.

Ostrom, Charles, and Dennis Simon. 1985. "Promise and Performance: A Dynamic Model of Presidential Popularity." *American Political Science Review* 79 (June): 334–58.

Perrow, Charles. 1986. *Complex Organizations*. 3d ed. New York: Random House.

Peterson, Mark A. 1990. *Legislating Together*. Cambridge: Harvard University Press.

Pika, Joseph. 1981. "Moving Beyond the Oval Office: Problems in Studying the Presidency." *Congress and the Presidency* 9 (Winter 1981–1982): 17–36.

Pious, Richard. 1979. *The American Presidency*. New York: Basic.

Pratt, John W., and Richard J. Zeckhauser. 1985. *Principals and Agents*. Boston: Harvard Business School Press.

President's Committee on Administrative Management. 1937. *Report with Special Studies*. Washington, D.C.: U.S. Government Printing Office.

Rockman, Bert. 1984. *The Leadership Question*. New York: Praeger.

———. 1986. "Presidential and Executive Studies: The One, the Few and the Many," in Herbert F. Weisberg, *Political Science: The Science of Politics*. New York: Agathon.

Rourke, Francis E. 1984. *Bureaucracy, Politics, and Public Policy*. 3d ed. Boston: Little, Brown.

Seidman, Harold, and Robert Gilmour. 1986. *Politics, Position, and Power.* New York: Oxford University Press.

Shepsle, Kenneth A. 1986. "Institutional Equilibrium and Equilibrium Institutions." In *Political Science: The Science of Politics,* ed. Herbert F. Weisberg. New York: Agathon.

Skowronek, Stephen. 1984. "The Presidency in Political Time." In *The Presidency and the Political System,* ed. Michael Nelson. Washington, D.C.: Congressional Quarterly Press.

Wayne, Stephen J. 1978. *The Legislative Presidency.* New York: Harper and Row.

———. 1983. "Approaches." In *Studying the Presidency,* ed. George C. Edwards, III and Stephen J. Wayne. Knoxville: University of Tennessee Press.

Weingast, Barry, and William Marshall. 1988. "The Industrial Organization of Congress." *Journal of Political Economy* 96:132–63.

Williamson, Oliver E. 1985. *The Economic Institutions of Capitalism.* New York: Free Press.

Wilson, Scott A. 1991. "Presidents and Reorganization." Unpublished manuscript, Stanford University.

10

The Methodology of
Presidential Research

GARY KING

T HE ORIGINAL purpose of the paper this chapter was based on was to use the Presidency Research Conference's first-round papers—by John H. Aldrich, Erwin C. Hargrove, Karen M. Hult, Paul Light, and Richard Rose—as my "data." My given task was to analyze the literature ably reviewed by these authors and report what political methodology might have to say about presidency research. I focus in this chapter on the traditional presidency literature, emphasizing research on the president and the office. For the most part, I do not consider research on presidential selection, election, and voting behavior, which has been much more similar to other fields in American politics.

I am in an odd position in this task, since many of the various topics on which methodologists usually give advice do not apply here. In other fields, we are often asked how to estimate the parameters of a particular model with available data, how to develop a model from a more vaguely expressed theory, how to measure a concept more accurately, or how to avoid statistical biases when available data have a variety of specific limitations. Judging from the first-round papers, one might think that few presidency researchers pose questions like these. Although probably more has been written about the presidency than all other areas of American politics combined, most work in the field is not yet to the point where concepts are to be measured and theories tested systematically.

Yet, I do think that the presidency literature could benefit from some of the insights of political methodology. In this chapter, I address this state of affairs in presidency research in four increasingly specific ways. First, I directly discuss the *systematic* study of the American presidency, a subject about which presidency scholars often seem quite defensive, and I believe unnecessarily so. I argue here that the division between "rigor and relevance" made numerous times in these papers and in the literature is of limited value and that qualitative research can be as rigorous as quantitative research. Indeed, the rules of scientific inference apply to all areas of research equally, so we must hold qualitative presidency research to the same standards. Second, I discuss the explicit goal of the literature reviewed in every first-round presidency paper: increasing the richness of description and inclusiveness of theoretical perspectives. I take the position that this is not a productive direction for future research on the American presidency. Instead, we need much *less* inclusive and more *specific* theoretical concepts: a few very precise or even incorrect theories would serve the discipline much better.

Third, I argue that the famous $n = 1$ problem of presidency research is not at all specific to this literature and is indeed a perfectly general statement of the problem of causal inference. I also demonstrate in this section that the common practice of using the president as the unit of analysis is very unlikely to yield reliable inferences Although this problem is widely recognized in the presidency literature, its solution is not self-consciously understood even though much research does get around the problem. Finally, I make some very specific positive suggestions for the presidency literature by providing outlines of research projects that might help presidency scholars design research so they could learn what they desire to know and, at the same time, meet the standards of scientific inference espoused by political methodologists.

The Systematic Study of the American Presidency

Presidency research is one of the last bastions of historical, nonquantitative research in American politics. In this section, I argue that the frequent questions about whether we should use systematic approaches are moot. An area of research is not systematic just because scholars use numbers or nonsystematic because they do not. Indeed, there is no inherent nonstylistic difference between quantitative and qualitative research—in the presidency or in any other area. To the contrary, I have never heard anyone even argue that specific rules of inference are inapplicable in qualitative research; I see no reason, therefore, to treat qualitative research any differently than quantitative. Thus, we must apply these time-honored rules in order to evaluate and, where possible, improve presidency research.[1] It is from this perspective—using the rules of inference so clear in quantitative research to best understand the qualitative research in this field—that we can best evaluate inferences about the American presidency.

We should never permit a "balance" between rigor and relevance: we simply must demand both. Traditional presidency scholars are unquestionably correct in arguing that rigor without relevance is worthless: a good answer to a question no one cares about is of no value. Unfortunately, rigorous papers about irrelevant topics have appeared in the presidency literature, as elsewhere, so the criticism is to the point. By the same token, unconvincing analyses of important issues are equally suspect.

On the other hand, the presidency literature also contains countless books and articles with highly relevant arguments that are qualitative instead of quantitative. This is not necessarily troublesome at all, insofar as one should not automatically equate rigor and quantitative analysis. Although presidency researchers could bring methodologically sophisticated analyses to bear on relevant empirical questions in the presidency literature to a much greater extent then they currently do (see Edwards, 1983), much current work would not be improved by adding quantitative analysis. Rather, the standards for judging qualitative research must be clarified and scholars' qualitative work evaluated accordingly. The problem with this part of the presidency literature is *not* that scholars have failed to do something they did not wish to do, for we must judge these works on their own grounds. The problem is that the qualitative research that is done is not always as rigorous as it could be.

Precisely what about qualitative research in the traditional presidency literature could be improved? One could speak of many problems: incorrect inferences, misunderstandings of causality, measurement error, bias in case selection, spurious effects, and others. However, to some extent, all these problems afflict every kind of qualitative research—and much quantitative work as well. That these problems exist in the presidency literature does not make it unique or even unusual.

In my view, the signal problem with qualitative research on the presidency is its failure to appropriately judge the *uncertainty* of our inferences. One can make a valid inference in almost any situation, no matter how limited the evidence, but one should avoid forging policy recommendations out of thin data. The point is not that reliable inferences are impossible in qualitative research; rather, one should always report a reasonable estimate of the *degree of certainty* we have in each of our inferences.

For example, suppose you buy a house, move into a neighborhood, and shortly thereafter discover that ten of your neighbors have stomach cancer. A reasonable inference is that the water supply is badly contaminated. At this point, should you sell your house for a small fraction of its purchase price in order to move out of the neighborhood as quickly as possible?

You would probably want more evidence first, since the uncertainty of your original inference is too high for you to make such an important decision. (On the other hand, you might purchase bottled water for a while, a relatively low-cost decision.) The certainty of your inference would increase if you found that a river running through town looked polluted, and it would increase further if you found an industrial plant upstream dumping waste into the river. You might become very certain if you tested water in that river and found a known carcinogen present in high quantities. However, if you then found that drinking water for the town did not come from the river, the inference of a problem with the water supply would again become less certain. If a test of the town's water supply indicated no carcinogens, you might just be genuinely puzzled—no longer even willing to hazard a guess as to the cause of the high incidence of stomach cancer. Finally, if you discovered that your ten neighbors moved to town *with* the disease in order to be close to a major hospital that specializes in the treatment of these patients, the puzzle would be resolved, and you would dismiss your inference with a high level of certainty.

At each point in this ministudy, your estimate of the uncertainty of your inference about the water supply changed. If polled about your opinion at any point in this process, you would report both your inference—your best guess based on the available evidence—*and* an assessment of how good that best guess is. In no case would it make much sense to report the inference without also reporting a judgment about the uncertainty of the inference. Indeed, reporting the inference with an incorrect assessment of its uncertainty can be as bad or worse than if your best guess were wrong.

In quantitative research, scholars routinely calculate point estimates and standard errors. We can think of these as best guesses and the uncertainty of these guesses, respectively. Quantitative researchers sometimes fail to correctly calculate standard errors and sometimes fail to include them at all (and thus fail to judge the uncertainty of their inferences). However, qualitative researchers include this uncertainty estimate much more rarely.

Indeed, the problem in the traditional presidency literature is a fairly general tendency to avoid uncertainty estimates, and, when they are given, in most cases they are often far too low even to be taken seriously. It takes much more than a cogently argued point to verify an empirical claim about the world. We do not necessarily need quantitative analyses, but whatever analyses we have must be far more systematic.

Perhaps the most important consequence of incorrectly judging or failing to report estimates of uncertainty is the overwhelming urge many presidency scholars feel to make prescriptions—often suggesting fundamental changes in the structure of American democracy, electoral terms, White House organization, presidential policy making, the rules that govern the press, and virtually every other aspect of the subject. Wayne (1983) and others have written about the "almost evangelic tone of much of the literature." In presidency research, we have the luxury (and drudgery) of knowing that many of our recommendations will not be implemented. Nonetheless, prescriptions without adequate judgments of uncertainty are just as irresponsible. If we are listened to at some point, as we occasionally are, improper uncertainty estimates might cause policy makers to act too early, perhaps doing significant damage by creating political instability or even civil war.[2] Prior to making prescriptions, we should be asking ourselves whether we are willing to risk the unintended or unknown consequences of proposed institutional reforms.[3] Neustadt and May (1986, 274) propose a useful method of encouraging policy makers to judge the uncertainty of their conclusions. They ask, "How much of your own money would you wager on it?" The varying utility of money across individuals prevents this from becoming a universal metric for gauging uncertainty, but it does drive home the importance of the judgment.

Several of the first-round authors recognize a consequence of this problem when they complain that the subfields they are reviewing "conflate what is with what ought to be" (Hult, 1990, 52). Rose (1990, 52) even finds some situations in which the two should *not* be distinguished. In my view, presidency scholars should refrain from making prescriptive statements for some time—at least when it comes to most of the critically important problems we study. We should only move to prescription when we have reduced uncertainty far more than the current situation. If we followed *this* prescription, we would not conflate the two at all, but presidency researchers would still have plenty of important subjects to write about and aspects of the presidency to analyze.

I provide an illustration of this point below, albeit with some apprehension, since my purpose is to criticize a research tradition and to suggest possible improvements, not to pick on anyone in particular. In fact, most of the first-round papers meet the highest standards of the traditional presidency literature.

With this focus clearly in mind, consider Paul Light's chapter as an example of the general point. Light makes the argument that presidential policy is increasingly characterized by short-term rather than long-term policy making. Unfortunately, he provides no systematic empirical evidence for this claim but does recognize this in the following qualification:[4]

> Luckily for the poor researcher who would have to operationalize this variable, this distinction between short-term and long-term policy is offered less to create a new empirical category for research and more to illustrate the primary theme of this brief paper. . . . I am convinced that careful coding would find an increase in short-term policy vis-à-vis long-term policy over the past two decades, for presidential policymaking is increasingly characterized by a set of incentives and constraints which reward short-term policy and make long-term policy almost impossible. (Light, 1990, 6–7)

Light spends much of the rest of his paper exploring the *reasons* why presidential policy making is increasingly oriented to the short term, and he concludes with some wide-ranging prescriptions. These include "election reforms, more evaluation capacity, a sensitivity to the impact of monitoring on implementation," in addition to electing "an occasional prophet" (ibid., 42).

Light is prepared to accept the possibility that, if he is wrong about the prior empirical claim, most of his paper is superfluous. We might legitimately criticize him for climbing so far out on a limb not known to be anchored at all to the tree. Of course, this criticism is certainly correct, but a far more important point is the strategy of inquiry his paper represents. The strategy is one in which the author puts much effort into the interesting questions and does not always take sufficient time to verify the prior empirical claims on which these questions stand. Studying the prior questions would not be as exciting, but they are essential. Unfortunately, this research strategy is inherent in too much of the traditional presidency literature.

One of the key contributions of science is that it helps keep us from tricking ourselves. Human beings are extraordinarily good at pattern recognition, but we are not very good at verifying when patterns we perceive are more apparent than real. Is Light's basic assumption correct? Suppose for a moment that he is wrong, that the proportion of short- and long-term policy has not changed in the last two decades. How could we reconcile this supposition with the fact that we perceive a change toward short-term policy? Perhaps presidency scholars, like everyone else, remember events that happened yesterday more easily than events of twenty years ago. Perhaps we remember presidential policies from 1970 that *persist* to today—by definition, long-term events—and forget some of the short-term policies that have little bearing on today. From Nixon, we remember Vietnam more vividly than his politically expedient opposition to busing in order to placate the South, but from Bush we remember the flag-burning issue as easily as the end of the Cold War and the invasions of Panama and Grenada. Thus, perhaps our casual observation that short-term presidential policy making has increased is only a natural consequence of our necessarily limited memory. A more systematic analysis might indicate that no change has occurred at all.[5]

Light's argument seems plausible enough to me, but the point of science is that we should not trust our casual judgments about such matters. We should do the hard work implied in Light's above quotation. In addition to Light's preliminary analysis, someone should provide a clear definition of short-term and long-term policy and then catalog decisions from presidential diaries or even speeches.

(The process of collecting these data systematically will further define and thus strengthen the theory of short- and long-term policy.) Only with a replicable analysis such as this can we be sure of the basic empirical point. This sort of research might be less fun, and perhaps even less interesting, but its results would be no less important.

This argument is relevant to one of many interesting debates that has been ongoing among scholars in American politics (and was revisited several times during the Presidency Research Conference). The question was why the congressional literature is systematic and theoretically and empirically advanced, whereas the presidency literature seems to lag so far behind. Many reasons are offered for this puzzling difference: more data exist in the study of Congress; members of Congress are more accessible to scholars than is the president; the presidency literature is filled with books written by numerous participant observers without much systematic rigor. In my view, each of these is partially true, but in the end none can account for the difference between the two literatures: much data exist in presidency research too (King and Ragsdale, 1988); the president is not very accessible, but most of his staff are (as Kessel, Pika, Peterson, and others have repeatedly shown), and, regardless, most congressional scholars do not conduct personal interviews with the people they study—the congressional literature also includes participant observer reports, and numerous presidency scholars do research other than participant observation.

In my view, what accounts for the difference between the congressional and presidential literatures is that in the former, but not the latter, scholars spent considerable time recording systematic, but descriptive, patterns. For example, Erikson (1971) and Mayhew (1974) first identified the increasing incumbency advantage and corresponding decline in competitiveness of congressional elections. They did this with fairly systematic and quite careful research, but the literature did not stop there. Literally dozens of scholars published articles showing nothing more than the increase in incumbency advantage. The results were duplicated, replicated, verified, and made much more precise. After scores of descriptive articles, we were quite certain that congressional elections were becoming less competitive and that incumbents were getting a larger share of the vote just because they were incumbents. Only then could serious work begin on building theories to explain these phenomenon, and theory building did begin. The result is that we now have well-developed theories, reasonably strong evidence for them, and a vibrant and active literature on congressional elections.[6] However, I believe the key to the causal explanations we all admire was this prior systematic descriptive work.

I see no reason why we could not follow this same research strategy in the presidency literature. One important possibility is actually Light's suggestive research. For example, suppose that the systematic descriptive work I am advocating were to indicate that Light is correct, that presidents spend considerably more time on short- than on long-term policy making now than twenty years ago. This would be an incredibly important finding. Scholars in our sister subfield spent fifteen years studying a decline in the competitiveness of House elections because this was a key element of democracy. If we could show that Light is correct—that modern presidents spend more time on short- than on long-term policy—we would have a much more important discovery about American politics and American democracy. A whole industry of political scientists might form, trying to explain the newly discovered trend, just as it did in the congress subfield more than a decade ago. However, without this *systematic descriptive* work, Light's (and other's) suggestive but hypothetical speculations will only encourage other speculations and not lead to the kind of general explanation and understanding that we all seek.

Toward Incorrect Theories

I do not disagree with much of the substance in the first-round papers. In part, this is because they are all reviews and, in part, because all do a good job in their stated purpose. However, it is difficult to find much of anything in the literature these papers review that one could disagree with, even in principle. Indeed, from one perspective, the big problem in this literature is its goal: everyone seems to be searching for richer theories, more detailed contextual description, and more all-inclusive theoretical concepts. This goal is precisely what we need for some purposes but exactly the opposite for others. Before explaining these purposes, I provide a few examples.

In describing a "model of political personality," Hargrove (1990, 9) writes, "it must be sufficiently broad to permit its use by advocates of contending theories and those who do not use personality theory at all." He tells us repeatedly to "avoid psychological reductionism" (17) or "try to avoid reductionism" (23). Finally, his summary advice to the subfield is along precisely the same lines: "Avoid reductionism in explanations and look for congruence in motivation. Combine both person and context in explanations. Search for abstraction and generalization but respect the individuality of lives and styles. Compare presidents in ordinary language that will be consistent with diverging theories" (50).

Hult (1990, 12) also argues that, despite the richness of research on presidential advisory systems, we need more richness: "Other efforts to categorize whole advisory systems and to classify presidential management styles fail to 'capture the complexity and variation in advisory practices' (Greenstein, 1988: p. 351)." And at more length and even more explicitly, she writes:

> Scholars have considered numerous independent variables in trying to account for advisory arrangements and the impact of advice on presidential actions. These dimensions have ranged from presidential styles, ideology, and strategy to small group interactions and staff structures to prevailing values in the larger political system, fragmentation in Washington, and features of the relevant policy arena. Despite the richness of presidential, organizational, and environmental factors, much work concentrates on only one cluster of variables (Hult, 1990, 46).

In one way or another, every one of the first-round authors (and many other authors in the rest of the presidency literature) is arguing for additional richness of theory, explanation, and context.[7]

In judging this methodological advice, we must distinguish *social science* from *history and biography*. The difference I have in mind is not entirely disciplinary, since many historians make important contributions to social science and numerous social scientists describe themselves as primarily historians. Rather, I am interested in the specific purposes of our scholarship, and from this perspective, most of the traditional presidency literature is composed of first-class historical and biographical accounts of presidents and their administrations. The dominant goals include getting the facts right, chronicling the fascinating stories in and around the White House, and comparing and contrasting different presidents, their aids, policies, successes, and failures. In pursuing these largely descriptive goals, no field in political science or American politics is more developed. Few across the social sciences match the extent of our descriptions. The history of no other institution or person is as completely recorded as that of the American presidency and president. For this, presidency scholars should be justifiably proud. The frequently expressed pessimism scholars have about the presidency field cannot be about its main goal of history and description.

On the other hand, presidency research has a way to go in pursuing the goals of social science. As evidence of how far other fields have surpassed us on this score, consider that traditional presidency scholarship rarely even makes it into mainstream political science journals anymore. A parsimonious explanation, and not richer and richer contextual description, is the immediate goal of social science. Rich description is important for understanding what is to be explained by later systematic analysis; it is important for telling history, where we would prefer to know the facts as closely and perhaps even as completely as possible. But it is not particularly useful as theory or explanation.

To make the distinction between social science and history clearer in this context, let us analyze the scholarly benefit we would get from collecting a large number of explanatory variables. For historical purposes, this is a very useful activity, since it will help a scholar to provide a more accurate picture of a president or the presidency. However, *for social science, no reasonable argument can be constructed in which all conceivable explanatory variables could be used at once in making inferences.* In some specific cases, other explanatory variables will help. In general, however, they will not. (See King, 1991).

Take, for example, a very good and specific testable hypothesis given by Hult (1990, 9): "Staff units that span White House boundaries (e.g., press, congressional liaison) will be less influential in White House discussions, since the president and other staffers frequently view the contacts with outsiders with some suspicion. Whether this is so needs to be tested more systematically." The dependent variable in Hult's hypothesis is staff unit influence in White House discussions, by which she presumably means the influence the head of a staff unit has on the heads of other staff units and the president. It would take some work to measure this, but it seems feasible to measure it—perhaps with Kessel's (1984) interview and network analysis data or some other type of information. The unit of analysis is the staff unit, and the key explanatory variable is whether or not a staff unit spans White House boundaries.

How would it help us in assessing the effect of spanning boundaries on influence in the White House to simultaneously study the effects of other explanatory variables? For the answer to this question, I turn to the quantitative literature, where the problem is known as omitted variable bias. My point is not to turn this into a quantitative inference in this qualitative research project. Thus, for simplicity, I consider two other possible explanatory variables: (1) number of years in which the organization of a staff unit has remained the same, and (2) the quality and experience of the head of the staff unit.

It might be interesting to know the effect of the number of years since reorganization. Indeed, even listing the relative durations between reorganizations for each staff unit could provide a gold mine of descriptive information. It would even be easy to imagine a study trying to describe or explain these interagency differences. Moreover, this variable would seem to have an important effect on the dependent variable, because stable staff unit organizations will probably have deeper institutional relationships with other staff units, and influence will be easier and more frequent. Staff units that have recently had institutional overhauls will likely be more preoccupied with internal politics than with influencing other staff units.

However, it turns out that this variable is largely worthless in gauging the effect of spanning boundaries on staff unit influence, and it will therefore have no impact on tests of this hypothesis. The reason is that organizational stability is unrelated to the key explanatory variable, spanning boundaries, unless a particular president specifically set out to reorganize staff units that spanned boundaries more (or less) frequently than other staff units. Since this is not usually the case, any estimate (quantitative or qualitative) of the effect of spanning boundaries on a staff unit's influence in the White House will remain unbiased regardless of the number of years in which the staff unit's organization has remained the same. Gathering information on this variable might be interesting by itself, but it would be a waste of resources for purposes of examining Hult's hypothesis. Thus, however interesting this variable might be for descriptive purposes, we can and probably should omit it from our explanatory analysis, and our research will suffer no negative consequences.

In testing the effect of spanning boundaries on White House influence, we would probably not simply compare the influence of those staff units that spanned boundaries with those that did not. This would not be advisable, because the heads of these staff units are likely selected in ways that are related to their probable influence. For example, suppose that Hult is correct in postulating that staff units that span White House boundaries will be less influential. A logical consequence (or a rational expectation, in economics terms) would mean that the best staff members would be appointed to staff units that do not span boundaries. If one just compared the influence of the two types of staff units, we might find that those that spanned boundaries are less influential, but this might be due solely or primarily to the initial staff appointment process. Indeed, the better the initial appointment process was in incorporating these rational expectations, the more biased would be the estimate produced by this (naive) study.[8] One way to cope with this possible confounding problem is to measure the quality or experience of the head of each staff unit.

In a quantitative analysis, we might well include this second variable in a regression equation to avoid omitted variable bias.[9] However, the same bias would afflict a qualitative analysis if one did not somehow take into account the quality of the staff head. If one possessed some assessment of how good each staff head was—and we would have much better information on this variable in a qualitative rather than a quantitative study—one could choose cases where the head was very experienced or skilled for both a staff unit that spanned boundaries and one that did not. We might also choose both types of staff units with inexperienced or less skilled heads. If Hult is correct, we would find that the spanning boundaries variable still explained influence in the White House, even after we held constant the effect of quality and experience of the personnel.

Thus, collecting some types of additional explanatory variables will help us explore the implications and veracity of our key hypotheses. However, a wide-ranging collection of all possible explanatory variables will not help us achieve any relevant goal of social scientific causal inference. In fact, it is even worse, since each additional variable for which we simultaneously estimate a causal effect reduces

the precision of all of our causal estimates. Thus, "success" in amass-
ing a larger and larger number of variables will automatically produce failure in learning about any one causal inference. This strategy
would still be interesting and productive for descriptive or historical purposes, but it would not be very useful for social scientific
inference.

I underscore what we all probably know here, that good history is
not necessarily good social science (and vice versa). A theory that is
sufficiently broad, or an "explanation" with a huge number of explanatory variables, illuminates nothing whatsoever. A "theory" incapable of being wrong is neither a theory nor an explanation.
Philosophers of science might say that a theory or hypothesis should
be "falsifiable," but this concept confounds two separate criteria. The
first is that, in principle, any theoretical statement should be either
true or false; in particular, a theory that purports to combine every
perspective about a subject is unlikely to be capable of being false. In
other words, if one cannot imagine a series of events in the real world
that would convince one that a theory is wrong, then the theory is
useless from the start. Second, research methods capable of distinguishing whether a theory is true or false must be identified.

In my view, the first criterion is essential. The second should be
used to judge the veracity of particular theories, rather than these theories per se. Separating the two criteria is pivotal. Traditional presidency researchers are sometimes good at stating theories capable of
being false; they have rarely provided sufficient evidence to support
or oppose any particular theory. Completing the first step alone is
useful, provided it is recognized as only the first step—and as long as
one reports it with a fairly large estimate of uncertainty.

In order to state theories in such a way that they are capable of being false, we must choose theoretical statements that are *specific*. For
example, consider the following quotation from Hargrove's paper
(1990, 6), outlining the purpose of his review of the presidential
psychology literature. I emphasize those words or phrases in this passage for which the presidency literature provides an insufficiently precise means of understanding, much less measuring with any degree
of specificity:[10]

This essay will explore two areas in which the consequences of personality are very important:

1. Presidents who find themselves in situations which place *high stress* on them may *deal with the stress* by *responding to internal psychological needs* rather than *acting in ways appropriate to the external situation.*

There are difficult interpretive questions here because there is usually more than one appropriate response to a situation. *Ego defensive actions* that serve the *vulnerable person* may be identified in an individual if they occur often enough and are accompanied by *recognizable emotions* that *reveal the vulnerability.*

2. The *management of decision-making* among lieutenants and advisers is a manifestation of *style of authority* which is, in part, a reflection of *self-confidence* and *cognitive openness* as well as *beliefs about effective leadership.*

The problem with the emphasized words and phrases is not that quantitative measures have not been developed. For most of these concepts, this may never occur. Certainly the rules that do exist for defining these concepts are not adequately precise; a scholar from outside the presidency literature could not come along and identify "cognitive openness," "ego defensive actions," and the other terms, just from the definitions given and perhaps not even from a complete review of the presidential psychobiography literature. We must have rules so that other researchers can come along and apply the same rules and reach the same judgments.[11] Better theory will also come from more precisely laid-out rules.

One possible objection to my argument here is that these concepts, however fuzzy, are what interest presidency researchers. My response is that this could not possibly be true. What interests presidency researchers, by definition, are presidents and the presidency. How these concepts relate to presidents or the presidency is an argument for their proponents to make. Sometimes these arguments have been successful and sometimes not (as Hargrove makes clear in the rest of his paper). However, if the argument cannot be made in particular cases, of what use are fuzzy concepts? How can an ill-defined problem even be interesting in the first place without some specificity? In general, it cannot. However, in much of this literature, specific ideas do underlie much of the argument. The problem is that different scholars have used different psychological terms in the same way or the same psychological terms in different ways. This strategy has often been useful for description—perhaps its main purpose—but it has not always been helpful in arriving at reliable causal inferences.

The President as the Unit of Analysis

Perhaps the best-known methodological problem in the presidency literature is the $n = 1$ problem. This is the idea that only one president is in office at any one time, and so inference is inherently difficult if not impossible. How are we to use John Stuart Mill's methods of difference or agreement if we cannot find two presidents who are alike in all respects but our key explanatory variable? Too much of the world changes when the president changes. Franklin Roosevelt was something like John Kennedy, but how can we hold "things" constant in studying any explanatory variable when "things" include differences in age, health, a world war, the economy, and a myriad other factors. The $n = 1$ problem guarantees that this sort of difficulty will always come up in presidency research, perhaps even more frequently in this subfield than anywhere else.

The basis of the $n = 1$ problem is precisely correct, and it does have exactly these consequences. However, not only is the problem not unique to the presidency literature, but it is perfectly general. It is merely a clear statement of the very definition of causality. To be a little more general about this, Holland (1986) describes what presidency scholars call the $n = 1$ problem as "the fundamental problem of causal inference." To best describe this problem I provide a *definition* of a causal effect, entirely independent of the difficulties we might have in *estimating* this effect.

For simplicity, consider the causal hypothesis that presidents who were once members of Congress veto legislation less frequently. The precise definition of this casual effect is as follows. Consider one president, say Jimmy Carter, and observe the number of veto orders he signs during his four years in office. Then take the same president, turn the clock and the world back to 1976, alter Jimmy Carter so that he is alike in all respects except that he served as a member of Congress, make everyone (but you!) forget the first experiment, and run the world a second time. The causal effect is then the difference between the numbers of vetoes from these two experiments. It should be obvious that one cannot *know* the causal effect even in theory, since one of the values required (the number of vetoes for each experiment) is always unobserved. Thus, this is indeed a fundamental problem, and it should be clear that it is completely general—applying to all types of causal effects. Getting around this fundamental problem is difficult, perhaps even more difficult in the presidency literature, but the problem is not unique here.

In the remainder of this section, I show that the common practice of using the president as the unit of analysis for causal inferences is extremely unlikely to yield reliable empirical conclusions. I then provide some examples of research designs we can use to get around these problems. The president is used as the unit of analysis in studies of decision making, organizational style, and advice structures, but perhaps its most common application is in presidential psychology. Barber's (1980) famous work uses presidents as the unit of analysis; indeed, most analyses that put presidents in categories do the same. Probably the most important findings of the presidential psychology literature are based on this kind of research design. Such analyses predict that presidents with a particular personality profile (referred to in various forms as active-negative, ego-defensive, etcetera) will "rigidify" sometime during their terms in office. Woodrow Wilson and Richard Nixon are generally the two leading examples of this personality profile, and the League of Nations debate and Watergate, respectively, are generally provided as evidence of rigidification (see George and George, 1956).

Many object to these sometimes vague theoretical constructs in the political psychology literature.[12] However, in the analysis that follows, I make the very conservative and optimistic assumption that we have worked out all of the definitional problems associated with ideas like *rigidify* and *ego-defensiveness*. Nevertheless, even in this rosy situation, taking the president as the appropriate unit of analysis is still fraught with problems.

Let us take a very simple case. Suppose we have a single dichotomous explanatory variable. To fix ideas, let this variable be a presidential personality type, either "good" or "bad." Let the dependent variable be whether or not a president rigidifies during his or her term. The basic idea is that the probability of rigidifying is larger for "bad personality" presidents than "good personality" presidents, although I emphasize again that this logic applies for any research problem in which the president is the unit of analysis. In particular, the hypothesis is that the following difference in probabilities is positive and large enough to make a substantive difference:

$$\Pr(\text{rigidify}|\text{bad}) - \Pr(\text{rigidify}|\text{good}).$$

I refer to this difference in probabilities as the *causal effect* we are interested in. Note that it is also another example of the fundamental problem of causal inference, since we can never assess both probabilities for a single president. Furthermore, although we might estimate this effect with either quantitative or qualitative methods, the underlying logic of inference about this effect is essentially the same when you use the president as the unit of analysis: One does a number of case studies of presidents and calculates the proportion of bad presidents who rigidify and subtracts that from the proportion of good presidents who rigidify. This *estimated effect* is based on however many presidents are included in our study. Whether the study is quantitative, and measures are numbers, or qualitative, and measures are just verbal evaluations, this same inference is the goal of the analysis.[13]

My question is how good the estimated effect can possibly be when it is based on the small number of presidents we have available. To answer this question, we need to calculate the "statistical power" of this estimator. In particular, for a given effect size, standard methods of inference enable us to calculate the number of observations (presidents) necessary to find a .05 significant difference some fixed proportion of the time. This fixed proportion is referred to as the power, and the 0.05 significance level is just a reasonable (and arbitrary) convention in most of the social sciences. Table 12 reports some of these calculations for effect sizes of 0.1 and 0.2—reasonably large effects for political science and enormous ones for a field as necessarily imprecise and uncertain as the psychobiography of presidents (after all, presidency scholars rarely even get to interview presidents, much less psychoanalyze them in repeated individual meetings). For each of these effect sizes, the table reports the number of presidents we would need in order to find a significant difference at the 0.05 level 80 percent, 90 percent, and 95 percent of the time, respectively.

The results in table 12 should be somewhat disconcerting to anyone using the president as the unit of analysis to test any hypothesis. Even if we analyzed every existing president, we would still not come near the required number of observations necessary to make reliable inferences with a reasonable degree of certainty. In practice, of course, it takes considerable documentation to conduct a reliable psy-

TABLE 12
Required Sample Sizes to Use the President as the Unit of Analysis

	Difference in Proportions	
Power	.1	.2
.80	388	91
.90	515	121
.95	638	150

chological analysis of a president, and most researchers therefore use only postwar presidents. The table also shows that the lower the statistical power one is willing to live with, the fewer the presidents that would be necessary to find a significant difference at the .05 level. Also, the larger the true effect, the fewer presidents there would have to be; this is a more difficult criterion in practice, of course, since the purpose of the empirical analysis is to estimate the effect, so it cannot be known prior to that analysis.

To make this difficult situation somewhat more graphic, suppose we waited until enough presidents had served to enable us to use the president as the unit of analysis. Under the most optimistic of research circumstances, let us suppose that we had only one-term presidents from now on and we were somehow able to analyze every president beginning with George Washington. We would also have to assume that the basic structure and validity of the hypothesis, as well as the size of the causal effect, remains constant, and that no explanatory variables omitted from this analysis would cause any bias. If any of these rosy assumptions are incorrect (and most certainly are), then the conclusions of this section will be even more pessimistic regarding any efforts to use the president as the unit of analysis. Under these assumption, table 13 reports the approximate *year* in which a reliable analysis could be conducted, in that a significant effect would be found if it indeed did exist.

Waiting until somewhere from the year 2193 to the year 4378 is obviously not feasible for a dissertation project or any other scholarly endeavor! If the true effect were much larger than .2, we might be able to get away with a much smaller number of presidents in the analysis, but we should not choose a research design that is only

TABLE 13
Year in Which the President Can Be Used as the Unit of Analysis

	Difference in Proportions	
Power	.1	.2
.80	3378	2193
.90	3888	2313
.95	4378	2428

useful if the effect we are estimating is enormous or that requires us to wait until nearly the end of time.

In his first-round paper, Hargrove writes, "One cannot have it both ways, arguing that individuals are not important and then in the same breath arguing that the importance of individuals precludes systematic study" (1990, 2). This point about the critics of the presidential psychology is right on the mark. Indeed, it is almost certainly true that individuals are important *and* that presidents can be studied systematically. However, it is clear that the systematic study of individual presidents should not continue in the tradition of using the president as the unit of analysis. If it is advisable to give up this research design, one need not necessarily give up political psychology or the study of the other areas that rely on the president as the unit of analysis.

The solution is to look for ways of multiplying the number of observations—looking for additional observable implications of the same theory. For example, an obvious choice for political psychology and for decision-making research is to use the decision as the unit of analysis. One possibility is to use the president's decision about whether to endorse each piece of congressional legislation or to veto it. This is a set of easily identifiable decisions and might enable one to generate a larger number of specific predictions from a psychological perspective. Even twenty-five or fifty observations would provide a significantly improved research design. If this study goes well, one might be able to abstract the essential features of the psychological variables, making it easier to collect an even larger number of observations. Any prediction along these lines would obviously not be correct in every instance, and the more observations we collect and the less time we have to devote to any one, the more error there will

likely be. However, all we should expect is that the difference in proportions (the estimated effect) be large enough to be important and
detectable.[14]

Can the study of presidential personalities or decision-making
styles help us to predict decisions such as these? Since the president
is not offered exactly the same choice in each instance, the degree to
which each situation would generate ego-defensive behavior would
not be identical even for the same president.[15] The very process of de-
riving coding rules would help make the theory more specific and
useful, and the study itself would help us to know whether we are indeed right. If political psychology turns out not to be able to make
predictions in an area like this, where the decision context and possible outcomes are very clear, then perhaps one might conclude that
we should channel our efforts in more rewarding directions. Of
course, on the basis of the extensive literature in this area, I feel fairly
certain that this study would yield fairly strong effects, and if so, it
would give presidential psychology studies considerably more specificity and thus significantly more reliability.

A similar problem to that in the presidential psychology literature
is in the literature on leadership, as Sinclair ably argues in this volume
(chap. 5). She asks the basic question of whether presidents lead. Re-
stated in causal language, we might say, if another person were in the
same situation, would he or she decide something different? Because
of the fundamental problem of causal inference, this would obviously
be a particularly difficult problem to study in presidency research. It
would be very difficult to get around this problem even if we used decision points, instead of presidents, as the unit of analysis.

Perhaps, then, *we can look for a different set of observable consequences of the same theory.* For example, we might construct the following experiment. We could go into the archives of some president
and extract a number of cases where there were lots of evidence about
advice from presidential staff. We could then change a few key facts
in this situation so respondents would not remember what happened
in the actual historical event. Alternatively, and probably better, we
could find some ordinary presidential decisions. This would be better
because the experimental subjects would be less likely to remember
and especially because more presidential decisions are indeed fairly
ordinary. We could then give the set of advice from the various advisers to a few dozen people—perhaps randomly selected citizens, or

perhaps people who seek to understand the role of the president (such as graduate students or law students), or those who were close to presidents or would like to be president (such as former presidential staffers or members of Congress). There are many questions we could then ask. First, if there was very little variation in the decisions made by these people, then the evidence would be consistent with the idea that presidential leadership does not exist: anyone would make the same decision in the same situation. If the more likely situation occurred, where there is some variation, could we account for it? Is the variation due to the person's party affiliation, education, occupation, degree of ego-defensiveness, or something else? With a study like this we could generate a large number of observations and would likely learn many important facts about leadership, decision making, and even presidential personality.

One final way to increase the number of observations is to look for observable implications of one's theory at other levels of aggregation. For example, one of Aldrich's questions is the extent to which the presidential campaign matters. Our forecasting models seem to do quite well without any information from the campaign (see Rosenstone, 1983). Indeed, contrary to media expectations, Dukakis did better than our prediction models indicated in 1988. Because of the Fundamental Problem, in order to estimate the causal effect we obviously cannot measure the observed election result in 1988 *and* in a hypothetical election that was the same as 1988 except for certain key campaign events.

However, campaign events such as the Willie Horton ads presumably had different effects in different states. If the ads were successful at provoking latent racism among whites, then the electoral effect would presumably be different in Washington, D.C., with a very high proportion of blacks, than in New Hampshire, with almost none. Remember that we really do not care whether this effect is different in different states per se, but since this idea is consistent with the more general hypothesis, this study could provide the necessary critical evidence. This would not even necessarily be a full quantitative study, since we could learn an awful lot from a map with prediction errors in various states highlighted; one could then use our enormous base of qualitative knowledge about the campaign in different states to try to make sense of the results.

We could even go farther and look at individual level survey data. This might help us determine whether racist whites voted for Dukakis less frequently than other whites in similar economic and political circumstances. Again, if we are mainly interested in the effect of the campaign, a survey is not directly relevant, but its indirect relevance in possibly confirming an important implication of the more general theory is overwhelming.

Although one cannot use the president as the unit of analysis in order to derive reliable causal inferences, most of the theories that have been explored in this way could be studied in other ways too. Perhaps the most productive strategy is to search for numerous additional observable implications of one's theory. These implications may be at different levels of aggregation, in different political systems, at different times, or with different measures of the same variables.

Concluding Remarks

The traditional presidency literature has accomplished an enormous amount in the area of history and contextual description. However, progress in a social science of the American presidency is far less advanced.

Future research needs to emphasize not only quantitative analyses but rigorous and systematic qualitative research. We need to insist absolutely that any prediction or explanation must come with a fair assessment of its uncertainty. My example of research based on the president as the unit of analysis demonstrates just how uncertain some of our best work is likely to be even in the foreseeable future. Continuing research will undoubtedly reduce this uncertainty, but only if our qualitative research follows the standard rules of scientific inference.

Notes

1. This is a specific version of the argument in King, Verba, and Keohane (in progress).

2. Without more systematic research, there will be many situations where the world would be better off without any presidency literature. Florence Nightingale once said at a minimum, hospitals should not *spread* infection."

3. Perhaps it pays to remember that the goal of the academic members of the McGovern-Fraiser Commission was to increase party discipline and organizational strength—precisely the opposite of what happened.

4. This discussion characterizes the first version of Light's paper. He has subsequently revised his paper to include some quite suggestive empirical evidence, though still not conclusive even by his judgment.

5. Indeed, what president in modern times was more concerned with short-term political gain than Nixon? Watergate could easily be interpreted as a series of presidential decisions seemingly designed for no purpose other than short-term political gain.

6. The newest work in the congressional elections literature displays a similar trend designed to describe and explain the apparent increase in divided government at the federal and state levels.

7. Even Aldrich is arguing for more complete, realistic, and all-encompassing theories (1990, 48): "The division into who runs, who is nominated, who is elected, and how does all this affect the actions of the victor is, unfortunately, too tidy. . . . A theory of one component is necessarily incomplete. The theory of presidential selection must attempt to answer all four of these questions." Unlike the other presidency subfields, which I have been referring to as the traditional presidency literature, Aldrich's goal may actually be more immediately reachable, because scholars have been very specific along the way and have made considerable progress on separate theories and empirical analyses from each of the four parts.

8. This is the same kind of selection bias that occurs when one tries to predict success in graduate school on the basis of standardized test scores or undergraduate grades, using as data only those students who were admitted. It turns out that the better the admissions committee was in choosing the best students, the poorer job we would think they did.

9. More specifically, one can avoid omitted variable bias if the omitted variable is uncorrelated with the included one or the omitted variable has no effect on the dependent variable. If neither condition holds, then omitting this variable will bias one's estimate of the included variable's effect on the dependent variable.

10. Hargrove is quite aware of the problems with defining these concepts, as he makes clear from the first sentence of the third paragraph of this quotation. I certainly do not mean to blame him for problems in the political psychology literature!

11. Social scientists should not measure concepts the same way as the Supreme Court determines whether something is pornographic.

12. Did Nixon and Woodrow Wilson really rigidify? Or did they think that they could really get what they wanted? Many argued that the game was over, and yet these two pursued their goals (staying if office and in the League of Nations, respectively) relentlessly. Perhaps this is true, but if these goals were of incredible importance to them, perhaps it made perfect sense for them to keep pushing. From this perspective, Nixon was fighting to save face, to survive politically, and to keep a positive place in history. One would not have to stretch the bounds of rational choice modeling very far to fit in the behaviors of these two political actors. Wouldn't you fight as hard as Nixon? Perhaps he did not rigidify but instead became more and more flexible and creative about trying to get around a very big roadblock. If he managed to stall until the end of his term,

would we be calling this *rigidity* or *cleverness?* If we cannot agree on even vague measures of either the explanatory or the dependent variables, how can we expect to find a relationship among them that anyone would accept?

13. This procedure is valid so long as we are not omitting key explanatory variables that are prior to personality and correlated with it and also that affect the probability of rigidification in office. Since the theories of personality usually used in this literature assume that personality is formed at an extremely early age, the study would seem valid in design.

14. Another possibility is to use decisions to appoint and dismiss various White House personnel.

15. Bensel (1980) did an analogous study where he coded each piece of congressional legislation to see if it narrowed the discretion of bureaucrats.

References

Aldrich, John. 1990. "Presidential Selection," paper prepared for the Presidency Research Conference, University of Pittsburgh, 12–14 November.

Barber, James David. 1980. *The Presidential Character.* N.J.: Prentice Hall.

Bensel, Richard. 1980. "Creating the Statutory State: The Implications of a Rule of Law Standard in American Politics." *American Political Science Review* 74(3):734–44.

Edwards, George C., III. 1983. "Quantitative Analysis." In *Studying the Presidency,* ed. George C. Edwards, III and Stephen J. Wayne. Knoxville: University of Tennessee Press.

Erikson, Robert S. 1971. "The Advantage of Incumbency in Congressional Elections." *Polity* 3:395–405.

George, Alexander L., and Juliette L. George. 1956. *Woodrow Wilson and Colonel House, A Personality Study.* New York: John Day.

Greenstein, Fred I. 1988. *Leadership in the Modern Presidency.* Cambridge: Harvard University Press.

Hargrove, Erwin C. 1990. "Presidential Personality and Political Style." Paper prepared for the Presidency Research Conference, University of Pittsburgh, 12–14 November.

Holland, Paul, 1986. "Statistics and Causal Inference." *Journal of the American Statistical Association* 81:945–60.

Hult, Karen M. 1990. "Advising the President." Paper prepared for the Presidency Research Conference, University of Pittsburgh, 12–14 November.

Kessel, John. 1984. "The Structure of the Reagan White House." *American Journal of Political Science* 27:431–63.

King, Gary. 1991. " 'Truth' is Stranger Than Prediction, More Questionable Than Causal Inference," *American Journal of Political Science* 35 (November): 1047–53.

King, Gary, and Lyn Ragsdale, 1988. *The Elusive Executive: Discovering Statistical Patterns in the Presidency.* Washington, D.C.: Congressional Quarterly Press.

King, Gary, Sidney Verba, and Robert O. Keohane. In progress. *Scientific Inference in Qualitative Research.*

Light, Paul C. 1990. "Presidential Policymaking." Paper prepared for the Presidency Research Conference, University of Pittsburgh, 12–14 November.

Mayhew, David R. 1974. "Congressional Elections: The Case of the Vanishing Marginals." *Polity* 6:295–317.

Neustadt, Richard E., and Earnest R. May. 1986. *Thinking in Time: The Uses of History for Decision-Makers.* New York: Free Press.

Rose, Richard, 1990. "Evaluations." Paper prepared for the Presidency Research Conference, University of Pittsburgh, 12–14 November.

Rosenstone, Steven R. 1983. *Forecasting Presidential Elections.* New Haven: Yale University Press.

Wayne, Stephen J. 1983. "An Introduction to Research on the Presidency," in *Studying the Presidency,* ed. George C. Edwards III and Stephen J. Wayne. Knoxville: University of Tennessee Press.

III

Comparisons

Foundations of Power

ANTHONY KING

THERE ARE essentially two reasons for studying comparative politics. One, the more ambitious, has to do with the desire to develop well-supported empirical theory—about, for example, why some countries are liberal democracies while others are not, about the relationship between electoral systems and party systems, perhaps about the relationship between pluralist political systems and efficient and productive economic systems. For obvious reasons, such empirical theories are easiest to construct when the number of cases is large and there is therefore a high probability that a considerable number of both constants and variables will be available.

The second reason for studying comparative politics is more down-to-earth and is well captured by Rudyard Kipling's famous question, "And what should they know of England who only England know?" To recognize what are, and are not, the idiosyncratic features of one's own country, to understand why the institutions of one's own country work as they do, it is of inestimable advantage to know how similar institutions—or at any rate institutions that might be thought to be similar—work in other countries. The study of foreign countries can render the natural unnatural, the familiar mysterious. It can also give one a sense of proportion and help to put things in perspective. One's hometown traffic jams never seem quite so bad when one has seen those in the big city.

This chapter does not aspire to grand theory. It is meant to be more Kiplingesque in approach. Its purpose is to see whether, if students of the American presidency knew more about executive presidencies and prime ministerships in other countries, they might come to see the U.S. presidency in a new light. At the very least, they might want to ask new questions and pursue new lines of inquiry. At most, they might want to reconsider the presidency's place in the modern American political system.

Studying the American presidency comparatively is not easy. There are at least three difficulties; two practical, the third more intellectual.

The first practical difficulty—one that may come as a surprise to those who have studied the presidential institution in the United States—is that the academic literature on equivalent offices in other countries is virtually nonexistent. There is no book in French or any other language about the French presidency or the French prime ministership. There are very few books in German or any other language about the German chancellorship. The literature on the British prime ministership, although somewhat more voluminous, is still quite thin. And so on. More books and articles are published on the American presidency each year than on all of the other headships of government in the world put together. Why this should be so would make an interesting subject for inquiry, but for our purposes what matters is that it *is* so. Fortunately, a number of the gaps have recently been filled by a special issue of *West European Politics* devoted to western European prime ministers (Jones, 1991).

The other practical difficulty is the virtual nonexistence of comparative case studies of presidential and prime ministerial leadership (or, as the case may be, nonleadership). We never see the presidents and prime ministers of different countries in action in similar circumstances. This is partly because the circumstances seldom are similar; but it is also a reflection of the fact that headships of government in countries apart from the United States have been so little studied. All the same, excellent opportunities do occasionally present themselves. In August 1990 the governments of the United States, Great Britain, France, Germany, Japan, and many other countries had to decide how to respond to the Iraqi invasion of Kuwait. It would be fascinating to know in detail—and it would probably be possible to find out—how each of a wide range of political systems functioned in the course of the ensuing crisis and, in particular, what role the head of each country's government played in policy formation and decision making. The Persian Gulf crisis could be used as a single window onto a number of different political systems.[1]

The more intellectual difficulty arises out of the fact that the American presidency is indeed unique. All other headships of government

TABLE 14

Attributes of the Head of Government in Nine Countries

Country	Is he also head of state?	Is he "chief executive" on his own (as distinct from chairing a cabinet)?	Is he commander in chief of the armed forces?	Is he prevented from being a member of the national legislature?
United States	yes	yes	yes	yes
France (president)	yes	yes (?)	yes	yes
Germany	no	no	no	no
Italy	no	no	no	no
Japan	no	no	no	no
Great Britain	no	no	no	no
Canada	no	no	no	no
Australia	no	no	no	no
New Zealand	no	no	no	no

in the liberal democratic world, with the possible exception of the French presidency, resemble each other more than any of them resembles the presidency of the United States.[2] It is unusual for a head of government to be also his country's head of state. It is unusual for a head of government to be the head of his country's executive branch entirely on his own rather than being merely the principal figure in some more collegial decision-making body. It is unusual for a head of government to be, in addition, the commander in chief of his country's armed forces. It is fairly unusual for a head of government not to be a member of his country's national legislature. What makes the United States different is that the American president is all of: head of government, head of state, sole chief executive, commander in chief, and a figure set deliberately apart from the national legislature. Table 14 tells a vivid story of the United States' constitutional distinctiveness.

It follows that the U.S. presidency would hardly be a suitable subject for grand theorizing even if one were disposed in that direction. The intellectual strategy to be adopted must necessarily be less pretentious and to be of the "most dissimilar" rather than the "most similar" variety. That said, it would be surprising if there was nothing to be learned from a comparative study of the U.S. presidency. We shall see shortly whether there is.

One further—and very important—preliminary point needs to be made. When people say that a head of government is "powerful," they frequently fail to make clear what specific political context they have in mind. Do they mean that the head of government is powerful within his own government (so that he is able to make the government as a whole move in the direction he wants)? Or do they mean that he happens to be the head of a government that is itself powerful within its own territorial jurisdiction (so that, if the power of the government as a whole increases, so does the power of the head of government)? Or do they mean that he happens to be the head of government of a powerful country (so that, if his country becomes more powerful, he, by definition, becomes more powerful too)?

These three meanings are often elided, but they are obviously not the same. Someone may lead a weak country with an ineffectual government yet be very powerful within the limits of that ineffectual government. Someone else may lead a powerful country with a strong government yet in reality have little capacity to shape the actions of that government. One person may be the powerful leader of a banana republic. Another may be thought of as the "leader" of a great world power yet in practice be only one of a number of power holders within that world power's governmental system. General Alfredo Stroessner was probably a more powerful figure in the government of Paraguay in the 1960s than Lord Rosebery was in the government of Great Britain in the 1890s, yet Paraguay in the 1960s was internationally impotent, while Britain in the 1890s was at the zenith of its imperial power.

In this chapter, the focus will be on the power—or influence, or strength (the vocabulary does not matter)—that the head of government can exercise *within his or her own governmental system*. The question will be: To what extent is the head of government in a position to assert his or her will over the rest of the cabinet, the civil service, and the national legislature? Both the government's power to exert its will within its own national boundaries and the country's power to exert its will outside its own national boundaries will in effect, for our purposes, be held constant.[3]

With this as one's focus, it becomes meaningful to say, for example, that George Washington was probably a more powerful U.S. president in the 1790s than George Bush was in the 1990s—even though the "penetration" of the federal government inside the territory of the United States has increased immeasurably over the intervening two hundred years, and even though the power of the United States in the world has likewise increased immeasurably. The statement that President Washington was more powerful than President Bush may not turn out to be true, but in this context it is at least a reasonable hypothesis to test.

Against this background, the question of the present chapter becomes: How does the power (or influence or strength) of the president of the United States, within the American system of government, compare with the power (or influence or strength) of heads of government in other countries, within the national systems of government of those countries? From this point of view, such matters as the possession or nonpossession of nuclear weapons and the size of a country's gross national product are irrelevant.

It remains only to decide which countries are to be compared with the United States. The answer, for all kinds of fairly obvious practical as well as intellectual reasons, is: the major countries of western Europe (Germany, France, Italy, and Great Britain), plus Japan and the three Westminster-model democracies (Canada, Australia, and New Zealand). Taking in such a large number of comparators means that the analysis will inevitably be more loosely textured than it would have been otherwise; but what it loses in rigor it may gain and should gain in the opening up of new lines of thought.

A convenient way of gaining leverage on the problem is to consider what factors *might* conduce to a head of government's having power—or at least potential power—within his or her system of government. If a head of government wishes to exercise power, to steer events in a direction that they might not otherwise have gone in, what features of his or her country's political arrangements might—or might not—conduce to that end?[4]

Some Potential Sources of Head-of-Government Power

On the face of it, there would appear to be at least ten such potential sources of head-of-government power. Some of them could easily be subdivided so as to produce even more. At least one, as will appear, may not be a source of power so much as an institutional manifestation of lack of power. We shall consider each of the ten as they operate, or fail to operate, in countries outside the United States, then as they operate, or fail to, within the United States.

TERMS OF THE CONSTITUTION

Other things being equal, a head of government will be more powerful within his own system of government if the constitution of his country is taken seriously as a guide to political practice and if it explicitly assigns him a range of specified "powers" (in the sense in which *powers* is used in the U.S. Constitution).

In this respect, countries' constitutions vary enormously. Great Britain and the other Westminster-model countries do not have written constitutions that cover the distribution of authority among different agencies of national government, with the result that prime ministers under those systems do not have any formal powers (though of course they have many informal ones).

The Japanese constitution gives the prime minister the power to appoint and remove other ministers, but the constitutional balance of power in Japan is clearly meant to be tilted away from the prime minister as an individual and toward the cabinet collectively. Article 65 of the Japanese constitution states bluntly: "Executive power shall be vested in the cabinet," and under Article 73 the cabinet is given the tasks of administering the law faithfully, conducting affairs of state, managing foreign affairs, administering the civil service, and preparing the budget. Article 72 states that "the prime minister . . . submits bills, reports on general national affairs and foreign relations to the Diet and exercises control over various administrative branches," but it adds the important proviso that in doing so he is "representing the cabinet." Apart from the appointment and removal of ministers, the only formal power assigned to the Japanese prime minister is the requirement under Article 74 that he countersign all laws and cabinet orders.

The German and Italian constitutions are surprisingly similar in the very brief provisions they make covering the head of the government and the cabinet. Article 65 of Germany's Basic Law states: "The federal chancellor shall determine, and be responsible for, the general policy guidelines. Within the limits set by these guidelines, each federal minister shall conduct the affairs of his department autonomously and on his own responsibility. The federal government shall decide on differences of opinion between federal ministers." Article 95 of the Italian constitution is similarly terse:

The president of the council [i.e., the prime minister] conducts, and is responsible for, the general policy of the government. He maintains unity in general political and administrative policy and promotes and coordinates the activities of the ministers.

Ministers are jointly responsible for the decisions of the cabinet as a whole and individually for those of their own particular departments.

Both constitutions clearly create something of a formal tension between the chancellor or prime minister's overall responsibility for "the general policy guidelines" and "the general policy of the government" and the cabinet or the government's responsibility for, in the German case, deciding on "differences of opinion between federal ministers" and, in the Italian case, "the decisions of the cabinet as a whole." Neither constitution gives the head of government any further powers beyond the usual ones of appointing and dismissing ministers. The German constitution explicitly denies the chancellor the power of command over the armed forces and instead gives it to the defense minister. The Italian constitution gives it to the president of the republic.[5]

The French constitution, as is well known, is something of a curiosity, creating, as it does, an executive with two heads. Article 5 says vaguely:

The president of the republic sees to it that the constitution is respected. He ensures, by his arbitration, the regular functioning of the public authorities as well as the continuity of the state. He is the guarantor of national independence, of the integrity of the territory and of respect for Community [French Community, not European Community] agreements and treaties.

More precisely, Article 8 gives the president the power to appoint the prime minister, and the president also has the power to dissolve the National Assembly, to submit to a national referendum "any government bill bearing on the organization of the public authorities," and, at moments of grave national crisis, to assume emergency powers, which he then exercises personally.

Moments of grave national crisis apart, the French constitution's text appears to envisage a regime centered on the prime minister and the government rather than on the president; and the prime minister is clearly intended to be the dominant figure in the government. Article 20 states that "the government determines and directs the policy of the nation" and "has the administration and the armed forces at its disposal"; but Article 8 gives the prime minister the usual power to appoint and dismiss individual ministers, and the first two paragraphs of Article 21 are considerably more sweeping in their language than their equivalents in the Japanese, German, and Italian constitutions: "The premier directs the activity of the government. He is responsible for national defense. He ensures the execution of the laws. . . . [He] exercises the rule-making power and makes civil and military appointments. He may delegate some of his powers to the ministers." This assignment of powers to the French prime minister is, on the face of it, impressive, especially given the importance of the "rule-making power" in the French system.

Although several passages in the French constitution are vague, the constitution of France goes into considerably more detail concerning the president, the prime minister, and the government than do the constitutions of the other seven comparator countries. Where the other constitutions exist at all in a written form, the passages in them dealing with the position of the head of government are both brief and remarkably imprecise. Certainly they assign the head of government very few specific formal powers. The Japanese constitution appears to tilt the balance of authority toward the cabinet and away from the prime minister, while the French constitution appears to lean the other way. But in all of our comparator countries the head of government's position and power are left very much open, to be determined by factors other than the contents of written documents. Indeed, the absence of an allocation of formal powers, as in the Westminster-model countries, may allow heads of government in such countries to expand the limits of their office and, to some extent, to "write their own ticket."[6]

DIRECT ELECTION BY THE PEOPLE

Other things being equal, a head of government is likely to be more powerful within his system of government if he has been directly elected by the people rather than attaining the office merely as the head of his party or as the result of some intraparliamentary process.

The argument here is that in the democratic age a directly elected public official is likely to have acquired a degree of democratic legitimacy that an indirectly elected official lacks. He may be able to use this greater democratic legitimacy in his efforts to persuade others within the government to do what he wants them to do, or others may simply accord him greater respect and influence by virtue of his elected, as distinct from nonelected, status.[7]

Very little needs to be said under this heading for the simple reason that, outside the Western Hemisphere, directly elected heads of government (as distinct from heads of state) are virtually unknown. The only directly elected head of government in our eight comparator countries (he is also head of state) is the president of France, who has been elected by universal franchise since the French constitution was amended to that effect in 1962. President Charles de Gaulle had the constitution amended to provide for democratic election precisely because he believed it would increase the office's effective power.[8]

SECURITY OF TENURE

Other things being equal, a head of government will be more powerful if he enjoys a high degree of security of tenure in office.

This point is important and could easily be overlooked. Consider the position of a head of government who knows—and knows that others know—that he may at any time be deposed. The bargaining position of someone in this position is seriously compromised. He cannot make long-term threats or promises because he knows—and knows that others know—that he may not be in office for very long. Those around him are bound to think of him as someone they are likely to have to do business with for days or weeks rather than months or years; they will constantly have their eye not just on him but on his probable successor—or on each of a large number of people who may possibly succeed him. Moreover, he will have his eye on them too. In everything he does, he will be conscious that his first duty is self-defense. He will have to use such bargaining advantages as he possesses principally to remain in office rather than to advance disinterested policies or causes. Those around him who want his job—and there are likely to be many of them—will know that they have a vested interest in preventing him from building up his position. They will thwart him from time to time simply in order to prevent him from doing so. The question of "leadership" scarcely arises in such a situation. Endless compromise is the name of the game.

In our eight comparator countries, the French president and the German chancellor are normally highly secure, but the security of tenure of most of the others is variable. A Japanese prime minister or a prime minister of one of the Westminster-model countries is likely to be secure immediately after a successful election campaign, or when the country's economy is doing well, or when he and his party are riding high in the polls; but, absent one or more of these conditions, the prime minister's position is likely to be much less secure. Table 15 attests to the large number of prime ministers who have been forced from office in parliamentary systems; but what it does not show, and what is more important for our purposes, is the even larger number of prime ministers who have remained in office but have done so only at the cost of making compromises with their opponents and seeing their influence reduced. New Zealand prime ministers frequently govern in fear of their political lives, and even as powerful a British prime minister as Margaret Thatcher went through phases—for example, following the so-called "Westland affair" in 1986—when she had to adopt an unwontedly collegial leadership style. And, in the end, she fell.[9]

The extreme case is, of course, Italy. There were eleven Italian prime ministers and twenty-four separate Italian prime ministerships during the two decades covered by table 15. The longest single government lasted a mere 1,057 days (Hine and Finocchi, 1991). The cumulative consequences for the office of prime minister in Italy have been described in detail by Hine and Finocchi (1991, 79–80):

> This brevity of tenure, combined with the complexity of [Italian] coalitions, fundamentally affects the nature of the role. The emphasis is inevitably placed on administrative coordination, short-term conflict resolution . . . and coalition troubleshooting. The prime minister has little chance to impose a distinctively personal policy imprint on his government, still less to spend large amounts of time on longterm policy analysis. . . .
>
> The high rate of prime ministerial turnover inevitably reduces the status of the current incumbent. At any one time there will be several former prime ministers in active political life, some of whom still harbor aspirations to return to office. Some may be sitting together in the council of ministers (cabinet). Establishing a personal preeminence—whether in the esteem of colleagues or in the eyes of the mass electorate—is very difficult in such circumstances. The reduced status is self-fulfilling. Because prime ministers can be challenged and checked, such behavior falls within the range of the politically acceptable. Voters expect it, and the taboo against doing so is permanently lowered.

TABLE 15

Number of Heads of Government Between 1970 and 1990, Nine Countries

Country	Number of heads of government	Number who retired or died	Number who were forced from office	Number who left office after being defeated in an election
United States	5	1	1	2
France				
President	3	1	0	1
Prime minister	8	0	3[a]	4
Germany	3	0	1	1
Italy	24[b]	0	22[c]	1
Japan	10	4	4	1
Great Britain	5	1	0	3
Canada	5	1	1	2
Australia	5	0	1[d]	3
New Zealand	9	4	0	4

Note: With the exception of Italy, if a head of government held office for more than one term consecutively, all the terms are counted as one. For example, Thatcher had three consecutive terms of office, but the period 1979–90 is counted as a whole. "Retired" includes all heads of government who left office voluntarily. They may or may not have retired from active political life. "Forced from office" includes all those who were sacked, resigned amid a scandal, or who lost a crucial vote in their parliament and were required to resign.

a. Jacques Chirac resigned, but he had been at odds with President Valéry Giscard d'Estaing. In effect, he was forced from office by the president.

b. Each term of office served by an Italian prime minister is counted separately. Although a prime minister may have resigned only to be subsequently reappointed, the balance of the coalition will have changed. The prime minister then forms a new administration.

c. Italian prime ministers are usually forced from office because they have lost a crucial vote in parliament or because their coalition has broken up.

d. Australian Prime Minister Gough Whitlam was removed by the governor general of Australia when he refused to resign after he had lost a vote in the Australian Senate.

EFFECTIVE LEADER OF POLITICAL PARTY

Other things being equal, a head of government will be more powerful if he is the effective leader of a political party. His power will be further augmented if the party he leads is also large and cohesive.

The prime ministers of the Westminster-model democracies, especially Great Britain, Australia, and New Zealand, anchor one end of what might be thought of as a party-leadership scale. The prime ministers of those countries are usually in effective command of their party. Their party usually has majority or at least plurality backing in the country and also an overall majority in the lower house of the national legislature. And their party can usually be counted upon, within the legislature, to be cohesive, to act as a single, disciplined, united body. To be sure, the prime minister is not normally in a position to act as an autocrat; he or she must, and normally does, take into account strongly held views in the party. But, provided he does that, he can normally count on having a formidable political force behind him. Indeed, the prime ministers in those countries are usually prime ministers precisely because they have such a force behind them. In the Westminster-model systems, national government is, as Rose (1974) points out, to a large extent "party government."

German chancellors and French presidents in practice usually find themselves in the same position. The German chancellor since 1948 has always headed a coalition government, but since the 1950s the coalition has usually been made up of parties that have fought the previous election on the basis that, if they succeeded in winning a parliamentary majority, they would form a government together; and the resulting coalitions have almost always been stable, surviving until the next election. The German chancellor needs to bargain with the leader of the other party in his coalition, usually the Free Democrats, but he can normally rely on the support of both his own party and the Free Democrats as well. German government is only slightly qualified party government.

Since the early 1960s, the same has been broadly true of France. French presidents have either brought in a majority grouping with them or else have been able to use their power to dissolve the National Assembly in order to secure the return of a majority favorable to them. Only between 1986 and 1988, during the period of "cohabitation," when a Socialist president, François Mitterand, found himself saddled with a right-wing majority in parliament, has the president not been able to count on majority-party backing. Even then, the prime minister, Jacques Chirac, did have the backing of a majority; and, not surprisingly, for that short period effective power in the French system shifted from the president to the prime minister.

Japan and Italy, for somewhat different reasons, anchor the other end of the scale. The Japanese prime minister is always the leader of his party, and his party, the Liberal Democratic party, is always the majority party; but the LDP is not at all cohesive, except (sometimes) in the face of the opposition, and its leader is frequently leader only in name. Occasionally a prime minister, like Yasuhiro Nakasone in the 1980s, establishes a considerable degree of dominance over the government, but normally the influence of Japanese prime ministers is limited by the fact that they lead only one faction out of many in the LDP and by the presence in the party of numerous policy-oriented opinion groups. The LDP is more like a loose holding company than like a Westminster-style political party; and the prime minister is the head, in effect, of one of the holding company's subsidiaries rather than of the whole company. Richardson and Flanagan, in their standard textbook on Japanese politics (1984, 337), describe the consequences:

> Because the prime minister is chosen mainly by a coalition of Liberal Democratic party factions, his freedom of action is restricted by the endless play and counterplay of factional politics. . . . Japanese elite politics—in this case Liberal Democratic factional politics— involves frequent power moves by ambitious senior politicians. Typically, these manipulations focus on the recruitment process and involve attempts to place members or leaders of particular factions in leading positions. Factional in-fighting, though, spills over into the policy-making process at times. . . . The vulnerability of the prime minister, and the related vulnerability of his cabinet as well, to being pushed out of office in the factional game, is sufficient to restrict considerably their freedom of choice in policy matters.

In Italy the processes are somewhat different, but the consequences for prime ministerial power are the same. The Italian prime minister is always a leading party figure, but he is seldom the leader of his party. More to the point, whereas Japanese governments are made up of coalitions of factions, Italian governments are made up of coalitions of both parties and factions. Italy's dominant party, the Christian Democrats, is almost as factionalized as the Japanese LDP, with as many different faction leaders and ideological tendencies; and in addition, every Italian government, unlike governments in Japan, is an interparty coalition, with the Christian Democrats in temporary and more or less uneasy alliance with one or a number of minor parties. In Italy as in Japan, an occasional prime minister (like Bettino Craxi in the mid 1980s) manages to dominate his government, at least in presentational terms, but the Italian norm is for the prime minister to be not so much an assertive head of government as the man who happens to register in his person the equipoise that Italian politics happens to have reached at a given moment. Party leadership, unlike in the Westminster-model systems, can seldom be translated into governmental leadership.

CONTROL OF OR INFLUENCE
WITHIN THE LEGISLATURE

Other things being equal, a head of government will be more powerful within his system of government if he can exert a high degree of control over, or influence within, the national legislature. Indeed, to some extent this statement is tautologous since, by definition, not to exert a high degree of control over, or influence within, the national legislature is not to be powerful within one's system of government. This factor can be dealt with more briefly because legislative leadership is, to a large extent, a function of party leadership. The head of government who is at the same time the effective leader of a large cohesive party will usually be able, via his party and government, to dominate the legislature and the legislative process.

In Germany and the four Westminster-model countries, Great Britain, Canada, Australia, and New Zealand, the chancellor or prime minister can usually control, if he wants to, the gestation of legislation within the executive branch; and the government, via its leadership of the majority party in parliament, can usually control the passage of legislation through parliament. Governments in these systems are occasionally thwarted (or forced to back off even before legislation has been introduced), but not often. In France, since the early 1960s, the president and his prime minister have likewise been able to rely almost invariably on majority support in the National Assembly. During the period of cohabitation between 1986 and 1988, President François Mitterand largely disappeared from the legislative process, but Prime Minister Jacques Chirac at that time was fully as dominant as a Margaret Thatcher in Britain or a Brian Mulroney in Canada.

In Japan the government can usually (though not always) count on the Diet's support for its major legislative proposals; but the proposals themselves are best understood as being the work of the government as a whole since, as we have seen, the Japanese prime minister is not typically a strong policy leader. The same is broadly true in Italy, except that in Italy the government of the day can by no means count on majority support for whatever it proposes. On the contrary, the combination of multiparty politics and extreme factionalism in the Italian Chamber of Deputies means that the Italian parliament is the most assertive and least predictable of all the parliaments in our eight comparator countries.

CONTROL OF APPOINTMENTS

Other things being equal, a head of government's power will be greater if he effectively controls ministerial and other similar appointments and if such appointments are much sought after by other politicians in the system. The power of patronage is always useful. It is even more useful if patronage is something that a lot of people badly want.

In most countries the patronage power is at least nominally in the hands of the prime minister or other head of government. The only major exceptions are the insistence of the Australian Labor party and the New Zealand Labour party that prime ministers of their party appoint to government only men and women who have previously been elected by the parliamentary caucus. The prime minister merely decides which portfolios will be assigned to which ministers. Prime ministers under these arrangements are left some discretion in the firing of ministers, but no one in Australia or New Zealand seems quite sure how much (Weller, 1985). The British Labour party adopted a similar arrangement in 1981. An incoming Labour prime minister in Britain is now required to appoint to his cabinet all of the elected members of the old shadow cabinet who have been returned to the new parliament. It is left open to the prime minister only to add a few additional members and to allocate portfolios. A British Labour prime minister's power to fire ministers appears, however, to have been left intact.[10]

In seven of the eight countries the norm is that the great majority of ministers will be members of the national legislature. Only in France does the constitution, under the so-called incompatibility rule, bar sitting members of parliament from also serving as members of the government.

The extreme case of the power of prime ministerial patronage, at least historically, has been Great Britain. The British prime minister's power of appointment has until quite recently been virtually untrammeled. An incoming prime minister has some ninety posts to fill, and they do not have to be filled according to any regional, religious, ethnic, or other quotas. The prime minister's only concerns need be political or ideological. In addition, British politics has long been dominated by career politicians, by men and women for whom ministerial office is the ultimate prize, loss of office the ultimate deprivation. "It has been terrible," Ramsay MacDonald is reported to have said in 1929, when he was forming his second administration. "I have had people in here weeping and even fainting" (Dalton, 1953, 217). Subject to the usual vicissitudes of politics, the prime minister is thus in a position to use his power over ministerial appointments to discipline ministers, to discipline back-bench members of parliament and to influence profoundly the direction of public policy. Her single-minded use of her power of appointment in order to further her ideological objectives was one of the hallmarks of the Thatcher administration (see King, 1985, 118–19, 132–33; 1991, 37–38).

The prime minister's power of appointment in the other Westminster systems is more constrained. The Canadian prime minister is under an obligation to include in his cabinet francophones as well as anglophones and representatives from all the Canadian provinces. Many senior Canadian politicians also pursue business or other careers outside politics, so that the prime minister's hold over them is reduced. In Australia, as we have seen, Labor prime ministers have to live with whomever their parliamentary caucus elects, and both Labor and Liberal prime ministers, like their Canadian opposite numbers, have to make allowances for the country's regional diversity. New Zealand prime ministers, quite apart from the Labour party's special rules, are constrained by the fact that, in such a small country, the ratio of ministers to all members of the governing party in the House of Representatives is inevitably very high. Even National party prime ministers in New Zealand, although in principle they have full freedom of choice, do not have all that many potential ministers to choose from (Weller, 1985).

The French president—or, during periods of cohabitation, the prime minister—is in almost as strong a position as the British prime minister. The French head of government does not appear to be greatly inhibited in practice by the incompatibility rule, since most French members of parliament, offered ministerial office, appear happy, even eager, to accept it and to suspend their parliamentary careers (as they hope) temporarily. The French head of government can also, unlike his British counterpart, offer ministerial posts to experts and technocrats from outside parliament.

The German chancellor's room for maneuver is more restricted. He must make most of his ministerial appointments from among the members of the Bundestag, and he has no choice but to give several of the most important posts to men and women drawn from among his coalition allies. There is also in Germany a tradition that the leading figures in the cabinet should have some substantive expertise in whatever subject—foreign affairs, economics, education, agriculture—they are to be responsible for in government. This tradition both constrains the chancellor in his initial choice of ministers and makes cabinet reshuffles considerably more difficult than they are in, say, Britain.

In Japan and Italy, the power of the prime minister to choose and dismiss ministers is largely a function of the prime minister's standing with regard to the factions or parties that make up his current political power base. Ward writes of Japan (1978, 156): "Although largely free to choose whom he wants to serve in his cabinet, a prime minister is politically obligated to apportion these posts so as to maximize the support behind his own position. A very delicate weighing and balancing operation is involved."

Some Japanese prime ministers have been in a position to appoint and remove subordinate ministers more or less at will, but most have not. The Italian prime minister is even more hemmed in. His continuation and that of his government in office depend on the careful allocation of posts to the minority parties and to factions in the Christian Democratic party according to an almost mathematical formula.[11] The Italian prime minister is more a product of the selection process than the dominator of it.

STRUCTURE OF THE EXECUTIVE BRANCH

Other things being equal, a head of government will be more powerful if he can, on his own initiative, determine not merely who will serve in the government but the structure of the government itself. A head of government who can create and abolish governmental agencies at will is in a stronger position to exert his influence within the governmental system than someone who is not.

In most parliamentary systems, the government is the direct inheritor of executive power in the state, and it by itself controls the internal structure of the executive branch. If a new government department or other administrative agency is to be established, it is established by governmental decree, and there is no need for the government to go to the legislature for legal permission to act. The one exception in our eight comparator countries is Italy, where the constitution states explicitly (Article 95) that "the law . . . establishes the number, responsibilities and organization of the various ministries." Thus, except in Italy, if the government in a parliamentary system wishes to create, say, a new department of the environment, it merely needs to decide to do so and to announce its decision publicly.

Moreover, in most parliamentary systems decisions concerning the structure of government are normally taken by the head of government rather than by the whole government. The president of France acts by means of presidential decree, and the prime minister (usually acting on behalf of the president) determines the fields of responsibility of individual ministers. The power is used extensively. There are usually between fifteen and twenty ministries in France, but only seven—Foreign Affairs, Interior, Justice, Defense, Agriculture, Posts, and Veterans Affairs—have had a continuous existence since the Fifth Republic was established in 1958 (Elgie and Machin, 1991, 67). Governmental reorganizations take place equally frequently in Britain, and the British prime minister is solely responsible for them. They are less frequent in Germany, but again it is the chancellor who takes the decisions. Japan appears to be the only one of our eight countries (apart from Italy) in which changes in the structure of government require the cabinet's consent.

CONTROL OF THE CIVIL SERVICE

Other things being equal, a head of government will be stronger within his governmental system if he personally is in a position to control or influence the actions of civil servants. A head of government who controlled not only the political heads of departments but the departments themselves would be a very formidable head of government indeed.

In fact, the degree of head-of-government control of the civil service is limited and indirect in all of our eight countries. Departments and agencies tend to be fairly autonomous and more or less to run themselves. When they are subject to effective political direction, the direction is almost invariably provided by the political head of the agency and by the people he appoints rather than by the president, prime minister, or chancellor. Two partial exceptions are the French president and prime minister and the British prime minister. In France it is customary for both the president and the prime minister to identify certain fields of policy as being ones in which they will take a special interest and in which they will wish to intervene directly. When they do, senior civil servants in the relevant ministries often begin to function as, in effect, *their* civil servants rather than the minister's. The most conspicuous such fields since the 1960s have been foreign affairs and European Community affairs. The president of the republic in these connections has typically established himself as the head of a small subgovernment and has liaised directly with the relevant minister (often over the head of the prime minister) and with the relevant minister's officials.

In Britain a degree of prime ministerial influence is exerted by virtue of the fact that the prime minister is formally responsible for appointing all the civil service heads (as well as the political heads) of government departments. Indeed, the prime minister is formally "the minister for the civil service." Most prime ministers take only a passing interest in these appointments, but some, including Thatcher, have used their appointment power not to promote officials who shared their substantive or ideological opinions (which would be considered wholly illegitimate in Britain) but to promote ones who sympathized with their general approach to government—in Thatcher's case "gung ho" and "can do" rather than cautious and reflective (Royal Institute of Public Administration, 1987).

PUBLIC PRESTIGE

Other things being equal, a head of government will be more powerful within his system of government if the voters know who he is and if they respond favorably to him—or, more precisely, if other politicians in the system believe that voters respond favorably to him. Neustadt (1990) calls this factor "public prestige." It can operate via a "halo effect," with politicians thinking better of the head of government simply because they know that voters think well of him; or it can operate more instrumentally, with politicians, especially of the head of government's party, believing that their own electoral fortunes are bound up with his.

There is no need to dwell on this point at length because the factor of public prestige is obviously one that, for the most part, produces variation more within political systems across time than among different political systems at the same time. The head of government's public standing within his country is likely to be one of the main determinants of his power to persuade others in the system to do what he wants them to do. A popular British prime minister is, other things being equal, more powerful than an unpopular one; a German chancellor about to lead his party or coalition to victory in a national election is likely to be more powerful within his government and in the Bundestag than one who is thought to be about to go down to defeat dragging others with him.

That said, it is worth noting that in two of our eight comparator countries, Italy and Japan, the prime minister is often not sufficiently well known to the electorate for the factor of public prestige to operate one way or the other. As Hine and Finocchi say of Italy (1991, 87):

> The expected brevity of a prime minister's tenure, combined with the dual leadership that results from the prime minister/party secretary tandem, ensures that Christian Democrat prime ministers can rarely create an identity in voters' minds between their own political status and that of the party. There is thus no significant coattails' effect. Prime ministers cannot easily take personal credit for government performance, translate it into personal political popularity and use it as a resource.

The rare Italian prime minister who is not a Christian Democrat suffers from the fact that, like his Christian Democrat opposite numbers, he invariably leads an interparty coalition. Bettino Craxi is one of the very few Italian prime ministers in recent years to have succeeded in establishing a rapport with the electorate and to have traded on that fact in his dealings with fellow politicians. Similarly, in Japan, while some prime ministers, like Yashuhiro Nakasone, are well known, others come and go, leaving little or no trace in the public consciousness.

STAFF SIZE

Finally, it might be supposed that, other things being equal, a head of government would be more influential within his system if the office of head of government in the system was extensively staffed. The bigger the staff, it might be hypothesized, the more powerful the office.

As it happens, the size of head-of-government staffs varies enormously. It is hard to obtain figures that are strictly comparable from one country to another, but the following list conveys a sense of the range (Hess, 1988; Mény, 1990, 227, 229, 230; Ward, 1978, 161; King, 1991, 40; Weller, 1985):

United States
   White House, 900
   Executive Office, thousands
France
   President, 15–30
   Prime Minister, 100
Germany, 500
Italy, 1,600–1,800
Japan, 30,000
Great Britain, 24–30
Canada, 150
Australia, 400–450
New Zealand, 20–25

One fact immediately stands out. The size of heads of governments' staffs bears little, if any, relationship to the power of each country's office as it has started to emerge in the preceding pages. At one end of the range, the British prime minister and the French president have very few people working for them directly (at most, two or three dozen). At the other, the Japanese and Italian prime ministers have enormous staffs (or at least what are described as staffs in the sources). Heads of government who have substantial power resources in other respects appear not to need large staffs, while less powerful heads of government may seek to make up in staff for what they lack in real political clout. Mény observes of Italy (1990, 227): "It would appear that . . . the increasing size of these [prime ministerial] staffs is an institutional and structural reaction to the constraints of a system that is diffuse, fragmented and multipolar." The staff size hypothesis, in other words, may (or may not) be true of heads of government over time in any one system, but it is not at all a good predictor of the potential power of heads of government across systems.[12]

It goes without saying that this list of ten potential sources of power could be added to. Some systems of government, for example, are more collegial in their culture than others, with an emphasis on consultation and consensus building (even apart from any formal requirements that people be consulted and a consensus built). The hypothesis that might seem to follow would read: The head of government will probably, other things being equal, be more powerful within his system of government, if he is *not* required to obey, or at least accommodate himself to, a cultural "norm of collegiality." Another factor that would be worth taking into account in any more extensive comparative analysis would be the head of government's control (or, more commonly, lack of it) over his country's central banking institutions and the function of its monetary system. The list could be further extended, but the ten factors listed would certainly seem to be among the main ones.

The Power of the Head of Government

It is time to draw together the threads of this part of the argument. This chapter's focus is on the amount of power—or influence or strength (to repeat, the precise vocabulary does not matter)—that the head of government can exercise within his or her own governmental system. Specifically, it is on the substantially differing amounts of potential power that seem to be available to the heads of government in different democratic countries. The power referred to here is the power that the head of government possesses simply by virtue of being the possessor of the office, not power that may (or may not) arise out of the individual's personal attributes or current political situation. It hardly needs to be said that, within the boundaries of a single country, one head of government may be more powerful than another and the same head of government may be more powerful during some periods of his or her tenure of office than during others. Thatcher in Britain was more powerful than Sir Alec Douglas-Home in Britain; and Thatcher, as we saw earlier, was more powerful at some stages of her prime ministerial career than at others.

Unfortunately, no standard or precise metric is available for comparing the power of heads of government within their national political systems, and the absence, already referred to, of studies of the headships of government in countries apart from the United States is a considerable handicap. Nevertheless, a very rough rank ordering of our comparator countries does suggest itself. To those who would wield power within a single country's governmental institutions, some jobs are undoubtedly more desirable than others.

At the top of the batting order should probably come the president of France, at least when his grouping of parties has a majority in the National Assembly. The French president does not have a wide range of formal powers, but de Gaulle and his successors succeeded in making full use of the powers that are implied in the constitution, and France's informal, unwritten constitution is now highly presidential in orientation. The French president is directly elected, he has a high degree of security of tenure (his term lasts seven years), he is normally the leader of the majority party, he controls the legislature, he appoints the prime minister (who is normally, in effect, his deputy), he has a large influence in other ministerial appointments, he determines the structure of the government, he has as much influence over the civil service as he needs, and he has no need of a large staff. The president of France is not all-powerful; he has the same problems—and headaches—as the head of government in any liberal democratic country. Nevertheless, it is hard to quarrel with Suleiman's conclusion (1980, 103) that "the president of France is, in many respects, the most powerful executive in the western world."

Not far behind the French president would probably have to come the German chancellor and the British prime minister ("the power of the prime minister within the British state, if he or she chooses to exercise it, is immense" [King, 1991, 43]), followed at a little distance by the other three Westminster-model prime ministers, those of Canada, Australia, and New Zealand. The German chancellor's power is restricted chiefly by his need to work with his party's coalition partners. The British prime minister is, sometimes to a lesser extent, restricted by the norms of "cabinet government" in Britain. The Canadian, Australian, and New Zealand prime ministers are constrained by the norms of cabinet government operating in those three countries and also by the various specific factors mentioned above (including, in Canada and Australia, the impact of federalism on the national government).

At the bottom of the list should clearly come the prime ministers—or, more precisely, the prime ministerships—of Italy and Japan. For the reasons already given, both offices give their holders only very limited leverage on either the policies or the personnel of the governments of which they are nominally the head. All the advantages that a French president has, they lack. They have little formal constitutional power, they have no Gaullist history behind them, they are not directly elected, they have minimal security of tenure, they are not the leaders of political parties that are both large and cohesive, they have little control over the legislative process, they are constrained in making ministerial appointments, they have little control over either the structure of government or the civil service, and they are desperately in need of large staffs. From time to time, an individual Italian or Japanese prime minister, because of who he is or because of a favorable concatenation of political circumstances, will succeed in making a mark, but most Italian and Japanese prime ministers, compared with the other heads of government we have been considering, appear to be but ciphers.

If this rank ordering is roughly correct, which of the ten factors listed above are most important in contributing to the power of heads of government and at the same time in accounting for the disparities in the power of different heads of government? Suppose one had a dependent variable in the form of precise (or even not very precise) measurements of the power of different heads of government within their own countries. Which of the above independent variables, or combinations of independent variables, would best explain the observed variation?

This question is impossible to answer in the present context. It may be impossible to answer with any satisfactory precision in any context. The various national settings are too diverse; the number of political systems available for comparative study is too small (though not as small as in this chapter). A Kiplingesque approach is probably the best we can reasonably hope for. That said, however, and before we turn to the U.S. presidency, a number of points should be emerging from our analysis. It seems that formal constitutional "powers" matter less than a headship of government's total constitutional setting. It seems unlikely that direct election, in and of itself, is very important. Lack of security of tenure is probably more an indicator of the weakness of an office than a cause of it. The size of a head of government's staff appears to be neither an indicator nor a cause of head-of-government strength (at least across different countries). Having personal control over the structure of government does appear to be useful—but probably not very. High personal prestige provides the greatest benefits when others in the system are politically dependent on the individual whose prestige is high.

But the most important variables are almost certainly those having to do with party leadership and control of the national legislature, on the one hand, and control of appointments, to both ministerial offices and senior civil service posts, on the other. The head of government who is the effective leader of a strong, cohesive party is likely to be a powerful head of government, especially if that party has an overall majority or an otherwise dominant position in the legislature. Likewise, the head of government who can make or break the careers of both other politicians and senior civil servants is likely to be extremely powerful. Moreover, these two sets of factors—effective party leadership and the control of appointments—frequently (though not invariably) go together, the latter both stemming from and reinforcing the former. The French president or British prime minister, who typically control the party or formation having a majority in the national legislature and who also have wide and effective patronage powers, are not only more powerful within their systems than the heads of government of many other countries; they have little need, most of the time, of formal constitutional "powers", direct election, and control of the structure of government. Conversely, heads of government lacking control of party and appointments are likely to be heads of government only in name. Comparative research, while not neglecting any of the other factors, would do well to focus on these.[13]

The United State Presidency Compared

Against that background, we can now return to our checklist of ten factors and consider the U.S. presidency. How does the U.S. presidency compare as a headship of government with those in our eight comparator countries? We can consider the presidency in terms of each factor discussed.

TERMS OF THE CONSTITUTION

The powers of the American president on paper are very considerable—and they are his alone, not ones that he has to share with either a "cabinet" (which is not mentioned in the U.S. Constitution) or with a "government" (which is not mentioned either):

The executive power shall be vested in a president of the United States of America. . . . The president shall be Commander in Chief of the Army and Navy of the United States. . . . He shall have the power, by and with the advice and consent of the Senate, to make treaties, provided two-thirds of the senators present concur; and he shall nominate, and by and with the advice and consent of the Senate, shall appoint ambassadors, other public ministers and consuls, judges of the Supreme Court, and all other officers of the United States, whose appointments are not herein otherwise provided for and which shall be established by the law.

The only check on presidential power that is not to be found in any of our other countries is the limitation on the executive branch's power to make treaties and to appoint ambassadors, judges, and heads of executive departments ("other officers of the United States") without the agreement of one branch of the legislature. In none of the other eight countries are the executive's prerogatives circumscribed in this way.

Against that, the U.S. Constitution gives the American president an additional formal power that has no direct analog in any of our comparator countries: the power of veto over legislation passed by Congress. Only in France are there anything approaching similar devices. The French president may require the French parliament to reconsider laws it has passed. More important, Article 47 of the French constitution gives the government power to impose a national budget if parliament has been unable to agree on one within a specified time, and Article 49 gives the prime minister the power to impose the text of a bill unless the National Assembly, by an absolute majority of all its members, acts to censure the government (in effect, to oust it). The U.S. president's veto power, however, needs to be seen for what it is: a device for giving the president some additional leverage on an independent and often recalcitrant Congress. A large proportion of European and Westminster-model heads of government have no need of a veto power since the chances of the legislature presenting them with legislation that is unwelcome to them approach zero.

DIRECT ELECTION BY THE PEOPLE

The president of the United States is, for all practical purposes, directly elected. How much extra political influence this circumstance by itself gives the president is open to argument. It almost certainly gives him some. If a presidential election were thrown into the Electoral College, and if the Electoral College chose someone who was widely thought not to be someone whom the people themselves would have chosen, then the influence of the president within the system would probably be considerably diminished.

SECURITY OF TENURE

The U.S. president enjoys a high degree of security of tenure. He resembles the French president in this respect more than he resembles any of the other heads of government. Death apart, an American president can be removed from office only via impeachment or by failing to be reelected at the end of his first term. He need have no worries about parliamentary votes of no confidence or about being displaced by the leader of some hostile coalition of parties or factions. He has no need therefore to be constantly looking over his shoulder and making compromises in order to secure his position.

On the other hand, the U.S. president is unique among the heads of government in the countries being considered here in being limited to two four-year terms (a provision that, if operational in Britain, would have forced Margaret Thatcher from office as early as 1987). The two-term limit means that a second-term president is bound to lose some degree of influence toward the end of his second term. The only advantage to a president in knowing in advance that he cannot run for reelection may be that it gives him a degree of freedom to speak and act against the immediate wishes of the majority of voters. The Twenty-second Amendment imposes one constraint on a second-term president (he cannot run for reelection), but at the same time it frees him from another (the need to court electoral popularity in the course of so running). Neither Dwight Eisenhower nor Ronald Reagan, the only two-term presidents to have served since the ratification of the Twenty-second Amendment, chose to devote all or part of their second term to becoming "the teacher of the nation," but a future president might want to.

EFFECTIVE LEADER OF POLITICAL PARTY

As is well known, modern U.S. presidents do not benefit from being the acknowledged leaders of large, cohesive parties. To be sure, the Democratic and Republican parties are large (in so far as they exist as organizations), but the incumbent president is not the acknowledged leader of one of them, except in the most nominal sense, and America's parties are anything but cohesive. America is said to have a two-party system, but, as it actually operates, America's party system resembles the multipartism and hyperfactionalism of the Italian system much more than it resembles the two-party politics of Great Britain or even the two-bloc politics of France or Germany. Indeed, with regard to the United States it is probably too strong to speak even of factions. In the United States almost every politician is his or her own one-person faction.

In countries like France, Germany, and Great Britain, the fates of individual politicians and of whole governments are linked with one another and also with the parties. In the United States, thanks to the separation of powers and the increasing "separation of elections," these links do not hold. The principal consequence is that the U.S. president, unlike the French president, the German chancellor, or the British prime minister, cannot ask other politicians to accede to his will simply by virtue of the fact that he is their party leader; or, rather, the president can ask—but only very rarely, such as in the year immediately following Reagan's first election in 1980, is he likely to elicit a positive response.

CONTROL OF OR INFLUENCE WITHIN THE LEGISLATURE

Because of the separation of powers and because of the weakness of the parties, the president of the United States is only rarely (Roosevelt in the early 1930s, Johnson in 1963–1964, Reagan in 1981) America's "Chief Legislator" (Rossiter, 1960, 28). Most of the time America does not have a chief legislator. A recent book tends to emphasize the president's capacity to influence congressional action, but the author does not deny that

> presidents from Eisenhower to Reagan had trouble winning approval of the more controversial aspects of their legislative programs. A majority of these tough issues were decided by the most publicly confrontational forms of congressional action, and barely half were finally enacted with or without amendment. Only 40% of the most innovative presidential initiatives (those involving large and new departures in government activity) were passed. (Peterson 1990, 271)

The contrast with most of our eight comparator countries is stark. In France, Germany, Britain, and most of the Westminster-model countries, it is quite unusual for the head of government and the government as a whole to be defeated in the course of trying to introduce legislation. This is partly because governments in such countries, if they know they may be defeated, tend not to introduce the legislation in the first place; but it is principally because they can normally count on the disciplined loyalty of their parliamentary followers. Compared with them, the U.S. president is in a very weak position indeed.[14]

CONTROL OF APPOINTMENTS

The president does effectively control the American equivalents of ministerial appointments. He himself makes all the nominations, and the Senate seldom rejects them. The number of such nominations and appointments is, moreover, very large. Other heads of government might well envy the U.S. president his ability to fill many hundreds of patronage posts. At the same time, the uses to which American presidents put their power of appointment appear to be very similar to the uses that their opposite numbers make of theirs in the other countries: to impress voters and foreign governments, to ensure political loyalty and ideological conformity throughout their administrations, and to achieve at least some minimal degree of competence in the conduct of administration.

Compared with the heads of government in most parliamentary systems, the American president has the additional advantage that he can appoint to his administration people from any walk of life, politicians and nonpoliticians alike. What is less clear about the U.S. president's position, compared with that of his opposite numbers in other countries, has to do with the "demand," as distinct from the "supply," side of the appointments equation. Clearly the advantages that a president gains from his appointments power will be increased if large numbers of people want jobs in his administration and if, further, large numbers of those people want to stay in the administration and to be promoted within it, so that they become and remain loyal executors of the president's will.

Are there people in the White House "weeping and even fainting" in pursuit of office? No one seems to have studied this aspect of the president's appointments power in any detail, but anecdotal evidence suggests that, after a president's first year or two, enthusiasm for join-ing his administration tends to wane and that what begins as a power on his part ends up by being more of a duty. Career politicians do not normally seek appointments in the federal administration; others are likely to be deterred by the better pay and career prospects in other walks of life. Still, the differences in this connection between a U.S. president and other heads of government are probably not very great.

STRUCTURE OF THE EXECUTIVE BRANCH

In contrast to many other heads of government, the U.S. president has little control over the structure as distinct from the personnel of the executive branch. Whereas most other heads of government merely have to will the creation of new executive agencies and the dis-mantling of old, the president of the United States, in almost all in-stances, is forced to seek the agreement of Congress. Discussions in the United States, such as those during the Nixon and Carter admin-istrations, about the amount of power that the president ought to be given to reorganize the executive branch tend to obscure the fact that, compared with other heads of government, the U.S. president does not begin to be master of the design of his own house. The most am-bitious reorganization proposals in the United States would still leave the president in a far feebler position than, say, the German chancel-lor or British prime minister.

CONTROL OF THE CIVIL SERVICE

Most heads of government have little direct control over their country's career civil service. The U.S. president is no exception. The president's control over the U.S. civil service (and indeed his control over the heads of many executive branch agencies) is, in addition, fur-ther limited by the fact that executive branch departments and agen-cies in the United States, in contradistinction to those in almost all other countries, are forced to acknowledge the authority of two su-perordinate bodies and not just one: Congress and its committees in addition to the president or the cabinet. For most career civil servants in Europe and in Westminster-model systems, the two houses of the national legislature are merely "noises off." For civil servants in the United States, the House of Representatives and the Senate are fre-quently center stage, providers of financial as well as legal authorizations. Civil servants in most countries have only one boss. Civil servants in the United States have two. And of course one of them can always be played off against the other.

PUBLIC PRESTIGE

The American president, in contrast to the Italian and Japanese prime ministers, clearly moves in a political world where the factor of public prestige is potentially relevant. Who he is is known to almost every American. He, uniquely, is given credit for almost everything that goes right in America; he, uniquely, is blamed for almost everything that goes wrong. No American president can retreat into decent obscurity. Many scholars have testified to the importance of the halo effect of presidential popularity. The instrumental effect, however, is attenuated by the limited extent to which members of the president's party believe that they either benefit from the president's popularity or suffer from his lack of it. Neither coattails nor reverse coattails are as politically important in the United States as both of them are in a system like the German or the British in which the political fates of the head of government, the government as a whole, and the head of government's party in the legislature are all manifestly bound up together.

An American congressman or senator is quite pleased if a president of his party is well regarded by the American people and is likewise quite displeased if he is not; he identifies both himself and his electoral fortunes with the president. But the American politician's strength of feeling is as nothing compared with that of a British member of Parliament or a member of the German Bundestag. In a system of party government, the head of government's public prestige is much more likely than in the United States to be a matter of political life and death for those on whom he is dependent and who in turn depend on him.

STAFF SIZE

Little further need be added about the factor of presidential staffing. The president of the United States has an enormous staff (however the term *staff* is defined); each year he and his people take up several pages of the *United States Government Manual*. And there is no doubt that the president's influence within the American system of government is greater because he possesses a large staff than it would be if he did not possess one; but equally, as we have seen, there is no doubt that the president's large staff, by itself, does not make the U.S. president more powerful within the American system of government than another head of government who does not have such a large staff is within his. On the contrary, an observer of the American system is tempted to say, as Mény says of Italy (1990, 227): "It would appear that . . . the increasing size of these staffs is [primarily] an institutional and structural reaction to the constraints of a system that is diffuse, fragmented and multipolar." Hundreds of people at work in the White House, the Old Executive Office Building, and elsewhere in Washington may make a U.S. president look good and feel good. What they tell the political scientist about the president's actual power is more problematical.

Conclusion

All ten factors having been considered, we can now go back to the question we asked at the beginning: How does the power (or influence or strength) of the president of the United States within the American system compare with the power (or influence or strength) of other heads of government within their national systems? Or, as we can now pose the question: How does the U.S. president's power compare with that of the heads of government in our eight comparator countries? How does he rate?

Judgments on this matter will inevitably differ, but a reasonable approximation to the truth would be that, in terms of power within his own governmental system, the U.S. president probably belongs in the middle rank of heads of government, possibly toward the bottom of it. On the one hand, his control over the executive branch is probably somewhat greater than that of most heads of government (though not the French president's); on the other, his lack of control over the legislative branch puts him more on a par with the prime minister of Italy than with the prime ministers of Canada or Great Britain. Most recent American presidents have often looked extremely Andreotti-like.

What Suleiman says (1980, 103–04) of the French presidency would also, suitably qualified, appear to be true of at least the German chancellor, the British prime minister, and possibly also the Canadian, Australian, and New Zealand prime ministers:

> His constitutional powers are as important as those of the president of the United States, yet he does not face the same constraints on his power. He does not have to strike bargains for votes at Elysée breakfasts nor does he have to deal with unpredictable majorities in parliament, with legislators whose base of power is separate from that of the president, with parliamentary commissions that question his policies and ask his aides and policy makers to account for their actions, with a committee system that allows deputies to accumulate power to alter a bill beyond recognition if they do not lock it up in a drawer, with a powerful lobby group system (private groups as well as state and local governments) that acts directly on the president or indirectly through their representatives, or finally with the institutional constraints of federalism or of a Supreme Court. If the term "imperial presidency" can be applied with any degree of validity, one might choose to apply it to the president of France rather than to his counterpart in the United States.

One curious implication of Suleiman's remarks is that Ronald Reagan may have been right as president (up to a point) to emphasize his head of state role at the expense of his head of government role. If one is U.S. president, perhaps there is more fulfillment to be had saluting the flag and reviewing troops than trying to pass a budget or reform America's educational system. Perhaps Reagan knew something that Carter, his assiduous predecessor, overlooked.

This conclusion, that the presidency of the United States deserves to be placed in the second or possibly even the third rank among headships of government, may startle, perhaps even shock, some American readers. Americans tend to conflate the power of the president with the power of the country. Some are probably overimpressed with the mere trappings of the presidency (Air Force One, "Hail to the Chief," and the fact that people stand up when a president enters the room) as distinct from its political substance. Occasionally students of the presidency give the impression of thinking that because America is a wonderful country the presidency *ought* to be a wonderful office. But the one, obviously, by no means follows from the other.

In fact, the view that the U.S. presidency is an office of limited powers, with limited potential, ought not to cause consternation. It is what the Founding Fathers had in mind; they meant the office to be checked and balanced by powerful forces elsewhere in the system. And many scholars of the presidency have likewise been seized by the extent to which policy-oriented or action-oriented presidents were bound to be frustrated. Neustadt wrote his classic *Presidential Power* out of a sense of presidents' weakness, not out of a sense of their strength, and Heclo (1981) writes aptly of "the illusion of presidential government." Comparative inquiries like this one will serve a useful purpose if they make the presidency seem a less remote and less regal office. Individual presidents have long since been removed from their pedestals. The presidency itself now deserves to be taken down from its pedestal and examined alongside other exhibits in the political scientist's museum.

Notes

1. On the opportunities offered by the case study method in comparative politics, see Eckstein (1975).

2. There is a strong case for arguing that the term *head of government* applied to the U.S. presidency is itself a misnomer, since the U.S. president does not head a "government" in the European sense and since he is, at most, the head of the executive branch of the American government. The trouble is that there is no really satisfactory alternative. Phrases containing the word *executive* are misleading because they imply an American-style tripartite division of governmental powers. In addition, many heads of government outside the United States cannot really be described with any degree of accuracy as "executives." In the end, *head of government* is probably the least-bad term available.

3. The relationship is, of course, somewhat more complicated than is indicated in the text. The fact that someone is the head of government of a very powerful country may in practice augment the power of the individual in question within his own system. But that such is in fact the case needs to be demonstrated in each instance, not simply inferred. The international dimension of head-of-government leadership in the modern world has been generally neglected. A welcome (and important) exception in Rose (1991).

4. The focus in this chapter, it should be emphasized, is on the power potential of various offices considered as offices; i.e., considered apart from the skills and ambitions of the various individuals who may hold them from time to time. In practice, one person may be a powerful holder of an otherwise "impotent" office while another may be an impotent holder of an otherwise "powerful" office. This chapter's focus is on institutions, not individuals. As it happens, most of the institutions being considered here have changed little in their power relations with other institutions in recent years.

5. In Westminster-model countries the head of the armed forces is nominally the queen or her national representative. The Japanese constitution contains a provision renouncing war as a sovereign right of the nation, and in consequence the document is silent on who is to be the commander in chief of Japan's (con-

stitutionally nonexistent) armed forces. In practice it is clear that responsibility is vested in the prime minister and the cabinet.

6. For some comments on how Margaret Thatcher was able, within limits, to write her own ticket, see King (1991).

7. There is a slight complication that ought to be referred to. In Westminster-model countries and other countries where national elections are linked directly to the formation of governments, the leader of a party that has been victorious in an election has, in a loose sense, been directly elected and might hope to derive some political benefit from that fact. Against that, prime ministers in Westminster-model countries who have come to power between elections, such as John Major in Britain in 1990, do not seem to have had significantly less authority as a consequence.

8. For a brief account of the change to direct election in France, see Machin (1990).

9. On the circumstances of her falling, see, among many other things, Anderson (1991). A French prime minister under a strong president similarly cannot count on security of tenure. De Gaulle fired Michel Debré, Pompidou fired Jacques Chaban-Delmas in 1972, Mitterand fired Pierre Mauroy in 1984 and Michel Rocard in 1991. In the text, the distinction is alluded to between security of tenure and longevity or duration in office, and this distinction perhaps needs to be emphasized. Someone who lacked security of tenure could nevertheless remain in office for a very long time if he kept his head down, was ready to accede to the wishes of powerful others, and in general went out of his way to keep out of trouble. Long-serving prime ministers in a number of European countries fall into this category.

10. The new arrangement in the British Labour party has attracted almost no attention, even in Britain. For a brief discussion, see King (1991, 31–32).

11. On the "Cencelli handbook," which sets out the mathematical formula referred to in the text, see Mény (1990, 211).

12. This is not the place to explore in detail the subtle relationships between staffing and the actual or potential power of heads of government, but it is worth noting that, within any one system, the relationship could be a curvilinear one, with increased staffing being useful to a head of government up to a point but, beyond that point, becoming a positive hindrance. Iran-contra in the United States comes to mind; so does Margaret Thatcher's (almost certainly wise) insistence on keeping her staff small (King, 1991, 41–52).

13. The reader should not infer from any of the above that the present author is in any way advocating strong headships of government or equating good government with strong executive leadership. On the contrary, systems in which a number of different and mutually independent power holders have to bargain with one another and engage in mutual persuasion may in the long run produce better and more stable policy outcomes, and such systems may also be conducive to greater social stability. As the authors of *The Federalist Papers* recognized long ago, the balance of the argument is a fine one.

14. The references in the text are to recent U.S. experience, but, as is well known, the cohesion of American parties and the character of the relations between the president and Congress have been among the great variables of American political history. Someone writing on party leadership and the president's relations with Congress during much of the nineteenth century would have had a very different story to tell.

References

Anderson, Bruce. 1991. *John Major: The Making of the Prime Minister.* London: Fourth Estate.

Dalton, Hugh. 1953. *Call Back Yesterday: Memoirs 1887–1931.* London: Frederick Muller.

Eckstein, Harry. 1975. "Case Study and Theory in Political Science." In *Handbook of Political Science: Strategies of Inquiry,* ed. Fred I. Greenstein and Nelson W. Polsby. Reading, Mass.: Addison-Wesley.

Elgie, Robert, and Howard Machin. 1991. "France: The Limits to Prime Ministerial Government in a Semi-presidential System." In *West European Prime Ministers,* ed. G. W. Jones. London: Frank Cass.

Heclo, Hugh. 1981. "Introduction: The Presidential Illusion." In *The Illusion of Presidential Government,* ed. Hugh Heclo and Lester M. Salamon. Boulder, Colo.: Westview.

Hess, Stephen. 1988. *Organizing the Presidency.* 2d ed. Washington, D.C.: Brookings.

Hine, David, and Renato Finocchi. 1991. "The Italian Prime Minister." In *West European Prime Ministers,* ed. G. W. Jones. London: Frank Cass.

Jones, G. W., ed. 1991. *West European Prime Ministers.* London: Frank Cass.

King, Anthony. 1985. "Margaret Thatcher: The Style of a Prime Minister." In *The British Prime Minister,* ed. Anthony King. London: Macmillan.

———. 1991. "The British Prime Minister in the Age of the Career Politician." In *West European Prime Ministers,* ed. G. W. Jones. London: Frank Cass.

Machin, Howard. 1990. "Political Leadership." In *Developments in French Politics,* ed. Peter A. Hall, Jack Hayward, and Howard Machin. London: Macmillan.

Mény, Yves. 1990. *Government and Politics in Western Europe: Britain, France, Italy, West Germany.* Oxford: Oxford University Press.

Neustadt, Richard E. 1990. *Presidential Power and the Modern Presidents: The Politics of Leadership from Roosevelt to Reagan.* New York: Free Press.

Peterson, Mark A. 1990. *Legislating Together: The White House and Capitol Hill from Eisenhower to Reagan.* Cambridge, Mass.: Harvard University Press.

Richardson, Bradley M., and Scott C. Flanagan. 1984. *Politics in Japan.* Boston, Mass.: Little, Brown.

Rose, Richard. 1974. *The Problem of Party Government.* London: Macmillan.

———. 1991. *The Postmodern President: George Bush Meets the World.* Chatham, N.J.: Chatham House.

Rossiter, Clinton. 1960. *The American Presidency.* 2d ed. New York: Harper and Row.

Royal Institute of Public Administration. 1987. *Top Jobs in Whitehall: Appointments and Promotions in the Senior Civil Service.* London: Royal Institute of Public Administration.

Suleiman, Ezra. 1980. "Presidential Government in France." In *Presidents and Prime Ministers,* ed. Richard Rose and Ezra Suleiman. Washington, D.C.: American Enterprise Institute.

Ward, Robert E. 1978. *Japan's Political System.* 2d ed. Englewood Cliffs, N.J.: Prentice Hall.

Weller, Patrick. 1985. *First Among Equals: Prime Ministers in Westminster Systems.* Sydney, Australia: Allen and Unwin.

Evaluating Presidents

RICHARD ROSE

THE ROOT of the term *evaluation* is the idea of the intrinsic worth of something; intrinsic values cannot be reduced to a quantitative measure such as money. Evaluation involves normative judgments about what ought to be. As Neustadt (1960, 1) notes at the start of his classic study, "In the United States we like to rate a President. We measure him as 'weak' or 'strong' and call what we are measuring his 'leadership.'" The values underlying judgments of presidents as "weak" or "strong" or "good" are contestable (cf. Rockman, 1984, 11).

In the literature of the presidency, the normative dimension of evaluation is sometimes explicit; for example, Richard Nixon is frequently described as a "bad" president. Often, the normative dimension of an evaluation is almost explicit. For example, Franklin Roosevelt is described as a "great" president, a classification that is preferable to being undistinguished, and Dwight Eisenhower and John Kennedy are described as "popular," and popularity is preferable to unpopularity. Evaluating a president's performance by success in achieving campaign promises or legislation in Congress has a normative dimension, for doing so implies that the country is better off if the president of the moment achieves what he proposes. The examples emphasize that a normative element can be found in both quantitative and nonquantitative evaluations of the presidency.

Politics is concerned with values. In Easton's well-known definition, politics is about "the authoritative allocation of values for a society" (1965, 50). Much political activity is about the articulation and resolution of value conflicts. As a politician, the president is inevitably concerned with questions of fact and value; the two are intertwined, and their interpretation is contestable, between the White

House and other actors in the political system and within the White House itself. Contemporary political scientists, especially scholars of the presidency, also address issues where questions of fact and value are intertwined. A political scientist may respond by making statements of an if/then type, such as: If a president wants to do *A*, then he or she should do *X*. Or, the marshaling of evidence can be pursued until it leads to the point at which, as Edwards (1990, 39) notes, we "arrive at the point where our values dominate our conclusions."

The following pages demonstrate the importance of recognizing that evaluations of a political institution as important as the presidency cannot be value-free (cf. Weber, 1948). Recognizing this can expand our understanding of the office. The first section shows how conceptualizing the presidency implies evaluations of what is and is not important in situating the White House among institutions in time and space. The next two sections illustrate the normative implications of empirical data about public opinion and the empirical implications of perceiving presidential policy making as if the president were the only independent variable in the policy processes. As election campaigns demonstrate, presidents can be evaluated by conflicting criteria. Hence, the concluding section of this chapter outlines a *two-party* standard for evaluating presidents.

Clarifying the Concept of the Presidency

Clarity in defining concepts is necessary for a social science evaluation. But because the presidency is a familiar subject, many authors assume that the subject defines itself: presidents are the men who have held the office stipulated by the United States Constitution. The literature often uses a vocabulary that is ideographic. Words refer to specific institutional attributes of the White House, to a particular president, or to events or problems only meaningful within the term of a particular president. This is perfectly acceptable as history, and most people inside the Beltway think in terms of such specifics. But this is not social science, for the result is a set of "incomparable" statements that cannot reliably or validly be generalized.

Before we can evaluate presidents, we need to stipulate what we are looking for: is the object of analysis individual presidents or the presidency as an institution of government, or is it something less formal, such as political leadership? Without stipulating terms, we have only value-laden judgments, data sets of uncertain use as indicators, or journalistic descriptions that attempt "pure empiricism," which is, as Oakeshott notes (1951), "merely impossible." A social science definition requires concepts that can be applied generically. The minimum test is that terms used can be applied to more than one president with reliable results. But this minimum is insufficient to establish a concept as a scientific term. For this to be the case, it must have "legs," that is, it must be capable of application in more than one time and place. Scientific generalizations, as distinct from inductive observations, should not be limited to a single office in a single place.

Evaluation involves a double use of comparison. A president may be compared with an absolute abstract standard—for example, how high his opinion poll rating is on a scale that reaches to one hundred. Alternatively, a president may be evaluated by comparison with other national leaders across time, comparing his popularity with that of past presidents, or across space, comparing his putative power with that of leaders of other countries. Evaluation thus requires the specification of institutional, historical, and geographical contexts. An individual president may be evaluated differently depending upon whether the institutional focus is domestic or foreign policy making. Comparing a president with immediate predecessors covers a very brief time span; evaluating a president against all other incumbents of the office covers centuries. The geographical scope for evaluation is potentially vast, for a president can be set against leaders of other democratic systems, dictators, or leaders of nations perceived as enemies.

The institution of *leadership* is an example of a term frequently used in evaluating presidents without the user defining its meaning or specifying its context. If we think of presidential leadership in institutional terms, then this can differ depending upon the policy context, for a president does not seek to give a lead in everything that government does. Cronin's (1980, 276ff.) distinction between the inner and the outer cabinet delineates areas of executive branch policy of persisting concern to presidents, such as national security and economic issues, and those in which the White House is not interested, such as the departments of Health and Human Services, Housing and Urban Development, and Labor. The White House is even less concerned with giving a lead to bureau chiefs in operational control of specific programs. Kaufman (1981, 59) reports: "The extent of direct relations between the bureau chiefs and the cluster of presidential organizations, even for bureau chiefs who were presidential appointees, was modest."

Within areas of policy attracting White House attention, a distinction can be made between the institutions of the domestic presidency and the defense and foreign policy presidency. As commander in chief of the armed forces and spokesman for the United States in negotiations with other nations, the president is said to enjoy much greater authority than as a supplicant of congressional votes on matters of domestic legislation. Comparing evidence from congressional action on presidential proposals in the postwar era shows that the difference in congressional support on domestic and international issues is minimal (cf. Wildavsky, 1975; Edwards, 1989, chap. 4). But this leaves open the importance of international actions that the president can take without explicit authorization by Congress (cf. Nathan and Oliver, 1987; Mann, 1990; Koh, 1990).

The presidency is not the only position of leadership within the American political system. Governors and mayors hold elective leadership posts in state and local government. Insofar as presidential leadership is about exercising influence within government, then it should in principle be possible to evaluate behavior at all three levels of government. The greatest limitation upon generalizing from lower tiers of government to Washington does not concern institutions but policy. The chief policy concerns of a president, national security and macroeconomic policy, are not the responsibility of governors or mayors.

Within U.S. society, leadership is a phenomenon found in many institutions. Insofar as presidential scholars are concerned with leadership as a generic phenomenon, they could test hypotheses about the White House with reference to the leadership of chief executive officers of corporations, trade union officials, military commanders, church bishops, university presidents, or in small groups of any kind, as social psychologists do. A study by Cohen and March, *Leadership and Ambiguity* (1974), often cited as relevant to Washington because it invented the "garbage can model" of decision making was, in fact, based upon research about university presidents.

Presidential scholars are more inclined to evaluate leadership by comparing presidents at different points in time rather than comparing leadership in the White House and in other institutions. Historians can examine all presidents from George Washington to George Bush, assuming that there is an "essential," albeit unspecified, unity that makes it possible to apply the same criteria of evaluaton to the 1790s, the 1890s, and the 1990s (cf. Murray and Blessing, 1988). There are also attempts to define recurring cycles of behavior found in presidents as distant in time as James Polk and John Kennedy (see, e.g., Skowronek, 1990).

The further back in time that comparisons are extended, the more dubious is the underlying assumption that nothing has essentially changed over the centuries. Dodd (1991) argues that by its very nature the historical process creates qualitative change; it is therefore misleading to assume that generalizations apply for all time. Dodd recommends thinking in terms of the "transformational" analysis of circumstances in which the office of the presidency is fundamentally altered. Lyndon Johnson or Ronald Reagan cannot be evaluated by the same criteria that would be applied to Calvin Coolidge or Rutherford Hayes.

To speak of transformation between past and present is not to deny connections but to emphasize the significance of differences. The idea of the modern presidency, starting under Franklin Roosevelt in the 1930s, is a significant example of a concept that is inherently time-bound (Greenstein, 1988). The modern presidency, which initially concerned only domestic policy, became internationalized in the 1940s. Changes in America and in the world of which it is a part in the past half century raise the possibility of another transformation, of the terms in which we think of a postmodern presidency (Rose, 1991a). If, in effect, the past is another country, then it follows that the American presidency today may be evaluated more appropriately by comparison with political leaders in foreign countries than with presidents from America's distant past. The president's problem of giving direction to government is, after all, a common problem of every society, modern and premodern, democratic and nondemocratic (see, e.g., Bunce, 1981).

A striking feature of the presidency as an institution is that it is more often found in Third World than in First World countries. An international review by Riggs (1988, 249; see also Linz, 1990; Mezey, 1991) concludes: "Almost universally, Presidential polities have endured disruptive catastrophes, usually in the form of one or more coups d'état, whereby conspiratorial groups of military officers seize power, suspend the constitution, displace elected officials, impose martial law and promote authoritarian rule. . . . No country following a presidentialist model has been able to avoid at least one such disruptive experience." A comparative evaluation makes the American presidency appear a deviant case, because it is both democratic and stable. It also invites scholars to explain why this should be so. Riggs seeks to identify paraconstitutional features making the American presidency different.

Among democratic systems, the Fifth French Republic offers an obvious yet surprisingly neglected office for comparative evaluation. It has a president elected by popular vote through a two-ballot runoff system that is not unfamiliar in the United States, and personality is important as well as party. France differs in also having a prime minister appointed by the president to deal with a separately elected National Assembly. "Cohabitation," that is, the presidency and the National Assembly being in the hands of different parties, has a parallel in Washington. There is sufficient similarity between Paris and Washington for evaluating the office cross-nationally (Pierce, 1991).

Cross-national comparison offers an empirically grounded basis for evaluating the American Presidency as one among a class of leadership offices (see, e.g., Rose, 1980; Rockman, 1984). In most democratic systems the chief political leader is a prime minister accountable to Parliament. If one wants to evaluate political leadership on the basis of a large number of cases, the universe of parliamentary democracies covers more than twenty countries which differ in significant ways in the institutions of leadership and hundreds of prime ministers (Rose, 1991b). For example, in recruiting leaders parliamentary systems usually emphasize leaders learning first how to govern, whereas the American system tends to emphasize learning how to campaign (Rose, 1991a; chap. 6). To argue that it doesn't make sense to compare what happens in the White House with what happens in comparable offices in Bonn or in Copenhagen implies that the critical feature of the presidency is not the institution but the fact that it is American.

The fundamental point about evaluating the presidency is not whether the focus is narrow or broad, or the method quantitative, nonquantitative, or based upon explicitly or implicitly normative assumptions. The sine qua non for a social science evaluation of the presidency is clarity about concepts and context. (Rose, 1991c).

Public Opinion: Normative Implications
of Empirical Data

The analysis of presidential popularity normally focuses upon two types of quantitative evidence—election results and public opinion polls. Both are quantified, thus meeting the basic criterion of "hard-nosed" empiricism. However, the evaluation of such data has normative implications, whether the data examined consist of facts as hard as election results, public opinion poll data, or the outcome of periods of divided government.

EVALUATING ELECTION RESULTS

By definition, representative democracy requires free elections, but electoral institutions can take many forms, and empirical results may not necessarily fit with explicit or implicit assumptions about what is a "good" system or a "fair" outcome. Consider the following *factual* propositions:

1. The president is not always popularly elected. Three of the nine postwar presidents—Truman, Johnson, and Ford—succeeded to the office from the vice presidency, holding office by succession, not election, for a total of seven years.

2. The president often lacks endorsement by half the voters, and losers are normally endorsed by at least three in seven voters. In three of eleven elections since 1948, the president did not win half the vote, and the winner took 50.1 percent and 50.7 percent in 1976 and 1980 respectively. In the postwar era, the winning candidate for president has averaged only 53 percent of the popular vote.

3. The president never gains office with the votes of half the adult electorate. Given an average turnout of 58 percent in postwar presidential elections, the vote of the victor, on average, constitutes 31 percent of the total electorate.

The interpretation of each of these facts reflects normative values, and an unfavorable evaluation leads to proposals for reform. Writings on turnout and voter registration are full of controversy among academics about whether turnout is high enough or registration in America (which follows nineteenth-century English, not contemporary English or European, practice) is satisfactory (cf. Wolfinger and Rosenstone, 1980; Piven and Cloward, 1988, 1989, 1990; Bennett,

1990; Gans, 1990). The practice of presidential primaries has been attacked and altered substantially in recent decades and continues to attract proposals for reform. To argue that a reform is unlikely to be adopted may be correct as prediction, but this is not to be confused with evaluating the status quo as desirable.

EVALUATING PUBLIC OPINION: HOW POPULAR SHOULD A PRESIDENT BE?

Public opinion polls provide a plentiful amount of empirical data for evaluating postwar presidents (see, e.g., Edwards with Gallup, 1990). The standard Gallup Poll question is: Do you approve or disapprove of the way in which ——— is handling his job as president? The approval ratings of presidents fluctuate within their term of office and differ when compared (see table 16). From a statistical perspective, variation is welcome, providing a clear analytic task: to explain the causes of variations in approval. However, a statistical explanation begs the evaluative question: How much approval should a president have?

One standard of evaluation is that a president elected by a majority of voters should maintain this level of approval throughout his term of office. In principle, this is a standard that every president could attain. In practice, seven of the eight postwar White House incumbents fail to meet this standard. During their term of office, most office-

TABLE 16
Peaks and Troughs in the Popularity of Presidents

President	Gallup Poll			Historians' Rankings out of 36
	Average	High	Low	
John F. Kennedy, 1961–1963	71	83	56	13 Average +
Dwight D. Eisenhower, 1953–1960	65	79	48	11 Average +
Lyndon B. Johnson, 1963–1968	56	80	35	10 Average +
Ronald Reagan, 1981–1988	52	68	35	[a]
Richard Nixon, 1969–1974	49	67	24	34 Failure
Gerald Ford, 1974–1976	47	71	37	24 Average
Jimmy Carter, 1977–1980	46	75	21	25 Average
Harry Truman, 1945–1952	43	87	23	8 Near great
Average	53	76	35	[a]

Source: Gallup Poll, Princeton, N.J.; Murray and Blessing, (1988), 16f.).
[a]Not available.

holders have been, momentarily at least, minority presidents in terms of public approval. At the trough of their presidency, Carter, Truman, and Nixon were approved by less than one-quarter. The low point of postwar incumbents of the White House has averaged 35 percent. Only John Kennedy always held the approval of half the electorate during his truncated term of office.

An alternative standard is that a president's approval rating should, over his term of office, average endorsement by a majority of voters. Averaging peaks and troughs in monthly ratings and transitional periods raises to four the number of presidents who could, on this basis, be classified as successful. Yet four presidents—Nixon, Ford, Carter, and Truman—were, on average, endorsed by less than half the electorate interviewed by the Gallup poll.

Public opinion poll data by itself is insufficient for evaluation. King and Alston (1991, 254ff., 274ff.) argue that a concern with a good public opinion rating is actually harmful to American government because "the politics of high exposures" inclines the White House to "the avoidance of tough decisions" on such issues as the deficit, drugs, and the underclass. The only way in which poll data can justify a president's actions is by the tautological criterion that whatever is popular is right. Such a proposition is not only logically deficient but also politically contestable; for example, normative evaluations of the Vietnam War or the Korean War are not derivable from public opinion poll data (cf. Mueller, 1973).

More complex political and analytic issues arise if short-term popularity is compared with the judgment of history. Doing what is popular in the short term is not necessarily doing what historians will retrospectively judge to be right. A perennial issue facing every president is: How much popular approval should he risk, if only in the short term, in order to do what he believes is right in the longer term? The debate about the budget deficit is a familiar example of such a conflict. There is a widespread perception inside the Beltway that voting to raise taxes or cut public expenditure is immediately unpopular but maintaining a high federal deficit will be harmful to the economy in the longer run. While it is possible to identify the short-term calculations that lead politicians to make decisions to their perceived short-term advantage, this leaves open whether or not the short-term choices are in the long-term national interest (cf. Stockman, 1986; White and Wildavsky, 1989; Whicker, 1991).

American historians evaluate presidents in a very different time perspective than that used inside the Beltway or in overnight opinion poll evaluations. The Murray-Blessing survey of specialists in American history listed in the AHA's *Guide to Departments of History* (for details, and comparisons with other such surveys, see Murray and Blessing, 1988, chap. 2) is representative of the evaluation of historians. They were asked to rank all presidents, from George Washington through Jimmy Carter, on a six-point scale with positions ranging from *great* through *failure*.

There is no correlation between presidential rankings by American historians and public opinion rankings (see table 16). The one postwar president considered "near great" by historians, Harry Truman, comes at the bottom in contemporaneous public opinion. The president placed highest by opinion polls, John Kennedy, is ranked in the middle by historians. The three presidents grouped together as "average plus" by historians—Kennedy, Eisenhower, and Johnson—differ by fifteen percentage points in their Gallup Poll ratings and even more in the variability of popularity during their term. Richard Nixon, near the middle in poll popularity, is ranked a failure by historians.

EVALUATING DIVIDED GOVERNMENT

A distinctive feature of the Constitution is that it did *not* create a presidential system of government but a system of checks and balances with a separately elected Congress. The separation of powers was contested in the Constitutional Convention, and its evaluation is still contested today. Some political scientists evaluate the system as "too divided," whereas others defend the present situation as satisfactory.

When the White House and Congress are in the hands of different parties, constitutional divisions are reinforced by partisan divisions, producing what is now described as divided government. In the first half of this century, this rarely occurred. From 1901 to 1947, the same party controlled both institutions 87 percent of the time, and this was true for Republican and for Democratic presidents. In each of the three instances in which government was divided, this reflected a midterm election that heralded a change in party control of the

White House at the next presidential election. The period from 1947 to 1969 saw divided government becoming more frequent; it prevailed for eight years under Truman and Eisenhower (for details, see Jones, 1991, 40ff.).

Since 1969, divided government has been the empirical norm, prevailing for twenty of twenty-four years. The Democrats have always held one or both houses of Congress, and the Republicans have won five of six presidential elections. The counterpart to the political inadequacies of the Democrats in fielding a winning candidate for the White House is the difficulty that the Republican party has in winning House seats (cf. Jacobson, 1990). Election results do not provide a clearcut evaluation of divided government, for people do not vote on the composition of Congress as a whole but only for an individual member of Congress. Surveys indicate that the great majority of voters cast ballots along party lines when casting a vote for the president and for a member of Congress. From 1952 through 1964, an average of 86 percent reported that they voted a straight ticket. Since 1968, the proportion has averaged 72 percent (Wattenberg, 1987; 66). More than two-thirds of voters thus appear to support the same party winning control of both Congress and the White House. Divided government is a consequence of ticket splitting by about one-quarter of voters.

When opinion surveys ask whether people think it better for the country to have a president and Congress of the same party or different parties, there is no consensus. In 1981, 47 percent favored a single party in control of both ends of Pennsylvania Avenue, and 34 percent were opposed; in 1989, the balance had tilted in the other direction, 45 percent in favor of divided control and 35 percent supporting single-party control. In both instances, the median respondent was a "don't know" (Jacobson, 1990, 119). Political scientists are also divided about the evaluation of divided government (cf. Thurber, 1991). Single-party government has always had supporters, dating back to Woodrow Wilson's youthful days as a political scientist (for restatements, see, e.g., Schumpeter, 1942; for an empirical critique, see Rose and McAllister, 1992). The core assumption is that control of the executive and legislature by the same party is the best way for voters to hold elected officials accountable. A voter satisfied with how the country is governed can vote to keep the in party in, and a dissatisfied voter can vote to turn the rascals out. By contrast, in a system of divided government, each party can blame the other, and there is no clear method by which a voter can determine whom to hold responsible. A second strand of criticism is that divided government is an obstacle to effective action in Washington, since it is harder to get agreement on legislation and, particularly, for the president to secure support for his proposals (see, e.g., Sundquist, 1988; Mezey, 1991).

A negative evaluation leads critics of divided government to prescribe reforms. One set of reforms is intended to strengthen parties. A second set goes further, proposing changes in the institutions of the federal government designed to reduce friction between Congress and the White House. Sundquist (1986, 12, 16) admits that reform is a speculative gamble, but he argues that the disadvantages of the present situation require the introduction of new institutions (see also Robinson, 1989). The negative evaluation of divided government is challenged on two grounds. One asks a researchable question: What difference does it make to the actions of government if power is divided between the parties? Mayhew's systematic analysis of the postwar enactment of major laws and congressional hearings concludes that whether or not government is divided makes very little difference to these outcomes. Even when control of both branches is nominally in the hands of the same party, "enacting coalitions are hard to assemble even if party control is unified, and awkwardly stitched together compromises can occur anyway" (Mayhew, 1991). The implication is clear: reforms to reduce divisions in government would not make much difference to the way that Washington works (cf. Powell, 1991).

Another approach emphasizes normative arguments about what ought to be studied. Jones (1991b, 53; 1991a, 165) labels the separation of the presidency from the rest of the political system as "co-partisanship" and describes it as "a fact of contemporary political life." Jones argues against evaluating relations between president and Congress in terms of a party responsibility model because "the party responsibility model is of little or no explanatory or predictive value in contemporary politics, for all of the reasons Sundquist identifies." Normative and empirical issues are commingled, as Jones adds: "Comprehending co-partisan government begins with accepting its legitimacy and understanding its dynamics. To do otherwise typically encourages the analyst to propose recommendations for institutional reform" (Jones, 1991b, 63; 1991a, 165f.).

The debate about divided government illustrates the philosophical truism that propositions about what ought to be cannot be derived from propositions about what is. The statement, "Divided government exists" is not the same as the proposition, "Divided government is desirable." Reform politics is based upon dissatisfaction with the status quo. To argue that nobody should be dissatisfied with any feature of the presidency is tantamount to saying that there ought to be no politics in the evaluation of the presidency. Even if the majority of voters and political scientists evaluate favorably the workings of representative institutions in America today, there would still remain a dissatisfied minority.

The assertion that a dissatisfied minority can never become a majority is a speculative statement as incapable of empirical proof as are the future benefits promised by reformers. In the postwar era there have been major reforms in the presidency. The office that Harry Truman entered in 1945 was based upon caucus nomination of presidential candidates, a franchise that excluded blacks and many whites in more than one-fifth of the states, and a Congress in which power was centralized in committees controlled through seniority. This is very different from the system today. To dismiss all prospects of purposeful change (that is, reform) is to violate one of the oldest political maxims: Never say never in politics.

Perceiving Policy: Empirical Implications of Normative Assumptions

The incumbent of the Oval Office must deal with public policies. But the analytic framework within which the president's actions are perceived is not a given, nor is it lacking in normative assumptions. If the president is believed to be of primary importance, then studies are likely to perceive the president as *the* independent variable; his influence is the only influence considered. If the president is perceived as a major but not exclusive influence in the American political system, then studies can include other institutions and politicians inside the Beltway. A common practice of presidential scholars is to concentrate upon policy-relevant activities *within* the Executive Office of the President, for example, the Oval Office of the President, the National Security Council, the Council of Economic Advisers, OMB, and so on.

If the outcome of the policy process is deemed of primary importance, then the White House must be perceived as only one among a number of variables—foreign as well as domestic—exerting some influence on outcomes. Instead of asking, What did the White House do? the policy relevant question is, what or who influenced the outcome? To do this does not require abandoning concern with the White House but including actors outside the Beltway as well as inside it. Political scientists in smaller European democracies long ago became accustomed to seeing critical determinants of their national politics affected by events in larger neighbors, and prime ministers in all twelve member states of the European Community now take for granted that some of their powers are limited by Community obligations.

For half a century, two policy areas have been of continuing importance. National security, the conjunction of diplomacy and defense seasoned by CIA reports, come first. The economy is also a recurring concern. Both national security and the American economy are affected by what happens abroad as well as by what happens at home. Contemporary presidents spend an inordinate amount of time traveling abroad, talking with foreign leaders, or discussing what to do about problems in other continents. Yet to perceive America's economic policy and national security as no longer determined simply by actions of the president or actors inside the Beltway or inside the United States is tantamount to saying that America has lost its hegemonic power. This evaluation is disputed among academics and in Washington too. For the most part, presidential scholars continue to have a narrow vision, defining policy as what happens within the White House, inside the Beltway, and inside the United States.

INSIDE THE BELTWAY: THE PRESIDENT AS INDEPENDENT VARIABLE

Studies of presidential leadership treat the president as *the* independent variable. Greenstein says the first premise of the modern presidency is "American Presidents strongly influence public policy" (1988, 1). Analysis focuses upon the means of exercising influence.

The classic Neustadt (1960) view of the modern presidency emphasizes the president taking charge in Washington (see, e.g., Sperlich, 1975; Cronin, 1980, 121ff.). To influence policy the president first must influence Congress, the bureaucracy, and interest groups. Studies in this tradition have focused on within-the-Beltway politics, concentrating upon the ways in which the White House influences Congress, agencies within the executive branch, and the interest groups that often interpenetrate both. A typical study concerns a bill that the White House proposes to Congress; success is evaluated by whether or not the bill becomes a law.

Kernell's (1986) model of the president going public stresses the mobilization of public opinion, both as a means of winning elections and as a means of bringing influence to bear upon policy makers inside the Beltway who do not want to challenge a president who has successfully mobilized public opinion. If there is initial public indifference, the White House may shape media coverage of an issue and therefore shape public opinion and responses inside the Beltway, thus achieving a desired policy outcome.

Since World War II the White House has been continuously concerned with influencing international outcomes. Rossiter (1956) provides a vintage Cold War portrait of the president as the leader of a coalition of free nations. When the White House spoke, other nations were meant to listen. Their attention reflected the military and economic power of the United States and their own relative weakness. Studies in this tradition have concentrated upon the politics of foreign policy making within the White House (e.g., National Security Council studies) and relations between president and Congress or between the White House and the Pentagon. Similarly, studies of the president's role in economic policy making concentrated upon OMB or upon political interactions among the Executive Office, Congress, and the Federal Reserve Board, as if the United States was either a closed economy or could not be influenced by economic developments abroad.

Models treating the president as an independent variable are complementary and reinforcing. A president is evaluated as most successful if he simultaneously leads Congress, public opinion, and foreign governments. The view is White House–centric, for the focus of analysis is very narrow.

WHAT DETERMINES POLICY? THE PRESIDENT AS INTERVENING VARIABLE

If we take a policy-centered approach and ask, What determines policy outcomes? the president's significance is diminished. This perspective will normally show the president as only one among many intervening variables, including impersonal social and economic conditions and actions taken far outside the Beltway.

From a policy-centered perspective, the primary causes of a problem almost invariably predate the involvement of the incumbent president or the White House; they are inherited from predecessors (Rose, 1990). As Neustadt and May (1986, 106) emphasize, the first step in analyzing a problem is not to state goals but to find out its origins. A dynamic model of the making of a policy will focus first upon historical antecedents. A historian could trace causes of the problems of the urban underclass back to slavery, and an explanation of America's trade deficit today would require an understanding of changes in the world economy since 1945. The president must accept such influences as givens and act within a framework of inherited constraints.

At any given point in time, a multiplicity of influences affect the conditions that are the objects of public policy, many of which operate outside the Beltway. A social science explanation of the educational achievements of eighteen-year-olds emphasizes such independent variables as parents, class, race, urban versus rural residence, the role of teachers and classmates, local and state school system attributes, and educational expenditure. Except for the courts, the federal government has little role to play in education; it does not run schools, hire teachers, or test or accredit high school graduates, and provides very little of the money spent on primary or secondary education. Even though education is perceived as a local issue, its evaluation is becoming internationalized, as the educational skills of American workers become perceived as influencing the capacity of the American economy to compete internationally.

If only for electoral reasons, the White House is bound to be interested in the state of the economy, but a president does not manage an economy as one might manage a business or steer a ship (Rose, 1985). When the economy is booming, the White House is happy to take credit for the good news, but when it is faltering, it seeks to minimize its influence and blame others for what happens. Within the federal government, the White House shares responsibility for economic policy making with the Federal Reserve and Congress as well as with the Treasury and OMB. Decisions of investors, employers, and workers throughout the United States also influence outcomes.

The more complex the policy concern, for example, international macroeconomics or cooperation and discord in world politics, the less significant becomes the influence of the president. Both Gilpin's (1987) and Keohane's (1984) prizewinning studies of change in the international system have more index references to writings of American Political Science Association presidents on the primary causes of world change than to presidents of the United States, who cannot necessarily control changes that scholars can identify.

EVALUATION CANNOT STOP AT THE WATER'S EDGE

By definition, national security is the outcome of what happens within the United States and what happens outside it. The White House cannot afford the luxury of drawing rigid boundaries segregating domestic from foreign policy. A president must simultaneously think in terms of Washington, public opinion, and international influences, for what happens abroad affects what happens at home, as well as vice versa. As Putnam (1988, 433) emphasizes in describing presidential concerns as two-level games: "We need to move beyond the mere observation that domestic factors influence international affairs and vice versa, and beyond simple catalogs of instances of such influence, to seek theories that integrate both spheres, accounting for the areas of entanglement between them."

Interdependence describes the world of the contemporary postmodern president; he must accept that what other nations do influences the White House and that Washington influences events elsewhere (Keohane and Nye, 1989). This makes the president's involvement in big international issues a much more ambiguous attribute today than when Rossiter wrote. Analytically, it is not so difficult to analyze reciprocal causation, but politically it is much more difficult to emphasize the influence that other nations can exert on the White House and externally imposed limits on presidential power.

In an interdependent international system, the president is only one among a multiplicity of actors. President Bush has rightly referred to "other co-leaders in the alliance" (Rosenthal, 1990). The cast depends upon the problem at hand. The fluidity of the international system today makes it difficult to specify which influences will be most important in a given situation, and thus to rule many out of consideration (Berman and Jentleson, 1991, 95ff.). In a polycentric world there is no assurance that the United States will even be an intervening variable on matters of major White House concern. For example, the European Community is now empowered to take major decisions on trade and monetary policy without negotiations with the United States, and German reunification occurred in 1990 by direct negotiation between German Chancellor Helmut Kohl and President Mikhail Gorbachev. In such circumstances, the White House can monitor what happens but it is on the outside looking in.

The internationalization of the American economy has further diminished the influence of the White House; as President Bush noted in his inaugural speech, "we have the will, but not the wallet." In an interdependent world economy, inflation, unemployment, interest rates, and monetary policy are affected by events abroad as well as at home. The international economy is the result of the interaction of market processes dispersed throughout the world. Many decisions significant within the United States are now taken by foreign governments and enterprises from Tokyo and Taiwan to Brussels and Bonn. A major econometric study of the world economy concludes: "As economies become more closely intertwined, policy decisions in any single nation become more difficult to make" (Bryant et al., 1988, 1:3).

Just as the White House is trying to make the Washington system work, so heads of foreign governments are trying to make the German, Japanese, Russian, and Iranian systems work. Success requires a coincidence of interest between different countries; it cannot be imposed by any one national leader. The Gulf War demonstrates that the president can sometimes be of critical importance to outcomes abroad. However, the initial impetus—Iraq's decision to invade Kuwait—came from the Middle East, not Washington. The success of President Bush's military intervention rested upon building a global coalition involving Middle East nations immediately affected, such as Saudi Arabia, Iran, Egypt, and Syria; UN resolutions endorsed by a Security Council that included the Soviet Union, China, and nonaligned Third World states; and sanctions requiring countries such as Turkey to forgo oil revenue. The noninvolvement of Israel was also necessary. President Bush's unique contribution was to mobilize a coalition that reflected not only his diplomatic skills, but also the disposition of others to see cooperation as in their interests too. When the interests of nations are in conflict, then the White House can intervene on the losing side, as in Vietnam, or it can avoid intervention, as in Lebanon or Northern Ireland.

The openness of the international system is now calling into question the operational meaning of the national interest. In an interdependent world, lobbyists in Washington, whether representing the European Community, Israel, Japan, or a Third World nation, can become part of a policy network supporting like-minded American pressure groups. The White House can similarly seek to play upon internal divisions in other nations to find support for its initiatives abroad (see, e.g., Funibashi, 1988; Putnam, 1988). The fact of interdependence is neither threatening nor good in itself. But it does require a fundamental reorientation of the way the president's international influence is evaluated. A global assessment requires that we start by recognizing that foreign policy outcomes are not simply a reflection of what happens inside the Beltway but the product of an international process. In this process, the White House influences the event but so do other nations and transnational actors. If foreign influences are consistent with White House goals, this reinforces the probability of an outcome satisfactory to the president. If they are opposed, then the president's influence on events is problematic.

A president is *vulnerable* if his influence on American policy is high but his actions are opposed by other nations with comparable influence on the outcome. In an interdependent system in which no one nation can determine the outcome, for example, the Middle East or international trade, vulnerability leads to frustration, as the president is unable to get his way because of influences outside the control of the United States.

Under some circumstances, the White House may recognize that its influence is low and decide simply to support the goals of other nations determining events. In such circumstances, the president is a *spectator,* not a primary influence on outcomes. For example, the

United States has been a spectator of activities that have led to the broadening and strengthening of the institutions of the European Community. The White House may also adopt a passive role as spectator to avoid frustration or failure when its influence is low and no desirable outcome is likely, as in many trouble spots in Africa.

If the White House is involved in an issue and opposed by foreign influences that are much stronger than it, the outcome is *global failure*. President Johnson found, notwithstanding a massive 1964 election victory, that he could not mobilize national or international support for a war in Vietnam. Unlike leaders in many parts of the globe, an American president who fails globally is not threatened by a military coup but does risk electoral defeat.

A president is most likely to appear as a *world leader* if two conditions are met: the influence he exerts inside the Beltway, on American public opinion, and on foreign nations is reinforced by other nations acting in harmony to advance their own interests. The president can then take 100 percent of the credit domestically. But in such circumstances a president is not necessarily exercising power in Dahl's sense of making country B do something that country B would not otherwise do. He appears as a leader because the actions of a number of different nations reinforce the pursuit of goals that may reflect a modification of White House aims in response to foreign influence, as well as foreign acceptance of White House influence.

"Where you stand depends upon where you sit" is a familiar aphorism of public administration. The sociology of knowledge emphasizes that presidential scholars are also not immune from having their perceptions shaped by the conventional wisdom of the political science discipline. This can be summed up in the aphorism, "What you see depends upon where you look." As long as presidential scholars look only inside the Beltway or to public opinion for the determinants of policy, then such perceptions will exclude potentially more important influences. A paradigm shift is needed in the evaluation of the president as a policy maker. The best way to find out under what circumstances and to what extent the president is a primary influence in the international system is to subject the proposition to an empirical test of White House influence against the influence of other national and transnational actors and forces.

Toward A Two-Party Standard for Evaluation

In a competitive party system, it is hardly surprising that presidents differ in what they set out to do. It follows that an evaluation that compares presidential intentions with performance should allow for differences in intentions. The alternative is to impose a uniform standard upon the evaluation of the presidency, a standard that will be rejected by some presidents and many voters. Presidential scholars display a strong bias toward one alternative, activism.

ACTIVISM AS A VARIABLE, NOT AN OBLIGATION

There are partisan differences about how active a president ought to be. Liberals have favored the active use of the powers of the White House as part of a general preference for greater involvement by government in American society. For liberals, Franklin Roosevelt is the archetype of the modern president. This view was also enunciated by Democratic successors, such as Harry Truman, John Kennedy, and Lyndon Johnson. By contrast, conservatives favor on principle a limited use of presidential powers; this reflects a general preference for less involvement by government in American society. This is true even if they favor an active policy abroad. Dwight Eisenhower was a prime exponent of the conservative reaction against liberalism, and George Bush adheres to this view as well. Insofar as party labels correlate with different conceptions of the role of the president, then the White House since the departure of President Truman in 1952 has normally been occupied by a Republican who viewed the presidency conservatively, believing that he ought to be evaluated for what the government did *not* do, as well as for positive actions.

If presidential scholars divided like the national electorate, we would expect to find two competing criteria of evaluation, with as many books and articles propagating nonliberal theories of the presidency as those having activist assumptions. William Howard Taft would be considered important as a theorist of the presidency, for Taft (1916) saw himself as a chief magistrate, subject to the constraints of a strict interpretation of the Constitution (for a rare and unsympathetic treatment of Taft, see Barber, 1972, 174ff.). The Eisenhower presidency would be used as a criterion against which to assess Kennedy and Johnson rather than vice versa. Ford would have

TABLE 17
Political Views of Presidential Scholars and the Electorate,
1984 (percent)

	Presidential Scholars	Electorate	Difference
Vote			
Democrat	71	41	30
Republican	25	59	34
Other	4	0	4
Ideological orientation			
Liberal	58	23	35
Middle/moderate	21	39	18
Conservative	18	35	17
Other; don't know	3	4	1

Source: Bosso (1989, table); Stanley and Niemi (1988, table 5.3).

been praised for the absence of a large agenda and Carter damned for attempting too much.

However, presidential scholars do not divide politically like most Americans (see table 17). Ordinary Americans were more than twice as likely as presidential scholars to vote for Ronald Reagan than for Walter Mondale.[1] Presidential scholars are more than twice as likely as ordinary voters to hold liberal opinions and much less likely to hold conservative views. The median voter is a self-described moderate, whereas the median presidential scholar is a self-described liberal. Among the whole range of academic faculty, public affairs faculty, and political scientists are among the most liberal (Roper Center, 1991, 86). Political science writings about the presidency show a bias toward the activist conception of the presidency. The very idea of the modern presidency emphasizes presidential activism. In a poll asking historians to rank presidents in terms of greatness, Schlesinger defines greatness as "taking the side of liberalism and the general welfare against the status quo" (Nelson, 1990, 5; cf. Cronin, 1980, chap. 3). Neustadt (1960, 5f.) set a more perceptive yet still normative standard. After approvingly quoting Woodrow Wilson's phrase, that a president has the liberty "to be as big a man as he can," he added the important rider: "Nowadays he cannot be as small as he might like."

From an analytic perspective, Neustadt's epigram says no more than that the minimum threshold of presidential activity has been raised. It does not say whether the range between the most and the least that the president can do has been narrowed or widened. The range would be wider if the ceiling on a modern president had been raised more than the floor. Neustadt simply asserts that "all Presidents are leaders nowadays." From the perspective of a liberal Democrat, Neustadt evaluates President Eisenhower, the most electorally popular president since Roosevelt, thus: "The striking thing about our national elections in the Fifties was . . . the genuine approval of his candidacy by informed Americans whom one might have supposed would know better" (Neustadt, 1960, 194; cf. Greenstein, 1982, 3f., 228ff., 1988, 311ff.). Barber's (1972, 11ff.) typology for analyzing presidential character similarly emphasizes the active-passive dimension: "How much energy does the man invest in his Presidency?"

Soon after Neustadt penned his paean in favor of activism, political events in the 1960s and 1970s created a problem in evaluating presidents solely on this basis. The Vietnam War led its liberal opponents to attack the White House for being "too strong." Under Lyndon Johnson, and even more under Richard Nixon, the presidency was said to have become imperial. Schlesinger declared (1974, 12): "The Presidency has gotten out of control and badly needs new definition and restraint." President Ford did not satisfy liberal critics, for his conception of the presidency was not activist; he proclaimed himself "a Ford, not a Lincoln." The failure of the White House under Ford and Carter to promote a liberal agenda gave rise to the question of whether the presidency had become "too weak." At the end of the decade Neustadt asked (1980, 241): "Is the Presidency possible?" The Iran-contra hearings were a reminder that "imperial overstretch" remains a problem (cf. Orman, 1990).

ALTERNATIVE CRITERIA: INTENTIONS AND CONSTRAINTS

If social science evaluations of the presidency are to differ from normative judgments in use in political debate, then we need bipartisan criteria that identify two different ways in which a president may be described as a success, and two different ways in which he may be assessed a failure. A good starting point is each incumbent's own definition of the job. This allows each president to define the political value by which he is evaluated, rather than relying upon the implicit or explicit values of political scientists. Anchoring an evaluation in subjective intentions is consistent with the Michigan dictum that the behavior of those who vote for the president should be examined from "the point of view of the actor" (Campbell et al., 1960, 27).

In intent, presidents differ in the extent to which they actively seek to promote change. While every incumbent in the White House is compelled to react to major events, there is no requirement that a president have a major agenda for introducing changes in the direction of American public policy. While accepting that the office today imposes a minimum standard of action and reaction to events, a president is not obligated to be as big a man as he can—and may even have campaigned with a promise to do less, rather than more. In intent, Dwight Eisenhower cannot be evaluated as less successful than Lyndon Johnson because less active, but simply as different.

Intentions are not enough; achievements also count. The capacity of a president to achieve intended goals depends to a substantial extent upon political conditions that facilitate or constrain action (cf. Burke and Greenstein, 1989, 24; Mayhew, 1991). These conditions are much more changeable than the institutions that constrain the presidency. President Johnson's election victory of 1964 gave him a mandate and a Congress consistent with his activist goals for domestic policy. By contrast, although John Kennedy made extravagant use of activist language when running for the White House, once in office he was cautious in his initiatives, facing a Congress with many conservatives, having won election with less than half the popular vote, and concerned about the potential military menace of the Soviet Union. In an interdependent world, many constraints and opportunities affecting America's security and economy depend upon circumstances in other nations and other continents.

EVALUATING PRESIDENTS

Combining subjective intentions of a president with objective conditions that facilitate or obstruct leadership provides a bi-partisan means of evaluating a president (see table 18). Whether a president is evaluated positively depends upon the fit between intentions and political conditions.[2] An activist president requires a buoyant tax revenue to finance new domestic programs and the cooperation of allies

TABLE 18
Evaluating Presidents in Two Dimensions

	Political Conditions	
Intention	Facilitate	Obstruct
Active	Innovator	Frustrated
Limited, reactive	Guardian	Inadequate

abroad to support new international initiatives. A president who wants to preserve the status quo will feel less constrained by a Democratic Congress than will an activist who requires congressional approval of his initiatives.

If political conditions facilitate the president's active pursuit of his goals, then a president is an *innovator,* introducing important new directions to American government. Ronald Reagan is an example of the president as innovator. He was not a conserver of the status quo, but actively reactionary; that is, he wanted to roll back the size of government at home, and roll back Communist strength abroad. The 1981 Tax Act, supplemented by the 1986 Tax Act, has imposed a fiscal tourniquet upon federal expenditure that continues to constrain public spending. Internationally, the Reagan administration sought to achieve its goals by increasing the pressure of military expenditure. Changes within the Soviet Union under President Gorbachev created conditions that enabled the White House to negotiate significant foreign policy agreements in which there was great interdependence between Reagan and Gorbachev.

The presidencies of Harry Truman and Lyndon Johnson emphasize that political conditions are as important as personal intentions in evaluating a president's achievements. Both Truman and Johnson saw their role in the Roosevelt model of an active, innovative president introducing changes abroad and at home. The political vacuum at the end of World War II gave President Truman great scope for innovation internationally through such measures as the Marshall Plan, NATO, and the defense of South Korea. However, at home there was no political majority for New Deal legislation, and he was frustrated. Johnson, by contrast, was an innovator at home, making use of civil rights demonstrations and a massive 1964 election victory to promote Great Society programs. But internationally, Johnson was frustrated by inheriting from President Kennedy an unsustainable commitment to defend a regime in South Vietnam.

A president whose announced intentions are not achieved because of political constraints is *frustrated*. From an activist perspective, the president seeks major changes. But in terms of performance, the president fails to deliver as promised. The limits of personal leadership are shown by the international frustrations of Johnson and the domestic frustrations of Truman. Reagan and Roosevelt succeeded as innovators not only because of their intentions but also because they took office at a time when political conditions—in the case of Roosevelt, a severe economic depression, and in the case of Reagan, a popular reaction against federal taxation—facilitated change. By contrast, Kennedy's rhetoric in favor of innovation was not matched by political conditions supporting major change.

Guardianship describes the role of a president who limits actions in the belief that less government is better government and who is in office when political conditions facilitate a president doing less. The Eisenhower presidency offers an example of guardianship. Having been raised in rural Kansas at the end of the nineteenth century, Eisenhower rejected the political goals of New Deal Democrats—and Democrats from Stevenson to Neustadt evaluated him negatively because his political values led him to define his role narrowly. During his eight years in office, Eisenhower endorsed laissez-faire economic policies and took a laissez-faire attitude toward the implementation of the 1954 Supreme Court decision outlawing segregation. Eisenhower signed fewer pieces of major legislation (7.8 per Congress) than any other postwar president (Mayhew, 1991, 10). Abroad, his two main achievements also reduced government commitments; the Korean War was ended and the White House did *not* send troops to Vietnam when the French army withdrew (Burke and Greenstein, 1989).

George Bush entered the White House strongly committed to a limited definition of the presidency. His inaugural address explicitly rejected the Kennedy vision of "leadership as high drama, and the sound of trumpets calling." Repeatedly, President Bush has stated a preference for ad hoc reactions to difficulties. For four years he refused to give a clear lead on the budget deficit. The opposition of a Democratic Congress and constraints on public spending because of the budget deficit facilitated Bush's adoption of a limited role in domestic policy. In foreign affairs, a much higher level of White House activity is necessary; President Bush's characteristic policy stance is to react to events elsewhere, most notably, the Iraqi invasion of Kuwait, the breakup of the Soviet bloc, and German reunification (see Rose, 1991a, 309ff; Campbell and Rockman, 1991). However, when Bush failed to respond actively to economic recession, he appeared inadequate.

When political conditions force a limited president to react in adverse circumstances, then he appears *inadequate*. The inadequacy of Herbert Hoover's response to the Depression created political conditions that Franklin Roosevelt was to exploit as an innovator. Gerald Ford entered office in 1974 with a lifelong Republican's opposition to an activist White House and no agenda for action. In quiet times, this was sufficient to be a guardian president. However, during Ford's tenure political conditions created demands for action: the first OPEC oil crisis, price inflation, and a contracting instead of growing economy. His successor, Jimmy Carter, similarly entered office with a vague aspiration to make a government "as good as its people" but no active program. Carter's inability to overcome the problems presented by recurring inflation, the second OPEC oil crisis, and the seizure of American hostages in Iran made him appear inadequate.

The Nixon presidency illustrates that in the course of six years the evaluation of an individual president can alter with political conditions. In foreign affairs, President Nixon sought to be an innovator, appointing Henry Kissinger as his chief adviser on global strategy. The opening of diplomatic relations with China was an innovative achievement, but his pursuit of victory in Vietnam was frustrated. Nixon wanted to limit his involvement in economic policy, caring little about the intricacies of the dollar or the lira. But the accumulation of international financial pressures on the dollar revealed his laissez-faire approach to be inadequate, and in August 1971 the dollar was taken off the gold standard (see Odell, 1982). The failure of the Watergate cover-up (which, unlike the original break-in, Nixon actively supported) was the ultimate in a president being frustrated by political conditions outside his control.

Altogether, the two dimensions of evaluation in table 18 can lead to four different conclusions, two positive and two negative. A liberal president can be successful if political conditions facilitate activist intentions, and a conservative president can be successful if there are no untoward events to undermine limited intentions. Failure too can take different forms: a president can be frustrated by attempting too much when times are wrong or through inadequacy when there is a demand for action.

Evaluating a president by intentions and political conditions is the beginning, not the end, of analysis; it describes what must be explained. In order to understand a president's intent to be innovative or a guardian, a researcher can apply political, sociological, and psychological theories to biographical facts. To understand why a president succeeds in his intended goal, it is necessary to broaden our perceptions beyond the White House to the world outside the Beltway and outside the United States.

Notes

Thanks to Thomas E. Cronin, George C. Edwards III, and Bert Rockman for their constructive comments on this essay.

1. The curious reader may want to know that the author is a border-state Democrat from Missouri and cast his only presidential vote for Adlai Stevenson against President Eisenhower in 1956.

2. It also depends upon the events or policies that are deemed to characterize his presidency. The analytic distinctions made in table 18 are likely to vary from policy area to policy area; for example, the Camp David Agreement between Israel and Egypt was an innovative achievement of President Carter, whereas his intentions for energy policy were frustrated. However, holistic judgments are common in Washington and among historians. A president must thus take pains to define the parts that color his evaluation as a whole.

References

Barber, J. David. 1972. *The Presidential Character.* Englewood Cliffs, N.J.: Prentice-Hall.

Bennett, S. E. 1990. "The Uses and Abuses of Registration and Turnout Data." *PS* (June): 166–72.

Berman, Larry, and Bruce W. Jentleson. 1991. "Bush and the Post-Cold War World: New Challenges for American Leadership." In *The Bush Presidency: First Appraisals,* ed. C. Campbell and B. Rockman. Chatham, N.J.: Chatham House.

Bosso, Christopher J. 1989. "Congressional and Presidential Scholars: Some Basic Traits." *PS* (December): 839–49.

Bryant, Ralph C., D. W. Henderson, G. Holtham, P. Hooper, and S. Symansky, eds. 1988. *Empirical Macroeconomics for Interdependent Economies.* Washington, D.C.: Brookings.

Bunce, Valerie. 1981. *Do New Leaders Make a Difference?* Princeton: Princeton University Press.

Burke, John, P., and Fred Greenstein. 1989. *How Presidents Test Reality.* New York: Russell Sage.

Campbell, Angus, P. E. Converse, W. E. Miller, and D. E. Stokes. 1960. *The American Voter.* New York: Wiley.

Campbell, Colin J., S.J., and Bert Rockman. 1991. *The Bush Presidency: First Appraisals.* Chatham, N.J.: Chatham House.

Cohen, Michael D., and James G. March. 1974. *Leadership and Ambiguity: The American College President.* New York: McGraw-Hill.

Cronin, Thomas E. 1980. *The State of the Presidency.* 2d ed. Boston: Little, Brown.

Dodd, Lawrence C. 1991. "Congress, the Presidency and the American Experience: A Transformational Perspective." In *Divided Democracy: Cooperation and Conflict Between the President and Congress,* ed. J. A. Thurber. Washington, D.C.: Congressional Quarterly Press.

Easton, David. 1965. *A Framework for Political Analysis.* Englewood Cliffs, N.J.: Prentice-Hall.

Edwards, George C., III. 1989. *At the Margins: Presidential Leadership of Congress.* New Haven: Yale University Press.

————. 1990. "Studying the Presidency." In *The Presidency and the Political System,* 3d ed., ed. M. Nelson. Washington, D.C.: Congressional Quarterly Press.

Edwards, George C., III, with Alec M. Gallup. 1990. *Presidential Approval: A Sourcebook.* Baltimore: Johns Hopkins University Press.

Funibashi, Yoichi. 1988. *Managing the Dollar: From the Plaza to the Louvre.* Washington, D.C.: Institute for International Economics.

Gans, Curtis B. 1990. "A Rejoinder." *PS* (June): 175–78.

Gilpin, Robert. 1987. *The Political Economy of International Relations.* Princeton: Princeton University Press.

Greenstein, Fred I. 1982. *The Hidden-Hand Presidency: Eisenhower as Leader.* New York: Basic.

Greenstein, Fred I., ed. 1988. *Leadership in the Modern Presidency.* Cambridge: Harvard University Press.

Jacobson, Gary C. 1990. *The Electoral Origins of Divided Government.* Boulder, Colo.: Westview.

Jones, Charles O. 1991a. "The Diffusion of Responsibility: An Alternative Perspective for National Policy Politics in the U.S." *Governance* 4 (2): 150–67.

————. 1991b. "Meeting Low Expectations: Strategy and Prospects of the Bush Presidency." In *The Bush Presidency: First Appraisals,* ed. C. Campbell and B. Rockman. Chatham, N.J.: Chatham House.

Kaufman, Herbert. 1981. *The Administrative Behavior of Federal Bureau Chiefs.* Washington, D.C.: Brookings.

Keohane, Robert. 1984. *After Hegemony: Cooperation and Discord in the World Political Economy.* Princeton: Princeton University Press.

Kernell, Samuel. 1986. *Going Public: New Strategies of Presidential Leadership.* Washington, D.C.: Brookings.

King, Anthony, and Giles Alston. 1991. "Good Government and the Politics of High Exposure." In *The Bush Presidency: First Appraisals,* ed. C. Campbell and B. Rockman. Chatham, N.J.: Chatham House.

Koh, Harold Hongju. 1990. *The National Security Constitution: Sharing Power After the Iran-Contra Affair*. New Haven: Yale University Press.

Linz, Juan J. 1990. "The Perils of Presidentialism." *Journal of Democracy* 1(1): 51–69.

Mann, Thomas E., ed. 1990. *A Question of Balance: The President, the Congress, and Foreign Policy*. Washington, D.C.: Brookings.

Mayhew, D. R. 1991. *Divided We Govern: Party Control, Lawmaking, and Investigations, 1946–1990*. New Haven: Yale University Press.

Mezey, Michael A. 1991. "Congress Within the U.S. Presidential System." In *Divided Democracy: Cooperation and Conflict Between the President and Congress*, ed. J. A. Thurber. Washington, D.C.: Congressional Quarterly Press.

Mueller, John E. 1973. *War, Presidents, and Public Opinion*. New York: Wiley.

Murray, Robert K., and T. H. Blessing. 1988. *Greatness in the White House: Rating the Presidents*. University Park: Pennsylvania State University Press.

Nathan, James A., and James K. Oliver. *Foreign Policy-Making and the American Political System*. 2d ed. Boston: Little, Brown.

Nelson, Michael, ed. 1990. *The Presidency and the Political System*. 3d ed. Washington, D.C.: Congressional Quarterly Press.

Neustadt, Richard E. 1960. *Presidential Power*. New York: Wiley.

Neustadt, Richard E., and Ernest R. May. 1986. *Thinking in Time: The Uses of History for Decision-Makers*. New York: Free Press.

Oakeshott, Michael. 1951. *Political Education*. Cambridge: Bowes and Bowes.

Odell, John S. 1982. *U.S. International Monetary Policy: Markets, Power, and Ideas as Sources of Change*. Princeton: Princeton University Press.

Orman, John. 1990. *Presidential Accountability: New and Recurring Problems*. New York: Greenwood.

Pierce, Roy. 1991. "The Executive Divided Against Itself: Cohabitation in France, 1986–1988." *Governance* 4(3):270–94.

Piven, Frances Fox, and Richard A. Cloward. 1988. *Why Americans Don't Vote*. New York: Pantheon.

Piven, Frances Fox, and Richard A. Cloward. 1989. "Government Statistics and Conflicting Explanations of Nonvoting." *PS* (September): 580–88.

Piven, Frances Fox, and Richard A. Cloward. 1990. "A Reply." *PS* (June): 172–73.

Powell, G. Bingham, ed. 1991. "Symposium on Divided Government." *Governance* 4(3): 231–94.

Putnam, Robert. 1988. "Diplomacy and Domestic Politics: The Logic of Two-Level Games." *International Organization* 42(3): 427–60.

Riggs, Fred W. 1988. "The Survival of Presidentialism in America: Paraconstitutional Practices." *International Political Science Review* 9(4): 247–78.

Robinson, Donald L. 1989. *Government for the Third American Century*. Boulder, Colo.: Westview.

Rockman, Bert A. 1984. *The Leadership Question: The Presidency and the American System*. New York: Praeger.

Roper Center. 1991. "Politics of the Professoriate." *The Public Perspective* 2(5): 267–80.

Rose, Richard. 1980. "Government Against Sub-Governments: A European Perspective on Washington." In *Presidents and Prime Ministers*, ed. R. Rose and E. Suleiman. Washington, D.C.: American Enterprise Institute.

———. 1985. "Can the President Steer the American Economy?" *Journal of Public Policy* 5(2): 267–80

———. 1990. "Inheritance Before Choice in Public Policy." *Journal of Theoretical Politics* 2(3): 263–91.

———. 1991a. *The Postmodern President: George Bush Meets the World.* 2d ed. Chatham, N.J.: Chatham House.

———. 1991b. "Prime Ministers in Parliamentary Democracies." *West European Politics* 14(2): 9–24.

———. 1991c. "Comparing Forms of Comparative Politics." *Political Studies* 39(4): 446–62.

Rose, Richard, and Ian McAllister. 1992. "Expressive versus Instrumental Voting." In *Electoral Politics*, ed. Dennis A. Kavanagh. Oxford: Oxford University Press.

Rosenthal, Andrew. 1990. "Bush Declares He Does Not Feel Left Out by Gorbachev and Kohl." *New York Times International Edition.* July 18, 1.

Rossiter, Clinton. 1956. *The American Presidency.* New York: Harcourt, Brace.

Schlesinger, Arthur M. 1974. *The Imperial Presidency.* New York: Popular Library.

Schumpeter, Joseph A. 1942. *Capitalism, Socialism and Democracy.* London: Allen and Unwin.

Skowronek, Stephen. 1990. "Presidential Leadership in Political Time." In *Presidency and the Political System*, 3d ed., ed. M. Nelson. Washington, D.C.: Congressional Quarterly Press.

Sperlich, Peter. 1975. "Bargaining and Overload: An Essay on Presidential Power." In *Perspectives on the Presidency*, ed. A. Wildavsky. Boston: Little, Brown.

Stanley, Harold W., and Richard G. Niemi. 1988. *Vital Statistics on American Politics.* Washington, D.C.: Congressional Quarterly Press.

Stockman, David. 1986. *The Triumph of Politics.* New York: Harper and Row.

Sundquist, James A. 1986. *Constitutional Reform and Effective Government.* Washington, D.C.: Brookings.

———. 1988. "The New Era of Coalition Government in the United States." *Political Science Quarterly* 103: 613–35.

Taft, William Howard. 1916. *Our Chief Magistrate and His Powers.* New York: Columbia University Press.

Thurber, James A. 1991. *Divided Democracy: Cooperation and Conflict Between the President and Congress.* Washington, D.C.: Congressional Quarterly Press.

Tulis, Jeffrey. 1987. *The Rhetorical Presidency.* Princeton: Princeton University Press.

Wattenberg, Martin P. 1987. "The Hollow Realignment." *Public Opinion Quarterly* 51(1): 59–71.

Weber, Max. 1948. "Science and Politics." In *From Max Weber*, ed. H. H. Gerth and C. Wright Mills. London: Routledge.

White, Joseph, and Aaron Wildavsky. 1989. *The Deficit and the Public Interest.* Berkeley and Los Angeles: University of California Press and Russell Sage Foundation.

Whicker, Marcia Lynn. 1991. "Review of J. White and A. Wildavsky, *The Deficit and the Public Interest.*" *Governance* 4(3): 354–55.

Wildavsky, Aaron. 1975. "The Two Presidencies." In *Perspectives on the Presidency,* ed. A. Wildavsky. Boston: Little, Brown.

Wolfinger, Raymond W., and Steven J. Rosenstone. 1980. *Who Votes?* New Haven: Yale University Press.

Conclusion

THE Presidency Research Conference at the University of Pittsburgh in November 1990 that spawned this book generated deeply felt, even passionate, discussions about how to study the presidency. These discussions attained such levels of passion mainly because, while we often hold intense preferences as individuals about how best to study the presidency, considerable collective uncertainty persists as to the optimal approach. In essence, individual certainty is combined with collective uncertainty. Individual certainty derives in part from each scholar's cumulative past investments in research strategies and the paths that these investments open (and close) in the way of future research possibilities. Collective uncertainty results from rival individual certainties. No single research strategy is self-evidently dominant and capable of providing a paradigm that both satisfactorily defines and resolves existing puzzles. This collective uncertainty means that there is a potentially available market for convincing approaches to studying the presidency. Individual certainty, however, raises the paradox that this may be a market long on sellers and short on buyers.

Presidency scholars sometimes feel humbled by the company they keep. Like the comedian Groucho Marx, they wonder whether any club (subfield) willing to accept them is not already too inclusive. Many of the currents influencing research in American political science have been perceived by scholars both inside and outside the presidency subfield as having passed it by or, at best, only lightly grazed over it. Work on the presidency is often perceived as the gateway between journalism and political science. That is a plus in communicating with users of knowledge. But within the political science profession, scholarship on the presidency has only lately emerged from the status of a backward province.

Indeed, from within the political science community, questions have been raised as to whether there is a legitimate field of presidency research. Is there cumulativeness? Are there testable propositions? Is there a prevailing theory, or are there at least clearly articulated competitive theories? Such questions certainly were raised at the conference. Similarly, there was spirited debate as to whether obsessions with the abstract state of a subfield are relevant to tackling important research questions.

Theory and *rigor* were the watchwords of the conference. These are values to which all participants could subscribe, so long as they remained undefined. We are all convinced that theory is something we wish to achieve. We are less sure as to how we go about achieving it. The same is true of rigor. We think this too is a good. Yet, individually, we are apt to have different conceptions of it. One scholar's pristine logic is another's mere set of untested assumptions. One scholar's data base is another's atheoretical inductivism. We have been conditioned to salivate at certain symbols of scientific progress—*theory* and *rigor* are words that appeal to these glands. But behind our operant conditioning (who gets rewarded for saying they are atheoretical or impressionistic?) we have different images of what these words mean.

Differences Among Conference Participants

If we participants were in agreement on ideals and goals, how did we differ? Let us count the ways.

PARSIMONY AND DETAIL

Underlying this controversy is a view of how we best understand complex phenomena, whatever they are. Parsimony, it is argued, is essential to theorizing, for theories must reduce vastly the realities they seek to explain. A parsimonious explanation should yield consistent predictions. The proof supposedly lies in this pudding. But predictions may be consistent with more than one explanation. Hence, prediction as a theoretical criterion cannot by itself establish sufficiency in the validity of an explanation; it can, however, discard explanations inconsistent with the predictive yield.

There is no doubt that the presidency remains a subfield thicker in description and richer in texture that most. We have little interest, after all, in any particular voter's choices or even in those of any particular member of Congress. We do, however, have an interest in seeing the details of presidential behavior, whether this be with whom he spoke, how he decided, or what his assumptions seemed to be in the process of deciding.

There is, then, an obvious and perhaps irreconcilable tension between the functions of theoretical reduction and nuanced description. Which of these should take priority? Textured descriptions involving case studies of decision making, communications, and advice rendering often are regarded by their proponents as the building blocks of a larger theoretical enterprise. The proponents of thick description tend to emphasize the importance of understanding the logic in use by a president or his advisers. Externally imposed assumptions are weak or nonexistent. The proponents of parsimony are more likely to feel comfortable in a deductive world where logic can be reconstructed either on the basis of inferences drawn from a general pattern of findings or on the basis of axiomatic theory. Proponents of parsimony do not deny that much is lost when simplifications are introduced; they tend to question the value, however, of pursuing a richness that they find unproductive of more general theoretical conclusions.

To be sure, these differences stem from differences of temperament. Some like it thick; others prefer it thin. But they also stem partially from analytic focus as well. Thick description helps capture the ways (or styles) by which presidents decide. Alternatively, parsimonious and deductive models of explanation may work best with regularized and repetitive behaviors, for example, the institutional logic of conflict (and sometimes cooperation) between the executive and legislative branches.

INDIVIDUALS AND INSTITUTIONS

A second dispute is whether one should focus on individuals or institutions. Where should we begin? With the individual or with the institution? Which will take us farther?

Individuals are variable, and, within certain bounds, the role of the presidency is a fairly discretionary one. To consider just the last three incumbents of the presidency (Carter, Reagan, and Bush), for example, is to cross an expansive landscape of individual difference. One president (Carter) was consumed with crossing *t*'s and dotting *i*'s. His knowledge of Washington and politics in general was sparse. His devotion to hard work was legendary. This president's successor (Reagan) was, in all important respects, nearly Carter's exact opposite (other than in his contempt for Washington political institutions). Carter's obsession with hard work and detail was replaced by Reagan's indolence and instinct for situational politics. Carter's indecision was replaced by Reagan's stubbornness and principles. The inexperience of each with Washington political institutions was, in turn, replaced by (George Bush's) varied experience with these institutions. Nor has Bush had either Reagan's commitment to principles nor Carter's commitment to an active, if uncertain, agenda.

Now that we know all of these things about individual presidents, what do we know? We know there is individual variability. The question is, What does that knowledge mean theoretically? Does it parse in a manner that advances not simply what we know about any given president but also theoretically consistent generalizations across presidencies?

For some of us, what is most essential about the office is its occupant. To others of us, however, focusing on the individual incumbent cannot take us far, either theoretically or in terms of empirical rigor. Too many variables and too few cases is the concern here. Rather than think about the presidency in personal terms, trying to psyche out the individual with ill-defined analytics, one type of critique would emphasize that the presidency is best seen as an institution. From this standpoint, the presidency is an institution that fulfills a role within the particular logic of the U.S. system of government; it has a past with a set of routines and habits and a regularized set of relations with other institutions in its midst.

The presidency, of course, is both—people and institution. The issue is not whether it is one or the other but which perspective allows us to say more. We must recognize that, scientifically, a focus on individuals emphasizes their variability, at least as types, whereas a focus on the institutional aspects of the presidency emphasizes invariability. The institutional presidency presumably ought to work similarly for different presidents. This dilemma cannot be resolved here. Nor is it likely to be resolved merely by fiat. We will have to get down to the hard tasks of showing where differences make a difference and where invariabilities override the differences. And, even prior to this, we will have to conceptualize and operationalize what varies, how it varies, and what is invariant. In other words, we will have to move from discussions that have a quasi-theological status to the hard work of actual research.

ECONOMIC AND PSYCHOLOGICAL CONCEPTIONS
OF INDIVIDUAL BEHAVIOR

Psychologists search for motives and assume cognitive limits. Economists know motives (or, more properly, are unconcerned about them) and assume omniscience. These are stereotypes, of course. But they hold some meaning for the ways in which we can study the presidency. At least implicitly, an important fault line in studying the presidency might be described as the psycho-econo rift.

Psychological approaches emphasize the limitations of decision making. Personality approaches emphasize individual differences and locate the core decision-making limitations in individual dysfunctions. Cognitive approaches emphasize imperatives to find shortcuts or minimize information discrepancies. Accordingly, decision makers narrow the range of information they employ in making decisions and try to decrease the costs of processing it. Discovering just what factors most powerfully decrease these costs, of course, is at the basis of contending cognitive theories.

Viewed from an information processing perspective, the presidency is an institution long on stimuli and short on attention spans. The particles of information that get to top decision makers, and how these are dressed up and arranged, become vitally important to presidential decisions making—affecting what is noticed and how it is understood. Presidential preferences are usually seen as being in a state of formation rather than fixed, and the presidency, thus, can be conceptualized as a "garbage can". Which preferences are activated, then, depend on what stimuli are there to evoke them.

Economic theories of choice, by contrast, typically assume fixed preference schedules, more or less complete information, and utility maximization. As a consequence, interests provide the currency of rational action. In one sense, therefore, James Madison is the architect of a system built around rational choice assumptions; that is, actors will seek to maximize their interests and will do so unless inhibited by other actors seeking to do the same.

Defining interests precisely is no easy matter since that requires measuring actors' utilities. Consequently, it is assumed that people act in ways that reflect their interests. Hence, we know by their revealed behavior what it is that they really care about. However they behave, people are presumed to behave in ways consonant with their interests. The economic assumption that actors seek to maximize their interests leads to theories based on the logic of interests—a logic that is at the core of the design of American government.

Neither the psychological nor the economic perspective is right or wrong. Each leads us to distinctive sets of problems to be resolved, however. One tends to emphasize the role of communications, information absorption, and decision making; the other tends to emphasize the longer-term logic of institutional behavior and interinstitutional relations.

There is, of course, room to maneuver between these different conceptions of behavior. As the chapter by Gary Miller suggests, information asymmetries can lead to behavior in no one's interest. Indeed, the classic problem of when to storm the Bastille presents a paradigm for much presidential-congressional bargaining (especially under divided government) when neither actor wants to make either the first or definitive move in resolving an issue that each would like to resolve so long as each can avoid being identified as exclusively responsible for an unpopular solution. For example, see foreign aid. For another, see taxes.

Onward to Our Work Stations

Studying the presidency is sure to be ripe with controversies. These probably should be taken as vital signs rather than as evidence of morbidity. For too long, the study of the presidency seemed to be isolated from these essential controversies. Now it has become a part of the metropole. With this movement to the forefront, therefore, have come all of the controversies about how we study politics and government generally.

The ferment is healthy. The purpose of this book (and of the conference that generated it) is not, however, to have scholarly armies confronting one another across analytic divides. Its purpose is to explore complementarities—how one type of analysis might be different yet congruent with another. That, we believe, is how progress comes about.

There is much to do and much to be excited about. A lot of ground has been gained. New avenues of research and theory have opened up. Much of that has been the result of work by scholars assembled at the conferences and by those whose chapters are in this book. The book suggests that research and theory are about choices, and that choices have consequences. Our intent is to elucidate the variety of these choices and to explore their consequences. But the real payoff is not in what we have done in this book or what was done at the Pittsburgh conference. It is in what the book stimulates others to do. Here's hoping "a thousand flowers bloom." The most promising will be harvested, and these should contribute to a scientific and theoretical enrichment of presidency studies.

Notes on Contributors

John H. Aldrich is Professor and Chair of the Department of Political Science at Duke University, with interests in American politics, formal (or positive) political theory, and methodology. He received his Ph.D. from the University of Rochester and has taught at Michigan State University and the University of Minnesota. He has served as co-editor of the *American Journal of Political Science* and is author or co-author of such books as *Before the Convention* and the series *Change and Continuity* in national elections, as well as numerous articles. His interests include elections, political parties, and institutions. He is currently completing a book on U.S. political parties.

George C. Edwards III is Distinguished Professor of Political Science at Texas A&M University and director of the Center for Presidential Studies. He also holds the Jordan Professorship in Liberal Arts. He has written over a dozen books on American politics and public policy making, including *At the Margins: Presidential Leadership of Congress, Presidential Approval*, and *National Security and the U.S. Constitution*. He has served as president of the Presidency Research Section of the American Political Science Association and was an issue leader for the National Academy of Public Administration's Project on the 1988 Presidential Transition.

Martha S. Feldman is an Associate Professor of Political Science and Public Policy at the University of Michigan, Ann Arbor. Her research interests involve how people construct their social reality and how they act in a social context. Her particular focus has been on organizational decision making and how various forms of information and communication are involved in that process. She is currently studying organizational routines as a form of intelligence that is organizational rather than individual. Her publications include *Order without Design: Information Production and Policy Making* (1989), *Reconstructing Reality in the Courtroom* (with W. Lance Bennett), and *Information in Organizations as Signal and Symbol* (with James G. March).

Susan T. Fiske is Distinguished University Professor of Psychology at the University of Massachusetts, Amherst. After receiving her Ph.D. in social psychology from Harvard University, Fiske was Assistant and Associate Professor at Carnegie-Mellon University, 1978–1985. She is the author, with Shelley E. Taylor, of *Social Cognition* (1984, 2d ed. 1991). Her federally funded research on social cognition focuses on motivation and person perception. Her work in political cognition examines perceptions of political entities not encountered directly, such as politicians, nations, and nuclear war. Fiske is the 1991 winner of the American Psychological Association Award for Distinguished Contributions to Psychology in the Public Interest, Early Career.

Erwin C. Hargrove is Professor of Political Science at Vanderbilt University, with a principal interest in political and administrative leadership. His books on the presidency include *Jimmy Carter as President* (1988), *Presidents, Politics and Policy* (1984), *The Power of the Modern Presidency* (1973), and *Presidential Leadership, Personality and Political Style* (1966). He co-authored and edited *Impossible Jobs in Public Management* (1990) and *Leadership and Innovation, a Biographical Perspective on Entrepreneurs in Government* (1987). He is currently at work on a study of the leadership of the Tennessee Valley Authority from 1933 to 1990.

Karen M. Hult is Associate Professor of Political Science at Virgina Polytechnic Institute and State University. Her research interests are organization theory and its applications to the U.S. presidency and executive branch bureaucracy; she is currently studying the organizational evolution of the White House staff. Her publications include *Agency Merger and Bureaucratic Redesign* (1987), *Governing Public Organizations*, with Charles Walcott (1990), and articles in journals such as *Administration and Society*, *American Journal of Political Science*, *Policy Studies Journal*, and *Presidential Studies Quarterly*.

Gary King is Professor of Government and Director of the Government Data Center at Harvard University. He has authored, coauthored, or edited *Scientific Inference in Qualitative Research*, *Unifying Political Methodology: The Likelihood Theory of Statistical Inference*, *The Elusive Executive: Discovering Statistical Patterns in the Presidency*, *The Presidency in American Politics*, and numerous journal articles in political methodology, American politics, and other fields. He has served on the editorial boards of the *American Journal of Political Science*, *American Politics Quarterly*, *Journal of Conflict Resolution*, *Journal of Politics*, *Political Analysis*, *Public Opinion Quarterly*, *Sociological Methods and Research*, and the National Science Foundation political science panel.

Anthony King is Professor of Government at the University of Essex in England. He is the editor of *The New American Political System* and is currently writing a book on the British prime ministership.

Paul C. Light is Professor of Public Affairs and Planning and Associate Dean at the Humphrey Institute of Public Affairs, University of Minnesota. He served as senior advisor and authored the final report of the National Commission on the Public Service (the Volcker Commission). His primary interests are executive organization and management, the national policy process, aging and veterans policy, and U.S. political culture. He is the author of *The President's Agenda: Domestic Policy Choice from Kennedy to Carter* (1982; rv. ed. 1991), *Artful Work: The Politics of Social Security Reform* (1985), and *Monitoring Government: Inspectors General and the Search for Accountability* (1992).

Gary J. Miller is Taylor Professor of Political Economy at Washington University in St. Louis. He focuses his research, much of it experimental, on group decision making in committees and hierarchies. His research issues include the effects of institutional rules and social norms on coalition formation in committees and on leadership in hierarchies. Most recently, he has published *Managerial Dilemmas: The Political Economy of Hierarchy* (1992).

Terry M. Moe has been Professor of Political Science at Stanford University since 1981. His teaching and research are concerned most generally with American political institutions and theories of organization, and he has written extensively on a variety of topics, among them: public bureaucracy, the presidency, interest groups, and the educational system.

Richard Rose has published more than three dozen books on politics and public policy in the United States and Europe. He has pioneered the study of the presidency in comparative perspective in *Presidents and Prime Ministers* (1980) and *The Postmodern President: The White House Meets the World* (1991). Rose is Director of the Centre for the Study of Public Policy at the University of Strathclyde, Glasgow, Scotland. He has been a visiting fellow at the Brookings Institution, the American Enterprise Institute, and the Woodrow Wilson Center of the Smithsonian Institution, and is a fellow of the British Academy.

Barbara Sinclair is Professor of Political Science at the University of California, Riverside. She received her Ph.D. from the University of Rochester. Her publications include *Congressional Realigment 1925-1978* (1982), *Majority Leadership in the U.S. House* (1983), and *Transformation of the U.S. Senate* (1989), winner of the Richard F. Fenno Prize and the D.B. Hardeman Prize.

Pitt Series in Policy and Institutional Studies
Bert A. Rockman, Editor